THE
CULINARY
CRAFT

THE CULINARY CRAFT

BY JUDY GORMAN

A guide to
the how, what, and why of cooking,
plus more than 300 kitchen-tested
recipes.

A division of Yankee Publishing Incorporated, Dublin, New Hampshire

Edited by Sandra J. Taylor
Designed by Jill Shaffer
Illustrated by Pamela Carroll

Yankee Publishing Incorporated
Dublin, New Hampshire
First Edition
Second Printing, 1984
Copyright 1984 by Yankee Publishing Incorporated

Library of Congress Catalogue Card Number: 84-50427
ISBN: 0-89909-038-9

For Edmund

Contents

Introduction

This book is the result of a life-long fascination with how cooking works. Looking back, I can clearly remember how excited I was when, as a young teenager, I managed to turn blobs of batter into cream puffs for the very first time. It seemed an incredible, magical event, and I wanted to know how it happened — how it was possible for that thick, dense dough to be transformed into puffy spheres.

In the years since, I've continued to investigate many of the whys and hows of cookery. Consequently, my intention for this book is to provide the reader with an understanding of how foods react and interact, why ingredients behave differently under certain conditions, how the composition of various ingredients influences the final product, and how certain procedures are related to the chemical nature of foods.

With that in mind, the book has been arranged in two parts: the first section deals with specific cooking terms and techniques, chemical reactions, and the properties of significant ingredients. This portion of the book is arranged alphabetically, with many of the entries cross-referenced to help the reader locate closely related information. For the most part, each entry highlights a process, such as "Crust Formation"; a chemical reaction, such as "Coagulation"; a technique, such as "Kneading"; or a specific ingredient, such as "Butter." The entry for "Pots and Pans" discusses the essential characteristics of cooking equipment. The entry for "Sour-dough Starter" describes how the acids that give sourdough its tangy flavor are produced; readers wishing to learn more about this can easily turn to entries such as "Fermentation," "Carbon Dioxide," or "Yeast."

The second part of the book contains a variety of recipes that incorporate, in varying degrees, the topics discussed in the first section. The instructions that accompany the recipes emphasize a multi-sensory approach to cooking, because visual clues alone are seldom adequate for judging the progress of a particular procedure. To achieve consistently successful results, a cook needs to pay attention to the way food feels and smells and, occasionally, to how it sounds.

Since nothing can duplicate the lively flavor created by using fresh ingredients, I've repeatedly stressed the importance of using fresh produce, herbs, and spices. Salt, while not completely eliminated, has been listed in moderate amounts. Most recipes using butter can be prepared with either salted or unsalted varieties.

I hope that beginning cooks, as well as those who are accomplished, will become as intrigued as I am with how cooking works. A basic knowledge of food science can liberate a cook from the strictures of recipes and produce the confidence that is needed to be creative in the kitchen.

I am deeply grateful to my editor, Sandy Taylor, for her patience, attention to detail, and unfailing sense of humor.

Judy Gorman

CULINARY TECHNIQUES, TERMS, AND PROCEDURES

A

ACIDS

If you thought you had left the subject of acids back in those dreadful chemistry labs of your youth, just look around your kitchen. Acids are a part of every cook's daily life.

There are two categories of acids — those that occur naturally in food and those that are commercially prepared. Citric acid (in lemon juice) and acetic acid (in vinegar) are commonly recognized as kitchen acids, and both have a fairly pronounced sour taste, a characteristic shared by all acids.

Other acids that turn up in the kitchen include lactic acid (in sour milk, buttermilk, and cheese), malic acid (in sour apples), tartaric acid (in wine), benzoic acid (in cranberries), salicylic acid (in wintergreen), oxalic acid (in rhubarb and spinach), and ascorbic acid (the vitamin C found in fruits and vegetables). Measure for measure, some of these acids are more sour in flavor and perform more powerfully than others. The strength of an acid is expressed in terms of the pH scale, with a high level of acidity registering in the lowest numbers (see pH Scale).

Chemically prepared acids commonly used in home cooking include potassium acid tartrate (cream of tartar and a component of baking powder) and sodium aluminum sulfate, calcium phosphate, and tartaric acid — all used as reactive agents in baking powder.

Both natural and chemical acids can affect the flavor of food, as well as the way in which certain ingredients behave. Citric acid, particularly lemon juice, is often added to heighten or intensify flavors. Thus, you might squeeze a few drops of lemon juice into mushroom soup before serving. Acetic acid, the acid of vinegar, adds zing to salad dressing and Béarnaise sauce, and forms the basis for the complex taste sensation of sweet and sour sauce. Lactic acid in buttermilk, sour cream, and yogurt enhances the flavor of baked goods and sauces.

Chemical acids in baking powder play an important role in balancing flavors. Since acids neutralize alkalis (and vice versa), their distinctive tastes tend to cancel one another out. That's one reason why recipes containing acidic ingredients call for baking soda, which is an alkali. The citric acid and the baking soda neutralize each other and prevent the development of an overly sour flavor. The chemical acids contained in baking powder perform the same balancing act; without them, a soapy alkaline taste would result. Granted, baking powder and baking soda also affect the rising of baked goods (see Leavening), but they are important to the taste of food as well.

Besides balancing flavor, acids are important because they break down and dissolve carbonates. Baking soda (a *bi*carbonate) is just such a compound. In order to obtain the carbon dioxide needed to leaven bread and muffins, an acid must be added to baking soda. The chemical reaction that takes place produces carbon dioxide gas (see Baking Powder/Baking Soda).

Acids produce other chemical changes, too. If you've ever added lemon juice to milk to create your own sour milk, you've already witnessed one of them. Acids denature protein, which means they firm up protein molecules. So when you add 1 tablespoon of lemon juice to a cup of milk and let it stand at room temperature for 5 to 10 minutes, you'll notice that it becomes thicker, or more viscous, and that some of the protein molecules clump together to form solid particles. The acid has denatured the casein, or milk protein, causing it to coagulate (see Denaturing; Coagulation). This type of coagulation also occurs when you add acid in the form of cream of tartar to egg whites as you whip them. The protein molecules uncoil and become firm; the protein coagulates slightly and the egg-white foam easily whips to stiff peaks.

Acids have a denaturing effect on egg protein in other situations, too. A few drops of vinegar added to poaching water firms up the egg-white protein to produce a neatly poached egg (see Acidulated Water). When whisked with an egg yolk, the acid in lemon juice denatures the protein in the yolks to form a thick mixture (the first step in preparing mayonnaise), and in that way helps to stabilize the emulsion (see Emulsion).

The behavior of wheat protein is similarly altered by the presence of an acid. Acetic acid and lactic acid both weaken strands of gluten to produce outstanding pastries. Vinegar in pie crust is an old trick for producing flakiness, and for generations cooks have known that sour milk and buttermilk make cakes extra tender and biscuits more flaky.

Acids also help tenderize meat. That's why marinade recipes usually call for wine, lemon juice, or cider. The acid component in these ingredients softens the collagen that binds meat fibers together and makes the meat easier to chew (see Connective Tissue). (It is interesting to note that collagen is the fundamental element contained in gelatin, which explains why acids can interfere with the setting of gelatin salads and desserts.)

Acids not only affect proteins but they also modify the behavior of carbohydrates. Lemon juice, vinegar, cream of tartar, and powdered citric acid are all used at various times to create invert sugar from sucrose, which is important when making candy and certain frostings (see Sugar Cooking; Sucrose; Invert Sugar). Acids are notorious for reducing the thickening power of starches, a fact that determines to a great extent which thickener you'll use for fruit pie fillings (see Pie Baking: Dessert Pies).

Pectin, which is also a carbohydrate, is powerless without the aid of an acid. Combined with sugar and a strong acid (pH 3.5 or lower), the chainlike pectin molecules link together to form the three-dimensional framework that firms a pectin gel and creates jelly. Insufficient acidity results in soft, runny preserves (see Jam and Jelly Making).

A small quantity of acid is sometimes added to water to intensify the natural color of certain vegetables like cauliflower, parsnips, or cabbage. Applied directly to sensitive fruits and vegetables, an acid acts as an antioxidant by preventing the oxidation that causes them to turn brown.

Strong acids retard the growth of most bacteria, which is why vinegar is often used to preserve pickles and relishes. In this instance, the strength of the acid is all-important: the stronger the acid, the safer your preserved foods will be.

RECIPES: Béarnaise Sauce, Mayonnaise, Mushroom Soup, Sweet and Sour Sauce. ◄ঽ

ACIDULATED WATER

One of the ways to prevent browning caused by the action of enzymes is to submerge sensitive foods in acidulated water (see Browning: Enzymatic). Acidulated water is formed by adding either lemon juice (citric acid) or vinegar (acetic acid) to water. The usual proportions are 1 tablespoon of acid to

1 quart of water, but that's only a guideline. Stronger acids hold off browning for a longer period of time, so feel free to use a larger amount of acid accordingly (as long as the strongly acidulated water doesn't affect the final flavor of the food).

Acidulated water accomplishes its mission in two ways — it postpones enzymatic browning, by cutting off the supply of oxygen available to the cut surface of food, and it modifies the enzyme's environment. In other words, since enzyme action slows down in the presence of an acid, acidulated water will retard the browning caused by food enzymes. However, enzyme activity will continue, albeit at a reduced rate. Since water itself contains oxygen, acidulated water cannot create surroundings truly devoid of oxygen. Therefore, you can't use acidulated water to any great extent as a means of preparing food ahead of time.

Lightly acidulated water produces well-shaped poached eggs. This is because acids cause the protein molecules in egg whites to change their shape from round to elongated — a shape that does not dissolve easily (see Denaturing). Therefore, if you add a small amount of vinegar to the poaching water for an egg, the acetic acid will firm up the egg white just enough to prevent the white from drifting all over the place, and you'll produce a neater-looking poached egg.

The usual proportion is ½ teaspoon of vinegar, or 1 teaspoon of lemon juice, per quart of water. Resist the temptation to use more, because strongly acidulated water imparts an acidic flavor to poached eggs. (Poaching eggs in acidulated water also bleaches the color pigment, known as flavones, in egg white, so you get whiter-looking poached eggs. Likewise, adding lemon juice to the cooking water for vegetables such as potatoes and cauliflower bleaches out the flavones, and considerably brightens these white vegetables.)

Acidulated water may also be used to adjust the pH level of tap water. If your boiled potatoes are turning yellow or your beets or red cabbage are coming out sickly purple, chances are that alkalis in your tap water are to blame. Add 1 tablespoon of lemon juice to the cooking water to neutralize, or counteract, the alkalis (see Alkali).   ⊷

ALCOHOL

The alcohol used in cooking is called grain or ethyl alcohol. It's a product of the fermentation process and is present in wine, malt liquor (beer and ale), distilled liquor (brandy, rum, whisky, and vodka), and liqueurs.

Alcohol lends a harsh, unpleasant flavor to a dish if it's not evaporated off, so most recipes direct you to add wine or beer, then simmer for at least 10 minutes (and sometimes for as long as 3 hours). Recipes calling for whisky, rum, or one of the liqueurs are usually baked, flamed, chilled, or frozen. When heated, the alcohol evaporates quickly; when chilled, or frozen, it evaporates more slowly.

Alcohol boils at 173°F., a much lower temperature than water, and begins to vaporize around 130°F. — you can smell it. It is completely evaporated by 212°F., leaving behind the essence of the liquor without the harshness of the alcohol. Alcohol also freezes at a much lower temperature than water — a fact that's handy to keep in mind if you're using it in ice cream or a frozen dessert, for it may take longer to harden than you expected.

Years ago, before the availability of baking powder, alcohol was used to leaven cakes. The vaporizing alcohol leavened much like steam or carbon dioxide gas, except that it was quite weak. Today, although we cook with all kinds of beer, wine, distilled liquor, and cordials, it's generally the flavor of the liquor we're after. The alcohol itself doesn't play an important part at all, except in preserving fruits or flaming an entrée or dessert.

The percent of alcohol by volume is sometimes indicated on the bottle's label by an actual percentage (like wine, which is often 12.5 percent) or by its proof. To arrive at the actual percentage, simply divide the proof number by two. An 80-proof vodka, then, would contain 40 percent alcohol.

Knowing the percentage of alcohol is important in order to predict how a certain liquor is going to react. The higher the alcohol content, the more volatile the liquid, and the sooner the mixture will return to the boil. The sooner it boils, the more quickly the alcohol will evaporate.

Once you get the hang of it, you'll be able to tell just by smelling a dish when the alcohol has started to vaporize and when it has disappeared. This is particularly handy when you're flaming a dish because you'll want to be sure to ignite it at just the right time — just *after* it returns to the boil (see Flaming).

Flavor extracts also contain alcohol (some, like lemon, as much as 80 percent). This can cause you problems in two different respects. If you add an extract to a hot mixture, like a pastry cream for instance, the heat will vaporize the alcohol and concentrate the flavoring before it can be blended in evenly. Always allow a hot mixture to cool slightly before stirring in the required extract.

The second problem occurs when you add an extract or high-proof liquor to a warm egg-based sauce or mousse. The alcohol (when added to a mixture) generates heat of its own, and this increased heat can be enough to curdle or separate the egg-based mixture. If this happens to your chocolate mousse, splash a few drops of ice-cold water into the mixture, or grab a few slivers of ice from the ice cube tray. Whisk the water or ice into the curdled mixture to lower the temperature before any permanent damage is done; it will rapidly pull back together.

One approach to flaming desserts is to saturate cubes of sugar with lemon extract and ignite them. This works only if done at the last minute, since sugar cubes soaked ahead of time won't contain any alcohol by the time you light them — it will have completely evaporated. Alcohol will also evaporate from loosely capped bottles of extract, so be sure to screw the tops on tightly.   ◄ৡ

ALKALI

An alkaline substance, such as baking soda, can counterbalance or neutralize an acid. Hence, recipes using acidic ingredients, such as lemon juice or sour milk, include alkalis to offset the acidity and balance the flavor (see Acids).

Yet recipes frequently include acidic elements that are apt to go unnoticed. Brown sugar, molasses, most fruits and fruit juices, honey, yogurt, buttermilk, and sour cream are all acidic to some degree, and this is where problems can arise when you substitute ingredients. For example, if you use white sugar instead of the brown sugar listed in a recipe, following the rest of the instructions to the letter, you will have decreased the amount of acid by removing the brown sugar, and thus upset the acid-alkali balance. Consequently, the alkali flavor component will dominate in the final product and create an unpleasant taste.   ◄ৡ

ALUMINUM FOIL

Aluminum foil is made from a solid block of pure aluminum that has been repeatedly rolled and pressed until it emerges as a paper-thin, pliable sheet of metal. During this process, the action of the rollers gives the completed foil a dull side and a shiny side, but this fact is not as important as it is sometimes made out to be. The difference in the amount of heat reflected off the shiny side as compared to that of the dull side is insignificant.

More important is the fact that aluminum foil is nonporous. Since it *totally* prevents the escape of moisture and steam during cooking, food heated in foil not only cooks quickly, but comes out exceptionally moist. However, because it is nonporous, foil is less effective than parchment paper for cooking meat and fish *en papillote* (see Bag Cookery; Parchment Paper). To a limited degree, aluminum foil also acts as an insulator, slowing the loss of heat from hot foods and the warming of chilled foods.

Because it locks in hot, moist air, aluminum foil actually steams food, which explains why fresh vegetables cooked in foil packets are tender and full of natural juices. On the other hand, potatoes baked in foil are not so much "baked" as they are "steamed" (an unfortunate process that results in dense, soggy potatoes), and roasts wrapped in foil are not really "roasted." Be aware that too much moisture can toughen roast beef and give roast turkey an unpleasant, mushy texture (see Roasting). So, although foil is great for moist cooking, it is a good idea to keep its limitations in mind. ❧

ASPIC

An aspic is made from concentrated stock, so in that respect it can be considered a reduction sauce (see Sauce Making: Reduction Sauces). The natural proteins contained in bones and connective tissue leach out into the simmering stock during cooking. When the stock is reduced, the protein molecules link together and the sauce thickens. As the temperature decreases when the stock cools, the liquid becomes more viscous and finally gels — a process that eliminates the need for adding powdered gelatin.

A clear, sparkling aspic must be made from *absolutely* fat-free stock, so when you prepare a stock for use as an aspic, don't allow it even to *approach* a boil. Vigorous bubbling will break the fat drops into tiny droplets that stubbornly refuse to separate from the stock when it is chilled. If, however, in spite of all your precautions, your final stock is more cloudy than clear, you will have to clarify it in order to produce an attractive aspic (see Clarifying Stock).

Before refrigerating the reduced stock for an aspic, pour it through a sieve lined with a double thickness of cheesecloth to eliminate any stray particles, then chill it thoroughly. As it cools, the fat drops will join together and

rise to the top. (Extremely fine droplets lose the desire to coalesce, which explains why boiled stock becomes cloudy.)

When the stock is firmly set, remove the layer of cold fat that has risen to the top by scraping it off with a sharp-edged spoon. This is no time for false thrift — it's far better to remove some of the stock while skimming than to leave behind remnants of fat. Then, to pick up every bit of grease, moisten a paper towel with *hot* water and wipe the surface of the stock. At this point, you might want to reheat the stock and repeat the chilling and degreasing procedure in an attempt to avoid clarifying.

Always test the consistency of an aspic before using it, for if it isn't as firm as it should be, your final product will be ruined. Pour ½ cup of stock into a small mold or custard cup and chill for 15 to 45 minutes. (The length of time it takes to set indicates the strength of the gelatin.) Turn out the aspic and break it with a fork. It should be firm but not rubbery, and capable of standing at room temperature for 10 minutes without oozing.

If you find that your aspic is too thin (fish stock seldom contains enough natural gelatin to set firmly), either reduce it further or soften a small amount of powdered gelatin (½ teaspoon for 2 cups aspic) and add it to the aspic. Heat to dissolve the gelatin and chill until firm. Aspic that is rubbery can be adjusted by thinning with additional stock, reheating the mixture, and chilling until firm.

Aspic should be applied to cold food in thin coats, allowing each application to set completely before spooning on the next; otherwise, the final result will have a rippled texture. Spoon on each successive coat or gently brush on with a goose feather — a pastry brush is too harsh.

Cream can be reduced along with the stock to form an aspic cream, or chaud-froid sauce. The classic method of preparing this includes a velouté sauce as a thickener, but the butter used to form the roux often causes the final coating to develop a pitted, granular look. For a lighter sauce with better coating ability, see the recipe for Chaud-Froid Sauce. This omits the velouté and uses powdered gelatin as a thickener.

RECIPE: Chaud-Froid Sauce.

AU GRATIN

A funny thing happened to this term. It grew to mean so many things that the important aspects of the method involved got lost in the shuffle. But one thing is certain — that ubiquitous heap of cooked potatoes and cheese sauce that shows up at every third political banquet is not necessarily potatoes "au gratin."

First of all, the term "gratin" means crust — the browned surface that forms on a dish when it is either baked or heated under a broiler (see Browning — Maillard Reaction). The crust can consist of bread crumbs, melted cheese, white sauce, whipped cream, or coagulated cream, but the ingredients aren't the important part — it's the crust itself that makes a dish a gratin. Contrast is important to this preparation, however, so strive for a crisp, dry crust masking a soft, moist layer underneath.

The pan or dish in which the food is cooked is also called a *gratin*. Usually round or oval in shape, a gratin is always shallow, providing the maximum browning surface for its contents and making it possible for each serving to carry with it a generous portion of the beautiful crust. Because the shape of the dish makes it easy for food to dry out, doing all the cooking in a gratin dish can be tricky. One solution is to lower the oven temperature to 350°F. after baking 10 minutes at a higher setting; then raise the temperature at the end of the cooking time to brown the surface — or place under the broiler. You can also cover the gratin dish with aluminum foil to help retain the moisture, bake it at 400°F., and remove the foil towards the end so a crust will form on top.

RECIPES: Creamed Leeks au Gratin, Flounder Quenelles au Gratin.

B

BAG COOKERY

A few years ago, a new product appeared on supermarket shelves — a plastic bag for cooking. Guaranteed to produce moist and tender meat from bargain cuts, plastic bags would also roast a chicken or turkey without basting and keep your oven clean.

What nobody bothered to point out was that the same results could be achieved by using any heavy pot with a tight-fitting cover on it. Not as much fun maybe, but braising is braising no matter what you do it in (see Braising).

As for roasting in a plastic bag — it can't be done. Food cooked in a closed environment with a small amount of liquid is actually steamed, and though steamed turkey may be moist, it's mushy, not tender. A *real* roasted cut of meat is cooked by dry heat, no other way (see Roasting).

Brown paper shopping bags are used in another form of bag cookery that has its following of enthusiastic fans. Turkey roasted in a shopping bag and brown-bag apple pie have both been popular fads, but I strongly discourage cooking in shopping bags at all. Today, most of these bags are made from recycled paper, and the toxic chemicals used in the paper-making process are apt to contaminate food. In addition, the glue used to hold shopping bags together contains a substance that attracts tiny bugs and weevils, not to mention mice and rats!

Another, more sophisticated, method of cooking in paper utilizes baking parchment (see Parchment Paper). Known as cooking *en papillote,* this technique involves wrapping or sealing food inside parchment paper and placing it in the oven. When the package heats, the water naturally contained in the food converts to steam, and the package puffs up as the steam billows around inside. Meanwhile, the food cooks gently by a combination of steam and the heat of its own internal moisture. Any recipe designed to be baked in a paper grocery bag can be prepared more safely by stapling sheets of parchment paper together to form an enclosure.

RECIPE: Halibut Steaks en Papillote.   ❧

BAKING

Why is it said that you "bake" a cake, but "roast" a turkey — especially since the cake and the turkey are subjected to the same cooking process?

Perhaps, long ago, when huge pieces of meat were roasted over an open fire, the distinction between baking and roasting was clearer than it is today. Roasting took place without a trace of moisture or humidity. Meat juices just dripped into the fire or evaporated immediately into thin air. Baking, on the other hand, took place in a closed chamber where small amounts of moisture turned to steam. That's what produced the wonderful, crispy crust on brick-oven bread.

When gas and electric ovens became available, people started cooking large cuts of meat in them. Strictly speaking, they were baking their meat, since there was a degree of steam present in the closed oven. Today, the terms baking and roasting have come to signify the same process — cooking in an oven, using an uncovered pan. (Casseroles and vegetable dishes that are covered for a portion of their cooking time are actually braising during the time they are covered.)

The term roasting, which is commonly associated with poultry and large cuts of meat, suggests a dry, ambient heat (see Heat). Therefore, meat and poultry should be set on an elevated rack in a roasting pan to promote the circulation of hot air. Basting is usually required during the roasting process to counteract the drying effects ambient heat has on the skin and flesh of most meat. Ham is a remarkable exception, for, although it is often referred to as baked, it may or may not be basted, and is often topped with a glaze.

The term baking is now assigned to desserts and pastries, such as cakes, pies, and cookies, and to vegetable dishes and layered casseroles that are cooked uncovered. While the presence of steam does play a limited role in most baking, any differentiation between the terms roasting and baking is more the result of common usage than any significant technical variance.   ❧

BAKING POWDER/ BAKING SODA

Have you ever wondered why some recipes call for baking soda, some for baking powder, and some for a little of each?

Not so long ago, baking soda (sodium bicarbonate) was the only non-yeast method cooks had of leavening baked goods with carbon dioxide (see Leavening). They knew that in order for the soda to react it had to come in contact with an acid. That was no particular problem at the time, since refrigeration was still rather unreliable and soured milk and cream were almost always on hand. Also, cooks were always eager to find new ways to use up the buttermilk they accumulated from churning butter.

The problem was that acidity levels, too, were not reliable; sometimes things turned out well and sometimes they didn't. What was needed was a way to ensure that the amount of acid present was always sufficient to react with a given amount of baking soda.

Cooks experimented with adding small amounts of acidic ingredients, such as tartaric acid and cream of tartar (potassium acid tartrate). They were on the right track, but the procedure still wasn't dependable. Then baking powder, a pre-measured combination of baking soda and a powdered acid such as cream of tartar, became available to the public. A small amount of cornstarch was added to the mixture to absorb any moisture present in the environment, so that the powder could be kept on the shelf for some time without reacting inside the can and losing its "oomph."

Recipes calling for baking soda invariably include an acid — be it sour cream, sour milk, buttermilk, molasses, vinegar, wine, lemon juice, or cream of tartar. If the proportion of that acid isn't high enough to react with the amount of soda needed to leaven the batter, a recipe will call for a small amount of baking powder, too. If a recipe contains no acid at all, baking powder is used because it already contains the correct amount of acid needed to ensure leavening.

When baking soda meets a liquid (or any form of moisture) in the presence of an acid, carbon dioxide gas is given off. The gas forms tiny bubbles within a batter, much like those in a glass of club soda. When the batter is heated, the gas bubbles expand, leavening your cake or muffins or quick bread. That's why it's important to get baked goods into a preheated oven immediately. If you delay,

most of the carbon dioxide will dissipate into the air; the walls of the bubbles will cave in and the food will be dense and heavy.

To help alleviate this problem, scientists came up with double-acting baking powder. It contains a second acid, sodium aluminum sulfate, which reacts only when heated. So you get two reactions: first, when carbon dioxide is given off because a liquid is added; and second, when the gas is given off because the batter is warmed.

There are three different types of baking powder available — tartrate, phosphate, and double-acting. All contain baking soda (sodium bicarbonate) as a base and some kind of starch, either cornstarch or flour, to absorb moisture. The difference between the types of powders has to do with the acid used. The tartrate type contains cream of tartar and sometimes tartaric acid; the phosphate type contains some form of acid phosphate; the double-acting type, which most cooks use today, contains two acids — a phosphate acid, usually calcium acid phosphate, and sodium aluminum sulfate.

Using a double-acting powder gives you a certain time advantage. You don't have to feel as rushed about getting your batter into the hot oven, since double-acting powder reacts mostly to heat. You can even prepare some batters ahead and refrigerate them for later use, though some leavening is lost in the process. Therefore, keep in mind that batters prepared ahead will never compare in lightness to those that are baked immediately, because the carbon dioxide produced in the first acid reaction will have vanished. ❧

BARDING

Barding, like larding, is a culinary sleight of hand designed to make lean cuts of meat more tasty and moist (see Larding). It involves tying a sheet of fat to the outside of a roast with kitchen string. As a roast heats in the oven, the fat melts, providing continuous basting for the meat.

Roasts with little or no fat of their own benefit most from barding. A beef sirloin tip, beef fillet, veal roast, or pork loin all taste better when cooked under a blanket of melting fat.

Many recipes recommend barding all types of meat with pork fat, or fatback, because it's so easy to work with — it comes in thin, pliable sheets and can be pounded even thinner without crumbling. However, pork fat imparts a distinctly pork flavor, so I use it only when barding pork. (I can't see any point in spending a month's rent for a beef fillet to have it come out smelling and tasting like pork.)

Use fresh, *unfrozen* pork fat to bard lean pork roasts, such as cuts from the loin, or a blade roast. (Pork fat doesn't freeze well and becomes crumbly when defrosted.) Pound it thin between sheets of waxed paper, then tie it around the roast or drape it over the top. Pork fat browns beautifully and turns crackling crisp, lending a festive aspect to any plain pork roast.

To obtain a beefy flavor, bard with beef fat. Ask the butcher for beef fat cut either from the flank or from the outside of a rib-section or loin-section roast. It's not quite as pliable as pork fat, but you can pound it thin between two sheets of waxed paper and secure it to the outside of a roast with a string. Don't make the mistake of asking for suet. Suet is the hard, crumbly beef fat that surrounds the kidneys. It has an unpleasant flavor and is impossible to work with.

You can accumulate your own supply of beef fat by trimming pieces of fat from steak and roasts and storing them in the freezer. Pound the fat scraps, either before or after freezing, to thin them slightly. Beef fat freezes well because it doesn't absorb a great deal of moisture. Consequently, defrosted beef fat can be pounded without crumbling.   ◄૭

BASTING

There's more to basting than taking a swipe at the holiday turkey. Basting improves the flavor, texture, and appearance of many foods, in addition to preventing them from drying out in the oven.

Take fruits and vegetables, for instance. If you cut up potatoes, carrots, or onions and scatter them around a roast, they will be far more flavorful and develop crisp outer skins if you brush them with some of the meat's juices as they cook. Winter squash, cut in half and baked, tastes out of this world when the exposed flesh is basted with a mixture of melted butter and maple syrup. Baked potatoes develop exceptionally crisp skins if basted occasionally with vegetable oil, and baked apples won't have shriveled skins if brushed with melted butter while baking.

Basting is particularly important in broiling and barbecuing, for, in these two methods, the heat is so intense that food will dry out quickly if not protected by fat or moistened with oil. That's why it's a good idea to rub the surface of meat or vegetables with vegetable oil, melted butter, or rendered fat before cooking, then to continue basting occasionally. (If you've marinated the food, reserve the marinating liquid and baste with this.) However, always remember to baste with care when broiling or barbecuing. If you apply too much fat, it will drip down onto the coals and cause flaming, and too much marinating liquid can put out the fire. If you're broiling in the oven, excess fat is apt to catch on fire, so baste with moderation.

Thick, spoon-on barbecue sauce presents a unique basting dilemma. It's applied to flavor meat and keep it from drying out, but most sauces of this type contain a large amount of sugar and tomato sauce, both of which burn very quickly. It's best to brush on this kind of sauce during the last few minutes of grilling; then, if you want a heavier coating than that provides, you can complete the cooking by brushing on additional sauce and placing the meat in a 400°F. oven for 10 to 15 minutes.

Duckling and goose both possess an abundant layer of fat between the skin and flesh that melts during roasting, continuously bathing the meat in moisture. Hence, the only reason for basting either one is to create crisp, attractive outer skin. Turkey, chicken, and capon, on the other hand, lack this protective layer of fat, so they must be basted often to ensure moist, succulent meat and to produce an attractive appearance.

For a truly outstanding chicken or turkey, begin your ministrations by rubbing the entire surface of the skin with vegetable oil. If you want exceptionally crisp skin, continue brushing with oil every 45 minutes until the roast is done. You can also make a broth by cooking the neck and giblets in enough water to cover, then baste with that. The skin won't be as crisp, but the meat will certainly be moist.

The absolute pinnacle of perfection is attained by basting the bird with melted butter. Brushed on during the last 2½ hours of cooking, melted butter creates a deep golden skin with a crispy texture, and contributes a delicate buttery taste to the flesh. Just before bringing the roast to the table, brush on a final coat, and your golden bird will shimmer in the candlelight.

I haven't said anything about self-basting turkeys because, frankly, I don't think much of them. Glowing declarations on the label that claim the meat is "butter basted" or "deep basted" don't tell you that the basting liquid (which is, by the way, mostly oversalted broth) is injected directly into the flesh. This procedure can disturb the meat fibers and discolor the breast meat. In fact, when you cut into the breast of a self-basting turkey, you'll frequently find that the fillet has separated from the remainder of the breast, and that traces of a dark, frothy substance outline the area of separation. That's the area where the basting broth collects during roasting. As a self-basting turkey cooks, the broth bubbles around the meat fibers. Some evaporates through the skin, and the rest runs out when you carve, giving the impression of great juiciness. However, all that bubbling broth and steam only produce a mushy-textured turkey.

Basting can be done with a spoon, brush, or bulb baster. The object is to supply moisture to the surface of food, so it makes little difference how you go about it. A bulb baster works well with large quantities of basting liquid, but it's a devil to clean; a brush does a good job with limited quantities of fluid, such as melted butter, because a brush will hold the liquid and apply it in a thin coat. Incidentally, when you're purchasing culinary brushes, consider those with dark colored bristles; all brushes shed to some extent, and dark stragglers will show up more clearly then light ones, allowing you to find and remove them more easily.　　　　 ◣

BATTER COATING

Frying food with a batter coating can be a big disappointment. The coating frequently parts company with the food and floats around in the fat, or else the final product turns soggy in seconds and lies on your plate like a limp dishcloth.

The surface of food that is going to be batter-coated must be absolutely dry. If it's not, the coating will fall off as soon as the food hits the hot fat. It's to your advantage not only to pat food dry with paper towels, but also to dredge it in a mixture of flour and cornstarch, even if the recipe doesn't say so. The layer of flour and cornstarch forms a moisture barrier, absorbing drops of moisture that may be released from the food when it's heated.

Batter recipes vary widely in the ingredients they call for and the consistency they produce. Thin batters fry up crispier than thick batters, but they don't adhere to food as well as thick batters, so they're apt to break apart in frying.

Batters consist of dry ingredients, liquid ingredients, and an egg or two. Cornstarch promotes crispiness, so a recipe calling for equal proportions of flour and cornstarch will be crispier than an all-flour recipe. Water in the batter produces a lighter crust than milk, and a separated egg, with the beaten white folded in, produces a puffier coating than a whole egg.

Carbon dioxide is often added in one form or another to encourage puffiness. Yeast, beer, baking powder, and baking soda all produce light, crispy coatings. In fact, you can substitute club soda, which is carbonated water, in any batter recipe that calls for tap water, and you'll achieve a crunchier texture.

Batter should be beaten only until blended and allowed to sit at room temperature for 1 hour. Any lumps will break down as the batter rests. During that time, the starch molecules will swell and absorb as much liquid as possible (see Starch Molecules). This gives the batter cohesiveness — it will coat food more completely and be less apt to fall apart during frying.

Since all foods contain moisture, some to a much greater degree than others, a certain amount of sogginess is inevitable. Fish, for example, is an exceptionally moist food. You can dry it with towels, dust it with flour, and coat it with the most fantastic batter known to man, but the inner moisture will still affect the coating. As the fish fries, the coating crisps up, protecting the delicate flesh and locking in the succulent flavor. It also locks in the inner moisture, which turns to steam and eventually makes the coating soggy. The only solution is to serve batter-coated fried fish immediately. Other batter-fried foods like onion rings, vegetable fritters, chicken, and pork, which don't contain excessive moisture, will stay crisp longer.

RECIPES: Batter-Fried Cauliflower, Batter-Fried Nuggets of Cod.

BEANS (Dried)

Many recipes for dried beans instruct you to soak them in water for 8 to 10 hours or overnight before cooking. Others suggest a quick-soak, or simmering step, to soften the beans. The question is, which method should you use?

The reason for soaking beans is to rehydrate them, so they will readily absorb the flavorful liquid in which they eventually are cooked. Because whole dried beans, as opposed to split peas, for example, are covered by an impermeable skin, liquid can enter only through the hilum — the tiny hole where a small stem once attached the bean to the inside of its pod. Consequently, softening beans is a lengthy process.

Beans that are softened slowly will be uniformly soft; this enables them to absorb evenly the flavorful cooking liquid. Rushing the soaking step, however, results in beans of irregular texture and flavor. This could be important if you're responsible for upholding the reputation of great-grandmother's baked bean recipe, but it may not matter at all with some other preparations. Quick-soak beans can be added to soups and most casseroles without any significant change in the final dishes. (Directions for preparing beans by the quick-soak method appear in the recipe for *Baked Beans with Bacon* under step 1; directions for soaking beans overnight appear in the recipe for *White Beans Baked with Fruit* under step 1.)

People often avoid cooking with beans because of experiences with intestinal discomfort. In fact, the latest word on dried beans is that they contain a high level of toxins that can cause stomach cramps, nausea, and diarrhea. The high temperature of boiling water destroys these toxins, so it's possible to eliminate intestinal upset by gently boiling dried beans for 10 minutes after the soak step. (Place them over moderate heat and boil gently; vigorous boiling tears the skin on beans.)

Another method of civilizing beans is to discard both the soaking water and the water in which they were simmered. The loss of flavor and nutritional elements is very slight, and the fact that you've eaten beans won't come back to haunt you a few hours later.

RECIPES: Baked Beans with Bacon, Mexican Pinto Bean Casserole, White Beans Baked with Fruit.

BEATING

Beating is probably best defined as a vigorous version of stirring. It is done in order to blend ingredients, incorporate air, and distribute heat.

If the directions for making a cake say to "cream butter and sugar," you mix the two together with rapid movements of a sturdy spoon or with an electric mixer at fairly high speed. In the process, you're not only combining ingredients, but trapping air bubbles as well.

Beating, for the purpose of incorporating air, is referred to as "whipping" or "whisking." The latter term is no doubt employed in the hopes of encouraging the cook to use a wire whisk, for numerous wire loops are far more efficient at trapping air than are rotary-type hand beaters or conventional mixers.

Distributing heat by beating rapidly is the procedure you rely on when you want to warm a mixture gradually, prevent curdling, or set an egg-based mixture by slightly coagulating it. In making the filling for *Lemon Meringue Pie,* for example, a sizeable portion of hot mixture is beaten quickly into egg yolks. Whisking, or vigorous beating, distributes the heat so that curdling won't take place. At the same time, gentle heat warms the egg yolks, coagulating them slightly and causing them to thicken the pie filling.

When preparing *Italian Meringue,* you beat hot sugar syrup into the egg whites. The object is to distribute the heat quickly and evenly in order to coagulate the whites to the slightest possible degree — a technique that sets the whites, enabling them to form a particularly stable meringue.

Beating by hand is best done with a wooden spoon, not so much to avoid any chemical reaction that might take place, but because wood is resilient and easier on your bowls and ingredients; it also eliminates the unpleasant noise that accompanies beating with a metal spoon.

Beating is most comfortably done by holding the bowl at a 45° angle, wrapping your arm around it, and supporting it with your body. Use wide, circular, up-and-over motions to bring the mixture from the bottom of the bowl to the surface. Beat only as long as your recipe specifies — overbeating agitates gluten, which toughens delicate baked goods (see Gluten).

When incorporating air is the object, beat with a wire whisk, which draws in air bubbles each time it breaks the surface of the mixture. Use one that fits comfortably in your hand or that can be attached to an electric mixer.

If you're beating by hand and both hands are busy (as in making mayonnaise, for instance), fold a damp kitchen towel into quarters to form a skid-proof mat for your bowl, which, when set on top, won't roam around the counter as you beat.

For other methods of combining ingredients see entries for Creaming, Folding, Stirring, and Whipping.

RECIPES: Italian Meringue, Lemon Meringue Pie.

BEURRE MANIÉ

Kneaded butter, or beurre manié, is a paste, consisting of butter and raw flour, used to thicken stews and soups. It's also excellent first aid for sauces that come out thinner than you had expected.

To make a beurre manié, allow some butter, say 3 or 4 tablespoons, to come to room temperature. When it's soft and pliable, but not yet oily (no warmer than 60°F.), measure the same amount of flour onto a large plate or flat work surface. Work the flour and softened butter together into a smooth paste, using your fingertips or a fork.

Drop the paste by lima-bean-size bits into a *boiling* sauce and whisk vigorously after each addition, because the heat will immediately open up the starch particles. The particles will absorb liquid and the sauce will gradually get thicker. Cook only until the sauce thickens and returns to the boil. Always add as little of a beurre manié as possible to achieve the desired consistency — too much will affect the flavor.

If the paste is smooth, a beurre manié works like a charm, thickening the sauce without a single lump. There are, however, two disadvantages to using a butter-flour paste. A raw flour taste is discernible in all but the most robust sauces. Pot roast, stew, and hearty soups can handle a beurre manié, because they contain wine or some other flavor element strong enough to compete with the taste of uncooked flour. Don't use it for thickening anything more delicately flavored than these dishes unless you absolutely have no choice. Furthermore, a sauce thickened with uncooked flour will thin out if allowed to boil too long, or even if simmered for any length of time. It's better to use cooked flour (see Roux) whenever you need a thickener that will hold up well.

You can easily freeze beurre manié to keep on hand for thickening emergencies. Shape the paste into teaspoon-size balls and place on a flat pan in a single layer. When frozen, transfer to a plastic bag and close securely. Add only one frozen ball at a time to a *boiling* sauce, and whisk until completely dissolved before adding another.

RECIPE: Savory Pot Roast.   ⋖⋗

BISCUITS

The secrets of creating tender, flaky biscuits are the same as those behind tender, flaky pie crusts — lots of butter or shortening

cut into the flour, a small amount of liquid to bind the dough together, and a minimum of handling. The only difference is that biscuits are made using a chemical leavener, so a few light strokes of kneading help them stand up straight and tall (under-kneaded biscuits develop bulging sides).

All-purpose flour makes an excellent biscuit, for it contains just the right amount of gluten-producing proteins to yield flaky layers and straight sides (see Flour). However, if you tend to be heavy-handed, or you've come out with tough biscuits in the past, try substituting ¼ cup of cake flour for the all-purpose flour in your recipe. That will lower the overall gluten content of your dough and compensate for possible overhandling.

Sift the dry ingredients into a bowl and combine thoroughly by blending with a wire whisk or fork. Add chilled butter or other fat and cut it in using one knife. This single-knife method is a bit unusual; most recipes direct you to use either two knives or a pastry cutter, but I've found that you can work much more quickly by holding the bowl at an angle, turning it frequently, and cutting the butter into smaller and smaller pieces with a knife held in the other hand (see illustration). In fact, I do the entire biscuit and pie crust procedure using one knife.

Continue cutting in the fat as you would for pie crust (see Pie Crust; Cutting-In). When the mixture resembles tiny peas, gradually add the liquid, blending in with light cutting motions of the knife. Add only enough liquid to form a soft, workable dough. When it begins to hold together, gather it into a ball with your fingertips and swipe the sides of the bowl to pick up the remaining pieces of dough.

As soon as the liquid moistens the dry ingredients, work quickly and lightly. You don't want the carbon dioxide in the leavener to dissipate into the air, nor do you want to agitate the gluten by excessive manipulation and the heat from your hands.

Turn the dough out onto a lightly floured board and knead with 20 to 25 strokes. This activates the gluten and gives the fat a final

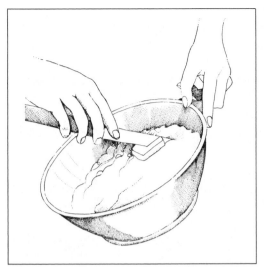

The single-knife method of cutting fat into dry ingredients allows greater control over the mixture's consistency and prevents over-softening of the fat.

blending. The dough should feel like fresh clay — moist and pliable, but not sticky.

Press the dough lightly into a flat circle. Roll with a rolling pin to smooth the top if you want to, but it's not necessary. A rough, slightly irregular texture on the top is very attractive. The traditional thickness for the dough is ½ inch. Biscuits will nearly double their height as they bake, so pat or roll your dough accordingly. If you want taller biscuits, cut them from thicker dough, but anything over ¾ inch doesn't bake up as light and flaky.

Cut out any size rounds you like, dipping the cutter into flour after each biscuit. Use a firm downward pressing motion and do not twist the cutter or move it from side to side, for that produces lopsided biscuits. If the cut is incomplete, remove the unwanted dough with a knife.

Place the biscuits on an ungreased baking sheet. (Biscuits and cookies bake more efficiently on a pan without sides.) If you prefer biscuits with soft sides, arrange them so that the sides touch; for biscuits with browned-crusty sides, place them 1½ inches apart. Brush the tops with a beaten egg or milk to produce a deep, rich color.

As the biscuits bake, the tiny bits of fat inside melt and are absorbed by the flour. The liquid turns to steam and fills the space once occupied by the fat. The steam expands and, with the help of the carbon dioxide, creates light, flaky layers. When the steam and carbon dioxide are completely dissipated, the biscuits are cooked.

RECIPES: Buttermilk Biscuits, Ham Biscuits, Shortcake Biscuits.

BLANCHING

Blanching and parboiling are similar techniques involving a short cooking period in boiling water. The essential difference is that parboiling is done to precook food and blanching is not (see Parboiling).

Blanching enables you to remove excess salt from bacon and ham, draw fat from sausage and marrow, and whiten variety meats, such as sweetbreads. A quick dip in boiling water also extracts strong flavors from vegetables such as cauliflower and turnips, and makes it possible for you to remove the skin from fruit and vegetables without marring the surface of the flesh.

The length of time needed to facilitate peeling varies with ripeness. A less-than-ripe tomato might require blanching for 30 to 45 seconds; a tomato at its peak, only a brief plunge. In fact, if you have a large batch of ripe tomatoes to peel, here's a speedy way to do it: Place 6 or 8 tomatoes in the kitchen sink, stem-end down, and pour a kettle full of boiling water over them, allowing the water to run down the drain. Peel immediately.

Blanching is also a necessary step in preparing most vegetables for the freezer because it halts potentially destructive enzyme activity. Enzymes are a special group of proteins that provoke chemical reactions in food. Some of these reactions are desirable, others are not.

If you freeze vegetables without deactivating the enzymes, the vegetables will slowly but surely deteriorate. Temperatures below zero slow down the action of many enzymes, but vegetables contain a particularly stubborn bunch that continue to work even when food is frozen. Blanching vegetables before freezing shocks enzymes into a state of "suspended animation"; when the vegetables thaw, however, enzyme activity resumes, so it's a good idea to cook frozen vegetables before they defrost.

Time is of the essence when it comes to blanching vegetables for freezing. If you don't blanch them long enough, the enzymes will remain active; if you blanch them too long, you'll soften the flesh. The ideal situation is to blanch only a small amount at a time, so that the water never leaves the boil. That way, you can begin timing as soon as the food hits the water. (If you find it necessary to add a large quantity and the boiling stops, wait until the water returns to the boil before you begin to time the blanching period.)

Freezing instructions usually tell you to submerge blanched vegetables immediately in a pan of ice water and leave them there for a matching period of time. For instance, green beans blanched for 2 minutes get 2 minutes in the ice-water bath. The purpose of this step is to eliminate residual heat so the vegetables won't continue to cook and turn soft. An ice-water dunk also sets their color nicely. Don't hesitate to reuse the blanching water and ice water five or six times.   ◅৶

BOILING AND SIMMERING

The two culinary terms "boiling" and "simmering" are commonly misunderstood, and, to compound the problem, recipes often recommend that a mixture be brought to a boil, without specifically stating what *kind* of boil. Consequently, cooks can be left unsure of just how to proceed.

In discussing the points that differentiate simmering and the various stages of boiling, it is helpful to visualize what happens to a pot of water placed over heat. When the burner is turned on, water molecules at the bottom of the pot, nearest the heat source, become warm and begin to rise. This sets up a pattern of circulation in which rising hot molecules nudge aside cold molecules, which fall to the bottom of the pot. When they in turn become hot enough to rise, they displace other molecules that have since become cool, and the result is a continuous movement of circulating water molecules. It is the circulation of hot molecules that makes this method of heating similar to the one that takes place inside a hot oven; this explains why boiling and simmering are considered types of convection cooking (see Heat: Convection).

As the temperature of the burner increases, the water molecules heat and rise at a faster rate, causing the water to exhibit various degrees of movement. The first stage, which is characterized by a slight shiver, occurs between 180° and 190°F. and is perfect for poaching. At the second stage, around 190°F., a limited number of bubbles begin to break the surface. Then, between 195° and 200°F., a sizeable number of air bubbles gently break the surface and the water is said to be simmering. It should be noted, however, that this third stage might also be referred to as a slow boil or a gentle bubble, a point that frequently leads to confusion in interpreting recipes.

When a recipe directs you to bring something to a boil, and no further specifications such as "moderate" or "vigorous" are given, it is intended that you heat the mixture until bubbles *begin* to appear in sizeable numbers. Generally, when the term "boiling" stands unmodified, it indicates gentle bubbling.

A "moderate" or medium boil occurs when water is heated to around 205°F. At this stage, the surface of the water is moderately turbulent, and the conversion of water to a gas is beginning to be evident as vapor rises slowly from the surface. With further heating, the water begins to boil rapidly, the surface becomes extremely turbulent, and generous quantities of steam are given off. This stage is considered a "full" boil and is commonly described as "boiling vigorously."

For the most part, cooking is done in simmering or slowly boiling water. Notable exceptions are green, leafy vegetables, which do best at a moderate boil, and pasta, which some recipes advise cooking at a vigorous boil. However, the turbulence of the water breaks certain types of pasta apart, so a moderate boil is nearly always a better approach.

Water boils vigorously at 212°F. at sea level, and no amount of additional heat can make water hotter than that under normal conditions. This is referred to as the boiling point; however, it is important to keep in mind that this temperature applies only to water (or to mixtures high in water). It should not automatically be assumed that other mixtures, especially those that are low in water, have a boiling point of 212°F.

Atmospheric pressure can raise or lower the boiling point of water. This becomes particularly important when you're cooking at high altitudes, which can lower the boiling point so dramatically that tea made from vigorously boiling water feels only mildly hot to the lips. On the other hand, the addition of salt or sugar raises the boiling point of water, as does the use of a pressure cooker. In fact, the temperature of water boiled in a pressure cooker can reach as high as 250°F. ◄₂

the fresh parsley in a pouch with the dried herbs, or should you toss it in separately?

Dried herbs take longer to impart their flavor fully, so they should be added earlier in the simmering period than fresh herbs. Fresh herbs lose their flavor if simmered as long as dried herbs, and some develop an unpleasant flavor if overcooked. Therefore, combining fresh and dried herbs in the same bouquet isn't a good idea. Instead, crush the dried bay leaf and combine it with the dried thyme in the center of a 4-inch square of double-thickness cheesecloth. Bring the sides of the cloth up together, tie securely with a piece of string, and drop the bundle into the simmering liquid at the start of the cooking period. About 45 minutes before the end of the cooking time, tie 2 or 3 sprigs of fresh parsley together and add to the simmering liquid, or just toss them in separately if you don't mind fishing them out later.

When a recipe calls for a bouquet garni, use 1 medium-size bay leaf, ½ teaspoon dried thyme, and 2 or 3 sprigs of fresh parsley. Use finely woven cheesecloth — not muslin or percale or some other scrap of cloth you might have lying around. Only cheesecloth has pores large enough to let all the flavor out, but not so large as to allows bits of herb to escape. Never, *never* use a first-aid gauze bandage. I came across this unsettling "hint" in a magazine one day. Yes, they're sterile, but the antiseptic smell belongs in a hospital, not in food. ◄₂

BOUQUET GARNI

A bouquet garni is a bunch of herbs, tied up with a string or enclosed in a cloth bag. It is used to add flavor to a simmering concoction like soup or stew. Recipes sometimes specify what the bouquet should contain. If not, it's taken for granted that you'll add parsley, bay leaves, and thyme.

In most kitchens, this presents a dilemma. Since fresh parsley is readily available and fresh bay leaves and thyme are not, do you tie

BRAISING

Braising doesn't seem to be a very popular method of cooking in the United States. Maybe that's because we're always in such a hurry, and good braising can't be rushed.

In much of cooking the object is to preserve individual tastes and textures, but the purpose of braising is exactly the opposite. What you're after in a successful braise is a concentrated *blend* of flavors. This blend occurs because meat or fish is simmered with chopped vegetables and a limited amount of liquid. During cooking, the vegetables exchange their flavors with the meat or fish, which then gives flavor to the liquid, which in turn flavors the vegetables. On it goes — each component of a braise exchanges flavors with the other ingredients. The result is a moist, flavorful dish. To serve, spoon the cooked vegetables and whatever broth remains over the meat, or purée the vegetables and broth to form a smooth sauce.

The secrets of ensuring a successful blend of flavors when braising are: chopping the vegetables finely and precooking them a bit, so they'll be done at the same time as the meat or fish; using a small amount of liquid, so the components are braised rather than boiled; and cooking slowly for a long period of time in a tightly closed pot, just large enough to accommodate the contents.

The size of the pot is crucial when you braise on top of the stove, where the heat source is at the bottom of the pot. If you keep the heat down as low as you should to provide slow, gentle simmering, and the pot is a lot larger than the contents, the air inside the pot will never get warm enough to cook the meat that extends above the liquid. Consequently, the meat sitting in the liquid will cook faster than the rest. When the contents fit snugly in the pot, more even cooking can take place.

If you want to experiment with this technique, and you don't have exactly the right size pot, plan to braise in the oven. There, the ambient heat will warm the air above the liquid, cooking the entire piece of meat at the same rate of speed.

Some cooks have an additional reason for using a compact pot — both in the oven and on top of the stove. They feel that excess air space inside the pan causes the braising liquid to condense on the inside of the lid and drip back onto the meat, resulting in meat that is more steamed than braised.

On the other hand, there are cooks who go out of their way to encourage a certain degree of condensation by using a special pot called a *doufeu*. Intentionally designed for braising, this peculiar-looking pot has a deeply recessed cover in which ice cubes are placed, thus cooling the lid and causing condensation on the underside. When drops form, they fall back onto the meat in a sort of self-basting process.

No matter what your preference, braising is best accomplished in a hot, moist environment. If a small amount of liquid is used, and the heat is kept low enough so that cooking takes place slowly and gently, you're not going to get great billows of steam inside the pot. In any case, a few drops of condensation aren't going to make much difference one way or the other. You can expect to be successful if you use a reasonably sized pot with a tight-fitting lid.

If you're braising meat, you might want to brown it, marinate it, or provide it with extra fat by larding or barding it first (see Larding; Barding). The best pieces of meat to use for braising are the lean, working-muscle cuts like those from the rump and shoulder. They contain very little fat, so some recipes suggest larding or barding them for extra flavor. However, that's an unnecessary embellishment, and one you might be better off skipping if you're at all cholesterol-conscious — the braising process does a fine job of producing flavorful, moist meat without the use of excess fat.

Marinating meat contributes an additional element of flavor, but unless it's a basic characteristic of the dish, as in sauerbraten, for example, it, too, isn't really necessary. Vegetables, herbs, and an assertive liquid provide plenty of flavor, and moist, slow cooking tenderizes the meat.

Browning is a step that some cooks omit, but I consider it essential. I always coat the meat with flour, then brown it in a small amount of fat — half butter, half vegetable oil. Browning the meat seals in the juices, heightens the flavor, and intensifies the color. Also, the browned flour disperses through the braising liquid and thickens it slightly, improving the consistency of the final sauce without the addition of another thickener.

Be careful not to overbrown (beef and lamb can be seared a deep brown; pork and veal should turn only light brown) and avoid any trace of black — that's burning, not browning, and it imparts a harsh, unpleasant flavor to the braising liquid.

Vegetables are important to the success of a braise, and should be chosen to complement the meat or fish with which they will share their flavors. Mushrooms, carrots, celery, spinach, and lettuce are all versatile and can be cooked with the most delicate fish or veal. Onions, green peppers, tomatoes, garlic, sorrel, and romaine are more assertive and go well with full-bodied fish, such as tuna or sword, and pork or beef roasts. Vegetables not only contribute flavor and moisture, but also serve as a protective bed on which to place delicate meat or fish, shielding it from direct heat when you braise on top of the stove.

In addition to meat and fish, vegetables themselves benefit from being braised. The object is still a transfer, or merging, of flavors, but there are only two components to this braise — vegetables and liquid. Braised endive is probably the most well-known vegetable prepared in this fashion, but carrots, onions, leeks, green and red peppers, and Brussels sprouts are also possibilities.

RECIPES: Braised Endive with Grapefruit Sauce, Braised Veal Shanks, Cabbage Braised in Apple Juice, Citrus-Braised Pork Chops, Pork Chops Braised in Beer.   ❧

BREAD BAKING
Yeast Breads

The process that occurs as yeast bread bakes is quite similar to what takes place during the baking of a cake (see Cake Baking). Air pockets, created by carbon dioxide, are surrounded by a weblike network of strands made up of starch and gluten. As the dough heats, the carbon dioxide produced during fermentation expands the air pockets, giving the bread a final, dramatic rise called "oven spring." Moisture in the dough turns to steam, which acts as an additional leavener as it rises to the surface of the loaf. There the steam evaporates, as does alcohol, another by-product of fermentation that gives baking bread its unparalleled aroma.

When the temperature inside the bread approaches 120°F. the yeast cells start to die. By the time the temperature increases to 140°F., all the yeast cells are destroyed and crust formation begins (see Crust Formation). The flour starch gelatinizes at around 150°F. and the weblike structure becomes firm. The crust begins to turn brown as more and more moisture evaporates (see Browning). Finally, the crust is crisp and the loaf sounds hollow when tapped, which means the bread is done.

In addition to flour, yeast, and liquid, yeast bread often, but not always, contains salt, sugar, eggs, shortening, and various flavorings. Salt flavors bread and regulates the growth of yeast, slowing down its action to prevent bread from developing a large-pored texture. Sugar is food for yeast to convert into carbon dioxide. A limited amount contributes to a light, airy loaf, but excessive sugar puts yeast to sleep and is apt to produce a heavy, dense loaf (see Yeast). Eggs contain fat and are high in protein; the protein helps strengthen the bread's weblike structure and the fat lubricates the strands of gluten, increasing their ability to stretch. Bread made with eggs and shortening has a smoother crust and a more cakelike crumb, and stays fresh longer than other bread.

The most common error that occurs in making yeast bread is the incorporation of too much flour. Since the ratio of liquid to flour determines the consistency of the final loaf, a high moisture level produces a light, airy loaf, and a low moisture content results in a dense, heavy one.

To make matters more difficult, it's nearly impossible to state accurately how much liquid a given amount of flour will absorb. This uncertainty arises because flour is capable of absorbing significant amounts of moisture from the air (which explains why flour should always be stored in an airtight container). On a humid day, flour may have already absorbed a considerable amount of atmospheric moisture and therefore be unable to take in the expected quantity of liquid. Consequently, it is often necessary to use more flour in creating a nonsticky dough on a humid or rainy day. On the other hand, during the cold, dry days of winter, flour releases its moisture into the atmosphere and becomes extremely receptive to liquid ingredients. In that case, less flour is needed to balance the liquid ingredients and form a well-textured dough. This wide fluctuation in moisture content is the reason why flour proportions in yeast bread recipes are frequently given in approximate amounts.

The best way to deal with the varying moisture level of flour is to always add less flour to yeast dough than the recipe calls for. One cup less than the total amount required is a good rule of thumb. Instead of blending it in, set that last cup aside. Then sprinkle the reserved flour over the dough as you knead, but *only* if the dough is sticky and willing to absorb it. Once the dough becomes smooth and feels resilient under your hands, don't force it to accept additional flour.

RECIPES: American-Style Italian Bread, Country-Style Italian Bread, Hawaiian Sweet Bread, Maple Whole Wheat Bread, One-Hour French Bread, Sour Caraway Rye, Sourdough French Bread.

Quick Breads

Quick breads, which are leavened by baking soda or baking powder, are made in much the same way as muffins (see Muffins). Dry ingredients are blended thoroughly to disperse the leavening agent, then the combined liquid ingredients are added.

Since quick-bread batter is a bit more cumbersome than muffin batter, you'll probably want to use an electric mixer, but don't turn your mixer on and walk away — overbeating causes a coarse texture and a tough consistency. Mix only as much as necessary to blend the liquid and dry ingredients.

It's perfectly acceptable for a loaf of quick bread to develop a crack down the middle. However, if your favorite recipe cracks more than you want it to, it probably means that it contains too much flour; reduce the amount by 2 tablespoons the next time you make it. Covering the loaf with aluminum foil during the last 15 minutes of baking also helps reduce cracking by preventing some of the moisture from evaporating.

To produce a loaf with a nicely rounded top — one that doesn't hump up — distribute the batter evenly in the pan by drawing the blade of a knife through the batter from one corner of the pan to the opposite corner. Then place in a preheated oven and bake at a moderate temperature (around 350°F.).

If the bread still humps up excessively, it may be that the oven temperature needs to be lowered 25°. Since quick bread cooks by conduction, the outside of the batter heats first (see Heat: Conduction), and it may even heat to the point where the structure around the perimeter of the bread begins to set. Then, when the center of the batter heats, it has no place to expand but upward, thus causing a misshapen loaf. Lowering the temperature slightly gives conductive heat time to reach the center before the perimeter sets.

Quick-bread batter is not as susceptible as yeast bread dough to variations in flour moisture; the quantities of flour involved are smaller, and so the amount of flour incorporated is less. You may still want to be alert to the possibility that during the summer months quick-bread batter might turn out a little on the wet side, but that's no cause for alarm — any excess liquid not absorbed by the flour will simply evaporate as steam. During the winter, when flour is drier, and therefore more absorbent, the batter will have a thicker consistency.

RECIPES: Gingered Pear Bread, Orange Quick Bread, Sourdough Banana Bread. ❦

BREAD CRUMBS

Carefully written recipes specify certain types of bread crumbs for different textural effects. There are fresh bread crumbs (sometimes referred to as soft bread crumbs), dry bread crumbs, buttered or browned bread crumbs, and seasoned bread crumbs.

Fresh bread crumbs are the soft, somewhat fluffy crumbs of *undried* fresh bread — minus the crust. These are a little tricky to make, because undried bread tends to get gummy when whirled in a blender or food processor. The secret to maintaining a light texture is to process only small amounts at a time, pulsing briefly.

Use nonsweet, French-style bread. Trim away the crusts and tear the bread into large chunks. If it's especially fresh, or has a lot of spring to it, let the bread chunks air dry until they feel less moist; or preheat the oven to 350°F., slide them in on a cookie sheet, and turn the oven off. They will lose their excess moisture in 5 to 10 minutes. Then place 3 or 4 chunks of bread in the blender or processor, pulse briefly five or six times, empty out the container, and start again. Don't expect fresh bread crumbs to be as fine as dry bread crumbs; in fact, they resemble shredded bread bits more than they do crumbs.

Fresh bread crumbs are especially good for sprinkling on fresh vegetables, topping casseroles, and lending flavor to fillings and stuffings. However, because they're extremely absorbent, they soak up a great deal of fat and aren't the best choice for coating foods that are going to be fried.

Dry bread crumbs are best for this purpose. Use fresh, nonsweet French-style bread. (Stale bread makes stale-tasting crumbs, so use it for something else.) Break the fresh bread, crusts and all, into small pieces and place in a 350°F. oven for 15 to 20 minutes or until they are completely dry but not toasted. Toasted crumbs, which taste different from dried crumbs, make a delicious topping for casseroles or garnish for fried fish.

Buttered crumbs are simply bread crumbs either coated with melted butter or browned lightly with butter in a frying pan. Using your own dry crumbs or unseasoned crumbs from a package, melt 3 tablespoons of butter for every ½ cup of bread crumbs and toss together with a fork until the crumbs are well coated. Use as is, or cook over medium heat until they turn light brown. Buttered crumbs are often sprinkled over freshly cooked vegetables, and they do a great job of forming a crust on top of a casserole. Since they've already absorbed a good deal of butter, they won't absorb liquid from the casserole, and your crumb crust won't be soggy on the underside.

Seasoned bread crumbs are typically used to coat meat or chicken for frying. They're readily available in packages and cans, but a commercially prepared product can't begin to compete with the flavor of your own freshly made seasoned crumbs. Start with dry crumbs, and for every cup add ⅓ cup grated Parmesan cheese, 1½ teaspoons dried basil, 1 teaspoon dried oregano, ½ teaspoon ground sage, and ½ teaspoon dried rosemary (the latter ground in a mortar and pestle before measuring). Blend thoroughly, tossing with a fork.

The type of bread you use for making crumbs influences the flavor and texture of the completed dish. The best fresh crumbs are made from French-style bread — the kind made without milk or sugar — because it produces a light, fresh crumb. For dry crumbs, any white bread that hasn't gone stale will suffice. If you're adventurous, you might like to include some whole wheat or rye bread when making crumbs to top a casserole — either one will contribute an interesting flavor to the crust.

All types of bread crumbs can be frozen in plastic containers or freezer bags for up to 2 months, or stored in the refrigerator for 7 to 10 days. Longer storage periods result in a stale flavor. Dry bread crumbs, from which all traces of moisture have been removed, may be stored at room temperature. (Since moisture encourages mold and bacteria to grow, be sure to thoroughly dry crumbs that will be kept at room temperature.)   ◄ᶾ

BREADING

Breading, like batter, gives food an interesting combination of textures — a crispy outside crust with a moist, succulent interior. A coating of bread crumbs also protects tender meat and fish from intense heat that would toughen them or cause them to dry out. In addition, a crumb coating seals in juices and locks out fat, so fried food remains moist and doesn't become heavy with grease. You can also use other types of crumbs for breading, such as cracker crumbs or crushed cereal.

To apply a bread-crumb coating, begin by dredging the food with flour. This helps seal in moisture that could seep out during frying, causing the breaded crust to fall off; it also provides a surface for beaten egg to cling to, which is generally the next step when coating with crumbs. Dip the flour-covered food into egg blended with a bit of liquid. (Use 1 teaspoon of water for each egg, but don't beat to the point where bubbles form; if you do, the crumbs won't stick when the air bubbles

break.) Then coat the food with bread crumbs, pressing down firmly with your fingertips to encourage the crumbs to adhere.

Shake off any excess crumbs, then place the coated food on a rack set inside a jelly roll pan so the air can circulate under the food and prevent the bottom from becoming soggy. (If you spray the rack with vegetable oil first, the coating won't stick to it.) Refrigerate, uncovered, for 30 minutes (or allow to stand at room temperature for 10 minutes) to give the flour undercoating time to absorb as much moisture as possible. This waiting period also firms up the beaten egg and allows it to dry partially, producing a crispier crust.

Some foods, such as deep-fried cheese, benefit from a double coating of egg and crumbs. Since the cheese is going to melt when plunged into hot fat, a double coating protects it from the heat longer than a single coating, and gives the crust time to firm up and brown before the cheese has a chance to ooze out.

Croquettes, and other preparations that are apt to disintegrate, also do better if given a double coating. First, dredge the food with flour to provide a dry surface. Then, dip it into beaten egg, coat it with crumbs, and refrigerate on a rack for 30 minutes. Dip into beaten egg and coat with crumbs a second time, then chill for another 30 minutes before cooking.   ◄ᶾ

BROILING

Broiling, grilling, and barbecuing all involve cooking with radiant heat, which can come from an electric coil, gas flame, wood, or hot coals (see Heat: Radiant). For the most part, broiling takes place *under* a heat source; grilling and barbecuing, *over* the heat.

One of the most frequent complaints I hear about cooking is the dissatisfaction people experience when broiling steak at home in the oven. Why do steaks cooked inside, under the broiler, taste so inferior to restaurant steaks or steaks cooked outdoors on the grill?

To begin with, home broilers can't even come close to giving off as much heat as a charcoal grill or a restaurant broiling unit. Home broilers go only to 550°F., but professional units can achieve temperatures from 700° to 1,000°F. This extremely high heat sears the meat instantly, forming a firm crust on the surface and contributing to that unique "broiled" flavor. The intense heat of a restaurant broiler also cooks exceptionally fast, which means that there is little time for juices to escape. (It's becoming more and more common for restaurants to install gas or electric briquette grills, so their steaks are actually grilled rather than broiled.)

In addition, meat cooked under a heat source misses out on the flavors contributed by a charcoal or wood fire (such as those created by burning hickory or mesquite) and the charred taste that results when melted fat and meat juices drip down onto a pile of hot coals, causing them to flare. The lower heat level in a home broiler creates a less-than-perfect situation, too — as the meat cooks, it gives off moisture as steam. However, the temperature in the oven isn't hot enough to dispel the steam quickly, so it begins to accumulate inside. Intensely hot, moist air only serves to toughen muscle fibers and give meat a steamed quality. (Leaving the oven door ajar while broiling allows some, but not all, of the steam to escape.)

In spite of these handicaps, it's still possible to produce a tasty piece of meat by cooking it under the broiler in your oven. For the best results, choose meat that's 1 to 2 inches thick and make sure it's a tender cut with generous streaks of marbling (see Marbling). Remove most of the fat, or rub it with lemon juice to prevent excessive flaring. Then make vertical cuts at 1-inch intervals through the remaining fat and connective tissue around the outside edge of the meat. (Unless connective tissue is slashed to make it lie flat, it contracts when exposed to high heat, causing a piece of meat to ripple and cook unevenly.)

Rub both sides of the meat with oil, melted butter, or rendered fat. In fact, you can improve the flavor of a steak immeasurably by trimming off the excess fat, melting it down in a small saucepan, and using it to baste the steak as it cooks. Preheat the broiling unit (but not the pan), then slide the meat under the broiler about 3 to 4 inches away from the coils. Broil the first side until well browned, then turn and brown the second side, basting generously. Use tongs to turn the meat, because a fork will pierce it and allow precious juices to escape.

A 1-inch-thick piece of meat is cooked to the rare point after approximately 2½ to 3 minutes on each side. Since you don't want the surface to dry out before the interior is cooked, any piece of meat thicker than 2 inches should be broiled farther away from the heat. Start the broiling process 3 to 4 inches away from the coils, and, as soon as both sides are thoroughly browned, lower the broiler pan to a rack 5 to 8 inches below the coils. Continue broiling until you reach the desired doneness. This far from the heating coil, a 2½-inch piece of meat will need to cook 6 to 10 minutes on each side before it reaches the rare stage.

Broiling is used in the preparation of other food besides meat. Dishes topped with cheese are often placed under the broiler for melting, cream-sauced and crumb-topped gratin dishes are given a final browning, and sugar-coated desserts are caramelized under the broiler. These finishing touches are best accomplished 5 to 6 inches away from the broiler to avoid subjecting delicate ingredients to excessive heat.

BROTH
See STOCK.

BROWN SAUCE

Brown sauce is something many cooks don't have the time or patience to cope with, and to make matters worse, the whole concept of brown sauce has become muddled and confused.

Put as simply as possible, brown sauce is formed by thickening brown stock with a brown roux (see Stock; Roux). The consistency of the resulting sauce depends on the proportions of roux to stock and the extent to which the sauce is reduced. A properly constructed sauce should be thick enough to coat food, but not so thick as to overwhelm it. Sauce that is too thick can be thinned by adding additional stock; sauce that is too thin can be thickened by reduction or, if absolutely necessary, by the addition of a beurre manié (see Reduction; Beurre Manié).

When you blend brown stock with a brown roux, you create a lightly thickened sauce called Espagnole. If you add an equal portion of brown stock to the Espagnole and simmer it further, reducing the mixture to a fairly thick consistency, the result is a sauce known as *Demi-Glaze.*

Here you come up against one of the enigmas in cooking terminology. Demi-Glaze is so named because it is half the thickness of meat glaze, or *Glace de Viande.* The confusing point is that Demi-Glaze is thickened with starch but Glace de Viande, which is brown stock reduced to a syrup, is thickened by natural gelatin. Glace de Viande, therefore, should not be thought of as a further reduction or derivative of Demi-Glaze; it is a totally separate preparation (see pages 347 and 350).

In classic French cooking, Espagnole is considered the grand, or fundamental, brown sauce. Other brown sauces (called small sauces), such as *Bordelaise, Chasseur, Robert,* and *Demi-Glaze,* are created by adding specific ingredients to an Espagnole. This brings us to another confusing issue. When a recipe

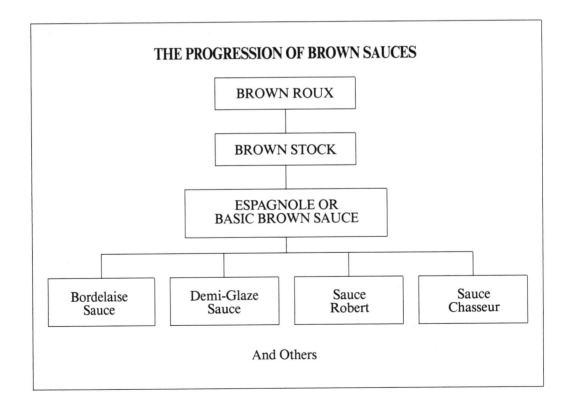

THE PROGRESSION OF BROWN SAUCES

BROWN ROUX

BROWN STOCK

ESPAGNOLE OR
BASIC BROWN SAUCE

| Bordelaise Sauce | Demi-Glaze Sauce | Sauce Robert | Sauce Chasseur |

And Others

calls simply for brown sauce, it leaves you at loose ends — should you use Espagnole or Demi-Glaze? The important thing to remember is that Demi-Glaze is a thicker, richer, more deeply flavored spin-off of Espagnole, so take those factors into consideration when deciding which to use.

To simplify matters, it helps to think of Espagnole as a basic brown sauce, so in this book I refer to it as just that — *Basic Brown Sauce*. It's the sauce I make (and freeze) for developing into other sauces at a later date.

RECIPES: Basic Brown Sauce, Basic Brown Sauce from Soup Mix, Bordelaise Sauce, Dark Brown Stock I, Demi-Glaze, Meat Glaze, Pork Scallops Chasseur, Sauce Chasseur, Sauce Robert.

BROWNING

Enzymatic Browning

There are two types of browning — the kind you try to encourage and the kind you take all sorts of measures to avoid. The latter, called enzymatic browning, is caused by the activity of enzymes, which turns the exposed flesh of certain fruits and vegetables an unappealing brown. Enzymes contained in these fruits and vegetables react with oxygen, setting off a series of chemical changes that produce a brown pigment called melanin. Fruits and vegetables that don't contain these particular enzymes (like melons, strawberries, carrots, and tomatoes) don't turn brown when exposed to the air.

Since enzymes are sensitive to extremes in temperature, you can slow down discoloration by chilling cut fruit and vegetables. You can also prevent unwanted browning by blanching food, since high heat inactivates the trouble-causing enzymes (see Blanching). Blanching, however, isn't always a practical solution — blanched bananas don't sound too appetizing to me — and chilling only slows the enzymes down. What's really needed is a way to keep the melanin from forming for an extended period of time.

One way to stall enzymatic browning is to prevent oxygen from coming in contact with the flesh of susceptible fruits and vegetables. You can do this by submerging them in water, coating them with dressing or sauce, or covering their surfaces with syrup (or anything else that will keep air away).

Since enzymes are not as active in an acidic environment, you can also deal with unwanted enzymatic browning by using an acid. This explains why recipes calling for sliced fruit often suggest that you sprinkle on lemon juice, and why recipes for guacamole require a small amount of lemon juice blended into the mashed avocado. You can also add lemon juice to a bowl of water during the preparation of artichokes (see Acidulated Water). After each artichoke is peeled and trimmed, drop it into the acidulated water; the cut edges won't turn brown and it's much easier than trying to rub every nook and cranny with lemon juice.

Nonenzymatic Browning (Caramelization and the Maillard Reaction)

Nonenzymatic browning is the kind you *want* to cultivate, and it includes two different processes: caramelization and the Maillard reaction. Caramelization occurs when sugar is heated and the water it contains is given off as steam, resulting in a complex chemical reaction. During this reaction, chemical compounds are formed which are brown in color (or even black if the heat is excessive). The substance loses its sugary taste and develops a totally different flavor that we identify as caramel.

You can cause sugar to brown by heating it alone or with water — a technique used when preparing caramel syrup (see Sugar Cooking)

— or when sprinkling sugar over onions during the last few minutes of cooking to give them a golden haze.

Some cookbooks use the term caramelizing to refer to all nonenzymatic browning, such as the coloring that takes place when meat juices coagulate and darken on the bottom of the roasting pan, but that's not entirely accurate. Caramelization is the browning that occurs as a result of the effects of intense heat on sugar and the subsequent evaporation of the water contained in sugar.

The browning that results when sugar and certain amino acids in protein are heated together is caused by the Maillard reaction. Named after the French chemist who, from 1912 to 1918, studied the phenomenon of food browning, this process involves an extremely complex set of chemical changes. Simply stated, when foods containing amino acids (the building blocks of protein) and certain forms of sugar are subjected to dry heat, the proteins and sugar react with each other, causing food to turn brown and to develop a unique taste sometimes referred to as "brown" flavor.

The workings of the Maillard reaction explain, for instance, why beaten egg brushed on pastry causes it to brown. The natural sugars present in the egg combine with egg proteins, which in turn are joined by the protein in flour and any sugar that may be in the pastry. As the pastry heats in the oven, the proteins and sugars interact and create an appealing brown finish.

The degree of browning you can achieve increases with both the temperature level and the amount of each element used. Hence, an egg-white wash will produce less browning than a whole-egg wash, which contains more protein. An egg-yolk wash, containing the most protein of all, will create the darkest browning effects (see Egg Wash), and if you increase the temperature of the oven, your pastry will brown even more.

You've probably used a combination of proteins and sugars to brown food many times without giving it much thought. When you pour cream over sliced potatoes, then slide them under the broiler, or dot an au gratin dish with butter or cheese in order to brown the top, you're supplying the ingredients necessary to encourage the Maillard reaction to take place.

Frying, which is considered a dry-heat method of cooking, is another example of the Maillard reaction at work. French-fried potatoes, doughnuts, and corn fritters all turn brown as a result of natural sugars interacting with proteins in the presence of heat. A loaf of bread will brown as it bakes, even without any glaze being applied, because of the natural sugars and proteins contained in flour. Barbecue sauce, usually quite high in sugar, creates a brown crust when exposed to the heat of the grill. Roasting meat forms a gorgeous brown exterior when its natural sugars and proteins interact with the heat of the oven.

Despite the fact that Maillard browning and caramelization often occur at the same time during cooking, the following features set them apart: caramelization is initiated by dehydration, or the removal of water from sugar. The sugars sucrose, glucose, fructose, and lactose may all be involved; however, proteins need not be present for the chemical reaction to take place. Maillard browning, on the other hand, is caused by the *interaction* of proteins and sugars in the presence of heat, and, although it occurs more rapidly in food with a low moisture content, the chemical reaction is not dependent upon the removal of water.

Sucrose (granulated sugar) is one of the few sugars that will not interact with protein to brown food in a Maillard reaction. Glucose, fructose, and lactose all perform without difficulty. However, this doesn't mean that you can't add granulated sugar to either initiate or increase browning. When the interior temperature of the outer layers of food reaches 320°F., the sucrose begins to break down into its simpler components — glucose and fructose — both of which interact readily with amino acids to cause browning.   ◅

BUTTER

There has been a great deal of talk recently about the use of unsalted versus salted butter, and an increasing number of recipes are now appearing in print with specific instructions to use the "sweet" or unsalted variety. All this publicity has had at least one beneficial effect — unsalted butter is much more readily available now than it used to be, and it even goes on sale occasionally, which was something that never happened years ago. However, the difference in price between the two types of butter is still significant, so it's helpful to realize that you needn't obey every directive recommending unsalted butter.

When cream, a fat-in-water suspension, is mechanically churned to produce butter, the agitation causes fat droplets to coalesce and form clots. Continued agitation produces increasingly larger clots until, finally, the separation of butterfat and liquid is complete. At that point, the liquid byproduct is drained off, and the clumps of fat are washed thoroughly to rinse away excess lactic acid. The result is a water-in-fat suspension, a complete reversal of the original state. Butter consists of tiny droplets of watery liquid that are suspended in fat.

Here in America, we have a standard that legally prescribes that the proportion of fat in butter must be at least 80 percent. That leaves the nonfat portion of butter at 20 percent, 16 percent of which is moisture. (The

remaining 4 percent consists of milk solids and salt, if it is added.)

The droplets of water suspended throughout butterfat contain proteins that attract certain bacteria, eventually causing rancidity. In order to combat these bacteria and protect butter from deterioration, manufacturers add salt. Consequently, because salt is used as a preservative, salted butter has come to be thought of as less fresh than unsalted butter.

Before cream is churned into butter, it is treated with a bacterial culture that reacts with the natural citric acid present in cream, producing diacetyl, butter's main flavor component. (To a lesser extent, lactose in cream is fermented into lactic acid, creating a secondary flavor element.) This is true for both salted and unsalted butter. The overwhelming difference in taste between the two varieties of butter is principally determined by the presence or absence of salt.

Salted and unsalted butter have nearly identical characteristics and behave in the same manner in the cooking process, with one notable exception. Since salt draws moisture from meat, sautéing it in salted butter causes more juice to be extracted. Consequently, a larger amount of brown coagulated particles form on the bottom of the pan in which you cook the meat. Should you go on to deglaze the pan and create a sauce, the result will be quite different in color, flavor, and aroma from that achieved by sautéing in unsalted butter.

Salted and unsalted butter can be used interchangeably, as long as you keep in mind the tremendous difference in flavor. Salted butter lends an abrasive edge to certain foods, particularly pastries, icings, and custard creams. Delicately flavored sauces, such as *Hollandaise* and *Whipped Butter Sauce,* usually exhibit a degree of harshness when made from salted butter, but there too, it's strictly a matter of personal taste. And taste is the basis on which to determine the type of butter you want to use.

Puff pastry has traditionally been prepared with unsalted butter, and, in a bit of convoluted reasoning, this fact has engendered the myth that salted butter contains more moisture than unsalted butter. This isn't true.

The confusion surrounding this issue occurred because butter available in France is, for the most part, unsalted. It also has a much lower moisture content (approximately 10 percent) than the butter available in America, and creates excellent puff pastry with a light but sturdy texture. Over a period of time, the attributes of French butter became associated with American unsalted butter, and the assumption that unsalted butter is superior for baking puff pastry caught on. In fact, American unsalted butter contains the same amount of moisture as its salty counterpart; it's superiority in the making of puff pastry is due entirely to its nonsalty taste.

The relatively high moisture content of American unsalted butter poses certain problems in the making of multileaved pastry. When the moisture heats in the oven, it produces too much steam, which puffs the layers excessively and weakens them. For this reason, recipes designed for use with American butter usually direct you to work a small amount of flour into the butter before beginning, in order to take up some of the surplus moisture.

Since unsalted butter is without the benefit of salt as a preservative, it doesn't keep for a long period of time. When you purchase it, choose a brand that is wrapped in foil. Foil is impermeable, so it does the most effective job of locking out air and errant odors. Unsalted butter does freeze well, so stock up when the price is most favorable.

RECIPES: Hollandaise Sauce, Unsalted Butter, Whipped Butter Sauce.   ◄շ

BUTTER SAUCE

Butter sauce has grown in popularity recently; maybe because it's so versatile and lightly textured. It can, however, also be quite tricky to handle.

Butter sauce is a temporary suspension with a twist (see Suspension; Sauce Making): A concentrated acid interacts with the natural emulsifier in butter to produce a rather thick, creamy consistency without the help of the lecithin contained in egg yolks. The whipping motion of a whisk also helps to promote stiffening of the sauce by breaking fat drops into droplets.

The basic pattern that underlies all butter sauces consists of cold butterfat blended with a reduced acid. You begin a butter sauce by rapidly reducing a certain amount of wine, vinegar, or lemon juice. Then you remove this liquid from the heat and whisk cold chunks of butter into the hot concentrate. (I place the chunks of butter in the freezer for 30 minutes first to make them extra cold.)

As the butter softens, the mixture develops a creamy consistency. The trick is to blend in the remaining butter, applying only enough heat to soften it, and retain the creamy consistency of the sauce as the butter is incorporated. Excessive heat will turn the butter oily and ruin the sauce.

The safest approach is to use a thick-bottomed saucepan and a heat diffuser, which gives you the closest possible control over the temperature (see Heat Diffuser). Hold the pan over the heat diffuser and whisk in a chunk of cold butter. As soon as the butter begins to soften, pull the pan away from the heat, whisking the mixture until the butter disappears. Drop in the next cold chunk and return the pan to the heat. Hold it only as close to the diffuser as necessary to soften the butter. Continue whisking, removing the pan from the heat each time the chunk of butter softens. The result should be a light, creamy, butter-colored sauce.

Maintaining a butter sauce is next to impossible, due to its extreme sensitivity to heat. If you must keep a butter sauce warm, pour it into a thermos bottle and seal tightly. (Do not heat the inside of the thermos with hot water.) If you have any butter sauce left over, refrigerate it to use as a flavored butter on grilled meat or hot vegetables. Don't attempt to reheat the sauce; it will separate.

Classic variations on a butter sauce include beurre au citron, in which reduced lemon juice provides the acid base, and beurre noir, in which the butter is clarified and browned before it is added. You can create your own variations by cooking minced shallots or garlic in the acid. Use an aromatic vinegar or reduced orange juice as the acid base, substitute red wine instead of the traditional white, or flavor the finished sauce with chopped fresh herbs or freshly grated nutmeg.

RECIPE: Whipped Butter Sauce.

BUTTERMILK

Natural buttermilk used to be the liquid residue left behind when nonhomogenized milk was churned into butter. Nowadays, buttermilk is produced by a fermentation process, and tiny particles of butter are added at the end to make it look authentic.

During the preparation of buttermilk, low-fat or skim milk is pasteurized and cooled. The cooled milk is then inoculated with certain bacteria that feed on lactose, or milk sugar, and give off lactic acid as a waste product (see Fermentation). Known as *Streptococcus lactis* and *S. cremoris*, these helpful bacteria are the same agents that ferment light cream, transforming it into sour cream (see Sour Cream).

Lactic acid is the element responsible for the sour or tangy taste of buttermilk, and because it acts like other acids, such as vinegar and lemon juice, it also enables buttermilk to produce exceptionally tender cakes and flaky biscuits.

Recipes that call for buttermilk invariably use baking soda as a leavener. Since lactic acid reacts with the carbonates in baking soda to produce carbon dioxide, the acid in baking powder isn't needed. There's also the matter of balancing flavors — an acid ingredient, like buttermilk, is usually paired with an alkali leavener (baking soda) rather than an acid-alkali combination (baking powder), so that the end product won't taste overly acidic (see Baking Powder/Baking Soda).

Buttermilk can be substituted for sour milk, sour cream, or yogurt without any change in quantity or type of leavener. Using it in place of sweet cream or milk is a different story, however. When you substitute buttermilk in a recipe originally formulated for sweet milk, you have to replace the baking powder with baking soda, thereby balancing the acidic flavor of the buttermilk with an alkali. The customary proportions in chemically leavened baked goods are 1 teaspoon of baking powder for every ½ cup of sweet milk. Since ¼ teaspoon of baking soda does the job of 1 teaspoon baking powder, use ¼ teaspoon baking soda for every ½ cup of buttermilk.

To reverse the procedure, substituting sweet milk for buttermilk, use 1 teaspoon baking powder in place of every ¼ teaspoon of baking soda called for in the recipe.

RECIPES: Blueberry Buttermilk Muffins, Herbed Buttermilk Dressing.

C

CAKE BAKING

When it comes to baking a cake, all cooks want the same thing — light layers with a tender, uniform crumb. Understanding what happens when cake batter heats up and bakes can help you to make a light, delicate cake.

Lightness is created by bubbles of air or carbon dioxide in cake batter (see Leavening). When batter is placed in a hot oven, the air or carbon dioxide expands as the batter warms, causing the bubbles to increase in size. Meanwhile, liquid contained in the batter turns to steam, replacing the air or carbon dioxide as it dissipates, and taking over the job of filling the air bubbles.

Each bubble, or pocket of steam, is surrounded by batter, usually containing eggs, milk, and flour. As the batter heats up, protein in the eggs and milk coagulates, changing from a liquid to a solid state. The flour starch gelatinizes, and soon the batter is set into a firm, weblike network. When most of the moisture has escaped from the bubbles and evaporated off as steam, and the crumb structure is set, the cake has finished baking.

The lightness of a cake is such an important characteristic that nearly all cakes can be divided into two main groups based on the way they are leavened: those leavened by carbon dioxide and those leavened by steam.

Cakes leavened chiefly by carbon dioxide are those to which baking soda, baking powder, or yeast have been added. They include the familiar two-egg yellow cake, devil's food cake, carrot cake, and all the packaged mixes except angel food. Cakes that use yeast as their source of carbon dioxide include German kugelhopfe and the rich, dense babas and savarins of France.

Cakes in the steam-leavened category include génoise, made with a foam of whole eggs, and angel food cake, which is based on a foam of egg whites. European-style tortes, constructed of meringue layers, and pound cakes, which are lightened only by air whipped into butter and eggs, also belong in this group.

Sponge cakes and chiffon cakes are a hybrid variety, relying almost equally on both carbon dioxide and steam for their leavening.

Recipes that call for carbon dioxide as a leavener invariably begin by beating air into butter or shortening until it becomes fluffy. Sugar is then added, using a beating technique known as creaming. Since sugar crystals encourage fat to hold bubbles of air, the creaming procedure is an important factor in the eventual lightness of a cake. The more air bubbles you incorporate during this step, the lighter your cake will be (see Creaming).

At this point, eggs are usually beaten in. This may involve adding whole eggs, or the yolks alone, with the whites being whipped separately and folded in at a later time to create an increased degree of lightness. Whichever the case, the fat in the egg yolks traps additional air bubbles as the mixture is beaten and adds to the airy consistency.

Next, baking powder or baking soda is added to the cake batter along with any other dry ingredients, usually by alternating dry and liquid ingredients. When the powder or soda comes in contact with moisture, it begins to release carbon dioxide gas. The gas forms bubbles in the batter much like the bubbles you see in a glass of club soda.

These carbon dioxide bubbles expand as the batter is heated and the gas warms. Gradually, the carbon dioxide dissipates and is replaced by steam, until nearly all the moisture has evaporated off and the structure is set. (To this extent, all cakes, even those leavened principally with carbon dioxide, are leavened also by steam.)

Recipes that depend solely on steam as a leavener usually contain more eggs than carbon-dioxide–leavened cakes. That's because eggs must perform the entire job of trapping the air bubbles that will ultimately support the cake. Air whipped into whole eggs produces a whole-egg foam, air whipped into egg whites forms an egg-white foam, and air whipped into yolks forms an egg-yolk foam. In all types of egg-foam cakes, moisture in the eggs turns to steam as the batter is heated. The steam fills the pockets of air created by the whipping process, causing them to expand. Meanwhile, flour that has been folded in lends strength to the egg protein, as it coagulates into a weblike network around each air pocket.

This is a good place to explain why cakes fall. Just as warmth causes air and carbon dioxide bubbles to expand, a cold draft will make them contract. If you open the oven door before the crumb structure is set, the bubbles will contract. Steam inside the bubbles will condense and revert to liquid, and the weblike structure will collapse.

The tenderness of the crumb in a cake is affected mainly by four things — the type of shortening, the type of flour, and the amount of sugar you use, plus the amount of beating you do.

Solid vegetable shortening is 100 percent fat, and thus, measure for measure, holds more air when beaten than butter. Furthermore, an emulsifier added during the hydrogenating process enables solid shortening to hold an increased amount of moisture and air. For that reason, solid vegetable shortening produces a more tender and delicate crumb than either butter or margarine.

Butter, of course, contributes far more flavor to a cake. Margarine, while it has nearly the same chemical composition as butter and behaves the same way in batter, lends far less flavor. Vegetable oil creates moist cakes, but it has no creaming ability, so it can't contribute to promoting lightness. For that reason, cakes made with oil tend to be heavy and dense. Oil-based cake batter requires more beating than other types of batter because oil is reluctant to disperse evenly; insufficient beating results in tiny pockets of oil.

Cake flour, which is higher in starch and lower in gluten-producing proteins than all-purpose flour, is frequently used in cake baking to help create a tender crumb. It is finely ground and also highly bleached, a factor that may be important to you if you're baking a white cake and want it to come out as white as possible.

The quantity of sugar that a recipe calls for indicates how delicate and tender the crumb will be. Cakes high in sugar are often called "high ratio cakes." High ratio cakes contain more sugar than flour by weight, and as a result are sweet, tender, and finely textured.

Probably the most crucial factor in determining tenderness is the amount of beating you do in order to incorporate the flour. If you beat too much, you'll overdevelop the

gluten and toughen the cake; if you don't beat enough, the gluten will fail to develop sufficient strength to support the weblike structure, and the cake will fall. The best approach, which some recipes mention and others don't, is to alternate one-third of the dry ingredients with one-third of the liquid ingredients until both are completely blended in. This procedure seems to provide just the right amount of beating needed to develop the gluten enough to support the cake, but not so much as to toughen it.

In addition to toughening a cake, overbeating produces a nonuniform crumb. The overworked gluten strands resist the leavening action of the carbon dioxide, forcing the gas bubbles into irregular shapes or tunnels. This is most obvious in overbeaten muffins, because they are low in sugar, but it can also occur in overbeaten cakes. You should never allow your electric mixer to run willy-nilly; by all means turn it off while you answer the phone or let out the dog.

RECIPES: Génoise, Holiday Spice Cake, Sachertorte.   ❧

leavening the batter (see Baking Powder/ Baking Soda). In a like manner, when yeast ferments sugar into alcohol and carbon dioxide, tiny gas bubbles are distributed throughout the dough and expand as the dough warms and rises.

Carbon dioxide is capable of being held in solution by a small amount of pressure, thus forming soda, or carbonated, water. Since soda water is actually dissolved carbon dioxide, you can use it to create some interesting leavening effects. Experiment with substituting soda water (measure for measure) for some of the liquid in pancake batter, biscuits, pie crust, and the batter used to coat deep-fried foods. Even though the bubbles of gas dissipate quickly, you'll be surprised at the light, puffy effect they create.

Dry ice, which is the solid form of carbon dioxide, is a powerful cooling agent. It's often used to stage spectacular culinary effects, because it condenses to white vapor when it comes in contact with warm air. Caterers frequently take advantage of this feature to create the illusion of intense cold or to construct a facsimile of a smoldering volcano.   ❧

CARBON DIOXIDE

Carbon dioxide, a colorless, invisible gas, is one of the most helpful chemical compounds cooks have at their disposal. Anytime you use yeast, baking powder, baking soda, soda water, or even dry ice, you are relying on some form of carbon dioxide to do a job for you.

Carbon dioxide is produced wherever there is fire. It's also a byproduct of such natural processes as respiration, decay or decomposition, and fermentation (see Fermentation). When an acid meets a carbonate, such as sodium bicarbonate, the acid decomposes the carbonate and carbon dioxide is given off. The invisible gas then disperses (throughout a batter, for example), forming tiny bubbles along the way. When the carbon dioxide in the bubbles gets warm, it expands,

CELLULOSE

Cellulose is a carbohydrate that lines the plant cells of all fruits and vegetables. It strengthens the cell wall and forms long supportive fibers in stems and the ribs of leaves.

When fruits and vegetables are young, their cell walls are exceptionally thin and composed almost entirely of cellulose. These walls surround a material that contains a high percentage of water. As plants mature, the cellulose layer thickens and becomes encrusted with lignin — an element that causes fruit and vegetable tissues to develop a stringy or woody texture.

The cooking process softens fruits and vegetables by changing the condition of the cellulose-lined cells. When heated, the cell walls rupture, separate from one another, collapse, or experience some combination of these three forms of breakdown. Meanwhile, the water contained within the cells is released, and the consistency of the fruit or vegetable changes from firm to soft. However, prolonged cooking does not tenderize vegetables, it merely *softens* them. Since neither cellulose nor lignin is soluble in water, the cooking process can only break down cellulose, not dissolve it. In other words, if you start out with overly mature yellow squash that's woody and stringy, the best you'll turn out is yellow squash that's *pulpy* and stringy, no matter *how* long you cook it.　　　&ª

(it makes a terrific polishing cloth), or you can always order it by mail (see Appendix).

By the way, when a recipe suggests using a double thickness of cheesecloth, it means to fold the cloth, as is, into two layers. (It usually comes already doubled, and sometimes tripled.) The idea is to reduce the size of the openings so that fine particles can't sneak through. Occasionally a recipe will direct you to wet the cheesecloth before straining with it, in order to prevent the cloth from absorbing whatever liquid you're pouring through. I've found, however, that dry cheesecloth doesn't absorb *that* much liquid, and that wet cheesecloth is a real nuisance to work with.&ª

CHEESECLOTH

We all have our indispensable companions in the kitchen — things we simply couldn't do without. One of mine is cheesecloth, a loosely woven, gauzelike fabric.

Porosity combined with great strength is the outstanding characteristic of cheesecloth. The openings in the weave are wide enough to make it the perfect pouch for herbs in a bouquet garni (see Bouquet Garni), yet a double thickness provides a way to strain out even the tiniest particles in a broth or stock.

I particularly like to use cheesecloth to hold things together. For example, if I'm going to poach a stuffed breast of veal, I wrap it in cheesecloth to help preserve the shape of the meat and keep the stuffing from bubbling out. A cheesecloth wrapper also gives you something secure to latch onto when you're lifting a sizeable item — like a poached fish, or a large stuffed pasta roll — in and out of the pot.

You can purchase a medium grade of cheesecloth in most large supermarkets, but the trick is in locating it. It might be in the gourmet section, the housewares department, or the floor-wax aisle. Hardware stores sometimes carry it, as do automotive shops

CHOCOLATE
Melting

One of the many traps awaiting unsuspecting cooks involves the melting of chocolate. For one reason or another, it's a step that gets people into a lot of trouble.

Recently, it's become fairly common for recipes to be quite explicit about the procedure. The usual wording is apt to be, "melt chocolate over hot, but not boiling, water." Older recipes didn't even offer that much advice; they simply said, "Melt the chocolate." Clearer directions are a definite help, but understanding the nature of chocolate gives you a better idea of why it behaves as it does.

All baking chocolate contains a small amount of starch and about 2 percent water. If you subject chocolate to high heat, the water and starch will begin to interact; the starch will gelatinize and actually thicken the chocolate (see Gelatinization). This results in the phenomenon referred to as seizing — the liquid chocolate suddenly develops a stiff, pasty consistency that no amount of stirring or beating can undo.

Seizing can also take place at lower temperatures if a large amount of moisture is present. This explains why liquid ingredients such as cognac or various liqueurs should never be added directly to melting chocolate, but instead be incorporated at some other point in the recipe, unless a buffering agent like cream or corn syrup is included. Melting chocolate in a double boiler is a frequently suggested method, but probably the riskiest approach. If you allow the water in the bottom of the pan to heat to the point where steam is given off (and this can be well below the boiling point), droplets of water in the steam can easily combine with the chocolate and ruin its consistency. Covering a pan of melting chocolate can likewise cause seizing when drops of water condense on the inside of the lid and fall into the chocolate. Also, beware the damp spatula or spoon — seizing can be caused merely by stirring melted chocolate with a wet implement.

Occasionally you can rescue seized chocolate by vigorously beating in 1 or 2 tablespoons of solid vegetable shortening, and depending on the nature of your recipe, it might be worth a try. The wisest move, of course, is simply to avoid the problem of moisture in the first place. There are two ways to accomplish this — over direct heat or in the oven.

Melting chocolate in the oven is the easiest and safest approach, although it takes about half an hour. Break up the chocolate (the smaller the pieces, the faster the melting), and drop into an ovenproof bowl. Place the uncovered bowl in an oven set at 275°F. Check its progress after 10 minutes by stirring with a dry spatula. Be patient, and resist the temptation to increase the oven temperature. Continue to check and stir until all is melted.

You can also melt chocolate over direct heat. The danger, of course, is that you might heat it too much and cause seizing. Keep in mind that chocolate melts at only 110°F. and follow these steps carefully: 1) Using a sharp knife or the steel blade in a processor, coarsely chop the chocolate. 2) Place half the amount in a medium-size, thick-bottomed saucepan and set over the lowest heat possible. 3) Stir continuously until the chocolate is

almost completely melted. 4) Remove from the heat and dump in the remaining chocolate. As you stir, the heat from the melted chocolate will melt the rest. If you feel you absolutely must return the pan to the heat, avoid letting the bottom get too hot — it should only feel warm to the touch. Now you see why melting in the oven is easier.

Another method of direct-heat melting is done over a heat diffuser. This gizmo, sometimes called a "simmer ring" or "flame tamer," looks like a metal platform with holes. Placed on top of a burner, it reduces and evens out heat in much the same manner as a double boiler (see Heat Diffuser).

Chopping the chocolate is a good idea in this method too, but since the heat is so gentle, it's not a necessity. Simply break the chocolate up into a saucepan, place the pan on the diffuser, and turn the heat to medium-low. Stir occasionally.

If, however, you still feel you want to use the double-boiler method, follow these safeguards: 1) Put a small amount of water in the bottom pan — it should *never* touch the bottom of the upper container. If it does, the chocolate at the bottom will overheat. 2) Bring the water to a boil, remove the pan from the heat, and wait for the steam to disappear completely. A water temperature of 140°F. is ideal. Position the container holding the chocolate over the hot water and allow it to melt. Stir occasionally, but do not return the double boiler to the heat. 3) Do not cover the chocolate at any time, because condensation will form and drop down, causing the chocolate to seize. 4) Wipe the bottom of the upper container as soon as you lift it out. Drops of moisture could possibly fall into the melted chocolate as you tip the container to pour it out.

One last precaution: when you're going to add melted chocolate to other ingredients, always allow the chocolate to cool to 80°F., or to room temperature. Chocolate that is too hot can melt shortening, curdle eggs, or otherwise upset the delicate balance of a mixture. Don't, however, try to rush things by cooling melted chocolate in the refrigerator. Cool temperatures can condense rising steam into droplets of moisture, and rapid cooling can cause the fat contained in chocolate to solidify, making it difficult to blend in.

Tempering

If you're planning to melt chocolate to coat strawberries, pineapple, or other fruit, or to mold chocolate into decorative leaves, shells, or cups, you'll want to use the specialized melting technique called tempering. Used as a matter of course by candy makers, this involves a slow melting process, a closely supervised cooling step, and a carefully monitored rewarming. The goal of tempering chocolate is to produce a chocolate coating with a smooth, nongrainy consistency and a highly glossy sheen.

Chocolate contains a high percentage of fat, specifically cocoa butter. If you could examine cocoa butter through a microscope, you would see that it's made up of tiny crystals arranged in a three-dimensional network; this gives chocolate its firm character. When chocolate is heated, these fat crystals liquefy and the network collapses, forming liquid chocolate. As liquid chocolate cools, the fat recrystallizes, and the chocolate again takes on a solid form.

The problem is that the fat crystals in co-coa butter don't all melt or set at the same temperature. Consequently, as chocolate cools, some fat crystals will solidify faster than others. Those that are the last to recrystallize appear at the surface, producing a dull finish, a grainy texture, and occasionally greyish streaks. By using the process of tempering, you can even out the rate at which cocoa-butter crystals set.

During tempering, the chocolate is first melted slowly over hot, but not steaming, water. Throughout the entire project, it's absolutely essential that no water come in contact with the chocolate. Watch out for steam, and make sure that all utensils, including your thermometer, are bone dry (see Chocolate: Melting).

As the temperature of the chocolate increases, the fat crystals will begin to liquefy. The chocolate will soften and then become a liquid. Stir occasionally to distribute the heat, until the temperature of the chocolate registers 115°F. on an instant-read thermometer. Immediately remove the upper container from the hot water, wipe the bottom dry with a towel, and begin to stir slowly, but continuously. The object is to control the reformation of the fat crystals by keeping them in motion as the chocolate cools.

Monitor the temperature closely. As it drops, the fat will begin to recrystallize and re-establish the structural network that causes the chocolate to thicken. The first crystals to form are called beta crystals, which have the unique capability of acting as seeds: beta fat crystals promote the creation of other beta crystals. Since beta crystals are stable, their presence throughout the chocolate contributes a steadying influence.

Allow all types of chocolate, except milk chocolate, to cool to 86°F. Milk chocolate, which contains about 4 percent milkfat, needs to be cooled to 83°F. (Milkfat has a lower melting point than cocoa fat, thus milk chocolate must be cooled to a lower temperature in order to solidify sufficiently.)

When the chocolate has cooled, it is considered tempered. However, because its consistency has thickened to the point where it's too stiff for pouring or coating, a second warming is necessary. Here's where you have to exercise special care — a tad too much heat will untemper the chocolate.

Place the pan of cooled chocolate over water that registers 95°F. on an instant-read thermometer, then slowly warm the chocolate. Since milk chocolate has a lower melting point, it only needs to reach 86° to 88°F. At temperatures higher than that, too much milkfat will melt, and the chocolate will thin out. The best temperature for all other types of chocolate is 88° to 90°F. If the temperature of the chocolate goes above this point and the consistency gets too thin, retemper it by cooling and stirring as you did before.

Incidentally, a thermometer designed specifically for working with chocolate has just appeared on the market. Since it registers heat in one-degree intervals, it's much easier to use for tempering than other models (see Appendix).   ◄₂

CLARIFYING BUTTER

Clarifying butter is a procedure that enables you to separate milkfat (also called butterfat) from milk solids. Why would you want to? One reason is because pure fat can be heated to much higher temperatures for frying or sautéing once the milk solids, which would burn and give off an unpleasant flavor, have been removed.

Another reason for clarifying butter is that, during the process, water contained in the butter is evaporated off as steam. This can be particularly important if you're working with a cake recipe that depends on a finely balanced moisture content. Butter that has been clarified contains very little water, so the amount of steam created during the baking process will be significantly reduced. For that reason, the success of certain cakes may rely on the use of clarified butter.

Finally, there's the difference in taste. Clarified butter has an extremely mild, delicate flavor due to the fact that the milk solids, which contain most of the buttery-tasting elements, have been separated out. This factor could also be important in cake baking, where you might not want as pronounced a butter flavor, or when you're serving drawn butter with baked, stuffed shrimp or lobster. On the other hand, there are times when a more assertive butter flavor is desirable. When you're following a recipe that calls for clarified butter, keep in mind that removing the milk solids attenuates the buttery flavor.

Butter is an emulsion of butterfat and water that contains the supplementary elements of milk, such as proteins and carbohydrates (see Emulsion). When you melt butter, you break the emulsion. In other words, the water and butterfat separate. At the same time, the other milk elements solidify — if you listen and watch closely, you'll see it happen.

To clarify butter, begin by cutting a stick or two into chunks of uniform size, so they will melt evenly. Always melt more than you need because some of the butter will be lost in the form of solids and some will evaporate. (You'll lose about 2 tablespoons of water and solids out of every 8 tablespoons of butter you melt.) Also, don't attempt to clarify frozen butter unless you've first defrosted it.

Place the chunks of butter in a heavy saucepan and set over medium heat. As the butter warms, it will begin to sputter noisily. (Water and fat, heated together, always produce this sputtering sound.)

Water bubbles will rise to the top, carrying with them particles of milk protein (casein). As these protein particles are heated, they denature and coagulate, forming a foamy curd on the surface of the hot butter. Meanwhile, the carbohydrates, which are mostly lactose or milk sugar, become saturated with water and fall to the bottom, because they're heavier than the fat.

In a fairly short time, three distinct layers appear: a thin, white, foamy curd on top; a sizeable layer of clear, yellow fat in the middle; and a layer of sediment and water on the bottom. It's important to stop heating the butter at this point, before the particles on the bottom layer begin to turn brown. These are milk solids, and they give off a bitter, unpleasant taste if allowed to color.

The middle layer of pure fat is what you're after, so remove the pan from the heat and allow the butter to cool slightly. Skim the top layer off with a fork, then pour or spoon off the pure fat, taking care not to disturb the bottom layer of sediment and water.

You can store clarified butter in a tightly closed container in the refrigerator for 3 to 4 weeks or freeze it for up to 6 months, so plan to clarify a large quantity at a time. If you process half a pound or more, you'll end up with a sizeable amount of sediment. Don't throw it away; it, too, can be stored in the refrigerator or freezer and used to grease pans. Since this sediment contains the concentrated flavor of butter, it's great for enriching soups or buttering vegetables, unless of course, it has turned brown. In that case, get rid of it.

Occasionally, you may come across directions for clarifying butter that recommend you simply melt, then strain the liquid butter into a container. If these instructions appear easy and uncomplicated, it's only because they are oversimplified. In order for the melt-and-strain method to work, you must warm the butter over the gentlest heat possible, not rushing it at all.

The water contained in the butter will be released slowly and evaporate from the surface. The protein molecules will denature, but because there are no rising water bubbles to carry them to the top, the proteins will fall to the bottom. Consequently, very little curd will appear on the surface. Continue heating the butter until the layer of yellow fat becomes clear. (Melted butter that is not clear still contains moisture and milk solids.) Strain the yellow fat through a double thickness of cheesecloth, but pay close attention as you pour because some of the milk solids are fine enough to pass through the openings of the cheesecloth. Be sure to stop pouring when you get to this milky residue.

Which brings us to the next point. There is a cookbook available in which the author suggests that you continue heating the butter until the particles in the sediment turn "golden brown." I think that's not only unnecessary, but rather poor advice. Browned milk solids lend an unpleasant taste and aroma to clarified butter. You will get a cleaner, fresher flavor if you heat the butter only until the foam on top becomes curdlike in texture and the middle layer of yellow fat becomes clear.   ·ϡ

CLARIFYING STOCK

The reason for clarifying stock is to remove traces of fat or other impurities from the liquid, in order to create an absolutely crystal clear broth. It's a time-consuming procedure that you can usually avoid by heeding the warning not to let stock boil before the fat has been removed. Vigorous bubbling breaks up fat drops into droplets so small that they lose their desire to coalesce. They remain diffused throughout the stock even after chilling, giving the finished product a cloudy appearance and an unpleasant flavor. (In fact, stock that is flawed in this manner is apt to turn rancid after just a few days in the refrigerator.)

Straining stock through a double thickness of cheesecloth will remove most of the tiny particles of meat and other debris, and this method works well for stock that's to be used as the basis for flour-bound sauces that don't have to be perfectly clear. However, for particular preparations like aspic and chilled consommé, where clarity is of the utmost importance, you may have to clarify stock with beaten egg white.

In addition to being a useful technique to know, the process of clarifying stock also involves an interesting chemical reaction. When beaten egg white is stirred into liquid stock, a colloid is formed. In other words, since egg proteins are so large, they never truly dissolve; instead, they remain suspended throughout the stock (see Suspension). As you gradually increase the temperature of the stock, the proteins denature — or uncoil like little balls of yarn — into long, thin strands. Although the protein strands are still invisible at this point, they won't be for much longer (see Denaturing).

When the stock-and-egg-white mixture reaches 165°F., the protein molecules begin to join together, forming a weblike network that traps fat droplets and other particles in its interstices, or pockets. The egg-white strands begin to solidify and you can see traces of solid egg white in the stock.

Continued heating creates a complex of coagulated protein throughout the entire pot of stock. (It's important to stir continuously to ensure even distribution of the molecular structure and to prevent the coagulated protein from falling to the bottom of the pan.) The protein complex will trap all the fat drops and other stray particles, so that when you pour the mixture through a cheesecloth-lined sieve, the coagulated protein and debris remain behind.

RECIPE: Light Brown Stock.   ⋘

COAGULATION

Coagulation is the firming up of a protein network, and, when kept under control, it causes a mixture to thicken smoothly and evenly.

Coconut Custard Cream Pie and *Caramel Flan* are two examples of coagulation. When protein molecules contained in eggs and milk are denatured by heat, the molecules join together and become firm, causing the pie filling and the flan to set (see Denaturing).

Scrambled eggs are another example of coagulation. As the heat under the liquid eggs increases, the egg protein denatures. Eventu-

ally, the eggs change from a liquid to a solid state and curds form. If you continue to heat the eggs, the protein molecules will aggregate and a watery liquid will be released (which explains why overcooked scrambled eggs are said to weep).

The trick to dealing successfully with coagulation is to keep everything under control. Excess heat or acid can cause the protein molecules to lump together, which is fine for scrambled eggs, but not for a smooth custard sauce. Keep in mind that a thickening egg-based mixture is actually a controlled coagulation in progress. If you use moderate heat, gentle stirring, and a limited amount of acid, you should be able to avoid the exuberant kind of coagulation that results in curdling (see Curdling).

Coagulation is also partly responsible for the way a cake bakes and a cream puff puffs. As the weblike network of egg and milk proteins heats, it coagulates to form the solid skeletal structure that is the crumb of the cake or the texture of a popover or soufflé.

RECIPES: Caramel Flan, Coconut Custard Cream Pie.   ⋘

COATING PANS

There are several reasons for coating baking pans. The most obvious is so you can get out what you put in — without leaving half of it behind, that is.

The easiest coating is simply a film of fat. Recipes that say "grease generously" or "grease lightly" are telling you to apply either a thick or thin layer of shortening to the surface of the pan so the contents won't stick during and after baking. For yeast breads, quick breads, and cookies, a casual approach will get the job done. You can smear the surface of the pan with solid shortening using your fingertips or a piece of waxed paper.

Beyond that, things can get a little more complicated. Cakes, for example, demand

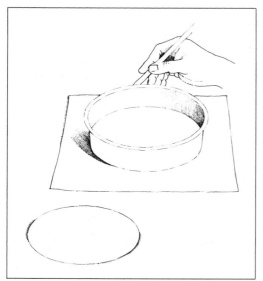

Lining the bottom of a cake pan with parchment paper protects the cake from absorbing fat during baking and from developing a soggy bottom.

special consideration. Sponge cake, génoise, or any cake that contains separated eggs needs ungreased sides to cling to during baking in order to reach maximum height, so you only need to grease the bottom of the pan. However, because you don't want the bottom of the cake to absorb a lot of fat, you have to be more fussy about how it's applied.

Your best bet is to brush the bottom of the cake pan with melted butter or shortening, using a pastry brush. Then sift a light dusting of flour across the bottom of the pan to protect the cake from absorbing fat during baking. Tilt and shake the pan to distribute the flour evenly, tap firmly to release any excess flour, and empty it out. The object is to create a thin, even coating — one without blobs of fat or flour. (For a deep brown bottom on a chocolate cake, sift on cocoa instead of flour.)

An alternate plan is to line the bottom of the cake pan with parchment or waxed paper (see Parchment Paper). First set the pan on top of the paper, then trace around the outside (see illustration) and cut out with scissors. You'll still need to apply a bit of grease to the pan bottom so the paper will lie flat

and smooth, but only a few small dabs here and there are enough.

Parchment works better than waxed paper because it's slightly porous, yet sturdy, and has no coating. Waxed paper, when hot, is flimsy, tears easily, and gives off an oily residue. Also, waxed paper cannot absorb moisture, but the slight porosity of parchment paper allows it to take in some of the moisture that's released during baking. Consequently, cakes baked in parchment-lined pans are less apt to have soggy bottoms.

Cakes that are made by first creaming together shortening and sugar rise less than separated-egg cakes. They usually contain more sugar, too, which means they are more apt to stick to the sides of an ungreased pan. When preparing a pan for these cakes, be sure to grease and flour both the bottom and sides of the pan. If you want to use parchment, omit the flouring step and cut a covering for the bottom and a strip to fit the sides of the pan. Again, lightly grease the pan bottom and sides first to give the paper something to stick to so it won't bump up when you pour in the batter.

Cakes or cookies made from a meringue base come out best when baked on parchment, for they stick relentlessly to a greased surface. Flouring the greased surface doesn't improve matters much, and using aluminum foil creates a disaster.

A cookie sheet presents special problems because it is usually used three or four times in the process of baking a batch of cookies. If it's coated with shortening, it must be wiped off and re-greased every time it comes out of the oven. Even so, you tend to get a build-up of brown, gummy, hard-to-clean shortening. Here again, parchment paper is a neat solution. It eliminates greasing and it can be used over and over. Lay it directly on an ungreased cookie sheet and place your unbaked cookies right on the paper. At the end of the baking period, it's easy to pull off the paper, cookies and all, onto a cooling rack, allowing the cookie sheet to cool quickly to room temperature before adding the next batch.

Coating pans and baking dishes improves the flavor, texture, and consistency of certain foods. The proper consistency of a soufflé depends on its ability to rise, so having something to grab on to as the batter climbs up the sides of the baking dish helps enormously. That's why recipes for sweet soufflés suggest that you coat the sides of the dish with sugar or fine cake crumbs, and recipes for savory soufflés call for preparing the dish with bread crumbs or grated cheese. These coatings also contribute flavor and create an interesting texture on the sides of soufflés.

For certain puff pastries, a special textural effect is created by coating baking sheets with butter and sugar. During baking, the sugar caramelizes, producing a sugary glaze on the underside of the pastries. However, since butter, sugar, and flour all burn at high temperatures, it isn't wise to flour or butter baking sheets used for most pastries and cookies; the coated surface of the pan that's exposed to the heat of the oven will burn, and the outer edges of the baked goods will acquire a burnt flavor. Solid vegetable (hydrogenated) shortening is the best choice for greasing exposed surfaces, because it can stand higher temperatures without burning.

Use butter for coating pans only when flavor is important, as in delicate buttery cakes. Most of the time, solid shortening is the best all-purpose grease for preparing pans. Vegetable oil in spray cans comes in handy if you want to bake muffins or cupcakes without paper liners, and a pesky casserole dish won't need scrubbing if you spray the inside lightly before filling.

Pie pans don't need to be greased because during baking the pastry releases fat, which prevents pie crust from sticking to the pan. Sometime, though, try buttering your pie pan, chilling it until the butter is firm, then laying in the pastry and adding the filling. The butter will heat quickly during baking to seal and crisp the underside of the bottom crust, thus preventing a soggy bottom.   ❧

CONNECTIVE TISSUE

If you've ever tried chewing a gristly piece of meat, you already know about connective tissue. You also know that its presence has a lot to do with how tough or tender a piece of meat will be (see Meat).

Connective tissue is what holds meat together. It can vary from extremely thin and fragile to tough and strong. It can be white or yellow, elastic or nonelastic; it is capable of being melted and liquefied or of remaining solid and firm. Connective tissue attaches one fiber of meat to another, binds groups of fibers into large bundles, and holds bundles of fibers together to form a whole muscle.

The kind of connective tissue that's of most concern to cooks is the white, semi-transparent tissue that runs between individual muscle fibers like thin white threads. Often it appears as the thicker streaks of white that delineate and separate bundles of fibers, or as the silvery sheath of tissue that surrounds an entire muscle.

This whitish connective tissue consists mainly of a protein called collagen. Fibers of collagen are strong and nonelastic, so it's no surprise that improperly cooked meat containing a significant amount of collagenous tissue is apt to come out tough.

The outstanding characteristic of collagen is its ability to break down and form gelatin when you heat it with water. Melted collagen is the substance that appears as pale yellow jelly when you pull apart a cold leg of chicken. Dissolved collagen, given off during the slow cooking of a pot roast, mingles with the cooking liquid and increases its viscosity, causing it to solidify when cooled. Because collagen is more abundant in pieces of meat that contain joints where bone connects with bone, stock made from these cuts (particularly the neck and breast of veal, an oxtail, or a calf's foot) will firm up when chilled without any help from packaged gelatin.

A second type of connective tissue is composed chiefly of elastin, a protein that forms yellowish, elastic fibers. Unlike collagen, elastin is extremely resistant to moist heat and cannot be softened or liquefied by cooking. The good news is that elastin exists mostly in tendons and ligaments that are trimmed away when meat is prepared for market. ✑

COOKIES

Have you ever wondered how two cooks can follow the same cookie recipe and come out with entirely different results? The main reason is shortening — the type of fat you use in making cookies has a significant impact on their flavor and texture. Butter produces a finely grained, almost sandy-textured cookie with an outstanding flavor; margarine gives cookies a chewy quality; and solid (hydrogenated) shortening turns out cookies that are soft and moderately moist, with a somewhat flaky texture.

Considering the exquisite flavor of butter and the texture it creates, it's unquestionably your best bet for delicate pressed cookies, ball cookies, or any type of plain wafer that uses butter as its chief source of flavoring. Solid vegetable shortening is hydrogenated (a process that incorporates air into shortening and enables it to hold larger amounts of sugar without weakening the skeletal structure; see Shortening). It's therefore an excellent choice for producing drop cookies with nicely rounded tops and a light, airy texture. Hydrogenated shortening also creates excellent refrigerator cookies and bars. Margarine is best reserved for chewy cookies, such as hermits or molasses cookies.

Flour is another variable to take into account when preparing cookie dough. Since excess flour is the most common reason for hard-as-a-rock drop cookies, the best way to prevent this is by adding less flour to a drop cookie batter than the recipe calls for. (You can always correct for too little, but you're stuck if you've added too much.) After blending in most of the flour, touch the dough with an unfloured finger. If it comes away sticky, slowly blend in a tad more flour. The object is to reach a consistency resembling moist sand. When an unfloured finger comes away clean, you've added enough.

Rolled cookies, too, often suffer from a surplus of flour. The batter is meant to be quite a bit stiffer than drop-cookie dough, but problems can arise during the rolling-out process. The flour you sprinkle over the work surface and rolling pin is absorbed by the dough, and can easily toughen the cookies. It helps if you dust lightly with sifted flour or, better still, confectioners' sugar. Chill rolled-cookie dough for only 15 to 20 minutes, for dough that's too cold is difficult to work with. Since small amounts of dough are easier to handle, divide the chilled dough into two or three portions. Also, keep in mind that the thinner you roll the dough, the crispier your cookies will be.

All types of cookie dough should be mixed with as little beating as possible, to avoid agitating the gluten. Just as in muffins and quick breads, overdeveloped gluten can cause tough cookies. For the same reason, don't allow cookie dough to become warm. Set it in a cool spot between batches, or refrigerate it if your kitchen is warmer than 75°F. Drop-cookie batter should be pushed from a spoon; avoid the temptation to roll the dough between the palms of your hands, because the warmth will encourage gluten to develop. Ball cookies, which must be shaped this way, should be rolled between your palms with the quickest, lightest strokes possible. Rolled cookies present a problem all their own — since repeated handling means overdeveloped gluten, you can never expect cookies cut from rolled scraps to be as delicate as those cut from the initial rolling.

To help you cope with this dilemma, there are cookie cutters available that are shaped like interlocking pieces of a jigsaw puzzle. With one of these cutters, it's possible to cut out several shapes at one time and pull them apart with no scraps left over (see Appendix).

Prepare your cookie sheets by greasing them with solid shortening rather than butter, because shortening can be heated to a higher temperature for a longer period of time without burning. You can also line your pans with parchment paper (see Parchment Paper; Coating Pans). Brushing a cookie sheet with oil creates a hard-to-clean residue, but spray-on vegetable oil works well. A warm pan causes batter to spread, creating tough, flat cookies with hard bottom crusts, so be sure to cool cookie sheets between batches. In fact, if you enjoy baking cookies, it's worth the investment to purchase at least three pans — while one cools, the second bakes, as you prepare the third for the oven.

Although it isn't always practical, the best approach is to bake only one pan of cookies at a time. A second baking sheet placed on a lower rack acts as an insulator and impedes the flow of hot air circulating under the upper pan. This can change the way in which the bottoms of the cookies on the upper sheet bake. Instead of crisp, lightly browned bottoms, you're apt to get soft, pale undersides that become tough as the cookies cool. There's also a great temptation to overbake cookies when the bottom doesn't brown properly. (Conversely, the upper baking sheet affects the way in which the tops of the cookies on the bottom rack develop.) Baking two sheets of cookies at one time also increases the amount of moisture and steam present inside the oven. This can adversely affect the final texture of your cookies, particularly if you're wanting them to be light and crisp.

RECIPES: Almond Butterballs, Applesauce Chocolate Chip Cookies, Chips of Chocolate Toll House Cookies, Forgotten Cookies, Sourdough Oatmeal Cookies.   ⤙

COOLING RACK

I'm willing to bet that the most frequently ignored directions are those at the end of bread and pastry recipes that say to "cool on a rack." Soggy cakes, cookies that don't crisp, and pies that weep are all victims that could have been saved by using a cooling rack.

When you take a cake from the oven, it contains a great deal of warm, moist air. If you set the cake directly on a solid surface, the water vapor at the bottom of the cake can't escape quickly enough, so it condenses, forming drops of water that collect at the bottom of the pan and make the cake soggy.

On the other hand, a cake placed on a cooling rack is exposed to air on all sides. The fact that it is elevated means that air can pass under the cake, cooling it evenly.

All baked goods can benefit from being placed immediately on a cooling rack. (The tiny beads of moisture that invariably appear on the counter under the rack are sufficient proof of that.)

While we're on the subject, here are two cooling-rack hints. To eliminate unsightly rack marks on the sides of loaf cakes and breads, position baked goods so that the cooling rack is in contact with the undersides. Also, apply solid shortening or spray-on oil to a cooling rack to help prevent the surfaces of cakes and breads from sticking.   ⤙

CRACKING

Cracked pumpkin pies and cheesecakes are high on every cook's list of bugaboos. In both cases, the reason cracks appear is generally overcooking, too rapid cooling, or a combination of the two. To make matters worse, many recipes instruct you to test for doneness by inserting the blade of a knife, which does a fine job of giving a crack a place to start.

To avoid overcooking custard pies, like pumpkin, you should halt the baking process before the filling is completely set. The residual interior heat will complete the job of cooking as the pie rests.

Rely on the "jiggle test." Since pie filling cooks by conduction, the center is always the last to cook (see Heat: Conduction). Toward the end of the recommended baking time, give the pie a nudge. You'll notice that a round area in the center still quivers. When this jiggly spot is reduced to the size of a quarter, turn the oven off and leave the door ajar. Do not test for doneness by inserting anything. The filling will continue to cook as the residual heat moves to the center. Allow the pie to remain inside the oven for several hours to cool to room temperature. This step provides the most gradual cooling possible. If, in spite of these precautions, your custard pie still cracks, you may have cooked it at too high a temperature (see Custard).

Creating humidity inside the oven while a cheesecake bakes can reduce its tendency to crack. (This won't work with a custard pie, by the way, because it would make the pie crust soggy.) You can supply this humidity by placing a pan containing 2 inches of boiling water on the rack under the cake, or, better still, by placing your cheesecake in a hot-water bath, which also acts as a buffer in the baking process. If you're using a springform or removable-bottom pan, be sure to wrap the pan with extra-heavy aluminum foil in such a way as to prevent water from seeping in and ruining the crust. Set the foil-wrapped pan inside a larger pan and pour in hot water to a depth of 1 to 2 inches. (The foil also serves an additional purpose: it retains heat and slows the cooling process to help prevent cracking.)

As the cheesecake approaches the end of the suggested baking time, give the pan a nudge. The area that quivers will be less defined than that of a custard pie, but it is still a reliable indicator of doneness. Many cheesecakes remain quite liquid in the center even well into the cooling period. This is because, unlike a custard pie, which sets from residual heat, the final setting of a cheesecake takes place as it cools.

Avoid inserting skewers or knives to test for doneness. When the jiggly spot in the center is the size of a quarter, turn the oven off and leave the door ajar. (Resist the urge to continue baking until the surface puffs; a puffed cheesecake has overcooked.) Contin-

ued cooking will take place from residual interior heat and the heat rising from the water bath. Allow the cheesecake to remain inside the oven for several hours to cool to room temperature, then refrigerate.

If you can do so without damaging the crust, run a knife around the top of the cake to release it from the sides of the pan. This alleviates the stress that occurs as a cheesecake contracts during refrigeration.

Cracking also causes problems with yeast breads, yeast pastries (like nut rolls), and quick breads. Although a limited amount of cracking is normal and even attractive in quick breads, excessive cracking is undesirable. Generally the cause is too much flour.

If a quick-bread recipe is giving you trouble, experiment with reducing the amount of flour by 2 tablespoons. Yeast bread and pastry recipes often call for excessive flour, which partly explains why beginning bread bakers tend to produce dry, heavy loaves. Always add less flour than the recipe calls for, kneading in the remainder. The dough will absorb only what it needs, and your loaves will be less apt to split and crack (see Bread Baking).

RECIPE: New York-Style Cheesecake. ✑

CREAM (Sweet)

Cream is a natural emulsion consisting of butterfat particles suspended in water, the liquid component of milk. Like milk, cream also contains numerous proteins, and those proteins are the source of most cream-related cooking disasters.

Since heat and acid denature protein, causing it to coagulate, you must be extremely careful when adding cream to a sauce, gravy, or soup (see Denaturing; Coagulation). It's a good idea to warm cream (even sour cream) before adding it to a hot mixture. Warm it slowly in a saucepan with a small amount of water (to dilute the protein content), or gently stir a sizeable portion of the hot mixture into it. Then remove the hot mixture from the heat and slowly stir in the warmed cream. (Occasionally you may run across recipes that instruct you to stir medium or heavy cream directly into a hot sauce. Although this sounds like a contradiction, it is technically possible because these two creams are high in fat, which surrounds the protein molecules and protects them from the heat.)

The proteins in cream and milk denature in much the same manner that egg-white protein does: firm clots appear that are impossible to dissolve. When you add cream to a sauce or gravy at too high a temperature, the proteins clump together, releasing liquid butterfat, and the sauce develops an oily, grease-streaked texture. This predicament is often described as curdling or separation (see Curdling).

You can sometimes remedy this situation by swirling in a lump of cold butter or, if more drastic action is called for, tossing in an ice cube. The sudden drop in temperature may halt the coagulation.

Acid, especially in tomato soup, causes the protein in cream to coagulate. Sauces to which lemon juice has been added are also vulnerable. For the same reason, the acid content of potatoes (Idaho potatoes contain a significant amount of citric acid) is apt to provoke curdling in scalloped potatoes. The best way to handle the troublesome combination of heat, cream, and acid is, again, to temper its exposure to heat. In the case of creamed tomato soup, heat the cream separately over medium heat and add it to the tomato base just before serving, or chill the tomato base (this works well for all creamed soups), add chilled cream, and gently warm the mixture.

A heat diffuser is a great help in preventing cream-enriched mixtures of all types from curdling on the stove top (see Heat Diffuser), and a water bath performs the same function for dishes cooked in the oven, for it protects food from the shock of excess heat. If you have had poor luck with scalloped potatoes,

next time you make them set your baking dish in a larger pan, add boiling water to the pan to a depth of 1 inch, and bake at a moderate temperature.

The amount of butterfat contained in cream is the chief factor in determining which type you choose. If you're going to whip cream, you'll undoubtedly want the highest fat content available; however, a lower fat content is better for most soups.

The descriptive titles given to the various thicknesses of cream aren't tremendously helpful. "Whipping cream" is a label that causes the most distress, because the fat content can vary anywhere from 30 to 40 percent. Too often people get 30-percent cream home, only to find out it won't whip. Your best bet is to check the side of the container for the percentage of butterfat before you buy. Standards differ from one state to another, but generally speaking, there are three levels of richness: heavy, also called heavy whipping, contains 36 to 40 percent fat; medium, also called table cream and light whipping, contains 30 to 36 percent fat; and light, which contains 18 to 20 percent fat.

Recently, another bit of information has appeared on the sides of cream containers. It's the word "ultrapasteurized," and it refers to a new high-heat method of pasteurization, in which cream is heated to 280°F. for 2 minutes. When you compare that with the traditional process, wherein cream was heated to only 166°F. for 15 *seconds*, you can see why people complain that ultrapasteurized cream tastes cooked.

This new process enables cream to stay fresh for an extraordinary length of time — a fact that certainly pleases supermarket managers, even though many cooks don't share their enthusiasm. High-heat pasteurization changes the way milk protein acts and gives the lactose, or milk sugar, an off taste.

As small, independent dairies go out of business, old-fashioned cream gets harder and harder to come by. Unless you have a cow next door, you may soon find it almost impossible to obtain cream that hasn't been ultrapasteurized. Don't despair — there's a new gizmo available that actually homogenizes milk and unsalted butter to produce exquisitely flavored, natural cream in your own kitchen. By merely adjusting the ratio of butter to milk, you can create various degrees of richness. For example: 4 ounces of melted butter to 4 fluid ounces of milk gives you medium cream; 3 ounces of butter to 4 ounces of milk gives you light cream; and 5 ounces of butter to 4 ounces of milk produces heavy cream.

I have to admit that standing there churning my own cream makes me wonder just how far we've really come. Nevertheless, I highly recommend this ingenious device. It's called the Bel Cream Maker and it's readily available in specialty cookware shops or through gourmet catalogs (see Appendix). ◄߭

CREAM PIE FILLING

Among the most annoying culinary situations is when cream pie filling thins out as it cools, or separates and weeps. All too often your beautiful creation must be eaten within a few hours, or it will turn into a soggy mess.

There are several reasons why thinning and weeping occur. Cornstarch is part of the problem, for while it thickens easily and smoothly, it isn't particularly stable when heated too long or at too high a temperature.

Yet the majority of cream pie recipes invariably call for cornstarch.

Flour, which is used in making classic French pastry cream, is far more reliable, and will produce an egg-enriched cream filling that holds together for days without releasing any moisture. For that reason, the recipes for cream pie filling that appear in this book rely on flour as the thickening starch.

One of the other troublemakers is sugar. It tends to interfere with the thickening power of starch, so for best results, most of it should be added after the starch reaches its full thickening capacity.

Then there are the eggs, which can cause all kinds of difficulty. They do, however, add richness and improve the texture of custard cream — without them, all you would have is pudding pie. Eggs curdle if heated too quickly, but in the presence of flour they can be brought to a boil. In fact, if they're not, an enzyme contained in the yolk will break down the starch and cause the custard cream to thin out (see Pudding: Stirred).

How do you cope with all these potential problems? The first step is to use a candy thermometer as a guide, particularly after the eggs have been added. Most enzymes become inactive at 180°F.; so when the mixture reaches that point, you know you've eliminated one possible cause of thinning.

The remaining difficulties can be handled by using a somewhat more time-consuming, but weep-proof, approach. The following steps outline the reasons for combining the customary eggs, milk, sugar, flour, and salt in a rather unusual way. (For specific recipes, see Index.)

1. A lumpless slurry is absolutely essential for the success of this method (see Slurry). Begin by dispersing the flour with the salt and a small portion of the sugar (see Dispersion). Slowly whisk in part of the milk, then heat the slurry slowly, stirring constantly to prevent the lactose in the milk from scorching. Continue cooking until the mixture reaches 194°F., at which point the flour will have attained its maximum thickening power. You

can then add the rest of the sugar, knowing that it no longer poses a threat to the thickening power of the starch.

2. Whisk the remaining portion of the milk into the egg yolks (this reduces their sensitivity to heat by diluting them). The hot flour mixture can then be added gradually without fear of curdling. A word of caution: since extreme agitation can cause a starch-thickened mixture to break down, do not use a whisk. Stir in the hot mixture with a rubber spatula or wooden spoon (which will also help to avoid the incorporation of excess air that results in a grainy texture).

3. The next step is to heat the egg yolk-flour combination. At 140°F., the milk proteins will begin to coagulate. The egg proteins will start to solidify at 144°F., and some visible thickening will begin to take place around 160°F. You must continue heating the mixture until it reaches 190°F. to be sure that the thinning agent in the egg yolk is destroyed.

Stir the mixture slowly, but continuously, over moderate heat, watching the thermometer. As the temperature approaches 180°F., lift your spatula frequently. Listen for the plopping sound that indicates the first bubble has broken the surface. On the second plop, immediately remove the pan from the heat. Prolonged cooking will cause the egg proteins to aggregate and force out whatever water they have been holding.

4. Cool the custard cream by pouring it into a bowl, but don't attempt to speed things up by stirring it. Cool air, incorporated into the mixture, causes it to give off liquid. Also, do not cover the bowl, for steam rising from the hot custard cream will condense and form into drops. As the mixture cools, these drops of water will fall back onto the custard cream, lying on top or oozing down to the bottom. Either way, the result is a watery consistency.

If you don't cover the mixture, though, steam will evaporate and a skin will form, so take the middle of the road: lay a piece of plastic wrap directly on the surface of the hot custard cream. Smooth out any air bubbles by pressing with your fingertips and push the excess wrap up against the sides of the bowl. This procedure allows enough steam to escape so that condensation won't take place, yet prevents the evaporation from the surface that causes a skin to form. Refrigerate the custard cream until completely cooled before adding it to a prepared pie shell.

RECIPES: Banana Custard Cream Pie, Butterscotch-Pecan Pie, Coconut Custard Cream Pie, Triple Chocolate Cream Pie. ◄₂

CREAM PUFF PASTRY

Cream puff pastry, or *pâte à choux,* is dough that, as it bakes, puffs up into cabbage-shaped pastries called cream puffs. That's also how it got its name — *choux* means cabbage in French.

The success of cream puff pastry depends on perfectly proportioned ingredients, thorough cooking of the *panade,* and enough beating to completely develop the elasticity of the gluten.

Start out by combining cold liquid (water, stock, or a milk-water combination) and cold butter in a deep saucepan. The object is to melt the butter and disperse it evenly throughout the liquid without losing too much of the liquid through evaporation. To speed melting, the butter should be cut into small chunks. Stir the mixture as it cooks to disperse the butter throughout the water. If sugar and salt are to be included, add them to the cold liquid so they will dissolve as the liquid heats. As soon as the butter and water reach a rolling boil, remove the pan from the heat and dump in the flour all at once. Beat vigorously with a wooden spatula until completely blended. Don't worry — this sudden dumping of flour won't result in lumps, because the butter, dispersed throughout the water, greases the flour particles so they won't stick together.

Butter lubricates the strands of gluten so they stretch as much as possible, and it contains moisture that converts to steam and contributes to puffing the pastry as it cooks. Generally speaking, for the puffiest pastry the amount of butter used should be half the amount of flour by weight (4 ounces of flour, or 1 cup, to 2 ounces of butter, or ¼ cup).

Return the saucepan to the burner and cook, stirring continuously over medium-low heat. As it cooks, the batter will begin to pull together into a smooth mass with a satiny finish. Continue cooking and stirring until the dough comes away from the sides of the pan. To test for doneness, pinch the dough — a thoroughly cooked *panade* will not stick to your fingers.

By the time the *panade* is completely cooked, a thin crust will have begun to cook to the bottom of the pan (see Panade). To avoid getting any of these particles in your pastry, empty the *panade* into a bowl before beating in the eggs. Let the *panade* cool for 5 to 10 minutes, or until its temperature drops below 140°F. Stir occasionally during this period to hasten cooling and to prevent a crust from forming on the surface.

The next step is to incorporate the eggs into the cooled *panade*. (Beating eggs into an excessively hot *panade* causes a portion of the egg to coagulate, reducing the amount available to strengthen and puff the pastry.) As the eggs are beaten in, the gluten strands will become more and more elastic. For this reason, it's a good idea to beat with a wooden spatula or the paddle attachment on an electric mixer. The regular beaters of an electric mixer tend to sever the gluten strands rather than develop them.

Under optimum dry conditions, 1 cup of flour will absorb 1 cup of eggs. That usually turns out to be 4 or 5 large eggs. Since the ratio of ingredients is crucial to the success of this pastry, measuring the eggs is a sensible approach. Lightly whisk the eggs and pour them into a measuring cup. If they don't equal the amount of flour used, whisk another egg, adding as much of it as necessary to make it equal. Beat one-quarter of the eggs into the *panade* at a time. At first, the mix-

ture will seem as though it won't accept the eggs, but don't give up. As you continue to beat, the eggs will be taken in and the mixture will smooth out.

The final quarter of whisked eggs should be added with caution: Beating vigorously, add it in a thin stream. You can test for proper consistency by lifting the beater or allowing the dough to drop from a spoon. It should fall in a thick, heavy ribbon and leave a peak that stands stiff. Keep in mind that the goal is to add as much egg as possible without thinning the consistency of the dough. This procedure differs from the classic technique of beating in whole eggs, but it enables you to incorporate the maximum amount of egg.

Completed cream puff pastry can be used for a variety of dishes. Baked, it can take on many forms, from tiny appetizer puffs to dessert eclairs, cream puffs, and profiteroles; dropped by spoonfuls into hot fat, it emerges as *beignets;* mixed with an equal amount of potato and fried in deep fat, it becomes *Potatoes Dauphine;* and when added to a meat, vegetable, or fish purée and poached, it turns into quenelles.

RECIPES: Beignets with Lemon Sauce, Cream Puffs, Flounder Quenelles au Gratin, Goat Cheese Beignets, King Crab Puffs, Mushroom Beignets, Potatoes Dauphine. ◀

CREAMING

When a recipe begins by instructing you to cream solid shortening (butter or hydrogenated [vegetable] shortening) and sugar together, it indicates that you're to combine the two. If performed correctly, though, the procedure involves far more than just dumping both ingredients into a bowl and beating the daylights out of them.

The reason for creaming solid shortening and sugar together in the first place is to incorporate as much air as possible into the batter. Since this is best accomplished by allowing the shortening to soften before beating, remove the necessary amount of butter from the refrigerator before you begin. (Hydrogenated shortening, which is customarily stored at room temperature, can be creamed immediately.) Cut the chilled butter into chunks, place in a large mixing bowl, and allow it to warm for 20 minutes. Depending on the warmth of your kitchen, it should by that time have softened enough to proceed.

The optimum temperature for beating air into butter is 60°F. Here's where an instant-read thermometer comes in handy — you can tell in seconds if your butter is ready by inserting the end of the thermometer into the center of a large chunk. If you don't own an instant-read thermometer, you can judge when the butter is ready by pressing your finger against it. Your finger should make a sizeable dent, but the butter should feel cool.

Be careful not to let the butter get too warm. Warm butter turns oily and refuses to hold air, so your final product comes out heavy and densely textured.

When the butter warms to 60°F. and is malleable, begin to beat it slowly, with your mixer set at low speed, with a wide wooden spoon if you're really full of pep, or with a large balloon whisk (either hand-held or attached to the mixer). Be attentive: it's very easy to overbeat, causing the butter to turn oily.

In any event, the creaming procedure should start slowly and gradually increase in speed. As air is drawn into the butter, it will be trapped and distributed as tiny air bubbles, and a fluffy consistency will develop. At that point, it's time to *sprinkle* in the sugar — don't dump it in all at once.

Sugar crystals have sharp edges that cut into the butter and create more air pockets as the sugar is blended in, so it's to your advantage to add sugar gradually. Continue beating only until the sugar is incorporated. Here again, it's important not to overbeat and turn the butter oily. (Oily butter does a poor job of accepting eggs, which is usually the next step in a recipe.)

A successfully creamed mixture should be light, fluffy, and nearly double in volume.

Only a slight graininess can be detected when you rub a small amount between your fingers. If you have used butter, the mixture will be pale yellow in color. A well-creamed mixture will readily accept eggs and other ingredients.   ◦ᢒ

CRÈME FRAÎCHE

Crème fraîche has always been an important element in authentic French cooking, and, with the recent popularity of nouvelle cuisine techniques, this ingredient is receiving more attention now than ever before.

Containing around 35 percent butterfat, *crème fraîche* is similar to American heavy cream, but there the likeness ends. *Crème fraîche* has a thicker, heavier texture due to the same kind of fermentation and denaturing that makes buttermilk and sour milk slightly viscous. Its flavor is somewhat sour, yet nutty. When heated, *crème fraîche* retains its thick consistency and resists curdling, even in the presence of an acid like wine, so it's unsurpassed when it comes to finishing sauces.

In its liquid form, *crème fraîche* is often poured over fruit and other desserts. Its slightly sour flavor provides an interesting foil for sweetness. Because of its high fat content, *crème fraîche* can also be whipped.

Commercially prepared *crème fraîche* is beginning to appear in large supermarkets, but you can also create an acceptable homemade substitute. This is done by adding a fermented or cultured dairy product to heavy cream, then leaving the mixture at room temperature; under these conditions, the bacteria that produce lactic acid will reproduce and infiltrate the heavy cream.

There is great disagreement over which cultured product makes the best *crème fraîche*. Sour cream, buttermilk, and yogurt can all be used, but each produces a different result. There is also a lack of consensus about how much of the culturing agent to use; formulas vary from as little as 1 teaspoon per cup to as high a ratio as cup-for-cup. In the long run you just have to decide for yourself.

Sour cream, which is made from light cream, and buttermilk, which is made from skim milk, are cultured with the same lactic acid-forming bacteria and therefore tend to contribute similar flavor elements. Sour cream produces a more mellow *crème fraîche,* but, if used in significant amounts, its higher fat content increases the number of calories in the final mixture. Depending on the proportions used, *crème fraîche* made from buttermilk is lower in calories and has a more acidic flavor. Yogurt, which is cultured with a different bacteria (see Yogurt), produces *crème fraîche* with the most assertive flavor (see recipes for *Crème Fraîche*).

Some recipes tell you to use heavy cream that's only pasteurized, not ultrapasteurized; others specify raw or unpasteurized. Actually, it's a matter of personal preference, for the final flavors will differ only slightly. You can successfully achieve thick, full-bodied *crème fraîche* with all types of heavy cream — raw, regular pasteurized, and ultrapasteurized.

The length of time you allow fermenting *crème fraîche* to stand at room temperature depends on the temperature in the room and the ratio of culturing agent to cream you use. Eight to 12 hours is usually enough time for the cream to thicken and develop an acidic tang, if you've mixed at least 1 part culturing agent with 2 parts heavy cream. Less culturing agent than that may require up to 24 hours. A chilly room (68°F. or lower) will slow fermentation, and the heat of a summer day will speed it up, so to regulate hot or cold conditions, use a thermos bottle. To compensate for a chilly room, allow *crème fraîche* to mature in a thermos rinsed with boiling water; for an overly hot room, pour *crème fraîche* into a thermos rinsed with ice water. (Temperature can also be controlled with a new gadget called the Solait Kitchen Dairy. This is a plastic insulating container surrounding a glass culturing jar that enables you to transform cultured cream or milk into *crème fraîche,* yogurt, buttermilk, or fresh cheese; see Appendix.)

Regardless of the culture you use to initiate fermentation, *crème fraîche* will keep in the refrigerator for 7 to 10 days. You can also freeze it, but it separates and thins out as it defrosts. The flavor remains good, so you can use it in some dishes, but because the consistency has been ruined, you can no longer rely on it to thicken sauces.

RECIPE: Crème Fraîche.

CRUST FORMATION

When baking yeast bread or rolls, two of the characteristics you want to be able to control are the texture and appearance of the crust. For example, you expect a water-based French- or Italian-style loaf to have a light brown, crisply textured crust with a chewy consistency. On the other hand, a pan of sweet dinner rolls should develop a deep brown, soft exterior that offers little resistance to the teeth.

As yeast bread bakes, the heat of the oven permeates the interior of the dough, transforming water to steam (see Bread Baking). The weblike network of protein and starch begins to set, and the loaf becomes slightly firm. Since the outer layers of dough are in direct contact with the heat of both the oven and the pan, they set first, release their moisture, and form a crust.

Several things determine how much interior moisture will be lost during evaporation and therefore what the final texture of the crust will be. If, before baking, you brush the surface of yeast dough with an egg glaze, you seal in considerable moisture and create a soft crust (see Egg Wash). At the opposite extreme, if you lightly dust the entire surface of the dough with flour, you achieve a crisp, crackly crust. The flour acts like a blotter, drawing moisture from the outer layers as the crust forms. This technique is particularly effective on free-standing peasant-style loaves, creating a hearty, robust exterior.

Brushing rolls or bread with milk before baking produces a thin, soft crust; using water forms a thin, crisp crust; and adding salt to the water flavors the crust and further increases its crispiness. A delicately crispy crust can be achieved by applying an egg-white wash to bread dough before baking, or, for a somewhat thicker exterior, try a cornstarch finish. In a small saucepan, dissolve 1 teaspoon of cornstarch in ½ cup cold water. Bring the mixture to a boil. Allow to cool slightly and brush over the surface of the unbaked bread. After the loaves have baked for 10 minutes, apply a second coating.

If you don't apply anything to the outer surface of yeast bread, the crust that ultimately develops will be determined by the heat and humidity inside the oven and the ingredients in the dough. Breads baked at high temperatures (425°F.) develop crisp crusts; those baked at moderate temperatures (325° to 375°F.) come out with relatively soft crusts. Creating humidity inside a hot oven is a popular method for attaining a crisp crust. This can be done by occasionally spraying the inside of the oven with a fine mist, or by placing a pan of water on the rack nearest the heating element. Soft crusts can be enhanced by applying a glaze after baking (see Glazing).

Yeast dough that is high in fat and sugar retains more moisture during baking than dough that has little of either, so don't expect bread containing shortening, milk, eggs, or a sizeable portion of sugar to develop a crisp crust on its own. However, water-based dough, which contains no fat, sugar, or eggs, readily gives up moisture in the form of steam. Consequently, its final exterior will be firm and crisp.

You can influence the color of bread crust by applying an egg wash; the type of wash you use will determine the depth and intensity of the color. A whole-egg wash produces a medium golden hue; an egg-yolk wash creates a rich, deep brown.

Bread dough will color naturally as it bakes without any help at all. The proteins and sugar present in flour interact with the dry heat to bring about the browning process known as the Maillard reaction (see Browning — Maillard Reaction). A loaf of water-based bread baked without anything applied to its surface will turn a pale, dusty brown, but a dough containing sugar and eggs will develop a browner crust due to the increased amount of protein and sugar available.

The bottom crust of yeast bread is greatly influenced by the material it's baked on. Shiny metal pans produce soft-crusted bottoms, so they are usually used for soft breads and dinner rolls. Black or dull metal absorbs heat and gives the bottom of bread a crisp texture. The crispiest crust of all is produced by baking bread on a ceramic baking stone, making it the best choice for peasant-style, free-standing loaves. A glass loaf pan produces a surprisingly crisp bottom crust, as does a round Pyrex dish, which is also an excellent container for baking a round loaf that doesn't have quite enough strength to stand on its own.

After all this talk about crust formation, it seems only fair to mention bread that doesn't have crust. A uniquely designed pan, called a Pullman loaf pan, turns out bread with the barest hint of a crust. The secret is a removable lid that you slide over the dough. As the loaf bakes, the dough is forced to conform to a neat rectangular shape, and because the lid prevents moisture from evaporating, the outer layers of dough don't have the opportunity to form a crust. It's just the thing for canapés and fancy sandwiches.   ◄

CURDLING

Anyone who has ever experimented with fairly intricate recipes has almost certainly encountered the cooking disaster known as curdling. The first stage of curdling appears as a kind of separation — the mixture takes on a grainy or streaky texture, and the surface looks oily and separated. Advanced curdling is evident as tiny lumps of egg yolk or clots of cream that refuse to dissolve. Heat, acid, salt, and the alcohol in liquor, wine, or flavoring extracts can each be held to blame for this predicament.

Curdling is apt to occur during the preparation of hollandaise sauce, cream pie filling, stirred custard, egg- or cream-enriched sauces, and cream soups. In fact, just about any time you heat a mixture containing eggs, milk, or cream there's a possibility it could curdle.

Eggs, milk, cream, and sour cream all contain a significant amount of protein. When protein molecules are heated, they gradually change from a liquid to a solid state (see Denaturing). During the initial phase of this process, the slowly firming molecules have the ability to trap and hold liquid, and are capable of thickening a mixture.

Denatured protein molecules tend to link together, forming a network of firm bridges, in the process known as coagulation (see Coagulation). As long as coagulation is kept under control, the protein molecules will thicken a mixture smoothly and evenly. But if too much heat is applied, or the molecules come in contact with excess acid, alcohol, or salt, coagulation will occur too fast — the proteins will then aggregate and release whatever liquid they had been holding. This is an irreversible situation. Protein molecules that have grouped together will not hold liquid, so you end up with a thin, runny sauce full of lumps, or curds, that you can't rescue.

To avoid curdling, use low heat. Stir gently to distribute the heat and to promote even thickening, by keeping all the molecules at the same level of firmness throughout the mixture. (You want to discourage groups of molecules from joining together and forming pockets of molecular networks before the entire mixture is thoroughly heated.)

Acids can help the thickening process because, like heat, they also denature protein molecules. So do alcohol and salt, but all

these elements must be added with care. Always keep in mind that uncontrolled coagulation leads to curdling.

For example, don't be surprised to see a smooth stirred custard separate if you add the vanilla extract before the mixture is cool enough to accept it (it should be allowed to cool for 10 minutes). This is the initial phase of curdling, and the combination of excess heat and alcohol is responsible for it.

You can often rescue a mixture at the earliest stage of separation by whisking in a few drops of ice water or slivers of ice. The quick drop in temperature will halt the curdling in most instances.

One of the trickiest maneuvers in cooking is adding eggs or cream to a hot mixture for the purpose of thickening it — a step that occurs in the making of various pie fillings, sauces, and soups (see Liaison). The key to success is to blend a sizeable portion of the hot mixture into the cooler eggs or cream. Initially, do it drop by drop, no matter what your recipe says. After you've blended in about 3 tablespoons of the hot mixture, you can add the remainder in a slow, thin stream.

This procedure gradually warms the protein in the eggs or cream and gives the denaturing process a chance to begin slowly. Two things happen simultaneously: the drops of hot liquid are quickly cooled by the cold eggs or cream to the point where they can't do any harm; at the same time, the eggs and cream are slowly warmed by successive drops of the hot liquid.

Remember that a drop of hot liquid can be dispersed and cooled very quickly by stirring it through the unheated eggs or cream. On the other hand, if you pour a drop of beaten eggs or cream into a hot mixture, it will curdle upon contact. That's why the rule of thumb is: always add slowly a hot mixture to a cooler mixture to avoid curdling or separating.

The warmed eggs or cream are subsequently added to the remaining hot mixture and this is returned to the heat for additional warming. At this point, everything should go along smoothly if the mixture is kept over low heat.   ◅〉

CUSTARD

Stirred custard and baked custard are thickened and firmed solely by the coagulation of proteins — not by starch. Although the two procedures for making these custards are slightly different, the chemical process that takes place inside the mixtures as they cook is very much the same.

In preparing a stirred custard, or custard cream, you combine eggs, milk, sugar, salt, and vanilla and cook over gentle heat until the mixture thickens and coats the back of a spoon. The whole idea is to denature the protein molecules slowly so they will unwind and join together, coagulating and forming a firm, weblike network (see Denaturing; Coagulation). The coagulation must be carefully controlled, however, since excess heat can cause the protein molecules to group together, release water, and result in a lumpy, weepy custard.

Success with stirred custard depends on first warming the milk, then gradually warming the eggs by stirring in the warm milk. At that point, the sugar and salt are blended in and the entire mixture is heated gently. Salt promotes coagulation, but sugar tends to interfere with the denaturing of proteins, so if a recipe requires a large amount of sugar (more than 1 tablespoon for every 2 egg yolks), it's

best initially to add only a portion of the full amount, then add the rest when the mixture has started to thicken.

Vanilla extract presents a different problem. Since it contains alcohol, vanilla generates heat, which can cause curdling if stirred into a hot mixture. For that reason, it's a good idea to combine the vanilla with the cold milk that is added during the final stage of the recipe.

In order to keep coagulation under control (and prevent the eggs from scrambling), custard must be cooked gently. If you decide to use a double boiler, regulate the temperature of the burner so that the water in the lower pan never rises above a simmer. Don't allow the water to touch the bottom of the upper container — if it does, the custard at the bottom will overheat.

It is possible to prepare stirred custard without a double boiler, but it requires constant attention. Use a thick-bottomed pan and set it on a heat diffuser to even the distribution of heat (see Heat Diffuser). Stir continuously with a heat-resistant rubber spatula (it does absolutely the best job of clearing the bottom of the pan) or wooden spoon (see Stirring). As the mixture reaches 144°F., the egg proteins start to solidify, and coagulation begins. Visible thickening takes place as you approach 160°F. Continue stirring slowly. To test for doneness, coat a spatula with the custard and draw a finger through the coating to create a path. When the path remains open for a few seconds, the custard is properly thickened (see illustration).

Remove the thickened custard from the heat and immediately add the cold milk and vanilla. Blending in cold milk at this point prevents residual heat from overcooking the mixture. The cold milk also lowers the temperature of the custard enough to eliminate the weeping that often occurs as a custard cream cools. Some recipes instruct you to stir or beat in order to hasten cooling. However, stirring or beating draws in bubbles of cool air that cause the mixture to exude liquid due to condensation.

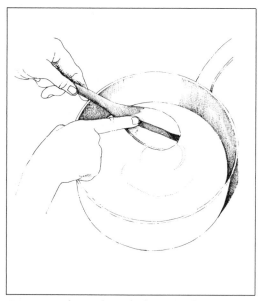

Draw your finger through the custard coating the spoon; if the path remains open for a few seconds, the custard has cooked long enough.

After the cold milk is incorporated, strain the custard cream into a chilled bowl and cover by laying a piece of plastic wrap directly on the surface. Smooth out any air bubbles by pressing with your fingertips and push the excess wrap up against the sides of the bowl. This covering prevents evaporation, which would otherwise cause a skin to form on the surface. Refrigerate until completely cool.

Baked custard is also made by combining eggs, milk, sugar, salt, and vanilla. The difference is that coagulation takes place in the oven rather than on top of the stove. In many ways, baked custard is easier to make than stirred custard; you simply combine all the ingredients and pour them into baking cups or a flan mold. There are, however, still a few tricks to the trade.

Warming the milk and gradually blending it into the eggs is not a necessary step, but it does give coagulation a head start and produces a smoother baked custard (see Scalding Milk). Do not beat or whisk as you combine the warm milk, eggs, and other ingredients. Stir gently; if you incorporate air, the custard will exhibit a bubbly, pockmarked texture. (On the other hand, if you prefer a porous custard with a frothy-looking top, whisking is the way to achieve it.) It's also a good idea to strain the egg yolks before adding them, in order to remove the large bits of egg white known as chalazae, which anchor the yolks to the whites and often remain even when eggs are separated. When chalazae coagulate, they mar the texture of baked custard by creating small watery pits.

Bake your custard surrounded by water to buffer it from the heat. Place the custard cups or flan mold on a rack set inside a large pan. Pour hot, but not boiling, water into the pan to the depth of 1 inch. (Boiling water shocks the custard mixture and is apt to result in a grainy texture.) If the use of a rack seems precarious to you, line the waterbath pan with a dish towel folded in quarters. The object is to elevate the bottom of the custard dish, or in some way prevent it from coming in direct contact with the hot pan, which can overheat the bottom of a baked custard.

A baked custard that exudes liquid has probably been overheated. When protein molecules are subjected to too much heat, they group together, squeezing out whatever liquid had previously been held in the pockets of the molecular network. Therefore, if you bake a custard too long, or at too high a temperature, it is apt to weep. Overheating can also cause cracks to develop during cooling, which fill with the liquid released earlier by the aggregating proteins.

Instead of testing for doneness by inserting the blade of a knife, take it from the oven while a spot in the center is still jiggly (see Cracking). For individual custards, the undercooked spot should be the size of a dime; in a large single custard or flan, the size of a nickel. Allow the custard to sit in its waterbath until cooking is completed by the residual heat.

RECIPES: Banana Custard Cream Pie, Caramel Flan, Coconut Custard Cream Pie, Crème Brulée, Roasted Red Pepper Flan.   ↝

CUTTING-IN

Everyone has a different opinion about what constitutes *the* perfect pie crust. Some prefer a short-flake, or mealy, crust — the type that breaks evenly when pierced with a fork; others like a long-flake crust that shatters into flakes. Cutting-in is the procedure that determines, to a great extent, whether your crust will be short-flake, long-flake, or something in-between.

Most pie crust recipes (and occasionally recipes for other types of pastry) start off by telling you to cut a certain amount of fat into flour. The object is to break the fat into tiny pieces, each coated with flour. Later, when the pastry bakes in the oven, the heat melts the fat, which is absorbed by the flour, and tiny pockets are created. Moisture in the pastry turns to steam, which fills the pockets and puffs them up, lightening the crust.

The size of the bits of fat is going to determine the size of the steam pockets. Therefore, if you want a short-flake, or mealy, consistency to your pastry, cut in the fat until the bits are very small and the mixture has a fairly homogeneous, crumbly look to it. For a long-flake crust, the kind that shatters when you break it, stop cutting in the fat when the bits are quite large — about the size of navy beans. This mixture will not be homogeneous at all. In fact, it will look downright peculiar, but don't be afraid to leave the pieces of fat a little larger than you think they should be.

Cutting-in occurs as each stroke of the knife, or other utensil, slices through the fat, breaking it into smaller and smaller pieces. The continued motion of the knife tosses the bits of fat, coating them with flour — a detail that's every bit as important as the actual slicing.

You can cut fat into flour with a wire pastry blender, one knife or two (one in each hand), a paddle-type attachment to an electric mixer, a food processor, or your fingertips. The food processor creates a crust with an extremely short flake because it cuts the shortening into such fine pieces. An electric mixer with a paddle beater is somewhat easier to control, but it also produces a rather mealy pie crust. A wire pastry blender is an efficient tool, but it doesn't cut so much as it mashes — a movement that can oversoften some of the fat before the procedure is completed.

Oversoftening is a disadvantage to using the fingertip method, too, and unless you're an old hand at this operation, it's better to skip it. The warmth from your hands can soften the fat to the point where it becomes oily. Oversoftened, or oily, fat coats an excess number of flour particles, which means that when water is added not enough gluten will develop. The result is a hard, heavy pie crust.

I've found that the very best approach to cutting-in is to use one knife and actually slice the fat into bits, tilting and turning the bowl with one hand while cutting with a knife in the other. Using this by-hand method, you have absolute control over what goes on. When you see a piece of fat that's a little too big, you can tackle that one piece, without demolishing several others around it.

Use the biggest bowl you own, too, so you'll have plenty of room to move around. Cut cold butter into small chunks, or scoop out shortening by tablespoonfuls, and drop onto the flour. Then, with an ordinary table knife, or an 8-inch palette knife that fits comfortably inside your palm, slice through the fat. Toss the flour as you cut to make sure that each bit is flour-coated. Stop cutting when you've reached the consistency you need for the type of crust you want (see Pie Crust). ✑

D

DEGLAZING

When you roast or sauté meat, fat and water rise to its surface. The water carries with it various protein compounds that denature and coagulate on the bottom of the pan. During cooking, the water evaporates off as steam and the coagulated protein turns brown and hardens into small particles (see Browning — Maillard Reaction).

These small brown particles are actually concentrated meat juice, and deglazing is a method of extracting their flavorful essence to use as the base for a gravy or sauce.

Successful deglazing depends, of course, on having particles to deglaze. Roasting doesn't seem to present any problems in this area, but sautéing does (see Sautéing). To achieve the maximum number of browned particles in a sauté, use the smallest amount of oil possible, and make sure the meat is dry when it enters the hot fat. (Meat may be coated with flour or blotted dry with paper towels. If flour is used, it contributes an element of thickening power to the particles that form.) Don't crowd the pan, because that produces excess steam, which in turn hinders particle formation. Cook over high heat and, above all, avoid using a pan with a nonstick surface. (Food doesn't adhere to the bottom of these pans, so particle formation is almost nonexistent.)

Carefully spoon or pour out most of the fat from the pan, taking care not to lose any of the browned particles. Then add some form of liquid, such as wine, stock, or water, to the pan and bring to a brisk bubble. Scrape the bottom of the pan with a wooden spoon to release any stubborn particles.

Some, but usually not all, of the particles will dissolve. Stir continuously to break them up, so they will transfer as much flavor as possible to the liquid. Continue cooking until the liquid is richly colored and slightly thickened. The undissolved particles can be strained out, or whirl the liquid in the blender to smooth out the consistency.

DEGREASING

Chilling is the most thorough and efficient way to remove the grease from any mixture, because cool temperatures encourage droplets of fat to join together in a group. When the group becomes large enough, the fact that the fat is lighter than the substance it's in causes it to rise to the surface. As the temperature drops further, the fat solidifies and can easily be lifted off with a spoon.

A version of this technique is sometimes used in gravy making. After you remove the roast from the pan, toss 8 to 12 ice cubes into the pan drippings. Place the pan in a cool spot, and, in 15 to 20 minutes, the fat will solidify in circles around the partially melted ice cubes. Lift off the firm fat and proceed to make gravy in your usual manner. Just remember to cook it a bit longer in order to evaporate the excess water created by the melting ice.

The principle of fat coalescence explains the workings of a new gadget designed for degreasing meat juices. Some imaginative person invented a container with a spout at the bottom instead of the top (see Appendix). When you pour your pan drippings into the container, and let them cool a bit, the fat drops join together and rise to the surface. Then when you tilt the container, grease-free meat juices pour out through the spout. A brilliant idea, except that I can never get the spout completely clean.

In some instances, liquid grease appears on the surface of simmering mixtures, like stew and spaghetti sauce. This is nearly always the result of a sautéing step performed earlier. When vegetables or meat are cooked in oil or butter at the beginning of a recipe, liquid grease will invariably show up later on, unless it is drained after the sautéing step. If a recipe doesn't tell you to drain the grease, it may be that the fat is expected to contribute flavor to the dish. In any event, I always skim it off with a shallow spoon before serving. Nobody needs those calories.   ◅ৈ

DENATURING

Many of the transformations that occur during cooking can be attributed to the chemical process known as denaturing. Protein molecules, particularly in eggs and milk, have the tendency to change shape when they are heated. In their natural state, protein molecules look like tightly coiled bundles of fibers, a compact shape that makes them fairly easy to dissolve (actually protein molecules are so large they never truly dissolve, but instead remain in suspension). When heat is applied, the molecules begin to uncoil into long strands. This change in structure affects their solubility: they are no longer capable of being dissolved and they also become firm.

With continued heating, the strand-shaped molecules begin to link together in a firm, weblike network. You can easily see this transformation take place when you prepare a stirred custard. As the protein molecules heat and change shape, the custard firms, or coagulates (see Coagulation). The denaturing process is the reason you must stir a custard gently. As you bring the denatured molecules up from the bottom of the pan (where they uncoil first) and distribute them throughout the mixture, they begin to link together. Vigorous stirring would disturb the network that is being formed.

Acids, salt, and mechanical agitation can also denature protein molecules. When you beat egg whites, they become light and fluffy because you're incorporating air bubbles (see Whipping: Egg Whites). But they become stiff because you're agitating them. If you add a dash of salt or a pinch of cream of tartar (an acid), you're supplying additional elements to encourage the egg-white proteins to denature and become firm (which explains why salt and cream of tartar are said to "stabilize" egg whites).

The denaturing of proteins is often a helpful procedure, but it can easily get out of control. Protein molecules have the ability to hold water to themselves, and also within the pockets of the network they form. This, however, is a tenuous arrangement. Too much heat, too much acid, or excessive beating can cause protein molecules to aggregate. As the molecules move toward each other, the pockets of the network become smaller and any water held there is squeezed out. You've seen this happen if you've ever overbeaten egg whites. The molecules group together, creating a grainy texture, and the water that is squeezed out appears on the sides and bottom of your bowl.

Then there are those times when curdling occurs (see Curdling). When eggs, milk, or cream are heated in the presence of an acid, denatured protein may produce unpleasant lumps. For this reason, recipes are usually very explicit about when and how to add acidic ingredients such as wine, lemon juice, or vinegar to mixtures containing eggs, milk, or cream.

It's interesting to note that milk is higher in protein than cream, and as cream increases in fat content, it decreases in protein. Milk contains 3.5 percent protein but heavy cream only 2.2 percent. This partially explains why heavy cream can be boiled without curdling. Heavy cream is also slow to curdle because butterfat surrounds the protein molecules, making it difficult for them to group together and form lumps.

In addition to a change in solubility, the denaturing of protein also brings about modifications in density. A very obvious example occurs during the baking of popovers. The network of protein molecules created by combining eggs and milk puffs up when the batter is heated. The interstices of the network, supported by flour starch and gluten, become air pockets, which grow larger as the hot air expands. When a certain temperature is reached, the protein denatures and the resulting increase in density causes the network to coagulate and become stiff, creating the weblike interior of the popover.

Meat protein denatures in a similar fashion. As you heat a piece of meat, the texture begins to change from pliant to firm at about 135°F. The network of protein molecules becomes firm and dense, affecting the texture and the moisture of meat. However, the denaturing of protein plays a relatively small part in the process of cooking meat, and many other factors contribute to its final toughness or tenderness (see Meat).

DISPERSION

A dispersion is a specific kind of mixture in which one element, or ingredient, is evenly distributed throughout another. Three types of dispersions are important to cookery: solid-in-solid dispersions, such as the mixture of sugar and flour you use to prepare a cream pie filling; solid-in-liquid dispersions like a roux of flour in melted butter; and liquid-in-liquid dispersions like oil and vinegar in vinaigrette dressing.

Solid-in-solid dispersions are often formed to ensure that dry ingredients, such as spices and leavening agents, are evenly incorporated when they are added to a batter. However, the predominant reason for using solid-in-solid dispersions is to prevent lumps from forming (see Lump Formation).

The usual approach to creating a solid-in-solid dispersion is to thoroughly distribute, or disperse, a readily dissolvable ingredient throughout one that is more difficult to dissolve. The combination of sugar and flour provides a good example. If you add liquid to a quantity of flour, a number of starch particles will spontaneously stick together and form lumps. (This is especially true when the liquid is milk, because the butterfat in milk retards the dissolving action.) If, however, you disperse sugar, which is easy to dissolve, throughout the flour, you will separate the flour particles from one another, making it possible to stir in a liquid without causing the flour to lump.

Solid-in-liquid dispersions are also used to avoid lumping. When you create a roux by melting butter and stirring in flour, you're separating the difficult-to-dissolve flour particles with liquid fat. Then, when milk or stock is added, the flour particles are far less likely to lump together (see Roux; Gravy).

Just as flour mixed with melted butter is not considered a solution because the flour doesn't dissolve, other solid-in-liquid dispersions aren't solutions either, even though they appear to be. A slurry of cornstarch or flour and water is a solid-in-liquid dispersion, because the granules of protein and starch aren't completely dissolved — they're merely separated. This becomes obvious if you let a slurry stand for any length of time; the solids will precipitate, or settle to the bottom. Milk and cream are naturally occurring solid-in-liquid dispersions. Even an egg white whisked with water, while it looks like a solution, is, in fact, a mixture of protein solids dispersed in a liquid.

Protein molecules are so large that they don't mix with liquids to form a true solution. In other words, they are not completely dissolved, but rather dispersed throughout the liquid. This explains why coagulation happens easily when milk or cream is heated, and why an egg white-water combination is used for clarifying stock (see Coagulation; Clarifying Stock).

A solid-in-liquid dispersion like milk, where the solid particles are so fine they remain permanently suspended, is often referred to as a colloidal dispersion, or colloid. A solid-in-liquid dispersion can also be considered a fine suspension, a term that I prefer to use because it emphasizes the fact that one element is held, or suspended, in another (see Suspension).

A liquid-in-liquid dispersion is a mixture of two ingredients, neither of which will dissolve in the other. When you combine oil and vinegar, for example, you've created a liquid-in-liquid dispersion (not a solution). If you shake the mixture, the oil droplets will disperse throughout the vinegar to form a vinaigrette dressing, but this is only a temporary situation. When you stop agitating the mixture, the oil droplets will group together and rise to the surface. Should you decide to add an emulsifying agent to a liquid-in-liquid dispersion, you can link the two ingredients together to create a permanent liquid-in-liquid dispersion, also called an emulsion (see Emulsion).

The concept of liquid dispersions is a bit tricky, so just to reiterate: a solid-in-liquid dispersion is not considered a solution, because the solid element doesn't dissolve. A liquid-in-liquid dispersion is also not considered a solution, since neither liquid element is capable of dissolving the other.   ❧

DREDGING

Dredging food in flour is often a preliminary step to coating it with beaten eggs and crumbs or dipping it in batter, so it might seem like a waste of time. Dredging, however, performs several very important functions.

First of all, it provides a dry surface for a beaten egg or batter coating to cling to. Dredging with flour insulates food from the high heat of frying so food doesn't dry out; it also forms an effective seal, so that fat can't get in to saturate food and make it greasy. In addition, the thin layer of flour creates a moisture barrier, absorbing traces of moisture that are given off as food cooks. This is extremely important, because this moisture can cause a batter coating to break apart during frying or turn a crisp coating limp (see Batter Coating). Last but not least, a light covering of flour eliminates spattering when you sauté meat or poultry.

Dredging food with flour requires a covering more substantial than a dusting, but lighter than a coating. (In connection with sugar, it implies a fairly heavy sprinkling — more than just a dusting.) Dredging can be accomplished by sprinkling flour, or a mixture of half flour and half cornstarch, over the food and distributing it evenly with your fingertips. You can also lower the food directly into a container of flour, turning it over and over until the surface is completely covered, then gently shaking off any excess flour.

I usually use a deep pie dish when dredging, but a plastic storage bag also works well and eliminates a lot of mess. Simply put some flour in a strong plastic bag, add one or two pieces of food, hold the bag closed, and shake to dredge. Avoid dredging food ahead of time, since the flour will absorb moisture from the food and turn gluey.   ❧

E

EGG WASH

Want to produce a pan of rolls with a deep, golden crust? Or make sesame seeds stay on your homemade breadsticks and not fall off? Try using an egg wash.

An egg wash, or glaze, is a classic culinary technique used to color yeast breads and pastries, to seal one layer of pastry dough to another, and to provide a kind of adhesive, so that seeds, nuts, or coarse salt will stick to the surface of baked goods.

You can use an egg wash any time you want to enhance the appearance of something you're baking — whether the recipe suggests it or not. Pie recipes, for example, often overlook this detail, but don't let that stop you. Brushing the top crust of a pie with a whole-egg wash furnishes additional protein and amino acids so the Maillard reaction will occur at an increased rate (see Browning — Maillard Reaction).

Depending on the egg wash you choose, you can create a variety of effects:

An *egg-white wash* consists of 1 egg white plus 1 tablespoon of water. Whisk until the mixture loses its viscosity and is easy to brush on. This wash produces a transparent sheen rather than color. Use it to give sparkle to puff pastries, Danish pastries, and dark breads like pumpernickel. You can also brush it on the surface of rolls, breadsticks, crackers — anything you wish to sprinkle with seeds, nuts, or coarse salt.

A *whole-egg wash* combines a whole egg with 1 tablespoon of liquid, either water or milk. It gives bread, rolls, and pastry a medium golden hue. A whole-egg wash containing milk softens the crust, so you might want to brush it on sweet rolls or dinner rolls. A wash containing water produces a crispier texture and is therefore better for pie crust and other pastry.

An *egg-yolk wash* is a mixture of 1 egg yolk and 1 tablespoon of water. This creates an assertive, deep brown color and is best used for meat pies and hearty, egg-enriched breads like brioche. An egg-yolk wash is apt to streak, so take care in brushing it on.

All types of egg washes can be brushed on with a pastry brush or swabbed on with a cotton ball or a small piece of soft cloth. You can also use your fingers or, for especially delicate work, a goose feather (imported from Hungary and sold in gourmet shops — see Appendix). To achieve a deeper, more even glaze, apply two coats when using either a whole-egg or egg-yolk wash. After the first application, allow the surface to dry slightly — about 2 or 3 minutes — then brush on the second coat.

Don't let an egg wash seep into any seams when you are glazing intricately shaped or braided breads or drip down the sides of cream puff dough and certain pastry. An egg wash seals dough together, so it's apt to hamper the oven rise of yeast breads and the puffing of air-leavened pastries.

Applying an egg wash is not a do-ahead project. On one occasion, I prepared a wheel of camembert wrapped in puff pastry as an appetizer for a dinner party and thought I was smart because I had it ready for the oven at ten o'clock in the morning — egg wash and all. Unfortunately, the pastry absorbed most of the egg wash and came out soggy; what hadn't been absorbed ran down the sides and oozed underneath, so the bottom of the pastry not only stuck to the pan but burned there. The sad lesson I learned was never to brush pastry with an egg wash until just before baking.   ◄᠗

EGGS

Eggs perform an amazing number of culinary tasks. They leaven delicate cakes, bind ground mixtures such as croquettes, glaze pastries, and lend richness to bread. The protein in eggs firms custards and flans, provides strength for the framework of popovers and cream puffs, and coagulates to trap impurities in the clarifying of stock. Notably rich in lecithin, egg yolks emulsify sauces and thicken soups. It goes without saying that eggs are an invaluable ingredient.

The actual cooking of eggs, however, presents a few problems; to understand their behavior, it's important to consider their chemical make-up. A whole egg consists of 11.5 percent fat, 12.9 percent protein, and 73.7 percent water. However, there is almost twice as much egg white as yolk, and the two differ considerably in composition. Egg whites contain only traces of fat (which is a good thing, since fat impedes the formation of whipped whites), 10.9 percent protein, and 87.6 percent water. Yolks, on the other hand, are high in fat (30.6 percent), most of which is lecithin. In addition, yolks contain 16 percent protein, 51.1 percent water, and various vitamins and minerals, including a significant amount of iron. The porous shell surrounding the egg is composed mainly of water and a small amount of protein and calcium.

Boiling

The fact that an eggshell is porous helps to explain one of the most common complaints among cooks — the cracking of shells during boiling. (In actuality, you shouldn't really *boil* an egg, but the term is generally understood, so let's stick with it.) When air enters through the pores of the shell, it gathers in a pocket at the blunt end of the egg — the older the egg, the larger this air pocket becomes. As you heat an egg in water, the air inside begins to expand. This expansion may or may not create enough pressure to crack the eggshell. If the expansion occurs rapidly, as it will if you submerge an egg in boiling water, chances are the shell will crack; if it occurs more slowly, the air has time to find its way out through the pores of the shell.

Some cookbooks suggest pricking a pinhole in the blunt end of an egg to reduce the buildup of air pressure. This method works if you don't make the same mistake I once did — salting the water too soon. Dissolved salt causes egg-white protein to coagulate faster than usual. It's true that this helps prevent boiling eggs from leaking out of their cracked shells in long white streamers, but it also seals up the pinhole.

When you first apply heat to a pan of pricked eggs (and if the eggs are more than a week old), you should hear high-pitched pinging sounds as a steady procession of air bubbles wends its way from each pinhole up to the surface of the water. After this activity ceases, you can safely salt the water to protect against any cracking that might still occur.

Other complications can develop when preparing hard-boiled eggs — that infamous green tinge around the yolk, for instance. During cooking, some of the proteins in the egg white give off hydrogen and sulfur, which combine to form hydrogen sulfide. If you cook the eggs too long, iron in the yolk will attract the hydrogen sulfide and create iron sulfide, the unattractive greenish deposit surrounding the yolk.

Since hydrogen sulfide prefers to go where

it's cool, you can prevent the formation of iron sulfide by cooling the surface of cooked eggs. When they are finished cooking, immediately submerge hard-boiled eggs in cold water. The drop in temperature will lure the hydrogen sulfide in the opposite direction from the iron in the yolk and prevent iron sulfide from forming.

Peeling

Pricking the shell before cooking helps you out in this department, too. During cooking, a small amount of water oozes in through the hole and sneaks around inside, loosening the membrane between the shell and the egg white, thus allowing smooth peeling. Using older eggs (over 4 days) also makes for easier peeling because as air passes in through the pores of the shell, it weakens the membrane that makes peeling difficult.

The alkalinity of egg white is another factor that influences ease of peeling. The problem is, fresh eggs have a pH of 7.6 — too acidic for easy peeling. After 4 or 5 days, though, the acid/alkaline balance changes, and the whites become more alkaline. At a pH level of 8.7, eggs tend to peel without any problem (see pH Scale).

Peeling eggs while they are warm works better than when they're cold and peeling from the blunt end first helps, too; so does holding the egg under a gentle stream of water from the tap.

Poaching

Poaching is another troublesome area of egg cookery. Despite all the gadgets and contraptions that claim to poach eggs, I still receive requests from people who want to know how to make a "real" poached egg — one that is cooked right in the water.

The main difficulty is producing a poached egg that neither overcooks nor falls apart. Since both salt and acid coagulate egg white, you could add a pinch of salt or a dash of vinegar to the cooking water. This helps to set the egg white, but many people have either cut salt from their diets or object to the smell of the vinegar.

The trick to poaching an egg is using gently heated water, and nothing could be more gently heated than a skillet of water that's been removed from the burner. Bring some water in a skillet to a rolling boil, then take the pan off the burner. After the bubbling has subsided and the sloshing has stopped, slip in an egg. Cover the pan immediately, and in the time it takes to make a piece of toast, you have a perfectly poached egg.

Scrambling

Problems with making scrambled eggs are usually caused either by applying too much heat or by trying to cook too many eggs at one time. Never cook more than 2 large eggs, or 3 of a smaller size, in an 8-inch pan. Four or 5 eggs do well in a 10-inch pan; 5 or 6 eggs, in a 12-inch pan. Mix the eggs with milk or water. (Milk is 87 to 90 percent water and contains coagulable proteins of its own; consequently, water produces a lighter, fluffier scrambled egg.) Cook over moderate heat in a thick-bottomed pan. You might even want to try using a heat diffuser to guarantee even cooking (see Heat Diffuser).

As the eggs heat, the protein molecules denature and curds begin to form (see Coagulation). The liquid you've added, plus the water naturally contained in the eggs, turns to steam and produces a light, puffy consistency. Maintain a gentle level of heat. Keep in mind that when protein molecules are overheated, they group together and squeeze out whatever water there had been in the spaces between them. This is what causes overcooked scrambled eggs to weep.

Whipping

For instructions on whipping egg whites and whole eggs, see the entry for Whipping.

RECIPES: Curry-Stuffed Eggs Baked in Shrimp Sauce, Eggs Benedict, Huevos Rancheros.

EMULSIFIERS

Emulsifiers are elements that have the ability to keep fat (or oil) droplets suspended in water, or water droplets suspended in fat. They function in two different ways, both of which are fascinating, since they involve a kind of duplicity.

Keep in mind that, because oil droplets are nonpolar, they have a strong desire to coalesce, a tendency that causes oil and water to separate almost immediately. One type of emulsifier deals with this situation by coating the surface of the oil droplets with a fine film. Since the film creates a physical barrier between the oil droplets, they are deceived into thinking they are alone and, consequently, they lose their desire to group together. Dry mustard, prepared mustard, and paprika are all examples of ingredients that emulsify oil and water in this fashion. If you add a small amount of either mustard or paprika to vinaigrette sauce and whisk vigorously, the oil will remain suspended in the water (that is to say, in the lemon juice or vinegar) for 5 to 10 minutes.

Another type of emulsifier works by creating a series of molecular bridges between droplets of oil and water. Lecithin, the powerful emulsifier contained in egg yolks, is the most frequently used emulsifier of this kind. It effectively links oil and water together by practicing a bit of chemical trickery. Lecithin molecules have two different kinds of endings. One is strongly attracted to oil and is therefore referred to as lipophilic; the other is similarly attracted to water and is referred to as hydrophilic. By deceiving oil droplets into joining its lipophilic end and water droplets into bonding with its hydrophilic end, a lecithin molecule can trick oil and water into linking together.

An additional dimension to this phenomenon involves electrical activity. The hydrophilic end of a lecithin molecule is polar, which means that, like water, it is electrically charged. On the other hand, the lipophilic end of a lecithin molecule is nonpolar and therefore, like oil, it is not electrically charged. During emulsification, the nonpolar ends of lecithin molecules move toward a nonpolar droplet of oil and attach themselves to it. Eventually the surface of the oil droplet is completely covered with the lipophilic endings of lecithin molecules.

Picture an orange with thousands of toothpicks sticking out of it. The ends sticking out represent the polar, hydrophilic ends of the lecithin molecules. Since the exposed ends of the lecithin molecules are all polar, the surface of the oil droplet is disguised as being polar, or electrically charged. The result is that the polar molecules of water are attracted toward the exposed hydrophilic ends of the lecithin molecules, while the nonpolar molecules of oil are repelled. They move off in other directions seeking the endings of nonpolar molecules to attach themselves to.

Chemically prepared emulsifiers also play an important role in the behavior of certain ingredients. Of particular interest are the mono- and diglycerides that are added to solid vegetable shortening during hydrogenation, because they enable the shortening to hold a greater amount of water in cake batter than other types of fat (see Shortening).

RECIPES: Hollandaise Sauce, Mayonnaise, Mayonnaise by Blender or Processor, Saucepan Hollandaise, Basic Vinaigrette Sauce. ❧

EMULSION

An emulsion is formed when an emulsifying agent is added to two liquids that would not mix under ordinary conditions. The emulsifying agent acts as a bridge, linking the two incompatible liquids together. Emulsions are important to cooking because they are the basis for two large groups of sauces — cold emulsified sauces and warm emulsified sauces. The most efficient emulsifier for sauce making is the lecithin contained in egg yolk (see Lecithin).

Three important factors in successfully making an emulsion are temperature, the amount of lecithin available, and the speed at which you whisk the ingredients together. Under optimum conditions, one large egg yolk will emulsify 4 to 6 ounces of oil, or 4 ounces of melted butter. For best results, don't try to incorporate any more than ½ cup of melted butter or ½ to ¾ cup of oil per yolk. Since emulsions form best between 78° and 120°F., have all your ingredients at room temperature when making cold emulsified sauces and use very low heat when making warm emulsified sauces. Whisk the ingredients continuously at as brisk a pace as you can manage.

Acids, such as lemon juice, lime juice, vinegar, and wine help to stabilize emulsions by slightly firming the protein molecules in egg yolks, butter, and milk (see Denaturing). For that reason, an acid is almost always included in recipes for emulsified sauces. Salt helps to stabilize an emulsion in much the same manner, which explains why cooks may have difficulty forming a salt-free mayonnaise.

When an emulsified sauce separates, it is said to have "broken," because certain conditions destroy, or break, the linking system. Heat intense enough to coagulate the protein in an emulsion (140°F.) will cause the sauce to break, which is why recipes warn you not to overheat hollandaise sauce. Excessive agitation, much more than you could ever create by hand, can also break an emulsion — that's why blender-made mayonnaise sometimes separates. Time and too much fat can similarly break an emulsion. If a mixture isn't sufficiently stabilized, or excessive fat has been added, an emulsion will separate after standing awhile.

Speaking of breaking an emulsion, there's a familiar axiom that warns against attempting to make mayonnaise during a thunderstorm, because it will refuse to bind. That admonition is based on the fact that the chemical bonding that takes place during emulsification involves electrical activity (see Emulsifiers). Since a thunderstorm upsets the normal activity of positive and negative electrical charges in the air, it can interfere with the formation of an emulsion such as mayonnaise.

RECIPES: Hollandaise Sauce, Mayonnaise, Mayonnaise by Blender or Processor, Saucepan Hollandaise.   ◄ঽ

EVAPORATION

Evaporation is the process during which water changes from a liquid to a gas. Since water molecules have a natural tendency to escape into the air, evaporation can take place over a wide range of temperatures.

At room temperature, evaporation takes place so slowly that it displays no visible signs of activity. A glass of water left standing on the kitchen counter will just slowly disappear. When water is heated, however, evaporation takes place so quickly that you can actually see the water vapor rising from the surface. Vigorous boiling causes evaporation to occur even more rapidly, because the water molecules rise to the surface in great numbers and clouds of water vapor are produced.

The principle of evaporation has several applications in the process of cooking. The most familiar use of evaporation occurs when you reduce a sauce or stock. As the mixture heats, water molecules rise to the surface and escape as vapor (which explains why reduction takes place more quickly in a wide pan). With continued heating, more and more water evaporates. The result is a thicker consistency and a concentrated flavor. Keep in mind that when doubling a recipe in which reduction is a factor the time needed to evaporate the liquid will also need to be doubled.

The principle of evaporation can be used to rescue dishes and head off culinary disasters. Since water can be added to a mixture and cooked off again without any damage to the flavor, you can always add water to sauces or stocks that are too thick or concentrated. In egg cookery, you can use water as a means of keeping coagulation under control. For example, a small amount of cold water (1 tablespoon water to 2 egg yolks) stirred into the yolks during the initial steps of a hollandaise sauce will forestall curdling. When scrambling eggs, a teaspoon of water per egg helps create a smooth texture, because the water lessens the curdling effects of heat.

It's interesting to note that evaporation occurs, although at a much slower rate, at below-freezing temperatures. When the moisture in frozen food evaporates, it causes the condition known as freezer burn, which ruins the texture of food and destroys its nutritional value. Thus, it's important to store frozen food in airtight bags or containers.   ❧

F

FATS

Fats can be divided into two major groups: those that are solid, or plastic, at room temperature, such as butter, margarine, hydrogenated shortening, and lard; and those that are liquid at room temperature, namely, the various oils. Each fat has its own unique set of characteristics; fats differ from one another in flavor, texture, moisture content, and their propensity to become rancid (see Butter; Lard; Margarine; Oils; and Shortening).

Fat performs several essential functions in cooking. Probably its most outstanding contribution is to flavor, but the ability of solid fat to trap and hold both moisture and air is also of great importance — it increases the lightness of baked goods and helps to retard the staling process. Fat is also valued in baking for its shortening capability. Used in large proportions, it tenderizes baked goods by deterring the gluten strands from linking together to form a cellular framework; in small quantities, fat lubricates the gluten strands so that they slide against one another to facili-

tate kneading and rolling (of breads and pasta), while still permitting the formation of a weblike network.

In addition to its role in baking, fat is used as the medium for heat transferral in deep-frying and sautéing. It is also an essential component in salad dressings and emulsion sauces.

When deciding which fat to use, keep in mind the type of results you're trying to achieve. Among the important features to consider are the smoke point, melting point, plasticity range, and creaming ability of various fats (see Creaming). The smoke point, important in the frying process, is that stage at which heated fat gives off thin, bluish smoke and begins to decompose. The melting point, that stage at which solid fat becomes liquid, is particularly significant to the preparation of baked goods.

Solid fats are said to have plasticity — a quality that makes them spreadable and capable of being whipped, though the temperature range over which they remain plastic differs from one solid fat to the next. For example, butter and margarine have a relatively narrow plasticity range, which is illustrated by the fact that they harden when refrigerated (at 40° to 45°F.), soften at room temperature, and melt in your mouth (at 98.6°F.). Hydrogenated shortening, on the other hand, exhibits a much wider range of plasticity, since it stiffens only slightly when chilled, barely softens at room temperature on the hottest summer day, and melts at around 109°F.

In the cooking process, there are advantages and disadvantages to both wide and narrow plasticity ranges. When you're working with puff pastry, for instance, butter is the fat to use, not only because of its flavor, but because of its narrow range of softening properties. This permits the butter to be rolled into the pastry dough while the butter is still in a semirigid state. Furthermore, when the pastry enters the oven, the fat melts almost immediately, allowing it to be rapidly absorbed by the flour — two important factors when making puff pastry.

The plasticity range of fats also plays a role in cookie baking. Since butter and margarine melt at a relatively low temperature, drop cookies containing either fat have the tendency to spread out and flatten before the crumb structure is set, but cookies made with hydrogenated shortening retain their rounded shape because the fat doesn't melt as quickly.

Butter is the most flavorful of all fats, so cooks often prefer to use it in cakes and pastry. On the other hand, it is not a particularly good choice for frying or sautéing because the milk solids burn easily, creating an unpleasant flavor. Even clarified butter, from which the solids have been removed, deteriorates rapidly at high temperatures due to its low smoke point. In order to give a buttery taste to sautéed food, you can combine equal amounts of butter and vegetable oil, which allows you to heat the fat to a higher temperature without burning the butter. (Recipes that instruct you to sauté mushrooms in butter alone seem to contradict this advice. However, because mushrooms are exceptionally absorbent, they soak up the butter almost immediately, precluding the problem of burnt milk solids.)

Most hydrogenated shortening is tasteless, so in instances where flavor is important, it's better to use something else. Shortening does, however, have a wide plasticity range and excellent creaming properties; in fact, it traps and holds more air than butter does, and the emulsifiers added during processing make it a fine candidate for high-sugar cakes and soft cookies. These same emulsifiers, though, cause hydrogenated shortening to break down when exposed to high heat, which makes it a poor choice for deep frying. When baking cakes, some cooks use part butter, part hydrogenated shortening, to take advantage of the qualities of both. Keep in mind that butter contains about 16 percent water and hydrogenated shortening contains none at all, so substituting one for the other necessitates an adjustment in the amount of liquid used in a recipe.

Margarine has a physical composition similar enough to that of butter so that it can often stand in as an adequate substitute. There's no question that margarine is flavorful, but how closely that flavor resembles butter is a matter of opinion. Just as in the case of salted versus unsalted butter, you must decide whether or not the flavor of margarine is pleasing to you. Like butter, margarine has a low smoke point and therefore does not hold up well when subjected to the high temperatures required for frying or sautéing.

Lard is composed of 100 percent animal fat. It possesses a distinctive and assertive flavor. Since it remains plastic over a wide span of temperatures, lard is a versatile fat. It is semisoft when refrigerated yet firm enough at room temperature to produce excellent pie crust. Lard creams well and can be heated to high temperatures for extended periods of time, making it an excellent choice for frying. Lard also has a slightly grainy texture, which tends to cut through gluten strands to create exceptionally flaky pastries and biscuits.

Other animal fats, such as chicken fat, bacon fat, and roast beef drippings, lend unique and individual flavors to food. For this reason, they are most often used in ethnic and country-style cooking.

Vegetable oils range in flavor from the full-bodied, fruity-tasting olive oil to the nearly tasteless corn oil. Olive oil and the various nut oils contribute interesting flavor to salad dressings and specialized dishes; most of the mild-flavored oils are excellent for frying foods because they can be heated to high temperatures without breaking down. Pastries made with vegetable oil tend to be greasy and mealy-textured (see Pie Crust). Cakes containing large amounts of oil are tremendously popular because they are quick and easy to make (inasmuch as the creamed shortening step is eliminated), and the substantial quantity of oil they contain creates the sensation of moistness. Oil, however, does not disperse well in batter (the lack of emulsifiers is one of the reasons why); thus all too often it gathers in pockets or sinks toward the bottom of the cake. Oil-based cakes also tend to be excessively dense with weak crumb structures.

Many fats used in cooking can be classified as visible fats, that is to say, those you can see. But of equal importance are the invisible fats, those that naturally exist in foods such as meat, poultry, cream, eggs, fish, fruit, vegetables, grain, nuts, and cheese. The fat content of these foods often determines how they will behave as ingredients. Of particular significance to the cooking process are the fats contained in milk, cream, and egg yolks (see Lecithin).

All fats are insoluble in water; however, there are elements in certain fats called phospholipids that often act as emulsifiers and help the fat to combine with water and water-soluble ingredients. Butter, for example, contains natural emulsifiers, which help to unify a sauce when you swirl in cold butter just before serving (see Finishing A Sauce). Margarine is processed with lecithin made from soybeans, and hydrogenated shortening contains mono- and diglycerides that make it possible for fat to be evenly distributed throughout bread dough and cake batter. ◦⃗

FERMENTATION

Fermentation is a process of chemical change brought about by yeast or bacteria feeding on certain food elements. It's important to home cooks, because the waste products that are created have a definite effect on the outcome of certain recipes.

When you add yeast to flour and water, you're initiating one of the most familiar kinds of fermentation. Since yeast is a living cell, it needs to eat in order to live, grow, and reproduce — and sugar is its favorite food (see Yeast). The yeast breaks down flour starch into glucose, then proceeds to feed on it (see Glucose). Ethyl alcohol and carbon dioxide are given off as waste. These two products are important for successful bread baking; the alcohol contributes flavor and aroma while the carbon dioxide is responsible for leavening the dough (see Leavening).

Fermentation that occurs when yeast feeds on sugar is also important in the making of wine. There, too, yeast ferments, or changes, the sugar present in grapes into alcohol and carbon dioxide. However, in wine making, the alcohol is more important than the carbon dioxide.

By the way, there are directions in some bread recipes that instruct you to "allow the dough to ferment." That's just another way of saying "let it rise." Strictly speaking, the term "ferment" refers to the chemical change that takes place as carbon dioxide bubbles form and cause the dough to rise.

In addition to yeast-on-sugar fermentation, other changes occur in food when bacteria feed on milk sugar and on alcohol. Certain kinds of bacteria exist that prefer to eat lactose, the sugar contained in milk. These *lactobacilli* consume milk sugar and give off lactic acid as waste. Lactic acid contributes a slightly sour taste to milk; it also denatures milk protein, a process that causes sour cream, buttermilk, and yogurt to thicken, and curds to form in cheese.

When bacteria feed on alcohol, acetic acid is produced. This type of fermentation is often the second step in a double-phase process. One example of double-phase fermentation takes place in the making of cider vinegar. Here's what happens. Apples not only contain sugar, but also carry bacteria on their skins. After the first phase, where yeast converts the sugar into alcohol and carbon dioxide, bacteria on the apple skins go to work converting the alcohol to acetic acid (the essence of vinegar).

The creation of old-fashioned sourdough is also the result of bacteria-on-alcohol fermentation. Alcohol, a waste product of yeast-on-sugar fermentation, is in turn consumed by bacteria in the air, with acetic acid given off as waste. This acid lends sourdough its distinctive flavor (see Sourdough Starter). Contemporary sourdoughs that contain milk or yogurt are flavored by lactic acid, the waste product of bacteria-on-lactose fermentation (see Herman). ◄ᴣ

A sauce that begins to separate can often be saved by adding cold chunks of butter. Swirl them in by rotating the pan with your wrist, not by stirring.

add some cream (whipping cream, sour cream, or *Crème Fraîche*). Remove the pan from the heat and slowly stir in enough cream, to lighten the texture and improve the consistency, then return to moderate heat for a minute or two. You can also achieve an especially elegant effect by folding whipping cream or whipped *crème fraîche* into a gently heated sauce. The lightened result is generally referred to as a sauce mousseline.

Cream blended with egg yolks is another technique for finishing a sauce. This mixture, also called a liaison, thickens a sauce slightly and creates a richness and velvety-smooth consistency that is not attained by any other method (see Liaison).

A simple finish that you might see executed at tableside in fine restaurants is designed to smooth out the consistency of a sauce that has turned oily or begun to separate. It consists of swirling in chunks of ice cold butter (1 tablespoon per cup of sauce). The sudden drop in temperature that occurs when you take the pan off the heat and add the butter is sufficient to pull the mixture back together. The butter must be swirled in, with the pan off the heat, by rotating the pan with your wrist (see illustration). Stirring the sauce

FINISHING A SAUCE

Just before you serve a sauce, you might want to add a final flourish to refine the texture or embellish the flavor. One of the easiest ways to smooth out the texture of a sauce is to causes the butter to melt too quickly, and it must be incorporated slowly in order for this technique to work. Once the butter has disappeared, serve the sauce immediately; it cannot be reheated.

Sauces that are basically purées, such as *Buttered Tomato Sauce*, benefit from a butter enrichment, which contributes a more subtle flavor and an even texture. Add whatever amount you need to create a smooth sensation on your tongue.

RECIPES: Asparagus Timbales with Lemon Mousseline, Buttered Tomato Sauce, Crème Frâiche, Sauce Mousseline.

FLAMING

Flaming, also called flambéing, is a dramatic maneuver during which you ignite the alcohol in warmed spirits, burning off the sharp edge that alcohol carries with it and leaving the essence of the flavorful liquor behind (see Alcohol).

The procedure falls into two categories — flaming desserts and flaming entrées. The method of flaming is essentially the same in both cases, but the reason for the procedure differs just a bit.

Desserts are flamed to evaporate the harsh alcohol and concentrate the flavor of the spirits. Since alcohol will evaporate when heated anyway, flaming is not strictly necessary, but warmed fruit combined with a warmed liqueur tastes fantastic, and, when flamed, makes an outstanding presentation.

Flaming entrées, particularly meat, are a different story. While the point is still to evaporate the alcohol, the reason for intentionally igniting it (as opposed to simply letting the heat vaporize the alcohol) is to increase the temperature of the meat's surface to a high point as quickly as possible. This leaves the surface of the meat impregnated with the flavor of the spirits. (How wonderful that tastes is subject to opinion; some chefs feel that flaming meat results in a bitter flavor.)

Whether you're flaming a dessert or an entrée, at the table or in the kitchen, the main precaution is not to lean over the dish as you light it. Using an extra-long wooden match is also a good idea. The fire catches almost without warning and it may startle you if it's your first experience. Also, the flames can, although they usually don't, leap high enough to send your hairdo up in smoke.

Most of the time, the opposite happens — your dish won't flame at all or it fizzles out after a flicker or two. The secrets to successful flaming are using liquor with a high alcohol content and igniting the spirits at just the right temperature.

Since alcohol begins to vaporize around 130°F., the trick is to light it somewhere between that temperature and 173°F. — its boiling point. Alcohol evaporates very quickly, so although you must wait for it to warm in order to ignite it, you can't wait too long, or all the alcohol will disappear.

This might sound much too complicated to even attempt, but it really isn't. All you have to do is gently warm the spirits in a small pan until the liquid is warm to the touch. (After you get the hang of it, you'll be able to tell when the alcohol is ready by smelling: as soon as you can smell alcohol rising from the pan, it's warm enough.) Add the warmed spirits to the hot food. If that's a sauce, make sure it's bubbling; if it's meat, both the pan and the meat should be hot.

To flame a sauce, remove the pan from the burner and pour the spirits over the sauce; do not stir them in. Return the pan to the burner and ignite the alcohol by holding a lighted match just above the liquid as soon as bubbles begin to reappear, or when you can smell the alcohol rising. Stir the flaming sauce with a lifting motion to fan the flame.

In flaming meat, or nonsauced items, your nose is always your best guide to proper timing. Remove the hot pan from the burner, pour the warmed spirits over the cooked meat, then return the pan to the heat. Ignite it *before* the liquor bubbles or as soon as you can smell the alcohol vapors. Shake the pan gently to fan the flame. When the flame dies out, all the alcohol has burned off.

To ensure success, you should always use spirits that are at least 80 proof (or 40 percent alcohol). That gives you plenty of alcohol to work with (plus some to spare in case you lose a little before you get the match lit). Keep in mind that the higher the alcohol content, the faster the liquor will heat, and the sooner the alcohol will evaporate.

If you've tried flaming a few times and haven't been happy with the results, here are two suggestions. When flaming a dessert, sprinkle some superfine sugar across the top of the bubbling mixture. The sugar will absorb the liquor and hold it there for a few minutes.

You could also try using 1 tablespoon of pure grain alcohol for every ¼ cup of spirits. It's 190 proof — nearly 100 percent alcohol. It has no flavor and will burn off completely, giving a bit of a boost to the other spirits in the process. Do be careful, though, since it is extremely volatile and produces quite a high flame. One further word of caution: *Never pour pure grain alcohol onto hot food straight from the bottle.* Transfer it first to another container.

RECIPES: Bananas Foster, King Crab Flamed with Cognac.

FLOUR

When wheat is harvested, the combine separates the seeds, or kernels, from the stalk. The stalks are plowed back into the soil, and the seeds are sent off to be processed. At a milling plant, they pass through sets of rollers that break the seeds open. The bran, or hard outer shell, is flattened, the germ is pressed into flakes, and the endosperm (interior tissue) is ground into powder.

The endosperm contains both protein and starch. As it repeatedly passes between the rollers, the endosperm is ground into flour particles, which are then sifted and separated according to size: the larger particles are high-er in starch; the smaller particles are higher in protein. Then, in a process called turbo-milling, the particles of different sizes are custom-blended to form flours with specific ratios of protein to starch. For example, high-protein/low-starch flour is produced to meet the needs of bread baking; low-protein/high-starch flour is created for cake baking; and a balanced combination is formed for all-purpose cooking.

Wheat flour contains four major types of protein — albumin, globulin, gliadin, and glutenin. Of these, gliadin and glutenin, both complex protein mixtures, are the elements necessary for the formation of gluten. However, water must first be added to wheat flour, and the moistened substance must then be agitated by stirring or kneading before gluten is formed (see Gluten). As a side note, cookbooks and magazine articles often refer to certain types of flour as being "high in gluten" or "low in gluten," but this can be misleading. Gluten doesn't exist in any type of flour; it's only the *potential* for gluten that is present.

Wheat flour is unique in that it contains sizeable, and nearly equal, amounts of gluten-producing gliadin and glutenin. Other types of flour, such as oat, rye, barley, and corn, differ in the amount of these proteins they contain, and therefore in their ability to produce gluten. This is why yeast bread recipes based on rye flour, barley flour, or corn flour often instruct you to include a certain amount of wheat flour, in order to furnish the gluten-forming proteins that are lacking.

In selecting a flour to use for bread baking, your best bet is a high-protein blend. (This information is usually listed under "nutritional information" on the side panel of the bag. For example, one bag of all-purpose flour in my pantry lists 11 grams of protein per cup, while a bag of bread flour lists 14 grams of protein per cup.) Flour that is specifically labeled "bread flour" usually contains potassium bromate, a dough conditioning agent. Bromated flour can be a big help if you enjoy baking free-standing breads, because the dough conditioner strengthens the gluten, producing a firmer dough that will hold its shape without a pan.

Whole wheat flour presents a puzzling situation. Although this flour contains a full complement of gluten-forming proteins, bread made from it often comes out heavy and dense. There are two reasons for this. First, whole wheat and cracked wheat flours contain coarse particles of the wheat germ and bran, and the sharp edges of these particles interfere with the development of gluten strands. Second, the proteins needed to form gluten don't exist in the germ or bran, and since these particles displace a certain number of protein particles, a cup of whole wheat flour will contain slightly fewer gluten-forming proteins. To compensate, either knead the dough for a longer period of time to be certain you have fully developed the available gluten, or substitute ½ cup all-purpose or bread flour for ½ cup of the whole wheat for every loaf the recipe yields.

All-purpose flour is a well-balanced blend of protein and starch and is also an excellent choice for carbon-dioxide–leavened goods. All-purpose flour contains just enough proteins to form gluten with sufficient elasticity to stretch around the gas bubbles, but not so much as to produce a tough crumb. All-purpose flour is also the best blend to use as a thickener, because a high-protein flour will cause gumminess and a high-starch blend, lumpiness (see Thickeners).

Pastry cooks use all-purpose flour for some types of dough. The protein content is high enough to form the gluten necessary to produce pie crusts that can be rolled and handled without falling apart and pastries with layers of dough strong enough to be puffed up by steam without collapsing. For cakes, however, a low-protein/high-starch blend is the better flour to use. Cake flour contains only about 7.5 percent protein (all-purpose contains about 10.5) and is ground as finely as possible, which means it will form a delicately textured crumb.

It is often suggested when you substitute all-purpose flour for cake flour to simply remove 2 tablespoons from each cup of all-purpose flour. This advice misses the point. Since cake flour is higher in starch than all-purpose flour, a better approach is to increase the starch level in the all-purpose flour that's going to be used as a substitute. To do this, scoop measure 1 cup of all-purpose flour, remove 2 tablespoons of it, and replace with 2 tablespoons of cornstarch. Sift together and blend thoroughly with a whisk, then scoop measure the amount of flour specified in the recipe.

Self-rising flour, which is most often used for baking quick breads and cakes, contains a predetermined amount of salt and a leavening agent. As with any preblended mix, it's best to use self-rising flour only in those recipes that have been formulated with it in mind. Otherwise, you end up guessing how much salt or leavening agent to leave out, and the results are apt to be disappointing.

Another specialty flour that was recently developed (by General Mills and marketed under the Gold Medal label) comes in a granulated form and is known as "Wondra." The texture of this flour actually resembles granulated sugar, and, because the flour particles are discrete, they don't stick together when moistened. Therefore, granulated flour resists lumping and is easy to use in making gravy and for last-minute emergency thickening. For example, you can sprinkle it lightly over a bubbling stew and stir it in without the bother of first blending it into butter as you would for a beurre manié.

Granulated flour is a time saver, too, because it doesn't need to be sifted. It's great for quick breads and coffee cakes, and its granular consistency produces crisp, mealy-textured pie crust and sandy-textured drop cookies. However, granulated flour doesn't develop gluten efficiently, so I don't recommend it for popovers, flaky pastry, yeast breads, or other baked goods that rely on a certain degree of gluten development for their success.   ◄੭

FOLDING

Folding is the method by which a light, delicate substance, such as whipped cream or beaten egg whites, is incorporated into a heavier substance. The object is to blend the two substances thoroughly, yet break as few air bubbles as possible. For the best results, use a very large bowl and a rubber spatula. This is strictly a by-hand procedure.

First, lighten the heavy batter by *stirring* in about one-eighth of the light substance (a heaping serving-spoonful is a good rule of thumb). Stir until completely blended. The resulting mixture will look lighter in color, feel lighter in texture, and will fold much more easily.

Pour in the rest of the light substance. Position the flat side of the spatula on top of the mixture and slide it across and down through the batter (see illustration). Let the spatula turn in your hand as you bring it up to complete a circle. Some of the batter from the bottom of the bowl will come up with the spatula.

Simultaneously, turn the bowl with the other hand and repeat the over-and-down strokes until the batter is blended, but don't

Always fold a light substance into a heavy one. As you repeat the over-and-down strokes with the spatula, turn the bowl with your other hand.

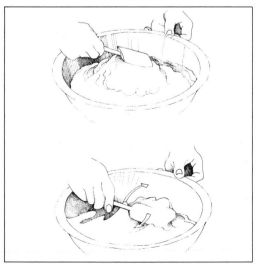

overdo it. It's better to leave a few streaks of the lighter mixture than to jeopardize fluffiness. No matter what your recipe says, *always* fold light into heavy. Pouring a heavy mixture on top of a light one will press the air right out of it.

FRUCTOSE

Like glucose, fructose is a monosaccharide. It is a single-molecule sugar that pairs with glucose to form sucrose, or granulated sugar. Conversely, fructose is one of the simple sugars that results when heat and an acid (or an enzyme) are applied to sucrose and break it down (see Invert Sugar).

Fructose is the sweetest and most soluble of all sugars. It is the natural sugar in fruit and is also found in honey. An outstanding characteristic of this simple sugar is its sensitivity to heat. It interacts with proteins at a faster rate than any other form of sugar, causing the Maillard browning reaction to take place rapidly and at a lower temperature. Consequently, baked goods made with fructose overbrown or burn easily.

(See Glucose; Lactose; Sucrose.)

FRYING
Deep-Fat Frying

Deep-fat frying, like boiling, involves cooking by convection. Molecules of fat nearest the heat source (at the bottom of the pan) become warm and rise to the surface, nudging cool molecules aside. These cool molecules fall to the bottom of the pan. When they, in turn, become warm, they then rise to the surface, creating a pattern of circulating fat molecules (see Heat: Convection).

As you increase the heat under a pan of hot fat, the fat molecules circulate faster and faster. Look closely and you'll see the fat appear to shiver or ripple. This is as turbulent as fat should get. Any bubbling that may occur is caused by water and air being extracted from food during cooking. (Fat that's been used too long foams readily.)

The circulating molecules of hot fat heat the exterior layer of food molecules, which in turn heat the interior food molecules by conduction (see Heat: Conduction). For example, when you lower an egg roll into a pan of hot fat, the outer surface is heated by the hot fat molecules, but the filling inside cooks by conduction. Meanwhile, the egg-roll wrapper is browning. Keep in mind that frying is a dry-heat method of cooking because there is no water involved. This means that the browning taking place is the same coloring process that occurs when you roast meat or bake a loaf of bread. The natural sugars and proteins in the egg-roll skin, heated by the hot fat, interact and turn brown (see Browning — Maillard Reaction).

Correct temperature is the key to successful deep frying. When fat is too hot, the outside of food browns before the inside is cooked; when fat is too cool, it won't seal the surface of food quickly enough to lock out excess fat. The best way to ensure the correct temperature is by using a deep-fat thermometer (see Thermometers). Don't rely on the oft-quoted technique of temperature testing that consists of frying a cube of bread. Even if you precisely measure and cut the bread to comply with the directions, you have no way of compensating for other variables involved — specifically, the freshness or staleness of the bread and the sugar content, both of which have a direct bearing on how quickly the cube will brown.

A thermostatically controlled fryer gives you some indication of what's going on, but it isn't as reliable as a thermometer because it only tells you that the fat is or is not at a set temperature (not to mention that thermostats are notorious for going out of whack). A thermometer lets you know exactly how hot the fat is, and how drastically the temperature drops when you put the food in. If the drop is severe, lift the food out for a few minutes to give the fat a chance to recover. Fry only a few pieces at a time, for overcrowding will also cause a drop in temperature.

Deep-fat frying, done properly, seals in moisture. When the moisture turns to steam, it helps cook the inside of food, such as French fried potatoes or the filling of egg rolls, and it contributes to the leavening and the puffing-up of food, such as doughnuts and *beignets*. Yet, even though moisture plays an important part in cooking deep-fried foods, it can also be a nuisance (see Batter Coating). Food that is to be deep-fried in a batter is often first coated with flour or bread crumbs (see Dredging). The flour or crumbs absorb moisture that's given off as food cooks, preventing the moisture from bubbling through the batter coating and breaking it apart.

Recipes frequently remind you to use a slotted spoon or tongs instead of a fork when transferring food in and out of fat. That's because a fork can easily pierce the coating, making a hole through which moisture can get out and fat can get in. When fat seeps in, food becomes heavy and greasy; when moisture seeps out, it speeds the deterioration of the fat.

RECIPES: Batter-Fried Cauliflower, Batter-Fried Nuggets of Cod, Beignets with Lemon Sauce, Fried Pork Packets, Mushroom Beignets, Shrimp-Filled Egg Rolls.

Shallow Frying

Here we enter an area of lively controversy. When is cooking in a small amount of fat considered frying, and when is it sautéing? Some cookbooks, and many prominent authorities in the field, point out that all pan-frying falls under the definition of sautéing (see Sautéing). That may well be, but I think no matter how long and furiously the argument rages, American cooks are still going to consider pan-frying a separate technique. It has become customary to think in terms of pan-fried liver, pan-fried steak, and pan-fried pork chops.

Pan frying is done relatively slowly in a

small to medium amount of moderately hot fat. The food is turned carefully, and only as often as necessary to prevent burning — all in all, a more gentle heating process than sautéing, which is done very quickly in a small amount of extremely hot fat. Also, sautéed food is shaken or tossed continuously while it cooks, and it must be sliced thin or cut into small portions so it cooks quickly; pan-fried food is apt to be as thick as 1½ inches.

You begin to pan fry meat by heating fat in a skillet or frying pan. Use enough to coat the bottom of the pan — or more if you're directed to have the fat come halfway up the sides of the meat. When the fat is sizzling hot, carefully place the meat into it. (If you want to test with an instant-read thermometer, 160°F. is the best temperature at which to initially add food to shallow fat. The temperature will drop briefly, then rise. Regulate the heat so that the fat maintains a temperature of approximately 200°F. for the remainder of the cooking time.) It's a good idea to allow meat to come to room temperature before you begin, so the temperature of the fat won't drop too far.

When the meat touches the hot fat, the fibers on the exterior surface contract immediately, sealing the bottom of the piece of meat. However, if the meat is damp or contains excess moisture (as frozen meat often does), the water droplets will be fiercely rejected by the hot oil, causing a great deal of spattering to occur. That's why recipes often suggest that you pat meat dry with paper towels before frying. A light dusting of flour also helps prevent spattering, because it absorbs moisture that paper towels can't reach.

As the fat warms up again, reduce the heat of the burner, so that the fat will be held at a moderate temperature. The hot fat cooks the outer layer of meat molecules, which in turn pass the heat along in the process known as conduction, and the heat begins to travel upward through the meat (see Heat: Conduction). At the same time, moisture inside the meat is working its way to the surface, where it will eventually appear as lightly colored juice. Some of this juice will run off the meat into the pan and the rest will turn to steam. As cooking continues, interior fat melts and drains into the pan, where it joins the exuded meat juice.

When the bottom surface is browned, turn the meat over to prevent the bottom from burning and to expose the other side to the heat, so the meat fibers there will contract and seal in whatever juice remains. With continued cooking, bits of meat will begin to adhere to the pan. They'll mingle with the traces of charred exterior fat, the meat juice that's been given off, and browned flour, if you used any; these elements form the basis for a gravy or sauce, should you decide to make one.

Fish is often pan-fried, as are certain vegetables like sliced potatoes and onion rings. They heat and cook in much the same way that meat does — the fat is held at a moderate temperature, and stirring or turning is frequent, but not continuous.

RECIPES: Beef Patties in Cognac Cream, Burgundy Beef Patties, Perch Fillets with Chive Butter, Veal Patties Stuffed with Herbed Cheese.

G

GEL

Frequently a liquid substance thickens, congeals, or becomes rigid due to the fact that a gel has formed. In other words, the protein or carbohydrate molecules have joined together to form a weblike network, resulting in a viscous consistency.

The gel you are probably most familiar with is the one you create when you make a gelatin dessert. This is called a protein gel, since the firming process is caused by protein molecules linking together to form a stiff, three-dimensional network. The unique characteristic of a protein gel is that thickening increases as the mixture cools, which is why gelatin sets when you refrigerate it.

Another example of a protein gel occurs during the cooking of a pot roast. When the meat is subjected to moist heat, water molecules attach themselves to protein molecules in the bones and connective tissue. This causes the collagen (protein) to hydrolize and become liquid. The liquefied protein blends into the pot roast sauce where it forms a protein gel and slightly thickens the sauce. If you refrigerate the leftovers, the protein gel will become semirigid and the sauce will set.

Coagulated proteins in eggs and milk are another type of protein gel. Stirred custards and pastry cream thicken as they cook, but become even more firm when you chill them. (Occasionally, powdered gelatin is added to both these creams to increase the firmness of the protein gel.)

Pastry cream has something else going for it, too — a carbohydrate gel. A small amount of flour is usually added to pastry cream to provide additional thickening. Starch gels are very similar to protein gels in that the molecules hold water and link together, forming a three-dimensional network. However, a starch gel will often deteriorate as it cools, separating and releasing liquid (see Starch Molecules).

All the starch-thickened sauces are made viscous by the formation of a carbohydrate gel (see Sauce Making: Gel Sauces). When starch granules swell and burst, they release the molecules inside. These molecules proceed to link together and gelatinization occurs (see Gelatinization).

Pectin, which is also a carbohydrate, firms fruit jelly. A pectin gel is sometimes referred to as a sugar-acid gel, because sugar and an acid are both needed in fairly high quantities before a pectin gel can form (see Jam and Jelly Making). Like starch and protein gels, a pectin gel is the result of molecules linking together to form a three-dimensional network that holds water in its interstices (see Molecular Network).

GELATIN

When you prepare a stock, especially one that contains a large number of bones, the moist heat transforms the collagen proteins in the meat and bones into liquid gelatin. Its presence becomes particularly obvious if you chill the stock, because a firm, jellied consistency then develops. Reducing the stock results in a concentrated glaze with a syrupy consistency, which is created by the high ratio of gelatin to water (see Sauce Making: Reduction Sauces).

Commercially prepared gelatin is one of the by-products of the meat industry. The same collagen proteins you cook out during stock making are extracted from animal bones, cartilage, and skin. The liquid gelatin is dried and formed into sheets or powdered granules. The powdered version is readily available, easy to use, and extremely reliable.

In working with dry gelatin, you must first disperse it in cold water before heating, to prevent the granules from sticking together and forming lumps (see Dispersion). Then, when you heat the gelatin-water mixture, the granules will liquefy, and the mixture will become a clear solution. Allowing the liquid to cool causes it to thicken until it eventually forms a gel (see Gel). This condition is almost endlessly reversible — you can melt firm gelatin by heating it and set liquid gelatin by cooling it. This comes in handy when you're applying aspic coatings or other gelatin glazes and their consistency becomes too firm or too runny for you to work with.

Occasionally you may run across a carelessly worded recipe that directs you to "dissolve gelatin in cold water." This is a physical impossibility, since gelatin will not dissolve without the application of heat. Added to a cold liquid like water, fruit juice, or stock, gelatin granules will soften, but not dissolve. If no provisions for heating the softened gelatin are made in the recipe, set the container in which you softened the gelatin inside a saucepan. Add water to a depth of 1½ inches and heat until the gelatin granules dissolve and the mixture turns clear.

In addition to using gelatin to set fruit molds and dessert creams, include it whenever you want whipped cream to hold up for a while, or use it to stabilize whipped egg whites in a chilled mousse. You can also add gelatin to ice cream (1 package to 4 cups liquid) to impede the formation of ice crystals and produce a smoother texture. ◀₂

GELATINIZATION

While protein-thickened mixtures, such as custards, are usually said to coagulate, and pectin mixtures are thought to gel, many cookbooks refer to the thickening action of starch as gelatinization. Therefore, it's helpful to understand what this specialized type of thickening involves.

When starch granules are heated in the presence of water, they absorb and hold a remarkable amount of moisture, which causes them to swell. As more and more water is taken up, the mixture becomes increasingly viscous due to the swelling of the starch granules. It is this swelling process that constitutes gelatinization.

There's more to it than that, however. If you could watch a starch-water mixture as it heats under a microscope, you would notice three distinct phases. The first phase takes place when the starch granules are dispersed in cold water. Some water is taken up (about 25 percent), but not enough to change the viscosity of the mixture. This phase is reversible in that a starch-water slurry can be dried, returning the starch to its original form.

The second phase occurs when the mixture is heated. At approximately 140°F., starch granules begin to absorb water rapidly. As heating continues, the appearance of the granules changes. They become extremely swollen, and, because the amount of available water has decreased significantly, the mixture thickens. This phase is not reversible.

During the third phase, as the mixture reaches the boiling point, the starch granules rupture and release amylose and amylopectin molecules, which, in turn, begin to take up water and swell. The amylose molecules uncoil and intertwine, while the amylopectin molecules extend their branches to form the three-dimensional network that finalizes the thickening process (see Starch Molecules).

The speed at which gelatinization takes place is influenced by the presence of sugar, the pH level of a mixture, and the size of the starch granules in the type of starch used. For example, potato starch granules are quite large, cornstarch granules quite small, and starch granules of wheat flour are of assorted sizes. Large granules tend to swell at lower temperatures, so potato starch can thicken a mixture at far below the boiling point. The presence of an acid and the addition of sugar to a starch-water mixture both retard the swelling process, and therefore hinder gelatinization.   ◄ð

GLAZING

A glaze is applied to the surface of food to enhance its appearance, to alter its texture, to provide an interesting flavor accent, or for a combination of these reasons. Certain glazes are most effective when brushed on hot food; others are meant specifically for cold food.

GLAZING FOR SHIMMER: There are a number of ways to give food a clear, sparkling surface. An egg-white wash adds luster to yeast breads and pastries (see Egg Wash), a clear aspic makes cold foods glisten (see Aspic), and a sugar-water solution lightly glazes vegetables such as carrots and onions while they cook. For a show-stopping roast turkey, dilute ½ cup of corn syrup with 2 tablespoons of water. When the turkey is nicely browned and is almost ready to come out of the oven, lightly brush the skin with the corn-syrup mixture. Cook 10 to 15 minutes more, and your turkey will gleam like mahogany.

GLAZING FOR COLOR: A whole-egg or egg-yolk wash adds color to the surface of food, as does a mixture of sugar and water. Other, more glamorous coloring effects can be obtained by applying coats of liquefied

jam or jelly to certain foods. Apricot jam, brought to a boil and forced through a sieve, forms a clear, golden glaze when brushed over pastries. To make fruit sparkle like precious jewels, select a jelly of the appropriate color and flavor (strawberry jelly for strawberries and so forth, or use apple jelly for a transparent shine and neutral color). Heat until liquefied, cool slightly, and pour or spoon over fruit. First take the precaution, however, of allowing the fruit to come to room temperature, for a hot glaze applied to cold fruit will cause it to ooze juice.

Cold food can be masked with a white or brown sauce known as chaud-froid. New versions of the more popular white sauce consist of mayonnaise with gelatin or reduced heavy cream with gelatin. This sauce is poured over cold ham, poultry, or fish, decorated with vegetable flowers or other attractive designs, and then allowed to set.

GLAZING FOR TEXTURE: Yeast breads and rolls brushed with milk or melted shortening after baking exhibit a glossy, soft crust. You can soften the top crust of whole wheat bread and add color by glazing the warm surface with a mixture of 2 tablespoons melted butter, ½ teaspoon water, and ⅛ teaspoon instant coffee. To add an appealing color to baked quick bread, brush the warm surface with a mixture of 1 tablespoon cream sherry and 2 tablespoons melted butter.

GLAZING FOR FLAVOR: For fantastic flavor, not to mention appearance and texture, no glazing procedure can beat the fruit- and tomato-based sauces applied to meat as it roasts or grills. These fruit glazes and barbecue sauces invariably include the sugar and acids necessary to react with meat protein to produce spectacular browning and crisping (see Browning — Maillard Reaction). Glazed meat is not only gorgeous, but also moist and flavorful, because the glaze seals in meat juices.

Another example of glazing for flavor is the application of caramel syrup to cooked fruits, pastries, and chilled cream-based desserts. Caramel syrup, which is made by cooking sugar to high temperatures, hardens to a brittle, crackly film as it cools, contributing not only its distinctive "caramel" flavor, but an interesting textural note as well.

GLAZING FOR PROTECTION: A recipe that instructs you to apply a fruit glaze to cake layers before the icing goes on may seem to be overdoing it, but a fruit glaze does serve two purposes. In the recipe for *Torte Sylvia*, for example, an apricot glaze protects the cake layers from moisture in the icing that might render them soggy; in the recipe for *Sachertorte*, the fruit glaze gives the icing something to cling to, which makes for a neater-looking final product. A fruit glaze can also be used to protect the bottom crust of pie shells and puff-pastry cases against sogginess. In cream pies, or fresh fruit pies like *Double Strawberry Pie*, a light film of liquefied jam or jelly (of the appropriate flavor), spread over *cooled* pastry, will form an effective moisture barrier between the pastry and juicy fruits or moist cream fillings.

RECIPES: Butter-Glazed Finger Carrots, Chaud-Froid Sauce, Double Strawberry Pie, Sachertorte, Torte Sylvia. ◄ঃ

GLUCOSE

Glucose, a monosaccharide, is one of two simple sugars that link together to form sucrose, or granulated sugar. Frequently referred to as dextrose, it is also one of the components of corn syrup. Glucose is sweeter than lactose, but not as sweet as sucrose, and it readily interacts with proteins to bring about the browning of food known as the Maillard reaction. Glucose is an essential element of invert sugar, which is important in the making of candy and various frostings (see Invert Sugar).

One of the most important functions of glucose is its role in the leavening of yeast breads. Since glucose is yeast's favorite food, it is quickly and directly converted during the fermentation process to ethyl alcohol and carbon dioxide, the gas that causes yeast bread to rise.

(See Fructose; Lactose; Sucrose.) ◄ঃ

GLUTEN

When wheat flour is moistened with a liquid, two complex protein mixtures, called gliadin and glutenin, join together to form gluten. If the moistened flour is then agitated, the gluten particles develop into strands (see Kneading). Continued agitation causes these strands to link with one another in a tough, elastic, weblike network.

Well-developed gluten possesses extraordinary elasticity, a feature that makes possible high, light loaves of bread and sheets of dough, such as pasta, filo, and strudel, which can be stretched or rolled so thin that they are nearly transparent.

Gluten is often as much a culinary enemy as a friend. Overhandling, or agitation, of dough and batter encourages gluten to develop when you don't want it to. The result is tough pie crust, heavy pancakes, or leaden muffins. When a recipe directs you to "handle lightly" or, as in the case of pancakes and muffins, to "stir only until moistened," it is warning you not to overagitate the gluten.

The amount of gluten you have to work with differs from one type of flour to another, and once you become aware of the gluten potential of different flours, you can use this information to your advantage (see Flour). ◄ঃ

GRANULATED SUGAR

See SUCROSE; SUGAR. ◄ঃ

GRAVY

I've often thought that cooks have poor luck with pan gravy because it's usually made on holidays. With a house full of guests and kids and dogs, it's difficult to pay attention to the gravy. I solve the problem by making my gravy ahead, but I'll get to that later.

The major complication seems to be a lumpy consistency. Gravy is essentially a starch-thickened brown sauce (see Brown Sauce), and a critical step in gravy making is the dispersion of starch particles in fat or water to eliminate the risk of lumping.

When you transfer a cooked roast to a platter or carving board, you're left with a pan containing a generous amount of grease, a smaller amount of dark brown juice, and darker brown bits of coagulated protein cooked to the bottom. At this stage, there are two courses of action you can take.

For a richly colored, opaque gravy, pour off most, but not all, of the fat. What remains will form the basis of a roux. Add flour to the pan, dispersing it throughout the fat to separate the starch particles (see Dispersion). Stir over medium heat until the flour turns brown and the roux foams. Remove from the heat and add hot broth all at once. Return to the heat and whisk until smooth, picking up the cooked bits from the bottom of the pan and incorporating them into the gravy. Cook till thick and serve strained or unstrained.

To achieve a fat-free gravy with a lighter color and a transparent finish, pour all the liquid left in the roasting pan into a 1-quart measuring cup. Immediately add 6 ice cubes and place in the refrigerator or freezer. The cold will encourage the fat drops to coalesce and harden.

Meanwhile, make a slurry by dispersing cornstarch in water, and set this aside (see Slurry). Pour either hot or cold broth into the roasting pan and place over medium heat, stirring to dislodge the cooked-on particles. When the mixture boils, remove the pan from the heat.

Take the container of meat juice and fat from the refrigerator, lift off the hardened fat, and discard it. If any ice cubes are still intact, remove them too. Stir the meat juice into the broth in the pan and blend in the cornstarch slurry. Return to the heat and cook, stirring continuously, until thickened. Serve as is or strain.

The quality of the broth you use affects the quality of the gravy. Homemade beef or chicken stock is always the best choice, but canned broth can also be used.

One of the most frequent complaints I hear about gravy making is that there's never enough. Cooks roast a 22-pound turkey to feed 12, and then don't have ample gravy to drizzle over 12 plates of mashed potato, stuffing, and turkey.

To be sure you have plenty of gravy the next time around, make it ahead and freeze it — just like any brown sauce. Not only will you have as much as you need, but you won't have to make it at the last minute.

RECIPES: Do-Ahead Gravies (Turkey, Chicken, or Roast Beef).

H

HEAT

Heat causes several different chemical changes in food that are commonly thought of as "cooking." When heat is applied, meat fibers firm up, connective tissue softens, the cellulose in fruit and vegetables breaks down, and egg protein coagulates.

Heat improves the appearance and flavor of food by causing it to turn brown. It also makes food safe to eat by killing harmful bacteria.

In order to effect these changes, heat has to travel from its source to the food. Its route can be direct, or it can travel through a medium, such as air, water, or liquid fat. Heat can also get from its source to the food through various conductors.

Ambient heat surrounds food while it cooks; direct heat approaches food from one direction. A roast of beef set on a rack inside a roasting pan, then placed in a hot oven, will cook by ambient heat — the hot air surrounding the roast. On the other hand, a sirloin steak, set on a broiler pan placed under the broiler, will cook only on the side exposed to the heat.

Radiant Heat

Cooking by radiant heat takes place when heat is transferred directly from a heat source to food. It is the fastest method of heating food because it doesn't depend on a medium, such as the molecules in air or water, to per-form the task of transporting heat (see Convection, this entry).

Waves of radiant heat travel from a hot coil, gas flame, or a charcoal fire. When they come in contact with food, the food absorbs the heat waves and cooking begins.

Food cooked by radiant heat is usually no more than 3 inches thick. A broiled steak, a barbecued hamburger, a piece of toast — all are examples of food cooked by radiant heat. It's worth noting, however, that radiant heat waves affect only the surface of food. Interior cooking takes place by conduction.

Conduction

Cooking by conduction occurs when heat is transferred from one molecule to another. It takes place in virtually a straight line, with one molecule touching the next. As the first molecule gets hot, it warms its neighboring molecule in a sort of pass-it-on reaction.

Metal molecules conduct heat very rapidly, but food molecules pass on heat quite slowly. This is demonstrated during the baking of a potato. Hot air inside an oven heats the molecules of the potato skin by convection, and they, in turn, heat the potato molecules directly under the skin. One potato molecule passes heat to the next potato molecule until the very center of the potato is hot. If, however, you insert a metal "potato nail" into the center of the potato, it will cook faster, because the metal molecules conduct heat to the center of the potato faster than the food molecules can.

Convection

Unlike conduction, which is a stationary sort of heat transferral, heating by convection involves movement — the circulation of hot air molecules or hot liquid molecules. Convection cooking that involves the circulation of hot liquid molecules occurs during boiling, simmering, poaching, and frying, when molecules of hot liquid travel around inside a pot or pan, transferring their heat to food.

Convection cooking by hot air molecules takes place in a conventional oven. The heating element, usually located at the bottom of the oven, heats the nearest molecules of air. Since warm air rises, the heated molecules circulate to the top of the oven, giving the cold molecules a nudge. The cold molecules then fall to the bottom, where they in turn are warmed, and a pattern of circulating air molecules is formed.

Anything that gets in the way of these roaming hot molecules becomes heated. A casserole dish placed in an oven is warmed by convection. The hot dish then passes on its heat to the food inside, where further cooking takes place by conduction.

There are ovens available that are especially designed with an interior fan to circulate the air molecules at an increased rate of speed. Specifically referred to as "convection" ovens, they also have the ability to cook more evenly and produce crisply textured crusts, because the fan encourages the molecules of hot air to circulate in an even pattern and dispels the humidity that builds up during baking. If you enjoy making pastry and bread, you might want to consider the advantages of a convection oven.

Most cooking involves more than one type of heat transferral. For example, consider a pot of boiling turnips. First you turn on the heat source — the stove-top burner. The heat travels from the burner to the bottom of the pan, where metal molecules conduct the heat to other metal molecules until the bottom of the pan is hot — a process of heating by conduction.

Then, the hot pan warms the water molecules, which begin to circulate, carrying the heat to the turnips — a process of heating by convection. In addition to circulating, though, the water molecules are also passing heat from one to another, so heating by conduction is taking place at the same time. Meanwhile, the inside walls of the pot are radiating heat they have absorbed.

Once the surfaces of the turnips get hot, the surface molecules transfer their heat to the molecules inside the turnips. They, in turn, pass the heat along until the turnips are heated through — a process of heating by conduction.

The combination of heat and moisture eventually breaks down the cellulose, the element that makes a turnip firm, and the turnips become tender.

With or without pots and pans, people have been cooking food by conduction, convection, and radiation for centuries, and now there's a new method of heating food — by molecular agitation. Better known as microwaving, this type of heating occurs when molecules near the surface of food are stimulated by very short (hence "micro") waves of electromagnetic energy. The friction caused by the molecules rubbing against each other results in tiny pockets of heat, which then cook the food (see Microwave Cooking).

HEAT DIFFUSER

A heat diffuser is a clever and efficient approach to the problem of controlling heat. Shaped like a Frisbee with holes around the outside rim, this round metal platform (see illustration) sits on a stove-top burner, distributing the heat and toning it down.

A heat diffuser works on the same principle as a double boiler. When you use a double boiler, a layer of water modifies the heat coming from the burner and spreads it out evenly. In like manner, the holes in a heat diffuser allow air to circulate inside the metal

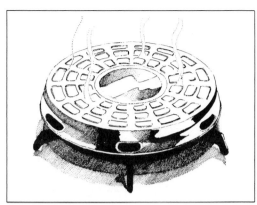

A heat diffuser is set over a stove-top burner to help distribute the heat as well as tone it down.

platform, creating a cushion of warm air between the pan and the burner. This cushion of air moderates the heat coming from the burner and diffuses it evenly across the bottom of the pan.

Once you've used one of these gadgets, you won't know how you ever lived without it. A heat diffuser allows you to prepare the most delicate custard cream without fear of scorching or curdling. Chocolate melts gently without seizing (see Chocolate: Melting), and you can keep a covered casserole warm for hours by setting it on a heat diffuser over a moderately warm burner. Most of the time, you don't need to wash a diffuser, either, which makes it far simpler to use than a double boiler.   ✍

HERBS

Without a doubt, the flavor of fresh herbs is far superior to that of dried, but not everybody has the time or the conditions for growing them year-round. The solution is to grow as many herbs as you can during the summer and preserve them for winter use. You don't need to cultivate a whole corner of the yard, either — a few giant pots will do the trick. I've got the blackest thumb that ever held a trowel, but every summer I successfully grow

basil, oregano, rosemary, and thyme — each in its own big pot.

Many cookbooks extol the virtues of drying herbs or preserving them in oil, but I much prefer to freeze them and have had fine results with basil, oregano, rosemary, thyme, tarragon, dill, chives, and parsley. All you have to do is wash the leaves and pat them dry with a paper towel; then place the herbs in plastic bags, secure airtight with wire twists, and store them in the freezer. When they become frozen and brittle, you can crush them by squeezing the bags with your fingertips, or leave them whole to chop or crush just before using. Frozen herbs retain their bright green color, and taste so close to fresh, you'll hardly notice the difference.

Store separate herbs in separate bags, or prepare and freeze small bouquets (see Bouquet Garni). It's a good idea to label and date each bag so you will know which one to use up first. The only thing frozen herbs don't do well is garnish — they turn limp and tired-looking as they defrost.

When freezing fresh parsley, prepare a bunch or two at a time. Separate the bunch, and wash the leaves by holding the parsley stems and plunging the leaves up and down in a bowl of cold water. Break the leaves off the stems and scatter the leaves over a clean kitchen towel. Pat with absorbent paper and air-dry for 30 minutes. Chop the leaves by hand, or dump them into the bowl of a food processor and pulse briefly eight to ten times. Transfer to an airtight plastic container, store in the freezer, and use (while still frozen) as needed. Don't hold the container of frozen parsley over a pan of hot food, because heat rising from the pan will cause condensation to form, and you'll soon have frost build-up all over the surface of your frozen parsley, which destroys its flavor. Tip the container over a bowl or plate when removing the amount you need, then immediately return the container to the freezer.

Dried herbs can never duplicate the flavor of fresh, but they can still do a fine job of flavoring — particularly if you are careful about choosing and storing them. Look for tightly sealed packages. Nontransparent containers are better than glass jars, because strong light can filter through glass and destroy the herbs' vitality. Buy small quantities, and replace them every six months.

Store dried herbs in tightly sealed containers in a cool, dry place (away from the stove, sink, and dishwasher, where heat and moisture will ruin them in no time).

Dried green, leafy herbs taste fresher if they're more green than grey, except for bay leaves, where the green leaf is known as California Bay, and the grey is called Turkish Bay. They are separate varieties and have distinctively different flavors.

Always break bay leaves in half before using them in order to release all their flavor. Crush most other types of dried herb leaves between your thumb and the palm of your hand, or between both palms. Dried rosemary leaves, which resemble pine needles, should be crushed to a powder with a mortar and pestle, not only to release flavor, but also to prevent a spiky needle from lodging itself between the teeth.

Substituting fresh herbs for dried always raises the question of how tightly packed they should be. Flavoring with herbs is so much a personal part of cooking that setting down a rule is difficult. Some cookbooks suggest using two to three times the specified amount if you're substituting fresh herbs for dried, since fresh leaves take up more room on the measuring spoon than dried, shriveled leaves. One reliable approach is to place the chopped herb in a bowl, then scoop measure what you need without packing the leaves down. If the flavor isn't assertive enough, you can always add more. Your nose and taste buds are still your best guide. Sometimes fresh herbs are so intensely flavorful that automatically doubling the amount can ruin a dish.

Add dried herbs as early in the cooking process as possible to give them time to absorb moisture and release all their flavor, for if they aren't cooked long enough, they impart a harsh taste and aroma. Fresh herbs (or frozen) should be added near the end of the cooking process. They don't need to absorb any moisture in order to give up their essence, and fresh herbs contribute a burst of flavor that overcooking can eradicate.

Recently, a small number of processors have been experimenting with freeze-drying herbs and other flavoring agents like onions and shallots. During the freeze-drying procedure, food is frozen and then exposed to a vacuum drier, which removes all traces of moisture. Vacuum drying is an exceptionally gentle process, so the flavor, color, texture, and vitamins of food are retained. I've cooked with freeze-dried chives, chopped green peppers, leeks, and shallots, and they have all produced excellent results. However, since green peppers and leeks are available year-round in many supermarkets, I can't see much point in using the freeze-dried variety; chives and shallots are another story — particularly shallots, which are not only hard to find fresh, but are also often flavorless. Consequently, I frequently use freeze-dried shallots and recommend them highly. The only drawback is that you can't sauté freeze-dried shallots as you might like, but I find even their unsautéed flavor superior to that of onions, often the suggested substitute.

Store freeze-dried products in an airtight container in a cool, dry place. Crush them with a mortar and pestle if you find the pieces are too large, and rehydrate by covering with water, wine, or another liquid included in your recipe (see Appendix).   ✑

———————

HERMAN

One of the most popular recent food fads is a type of sourdough fondly nicknamed "Herman" (see entry for Sourdough Starter). Enthusiastic fans feed him, stir him, generally fuss over him, and share him with friends. Herman can be used as the basis for breads, cakes, pancakes, and muffins.

This sourdough starter derives its unique flavor from the presence of lactic acid, which is given off when bacteria react with the lactose, or milk sugar, found in milk, yogurt, or sour cream. Sugar and yeast may or may not be included in this starter. If they are, yeast-on-sugar fermentation takes place and carbon dioxide is created, giving the mixture a bubbly consistency (see Fermentation). However, the essential process, the one that creates the flavorful lactic acid, is the result of bacteria-on-sugar fermentation.

Streptococcus lactis, and bacteria belonging to the group known as *Lactobacillus,* are attracted to lactose. When these bacteria feed on lactose, lactic acid is produced. Yogurt and sour cream are cultured with these bacteria, which explains why it's easier to form a Herman starter by using one or the other of these. Since this particular type of fermentation is an anaerobic process, many recipes instruct you to tightly cover milk-based sourdough starters.

RECIPE: Herman Starter.

HOLLANDAISE SAUCE

Emulsified sauces can be divided into two groups — cold emulsified sauces and warm emulsified sauces. Each of these two groups is anchored, so to speak, by a basic sauce — one that can be transformed into other sauces by the addition or substitution of various ingredients.

Hollandaise sauce is the basic sauce in the warm emulsified group; mayonnaise is the basic sauce in the cold emulsified group (see Mayonnaise).

Hollandaise sauce is basically an emulsion of oil and water — two elements that will not mix at all under ordinary conditions. In order to hold these two ingredients together in a permanent suspension, an emulsifying agent is added. The oil in a hollandaise is in the form of melted butter; the water is contained in the lemon juice, the egg yolks, and also in the butter; and the emulsifier is the lecithin present in the egg yolks.

Preparing a warm emulsified sauce like hollandaise is very similar to making mayonnaise. The technique is exactly the same except that in a warm emulsified sauce you cook the egg yolks ever so slightly. This is a plus in one sense, because slightly cooked egg yolks hold a greater amount of melted butter in suspension than raw yolks, and cooked yolks also give the sauce an extremely smooth, custardlike quality.

On the minus side, however, is the fact that heat can become a troublemaker. You must heat the yolks just enough to cook them slightly, but not so much that you cause them to curdle. You have to maintain that fine line between coagulating the egg yolks, so as to promote thickening, and overcoagulating them into scrambled eggs.

How is this accomplished? Is it even possible for mere mortals? It's not only possible, but actually quite easy. The trick is to warm the eggs slowly and evenly over low heat. If you don't get impatient, you'll make out fine.

During the process of making hollandaise sauce, you combine egg yolks, lemon juice, salt, pepper, and a small amount of water in a heavy saucepan. (I know many cookbooks suggest using a double boiler, but we'll get into that later.) The salt and the acid in the lemon juice encourage the egg yolks to denature and coagulate. Pepper and salt are added before the butter because they don't dissolve efficiently in large amounts of fat. The water is used to dilute the egg yolks, in order to slow down the coagulation of the protein and provide a margin of safety against scrambling. As the mixture heats, the water will evaporate off, but in the meantime it will give you better control over the cooking of the egg yolks.

The next step is to place the saucepan over very low heat. If you're using an electric stove, notorious for hot spots, set a heat diffuser under the pan (see Heat Diffuser). Whisk the mixture until it's foamy and beginning to thicken slightly. This thickening occurs because egg yolks contain fat, so you already have all the ingredients necessary for an emulsion even before you add butter.

If you're following a recipe that calls for melted butter, remove the pan from the heat. Whisk continuously as you add the melted butter drop by drop. As you whisk, you're breaking the drops of fat into smaller and smaller droplets. Each droplet becomes coated with a thin film of egg-yolk mixture, and the lecithin in the yolks begins to form an emulsion. In other words, the lecithin holds the fat and water in a permanent suspension (see Emulsion). This subdividing of fat into smaller and smaller droplets also helps to thicken the sauce, and increases its volume as the surface area of the oil droplets multiplies (see Whipping).

As the sauce gets thicker, you can add the melted butter in a thin stream, but don't try this too soon. Oil drops would rather be together than mix with water. If you add liquid butterfat faster than it can be whisked into tiny droplets and coated with lecithin, the uncoated drops will seek out each other and form puddles of liquid fat.

Puddles of fat can also be an indication that your sauce is getting too hot. Egg yolks begin to coagulate around 144°F., so that's the best temperature at which to prepare a warm emulsified sauce. As it begins to heat past that point, the egg protein coagulates too fast; the lecithin loses its ability to function as an emulsifier, and traces of butterfat appear on the surface.

If the traces of butterfat grow to be puddles, you've got trouble. Your sauce has curdled because the emulsion has broken — the emulsifier is no longer able to hold the fat and water in suspension. Keep going and you'll have lemon-flavored scrambled eggs.

You can rescue a *slightly* separated hollandaise by whisking in a few pieces of crushed ice. The ice will cool the mixture, halting the coagulation and allowing the sauce to pull back together. A *severely* separated sauce can be recovered by giving it a fresh dose of

lecithin. As in rescuing a broken mayonnaise, put a fresh egg yolk in a large, warm bowl. Whisk it with 1 teaspoon fresh lemon juice and a dash of salt. When it becomes light in color, gradually whisk in the separated hollandaise. Place it, uncovered, over water that has been heated to 140°F., and warm it for a few minutes before serving.

You can also keep hollandaise warm by setting it in a bain-marie, but keep in mind that moisture in the sauce will evaporate, making the acid component too intense. It's not a good idea to hold hollandaise this way for too long a time. If you want to keep hollandaise warm for an extended period, pour it into a thermos bottle or insulated pitcher that has been rinsed with boiling water, and seal tightly. If you want to make hollandaise ahead of time and reheat it without curdling, you can stabilize the mixture by adding 2 tablespoons of béchamel sauce or a slurry of 1 teaspoon cornstarch dissolved in 1 tablespoon of water. Stir the slurry into the chilled sauce and reheat.

One of the tricks to a smooth, gorgeous-looking hollandaise is to put the yolks through a sieve *before* you add them to the sauce. No matter how carefully you separate eggs, or how much of an expert you are, traces of white remain. When they are heated, they coagulate into tiny white lumps floating around in the sauce. Some recipes cope with this problem by straining the completed hollandaise, but straining an emulsified sauce cools it down and introduces air bubbles that can alter its consistency. Straining the yolks first is a better approach.

Now back to the much-favored double-boiler method. This particular technique lulls cooks into a false sense of security and points them straight to failure. What the cookbooks don't tell you is that using a double boiler is much trickier than it looks. If the water in the bottom pan becomes too hot, or if the hot water is too close to the bottom of the upper container, the sauce at the bottom of the upper container will overcook and thus cause the hollandaise to curdle and separate. You're much better off using a sturdy, thick-bottomed saucepan and a heat diffuser.

RECIPES: Hollandaise Sauce, Saucepan Hollandaise.   ◄ℐ

HOMOGENIZATION

Homogenization is usually associated with the processing of milk. When milk is homogenized, it's forced through a small orifice that breaks fat globules up into particles so tiny they lose their natural tendency to adhere, and therefore do not rise to the surface of milk as a layer of cream. But now, with recent developments in sauce cookery, another dimension has been added to homogenization. It also refers to a new method for thickening a sauce, by whirling it in a blender instead of binding it with calorie-rich liaisons (see Liaison). The blending process accomplishes two tasks — it purées whole ingredients, such as chunks of onion and carrot, which thickens the mixture, and it breaks up the globules of butterfat or cooking oil used in preparing the sauce into particles so tiny they will remain in suspension (see Suspension). The result is a homogenized sauce of full flavor and excellent texture.   ◄ℐ

HONEY

If you've ever tried to substitute honey in a recipe that called for granulated sugar, chances are you ran into trouble, and there are a number of reasons why.

To begin with, honey is 17 percent water but granulated sugar is only .5 percent, so the liquid balance of a mixture is significantly upset by the substitution of honey. Another problem is caused by honey's viscous nature. Not only does it lack the rough texture that enables granulated sugar to incorporate air when creamed with butter or shortening, but its heavy, syrupy consistency weighs down batter and makes leavening more difficult. In addition, there's the matter of heat sensitivity. Fructose, the principal sugar in honey, is inordinately sensitive to an increase in temperature. Browning of the Maillard reaction type affects fructose at a more rapid rate than any other form of sugar, which means that browning takes place quickly and at lower temperatures (see Browning).

To cope with these characteristics, recipes that include honey (or granulated fructose, for that matter) direct you to use lower oven temperatures and more gentle stove-top heat. Most baking temperatures are in the 325°F. range, but it's not unusual to see recommended settings as low as 275°F. Mixtures containing honey also require a larger-than-usual dose of baking powder or baking soda to counteract honey's viscous quality, and a decreased amount of liquid to bring the moisture balance back into line.

In order to use honey in place of granulated sugar, substitute the same amount of honey measure for measure. If the recipe calls for ½ cup sugar, use ½ cup honey, but reduce whatever liquid there is by 2 tablespoons for every ½ cup of honey. To prevent an overly dense texture, increase the amount of baking soda by ¼ teaspoon (or baking powder by 1 teaspoon) per ½ cup of honey. And to prevent excessive browning, reduce oven temperatures at least 25°F. In fact, the heat of the oven should not exceed 350°F.

Now that we've covered *how* to substitute honey, let's talk about why people want to. A large number of cooks have adopted the notion that honey is far more nutritious than granulated sugar; that cookies, pies, and cakes made with honey are healthful and better for you. Here are the facts.

The first step in the production of honey occurs when bees gather nectar from flowers. Nectar is mainly sucrose — the same type of sugar as granulated sugar (see Sucrose; Sugar). During the trip back to the hive, each bee secretes an enzyme, called invertase, which converts the sucrose to a combination of glucose and fructose (see Invert Sugar). The honey is deposited in the hive as a natural form of invert sugar.

The same sort of transformation happens to sucrose, or granulated sugar, during cooking and digestion. Sucrose is broken down into its component parts — glucose and fructose — when it is heated, either with water at fairly high temperatures or with an acid at lower temperatures. If you bake cookies at 375°F., the internal heat of the cookies is high enough to split sucrose into glucose and fructose. Therefore, by the time you consume baked goods, the granulated sugar they were made with has been converted into the same simple sugars present in honey.

Then what about uncooked granulated sugar? Enzymes in the digestive tract convert sucrose to glucose and fructose. Your body ends up absorbing glucose and fructose and using it as energy regardless of whether you eat honey or granulated sugar.

Don't get me wrong; I'm not anti-honey. It just seems that granulated sugar has been unnecessarily maligned. Honey is composed of fructose and glucose; 1 tablespoon contains 64 calories and costs approximately 5 cents. Granulated sugar is also composed of fructose and glucose; 1 tablespoon contains 46 calories and costs about 1 cent. Honey contains only minute traces of vitamins and minerals: by all means, use it if you like its flavor or the moist, rich consistency it lends to baked goods and other foods, but don't deceive yourself by thinking that it's an outstanding source of nutrition.   ◄≳

I

INVERT SUGAR

There's an old saying among candy makers that a few drops of vinegar keep taffy from "going to sugar." Like many culinary maxims, it is based on a scientific principle. When you heat sucrose (granulated sugar) and an acid together, the sucrose splits into equal portions of glucose and fructose, and creates invert sugar. In the case of taffy, the vinegar acts as a catalyst to break down the sucrose into simple forms of sugar that are extremely slow to crystallize. Consequently, the taffy retains a smooth texture. Invert sugar not only retards crystallization, but also increases the sweetness of candy and other confections; because the glucose component is somewhat less sweet than sucrose, and the fructose component is twice as sweet, the sweetness level of invert sugar is greater than the sucrose from which it was produced.

Invert sugar can also be formed by the action of an enzyme called invertase, which breaks down sucrose into the simple sugars glucose and fructose. This is especially important in working with yeast, because yeast is unable to consume sucrose. However, since yeast contains the enzyme invertase, it is capable of transforming the sucrose in granulated sugar and the sucrose in flour to forms of sugar it *can* eat, thereby giving off the carbon dioxide that is necessary for leavening (see Fermentation).

The formation of invert sugar is also important in the browning of food. Sucrose is capable of caramelizing, but it doesn't interact with proteins to produce the type of browning caused by the Maillard reaction (see Browning — Maillard Reaction). However, acids, or the invertase in yeast, break the sucrose down into forms of sugar that will react with proteins to brown food.

Invert sugar is an essential element in the making of jams and jelly. Since most fruit preserves are made with a high proportion of granulated sugar, crystallization can be a problem (see Sugar Cooking). For that reason, recipes usually call for some type of acid, unless the fruit itself is exceptionally acidic. The acid's job is to create invert sugar by breaking down the sucrose. In turn, the invert sugar keeps the jelly smooth. (As an interesting side note, commercially prepared invert sugar is added during the preparation of liqueurs to prevent the sucrose from crystallizing and turning the liquid cloudy.)

Invertase and invert sugar are both produced commercially and are used by avid candy makers. One neat trick is the use of invertase to make chocolate-covered cherries. The cherry is first covered with a coating of fondant, a stiff mixture with a finely crystallized texture. The layer of fondant is then covered with melted chocolate. Then where does the runny, liquid center come from? A few drops of invertase, added to the fondant, inverts the sucrose to glucose and fructose. Invert sugar dissolves in the moisture of the fondant and liquefies, causing the stiff fondant to develop a smooth, flowing consistency as the candy sits at room temperature.

Invertase and invert sugar, which can be added to granulated sugar to ensure nongrainy candy, are available from candy-making suppliers (see Appendix). ◄ِ

J

JAM AND JELLY MAKING

Successful thickening of jam and jelly depends on establishing a delicate balance among three ingredients: pectin, sugar, and an acid.

Pectin is a gumlike substance found in and between the cell walls of fruit. In fact, it's the glue that holds plants together. Pectin is a carbohydrate that has the ability to thicken a liquid mixture by forming a three-dimensional framework of molecules similar to that of a protein or flour-starch gel (see Gel). When cooled, a liquid containing a large amount of pectin will become firm and stiff.

The hitch is that pectin works only in combination with sugar and an acid, and in narrowly balanced ratios at that. Pectin forms a gel most efficiently when the acidity level of a mixture has a pH of 3, and the mixture contains 65 percent sugar.

Thank goodness we don't have to stop to figure all that out — modern recipes have the formula perfected. The point is, many people find jelly making difficult because they either don't take the recipe seriously, or they substitute a low-pectin fruit for a high-pectin fruit.

If you in any way upset the sugar-acid-pectin balance, the mixture won't gel. Doubling a recipe can also lead to trouble, because the increased amount has to cook longer to heat the center of the mixture sufficiently. Conversely, the center of a larger amount cools more slowly, and proper cooling is critical to the final texture.

During jam or jelly making, fruit is cooked with sugar. Pectin is added to low-pectin fruits, and acid is added to low-acid fruits. This step is essential, both to compensate for a lack of either substance and to provide the high-pectin, high-acid combination needed for a pectin gel to form. Of course, it's best to follow a reliable recipe, but if need be, you can pretty well judge acidity by how tart the mixture tastes. If you want to test for pectin content, spoon out 1 teaspoon of the liquid fruit juice onto a plate. Let it cool, then add 2 tablespoons of rubbing alcohol. Swirl the two together. If the juice clumps together in a large, gooey mass, you have enough pectin. Small, separate clumps indicate the possibility of insufficient pectin.

As your mixture heats, long, chainlike pectin molecules disperse throughout the fruit

juice. The mixture is brought to a boil and cooked for a specific length of time based on the amount of fruit. One of the reasons for boiling jam is to inactivate pectic enzymes that attack pectin and break it down, causing soft, runny jam. (That explains why no-cook recipes for jam and jelly produce soft jam that becomes more and more liquid the longer it's stored.)

When the jam cools, the pectin molecules link together and create a weblike network that traps and holds liquid in its interstices. Further cooling causes the carbohydrate gel to become firm. It's important to note that, like other types of gels, a pectin gel will release liquid under certain circumstances, and weeping occurs. Excess acidity is the most common culprit, so resist the temptation to add more acid than the recipe calls for.

Acid performs a dual role in jam and jelly making. It not only reacts with pectin to thicken the mixture, but also inverts the sucrose present, breaking it down into fructose and glucose (see Invert Sugar). Since the resulting invert sugar is extremely slow to crystallize, acid serves to promote a smooth, noncrystallized texture.   ❧

K

KNEADING

Kneading is a free-form, creative activity, and all cooks have their own personal styles. Successful kneading, however, is far more than just pushing a mound of dough around — it's an important technique based on certain characteristics of dough.

The basic reason for kneading dough is to develop the elasticity of the gluten, although it also evenly distributes the yeast cells and bubbles of carbon dioxide (see Gluten).

Some cooks prefer to knead on a floured cloth, others on a wooden board or table, but you can do a good job on any flat, easy-to-clean surface, such as a Formica counter.

Kneading, unfortunately, has often been recommended as a therapeutic way of working out aggressions, and too much emphasis has been placed on strength and power. Just remember that it is the motion and direction of kneading that are important, not brute force.

When flour and a liquid are combined, gluten is formed. The slightest friction or agitation, such as stirring, beating, or handling the dough in any way, causes the gluten to shape itself into strands. Continued friction causes the strands to join together and form a network of gluten strands. The object of kneading is to rub the gluten strands against each other, increasing their length and elasticity. So as you can see, it has very little to do with strength.

To begin kneading, place the ball of dough in front of you. Using the heel of one or both hands, apply pressure to the upper half of the ball of dough and push it away from you in a sliding motion that is parallel to the counter (see illustration). As the dough rolls over on itself, the gluten strands will rub against each other. Gather the dough into a ball, rotate it by a quarter turn, and repeat the pushing motion in any manner that is comfortable.

The most comfortable and efficient position for kneading is to have your work surface at a low enough level so your upper arms fall from relaxed shoulders, and your lower arms slope downward just a bit, allowing you to use the weight of your entire body while working the dough. Most kitchen counters are too high for this procedure, so you might want to use a table top that is lower.

Kneading is generally done with the heel of one or both hands and is most comfortable when the work surface is slightly below waist height.

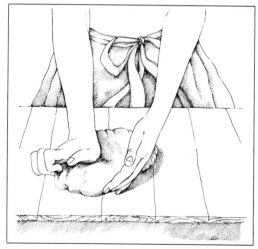

Some illustrations depict the kneading process as a pulling or tearing motion, with the hands going in opposite directions, but that is somewhat misleading. The idea is to stretch and lengthen the gluten strands, not to break them apart, which is counterproductive because that destroys rather than develops the gluten network.

Another important part of kneading is knowing when to stop. As you knead, the appearance and feel of the dough will change. It will no longer stick to the kneading surface and will adhere more to itself. Gradually, it will lose its tackiness and become smooth and shiny. When the dough feels resilient under your hand and springs back immediately if poked with your finger, you've kneaded long enough.

Occasionally, you may come across yeast bread recipes, such as the one for *American-Style Italian Bread,* that are based on a high amount of liquid. These recipes are designed to produce light loaves with an exceptionally airy texture. High-liquid dough tends to be sticky and moist, so if you knead according to the traditional technique, the dough will absorb too much flour and thus upset the high-liquid/low-flour ratio. The Press Method of Kneading, as described on page 225, allows you to develop the gluten without working in excess flour. You fold moist dough over on itself, then press down to distribute the bubbles of carbon dioxide; this repeated folding and pressing exercises the gluten and creates a remarkably high, light loaf with an open crumb structure.

L

LACTOSE

Lactose is the form of sugar that occurs naturally in the milk of all mammals. Like sucrose, it is a disaccharide, but it is less sweet and less soluble than sucrose.

Lactose is the substance that falls to the bottom of a pan of hot milk, forming a film that is difficult to wash off, or, even worse, that browns and ruins the flavor of the milk. Particles of lactose are also responsible for some of the off taste that results when unclarified butter is heated to the point where the milk solids burn.

Lactose is readily converted by certain bacteria into lactic acid, the component that lends a sour tang to buttermilk, yogurt, sour cream, cheese, and milk-based sourdough. It is not, however, one of the sugars that yeast feeds on, and therefore does not participate in the fermentation process in yeast dough. (See Fructose; Glucose; Sucrose.)

LARD

In the years prior to 1911, lard was *the* cooking fat preferred by cooks in the United States. It was much more available than butter and not nearly as expensive. However, cooks weren't the only consumers interested in lard — so were soap manufacturers. Eventually the overall demand exceeded the supply. At that point, hydrogenation was invented and lard took a back seat to solid white shortening (see Shortening).

The popularity of lard suffered a second blow when health experts discovered that animal fats were more saturated (and therefore less healthful to cook with) than the relatively unsaturated vegetable fats. Yet lard has a lot going for it — it has excellent creaming properties, it's exceptionally flavorful, and it's one of the best fats for frying, because it remains stable at high temperatures for long periods of time (see Fats).

Lard produces a full-flavored bread with a tender, yet sturdy, texture. During pastry making, lard maintains its firmness when rolled into thin layers — a factor that encourages flakiness. Also, its slightly grainy consistency shatters the gluten strands of pastry dough to create especially tender pie crusts.

RECIPES: Basic Pie Crust, Processor Pie Shell.   ❧

LARDING

Larding is a method of adding fat to lean cuts of meat. Unlike barding, which involves tying fat to the *outside* of a roast, larding involves adding fat to the *inside* of a roast (see Barding). As the meat heats in the oven, the inserted fat melts, moistening and flavoring the roast in much the same way that natural marbling creates juiciness — a sort of basting from within.

Larding is done with a long, sharply pointed instrument known as a larding needle, and there are several different kinds. The easiest to work with looks like a giant, hollow needle with the top half removed (see illustration). The U-shaped trough is where strips of fat are placed.

The fat is inserted into the meat by pushing the needle through the roast until it comes out the other side (see illustration). Then you

hold onto the fat with one hand, withdraw the needle slowly with the other, and the fat stays inside the meat. By repeating this procedure every 2 inches or so, you can create a symmetrical pattern that looks attractive when the roast is carved.

A larding needle is used to insert strips of fat throughout a roast. This adds moistness as well as flavor to the meat, and creates an attractive pattern when the roast is sliced.

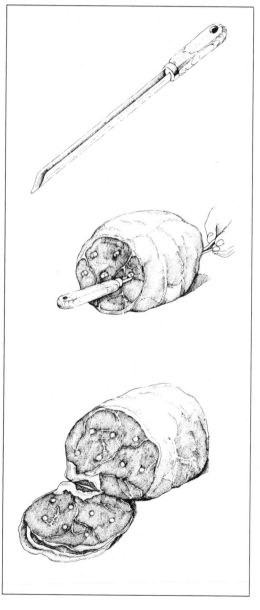

Insert the larding needle perpendicular to the direction in which you'll be carving. If you're working with a long, rectangular roast, like a loin of pork, and you plan to slice down across the meat (see illustration), then insert the larding needle through the length of the roast. In other words, if you're going to carve against the grain, which is the most common method, then lard *with* the grain. (Larding with the grain is much easier than against the grain, by the way.)

Fresh, unfrozen pork fat, also called fatback, is the easiest to use for larding. It is extremely pliable and cuts without difficulty. Make sure it's well chilled, then slice the fat into ¼-inch strips (called lardoons). For added flavor, you can marinate the lardoons in cognac or wine, or roll them in crushed, dried herbs or minced fresh herbs mixed with pressed garlic. If you can't get fresh pork fat, you can use salt pork or bacon instead, first simmering it in water for 10 minutes to modify its flavor and remove the saltiness.

With roasts of beef, I recommend using beef fat in order to maintain a beef flavor. It's more of a project to work with, though, for it isn't available in large sheets like fatback and it crumbles easily when you cut into it. It does, however, freeze well. I routinely trim excess fat from steaks and roasts and freeze it in a plastic bag. When I want to use it for larding, I allow it to partially defrost, then cut it into thin strips.

Cuts of meat that benefit most from larding are those that contain little fat, or marbling, of their own. A bottom-round roast of beef, a tip roast, and even an eye-of-round taste better if larded (or barded, which is less trouble, but produces different results). A loin of pork is my favorite candidate for larding with pork fat. The pork-fat flavor complements the meat and, since pork flesh is only lightly colored, you can create some very attractive and delicious effects by coating the lardoons with chopped fresh parsley, lemon zest, and garlic.

As a matter of fact, new trends in larding now tend to emphasize color and flavor rather than the addition of fat. You can achieve spectacular results by larding a light-colored veal or pork roast with strips of red and green roasted peppers, with a spinach-and-pine-nut paste, or with a thick onion-and-herb purée. The variations are endless — just use your imagination and experiment with all kinds of compatible combinations.

LAYERED PASTRY

Layered pastries have become strongly associated with individual nationalities. Mention filo and people think of Greece; strudel is commonly tied to Hungary and Austria; puff pastry is usually considered to be French; and Danish pastry is linked to the Scandinavian countries. Things aren't really as clear-cut as all that, though. All these pastries are historically interconnected, and the process by which they're prepared reveals a common thread.

Regardless of how it's constructed, layered pastry is principally leavened by steam (except for Danish pastry and croissants, which get an extra boost from yeast). During baking, butter trapped between the layers of dough melts and is absorbed by the flour starch. Meanwhile, moisture contained in the dough (and in the butter) turns to steam; the steam invades the airspace originally occupied by the butter and puffs the layers apart. The steam evaporates with continued baking and the dough dries out, creating a series of crisp, flaky layers.

It's interesting to note that layered pastry dough has its roots in the pasta dough of the Italian cuisine and in the dough used to make won-ton and egg-roll wrappers in the Chinese cuisine. Both the Italian and Chinese doughs are a mixture of flour, salt, water, and an egg. Kneaded until the gluten is highly developed and extremely elastic, these doughs are rolled until thin.

Strudel dough is basically noodle or pasta dough. In fact, the Hungarians and Austrians used the same dough for both entrée and dessert preparations; noodle dough, thinly stretched and brushed with melted butter, becomes strudel when it is rolled up upon itself to create numerous layers. The butter serves to separate the layers of dough during baking and to provide a space for steam.

Filo dough operates in much the same way. Produced by combining flour, salt, and water, filo dough differs from strudel dough in only one respect — it contains a substantial amount of olive oil to facilitate the thinnest possible stretching of the gluten strands. (Occasionally, recipes for strudel dough and pasta will include melted butter or olive oil for the same reason.) Thin sheets of filo are brushed with melted butter, folded, rolled, or stacked, and then baked to fashion layer upon layer of crisp, flaky pastry.

The Viennese took strudel dough one step further. Instead of rolling it thinly and brushing the surface with melted butter, they shaped the basic dough into a rectangle and wrapped it around a block of butter. This package was rolled and folded repeatedly to incorporate air and to form alternating layers of butter and dough. When baked, the pastry puffed into numerous crisp layers. (Incidentally, the basic dough, made of flour, water, and salt, came to be known as the *détrempe* when the French worked their special magic with puff pastry.)

Contemporary recipes for puff pastry usually recommend adding a small portion of oil or softened butter to the basic dough to make it easier to handle. Also, a small amount of flour is usually worked into the butter to make it more malleable at low temperatures and to offset the excess moisture found in American butter. Using salted or unsalted butter is entirely a matter of taste preference; their moisture contents are basically the same, so your choice has little effect on the baking process. The important point is that American butter is considerably higher in moisture than the European butter, for which puff pastry recipes were originally formulated. American butter, therefore, gives off more steam, which causes exuberant puffing and weakens the layers of pastry.

The inclusion of yeast produces another variation of layered pastry. The basic dough is once again wrapped around a block of butter, then rolled and folded repeatedly to trap air and form a layered effect. The final dough is then shaped into Danish pastries or croissants and allowed to rise. During baking, the carbon dioxide produced by the yeast helps the steam to puff the layers apart.

Several short-cut methods have been devised for creating multilayered pastries. There are mixer methods, processor methods, and new techniques for incorporating the butter; and the availability of frozen filo and strudel leaves has now made it possible for even the busiest cook to use these marvelous creations. No matter which approach you take, the fundamental principle remains the same — layers of butter separate layers of dough and prepare the way for stream leavening to take place.

RECIPES: Cream-Cheese Puff Pastry, Flaky Cheese Triangles, Zucchini and Fresh Tomato Strudel. ❧

LEAVENING

Leavening a dough or batter means lightening it with bubbles of air or carbon dioxide gas. As the dough or batter warms, the air or carbon dioxide expands, the bubbles get larger, and the dough or batter becomes lighter.

The source of the carbon dioxide gas is called the leavening agent or leavener. Yeast, baking powder, and baking soda are all leavening agents that produce carbon dioxide. When you use yeast, the carbon dioxide is produced by fermentation (see Fermentation); when you use baking powder or soda, the carbon dioxide is produced by decomposition — a process during which an acid breaks the sodium bicarbonate down into sal soda, water, and carbon dioxide (see Baking Powder/Baking Soda).

Both hot air and steam are also considered leavening agents and work the same way — air-filled bubbles expand when warmed. Yet air leavening is a much more delicate process than carbon dioxide leavening. Anyone who has ever made an angel food cake can attest to that.

Leavening by air and steam takes place whenever air is whipped into a batter: when butter and sugar are creamed together, eggs are beaten into a batter, or whipped egg whites are folded into a mixture. Air can act as a leavening agent on its own (see Cake Baking), but most of the time it acts in conjunction with carbon dioxide.

In air-leavened batters and most carbon-dioxide–leavened doughs, the object is to preserve the bubbles at all cost. Destroy the bubbles and you reduce the degree of lightness. Therefore, banging pans full of cake batter down on the counter to release large air bubbles is like throwing the baby out with the bath water. It's better to watch the batter for a few seconds before putting it in the oven. Any oversized bubbles will rise to the top, and can then be pricked with a toothpick.

Yeast dough is a little different story. It seems as though you are deliberately breaking carbon dioxide bubbles when you punch down risen dough or turn out the dough and knead it. What you're actually doing (in addition to developing gluten, which improves the texture) is subdividing and distributing the bubbles evenly throughout the dough. That's why a dough that is repeatedly allowed to rise and then punched down produces bread or rolls with a better texture than a dough that is simply shaped and allowed to rise once.   ◦⅋

LECITHIN

Lecithin, the strongest and most effective natural emulsifier, belongs to a group of molecules called phospholipids. Real Machiavellian characters, these molecules: one end re-sembles water, so it has an effect on water molecules; the other end resembles oil and exerts its influence on oil molecules. Consequently, lecithin is capable of holding oil and water together (see Emulsifiers).

Lecithin is present in large quantities in egg yolks, which are used in recipes for sauces such as hollandaise to bind the butterfat to lemon juice (water). Lecithin is also contained in milk, cream, and butter. The butterfat droplets in cream and also in butter are surrounded by a thin membrane or coating of phospholipids — lecithin among them. It's that small amount of lecithin that enables you to use cream or butter to slightly emulsify sauces or pull together sauces that have begun to separate.

You can also use lecithin to rescue cold and warm emulsion sauces, such as mayonnaise and béarnaise, but a much larger amount is needed. That's why directions for smoothing out separated mayonnaise instruct you to begin with a clean bowl and an egg yolk. The concentrated lecithin in the yolk will easily incorporate drops of the broken mayonnaise. You can't, however, repair mayonnaise by proceeding the other way around, because the lecithin becomes too diluted if you add the egg yolk to the mayonnaise.   ◦⅋

LIAISON

A liaison is a cream-and-egg-yolk combination used to give a final thickening and binding to a sauce or soup. Added at the last minute, a liaison also enriches the flavor and improves the texture. In fact, a soup or sauce finished with a liaison feels like velvet on your tongue.

A liaison does two jobs — it thickens by coagulation and binds by emulsion. The proteins contained in the egg yolks and cream denature when heated, forming a molecular network that thickens the sauce or soup (see Denaturing). As long as this process is kept under control, the mixture will coagulate smoothly and evenly. If the coagulation gets out of hand (because of too much heat, for example) the sauce will curdle.

Most fine sauces and soups contain some fat, usually in the form of butter. The second function of a liaison is to bind, or emulsify, this fat with the water-based ingredients such as wine or stock. So it often happens that a liaison performs two roles at the same time — while the protein molecules are denaturing, the lecithin in the egg yolks and cream is emulsifying the mixture to ensure a smooth, nongrainy texture.

When preparing a liaison, it's a good idea to let the egg yolks run through a sieve into the cream. This will remove the tiny bits of egg white, called chalazae, that invariably cling to the yolk and coagulate when heated, forming unsightly white specks. For every cup of sauce, whisk together 1 egg yolk and ⅓ cup of heavy cream. Blend in 1 tablespoon of cold water as insurance against curdling. (Light cream or whipping cream may be used, but the final result won't be as smooth or as rich. Also, since either cream is more apt to curdle than is heavy cream, be sure to include the tablespoon of cold water.)

Because the liaison is cool, and the sauce or soup is hot, you'll need to gradually warm the liaison, so that it will be accepted by the hot mixture without curdling. Do this by whisking one-third to one-half of the hot mixture into the liaison. Begin adding it drop by drop; then add the remainder in a slow, thin stream. Blend the warmed egg mixture into the remaining sauce or soup and return to low heat. Warm gently, but don't allow it to boil. Think of the mixture as highly diluted scrambled eggs that will thicken as they heat. Stir constantly to distribute the coagulating egg proteins (see Finishing A Sauce).

LUMP FORMATION

I would bet that anyone who has ever lifted a measuring spoon has encountered lumps somewhere along the line when cooking. They crop up in gravy, custard, cream pie filling, and white sauce. But you needn't resign yourself to accepting these frustrating episodes as inevitable. Once you understand why they develop, you should be able to banish them from your cooking for good.

Basically, there are two types of lumps — those that occur when starch granules fail to open properly, and those that appear as the result of uncontrolled coagulation.

When granules of starch are moist and warm, they develop a tendency to stick together, and often arrange themselves in a tightly knit group or clump. If you add a liquid to starch granules when they are in this condition, the liquid will be absorbed only by the granules around the outside of the group. This exterior layer of granules will proceed to swell, sealing other granules inside. You then end up with a sticky mass consisting of swollen starch granules locked around a number of unhydrated starch granules. In other words, a lump.

Increasing the temperature of a lumpy mixture solves nothing. Lumps of partially hydrated starch molecules are very stubborn; they won't dissolve or break apart. The only thing you can do is strain them out. Just keep in mind that a lumpy mixture isn't as thick as it should be, due to the number of unhydrated starch granules trapped inside the lumps. If you decide to rescue a lumpy mixture by straining it, then bring it to a boil and whisk in a beurre manié until it reaches the thickness you desire.

Prevention, of course, is the best approach. Since this type of lump formation occurs when starch granules group together, separate them right from the start by dispersing them in a second substance to separate starch granules from one another (see Dispersion).

When you blend flour or cornstarch with water to form a slurry, you have effectively separated the starch granules by dispersing them throughout water (see Slurry). In a beurre manié and a roux, the starch particles are dispersed throughout fat. And in recipes for stirred custard, custard cream, and cream pie filling, the starch granules in flour are dispersed with sugar before they are mixed with milk.

Another way to prevent the lumping of starch granules when blending ingredients is by "making a well." In this procedure, dry ingredients are pushed up against the sides of a bowl, forming a crater in the center. Liquid is then poured into the crater and stirred slowly. Recipes seldom mention it, but this method works best if only one-half the liquid is added at a time. As you stir the liquid, a small portion of the dry ingredients will be pulled in from the sides. If you proceed patiently, you'll produce a lump-free batter, because the liquid will take in only as many starch granules as it can incorporate smoothly. When the mixture in the center of the well is fairly thick, form an indentation for the remaining liquid. Then continue to stir.

Lumps that materialize when coagulation gets out of control are formed by protein molecules. Sometimes called curdling, this unfortunate predicament occurs in mixtures containing eggs, milk, or cream.

The gradual thickening of custards and cream fillings is brought about by the change in protein molecules called denaturing (see Denaturing). This particular thickening action, however, is successful only if it takes place gradually. If protein molecules are subjected to excessive heat or the abrupt addition of an acid, they become solid and form lumps. To avoid this kind of lump formation, be certain to heat protein molecules slowly and always add an acid gradually (see Curdling).

M

MARBLING

One sure way to judge how flavorful a piece of meat is going to be is by noting the amount of marbling it contains. It's easy to spot these rows of fat cells interspersed between the meat fibers; they look like little white blobs. You can distinguish them from the more threadlike connective tissue, because fatty deposits tend to be wider, shorter, and more irregularly shaped (see Connective Tissue).

Fat does two things for meat — it gives it flavor and creates juice. During cooking, the fat cells rupture, allowing melted fat to flow between the muscle fibers. As the liquid fat oozes around, it distributes flavor and moistens the meat fibers. This explains why a heavily marbled roast or steak seems very juicy when you cut into it.

Marbling alone is not a reliable sign of tenderness. Since fatty deposits tend to increase as an animal ages, it's entirely possible for a mature animal to exhibit generous streaks of marbling, yet not be tender at all. However, well-marbled meat of a young animal will almost always be tender.

MARGARINE

Margarine isn't exactly a recent invention. In 1869, the French government, faced with scarce pasture land and an increased demand for butter, offered a prize for an inexpensive butter substitute. The winner was a chemist by the name of Hypolite Mege-Mouries, who mixed a type of beef fat that melts at body temperature with milk, creating a spreadable fat that liquefied on the tongue. At the time, his discovery was named oleomargarine.

Now commonly called margarine, this butter substitute is remarkably similar to the real thing. Butter contains 80 percent animal fat and margarine consists of 80 percent vegetable fat. Both butter and margarine contain approximately 16 percent water, which exists in the form of droplets suspended throughout the fat by emulsifiers. They are, therefore, water-in-fat emulsions.

Because of these similarities in physical composition, margarine, like butter, possesses good creaming qualities, a low smoke point, and the ability to remain plastic over a fairly narrow range of temperatures. However, most margarines are formulated to remain plastic below normal refrigeration temperatures, for ease of spreading is a feature that consumers perceive as desirable. It's also interesting to note that commercial bakers of puff pastry have available to them a specially formulated margarine, one with a plasticity range that is so narrow it remains semirigid at room temperature, to facilitate rolling it into the dough.

During the manufacture of margarine, vegetable oils are first hydrogenated to create the proper spreading consistency. Then water, often in the form of milk, is added, and the same microorganisms used to produce the flavor in butter are introduced. Emulsifying agents are blended in, and the entire mixture is agitated to create an emulsion. Just as in butter, salt may be added to combat the growth of bacteria that occurs within the water droplets, causing rancidity. Margarine may also be left unsalted (see Butter).

The emulsifying agents added to margarine are soybean lecithins. Some processors also add the same mono- and diglycerides used in hydrogenated shortening to stabilize the emulsion. Consequently, margarine has nearly the same emulsifying ability as butter and solid shortening. Most margarine is fortified with vitamins A and D, and colored with carotene or annato.

Even though margarine and butter are chemically almost identical, there remains a significant difference in their effects on foods; this keeps me from recommending that they often be interchanged. Margarine gives off an unpleasant smell when heated, so it's a poor choice for sautéing meats and vegetables. Even when chilled, it lacks the hardness and firmness needed for successful pastry, and its flavor in baked goods is, to my mind, vastly inferior to that of butter.

On the plus side, margarine is less expensive than butter and, because of its soft texture, it creams without being warmed to room temperature. Margarine can be used as an acceptable butter substitute in recipes for coffee cakes, muffins, quick breads, brownies, or bars where a buttery flavor is not expected to come through.

MARINATING

Marinating is one of my favorite culinary techniques. It not only moistens and tenderizes meat, but also creates an enormous variety of interesting flavors. It's the perfect solution for those times when you're dying for the taste of something different.

Marinating consists of either rubbing the surface of food with a paste made from herbs and spices, or allowing food to soak in a flavorful liquid. Liquid marinades are probably the most familiar type. They are usually a combination of the same basic ingredients: oil to moisten, an acid to weaken meat fibers, and herbs or spices for flavoring. Occasionally, sugar is added to promote browning and to encourage the development of a thick, flavorful crust.

If you feel like being adventurous, concoct your own marinade. The basic formula is 3 parts oil to 1 part acid, plus whatever flavorings you like. You can use olive oil or vegetable oil. Blend it with red wine for beef; with white wine, lemon juice, lime juice, or vinegar for pork, chicken, lamb, and fish. Then add onion rings or crushed garlic cloves; crushed dried herbs like oregano, rosemary, and bay leaves; or chopped fresh herbs like basil, tarragon, or sage. For pork marinades, you might want to produce a sweet-and-sour crust by adding an ingredient that's high in sugar, such as ketchup, soy sauce, honey, or brown sugar.

The length of time you allow meat to marinate depends on the effect you want to create. If you're marinating to tenderize, it's a good idea to plan on 12 to 24 hours for thin cuts and cubes of meat, and 48 hours for thicker pieces. Exterior fat seals out a liquid marinade, so remove as much fat as possible. It also helps to pierce thick and fat-laden cuts with the tines of a meat fork to allow the marinade to penetrate.

Marinating for flavor can be done in less time. Just remember that the longer you marinate, the more assertive the flavor will be. To achieve moderately flavored meat, plan on marinating 1 hour at room temperature for every inch of thickness or 3 hours per inch in the refrigerator. Fish and shellfish spoil easily, so always limit their time at room temperature to 30 minutes.

It's best to marinate in a glass container or plastic bag, to avoid the chemical interactions that can occur when certain metals or unglazed pottery come in contact with the acid contained in a liquid marinade. Since most recipes seldom produce enough liquid to cover the meat completely, you'll need to turn whatever you're marinating several times to ensure even absorption. Marinating in a plastic bag greatly simplifies this chore. All you have to do is pour the liquid into a large plastic bag. Set the bag inside a pie plate or rectangular baking dish (in case the bag leaks), and arrange the meat in the liquid. Secure tightly with a metal twist. When it's time to turn the meat, just flop the bag over, meat and all.

Dry marinades are flavorful pastes you rub over food. Usually they consist of crushed, or finely chopped, herbs or spices and maybe a bit of grated lemon peel. Salt is sometimes included, and oil is often added to bind the mixture into a paste. Some recipes advise you to scrape away the marinade before cooking; others say to leave it on. The characteristics of certain dishes often hinge on the unique flavor that's created when a dry marinade cooks and forms a crust.

Recently, it has become a popular practice to marinate vegetables like onions, mushrooms, cabbage, and summer squash to create interesting appetizers and salads. This is basically marinating for flavor and takes a relatively short time.

RECIPE: Marinated Lamb Steaks.   ◄ঽ

MAYONNAISE

Mayonnaise, like its cousin, hollandaise, is a basic emulsified sauce. A member of the cold emulsified group, it can also be transformed into other sauces by the addition or substitution of various ingredients.

Mayonnaise is made by combining two incompatible elements — oil and water — with an emulsifier to form a permanent suspension (see Emulsion). The water is in the form of lemon juice or vinegar, and is also contained in the egg yolks used to emulsify the mixture (51 percent of an egg yolk is water).

Lecithin in the egg yolk performs the task of holding the oil and water together. As far as the oil is concerned, you can use corn oil, peanut oil, sesame oil, walnut oil, or safflower oil. All of the vegetable oils work equally well, but some, particularly olive oil, have more assertive flavors than others, so you may want to experiment a bit to find the oil you prefer. Some recipes suggest combining oils; 2 parts vegetable oil to 1 part olive oil makes a nice blend.

Other ingredients play important roles, too. Lemon juice and vinegar, besides containing water, are acidic, and acids help to form emulsions by denaturing protein. In other words, they firm up protein particles by causing them to change their shape, which contributes to the stiffness of the sauce (see Denaturing).

Mustard, frequently an ingredient of mayonnaise, is also an emulsifier, although a weak one. It's used to give a boost to the lecithin. Salt helps to stabilize an emulsion by encouraging protein molecules to denature.

The technique for preparing a cold emulsified sauce, such as mayonnaise, is almost exactly the same as that for making hollandaise, which is a warm emulsified sauce. The only difference is that hollandaise is composed of butterfat incorporated into slightly cooked egg yolks, while mayonnaise is made by incorporating oil into uncooked egg yolks.

As you whisk the oil into the egg yolks and lemon juice, you're agitating the mixture — a necessary step in forming an emulsion. Whisking breaks the oil drops into smaller and smaller droplets and disperses them throughout the egg yolk. Each oil droplet becomes coated with lecithin, and an emulsion begins to form, as the emulsifying agent links the oil and water droplets together in a permanent suspension.

It's essential that you add the oil very slowly at first, for it's much easier to form an emulsion when there's plenty of lecithin to surround each oil droplet. On the other hand, when oil is added too fast, the lecithin doesn't have time to coat all the droplets before they slither off to find one another.

If you do add too much oil for the emulsifier to cope with, puddles form on the surface of your mayonnaise, and your emulsion is said to have "broken." You can fix it by providing a fresh supply of lecithin. Simply place an egg yolk in a warm bowl, whisk in 1 teaspoon of fresh lemon juice and a dash of salt, and beat until the mixture is light in color. Then gradually whisk in the broken mayonnaise, adding it in small amounts at first to give the lecithin a chance to surround all the oil droplets.

To stabilize mayonnaise so that you can keep it for a week to 10 days, whisk in 1½ teaspoons of boiling water per egg yolk. Do this all at once, at the very end of the procedure. The heat from the water will slightly coagulate the egg protein and firm up the emulsion even further, to prevent it from separating as it stands.

Two important factors in successfully making mayonnaise are temperature and the amount of oil an egg yolk will hold in suspension. One large egg yolk can hold 4 to 6 ounces of oil. Just to be on the safe side, don't use any more than ½ cup of oil for every yolk until you're quite experienced. Also, since emulsions occur best at moderate temperatures, be sure to have all your ingredients and tools at room temperature. (However, since the optimum temperature for forming a cold emulsion is 78°F., you can speed things up a bit by running your bowl and whisk under hot water to warm them. Dry them thoroughly before proceeding.)

RECIPES: Mayonnaise, Mayonnaise by Blender or Processor.

MEASURING

Remember watching your grandmother cook? She started with two or three fistfuls of this, added half an egg shell full of that, then a capful of something else. If the "feel" wasn't right, she'd work in a smidgin of this or a little of that. She never seemed to measure anything. Maybe your favorite TV chef doesn't measure much, either. A splash of wine here, a pinch of herbs there. It's enough to give you the idea that measuring isn't important.

But let's be realistic — sometimes it is and sometimes it isn't. If you're an experienced cook, you can probably judge a teaspoonful of dried herbs by the size of the pile they make, so you pour a small mound in the palm of your hand and toss it into the sauce. Chances are you also know the extent to which a half-cup of wine decreases the amount in the bottle, so you pour it right into the sauce without using a measuring cup. People who cook a great deal do tend to develop their own personal measuring systems that are often remarkably accurate.

That's all well and good if you've been cooking since Hector was a pup, but cooking is as much a precise science as it is an art. Accurate measuring eliminates unforeseen disasters and helps you to achieve dependable results. Measuring carefully is especially important on your first experience with a recipe; it's the *only* way you can be sure you're duplicating the intended result. The second time around, you can add or subtract or get a bit creative.

Baking is one area where accurate measuring is absolutely indispensable. You can ruin a cake by using too much sugar, spoil cookies with too much shortening, and devastate popovers with too much flour. Some recipes specify a certain method of measuring dry ingredients and whether to sift before or after measuring (see Sifting). This is important information, because each method produces slightly different results.

If a recipe says to scoop measure flour, fluff it first by gently squeezing the sides of the flour bag, or by stirring it with a fork. Then plunge a measuring cup into the unsifted flour, lift it out, and without shaking or otherwise disturbing the contents, level off the top of the cup with the straight blade of a knife. If a recipe specifies using sifted flour, sift the required amount into a bowl, then plunge in a measuring cup and scoop measure in the same manner, unless, that is, you are instructed to sift directly into the measuring cup. This latter technique results in less flour per cup than scoop measuring because sifting incorporates a significant amount of air; therefore, it should only be used in recipes that specify this method of measuring. Avoid measuring flour by spooning or pouring it into a measuring cup unless directed to do so by the recipe. And particularly refrain from shaking, banging, or tapping — all are guaranteed to pack down flour inside the cup. (Recipes that don't specify a particular measuring method assume that you will scoop measure unsifted flour.)

There are two kinds of measuring cups, and their differences should be respected — don't use them interchangeably. Cups for measuring liquid ingredients come in many different sizes and are made of clear material — usually glass or plastic. They invariably have a spout to facilitate pouring, and the increment markings stop well below the top of the cup. The clear material allows you to see precisely the amount of liquid inside. But here a word of caution: use the measuring cup that most closely accommodates the amount you're measuring. In other words, don't measure ¼ cup of milk in a 2-cup or 4-cup measure. The wider the container, the greater the margin of error that exists in measuring small amounts.

Cups for measuring dry ingredients are usually made of metal or colored plastic. There are 1-cup, 2-cup, and 4-cup measures available with increments etched or punched on the side, but that negates the principle behind accurate dry measuring, which is to fill the cup to the brim, then level it off. You can't very well level off the contents if they're down inside somewhere. What ends up happening is that you shake the contents to see how much there is and pack the ingredients down in the process.

The best type of cup for measuring dry ingredients is the graduated style — where individual cups measure out ¼ cup, ⅓ cup, ½ cup, and so forth. Measuring liquid ingredients in this sort of cup leads to inaccuracies, because when the liquid reaches the brim, surface tension forms a kind of skin that allows you to overfill the cup (by as much as a tablespoon in a 1-cup measure).

When it comes to measuring small amounts of either liquid or dry ingredients, a set of individual spoons is a very reliable approach. Also, the cost is reasonable enough to allow you to invest in several sets, so you won't have to stop and wash out the shortening before you measure the sugar.

So far we've only discussed measuring by volume. But an extremely accurate method, one that's become increasingly popular with pastry cooks, is measuring by weight. For example, it's much easier and more precise to weigh a certain number of ounces (or grams) of butter than it is to soften the butter in order to fit it inside a cup, then be faced with waiting while it chills again. Measuring flour by weight is far more exact than measuring by the cup, because it eliminates errors caused by packing down. In essence, it's just plain handy to have scales in the kitchen, for there will always be times when you will want to

measure fresh herbs, which are fluffy, but you won't know how loosely or firmly to pack them, or other ingredients such as chopped nuts or shredded cheese that are often referred to in terms of ounces.　　　•⋑

MEAT
Selecting Cuts

Several factors determine how tough or tender a piece of meat is going to be. The most important consideration is what section of the animal the cut comes from. The more work a muscle does, the tougher it will be. Since animals stand and walk on four legs, the legs, rump, and shoulders get far more exercise than the back and rib area. Therefore, the meat of the legs, rump, and shoulder will be tough, and the meat of the back and ribs will be tender.

The major section of the animal is generally mentioned on the meat label. Terms such as steak, roast, and chops are not really helpful so look for the parts-of-the-body words like rib, rump, and round; they are the key to how tender meat will be.

With beef, the least developed muscles are located along the backbone and include the rib area. Loin and sirloin are from the backbone section; rib roasts and rib-eye steaks from the rib section. These meats are delicately flavored and finely grained (that is, the fibers are not easy to distinguish). The flesh contains very little connective tissue, but it is generously streaked with fat (see Marbling).

As muscle tissue becomes more developed, the fibers enlarge. Therefore, moving back toward the rump, the meat fibers become thicker, and there is an increased amount of connective tissue and less marbling (see Connective Tissue). Farther down the leg, the fibers of meat become even more obvious and connective tissue is abundant. If any part of the label says rump or round, it comes from this section.

Meat from the shoulder often has the word chuck or blade on the label. The muscle fibers in this section are extremely thick — more fibrous than those in the rump — and connective tissue is even more abundant. Cuts from the underside of the animal are called flank, plate, or brisket. They also contain a great deal of connective tissue and well-developed muscle fibers.

Generally speaking, meat with thick fibers has an assertive flavor, increased connective tissue, a greater degree of toughness, and less marbling, and it costs less than meat with thin fibers, which has a delicate flavor, less connective tissue, a greater degree of tenderness, and increased marbling.

With pork, the main body parts of the animal are nearly the same as those of beef. The rib (except spareribs), loin, and sirloin labels again designate the most tender parts — the back and rib cage. Any blade cut comes from the shoulder area, and arm or picnic shoulder denotes sections of the front leg. The hind legs become hams. Spareribs, bacon, and salt pork come from the underside. As with cuts of beef, the more developed muscles possess enlarged fibers and increased connective tissue. However, finely grained pork displays little marbling.

Lamb and veal are both quite tender in all sections, although the rib, loin, and sirloin cuts are still the most tender and finely grained. The leg and shoulder cuts have larger meat fibers and a greater amount of connective tissue, but it's not as tough as that of beef. Portions from the underside are called flank and breast, and the forearms are sold as shanks.

In addition to the amount of exercise certain muscles get, the toughness or tenderness of a piece of meat is also affected by the age of the animal, what the animal was fed, how it was slaughtered, and whether or not the meat was aged — conditions that not only are beyond your control, but often beyond your recognition as well. For example, yellowish fat can indicate beef that has been fed grass or that was slaughtered past its prime.

Cooking

Each section of the animal has unique characteristics that make it a good candidate for certain cooking methods but not for others, and this is where many cooks run into trouble. There's no point in trying to prepare a cut of meat in a way for which it's ill-suited. It's a waste of time and money.

Meat with fibrous muscle is extremely flavorful, but difficult to chew. Exposure to dry heat, like roasting or broiling, only increases the toughness of the fibers. Moist heat, however, softens the connective tissue that holds the fibers together and dissolves it, allowing the muscle fibers to separate and creating the sensation of tenderness.

Finely grained meat contains little connective tissue and doesn't benefit at all from moist heat. Since muscle fibers toughen when exposed to any kind of heat, and there is no collagen present to dissolve, the final product comes out extremely tough and dry even if it is braised or steamed. Use dry-heat methods of cooking for these tender, expensive cuts.

You can't go wrong if you roast or broil any cut that bears the term rib, loin, or sirloin as part of its label. Braise, stew, or otherwise cook in a pot those cuts designated shoulder, blade, chuck, breast, shank, brisket, flank, rump, or round. The exceptions are the hind legs of pork and lamb, which can be roasted.

Tenderizing

Since thin muscle fibers are easy to chew, it stands to reason that the way to cope with tough meat is to break or weaken the fibers. You can accomplish this by soaking meat in an acid (see Marinating) or by sprinkling on a commercial tenderizing powder. These powders contain enzymes that break down protein, thereby softening muscle tissue and making it more tender.

Other techniques for tenderizing meat by weakening or breaking the muscle fibers include scoring and pounding. For example, if you score a ½-inch-thick piece of beef round with a chef's knife, you can create home-made cube steaks that are more tender and less expensive than those prepared at the meat counter (see Scoring). Pounding thin meat with the smooth side of a mallet weakens muscle fiber to produce pork cutlets and veal scaloppine. More vigorous pounding can crush the connective tissue of fairly tough pieces of beef to make tender sandwich steaks. Pounding thicker meat with the serrated side of a metal mallet severs a certain number of muscle fibers to ensure a tender pot roast or Swiss steak (see Pounding Meat).

Carving against the grain, especially in rather thin slices, cuts the muscle fibers into easy-to-chew lengths. That's why London broil (from the shoulder, round, or flank), California blade steak, and other bargain cuts seem more tender when they're thinly sliced at an angle to the way the meat fibers run. ⁂

MERINGUE

There are three basic types of meringue — soft meringue, hard (or Swiss) meringue, and Italian meringue. All are a combination of whipped egg whites and some form of sugar.

The key to success is whipping the whites to their maximum potential, then slowly sprinkling in the sugar. Since sugar impedes the whipping process, it should be added gradually and at precisely the correct point. If you add it too soon, your egg whites will never achieve good volume; added too late, sugar won't completely dissolve (see Whipping: Egg Whites). When baking meringue, it's also important to preheat the oven, because meringue will break down if allowed to stand.

Damp weather is meringue's natural enemy. The excess moisture in the air is readily absorbed into meringue, causing it to develop a very unpleasant, gummy texture. If you make soft or Italian meringue on a humid or rainy day, plan to serve it within the hour. Hard meringue should be cooled in the oven, then transferred directly to the freezer without wrapping. Defrost by setting the unwrapped frozen meringue in a closed, cold oven for 2 to 3 hours.

Soft meringue is the version used to top pies and baked Alaska. Swirled or piped into intricate designs, it is then browned in a hot oven. Meringue applied this way acts as insulation, so that heat doesn't affect delicate cream pie fillings or melt ice cream.

When making soft meringue, it's a good idea to use either superfine or confectioners' sugar, because undissolved particles of sugar are what cause meringue to exude moisture. Confectioners' sugar not only is finely textured, but also contains a small amount of cornstarch, which will absorb any traces of moisture that exist in the whipped whites, thereby preventing beads of water from forming on the surface of baked meringue.

If you decide to use granulated sugar instead, whirl it around in the blender a few times to make it more finely textured, then add it to the beaten whites as usual. Check to see if it has completely dissolved by rubbing a bit of meringue between your fingers: grittiness indicates that the sugar is not completely dissolved.

Hard or Swiss meringue is made by incorporating larger quantities of sugar than are included in soft meringue. The result is an exceptionally stiff, glossy mound of meringue. This is the type used for making dessert shells, meringue-based cake layers, and macaroons, or for piping into fanciful pastries and cookie kisses.

Ground nuts, chopped glacéed fruit, or bits of chocolate can be folded into hard meringue to form an endless variety of sweets. Whatever form your meringue takes, it will be easiest to remove after baking if you cook it on a sheet lined with parchment paper, which releases baked meringue without any sticking (see Parchment Paper).

Recipes that direct you to bake hard meringue at a high temperature are striving to create a moist, sticky, somewhat marshmallowy consistency. Lower temperatures produce a meringue that is dry, crisp, and brittle.

A third approach is to dry, rather than bake, the meringue. This is done by placing the meringue in a preheated 350°F. oven, then turning the heat off and allowing the meringue to dry for 12 to 24 hours. The important point here is not to allow any browning — properly prepared meringue of this nature shouldn't even be tinged with beige.

Italian meringue is made by incorporating a sugar syrup into whipped egg whites. In this procedure, granulated sugar and water are cooked to form a syrup, so there is never a problem caused by undissolved grains of sugar. For that reason, some cooks prefer to use Italian meringue in place of soft meringue for topping pies and desserts. Italian meringue is exceptionally versatile; it can be piped into intricate shapes and baked or dried like hard meringue, or used as the foundation for numerous frostings and frozen desserts.

RECIPES: Forgotten Cookies; Italian Meringue; Meringue Shells Melba; Soft Meringue I, II, and III; Swiss Meringue.   ᴈ

MICROWAVE COOKING

Cooking by microwaves takes place when extremely short waves of electromagnetic energy come in contact with food molecules. Microwaves are high-frequency waves that pass through the air like ordinary radio waves (except that radio waves are anywhere from three feet to several miles long and microwaves are less than five inches).

Picture a typical microwave as a series of hills and valleys. For the sake of discussion, say that the peaks of the hills are emitting a positive electric charge and the valleys are giving off a negative charge. Keep in mind that food and water contain molecules that emit a positive electric charge at one end and a negative electric charge at the other. Since opposite electrical charges attract each other, the peak, or positive section of the microwave, acts as a magnet and pulls on the nega-tive end of food molecules; meanwhile, the valley, or negative section of the microwave, pulls on the positive end of the food and water molecules.

But the wave doesn't stand still. It travels through the air in the oven and enters food waiting to be cooked. As the microwave passes by the food and water molecules, the molecules twist around to align themselves with the nearest charge — positive ends moving toward negative charges and vice versa. Then, to keep things lively, the direction of the current changes. In fact, it reverses direction more than 2 billion times per second. Every time the direction of the current changes, the food and water molecules twist around again in a molecular Saint Vitus' dance.

The frenzied agitation of the molecules, as they vibrate back and forth, causes enough friction to create heat. In this way, microwaves, which possess no heat of their own, agitate food and water molecules into generating enough heat to cook food.

However, microwaves only penetrate food to a depth of 1½ inches. Consequently, it's necessary for two other types of heating to take place in order for food to cook thoroughly. When food is microwaved, heat generated by the vibrating molecules near the surface is passed to the interior by conduction (see Heat: Conduction). Meanwhile, the water contained in food heats and changes to steam, providing an additional form of heat for the interior portion of food.

Because of the way microwaving works, some foods are better suited to this method than others. Foods that benefit from steam cooking, such as vegetables and fish, microwave exceptionally well, because their interior moisture is converted to steam by the electromagnetic energy; the food literally cooks in its own steam, preserving all the natural flavor and nutrients. In the same vein, microwaving reheats leftovers beautifully, because their interior moisture converts to steam and warms the food, without drying it or changing its flavor in any way.

Food that is microwaved seldom browns, however. That's because the heat generated by the food molecules and steam doesn't reach a high enough temperature to cause the Maillard reaction to occur (see Browning — Maillard Reaction). Another disadvantage to microwave cooking has to do with the fact that food components differ in their ability to absorb microwaves. A piece of meat, for example, consisting of fat, bone, and meat fibers contains three different components that do not heat equally. This kind of difference in food composition causes many foods to cook unevenly.

To achieve the best results from this new cooking technique, enroll in a microwave cooking course and learn by doing it.

MOLECULAR NETWORK

The name sounds formidable, yet a molecular network is simply the skeletal structure that thickens a sauce, supports a cake, or firms a gelatin dessert.

Much of what goes on during the cooking process involves the building of weblike networks of molecules. In bread baking, for example, carbohydrate and protein molecules (in the form of flour starch and gluten) make up the molecular network that surrounds pockets of carbon dioxide and steam. As the bread bakes, the network sets, moisture dissipates into the air, and the network becomes increasingly firm. When nearly all the moisture has baked off, the bread is done.

Other networks of molecules form a series of bridges to thicken sauce and gravy. A skeletal framework of pectin molecules makes fruit jelly firm; a system of emulsifying molecules binds mayonnaise; and molecules of denatured protein coagulate to firm custard pie filling.

(See more at Coagulation; Denaturing; Emulsion; Gelatin).

MUFFINS

The secret to successful muffins is like the formula for tasteful decorating: less is more.

Nothing could be any easier to create than an excellent muffin, yet muffins are often poorly done — usually because people try too hard. Muffin making is an uncomplicated procedure that should be approached in a simple, straightforward manner.

The following two-bowl method produces the best results, because it reduces the tendency to overbeat. First, blend all the dry ingredients in one bowl and all the liquid ingredients in the other. Make sure that the leavening agent is well dispersed throughout the dry ingredients. If left in clumps, baking soda or powder will form tunnels as the batter is heated.

It's also a good idea to blend the egg and milk thoroughly by whisking them together. Beating them lightly with a fork, as some recipes suggest, tends to allow blobs of egg yolk to remain unincorporated, which gives the surface of muffins a mottled appearance.

To facilitate blending, make a well by pushing the dry ingredients away from the center of the bowl (see illustration). Then pour in the liquid ingredients and stir *by hand* until the dry ingredients are thoroughly moistened. The batter will be lumpy, *very*

Making a well facilitates the blending of a mixture. Dry ingredients are pushed away from the center of the bowl before liquids are added.

lumpy. Resist the temptation to smooth it out, because continued beating will develop the gluten and produce a coarse texture. Gently incorporate any fruit or nuts your recipe calls for. Here again, restrain yourself. Two cups of berries is not necessarily better than 1 cup. The success of your muffins depends on maintaining the correct ratio of flour to fruit or nuts.

Since the shape of your muffins is as important as the texture, fill the tins, or paper cups, no more than two-thirds full. If the batter rises and flows over the edge of the cup, it will either spread out and form a wide, flat top, or adhere to the lip of the cup and produce muffins shaped like sombreros. Partially filled cups are the only way to achieve nicely rounded tops.

Another important factor is heat. The best results are obtained by heating muffin batter quickly, so always place your pan in a preheated oven and *bake for a short period of time.* Twenty minutes at 400° to 425°F. is just about right.

Many people bake muffins in paper-lined tins, but try them without the paper. When muffin batter cooks directly in contact with hot metal, a hearty, crusty exterior develops. I use a preseasoned, cast-iron muffin pan with deep, straight-sided cups that produces wonderful muffins (see Appendix).

Grease the cups, and place the iron pan in the oven to preheat for 20 minutes. Then, when you fill the cups with batter, you'll hear a faint hissing sound, because cooking begins to take place immediately. To use aluminum muffin pans without paper liners, grease the cups generously and omit the preheating step. Bake your muffins until they start to pull away from the sides of the cups.

By the way, if you're disappointed because the tops of your muffins don't brown as beautifully as the ones you see in magazines, try baking them a few minutes longer; however, they will be somewhat drier and crustier.

RECIPES: Blueberry Buttermilk Muffins, Cranberry-Walnut Muffins, Fresh Raspberry Muffins.   ❧

N

NUTS

Nuts have always contributed a luxurious touch to baked goods and subtle nuances to salads and entrées. The oil they contain is responsible for their outstanding flavor. It's also responsible for the problems you encounter when grinding nuts finely for use in delicate pastries or as a substitute for flour in Austrian-style cakes.

The best way to prepare ground nuts is with a special nut grinder that transforms whole nuts to a powdery, flourlike consistency (see Appendix). The next best option is a Mouli grater fitted with a fine shredding cylinder. Some electric coffee grinders do an acceptable job, but avoid using a meat grinder or mortar and pestle, both of which press excess oil from nuts.

Recipes often direct you to prepare finely ground nuts in a processor or blender, but even if you exercise extreme care and operate the machine in the shortest spurts possible, nuts will still release a considerable amount of oil. Finely ground nuts that are going to be used in place of flour should be so dry they will flutter to the counter when dropped from between your fingers. The presence of oil causes nut particles to stick together, which hampers effective blending and produces dense, overly moist baked goods.

In the event that you must grind nuts in a processor or blender, place 2 tablespoons of sugar per cup of nuts into the container before adding the nuts. (Remember to deduct the 2 tablespoons of sugar from the amount called for in the recipe.) The sugar will help to absorb some of the oil that's released by the nuts. If bread crumbs are included in the recipe, they should be used instead of the sugar.

OILS

Most edible oils (cooking fats that are liquid at room temperature) are extracted from vegetable sources. Generally speaking, they are relatively lower in saturated fatty acids than fats from animal sources. Vegetable oils differ from one another in flavor, aroma, and "mouthfeel." You'll notice, for example, that safflower oil feels lighter and less greasy on your tongue than corn oil.

Flavor is the most outstanding characteristic of the various oils and determines to a great extent which oil you use for what purpose. Walnut oil, almond oil, and hazelnut oil possess distinctly nutty flavors. They are delicious when used in light salad dressings and in dishes especially designed to incorporate the nuts of their origins. Olive oil, with its intense fruity flavor, makes an admirable mayonnaise and lends unique overtones to sautéed meat, but the assertive results are not pleasing to everyone. Peanut oil is less potent and an excellent substitute for olive oil.

The mild-tasting, or nearly flavorless, oils are the best to use for deep-frying. Corn oil and cottonseed oil remain stable at high temperatures, and they can be strained and refrigerated so you can reuse them. Safflower oil and sunflower oil are light and virtually tasteless. You can use them for sautéing or frying, or blend them with assertively flavored oils if you want only a hint of flavor.

Vegetable oil can be heated to a much higher temperature than butter, which makes it a superior fat for sautéing and shallow frying. However, the flavor of butter is often essential to the character of a dish. For the best of both worlds, combine equal amounts of butter and oil. You will then be able to obtain the flavor of butter while taking advantage of the higher smoke point of oil.

A number of recipes exist that use vegetable oil as a shortening. They're enormously popular because they're quick — no creaming step, no messy melted butter pan to wash — and they produce moist cakes and manageable pie crusts. However, oil has no creaming ability at all and is not easily dispersed throughout batter. For that reason, oil-based cookies are often heavy and chewy, and cakes can turn out soggy and leaden. Pie crust made with oil is tender and crumbly (see Pie Crust), but tends to have an oily mouthfeel.

Substituting oil for hydrogenated shortening or melted butter is tricky. Butter contains approximately 16 percent water, but oil and hydrogenated shortening, which are 100 percent fat, contain no water. If you substitute oil for melted butter, you upset the liquid balance and the fat ratio. If you substitute oil for shortening, you eliminate the air- and moisture-trapping qualities that butter and hydrogenated shortening provide.   ❧

OVEN PLACEMENT

Did you ever wonder why an occasional recipe specifically directs you to "place the pan on the lowest rack" or "bake in the middle of the oven"? Does it really make any difference?

In order to realize the significance of those directions, it's important to understand what goes on inside a heated oven. Most ovens look alike. There's a heating element at the top and at the bottom, and four sets of rack supports on either side. Some ovens come equipped with two straight, or flat, racks; others have a straight rack and an offset, or U-shaped, rack. When the U-shaped rack is in place, the surface is located below the supports, which creates a placement option between one set of supports and the next — a sort of mid-level arrangement.

During baking, the source of heat is the element at the bottom of the oven. The heating element warms the nearby air molecules and, once heated, they rise to the top, where they nudge aside cooler molecules. The cooler molecules fall to the bottom, become warmed by the heating element, and rise to the top. In this manner, a series of circulating air currents is established (see Heat: Convection). It seems simple enough, but there's a hitch. Hot air molecules in an oven have no way to escape, as they do in a pot of boiling water, where they break through the surface as bubbles. So they tend to gather at the top of the oven, until they become cool enough to drop to the bottom again. This creates a layer of hot air at the top of the oven. Therefore, the highest and the lowest rack positions in an oven are hotter than the two positions in the middle. A cake baked on the uppermost rack will have a dark, dry, overcooked surface and an undercooked bottom; by the same token, if baked on the lowest possible rack, it will have an overcooked bottom crust long before the surface is completely set.

Cookies, cakes, and pastries bake well on the second rack from the bottom. However, the best situation is created by inserting a U-shaped rack in the *third* position from the bottom. The surface of the offset rack drops below the supports to a point that is just about the middle of the oven, the location where heating is usually the most even. Ovens do have their individual quirks, however, so the only sure way to establish the best baking position in your own oven is to use an oven thermometer. Set it on the rack as you would a pan and test several different locations. You may find as much as 15° to 25°F. difference between positions.

Air currents within the cavity of an oven travel in currents similar to those of a river. Where the riverbed is wide, the water meanders slowly, but where it is narrow, the water rushes through. When air molecules rush to get through a confined space, uneven baking results, because faster-moving hot air cooks food faster. For example, if you place two loaves of bread in the oven, side by side, and the space between them is narrow, that side of each loaf will cook faster than the other sides. To prevent this, many recipes for breads, pan rolls, and layer cakes remind you to leave 1 or 2 inches between pans.

Baking on two racks at the same time also

results in uneven cooking. If you place one pan directly over the other, the air currents can't effectively reach the top of the lower pan, nor the bottom of the upper pan. If you compensate by moving the bottom pan to the right and the top pan to the left to expose the troublesome areas, the heat from the walls of the oven will cook one side faster than the other. If you absolutely must bake on two racks (and only casserole-type dishes are flexible enough to stand up to this kind of treatment), stagger the pans — one to the left and one to the right — for half the cooking time. Then switch shelves and turn the pans around to even out the heating process.

Which brings us to hot spots. Most ovens, even the newest and fanciest, have an area where browning seems to take place faster. It's usually in the back and to one side. Once you catch on to where the hot spot is in your oven, don't hesitate to rotate baked goods during the last five or ten minutes to even out the browning. Just be sure that the crumb structure is firm and completely set before you move anything, so you don't precipitate a collapse. ◄ৡ

P

PANADE

A *panade* is a basic paste consisting of flour, water, and butter — the very same ingredients used in all types of pastry. The difference is that a *panade* is cooked to increase the elastic properties of the flour's gluten.

Eggs are beaten into a warm *panade* to form cream puff pastry (also called *pâte à choux*). The protein in the eggs strengthens the weblike network of gluten strands, and when heat is applied in the form of baking, frying, or poaching, the moisture contained in the eggs turns to steam. The steam permeates all the cavities in the gluten web, and the pastry puffs up (see Cream Puff Pastry). ◄ৡ

PANCAKES

Pancakes seem simple enough to make, but using the proper procedure guarantees the best results. Pancakes belong to the quick-bread family; the batter is blended together with a minimum of beating, and the leavening agents are carbon dioxide and steam (see Leavening). Sugar in a recipe isn't included so much for the purpose of sweetening as it is to give pancakes a rich, golden color (see Browning).

The texture of the pancake you end up with is determined to a great extent by the proportion of liquid to dry ingredients, so that thin batter produces thin pancakes and thick batter, cakey-type pancakes. Folding whipped egg whites into either kind of batter lightens the consistency and creates an airy texture (see Whipping: Egg Whites).

The best approach to mixing is to blend the dry ingredients in one bowl and the liquid ingredients in another. Then make a well in the dry ingredients and pour in the liquid. Stir with a spoon until blended, but don't beat. Too much activity at this point will agitate the gluten and produce a less-than-tender pancake.

The batter, which may be lumpy, should be the consistency of heavy cream; however, while it sits, the starch molecules expand, and as they expand, they absorb more liquid. Then they expand even more, the batter gets thicker and thicker, and you end up with doughy, heavy pancakes.

A solution to this problem is to allow the batter to rest for 10 minutes in the refrigerator. This not only relaxes any gluten that may have become overdeveloped during mixing, but it also gives the starch molecules time to expand fully. Don't worry about the fact that you've already added the leavening; cold air slows down the chemical action, so that only a small amount of carbon dioxide is released into the air.

At the end of 10 minutes, the batter will be quite a bit thicker than it was. Gently stir in as much additional liquid as you need to restore the original, heavy-cream consistency.

A good substantial griddle is essential in order to provide an evenly heated cooking surface. Flimsy griddles tend to warp and develop hot spots, so it's worth paying for a higher-quality item. A nonstick surface is a desirable feature, because it greatly reduces the need for using fat or grease.

Place the griddle over medium-high heat and grease the surface if necessary. When a drop of water hops vigorously across the surface and then evaporates, the griddle is at the correct temperature. (An even more reliable test is to cook a sample pancake or two.) The griddle should be hot enough to set the batter almost upon contact. Pour batter on with a ladle or large glass measuring cup.

The way to produce light, airy pancakes is to flip them at precisely the right moment. As the baking powder or soda gives off carbon dioxide, bubbles form on the surface of the pancake. When just about half the bubbles have broken, turn the pancake over, trapping some of the hot air inside. (If you are making *Blueberry Pancakes* or adding other types of fruit, you can achieve a more even distribu-tion by pouring plain batter onto the griddle, then sprinkling on the fruit as the first side cooks.)

After about 30 seconds, lift the pancake slightly and look underneath. If the bottom is browned, your pancake is done. Resist the temptation to flip more than once.

RECIPES: Blueberry Pancakes, Heavenly Pancakes.   ◆᙮

PARBOILING

Parboiling, like blanching, involves a brief period of cooking in hot water. However, parboiling takes longer than blanching, and its purpose is to partially tenderize food as a preliminary step to a second cooking method (see Blanching).

Pasta, rice, beans, grain, or anything else that is cooked in water prior to being sauced or combined with other ingredients and baked is said to be parboiled. Sturdy vegetables like cauliflower and broccoli are tenderized by parboiling before they are batter-fried. Giant mushrooms, large onions, zucchini squash, or eggplant that is going to be stuffed are often parboiled to reduce the cooking time of the final assembly. Cabbage is parboiled to soften the leaves, so they will be easier to stuff and roll. Potatoes, turnips, and other root vegetables are sometimes parboiled to give them a head start if they are going to be baked in a delicate sauce that would be ruined by an extended period of heating.   ◆᙮

PARCHMENT PAPER

Baking parchment looks and feels like the old-fashioned paper that important documents and proclamations used to be written on. Now, instead of writing on it, we cook with it.

Parchment paper comes in rolls of 20 or 40 square feet (15 inches wide) or in packages of

50 flat sheets measuring 10 by 15 inches. You can use it to line cake pans, cookie sheets, and even the bottom of messy casseroles. Absolutely nothing sticks to it, which makes parchment paper the only sensible way to line a surface for baking meringue shells, torte layers, or meringue-based cookies such as *Forgotten Cookies.* At the end of the cooling period, it peels away effortlessly, leaving your meringue creations intact.

There are other advantages to baking with parchment paper, too. When you're baking cookies, you can line your counter with sheets of parchment and get all the cookies ready to bake at one time. Then all you have to do is slide a sheet of baked cookies off the pan and replace it with a sheet of unbaked cookies. You'll find that cookies and cream puff pastries attain a better shape when baked on parchment, because they spread less during baking.

Lining cake pans with parchment paper enables you to turn the cakes out intact, and this is where parchment paper's advantage over waxed paper and aluminum foil becomes most obvious. Parchment paper is porous and ever so slightly absorbent; waxed paper and aluminum foil are not. Therefore, a cake baked on foil or waxed paper actually sits in a film of grease as it bakes, whereas parchment paper absorbs those traces of fat that are released as batter warms. This means that cakes, cookies, cream puffs, and other baked foods come out with a superior texture on the underside when baked with parchment paper.

Parchment paper can also be cut and formed into sturdy, disposable pastry bags (see Pastry Bag) or used for cooking food *en papillote* (see Bag Cookery). Because of its porosity, parchment paper allows a limited amount of steam to escape during cooking, an essential aspect of *en papillote* cookery.

Baking parchment is available in two styles — plain and silicone-treated. The silicone-treated is slightly more expensive, but it can be wiped with a damp cloth and reused (see Appendix).

A word of caution: *never* use brown paper shopping bags as a substitute for parchment paper. They contain harmful chemicals that could contaminate food.

RECIPES: Forgotten Cookies, Halibut Steaks en Papillote.

PASTA

There are basically two types of pasta — the flour-egg dough of Northern Italy and the flour-water dough of Southern Italy. The flour-water pasta of the South is more accurately referred to as macaroni. Firm and somewhat stiff, this dough is forced through molds of different shapes and sizes, then dried. The richer, more pliable flour-egg blend of the North, which is discussed here, is the dough that is stuffed and formed into intricate shapes.

Differing opinions exist concerning the merits of durum wheat and semolina flour. Milled from hard durum wheat, semolina flour is exceptionally high in gluten, which explains why commercial pasta makers use it. But semolina flour produces a dough that's too firm for convenient at-home handling (not to mention that it's quite expensive). Ordinary unbleached bread flour or all-purpose flour creates a gluten-rich, elastic dough that is easy to manage. It produces a fine, firm-textured pasta that requires no apology. (If, however, you're still determined to experiment with semolina flour, start with a blend of 2 parts all-purpose combined with 1 part semolina.)

Although some regions of Italy create pasta dough from flour and eggs only, the recipe on page 304 includes water and olive oil. Water activates the gluten in flour and results in a dough that is easier to knead. It also lends a degree of tackiness that enables you to shape and seal the dough efficiently. Olive oil lubricates the gluten strands to facilitate rolling and stretching the dough, and it also inhibits drying, which gives you extra time to fill and shape intricate pieces.

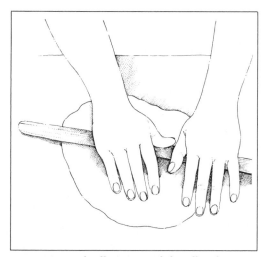

A conventional rolling pin with handles does not work well when rolling pasta dough. If you can't obtain a straight pasta pin from a local store, make your own from a 1½-inch dowel.

Generally, the most difficult step in making pasta is rolling out the dough. The crux of the problem is this: you must develop gluten to its fullest capacity, so it will stretch and stretch and stretch some more, enabling you to roll the dough to the desired thinness. However, when gluten is fully developed, the dough becomes as springy as a rubber band. Poke it, and it will jump right back at you. Attempt to roll it out, and it will contract as soon as you lift the rolling pin.

The solution is to let the dough rest, and what happens is an interesting phenomenon — the gluten retains its ability to stretch, but it becomes lethargic. If it rests long enough, it won't spring back. Some sources say that an hour's rest is long enough, but it isn't if you've fully developed the gluten. Twenty-four hours is more like it. In fact, the most manageable pasta is achieved by freezing it overnight, letting it defrost in the refrigerator, and then rolling it out while it's still cold.

Divide the dough into as many parts as you used cups of flour. A 1-cup batch rolls out to about an 18-inch circle. Anything larger than that would be wider than the average work area and quite difficult to manage. Keep any dough you're not working with in an airtight plastic bag to keep it from drying out. Once

pasta dough begins to dry, it's difficult to roll and impossible to seal.

Use a straight pasta pin for the best control (see illustration) — a conventional rolling pin with handles is not as efficient for this job. If you can't find a pasta rolling pin in a local shop, go to a lumber store and ask for an 18-inch length of 1½ inch dowel. Sand the cut edges and rub the dowel with mineral oil. This makes a terrific rolling pin.

Place the dough on an unfloured surface or, if the dough is excessively sticky, sprinkle the surface lightly with flour, preferably granulated (see Flour). A little bit of tackiness is helpful, though, for it makes it possible for the dough to adhere slightly to the work surface, so you can roll it out without it roaming all over the place.

Roll out the dough, using away-from-you strokes. Be fairly assertive, but don't press down and don't roll over the edge — it will begin to dry out if you do. Roll the dough, lift it and give it a quarter-turn, then roll again. After several turns, lift the dough (by rolling it up onto the rolling pin) and turn it over. Continue rolling on the other side. (If you see tiny air bubbles in the dough, that's a good sign — you have kneaded it sufficiently.)

How thin to roll pasta is pretty much a personal decision. Generally speaking, you should continue rolling until you can begin to see the wood grain on your work surface, or the color of your skin if you press your finger up against the underside.

Immediately begin to cut your dough into the desired strips or circles. Shape only a few at a time if you're a beginner, and cover the rest with damp paper towels. The thinner the dough is, the quicker it will dry out, so work as quickly as you can.

You can cook fresh, unstuffed pasta immediately, or dry it by hanging the strands over a rack, or by draping eight to ten strands into small nest-shaped mounds on a surface sprinkled with cornmeal. Short lengths of pasta, like farfalle or penne, can be dried on a clean kitchen towel. Depending on the thickness of the pasta, the drying process can take from one to three days. Unstuffed as well as stuffed fresh pasta may be frozen rather than dried. Arrange strands of pasta in nests, and shorter lengths or stuffed pasta, such as ravioli, in a single layer on a shallow, rectangular baking pan, lightly sprinkled with cornmeal. Freeze uncovered for 24 hours, then transfer to an airtight plastic bag. Do not defrost frozen pasta before cooking.

You can freeze pasta — stuffed or unstuffed, cooked or uncooked — for up to four months. Just keep in mind that the condition it's in when it goes into the pot determines how long it will need to cook. It takes longer to cook frozen, stuffed, or dried pasta than it does to cook freshly cut or unstuffed pasta.

You will notice several variations in color as you work with pasta dough. Freshly cut pasta is a bright, cheery yellow; dried pasta is a dark, rich yellow; and cooked pasta is almost white. This is one of the ways you can tell when your pasta is nearly cooked.

Test for doneness by inserting a metal skewer or toothpick. It should easily enter the pasta. If you're in doubt, taste it. The proper consistency of cooked pasta (often referred to as *al dente*) is such that your teeth meet some resistance — it should never be mushy.

RECIPES: Egg Pasta I, Egg Pasta II.

PASTRY BAG

Pastry bags are usually thought of in connection with decorating cakes, but there are other times when knowing how to manipulate one comes in very handy. Not to mention the professional touch that a bit of piping bestows on otherwise mundane fare.

You can buy pastry bags in various sizes, or make your own from pre-cut parchment-paper triangles sold in specialty shops. You can also cut your own triangles from a roll of parchment paper (see Parchment Paper).

For everyday use, you'll only need two different-size pastry bags — a large, 18-inch bag for piping bulky things like mashed potatoes and ricotta cheese, and a smaller, 12-inch bag

for stuffing eggs and celery or dressing up simple appetizers.

You'll also need a few basic decorating tubes, or tips. For smooth piping, such as filling pasta shells with cheese and forming eclairs or cream puffs, a large tip with a wide circular opening will do the job. For a ridged effect, buy either an open-star or closed-star tip. Use the open star for whipped cream and mashed potatoes; the closed star for more defined ridges, such as those on decoratively stuffed eggs.

Decorating tips are sized by number. The smallest round tips start with Number 1 and increase in size through Number 4; medium tips are sizes 5 through 12; large tips are numbered 1A and 2A. The open- and closed-star tips are sized by number in the same manner. In addition, they differ from one another in the number of cuts in the tips: the more cuts there are, the more ridges produced.

Don't bother to use a gizmo called a "coupler" unless you're decorating cakes. A coupler enables you to attach the tip to the outside of the bag so you can change tips without changing bags. For single-step procedures, all that is required is to drop the decorating tip down inside the bag.

When you're ready to fill the pastry bag, set it in an empty 1-quart mayonnaise jar to act as a holder. Fold the bag down on itself to form a cuff and make filling easier. Fill the bag a little less than three-quarters full. Any more than that will only back up and squish out of the bag as you pipe. Unfold the cuff and twist the top of the bag closed.

Hold the pastry bag with one hand at the top, and, with the twist held tightly closed by the pressure of your thumb and fingers, guide the bottom of the bag with your other hand.

Here's how to form your own pastry bag from a piece of parchment (see illustration on next page):

1. Cut a square piece of parchment paper (either 12×12 inches or 18×18 inches).
2. Fold the square in half diagonally to make a two-ply triangle. Hold the center point of the triangle at the top.

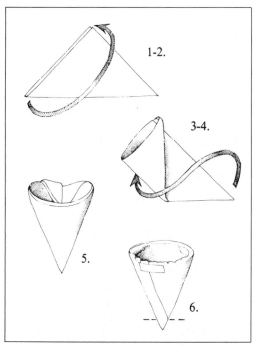

Making a pastry bag from parchment paper. The numbers refer to the steps in the directions.

3. Bring the left point around to meet the center point, forming a cone.
4. Wrap the right point over and around the cone so that the three points line up. Adjust the seam until the point is nearly closed.
5. Fold the points down and inside the cone, then fold in the side corners to make the mouth of the cone even. Tape the outside seam near the top to hold it securely.
6. Cut ¾ of an inch off the tip of the cone. Drop in a decorating tip. (Half of the tip should show. If it doesn't, trim more off the bag.)   ◄₹

PÂTE À CHOUX

See CREAM PUFF PASTRY.   ◄₹

PEELING FRUITS AND VEGETABLES

The greatest concentration of flavor and the largest amount of vitamins and other nutrients are located right beneath the skin of vegetables and fruit. For that reason, you should avoid peeling whenever possible.

Mushrooms don't need to be peeled. They may be rinsed briefly under cold running water and brushed lightly with a soft brush, but because they absorb moisture readily, do not allow them to soak. Many young unblemished vegetables such as green and yellow squash, carrots, and potatoes can get by with little or no scraping, and many fruits can be eaten unpeeled.

The tomato presents a contradiction — the more ripe and juicy the tomato, the tougher the skin, so you may want to peel these. If you're peeling a large quantity of tomatoes, you can speed things up by first plunging them into boiling water for 10 to 20 seconds, depending on ripeness. This method also works for soft-fleshed fruits such as peaches, plums, nectarines, and apricots.

Citrus fruits will shed their white membrane more readily if soaked in hot water before peeling. Bring a large pot of water to a boil. Remove from the heat and drop in lemons, limes, oranges, or grapefruit. Allow lemons or limes to soak for 3 minutes, oranges for 5 minutes, and grapefruit for 8 minutes, then peel. A great deal of the white membrane will lift off with the rind.

Certain vegetables improve with peeling because you have removed tough fibers or a strong-tasting outer layer. Asparagus and broccoli are both more delicately flavored and enjoyable when the stalks are peeled. Turnips lose much of their disagreeable odor when peeled before cooking.

The most efficient and easy-to-use implement for peeling is the swivel-blade peeler, commonly referred to as a vegetable peeler. Use it on everything but soft-fleshed fruit. Peel away from you in firm strokes, holding the peeler rather loosely in your hand.

Sometimes you're better off peeling after cooking. When hard-shell squash such as acorn or butternut is cut into chunks and then boiled, the skin is easy to remove. Beets retain their color and more of their flavor if you cook first and peel later.

Finally, there's the subject of onions. Ask 15 different cooks what they do to prevent tears while they're peeling onions and you'll get 15 different answers. You can peel (and chop) onions next to a lighted candle, or stand under an exhaust fan, or clench a wooden match between your teeth, or hold your breath until you're finished. You can even wear swimming goggles. All in an effort to avoid the sharp, stinging tears that well up in your eyes.

Recent scientific research turned up the fact that onions contain a substance called propanethial S-oxide that produces sulfuric acid when it comes in contact with the moisture in your eyes. No wonder it stings. Fortunately, there are ways to cope. The action of propanethial S-oxide is slowed considerably by cold temperatures, and it's soluble in water. Therefore, it's possible to eliminate, or at least greatly reduce, the tear-causing reaction by chilling onions in the refrigerator or freezer, and by peeling them under water.

It's a good idea to keep a small number of onions on hand in the refrigerator, so they will be chilled when you need them; store the rest in a cool, dark place. If you've forgotten to replenish your supply, simply place as many onions as you need in the freezer for 30 minutes, then peel under cold running water. If you work quickly, you'll be finished before the propanethial S-oxide is activated.

Peeling an onion under cold running water not only prevents tears, but also makes the job easier by lifting away the transparent membrane between layers. Most people don't remove enough of the onion when they peel. Take off at least one layer beneath the skin, and don't leave any tough, wrinkled areas or spots of brown. ◄╗

pH SCALE

The pH of a particular substance refers to its relative acidity or alkalinity. It is expressed as a number between 0 and 14 on the pH scale, with number 7, the midpoint, being neutral — neither acidic nor alkaline.

Numbers moving up the scale from 7 to 14 indicate an increase in alkalinity; numbers moving down the scale from 7 to zero, an increase in acidity. For example, a solution with a pH of 1 is about as strong an acid as you can get; a solution with a pH of 14 is an exceptionally strong alkali. Because the difference in strength between any two consecutive numbers amounts to a factor of 10, an acid of pH 3 is ten times stronger than an acid of pH 4. ◄╗

PIE BAKING

Dessert Pies

In striving for the perfect pie crust, it often seems that the filling gets neglected. Fillings can be cooked right along with the pie crust, or first cooked separately, then baked inside a crust. There are some fillings that are cooked separately and poured into a prebaked shell, gelatin pie fillings that are prepared and then chilled in a baked crust, and fresh fruit fillings that are simply tossed with a bit of sugar and added to a prebaked pie shell.

Fillings that bake inside the crust are mainly of the fruit and custard variety. There are also molasses- and sugar-syrup-type fillings such as *Louisiana Pecan Pie*, and dry-sugar fillings like *Canadian Sugar Pie*, but these don't present the baking problems that fruit and custard pies do.

Fruit pies have the potential to develop soggy bottom crusts and watery fillings. The consistency of the filling is determined by the amount of thickener used, how ripe and juicy the fruit is, and whether or not it has been frozen. Since the freezing process breaks down the structure of fruit, and also causes ice crystals to form, frozen fruit gives off more moisture during baking. Therefore, plan to add an extra measure of thickener to any fruit that has been frozen, or to fresh fruit inside a crust you plan to freeze and bake at a later date. (One-half teaspoon of additional cornstarch or tapioca per cup of fruit is usually sufficient.)

Flour, cornstarch, and tapioca are the thickeners most cooks use to bind fruit with juice. Approximately ¼ cup of flour, 2 tablespoons of cornstarch, or 2 tablespoons of quick-cooking tapioca will transform 4 cups of fresh fruit into a light, syrupy filling. Here's where personal likes and dislikes come in: Some people prefer a slightly runny filling; others, a firm filling that barely oozes at all.

Different varieties of the same fruit can vary widely in juiciness. So can the same variety grown under different soil and climatic conditions. Ripe fruit is juicier than underripe fruit, and overripe fruit is juicier still. Consequently, fruit pie recipes can only serve as guides. There's always going to be a certain element of guesswork involved in making a fresh fruit pie.

Here are some pointers to help you through the maze of variable conditions. First of all, taste the fruit. If it's sweet and excessively juicy, add less sugar than the recipe calls for. Sugar tends to increase the amount of juice, so adding as little as possible helps to create a more viscous filling.

Flour gives fruit filling an opaque appearance and, because the internal temperature of a pie is not intense enough to thoroughly cook the flour, it also contributes a raw, pasty flavor some people find unpleasant. Also, flour isn't particularly stable in the presence of an acid, so it's not the best thickener to use with tart or sour fruit.

Cornstarch and tapioca create a translucent filling, and both exhibit more stability than flour in the presence of an acid (tapioca is the more stable of the two, and should be used with extra-acidic fruits like cranberries and currants). Cornstarch and tapioca are usually mixed with ¼ cup of water. It's a good idea to let tapioca stand in water for 15 minutes to soften up a bit, but it isn't really necessary to blend cornstarch with water. In fact, some recipes direct you to sprinkle cornstarch or tapioca right over fruit and mix it in. This, of course, eliminates that extra water and produces a thicker filling. If you decide to add dry cornstarch to fruit, make sure you blend it with sugar first, to disperse the starch granules and ensure that they will dissolve evenly.

There's only one way to predict with any certainty what the viscosity of a pie filling will be — make it outside the pie. You can combine 4 cups of fruit, say blueberries, with ⅔ cup of sugar, add the juice of half a lemon, and cook over medium heat until the berries release their juice. Remove from the heat, and stir in 2 tablespoons of cornstarch dissolved in ¼ cup of cold water. Return to the heat and cook until bubbly and thick. Reduce the heat to simmer, and cook until the filling is almost but not quite as thick as you want. Remember, cornstarch-thickened mixtures become more viscous as they cool. Remove the filling from the heat and swirl in 2 tablespoons of cold butter. Pour into a prepared crust, top with a second crust, and bake until nicely browned.

Many fruit pie recipes call for lemon juice, because it accentuates flavor and retards discoloration in sliced fruits like apples, peaches, and pears. Besides that, it increases the acid and pectin content (lemon juice is high in both acid and pectin), so in those instances where lemon juice is added to high-pectin/ high-sugar fruits, the stage is set for a limited amount of sugar-acid thickening, the same kind of firming process that thickens jam (see Jam and Jelly Making).

It takes a certain amount of trial and error to arrive at the particular filling consistency you like best. After a while, you'll develop a knack for judging the sweetness and juiciness of fruit by taste testing. Then you can regulate the sugar — reducing the amount when it isn't needed, and perhaps adding an additional teaspoon or two of cornstarch when necessary, to compensate for excessively juicy or overripe fruit.

Once you get the feel for preparing a properly thickened filling, your soggy crust troubles may be over. However, crust turns soggy for other reasons, too. Cooking two or more pies at a time can create excessive steam inside the oven and result in soggy crusts, so it's better to cook only one pie at a time.

If you don't already own one, beg, borrow, or steal a metal pie pan — the murkier looking, the better. Dark metal absorbs and holds heat that crisps up a bottom crust. Also, be sure to cut enough vents in the top crust of the pie to allow steam inside to escape quickly; otherwise, steam trapped under the top crust will soften it and turn it soggy. Toward the end of the cooking period, check to see that the vents remain open, because thickening juices are apt to bubble up and seal steam vents closed.

By the way, you can set up an excellent venting system by using a small metal canapé cutter or a large round pastry tube, of the size used for piping out eclairs. Simply press the cutter, or the smaller end of the pastry tube, into the center of the pie crust. Remove the round of dough it cuts out, and ease the canapé cutter or the smaller end of the upturned pastry tube down inside the filling. As the fruit releases its juice, it will bubble up inside. This technique allows steam to escape and provides a way for heat to get to the center of the pie more quickly, by employing the same principle as that of a tube pan (see Tube Pan).

Just be sure to poke down inside the vent when the juices start to thicken. If the vent seals itself shut, steam pressure will build up inside the pie, causing the crust to crack and the filling to leak out.

Other precautions against soggy crusts are to brush the bottom crust with beaten egg white before you pour in the filling (see Egg Wash), or scatter crushed cookie crumbs over the bottom crust. The crumbs will absorb extra juices and give your pie an interesting change in flavor.

Apple pie, more than any other type of fruit pie, depends for its success on the variety of fruit you choose. Apples that can't stand up to excessive heat will break down and form a mushy filling. McIntosh apples, for example, make delicious eating out of hand, but are very poor candidates for pie. You're better off choosing a firm and slightly tart apple like the Rhode Island Greening, Granny Smith, Pippin, or Gravenstein.

You may have run across pie recipes calling for tart apples and wondered why they don't include a thickener. Tart apples, especially if they are unpeeled, contain enough acid and pectin to react with added sugar and form a sugar-acid gel. In other words, tart-apple filling sets in the same manner that jelly gels. A few other fruits, like currants, gooseberries, and sour plums are capable of doing this to a limited degree, but not as reliably as tart apples.

If you use a variety of apple that retains its texture, you won't have to worry about the shape of your apple pie changing during baking and cooling. It's apples that cook down and give off a great deal of moisture that cause the infamous collapsing apple pie. As the moisture turns to steam, it puffs against the top crust and weakens it. The apple slices shrink, then there's nothing left to hold up the crust, so it falls down in a heap.

Just in case you're absolutely attached to the flavor of one of these shrinking types and wouldn't change for the world, try this. Pour enough water into a large pot to barely cover the bottom. Add however many sliced apples you need, stir in the amount of sugar and spices called for, and cook slowly, so you don't break up the apples. When they are tender, and most of the moisture has evaporated, remove them from the heat and stir in 2 tablespoons of cornstarch dissolved in ¼ cup of water. Without further cooking, pour the mixture into a prepared bottom crust, and top with a second crust. Bake until nicely browned. You'll have the same apple flavor without the collapsing crust.

Custard fillings baked in the crust cause sogginess if they separate and give off liquid. This is called weeping, or syneresis, and the best way to avoid it is to heat the custard gently. For example, custard pies should never be baked at temperatures over 375°F. In fact, the safest approach is to partially bake the pie shell at 450°F., then add the filling and cook the assembled pie at 325°F.

Fruit pies should be baked on the lowest rack of a preheated 450°F. oven for the first 10 minutes of the cooking time. Placing a pie near the heating element like this sets the bottom crust before the fruit has a chance to give off any liquid. It's one more way to forestall a soggy bottom.

At the end of the 10 minutes, move the pie to the middle of the oven and reduce the temperature to 375°F. to complete cooking. (Fruit pies cooked at higher temperatures bubble too vigorously, which tends to weaken the upper crust.) Try to do without a drip pan, or at least wait until you absolutely need it. A drip pan placed underneath a pie interferes with the circulation of hot air. It may keep your oven clean, but the bottom crust won't cook as efficiently.

To enhance the appearance of your two-crust or lattice-topped pie, apply an egg wash and experiment with the various types until you achieve the look you like best (see Egg Wash).

RECIPES: Banana Custard Cream Pie, Blueberry Pie, Butterscotch-Pecan Pie, Canadian Sugar Pie, Coconut Custard Cream Pie, Double Strawberry Pie, Lemon Meringue Pie, Louisiana Pecan Pie, Triple Chocolate Cream Pie.

Main Course Pies

In one form or another, pastry-enclosed dishes exist in all the major cuisines of the world. Here we'll consider the basic points of two fundamental types of entrée pie — those with a single crust atop a filling, and those with double crusts.

Double-crust meat and vegetable pies are exceptionally prone to sogginess. Both the underside of the top crust and the inside of the bottom crust are vulnerable. Recipes that encourage you to make entrée pies a day ahead are overlooking this fact. To avoid soggy crusts, prepare the filling separately. By that I mean, all the ingredients should be fully cooked and combined with a cooked sauce or gravy of a sufficiently thickened consistency. This, of course, can be prepared ahead, as can the pastry. You can even roll out the dough, line the bottom and sides of the baking dish, and roll out the top crust. Place the lined dish inside a plastic bag, secure the bag with a metal twist, and refrigerate. Chill the top crust between two sheets of waxed paper lying flat on a cookie sheet. All you have left to do is the final assembly.

Preheat your oven, so the bottom crust will begin to firm immediately. Heat the filling until it bubbles and pay particular attention to the consistency of the sauce. If it seems runny, thicken it slightly by blending in a beurre manié (see Beurre Manié). Do not prick the bottom crust, as that would allow liquid to seep out. As extra protection against a soggy bottom, you might consider sprinkling the bottom crust with finely crushed bread crumbs, which will absorb any excess liquid.

Pour in the hot filling, top with crust, and bake. Many cooks like to use an open-lattice crust for the top of entrée pies. The advantages are obvious. With so many openings through which steam can escape, the underside of the top crust seldom gets soggy. If you prefer a solid crust, take pains to vent it well and to be sure the vents don't seal themselves shut during the final stages of baking.

A pie bird is a delightful way to vent an entrée pie. Shaped like a bird (usually a blackbird, for those who are up on their nursery rhymes), this ceramic ornament sits in the center of the pie and emits steam through its bill. It's not only clever and amusing, it does a darned good job of preventing soggy crusts (see Appendix).

Single-crust pies are a bit simpler to make, but they too are subject to the same problem — a soggy upper crust. They also need ample venting, unless you take the sly route. Roll out a top crust, using the top of a serving dish as a guide. Cut out a round of pastry ¼ inch larger than the dish (even the best-made pastry shrinks as it bakes). Crimp and decorate, and bake on a greased cookie sheet at 425°F. Meanwhile, heat the filling until it bubbles. When the crust is nicely browned, pour the hot filling into the serving dish, slide the hot crust on top, and return the assembled pie to the oven for 5 to 10 minutes before serving.

Whether you're making a single- or double-crust pie, it helps to have the filling hot before you put the pie in the oven. Then you only need to bake it long enough to cook the crust, thereby reducing the time the crust is in contact with the filling and consequently lessening the opportunity for sogginess. For the same reason, entrée pies should be served immediately. (Pies that are made ahead for picnics and such should be generously vented and thoroughly cooled on racks. Placing a hot pie in the refrigerator condenses the hot steam into water.)

The crust for entrée pies is customarily unsweetened, but beyond that, let your imagination run wild. I've seen pastry recipes calling for grated cheese, ground nuts, all sorts of herbs and spices, and a variety of flours and grains. Anything lusty and flavorful is fair game. Lard is often the fat of choice because of its assertive character, but butter, or a half-butter/half-lard combination, is also substantial enough to stand up to a robust filling. An all-butter or solid (hydrogenated) shortening crust is appropriate for subtly flavored vegetable pies. Bacon fat or chilled roast beef drippings contribute excellent flavor and are fun to experiment with. Start by substituting 2 tablespoons in place of the fat you ordinarily use. Blend in as usual, and bake with a hearty meat filling.

RECIPES: Pork and Apple Pie, Ratatouille Pie.

PIE CRUST

Even some experienced cooks cringe at the thought of making pie crust. Success seems to depend more on hocus-pocus than on a set of reliable rules, but there *are* reasons why pie crust comes out tender and flaky or tough as shoe leather.

If you could look inside a pie crust as it bakes, you would see little pieces of fat sandwiched between layers of flour-and-water paste. As the crust heats up, the bits of fat melt. The fat is absorbed by the flour, leaving small pockets of air where once there was fat. Meanwhile, the water is also getting hot and turning to steam. The steam fills the pockets of air and puffs them up a bit. Eventually the steam evaporates and the crust dries and becomes crisp.

All traditional recipes for pie crust start out by telling you to blend flour and fat together until a certain texture develops. Some say it should look like "coarse cornmeal" and others say "like large peas." Picture in your mind how the bits of fat melt and leave air pockets. The larger the lumps of fat, the larger the air

pockets, and thus the larger the flakes of crust. If you want a mealy or sandy-textured crust, blend until the fat is in smaller, mostly uniform pieces.

How you blend the flour and fat together makes a difference, too. Using your fingertips enables you to flatten the bits of fat between your fingers, and the warmth of your skin softens the fat ever so slightly, allowing it to coat a limited number of flour particles (which seals out the water required for gluten to develop). The fingertip method is probably the easiest way to distribute fat evenly, but the danger is that you may soften the fat too much and coat too many flour particles.

This is where the role that gluten plays must be considered. When water is added to the pie-crust mixture, gluten begins to develop. That's important, because without a certain amount of gluten your pastry wouldn't have the elasticity it needs to be rolled out. The flour particles that have been coated with fat are waterproofed — the fat seals water out and prevents gluten development. However, a certain amount of gluten development is necessary for pie-crust dough to be cohesive and manageable. The trick is to seal enough flour particles to keep gluten formation to a minimum, while at the same time leaving enough particles unsealed to provide the elasticity that makes rolling-out possible.

The best way to control this situation is to use the cutting-in method of combining the flour and fat (see Cutting-In). If you use a pastry blender or a knife to literally cut the fat into smaller and smaller pieces, or a food processor, which creates a more uniform mixture than doing it by hand, there's no danger of oversoftening the fat from the heat of your fingers.

The fat you decide to use in making pie crust determines the flavor and, to a lesser degree, the texture of the final product. Unsalted butter gives pie crust a delicate, sweet flavor; salted butter, while not quite as delicate, also provides a full, sweet flavor. Lard, bacon fat, and rendered beef fat make a richly flavored crust with meaty overtones, and hydrogenated (vegetable) shortening produces a rather bland-tasting pastry.

Both salted and unsalted butter and margarine contain about 80 percent fat and 16 percent water. Lard and hydrogenated shortening are 100 percent fat and contain no moisture. That's why recipes calling for butter usually include a greater quantity of fat than those which call for lard or shortening. Both lard and shortening produce a crust with a different texture from that produced by butter, not only because they're higher in fat, but also because they have no moisture to release as steam.

The water contained in butter and margarine makes working with them trickier than with lard or shortening, because it activates the gluten sooner, which leads more easily to tough pie crust. Lard and hydrogenated shortening can stand more handling and generally take more abuse, so they are good choices for beginners to use.

Water should be sprinkled in gradually so that no more is added than is absolutely necessary. As you add the water, toss the particles of pastry constantly. The dough will soon begin to adhere. Form it into a ball with your fingertips. When the dough holds together and will readily pick up the particles from the sides and bottom of the bowl, it's ready. The completed pastry should feel as damp and malleable as new clay. If it's too dry, the pie crust will crumble and fall apart as you roll it out. For that reason, it's better to err on the side of too much water rather than not enough.

Flatten the ball of pastry into a 5-inch disk, or if it's a double-crust recipe, divide into two slightly unequal portions (the larger one goes in the bottom of the pie pan) and form into two flattened disks. Drop into a plastic bag and secure, airtight, with a twist. Then chill. Many recipes suggest refrigerating pie dough for 1 hour to relax any gluten that may have been developed. I've found that 20 minutes is not only long enough, but that pastry chilled for 1 hour is extremely difficult to roll out because it's hard and it cracks as you roll it.

Dust a work surface with sifted flour and begin to roll out the dough using away-from-you strokes. Try to picture those little bits of fat being flattened out as you roll. Don't press down, press away! Start in the center and roll up to, but not over, the edge.

Lift the pastry, dust the work surface lightly if the dough is sticking, and turn it one-quarter of the way around. Continue rolling, lifting, and turning until the pastry is approximately ⅛ inch thick. If you've developed the right amount of gluten, the crust will stretch and roll without tearing. Trim off the jagged outer edges with a pastry wheel or ravioli cutter.

Buttering your pie pan is optional, but it does encourage the underside of the bottom crust to crisp up. Roll the dough up on your rolling pin (folding it in quarters can cause it to crack), and transfer it to the pie pan. Gently ease the dough down inside the pan. Don't poke, prod, stretch, or force the pastry in any way. It will shrink during baking if you do. Proceed to fill your pie shell and top with a second crust or bake blind (see Baking Blind, this page).

The basic proportions by weight for a single pie crust are 6 ounces (1½ cups) of flour, 4 ounces (½ cup) of fat, and 2 ounces (¼ cup) of water. If you're using butter, you may want to increase the amount you use, since butter is only 80 percent fat (and because it contains water, you may find you'll be able to reduce the amount of liquid, too). Recipes some-

times call for additional ingredients: sugar sweetens a pie crust and salt heightens flavor; egg yolks enrich and strengthen a crust; and an acid such as vinegar, wine, or lemon juice encourages crispiness.

If you've had poor luck with pie crust in the past, maybe you've been overmixing, overrolling, or in some manner overdeveloping the gluten. Try lowering the gluten content of the flour by substituting cake flour for one-fourth of the total amount you're presently using (see Flour). If you're unhappy with the texture you achieve, you may be breaking the fat into pieces that are too small (see Cutting-In).

Despite the fact that there are very popular recipes that call for hot water, the most dependable approach is to have all the ingredients cold. Even hydrogenated shortening, which is usually stored at room temperature, does better if it's chilled. The reason for this is those little pieces of fat I mentioned earlier. The flakiest, most tender crust depends on those fat bits holding their shape until the heat of the oven begins to convert water to steam. The colder the ingredients are, the better chances are that this will happen.

If your oven has a glass door, it's fascinating to watch a pie crust bake. After 10 to 15 minutes at 425°F., blisters appear all over the surface, heaving up and down, as the fat melts and the steam puffs the air pockets. The absence of this activity means that you either dispersed the fat through the flour too finely (in which case the crust will be sandy textured), or your oven isn't as hot as you think it is (see Thermometers).

Baking Blind

All types of pie crust will absorb liquid if given half a chance. That's why it's a good idea to prebake pie crust whenever you can. It's obviously out of the question when you're dealing with a two-crust pie, but any time you're making a single-crust pie, you can prevent a soggy bottom by partially baking the pastry shell.

This procedure, called *à blanc* in French, is also referred to as "baking blind." Whatever you call it, do it. Many recipes don't include this step, so you just have to go ahead on your own. Custard pies (including pumpkin), fruit tarts, streusel-topped pies — any and all single-crust pies can benefit from this maneuver.

Begin by buttering a pie pan and lining it with pastry. To prevent heaving, prick the entire surface of the pastry at ½-inch intervals with the tines of a fork, making the pattern go in one direction. (A pastry shell heaves because hot air gets trapped between the pan and the crust, so make sure the holes you make with the fork go all the way through to the pan.)

At that point, you'll need something to help prevent the bottom from bumping up and the sides from falling in. Hold a roll of waxed paper, parchment, or aluminum foil over the pie pan. Pull out a piece about 4 inches longer than the pie is wide. Tear off and fold into quarters, then diagonally into eighths. Holding the inside point of the folded paper over the center of the pie, cut the outer edge beyond the rim of the shell by using the curve of the pie pan as a guide (see illustration).

Unfold and fit inside the crust. Pour in 1 pound of dried beans (which you can save and reuse indefinitely) or those metal pie weights sold in specialty shops (see Appendix). Make sure the beans are distributed evenly and are exerting pressure against the sides of the pastry.

Place the pie shell on the middle rack of a preheated 425°F. oven. If you're planning to partially bake the shell and finish the baking with a filling inside, cook for 8 minutes. Remove the dried beans and the liner. The holes you made previously will have closed up; do not prick with a fork a second time because the filling will seep down into the holes. Instead, brush the bottom and sides of the crust with an egg-white wash as added protection against sogginess caused by juicy fillings (see Egg Wash). Return to the oven and bake at 400°F. for 3 more minutes. Remove and cool slightly. Pour in the pie filling, and bake at the

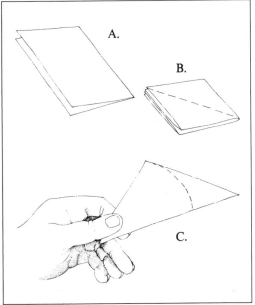

Fold the paper in half (A.), into quarters, and diagonally into eighths (B.) — along the dotted line. Hold the inside point of the paper over the center of the pan and cut the outer edge, using the curve of the pan as a guide (C.).

temperature recommended in your recipe until the filling is done.

For a fully baked pie shell, place in a preheated 425°F. oven for 8 minutes. Remove the dried beans and prick again at ½-inch intervals with the tines of a fork, this time making the pattern go in the opposite direction so you can tell where you've been. Brush the rim with an egg wash if you want it to develop a deep color, and return the crust to the oven. Bake at 375°F. for 15 minutes, or until pastry is nicely browned. Cool thoroughly on a rack before filling.

If you're planning to fill the pie shell with fresh fruit, you can prevent a soggy crust by spreading a thin layer of cream cheese over the bottom, or by sealing the pastry with a jelly glaze: Bring ½ cup of currant jelly to a boil. Continue to boil for 3 minutes or until it reaches 230°F. on a candy thermometer. Brush while hot over the bottom and sides of the cooled pie shell.

One of the most common culinary disappointments is a shrinking pie shell. Many cooks feel that, no matter how carefully they prepare and weight down pastry, it still shrinks as it bakes. First of all, a limited degree of shrinking is inevitable, so plan for it by shaping the sides a tad higher than seems necessary. Pie crust that shrinks more than a little has probably been stretched, poked, or prodded into the pan. Or perhaps the gluten was overdeveloped at some point. Since chilling relaxes the gluten, you can head off a shrinking problem by chilling the shaped shell for at least 1 hour before baking. Better still, freeze it for at least 6 hours. Freezing really knocks the wind out of gluten, so it practically guarantees a shrink-free crust.

To freeze an unbaked pie shell, slide it, pan and all, into a large plastic bag, and secure with a twist. Freeze for 6 hours or overnight and allow it to defrost (still wrapped) in the refrigerator, or bake while frozen, adding 4 to 6 minutes onto the baking time.

RECIPES: Basic Pie Crust, Egg and Vinegar Pie Crust, Processor Pie Shell, Water-Whipped Pie Crust.

PIZZA

If you've ever tried to reproduce pizzeria pizza in your own kitchen, you know how frustrating it can be. The problem isn't a lack of recipes — there are thousands of those — it's achieving a light, crispy crust.

Commercial pizza ovens are capable of reaching much higher temperatures than the oven in your home, so the first thing to consider is how to achieve a crisp crust at a lower oven temperature. The solution is to line the rack of your oven with unglazed quarry tiles or a baking stone (see Appendix). When the oven is heated, the tiles absorb and hold tremendous quantities of heat, effectively duplicating the conditions inside a brick oven. Placing the pizza directly on the hot tiles to cook causes the dough to puff slightly, while the crust browns and crisps on the bottom.

The other secret to light, crunchy pizza is a dough that contains a high ratio of water (2 parts flour to 1 part water makes the lightest crust). Although some recipes suggest adding olive oil, I don't recommend it. Incorporating oil of any kind makes pizza crust heavy and compact. However, if a thin-crust pizza is what you want, oil your hands as you press out the dough after its final rise. Then lightly oil the surface of the pizza shell — the oil will weigh down the dough just enough to keep it from puffing up.

Authentic pizza is always spread with sauce made from whole tomatoes, not spaghetti sauce. It's fairly easy to open a can of Italian-style plum tomatoes and add a few herbs with a clove of garlic. And it makes a world of difference in taste.

Top your pizza with sliced peppers, mushrooms, or whatever you like, but don't add the cheese until the last few minutes of the cooking time. Cheese that has cooked too long becomes tough and rubbery and loses its flavor. Experiment with other types of cheese besides the familiar mozzarella. Monterey Jack and Muenster both have a pleasing flavor and an excellent melting consistency, or try crumbled goat cheese (chèvre) for a Mediterranean flavor.

RECIPES: Pizza, Pizza Rustica.

POACHING

Poaching, like boiling, simmering, steaming, and stewing, is one of the moist-heat cooking methods. That is to say, water (or some other liquid) acts as a medium through which heat is transferred from a direct heat source (such as a stove-top burner) to food.

Poaching is an extremely gentle method of cooking. Molecules of liquid at the bottom of the pan, nearest the burner, become hot, and rise to the top of the liquid. At the same time, cold molecules at the surface are falling to the bottom of the pan. When they get hot, they will rise to the surface, nudging aside cooler molecules, which in turn fall to the bottom.

As hot molecules pass over food, some heat is transferred and the food becomes hot. However, this procedure takes place very slowly during poaching, because the heat of the burner is kept low. The molecules heat gradually and rise at a leisurely pace, moving constantly, but not rapidly. Air bubbles never break the surface, but the jostling water molecules cause a significant disturbance, so that a poaching liquid is commonly described as "shivering."

The most familiar application of this technique is poaching eggs, but fish and chicken are also frequently cooked this way; so are sausages, quenelles, and some fruits.

Poaching is an excellent treatment for fruit that isn't quite ripe. Peaches and pears, for example, can be poached in a sugar syrup or in wine. Such gentle cooking softens the fruit and intensifies its natural, fresh flavor without causing it to break apart. Fish and chicken are frequently poached because of their delicate texture. After they finish cooking, the poaching liquid can be reduced and thickened to form a sauce.

RECIPES: Eggs Benedict, Flounder Quenelles au Gratin, Huevos Rancheros, Poached Medallions of Salmon.   ⌊

POPOVERS

Popovers and cream puffs are similar in that they are both made with equal proportions of liquid to flour. Both also depend on the protein in egg yolks for the strength to rise to amazing heights.

Consequently, popovers "pop" in much the same way that cream puffs "puff." When the liquid and flour are combined, gluten is formed. Melted butter or oil lubricates the strands of gluten and allows them to stretch and form a web. As eggs and air are beaten into the batter, the friction caused by the beating motion develops the gluten into a complex network of air pockets surrounded by gluten strands. (In spite of the fact that many cooks swear by blender-made popovers, they tend to rise only to a limited degree, and exhibit a flabby interior due to the fact that the blades of the blender sever the gluten strands rather than develop them.)

During baking, steam continues to puff the gluten web until all the available liquid has evaporated. At that point, the popovers firm up and become crisp. That explains why you shouldn't open the oven door during the first three-quarters of the baking time. Cold air rushing into the hot oven destroys the steam and condenses it back into water, resulting in soggy, collapsed popovers.

To achieve tall, straight-sided popovers, use deep, straight-sided custard cups, or one of those new black steel pans especially designed to allow hot air to circulate around the outside of each cup (see Appendix). Regular muffin tins may be used, but their sloping sides don't produce the best-looking popovers. If you do use a regular muffin tin, fill only every other cup, so the popovers won't bump into each other as they rise.

A very hot, preheated oven does the best job of baking popovers, although recipes exist that recommend a cold-start technique. (Using an oven that has not been preheated creates popovers that rise successfully, but their interior texture lacks firmness.) If you like the inside of your popovers to be quite dry, make a small slit in the side of each baked popover with a paring knife. Turn the oven off. Loosen the popovers and tilt them in their cups. Return them to the oven and allow them to stand for 5 to 10 minutes with the door ajar.

Popover batter frequently assumes other forms. Baked in a square pan with roast beef drippings, it becomes Yorkshire pudding; cooked in a skillet or round shallow pan, it puffs into an oven pancake.

RECIPES: Bacon-Cheese Popover, Herbed Popovers, Individual Yorkshire Puddings. ⌊

POT ROASTING

What happens to a piece of meat that is cooked in a pot of water? If an inexpensive cut of meat makes a tender, flavorful pot roast, would a higher-priced piece come out even better?

Meat is made up of muscle fibers and connective tissue. The connective tissue wraps around bunches of muscle strands and holds them together. How tough or tender a piece of meat will be is partly determined by what happens to collagen, a protein contained in the connective tissue. When a piece of meat is placed in a pot of water and heated, the heat-and-moisture combination breaks down the collagen in the connective tissue. The melted collagen mingles with the water (or other liquid) to form part of the sauce.

A combination of heat and moisture helps dissolve collagen, but too much heat toughens muscle fibers. Therefore, the temperature must be high enough to melt the collagen, yet not so high as to adversely affect the muscle fibers. A gentle, scarcely moving simmer, where the temperature of the liquid reads about 180°F., is just about right for pot roasting and braising (see Braising). It should take at least 3 hours to cook an average-size pot roast.

Vegetables can be cooked separately or added to the liquid, which enhances the sauce. If the vegetables you're using are of various densities, add those that take longer to soften (like carrots and parsnips) early in the cooking process. Wait until near the end to add delicate vegetables such as mushrooms and peas.

Cover a pot roast during the first hour and a half, then uncover to reduce the liquid and concentrate the flavors (see Reduction). Always maintain the temperature at just under 180°F. (see Thermometers). The final sauce may be thickened or not, as you like — a beurre manié does the best job of thickening a pot roast sauce (see Beurre Manié)

Inexpensive cuts of meat are usually rather tough due to the fact that they contain firmer, more well-developed muscle fibers and more connective tissue (and therefore more collagen). They also contain more flavor than expensive cuts. Higher-priced pieces of meat, which are composed mostly of tender muscle fibers and very little connective tissue, come out tough when pot roasted, because moist heat toughens muscle fibers. An expensive cut of meat would lose its limited flavor if slow-cooked in a liquid, its comparatively small amount of collagen would dissolve before the meat thoroughly cooked, and the meat would fall apart in shreds.

RECIPE: Savory Pot Roast.

POTS AND PANS

If you've decided to treat yourself to a few new pots and pans, or if you're just starting to furnish a kitchen from scratch, you'll be faced with making decisions about price, quality, appearance, and the amount of time and money you're willing to spend taking care of them.

This is the place to think investment. Sturdy, reliable pans are at the least, moderately expensive, and at the most, outrageously so. But flimsy, lower-priced equipment cooks and handles poorly — it dents and warps, and burns food that you end up throwing away. Better to spend more money on higher-quality pots and pans in the first place, to ensure that they will last you a lifetime.

The important things to consider in choosing a pan are what it's made of, how it feels in your hand, and how practical it is. Each of the various metals has its advantages and disadvantages, and here's a brief rundown on what they are:

COPPER: Real, substantial copper pots and pans are beautiful to look at and also quite expensive. Copper conducts heat quickly, distributes it evenly, and cools rapidly. On the other hand, high-quality copper pans are usually lined with tin, which wears away and is costly to replace. To keep them free of carbon deposits that hinder heat distribution, they need frequent polishing.

Beware of inferior imitations. Pans with a very light coating of copper are not authentic copper cookware. Often lined with shiny or brushed nickel (tin has a distinctive dull finish), these impostors give the impression of great substance when you pick them up. That's because the handle weighs so much; the pan itself is actually quite thin and light in weight.

ALUMINUM: Heavy-gauge aluminum, that is to say, thick aluminum, is almost as proficient at heating and cooling as copper. However, acids such as wine and lemon juice react with aluminum, causing food to discolor. That's why more and more aluminum pans are appearing on the market with a greyish-black, anodized finish — anodized aluminum does not react with acids and is virtually nonstick.

STAINLESS STEEL: Stainless steel is durable, retains its bright, shiny appearance, and doesn't react with food in any way. But it's a very poor conductor of heat. Manufacturers, however, are beginning to use it in combination with other metals to take advantage of stainless steel's best qualities.

MULTI-METAL POTS AND PANS: In an attempt to have the best of all possible worlds, the makers of pots and pans are combining and sandwiching layers of different metals to capitalize on the good points of each. One or more layers of copper or aluminum provide optimum heat conduction and distribution; a layer of stainless steel or anodized aluminum on the inside prevents food from discoloring; and stainless steel on the outside looks attractive. These metals are being mixed and matched in such a variety of combinations that you need a scorecard just to read the advertisements.

CAST IRON: The first choice for many fried-chicken lovers, cast iron holds heat well and conducts it evenly, if somewhat slowly. Rapid cooling with cast iron, therefore, is out of the question. Iron pans are heavy and cumbersome and require extra care to guard against rust.

ENAMEL-COATED STEEL OR CAST IRON: This is a sandwich approach. An enameled interior and enameled exterior coat a steel or iron core, combining the positive features of cooking with cast iron and eliminating the problem of rust. Trouble is, enameled pans are heavy and will chip if dropped or banged around.

Success in cooking often depends on using the right pan. When a recipe says to use a "heavy" saucepan or skillet, it doesn't necessarily mean you should use a pan that weighs a lot. Rather, it indicates that a substantial pan with a sturdy, thick bottom is required for even heating. In this book, I've used the term "thick-bottomed" to emphasize that a pan of considerable substance is required for best results.

Another term that crops up in recipes is "nonreactive." This refers to the tendency of acids to interact with certain metals. Aluminum, uncoated cast iron, and unlined copper all produce a chemical reaction when they come in contact with tomatoes, vinegar, lemon juice, or wine. In the case of unlined copper, exposure to air and moisture causes a film of copper carbonate to develop on the surface of the pan. When it comes in contact with an acid, copper carbonate forms verdigris, a mildly poisonous substance that turns food green (and you sick). This explains why copper pans are almost always lined.

A recipe that specifically tells you to use a stainless steel or enameled pan is probably trying to help you avoid the chemical reaction between acidic ingredients and a metal that produces an off taste and discoloration. In such cases, you can also use nonreactive pans of tin-lined copper, enameled iron, anodized aluminum (such as Leyse or Calphalon), or glass.

In view of all that, multi-layered pots and pans are definitely worth considering, but the selection process can be complicated. Read the labels thoroughly and know what metal you're buying — it can have a significant impact on how food cooks. For example, a copper pan lined with tin will heat fast and evenly, but at high temperatures, tin is apt to melt. So perhaps you'd prefer copper lined with stainless steel — a durable, nonreactive coating that doesn't need to be replaced, but also doesn't heat efficiently. In fact, in some instances it may cancel out the advantages provided by the layer of copper. A copper pan lined with aluminum heats faster and more evenly, but aluminum reacts with acids.

To me, the best all-around pans are those made from anodized aluminum. Generally speaking, they are thick-bottomed and sturdily built. In addition, you get the quick, even heating and rapid cooling characteristics of aluminum, plus a nonreactive surface from the anodizing process. Whatever type of pan you decide to purchase, be sure to actually handle it first. The best pan in the world isn't much good if it's too heavy, or the handle is too long, or it's just plain uncomfortable to maneuver.

pork can take more vigorous strokes, but still shouldn't be pounded with all your might.

When you purchase a meat mallet, buy one that is hefty and wooden. It should sit comfortably in your hand and weigh enough so that when you pound, the weight of the mallet does most of the work. A metal meat mallet with a smooth side and a serrated side is fine for pounding tough cuts of meat or for working seasonings into the surface of a pot roast. But a metal mallet treats delicate meat too harshly. A wooden mallet is much kinder to veal and chicken.

If you enjoy dishes made with veal scallops, but seldom prepare them because of the high price of veal, use chicken breasts as a substitute. To make chicken scallops, bone, skin, and split a breast in half. Lay each half between two sheets of waxed paper, and, using a large, wooden mallet, pound the chicken with light downward/outward strokes. Be sure that only the flat side of the mallet hits the meat, because the edge will go right through and make a hole in the chicken breast.

Pound from the center to the outside, but don't directly pound the outer edge of the scallop or it will tear and become overly dry. Continue lightly pounding with downward/outward strokes until the scallop is about ¼ inch thick. The waxed paper offers some protection and is slippery enough to allow the meat to spread as it is pounded. (Plastic wrap, which is frequently suggested, prevents the meat from spreading as freely.) You should

POUNDING MEAT

Lean, boneless cuts of meat can be pounded with a meat mallet to produce delicate, tender scallops. I wish there were a better word for it, though. "Pounding" seems to imply walloping the daylights out of something, but that's not what the term is supposed to convey at all.

Although one of the reasons for pounding meat is to tenderize it by breaking some of the connective tissue and muscle fibers, veal and chicken are so tender to begin with that your strokes need only be gentle taps to flatten and shape them into scallops. Beef and end up with a scallop that's about half again its original size.

RECIPES: Beef Scaloppine, Chicken Breasts in Saged Cream, Pork Scallops Chasseur, Pork Scallops in Mustard Cream, Rolled and Stuffed Flank Steak, Veal Scallops Marsala, Veal Scallops Saltimbocca.

PREHEATING

Now that energy conservation is a priority in most households, cooks have begun to reconsider the preheating step in recipes, and sometimes eliminate it altogether.

If you're cooking casseroles, pot roasts, or stews, or roasting unstuffed poultry, it doesn't make a particle of difference whether you preheat the oven or not. The food heats up along with the air inside and no harm is done. But stuffed poultry is another story. To discourage the growth of harmful bacteria, it's necessary to raise the temperature of the stuffing as quickly as possible, so a preheated oven is an absolute must.

All baked goods (aside from the occasional cold-start recipe) do best when placed in a preheated oven. It's the initial blast of hot air that cooks the bottom crust of a pie before it can become soggy, that lifts muffins and cakes before the carbon dioxide dissipates into the air, and that allows yeast breads to rise properly before they set.

All cuts of meat roast better in a preheated oven, because the blast of hot air seals the surface and locks in moisture (see Roasting).

That takes care of the oven, but electric skillets, woks, and deep-fat fryers must be preheated, too. Food cooked in cool fat absorbs a great deal of grease, making it unpleasant to eat and nearly impossible to digest. So, under certain circumstances, what you save in energy costs by not preheating probably isn't worth what you give up in the quality of your cooking.

PUDDING

Steamed

The trick to producing a first-rate steamed pudding is to have clouds of hot steam billowing around inside a covered pot. That means a small amount of water, but lots of steam.

You'll come across recipes that recommend steaming in more than 2 inches of water — some say to add enough water to come halfway up the side of the mold; others say add water almost to the top of the mold. If you follow these directions, you are simmering the pudding, not steaming it, and the results aren't the same.

To steam a pudding you'll need a deep, large kettle, or a canning pot with a sturdy rack that fits down inside. Grease your pudding mold generously, and fill to within 1 inch of the rim, leaving room for the pudding to expand as it cooks. Cover with the pudding-mold lid or with aluminum foil to seal the pudding and to protect it against drops of water that condense on the lid of the kettle and drop down. (There should be at least 2 inches clearance between the top of the pudding mold and the lid of the steamer.) Secure the foil with a piece of string — tied into a bow knot to make it easy to undo when you want to check to see if it's done. Place the mold in the kettle, pour in hot water until it measures 1½ to 2 inches deep, and bring to a boil. Cover the pot, lowering the heat if necessary so the cover doesn't lift and allow steam to escape, but keep the water boiling at a good, brisk clip. The inside of the kettle actually becomes a steam chamber. Steam the pudding for 2½ to 4½ hours, depending on the density of the batter, the size of the pudding mold, and whether or not the mold has a center tube. Replenish the water from time to time, never going above the 1½- to 2-inch mark.

A cooked pudding is done when it takes on a cakelike appearance and firm texture. You can test for doneness by inserting a metal skewer into the center, and, as with testing a cake, you can tell it's cooked when the skewer comes out clean.

RECIPE: Steamed Pumpkin Pudding.

Stirred

The puddings in this category are cooked on top of the stove in a thick-bottomed saucepan that will distribute heat evenly, or in a double boiler. They are all thickened primarily with starch, although egg yolks are sometimes added for richness and a bit of extra thickening. Stirred puddings that contain egg yolks are usually thickened with flour because of its ability to stabilize egg protein, and puddings without eggs are commonly thickened with cornstarch. Stirred pudding can be poured into serving dishes and chilled, or used as pie filling, in which case it is called custard cream or cream pie filling (see Cream Pie Filling).

Because stirred puddings are thickened with flour or cornstarch, lumping can be a major problem; when eggs are added, curdling and separation upon cooling, often referred to as weeping, become additional bugaboos.

Cornstarch and flour both react to heat by expanding and absorbing liquid (see Starch Molecules), so it's important that they be heated gradually. Some pudding recipes instruct you to sprinkle a mixture of cornstarch and sugar directly onto hot milk, but that's not a good idea. In the presence of all that heat, some starch granules will absorb more than their share of liquid, then swell up and stick together, trapping undissolved starch in the middle and forming lumps. A better approach is to heat starch gradually after dispersing it in a cold liquid (see Dispersion).

Begin to make a stirred pudding by whisking together flour (or cornstarch), sugar, and salt in a thick-bottomed saucepan. Completely separating the starch granules by dispersing them throughout the sugar enables you to add cold milk and heat the pudding without forming lumps.

Stir in the milk and place over moderately high heat. As the mixture warms, the sugar will begin to dissolve, and the starch granules (which are floating around in the liquid completely separate from one another) will begin to open and spill starch molecules into the milk. As the starch molecules heat and absorb liquid, they will swell and thicken the pudding (see Gelatinization). Allow the mixture to come to a full bubble, so you'll know that the starch is thoroughly cooked. Boil gently for 1 minute, stirring to prevent scorching.

At this point you can either chill the pudding or go on to add egg yolks for a richer flavor and smoother consistency. This procedure is tricky, though, and requires close attention. In order to denature and coagulate egg protein, the mixture must be heated a second time. More specifically, it must be heated to the boil (which is *not* in this case 212°F.), because an egg-yolk–flour combination presents an interesting problem. On one hand, the flour stabilizes the egg yolk so it can be exposed to high heat, but egg yolks contain an amylase enzyme that breaks down starch if it's allowed to remain active. Consequently, the enzyme must be heated to the point where it is inactivated. This explains the maxim that states an egg-yolk–flour combination not only *may be,* but *must be* brought to the boil." If it isn't, the starch-destroying enzymes will go to work and your pudding will thin out.

The ticklish aspect of this procedure is that excessive heat causes egg proteins to aggregate, or bunch together, and force out whatever liquid they had been previously holding (see Denaturing). This results in syneresis, more commonly known as weeping. A thermometer is an indispensable aid in successfully performing this step.

Stirring slowly but continuously, warm the egg-enriched pudding over moderate heat. Monitor the temperature with a thermometer. As the temperature approaches 180°F., lift your spatula frequently and listen for a plopping sound as the first bubble breaks the surface. Wait for the second plop, then immediately remove the pudding from the burner. Do not allow it to heat over 190°F. (see Boiling and Simmering).

Most pudding recipes that include eggs call for using the yolk alone. That's because the protein in egg whites is not protected by any fat, so it coagulates at a lower temperature than the protein in egg yolks. Therefore, if you heat pudding that contains egg whites to 180°F., the proteins are nearly certain to overheat and aggregate, producing a pudding that weeps as it cools.

As a stirred pudding cools, a skin forms on the top, because moisture evaporates and the surface begins to dry out. The best way to avoid this skin is to lay plastic wrap directly on the surface of the pudding. Gently smooth out air bubbles with your fingertips and press the wrap up against the sides of the bowl. When the pudding is chilled, spoon it into serving dishes.

RECIPE: Maple-Bourbon Pudding.   ◄〉

PURÉE

To purée means to start with a solid food and reduce it to a smooth consistency. Mashed potatoes are a run-of-the-mill purée everyone is familiar with. So is tomato sauce. From there on, things can get pretty sophisticated — like lobster purée for a mousse and chestnut purée for a dessert soufflé.

There are several ways to purée. The method you choose depends on the consistency you want and whether or not you wish to strain out certain elements as you go along. The simplest form of purée can be done with a hand masher. It produces a rather coarse purée and can be used only when there are no tough skins or fibers present.

For a slightly smoother purée, you can press soft-textured food through a sieve or through a cone-shaped chinois using a wooden pestle (see illustration). To purée foods

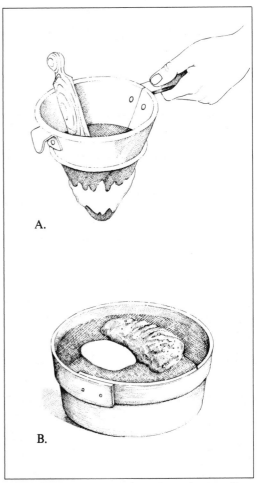

A.

B.

Puréed foods vary in texture, depending on the method used or consistency desired. The cone-shaped chinois (A.) produces a somewhat coarse purée; a drum sieve or tamis (B.), the smoothest.

with tough skins or fibers, or with a firm texture, your best bet is a food mill. Its metal blades help to break things up as they rotate.

A blender or food processor purées in the blink of an eye, but there are disadvantages. For one thing, both produce an unstrained purée; consequently, tomato sauce puréed in a blender or processor tastes slightly bitter, because the whirling blades pulverize seeds and all. There is also the possibility of puréeing to an excessive degree, so that starchy foods like potatoes or peas turn to paste.

The ultimate in puréeing is done with a drum sieve or tamis (see illustration). Its especially fine nylon mesh produces the smoothest possible purée, and at the same time strains out skins, shells, seeds, or other unwanted particles.

Food that's to be puréed is generally cooked first, then drained well. In some cases, as with pumpkin and squash, it is advisable to cook puréed food over low heat before using in order to evaporate any excess moisture that might ruin the final product.

RECIPES: Cream of Celery Soup, Summer Sauce.

Q

QUICK BREADS

See BREAD BAKING.

R

REDUCTION

Reduction is a culinary technique used to intensify flavor and to thicken the consistency of liquid substances.

When you heat a liquid in an uncovered pan, some of the water contained in the liquid will turn to water vapor and escape into the air. As this evaporation continues, the flavor of the concentrated liquid becomes more intense. If solid particles are present, the concentrated liquid also becomes thicker.

Always check the seasoning *after* you reduce a liquid, because salt doesn't evaporate during reduction and you can end up with an overly salty taste. On the other hand, fresh herb oils, which tend to be volatile, dissipate into the air when heated for too long or at too high a temperature; so briskly reducing a sauce that contains fresh herbs can sometimes cause a loss of flavor.

The instruction to reduce by one-half, or some other specific amount, should be taken seriously. Measure the liquid before heating, cook it down for a while, and then measure again. After some practice, you might be able to tell when you've reduced far enough by looking at the amount in the pan. If you reduce too much, you can correct this by replacing some of the water that has evaporated.   ◆◊

RICE

The trick to cooking rice is being able to produce the consistency you want when you want it. Served as an accompaniment to an entrée, rice should have firm, fluffy grains that show no trace of stickiness; as a casserole or pilaf style, it should also come out smooth with separate granules. Rice for a Chinese dinner should be just slightly sticky — a trait that's typical of oriental cooking, and which facilitates eating with chopsticks. Rice prepared for molded dishes, patties, cakes, or croquettes should be even more sticky so it will hold together.

Techniques for managing the stickiness of rice are based on the fact that rice kernels are 77 to 81 percent starch. When rice is combined with water and heated to 156°F., the starch granules begin to swell and absorb water. This is what causes rice to expand and become fluffy. As the rice continues to heat, the starch granules go on absorbing water and swell even further.

Inside the starch granules are amylose and amylopectin molecules — the same kind of starch molecules found in flour (see Starch Molecules). As the granules heat and expand, the molecules inside become moist and warm and they gelatinize. If you continue to apply excessive heat, the granules will begin to rupture — first on the outside of the grain, then on the inside. The gelatinizing molecules will spill out, and you'll end up with starch soup. Reducing the heat allows the rice to absorb moisture slowly and prevents turbulent cooking action that can break an excess number of exterior starch granules.

Cookbooks often warn against stirring rice as it cooks, because stirring creates abrasion against the kernels and ruptures the surface starch granules; the amylose and amylopectin molecules then tumble out and become sticky. You can, therefore, control the stickiness of rice by stirring or not stirring.

There are several different varieties of rice. Those that are higher in amylopectin starch cook up stickier, and are best used when a cohesive consistency is desired. Generally speaking, short grain rice, such as Italian rice, pudding rice, and glutinous rice, develops a sticky texture; long grain rice, like Indian, Carolina, and converted rice, retains a smoother, more separate character.

For firm, nonsticky rice, simmer long grain rice kernels in a measured amount of liquid on top of the stove, or bake slowly in the oven. In both methods, the total amount of water is absorbed by the rice, so no vitamins and minerals are poured out.

Converted rice is a long-grained, Carolina-style rice that has been subjected to a process called parboiling. During this process unhulled rice is steeped in hot water for various lengths of time (one example is 10 hours at 160°F.). The object is to infuse the kernel with the vitamins and minerals contained in the hull, bran, and germ that have been removed. In addition to enriching rice, parboiling changes the character of the kernels. They cook up into puffier, somewhat larger grains than unconverted rice, and because the parboiling process slightly sets the surface starch, the cooked kernels are more likely to be smooth with neatly tapered ends.

Carolina rice, which also comes from the states of Texas, Louisiana, California, and Arkansas, is often referred to in recipes as raw rice because it hasn't been parboiled. It has, however, been stripped of its brown layer of bran, polished to a high gloss, and enriched by a spraying process. (Brown rice is unstripped and unpolished, and doesn't need to be enriched because of the nutrients contained in the bran and germ.) During the milling and polishing process, a certain number of surface starch granules are broken, which leaves a starchy dust all over the rice kernels. This is particularly a problem in unenriched rice that hasn't been sprayed. Rinsing unenriched rice before cooking prevents this dust from cooking into glue.

Different varieties of rice absorb varying quantities of water. Generally, the accepted ratio for converted and Carolina rice is 2 parts liquid to 1 part rice, but you may want to adjust the proportions to suit your own taste — use more water for softer rice, less water for an *al dente* texture.

Whether you're cooking rice in the oven or on the stove top, select a wide pan that allows the rice to lie shallow. As rice cooks, the water level in the pan drops, which means that the rice at the top steams, while the rice at the bottom simmers. If you use a narrow pan, in which the rice is deep, the bottom level of rice cooks in water for a longer period of time, creating overly soggy rice on the bottom. Plus, when the rice lies deep, the heavier top layer packs down the rice on the bottom.

To cook either converted or Carolina rice on top of the stove, bring salted water to a rolling boil, pour in the rice, and stir once to separate the kernels. Immediately lower the heat to a simmer, and cover the pan. In 2 or 3 minutes, lift the lid to make sure the rice is not cooking too vigorously (particularly on an electric burner, which retains a great deal of heat.) Simmer gently from 17 to 20 minutes, depending on the consistency you want. When the kernels are tender, remove the pan from the burner and fluff lightly with a fork. Lay a double thickness of paper toweling over the top of the pan and replace the lid, using enough force to seal the pan tightly. As steam rises from the rice, the paper towel will absorb the moisture and dry out the rice. (This is also an excellent way to hold rice when you're faced with late-arriving guests.)

Cooking rice pilaf-style is another strategy for achieving a firm, smooth consistency. Oil, or a combination of butter and oil, is heated; rice is stirred in and then cooked until most of the kernels are opaque. The purpose of this step is to coat each rice kernel with hot fat, which sets the starchy surface and prevents one kernel from clinging to another.

At this point, a measured amount of hot liquid is added and stirred once. The pan is covered, and cooking is completed in the oven or at a low simmer. After 17 to 25 minutes, the kernels will be tender. Remove the pan from the heat, and place a double thickness of paper toweling between the pan and the cover to absorb excess moisture.

To prepare rice with a slightly sticky texture, start the rice in cold water. The gradual warming process tends to loosen surface starch granules and create stickier rice. Bring the water to a boil and cook briskly, until the water level has receded below the rice. Stir thoroughly and cover the pan. Reduce the heat and cook at a simmer for 17 to 25 minutes. When the kernels are tender, fluff with a fork and serve without drying.

Short grain rice can be cooked according to the methods described above, but since short grain rice is higher in amylopectin, the final product will be significantly more sticky. Glutinous rice, also a short grain variety, cooks up exceptionally soft and sticky. Frequently used in Chinese cooking, it develops a pleasant flavor often described as sweet (though not in the sugary sense) and it forms the basis for a variety of dishes, including both entrées and desserts. Glutinous rice contains no gluten, but rather derives its name from the gummy texture it exhibits.

RECIPES: American-Style Risotto, Cheese-Filled Rice Croquettes, Lemon Rice, Rice Fritters, Risotto Milanese.   ๛

ROASTING

When it comes to preparing an oven roast, all cooks want two things: tenderness and juiciness. You initially determine how tender your oven roast is going to be when you decide how much you're willing to pay for it. A tender piece of meat is expensive, but you *must* start with a tender cut to produce a tender oven roast (see Meat: Selecting Cuts).

Whether you're purchasing beef, veal, pork, or lamb, the best cuts for roasting are labeled rib, loin, or sirloin. (The only exceptions are the hind leg of veal and lamb, both of which are quite tender because these animals are slaughtered so young.) Cuts of meat from the shoulder, often called chuck roasts, and from the hind leg, usually called round or rump roasts, are less tender going into the oven, so they're going to be less tender coming out. In fact, chuck, round, and rump roasts do better when cooked according to a slow, moist procedure such as braising or pot roasting (see Braising; Pot Roasting).

There's an interesting paradox in meat cookery: heat, in the presence of a significant amount of moisture, softens and dissolves collagen and connective tissue; on the other hand, the identical combination of heat and moisture toughens meat fibers. Consequently, an inexpensive cut of meat, which contains abundant connective tissue, becomes tender when braised. (Moist heat doesn't actually tenderize meat; it causes the collagen and connective tissue to melt, which allows the muscle fibers to separate, and thus creates the sensation of tenderness.) Yet an expensive cut of meat, which contains relatively little connective tissue, becomes tough if roasted with water added to the pan. Meat fibers themselves contract and toughen, often becoming stringy. For that reason, naturally tender meat, which is composed mostly of muscle fibers, takes on a degree of toughness when exposed to moist heat.

The juiciness of an oven roast depends on several things: the presence of collagen (see Connective Tissue); the amount of natural moisture the meat contains; the amount of fat it has, both around the outside and interspersed between the fibers (see Marbling); and how the roast is cooked.

When you put a roast into a preheated oven, the hot air immediately surrounds the meat, coagulating the proteins on the surface and sealing in the moisture. The interior of

the roast begins to cook by conduction, a progressive form of heating in which one hot molecule heats the next, which heats the next, and so on (see Heat: Conduction). As the heat travels to the center of the roast, it turns the moisture to steam. Some of the steam makes its way to the surface of the roast and escapes; the rest softens and liquefies whatever collagen is present. During roasting, the melted collagen drips out of the roast as a mixture of gelatin and coagulable protein.

Meanwhile, the heat is rupturing fat cells along the way. Melted fat spills out and flows between the meat fibers, flavoring them and preventing them from drying out. Some of the fat eventually makes its way to the surface of the roast and drips down onto the pan, where it mingles with the gelatin and coagulable proteins. These are the elements that adhere to the bottom of the roasting pan and provide the basis for a sauce or gravy.

The melted fat and liquefied protein that come to the surface of the meat provide the natural sugar and amino acids necessary for the Maillard browning reaction to take place (see Browning — Maillard Reaction). Beef roasts, in particular, are high in the elements needed to form a dark brown crust. Veal, pork, and lamb roasts don't brown as well as beef, but browning can be promoted by basting them with a sauce that contains some sugar and an acid.

Once you understand what happens as a piece of meat heats, you can see that how you cook a roast affects its tenderness. Cuts of meat with little or no marbling are apt to come out dry and tough, particularly if cooked too long or at too high a temperature. Naturally tender, yet lightly marbled, meats like veal, pork, or lamb, and less-tender cuts of beef with little marbling need special attention (see Barding; Larding). They do best when roasted at temperatures low enough to soften and liquefy the collagen without toughening the muscle fibers (around 325°F. or below).

Cuts of meat that contain a large amount of interior fat (mostly beef) can be cooked at high temperatures to achieve a crisp, brown exterior with a red, rare center. Because the meat fibers are surrounded by liquid fat, they are protected from moisture, so they can stand more heat without becoming tough.

The fact that a roast cooks by conduction explains why high-heat roasting (at a temperature over 375°F.) produces a piece of meat that is well-done on the outside and rare at the center. High heat attacks the outer layer of meat, cooking it long before much heat can get to the center of the roast.

Low-heat roasting (between 275° and 325°F.), which is popular with cooks who prefer a medium degree of doneness, gives heat ample opportunity to wend its way to the center without overcooking the outside. The result is a more evenly cooked roast.

For best results with either the high-heat or low-heat method, set your roast on a roasting rack to allow hot air to circulate around the meat. If you cook a roast directly on the bottom of a pan, the portion of meat that touches the pan will actually fry. Then, as fat and meat juices appear, the meat at the bottom of the pan will become saturated with grease.

Avoid salting meat before roasting, for, as granules of salt heat and dissolve, they cause some of the meat fibers on the surface to pull together, leaving tiny gaps through which meat juices escape. Also, always preheat your oven, so the outer surface of the meat will firm up as quickly as possible, sealing in the juices.

A meat thermometer is an essential key to successful roasting. Multiplying pounds by minutes to calculate when a roast will be done is fine, if all you want is an estimate, but per-pound charts don't take into consideration the shape of a roast. (A long, narrow roast cooks in less time than a round, wide roast, because the heat travels to the center faster.) Cooking charts do not make allowances for the presence of bones either. (A boned roast cooks faster than the same size piece of meat with the bones left in.) A meat thermometer tells you the exact internal temperature of a roast, and no guessing means no more overcooked, dried-out, tough-as-shoe-leather roasts.

A roast should always stand for 5 to 20 minutes after it is removed from the oven. A large, highly marbled roast needs to stand longer than one that's small and lean. Consider the action going on inside a roast during the final stages of cooking — hot, liquid fat and melted collagen are gurgling around, bubbling to the surface. When you allow the meat to stand for a few minutes, it gives those juices time to settle down and retreat to the interior of the roast. A slight cooling also firms the meat fibers a bit, so carving is easier.

RECIPES: Rib Roast of Pork à l'Orange, Roasted Beef Tenderloin, Roast Rack of Lamb with Currant Sauce.

ROUX

A roux is a mixture of fat and cooked flour. The proportions of fat and flour are usually equal, and the extent to which the mixture is cooked depends on the character of the dish it will be used to thicken.

The first step in making a roux is melting a given amount of butter, or other fat, over medium heat — the temperature is important. If the fat is too hot when the flour is added, it will actually fry the flour, hardening the outside of the starch granules and sealing them closed. The object of this initial melting step is to provide liquid fat in which to disperse the starch granules. Each starch granule, evenly coated with fat, is then separate from every other starch granule, and the risk of lumping is eliminated (see Dispersion). Be sure to use a thick-bottomed saucepan so the heat is evenly distributed.

When the butter is melted, remove the pan from the heat and dump in the flour all at once. Return to medium heat and cook, stirring continuously. Allow the butter and flour to froth gently for 2 to 3 minutes. This cooks the flour, to do away with any raw, pasty taste, and warms the starch molecules, preparing them to receive and absorb a maximum amount of liquid.

At this point, the roux will be the color of melted butter. It's called a white roux and it is used as a thickener for all the various white sauces (see White Sauce). If you continue to cook the roux until it becomes deeper yellow or golden, you have created a blond roux to use as a thickener in specific veal dishes. Continued cooking produces a brown roux (see Brown Sauce).

The preparation of a brown roux is a bit tricky. First of all, if you use butter, it must be clarified. If you don't remove the milk solids, they will burn and destroy the flavor of a brown roux. Oil is a good fat to use if you don't have time to clarify butter, or you might want to try rendered pork fat or beef drippings, which add extraordinary flavor (see Clarifying Butter).

When browning a roux, continue to cook the mixture over low heat, stirring constantly. Once the mixture begins to color, it can quickly get ahead of you. The fat retains so much heat that the flour will continue to cook even after the pan is removed from the heat, so pull the pan off the burner before the roux reaches the desired shade of brown and allow the residual heat to complete the browning. Keep in mind that it's better to err on the side of underbrowning, for overbrowned roux can taste harsh.

S

SALAD DRESSING

Salad dressing is one of those things that most people would rather buy at the supermarket than try to make themselves. But once you start making your own, you'll be hooked — maybe not for every day of the week, but definitely for special occasions.

The trouble with store-bought salad dressing, especially cream-style, is the heavy dose of chemical emulsifiers manufacturers use to hold the dressing together. Chemical emulsifiers taste like plastic, but they're strong and reliable, and they prevent salad dressing from separating. The product looks good on the shelf, and that makes the manufacturer happy.

On the other hand, the stiffer and thicker the dressing, the more emulsifiers it contains, and the more it tastes like plastic. That makes consumers like me unhappy. But there are *natural* emulsifiers that can be added to homemade salad dressings to prevent them

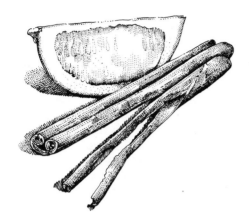

from separating. This makes it possible to create a variety of textures ranging from thin and pourable to thick and spoonable.

The simplest, easiest-to-prepare dressing is a basic vinaigrette — a combination of oil and vinegar or lemon juice. Since vinegar and lemon juice are essentially water, a vinaigrette, then, is a mixture of oil and water.

Oil and water don't mix unless they are agitated, which causes the drops of oil to get smaller and smaller and disperse throughout the water — temporarily. As soon as you stop mixing a vinaigrette, the oil and water will separate, because it's a liquid-in-liquid suspension and the oil droplets have a strong desire to reunite (see Suspension; Dispersion).

If you add bits of herbs or spices to a vinaigrette, it becomes a coarse suspension; the herbs and spices are heavy particles that fall readily to the bottom when you stop mixing or shaking the liquid.

In order to provide some stability to a vinaigrette, you can add a weak, natural emulsifier such as mustard (see Emulsifiers). This will bind the oil and water together for a short time, which explains why many vinaigrette recipes call for mustard. However, separation will occur soon after agitation ceases, because it's still only a temporary suspension.

Adding a strong emulsifier such as lecithin, which is contained in egg yolks, to a vinaigrette will hold the oil and water together for a longer period of time than will mustard,

and will create a thicker, creamier emulsion. It will be fairly stable, but may separate after a few days in the refrigerator.

A more stable cream-style dressing can be made by starting with mayonnaise (a prepared emulsion) and working backward, thinning it with additional vinegar or lemon juice, then adding herbs and spices at the end.

RECIPES: See Salads and Dressings.

SAUCE MAKING

The whole subject of sauces can seem intimidating, but once you know the reasons why certain procedures are followed and understand the surprisingly small number of steps involved, you will be able to prepare any number of sauces successfully.

Sauces are traditionally divided into six categories: white sauces, brown sauces, tomato sauces, oil and vinegar sauces, egg yolk and liquid fat sauces, and warm butter sauces. They can also be classified according to the method used to achieve their consistency and the reactions that occur during their formation. This creates three basic groups: gels, or starch-thickened sauces; suspensions; and reductions.

Gels, suspension sauces, and reduction sauces are often enriched with an egg-yolk-and-cream liaison (see Liaison), or finished by swirling in cold butter or folding in whipped cream (see Finishing A Sauce).

For a further explanation of the pattern underlying each type of sauce and some of its possible variations, see the individual entries: White Sauce, Brown Sauce, Vinaigrette Sauce, Butter Sauce, Mayonnaise, and Hollandaise Sauce. Also check the index under Sauces.

Gel Sauces

The gels are all those sauces thickened with some type of starch: uncooked flour (see Slurry; Beurre Manié); cooked flour (see

Roux); or others such as cornstarch, arrowroot, potato flour, or rice flour. This is the largest group of sauces; it includes all the classic white sauces, brown sauces, pan gravies, fruit glazes, and the translucent sauces of the Chinese cuisine.

Starch-thickened sauces are considered gels, because they are transformed from a liquid to a viscous state by the swelling of

---

A Sauce System

GEL SAUCES
(Starch-thickened sauces)

Uncooked } → slurry   → gravy
flour   } → beurre manié → gravy

Cooked } → white roux   → white sauces
flour   } → brown roux → brown sauces

Cornstarch }   { gravy, fruit
Arrowroot }   { glaze, and
Rice flour   } → slurry → { transparent
Potato flour }   { Chinese
                            { sauces

SUSPENSION SAUCES

Temporary   oil and vinegar or lemon
suspension   juice sauces (vinaigrette
                dressing); butter sauces

Permanent   cold and warm emulsion
suspension   sauces (mayonnaise and
(emulsion)   hollandaise)

REDUCTION SAUCES

Purée   Vegetable or fruit sauces (tomato,
        leek, sorrel, etc.)

Glaze   Meat glaze, chicken glaze, fish
        glaze of the nouvelle cuisine, and
        deglazed pan juices

---

starch molecules (and the three-dimensional network these molecules form when they join together). When making a basic white sauce, for example, the first step is to prepare a roux by melting a specified amount of butter and blending in flour, dispersing it throughout the fat to avoid the risk of lumps. As the hot butter coats the individual starch granules, they become warm — a condition that predisposes them to swell and absorb water, the major component of milk.

The next step is to cook the roux. The pouchlike starch granules become warmer and warmer and swell until they burst, allowing some of the starch molecules inside to escape.

When hot milk is added, the water contained in the milk is immediately attracted to the partially opened starch granules, and thickening begins. Then, as the sauce begins to boil, the pouches of starch open fully and spill their entire supply of starch molecules into the surrounding liquid.

At this point, two things happen. Some of the molecules (the amylose type) begin to uncoil and swell. Since they are attracted to water, and to each other, they attach themselves to water molecules and proceed to intertwine. The result is the three-dimensional network known as a gel (see Gelatinization). Meanwhile, the more numerous amylopectin molecules are also absorbing water and swelling. They thicken the sauce by reducing the amount of available water. Hence, the white sauce becomes more viscous for two reasons — water is trapped within a cellular network, and it is also held by molecules that have absorbed it (see Starch Molecules).

A properly constructed white sauce, or any starch gel for that matter, will remain fairly stable for a short period of time. However, amylose molecules have a tendency to group together as a sauce cools. As they move toward each other, they push away some of the water trapped between them. This water eventually makes its way to the surface of the sauce in the form of spidery cracks. Fortunately, amylopectin molecules are present in greater numbers, and they don't exhibit this annoying tendency.

Don't hesitate to freeze starch-bound sauces. In some instances, they may appear to separate, but they will smooth out quickly when stirred over moderate heat (see Separation of Sauces).

Suspension Sauces

Suspension sauces consist of temporary suspensions and permanent suspensions. In making a temporary suspension, such as a vinaigrette sauce, you blend oil and vinegar together by whisking lightly or by shaking. The two incompatible ingredients will mingle briefly, but separate upon standing (see Salad Dressing). Butter sauces, which are a combination of butterfat and water, are also temporary suspensions. However, they tend to be more stable than vinaigrette sauces, because butter contains a small amount of a natural emulsifier (see Emulsifiers).

The most stable suspension sauces are the permanent suspensions, or emulsions. In preparing this type of sauce, you add an emulsifying agent to the fat and water combination. The emulsifier, usually the lecithin in egg yolk, helps to create a smooth sauce by linking the incompatible elements together, but the way an emulsified sauce thickens depends on whether you're making a cold emulsion or a warm emulsion.

Warm emulsions, such as hollandaise and béarnaise, are stirred or whisked slowly over gentle heat. They are thickened by the same coagulation of egg protein that binds a custard (see Coagulation). Cold emulsions, like mayonnaise, are usually quite a bit thicker and stiffer than warm emulsions. This is because you vigorously whisk rather than stir a cold emulsion, and by whisking, you shatter the fat drops into millions of fat droplets.

When making mayonnaise, you whisk together lemon juice and an egg yolk, uniting the water and the emulsifier. Then, drop by drop, you whisk in oil. As the whisk passes through each oil drop, it breaks it into a number of smaller droplets, and each droplet becomes coated with a film of egg yolk.

As you continue to whisk, more and more oil drops are broken into droplets. Just as in whipping cream, where subdividing the drops of butterfat increases the volume and stiffness of the cream (see Whipping: Cream), the emulsion sauce begins to thicken as the total surface area of oil drops grows.

Soon you'll have thousands of tiny oil droplets, each coated with a layer of lecithin molecules linked to water molecules. As you continue to whisk, you'll break more and more oil drops into droplets, the volume will expand, and your emulsion will thicken. This also explains why the more oil you add, the stiffer your mayonnaise will become — until, that is, you run out of available lecithin.

Reduction Sauces

Reduction sauces are formed by evaporation, and rank among the most exquisite preparations in the entire culinary repertoire, because a reduction is achieved by concentrating natural flavors (see Reduction). Reduction sauces include certain aspics, tomato sauces, deglazing sauces, meat glazes, chicken glazes, fish glazes, and the reduced sauces of the nouvelle cuisine. Since these flavorful essences are thick and syrupy when hot, they can also be used to thicken other sauces. ❧

SAUTÉING

The term sauté has lost some of its punch. It has come to mean cooking over high heat, in a small amount of fat, using an uncovered pan. When a recipe instructs you to sauté onions, you probably stir them around in a little butter or oil and continue cooking them until they're soft. That's acceptable enough, but it's missing the true essence of sautéing.

Strictly speaking, to sauté means to cook in so little fat that you can shake the pan vigorously and none will slosh out. Sautéing should be done quickly. The food should be thinly sliced or cut into small pieces and completely dry. Then, when the fat is very hot, you toss in the food and shake the pan back and forth, using an upward flick of the wrist that causes the food to jump around in the pan (sauté is derived from the French verb "sauter" meaning to jump).

If you're not quite courageous enough for that maneuver, at least keep the food moving by lifting and stirring it with two hands as you would to stir-fry (which, incidentally, is a form of sauté). The object is to continuously lift the food away from the pan, so that steam doesn't have a chance to accumulate; any moisture that comes to the surface is quickly dissipated into the air by this rapid and continual motion.

Depending on what you're sautéing, you can use any thick-bottomed skillet that's light enough to zip around. Small portions of cubed beef or pork strips won't pose any problem, but larger pieces of meat like chicken segments will jump right out of the pan if you're sautéing with the proper degree of enthusiasm. For this, you need a high-sided pan, either a black steel frying pan with tall, flared sides, or the straight-sided sauté pan known as a *sautoir*.

Always sauté small quantities. The enemy of successful sautéing is moisture, so don't place too many items in the pan at one time. If you do, you'll create excessive moisture, which thwarts browning and makes it impossible for you to attain that special surface texture characteristic of sautéed food.

The fact that butter is often used for sautéing fresh mushrooms seems to contradict advice warning against cooking with butter at high temperatures (unless it has been clarified). However, since fresh mushrooms are exceptionally absorbent, the melted butter is completely taken in, thereby eliminating the question of burnt milk solids at the start.

A word of caution: sautéing over *consistently* high heat should not be done with mushrooms. Even though the butter has been absorbed, the constant high heat can cause mushrooms to burn. The trick here is to briefly pull the pan from the heat, shaking and stirring the mushrooms until they cool just to the point of releasing their moisture, then return them briefly to high heat. Repeatedly alternating this on-the-heat/off-the-heat procedure enables you to sauté mushrooms without burning them.

Sautéed mushrooms are considered done when they are tender but still offer some resistance to the teeth. Cooking them until they brown lightly around the edges is optional and a matter of personal preference.

RECIPES: Sautéed Cherry Tomatoes, Shrimp and Mushroom Sauté.   ◅

SCALDING MILK

Scalding milk has traditionally been considered a crucial step in preparing a variety of recipes. It's certainly true that it makes it possible to dissolve salt and sugar thoroughly, and provides you with an easy way to melt shortening. But when is scalding milk actually necessary?

Raw, unpasteurized milk contains *proteolytic* enzymes — microorganisms that break down protein. Proteolytic enzymes exist naturally in flour, yeast, and milk. (Also contained in flour are the essential proteins that unite to form gluten.) Therefore, if you use raw milk in making yeast breads, you're creating a situation in which protein-destroying enzymes will come in contact with flour proteins and break them down at a swift clip. The result will be sticky, gummy dough, because the gluten wasn't given a chance to develop properly. Scalding raw milk destroys the proteolytic enzymes that devastate gluten, so, in that regard, scalded milk produces yeast bread with a better texture.

However, the pasteurization process also destroys the enzymes in milk that interfere with gluten development. Consequently, there's no need to scald pasteurized milk when making yeast breads. The protein-destroying enzymes are still present in the flour and yeast, but they are active only to a limited degree. In fact, a balanced amount of proteolytic activity is desirable. There should be just enough to contribute to the elastic quality of gluten without interfering with its strength. A total lack of proteolytic activity would result in a dough that's very difficult to handle.

There are occasions when scalding does come in handy. Even though it's not necessary, I still warm milk when using it in yeast bread recipes that call for shortening. The milk has to be warm for maximum yeast growth anyway, and it's easier to warm the milk and melt the shortening all in one step.

Recipes for custards and other delicate preparations that contain eggs often suggest that you scald the milk before incorporating the eggs. Here again, since pasteurization takes care of inactivating proteolytic enzymes, the scalding is now done strictly to warm the milk in order to gently heat the eggs, so that further heat from the oven or stove-top burner won't be as much of a shock.

It's important to scald milk correctly to avoid the unpleasant flavor of cooked protein and milk sugar. Before you begin, rinse the pan with cold water; shake it out but do not dry. This discourages the lactose from sticking to the bottom of the pan, where it's apt to cook. It also makes the pan easier to wash.

Since you're only warming the milk, not heating it to destroy bacteria or enzymes, there's no need to wait until bubbles form around the outside edge of the pan (the classic description of the scalding point). Testing with your finger will tell you when the milk is sufficiently warm; if it's too hot for your finger, it's too hot for eggs. Use an instant-read thermometer if you like. You'll notice that as the milk reaches 130°F. a faint aroma is given off; at 150°F. the surface begins to wrinkle and the smell of cooked milk is quite prominent; at 160°F. the surface is covered by a skin that has wrinkled noticeably; and at 170°F. tiny bubbles form around the outside edge of the pan.

Heating the milk to 120°F. is sufficient for gently warming eggs. For those instances where shortening is to be melted in the hot milk, it's necessary to warm the milk to 140°F. Keep in mind that the skin formation on the surface of heated milk indicates that the protein has begun to coagulate, which gives milk a cooked flavor.

Stirring isn't necessary during the scalding process, unless you want to distribute the heat more evenly. But decide which you want to do and stick with it — either stir continuously or not at all. If the heat source is kept at a moderate level (and the pan has been rinsed with cold water), any lactose film that may collect in the bottom of the pan won't scorch. But intermittent stirring will dislodge it, lending a slightly grainy texture and cooked flavor to the milk. For that reason, it's not a good idea to use a spatula to get every last drop of milk out of the pan. Just pour it out and leave behind anything that clings.

The important point to remember about scalding milk is that it is no longer needed to destroy microorganisms, unless you're using raw milk. Any scalding done nowadays is solely for the purpose of providing a warm environment; therefore, I think the term "scalding" should be abolished altogether. Think of the procedure instead in terms of "warming" milk.   ✌

SCORING

Cooks often score the fat on a baked ham to make it look attractive, but there are other reasons for this procedure.

Scoring meat can tenderize it. A series of shallow slashes in the surface of meat actually cuts the fibers, breaking them down so they're easy to chew. Cube steaks are a common example of scoring to tenderize and they are very easy to make at home, using an economical roast, such as a tip roast, rump roast, or even an eye of the round. Freeze the meat for 30 minutes to make it easier to slice. Then, cutting against the grain, slice off pieces ½ to ¾ of an inch thick. Remove any connective tissue and fat from the outside edge of each slice. Next, make a series of parallel slashes across the top of the meat with a large chef's knife. Use a whacking rather than a slicing motion, letting the weight of the knife do the work. Turn the meat and make a second series of parallel cuts at a 90° angle. Repeat this on the other side of the meat.

Scoring thicker cuts of meat, like shoulder steak and round steak, allows a marinade to penetrate more deeply, and increases the amount of surface area exposed to the tenderizing liquid (see Marinating). It also speeds cooking by letting heat penetrate more quickly. When meat to be braised or roasted bears a thick coating of fat, as a ham often does, it's a good idea to score the fat so the braising or basting juices can penetrate through to the flesh.

Meat is sometimes scored to prevent it from buckling — especially if it contains connective tissue or cartilage, which seizes when exposed to dry, intense heat. For example, a pan-fried blade steak or shoulder lamb chop will often heave in the middle when the heat attacks the connective tissue. A few shallow cuts across the surface of the meat will help it lie flat and therefore cook evenly.

Fancy meat markets often make a series of cuts through the fat around the perimeter of loin and sirloin steaks, and the extra-large veal scallops used in Wiener Schnitzel are often scored for the same reason — to encourage them to lie flat when they're exposed to intense heat.

SEPARATION OF SAUCES

A sauce that separates at the last minute ranks among the most annoying of culinary predicaments.

Starch-bound sauces, especially those thickened with flour, are prone to separation as they cool. This condition is called syneresis, and is caused by the tendency of certain starch molecules to group together. As a starch gel decreases in temperature, the amylose molecules move toward each other, forcing out water that had previously been held in the spaces of the weblike network (see Molecular Network). The sauce takes on a grainy texture and tiny cracks appear. With a further decrease in temperature, water oozes from the cracks.

Syneresis, or weeping, of starch-bound sauces can be reversed by heating the sauce. But evaporation also plays a part in this type of separation, so stir in a small amount of water (1 or 2 tablespoons) to replenish what may have escaped. Starch-bound sauces that are frozen or refrigerated will nearly always exhibit a degree of syneresis. It disappears upon reheating.

A combination of evaporation and excess heat will cause butterfat or oil to separate out of deglazing sauces or sauces enriched with cream or a liaison (see Liaison). The loss of moisture through evaporation upsets the balance of the sauce, and the suspension breaks due to the heat. You'll see the solids go one way and the butter or oil go another. If the problem is slight, swirling in small chunks of cold butter may pull the sauce back together (see Finishing A Sauce). In the case of severe separation, swirl in an ice cube or two (smaller pieces of ice work best, but they're not always handy), holding the pan away from the heat. Then reheat the rescued sauce gently to evaporate the excess water from the melted ice.

Warm emulsion sauces, like béarnaise, are apt to separate if subjected to too much heat.

This is a signal that the protein molecules are on the verge of coagulating out of control. In other words, the eggs are about to scramble. Drops of cold water, or small pieces of ice, can be used to reduce the temperature quickly and rescue the sauce. Remove the sauce from the heat, and rapidly whisk in a few drops of ice-cold water. Any time a recipe advises you to have a pan or bowl of ice ready, it may be as a preventative measure against separation or curdling.

Adding alcohol in the form of liquor, wine, or flavoring extracts is another factor that can cause a mixture to separate. Reducing the temperature is again the way to cope with this. Plunge the container into a large bowl of ice or whisk in a few drops of ice water to pull the mixture back together.   ◆

SHORTENING

Commonly thought of as the solid, white fat in a can, shortening actually refers to all fats — butter, margarine, lard, meat drippings, and oil — because of the effect it has on strands of gluten.

When you incorporate fat into a pastry-type dough like pie crust, puff pastry, or biscuits, it intermingles with the gluten strands in such a way as to prevent them from joining together in the strong weblike network desired by bread bakers. Fat keeps the gluten strands from developing; it literally "shortens" them. For that reason, high-fat doughs are referred to as "short," as in short paste or short crust.

If you've ever analyzed different pie crusts, you've noticed that as your fork breaks through the crust, the texture varies. Some crusts crumble into uniform, mealy particles, while others break apart in layers of flakes. A truly short pastry is one in which the fat is so abundant, and so completely incorporated, that distinct layers of flour-and-water paste

don't occur. (Examples are hot-water pastry and pie crust made with oil. They are tender, yet mealy-textured, because the fat is blended in to such a fine degree.)

When less fat is used, or when bits of fat are left in larger pieces, some strands of gluten are left uncoated. They have the opportunity to develop to a limited extent, and will join to form the flat layers of flour-and-water paste that create the kind of texture that shatters or comes apart in flakes (see Pie Crust).

Shortening also determines the tenderness of cakes and cookies. Fat coats the particles of gluten, allowing them to slide against each other, so you can achieve a cellular structure that is strong enough to rise and hold up during baking, yet tender enough to crumble when you bite into it.

When a recipe calls for shortening, chances are you reach for the can of soft, white, partially hydrogenated shortening, also called vegetable shortening. Aside from the fact that it's flavorless (except for the newly developed version that is artificially butter-flavored), it's an excellent baking fat for several reasons.

During the hydrogenation process, liquid vegetable oil is heated in large vats, to which hydrogen gas is introduced under pressure. As the hydrogen is forced through the hot oil, the mixture is whipped, and the hydrogen molecules chemically attach themselves to the fat molecules. The substance is then cooled and whipped again to incorporate air, which gives it a smooth, creamy texture and turns it snowy white.

Most hydrogenated fats on the market today contain monoglycerides and diglycerides, elements that make it possible to produce the super-sweet, high-sugar cakes that have come to be regarded as American layer cakes.

Sugar has a great affinity for water. When mixed into a cake batter, it will compete with the protein and starch molecules for the available moisture. Therefore, in order to produce a cake that is both moist and sweet, it is necessary to find a way to increase the amount of liquid in the batter.

That's where the mono- and diglycerides come in handy. They act as emulsifiers, linking fat droplets to water so efficiently that you can incorporate a greater amount of liquid than usual in a batter (see Emulsifiers). The high ratio of water provides the moisture needed to balance a greater amount of sugar, and the result is a cake in which the weight of sugar is equal to, or even greater than, the weight of flour (½ cup of sugar equals 1 cup of flour by weight). A high-ratio cake is sweet, tender, and finely textured, with a cellular structure strong enough to resist collapsing during baking and cooling.

Many cooks use hydrogenated (or vegetable) shortening for deep-fat frying. It's less expensive than lard or vegetable oil, and it produces a pleasing, crisply textured crust. But the mono- and diglycerides, which are added during processing, decompose quite readily when the shortening is heated to high temperatures for prolonged periods of time. This lowers the smoke point of the fat, which means you can't heat it as long or reuse it as many times as you can oil and lard.   ❧

SIFTING

The problem with sifting is that it's such a pain. It takes time and energy and requires using another utensil that will have to be washed. So why bother with it?

Flour settles easily and quickly. In fact, flour packs down to such an extent that a cupful scooped from a supply that has been sitting around for a while can hold up to two more ounces than a cupful you've just sifted. The word "presifted" on the bag's label doesn't change that fact.

The majority of published recipes are formulated with sifted flour in mind, so if you use *unsifted* flour, you run the risk of upsetting the liquid-flour balance by adding too much flour. Inaccurate measuring of this nature can play havoc with delicate baked goods — especially pastry. That's why serious pastry cooks prefer to weigh their ingredients on a kitchen scale, for no matter how packed down the flour is, it still weighs the same.

Achieving the proper liquid-flour balance isn't the only reason for sifting. Putting flour through a sieve aerates the flour and separates the particles from one another — extremely important in baking light cakes. Unsifted flour tends to clump together when it hits the batter, resulting in tiny lumps of unincorporated flour. And cakes that require the flour to be folded in develop a more delicate texture if it is sifted directly onto the batter rather than spooned or poured on, which will deflate light batter.

Sifting flour over the surface of unbaked bread produces a thick, hearty crust and gives free-standing loaves an authentic country-style look. Pie crust, biscuits, and rolls also develop an interesting exterior when lightly dusted with flour before baking.

Pie crust and similar types of rolled pastry come out lighter and flakier when they are dusted with flour through a sieve. If, instead, unsifted flour is scattered onto the work surface or over the top of the pastry, it tends to lie in little heaps and get rolled in that way, which makes pastry heavy and tough.

The process of kneading and shaping bread is also better accomplished with sifted flour (although the actual dough can be prepared with unsifted flour), because a light dusting through a sieve guarantees the amount kneaded in will be the absolute minimum. When excess flour is incorporated into bread dough the result is a dense, heavy loaf.

A marvelous gadget for this light type of sifting is the new battery-operated sifter. It produces a fine shower of flour at the flick of a switch. It also takes only one hand to operate, so you can be turning, or folding, or otherwise attending to the dough with one hand while you sift with the other. I use mine strictly for flour, so I don't have to wash it. A firm tap or two clears out the wire screening, then I store it inside an unsecured plastic bag to keep the dust away (see Appendix).

Heavy-duty sifting is best carried out by using a spring-action sifter or a sifter with a rotary mechanism, or by shaking the flour through a strainer. Spring-action sifters do an excellent job, but the squeezing action sometimes makes the hand ache. For small quantities, shaking the flour through a sifter is a good alternative because it's far less tiring. A rotary-type sifter, which is operated by turning a handle, is capable of sifting large quantities with less effort than the spring-action style.

In addition to sifting flour, you might want to sift sugar, too — particularly if you live in a humid climate where sugar tends to lump. Tiny lumps of sugar can create a mottled effect on the surface of baked goods, but sifting sugar breaks up these lumps and enables the sugar to be more evenly dispersed throughout the other dry ingredients. Delicate pastries and meringues also come out better if you separate and aerate the grains of sugar (see Meringue).

Sifting has long been accepted as the best way to blend dry ingredients. Most recipes imply that to sift the dry ingredients together is sufficient. Spices, leaveners, and salt certainly do mingle better when sifted, but to ensure that they are completely dispersed throughout the flour, it's a good idea to toss the sifted ingredients several times with a dry wire whisk or fork.

There are times when sifting flour isn't absolutely necessary, such as when you're making yeast bread or pasta dough. The degree of humidity, or moisture, in the air has such a significant impact on how much flour you will use in these two doughs on any given day that it matters little whether you sift or not (see Bread Baking).   ✌

SLURRY

A slurry is a solid-in-liquid dispersion consisting of starch granules mixed with a liquid medium such as cold milk, water, or stock. When flour or cornstarch is stirred into the liquid, the starch granules separate from one another; once separated, they are far less likely to stick together and form lumps (see Dispersion; Lump Formation).

You can control the density of a slurry-type dispersion by adding liquid — the more liquid it contains, the farther apart the starch granules will be. Consequently, a slurry is very easy to work with. In fact, you can add a high-liquid slurry to a boiling mixture with absolutely no fear of causing lumps. Slurries are generally used when making gravies and sauces.   ✌

SOUFFLÉS

Soufflés come in two basic varieties — hot and cold. Hot soufflés can be either sweet or savory and are served as entrées or desserts; cold soufflés are customarily sweet and are usually reserved for dessert. While both types of soufflé have an ethereal consistency, their delicate frameworks set by entirely different processes.

When you prepare a cold soufflé, you whip egg whites or cream (or both) until they are swollen with tiny air bubbles. Then you fold in dissolved gelatin. The liquid gelatin surrounds the air bubbles, coating each one and forming a weblike network of protein molecules throughout the mixture. As the mixture cools, the gelatin network becomes firm and your cold soufflé sets (see Gelatin).

The framework of a hot soufflé sets in a somewhat more complicated manner. Most hot soufflés are a mixture of eggs and some sort of sauce base, plus a flavoring or purée. The eggs are usually separated; the whites are whipped, and the yolks are blended into the base. The flavoring or purée is then added to the base, and the whites are folded in.

During baking, the heat of the oven causes the air bubbles to expand; water contained in the mixture turns to steam, which puffs its way to the surface to evaporate. In the process, the steam also helps dilate the air bubbles. The base mixture surrounding the air bubbles consists of egg protein, milk protein, flour protein, and flour starch. When the protein and starch molecules are heated, they form a gel or weblike structure that becomes firm as the water evaporates (see Gel). The end result is a porous, three-dimensional network that we know as a soufflé.

Since the ultimate consistency of a soufflé depends on the presence of air bubbles, the manner in which you whip the whites and fold them into the base is extremely important. Many people make the mistake of over-beating egg whites, which produces a heavy, densely textured soufflé. Whites should be whipped only to the soft, droopy-peak stage (see Whipping: Egg Whites). At this stage, the air bubbles are numerous, easily visible, and moist-looking.

To preserve as many bubbles as possible, lighten the base by gently stirring in one or two generous spoonfuls of whipped whites. This procedure is a compromise — some bubbles will be broken, but lightening the base preserves many more bubbles during the folding step (see Folding).

Cold soufflés don't rise, so there's not much guesswork involved in selecting the right size dish. (Frequently a collar is used to enable the mixture to extend above the rim of the mold.) On the other hand, it's crucial that batter for a hot soufflé be in correct propor-

tion to the dish in which it's baked. Too much batter for the dish causes the soufflé to spill over the sides before the structure is set. (A collar can be used if necessary, but it doesn't produce as attractive a soufflé.) When you have too little batter for the dish, the soufflé won't rise beyond the rim. For best results, the dish should be three-quarters full. A mixture containing 3 or 4 egg whites does well in a 4-cup mold; for 5 egg whites use a 6-cup mold; for 6 to 8 egg whites, an 8-cup mold.

Choose a baking dish that's straight-sided. Curved or sloping sides impede puffability. The ideal shape is round, measuring approximately 5½ to 6 inches across, with sides about 3½ to 4 inches high. The bottom and sides should be generously buttered, then coated with bread crumbs, grated cheese, or granulated sugar. This provides a gritty surface that encourages the batter to climb up as it cooks.

Another factor that influences success is the condition of the soufflé base. A sauce base should be smooth and lump-free; strain it if necessary. Make certain that any purée to be added has been cooked until dry. Excess moisture in a purée can upset the balance of the mixture and produce a soufflé too weak to support its own weight. The sauce base should be warm, but not hot, when the egg yolks are added. As with cream puff pastry, allow the sauce to cool 5 to 10 minutes, or until the temperature drops just below 140°F. If you prepare the base ahead of time and refrigerate it, rewarm to this point before going on. A cool, congealed base produces a heavy soufflé.

Oven temperature is a critical element in baking a soufflé, too. It's absolutely essential that the oven be preheated, so that steam is produced as soon as possible. In fact, it's a good idea to give things an initial boost by preheating the oven to 425°F. Place the soufflé in the oven, and immediately lower the temperature. If you like your soufflé moist and creamy in the center, set the temperature at 375°F. for 20 to 25 minutes. For a firm, dry center, set the temperature at 350°F. and cook for 30 to 35 minutes, or until a skewer inserted into the middle comes out clean.

The best way to form a crown on your soufflé is by making a deep groove in the surface of the batter around the perimeter of the dish. Using your index finger, create a ½-inch depression in the portion of the batter around the rim. Deposit what you scoop up in the middle and smooth it over with a spatula. A crown will form better at 375°F. than at lower temperatures.

RECIPES: Cheese Soufflé; Fresh Corn Soufflé.　　　　　　　　　　　　　　&

SOUR CREAM

Sour cream derives its characteristic flavor from lactic acid, which is produced when certain bacteria feed on lactose (milk sugar) and give the acid off as waste. During the manufacture of sour cream, a bacterial culture is incorporated into pasteurized light cream. The culture consists of *Streptococcus lactis* or *S. cremoris* — both helpful bacteria that create a tangy flavor by converting lactose to lactic acid.

When you buy sour cream in the store, it contains these living bacteria. Like yeast, their activity is slowed by cool temperatures, encouraged by warm temperatures, and stopped by heat. The bacterial activity, which in this case is fermentation, continues at a slow pace during refrigeration. This explains why sour cream develops a slightly stronger flavor as it nears the expiration date on the package. Because warm temperatures speed up the bacterial growth and reproduction, sour cream, when left at room temperature, can be used to supply the bacteria needed to culture heavy cream and transform it into *crème fraîche* (see Crème Fraîche).

The consistency of sour cream resembles that of *crème fraîche*. However, unlike *crème fraîche*, which is thickened by the denaturing effect lactic acid has on milk protein (see Denaturing), commercial sour cream derives a good deal of its texture from gelatin and stabilizing gums. Since these elements thin when heated, you can't use sour cream to thicken sauces in the same manner as you would use *crème fraîche*.

Sour cream contains 16 to 20 percent butterfat and about 3 percent protein (only slightly less protein than milk). Since the fat content isn't high enough to adequately protect the molecules of protein, sour cream curdles easily (see Curdling). Therefore, before you incorporate it into a hot mixture, it should be warmed by gradually stirring spoonfuls of the hot mixture into the sour cream. When the sour cream feels warm to the touch, blend it into the main mixture and heat slowly to a gentle bubble, but don't allow it to boil.　　　　　　　　　　　&

SOURDOUGH STARTER

The distinctive, slightly sour flavor of sourdough is created by the presence of an acid. Contemporary sourdough, which often contains milk, yogurt, or sour cream, is laced with the flavor of lactic acid (see Herman); old-fashioned sourdough, made and replenished with water (milk was not readily available on pioneer wagon trains), is flavored by acetic acid.

Old-fashioned sourdough is a mixture of yeast (either trapped from the air or emptied from a package), flour, water, and maybe a bit of sugar to get things going. As the mixture sits at room temperature, enzymes in the yeast convert the sucrose contained in the granulated sugar and the flour to glucose (see Invert Sugar). The yeast consumes the glucose and gives off alcohol and carbon dioxide (see Fermentation). This is yeast-on-sugar fermentation, and is the process by which nonsour bread rises.

If you allow the mixture to sit at room temperature, certain bacteria will be attracted to the alcohol. When these bacteria consume alcohol in the presence of oxygen, acetic acid is given off and a slightly tangy flavor results. It's important to note that during the fermentation of sourdough the initial phase, or yeast-on-sugar step, continues to take place. Alcohol is still responsible for a portion of the flavor and aroma, and carbon dioxide is needed for leavening.

Since bacteria-on-alcohol fermentation is an aerobic process, you'll have greater success and develop a more assertively flavored sourdough if you allow air to come in contact with the starter. Draping a kitchen towel or double thickness of cheesecloth over the bowl will provide your starter with an abundant supply of oxygen. In addition to bacteria, wild yeasts will also infiltrate your mixture and give it a flavor totally unique to your kitchen. That's why you can't reproduce San Francisco sourdough bread on the East Coast. Even using packaged dried cultures won't recreate identical results without San Francisco air.

The only risk you run in allowing a starter access to the air is that molds occasionally drop in. The harmful ones will turn the starter pink. Toss it out and begin again. A greenish-blue mold is the same harmless fuzz that forms on cheese. Skim it off the surface and throw it away — the starter can still be used.

Sourdough starter can be refrigerated indefinitely, for chilling halts the bacterial action, but a starter won't develop in flavor unless you use it and replenish it regularly.

RECIPES: Herman Starter, Old-Fashioned Sourdough Starter.

SPICES

Spices, like herbs, are used to flavor and season food, but there's often some confusion as to which category a particular seasoning belongs in. One way to keep them straight is to remember that herbs are the leaves, stems, or flowers of low-growing plants that die down at the end of the growing season. Spices are (or are prepared from) the seeds, berries, bark, roots, fruit, or flower buds of taller plants, shrubs, and trees. Just to keep things interesting, there are plants, like dill, coriander, fenugreek, and fennel, that produce berries or seeds considered to be spices, though their leaves are regarded as herbs.

Some spice seeds and berries are used whole, such as poppy, sesame, caraway, and celery seeds; but in order for them to contribute much flavor, they need to be heated in some way. Fennel seeds are often simmered in sauces or stews, and sesame seeds are frequently toasted.

Other seeds and berries are ruptured to encourage them to release their flavor. Black and white peppercorns, cinnamon, cloves, nutmeg, and allspice are examples of spices customarily pulverized for maximum seasoning power.

Commercially prepared spices come already grated and ground, but so much flavor escapes during storage that their true essence is lost. Specialty cookware shops are beginning to carry a wide assortment of spice mills and graters, and larger supermarkets are stocking more and more whole spices, so now you can crack, crush, or crumble your own allspice, anise, black pepper, white pepper, cardamom, coriander, cumin, nutmeg, and countless other spices as you need them.

Like white peppercorns and black peppercorns, allspice can be ground in a pepper mill. Nutmeg can be ground in a specially designed nutmeg mill or grated with a small grater. Sesame seeds, mustard seeds, cumin, coriander, and anise seeds, which can be used whole or ground, have a more pronounced flavor and are easier to crush if they're lightly

toasted for 15 to 20 minutes at 375°F. When they have cooled to room temperature, you can grind them in an electric coffee mill or blender, or pulverize them with a mortar and pestle. Fennel seed and dill seed, customarily used whole, may be lightly toasted, then pulverized. Cardamom, which needs no toasting, comes encased in tiny pods. Crush the pods with your fingers to release the seeds inside, then pulverize with a mortar and pestle.

While whole spices can be ground by several different methods, I recently discovered a most efficient mill imported from France. Known as the Perfex pepper mill, it has an exceptionally smooth grinding action that easily pulverizes seeds and berries of all sizes. This mill also has a generous hopper, or wide opening, on the side that facilitates filling and emptying (see Appendix). ⇜

STARCH MOLECULES

Particles of flour, or any of the commonly used starch thickeners, contain starch granules that resemble tiny cellulose pouches. Each pouch holds a countless number of microscopic starch molecules.

When you mix a starch with cold water, the granules disperse throughout the liquid. They absorb a limited amount of the surrounding water and swell slightly.

As you heat the mixture, the granules begin to absorb water rapidly — at 60°F., they are already capable of absorbing 300 times their own weight. If you continue heating them, the granules will go on absorbing liquid. The more liquid they absorb, the larger they swell. Swelling increases until the mixture reaches the boiling point, at which time the cellulose coverings burst open, spilling starch molecules into the surrounding liquid.

Most starch granules release two types of starch molecules — amylose and amylopectin molecules. The amylose molecules are shaped like long chains coiled on themselves like balls of yarn. When uncoiled, they readily intertwine to form the three-dimensional network known as a gel (see Gel; Gelatinization). However, amylose molecules aggregate, or group together, quite easily. When they do, they push away the water previously held between them, which causes a starch-bound mixture to weep.

Amylopectin molecules are short and bushy with limbs like a fir tree. In the commonly used starches, they are more plentiful than amylose molecules. (In flour starch, for example, 75 percent of the molecules are of the amylopectin variety.)

Amylopectin starch molecules don't intertwine as efficiently as amylose molecules. Instead, they thicken a mixture by absorbing the surrounding liquid and swelling up. The branches of adjacent molecules fit in between one another. Whatever liquid has not been absorbed is held between the branches, and the mixture becomes viscous. ⇜

STIRRING

Stirring is a slow, gentle action done with a spoon, an electric mixer at low speed, a rubber spatula, or occasionally a whisk. The purpose of stirring is to combine ingredients in a manner that will neither create air bubbles nor agitate gluten (see Gluten). Stirring is also done to keep food from sticking to the bottom of a pan, and to distribute heat evenly throughout a mixture as it cooks.

Heat distribution becomes a problem whenever you cook on a stove-top burner, because the bottom of the pan, which is touching the heat source, can become intensely hot. Since the contents of the pan cook by convection or conduction, the upper portion of the mixture is always cooler (see Heat). Stirring promotes the circulation of hot molecules and evens out the temperature of the entire mixture.

Delicate preparations, such as cream fillings and egg-based sauces, must be stirred constantly to avoid overcooking near the heat source. Even when using a double boiler, you have to stir the mixture to lift it away from the bottom of the heated pan. Mixtures containing heavy ingredients need to be stirred so that items that have fallen to the bottom don't stick to the pan and overcook. These concoctions are usually not delicate, so an occasional stirring will do the job.

Recipes for stirred custard and other egg-based mixtures often suggest that you "stir in a figure 8." That indicates the slow, steady movement — in the shape of a numeral eight — of a spoon or spatula that is in constant contact with the bottom of the pan. This particular motion keeps the hot molecules circulating without drawing in air bubbles. The result is a velvety smooth mixture, free of any bubbles that might impart graininess.

If you have tried this figure-8 method with a wooden spoon and found that thickening often gets ahead of you, causing lumps or curdling, try stirring with a heat-resistant rubber spatula instead. The broad end of a spatula makes a much wider path than a spoon or a whisk, and does a better job of clearing the bottom of the pan.

Occasionally you may come across the suggestion to "stir in one direction." This is to encourage a slow, gentle, mixing motion in which the object is simply to combine the components of a recipe, not to incorporate air. In the case of yeast dough, stirring in one direction promotes the development of nice long gluten strands.

When stirring is done to blend ingredients together for muffins or quick bread, always use a slow, gentle mixing motion. Once again, the object is simply to combine elements of a recipe, such as dry and liquid ingredients, not to incorporate air. High speed on an electric mixer or vigorous, energetic arm movements are out of place here. You don't want to agitate the gluten, so keep your mixer at low speed (your hand mixing slow and gentle), and stir only "until well blended" or "until moistened" — whichever your recipe states.

One last precaution: Whenever you stir a thick mixture or a long-simmering sauce, be sure to make one final pass around the sides of the pan (preferably with a rubber spatula) to clear away any food that remains there. If you don't, whatever clings to the sides of the pan will dry out, or overcook and develop a bitter, unpleasant flavor, which it will impart to the rest of the mixture should it accidentally become incorporated.   ✍

STOCK

Stock (or broth) made from scratch, that highly praised darling of the culinary world, seems to suffer from an image problem. A great number of cooks avoid making it altogether, because they consider it to be a long, messy task, or have had disappointing results in the past. It really isn't a difficult procedure, although it does require some time.

There are several different types of stock. White stock, which is made primarily from unbrowned veal, is extremely versatile because its flavor blends with most meats. However, it's not very popular because of the high price of even the least expensive cuts of veal. Chicken stock, which can be considered a white stock if it's made from uncooked chicken, is often called chicken broth, and is used both for braising vegetables and as a foundation for some of the white sauces.

Chicken stock made from roasted, or browned, chicken is deeper in color and possesses a richer flavor. It is frequently used as a soup base. Fish stock, also called *fumet*, is made from the heads, bones, and trimmings of fish. It is used for poaching fish, and is incorporated into sauces used to complete fish preparations.

Beef stock comes in two tones — light brown and dark brown. Light brown stock is made from raw, unbrowned meat and bones. It's often called beef broth and is used for making soups, like consommé, and for braising rice and vegetables. Dark brown stock, made from roasted beef bones and meat, is used more frequently, and is the foundation for basic brown sauce (see Brown Sauce). Richness of color and flavor and ease of preparation are what many cooks want from a dark brown stock, and here's how to achieve just that.

First of all, plan to divide the task into two days' work — not so much because of the fuss involved, but because refrigerating the stock overnight allows you to remove the fat by simply lifting off the chilled layer that rises to the top.

You'll need a large roasting pan, a huge pot, a colander, meat scraps and bones, some vegetables, herbs, and wine, and about 9 hours. (Most of that time the pot can simmer unattended, so you can be off doing other things.)

Roasting the bones and vegetables not only enhances flavor and color, but also reduces the amount of scum that forms while the stock is simmering. However, it sometimes is necessary to skim the surface during the first hour, so don't add the roasted vegetables until later in the procedure, because they get in the way if you do have to skim.

You can use beef, veal, chicken, duck, or pork scraps and bones. In fact, a combination of various meats makes a more interesting stock. Turkey and lamb are strongly flavored, and liver becomes bitter from long cooking, so it's best to leave them out if combining

meats. For the best flavor, use as much meat as possible in proportion to bone.

Once you get the hang of stock making, you'll want to keep a plastic bag in your freezer to store meat and bone scraps as they accumulate, rather than spend money for them at the butcher's.

To roast the meat and bones, arrange them in a single layer in a large roasting pan. You may not be able to fit them all in, but that's okay; simply roast what is left over later and add them to the simmering stockpot. Cook in the oven at 425°F. until well browned. This can take 45 minutes to 1½ hours depending on the amount and size of the scraps. Stir a few times during cooking to promote even browning.

Transfer the roasted bones and meat to a large pot. If you're going to cook a second pan of bones, pour off the fat that has accumulated into a jar and refrigerate. If you're going on to roast the vegetables, leave the grease in the roasting pan. Add the cut vegetables, stir to coat with fat, and sprinkle on a pinch or two of sugar. The sugar will caramelize in the hot fat, and later dissolve in the stock to produce a deep, rich color. Roast the vegetables at 425°F. for 30 to 45 minutes, or until nicely browned. Don't allow them to blacken, for this will impart a bitter flavor to the stock.

To the bones in the pot, add enough cold water to cover them by 2 inches. Slowly bring to a boil, then regulate the heat so that a gentle bubble is maintained. Vigorous boiling causes the stock to become cloudy (see Clarifying Stock). Slow cooking gently softens the meat fibers and allows the heat to penetrate and melt the collagen into liquid gelatin (see Connective Tissue). The gelatin will later solidify, giving your completed, concentrated stock a jellylike consistency as it cools.

Skim the simmering stock with a shallow spoon to remove any scum that floats to the top. Add the herbs and spices and cook, uncovered. When the vegetables in the roasting pan are browned, transfer them to the pot and add more cold water to cover by 2 inches. Pour the fat from the roasting pan into a jar and refrigerate. This can be used for making *Basic Brown Sauce* (p. 346). Deglaze the roasting pan with water or red wine and add to the stock. Do not salt until later in the procedure, because salt doesn't break down or dissipate and its flavor can become too intensified when the stock is reduced.

From here on, the stock pretty much cooks itself. Regulate the heat so the liquid bubbles gently, and stir from time to time to be certain nothing is sticking to the bottom of the pan. Let the stock continue cooking for 5 to 8 hours, or until the meat falls away from the bones and the vegetables are soft enough to disintegrate.

Pour into a colander placed over a large bowl; reserve the liquid and discard the solids. If you pour the stock into a clear glass container, you'll see three distinct layers form — a dark brown layer of pure stock on the bottom, a light brown layer of stock and fat in the middle, and a layer of fat on the top. Refrigerate overnight. The fat in the middle layer will separate out, and the three layers will become two.

Now you'll be able to remove practically every bit of fat without having to clarify the stock. Lift the hardened layer off the top. Underneath, you'll see a soft, spongy layer of fat and debris; scrape that off with a spoon. Transfer the gelled stock to a large saucepan and heat gently to liquefy. Pour the warm stock through a cheesecloth-lined sieve and return to medium heat. Boil gently uncovered for 2 hours to reduce (see Reduction).

Taste to check for flavor. Adjust the seasonings by adding salt and pepper. Continue cooking until the stock develops the full-bodied flavor you're looking for. If you want to deepen the color, you can stir in a tablespoon or so of tomato paste, or add a small amount of caramelized sugar, which is what manufacturers of canned beef broth do.

Freeze the reduced stock in plastic containers or ice cube trays. (You can flip out the frozen cubes of stock and store them in plastic freezer bags to use when you need a small amount.) Stock can be frozen for up to 6 months.

RECIPES: Chicken Stock, Dark Brown Stock I and II, Fish Stock, Light Brown Stock.   ❦

SUCROSE

Sucrose, a disaccharide, is the form of sugar commonly used in cooking and baking. Highly soluble and moderately sweet, it is the sweetening agent usually associated with the term "sugar." Familiar forms of sucrose include granulated sugar, confectioners' sugar, and brown sugar. Sucrose is also the major component of molasses and maple syrup.

Sucrose is hygroscopic. In other words, it has an affinity for water and is capable of holding it in significant amounts. For that reason, sucrose, in the form of granulated sugar, increases the moistness of cakes and cookies. It also affects the consistency of whipped egg whites — when sugar is added to form meringue, it absorbs and holds a great deal of the moisture contained in egg whites. Consequently, a sweetened meringue will hold up for days, while unsweetened egg whites collapse in less than an hour.

Sucrose has the ability to delay protein coagulation. This can either be an advantage or a disadvantage, depending on whether you're baking bread or making custard. When sucrose is present in bread dough, the coagulation of the protein network slows down, which allows the dough to rise to greater heights before it sets during baking. (Keep in mind that this delaying tactic can also be achieved by using maple syrup, molasses, or brown sugar.) On the other hand, in custard containing a considerable amount of sugar, it is necessary to add an extra egg yolk to counterbalance the effect that sucrose has on coagulation.

Sucrose plays an essential part in the baking of yeast breads, although it is not directly consumed by yeast. It must first be broken down into the simple sugars glucose and fructose, which yeast cells readily ferment. Wheat flour is high in sucrose, so, consequently, there is plenty of sugar available in bread dough, even in those instances where recipes do not include granulated sugar.

Sucrose figures importantly in the browning of food, too. It caramelizes readily when heated in the presence of water (either its own inherent moisture or an additional quantity of water) and creates brown pigments called caramelans and caramelens. However, sucrose does not directly interact with proteins to bring about the brown pigments created by the Maillard reaction. Just as in its chemical interaction with yeast, sucrose must be broken down into simpler sugars in order for Maillard browning to take place (see Browning — Maillard Reaction).

Sucrose is found naturally in many vegetables, and its presence brings about some unwanted characteristics in harvested produce. For example, the sucrose in corn, peas, and lima beans rapidly converts to starch, so to maintain the quality of certain vegetables, it is necessary to retard this conversion by storing them under refrigeration.

SUGAR

Sugar plays an essential role in a number of chemical reactions that are related to the cooking process. These reactions involve not only granulated sugar (sucrose), but other forms of sugar as well, such as glucose, fructose, and lactose, which are naturally contained in food.

A fascinating aspect of sugar, and the one most significant to the cooking process, is the manner in which various forms of sugar are built up or broken down. Glucose and fructose belong to the group of sugars known as monosaccharides. They are simple, single-molecule units, but they possess the distinctive ability to link together, forming larger, more complex units called disaccharides and polysaccharides.

Simple sugars, then, are the building blocks of more complex sugars. When simple sugars join together like links in a paper chain, various other forms of sugar are created, according to the arrangement of the single-molecule units. This process, called polymerization, occurs when two or more small molecules of similar construction link together to form a larger molecule that consists of a repeating pattern of these smaller structural units.

Sugars progress in complexity from the monosaccharides to the disaccharides, a group that includes sucrose and lactose (the sugar in milk). More complex still are the polysaccharides, which include the dextrins, pectin, and starch.

Just as complex sugars are built up of more simple forms, so too, in a converse fashion, they can be broken down. When a cookbook states that starch heated too long will hydrolyze and lose its thickening power, it is referring to this decomposition process. The presence of acids, exposure to high heat, or a combination of the two will sever the links of the chainlike molecules and break them down into simpler sugars that lack the capacity for thickening.

Another example of this decomposition process occurs in the manufacture of corn syrup, where cornstarch is purposely hydrolyzed, or broken down, by the application of heat and an acid. The result is a combination of less complex sugars in syrup form. Invert sugar, which is created by the breaking down of sucrose into fructose and glucose, is also a product of sugar's unique ability to change form by shortening or lengthening its chain-like molecular structure.

All the various forms of sugar differ in solubility, sweetness, and the rate of speed at which they can be fermented by yeast. The simpler sugars, that is to say, the monosaccharides and disaccharides, dissolve easily in water, and the solution is sweet in taste; the complex sugars, such as pectin and starch, do not dissolve as readily, and the mixture produced is relatively tasteless. Glucose and fructose are fermented quickly; sucrose must be broken down into glucose and fructose in order to be consumed and fermented by yeast. Lactose isn't used as food by yeast at all; however, milk sugar is food for certain bacteria that ferment lactose. The lactic acid produced as waste during the fermentation process lends a slightly sour tang to buttermilk, yogurt, sour cream, cheese, and milk-based sourdough (see Fermentation).

Sucrose, glucose, and fructose are forms of sugar found in vegetables and fruits. As fruit ripens, the sugar content increases, which explains why ripe fruit is sweeter than fruit that isn't ripe. The sugar content in harvested vegetables does tricky things: in potatoes it increases dramatically if the potatoes are stored below 45°F., but doesn't increase at all when potatoes are stored above 50°F.; in sweet corn, peas, and lima beans, sugar quickly converts to starch, while in asparagus it turns to fibrous tissue. Chilling slows, but doesn't completely halt, this conversion of sugar to starch.

The natural substances used to sweeten food come in three different forms: granulated, powdered, and liquid. The form of sugar you use in a recipe affects not only the texture of the final product, but also the moistness, the flavor, and the sweetness.

Recipes call for specific types of sugar for a variety of reasons, and granulated sugar is the one most frequently used. Its crystalline texture helps shortening to incorporate air in the

making of cakes (see Creaming), and its ability to hold water contributes to the texture and moisture of baked goods. It caramelizes well, but it crystallizes easily (see Sugar Cooking). It also lacks the ability to react with proteins to brown food (see Browning — Maillard Reaction).

Brown sugar, also a form of sucrose, contains a small amount of molasses. For that reason, it contributes a different flavor from that of granulated sugar, and it tends to produce dense, chewy cookies and cakes. The molasses contained in brown sugar provides a trace of acid, which serves as a catalyst to invert the sugar as it heats (see Invert Sugar). Brown sugar is therefore less likely to crystallize during cooking; it melts to a golden syrup and produces caramel with spectacular coloring.

Confectioners' sugar, a powdered form of sucrose, contains a small amount of cornstarch. This makes it a good choice for sweetening whipped cream that's going to stand for a while. The cornstarch absorbs excess moisture that may be extruded, so the whipped cream remains stable for a longer period of time. Confectioners' sugar possesses a fine, grainy texture, so candy recipes often include it to encourage the formation of fine crystals.

Corn syrup is a liquid form of the simple sugar glucose. Usually flavored with vanilla, it's included in candy and frosting recipes to achieve a smoothly textured product. Since glucose is extremely reluctant to crystallize, it helps control the crystallization of mixtures containing sucrose.

Nearly flavorless, glucose is not as sweet as sucrose, so it can be incorporated in large quantities without resulting in something that's sickeningly sweet. Corn syrup retains even more moisture than granulated sugar and is sometimes used to create supermoist fudge and fondant, or, as in the case of peanut brittle, to prevent candy from drying out. Corn syrup also gives candy a chewy consistency and creates a confection that dissolves slowly in the mouth.

The other liquid forms of sugar are molasses and maple syrup, which are sucrose, and honey, which is fructose (see Honey). All are used primarily for their flavor and for their ability to contribute a moist, chewy quality to the texture of baked goods.

Pure glucose is available in either powdered or liquid form. It is used mostly by candy makers and cooks who prepare a lot of cooked frosting. If you like to make candy, you might want to try it. Either form is an excellent way to control the crystallization of sucrose. Powdered glucose is white and produces a soft fondant that's whiter in color than fondant made with granulated sugar (see Appendix).

Granulated fructose, which is a relatively new item on supermarket shelves, is often used by weight-conscious cooks. Equal to sucrose in calories per teaspoon, fructose is twice as sweet. Therefore, half as much is quite enough (and half the calories, besides). Some cooks use fructose in baking, but because only half as much is needed, the texture of foods made with it may suffer unless the recipe followed has been specifically formulated for its use. Other cooks feel that fructose loses its sensation of sweetness when heated, so they use it only with cold fruit and frozen desserts. Fructose is extremely sensitive to heat. It decomposes at 212°F., so recipes formulated for the inclusion of fructose suggest reduced oven temperatures and lower stove-top heat.

(See more at Fructose; Glucose; Lactose; and Sucrose.)   ◆

SUGAR COOKING

Cooking sugar is the basis for creating all sorts of wonderful things — candies, frostings, caramel glazes, and shimmering strands of spun sugar. So it's helpful to know how sugar behaves when it's heated.

One of the major concerns in cooking sugar is control over the formation of crystals. Sugar molecules have a maddening tendency to align themselves in symmetrical patterns that form crystals. This can be a help to you if you're making candy with a grainy texture like fudge and fondant. Unfortunately, it's all too easy for crystallization to get out of hand, resulting in a coarse, granular substance rather than the finely grained candy you had hoped for.

Then there are those preparations, like smooth frosting and nongrainy candy, where you want to avoid crystal formation altogether. Successful results from cooking sugar depend on your ability either to thwart crystallization completely or to control the production of tiny crystals.

The other great concern in the process of sugar cooking is the moisture content, which is controlled by evaporation. Sugar cooking is basically a matter of evaporating water from dry sugar or, more commonly, from a sugar-water solution. When heat is applied, the water escapes as steam and the resulting syrup becomes highly concentrated. It also becomes very hot. In fact, there's a direct relationship between the amount of water left in the syrup and its temperature. If you bring a sugar syrup to the soft-ball stage (say 238°F.) and you're not quite ready to use it, you can gain some time for yourself by adding a tablespoon of *boiling* water. The temperature of the syrup will drop slightly. But the really fascinating point is that when you bring the syrup back up to 238°F., you will have evaporated off precisely 1 tablespoon of water.

The characteristics of cooked sugar are determined by how much moisture remains. Syrup containing a considerable amount of water will be clear and fairly soft when it cools; that containing a small amount will be thicker, darker in color, and harder when it cools. To give you some idea of the relationship of moisture content to the hardness of cooked sugar, consider this: sugar cooked to the soft-ball stage contains approximately 16 percent water; when cooked to the hard-caramel stage, it contains almost no water at all.

The first step in cooking a sugar syrup is to combine a certain amount of granulated sugar and water in a saucepan. If you've ever followed a recipe that instructed you to do this, you might have noticed that, even though you stirred and stirred, the sugar stubbornly refused to dissolve completely. That's because the ratio of water to sugar is designed to be as low as possible, in order to reduce the amount of time needed for evaporation during cooking.

When you stir granulated sugar into cold water, a certain amount will dissolve. (Cold water can hold 1½ times its weight in sugar.) If you keep on adding sugar, you'll eventually reach a point at which the water refuses to accept any more, and the undissolved sugar falls to the bottom. This is called a saturated solution. No matter how much you stir a saturated solution, you can't force the water to dissolve any more sugar.

However, when you heat the mixture, more sugar begins to dissolve. That's because hot water can hold more sugar than cold water. This handy principle makes it possible for you to create a highly saturated solution, or one that contains four times more sugar than water, and avoid having to spend hours evaporating off the water.

The disadvantage of a highly saturated solution is that it crystallizes easily; as more water is lost to evaporation, crystallization becomes an even greater problem. Even in

candies that are supposed to exhibit a slight grain, you have to take special measures to control the formation of crystals, so the resulting texture will be only finely grained rather than coarse and granular.

One way to control crystallization is by using interfering agents. Acids, fats, and forms of sugar that rarely crystallize (see Invert Sugar) are considered interfering agents. Vinegar, lemon juice, and cream of tartar are the acids often used in recipes involving the cooking of sugar. They help control crystallization by transforming the complex sugar sucrose into two simple sugars — fructose and glucose — both of which resist crystal formation.

Some recipes handle the situation by including a form of fat or simple sugar. Fats, such as butter or cocoa fat, coat the sucrose molecules, making it impossible for them to join together to form crystals. Simple sugars like corn syrup, honey, and liquid or powdered glucose resist crystallization, and influence sucrose molecules to do the same.

Interfering agents make it possible to produce a completely smooth cooked sugar syrup. The next step is to develop a carefully controlled, finely grained texture. This is done in two ways — by agitation and by seeding. Recipes that instruct you to beat the cooked syrup, or to allow it to cool and then knead it, are using the agitation method of creating fine crystals. For even though sucrose molecules have been treated with an interfering agent, their desire to form crystals

can easily be rekindled. Any action that rubs sucrose molecules against each other does just that.

Seeding is another method of encouraging a controlled grain. Since sucrose molecules are easily influenced, you can add crystallized sugar, such as confectioners' sugar or previously prepared fondant, to cooked sugar syrup, and the crystalline substance will seduce the sucrose molecules into imitating its behavior. The entire mixture will take on a slightly grainy texture.

Unwanted crystallization can occur because of inadvertent seeding or agitation. When a recipe says "do not stir," pay attention. Stirring provides enough agitation to cause graininess. For that reason, a sugar syrup should never be stirred after the sugar is completely dissolved and the solution begins to boil.

Boiling, however, brings its own problems. Drops of syrup that collect on the sides of the pan will form sugar crystals. If these crystals fall back into the syrup, they will have the same effect as if you had deliberately seeded the mixture, and crystallization will take place.

You can handle this type of seeding in two different ways. Keep a pot of water boiling gently all the time you're cooking the syrup. As drops of syrup appear on the sides of the pan, moisten a pastry brush with hot water and run it around the sides of the pan. Rinse your brush in the boiling water and repeat as often as necessary to remove all traces of sugar syrup from the pan. Another method, which I don't really like because I can't check the temperature or see what's going on, involves covering the pan of bubbling syrup. The idea is to create steam inside the pan that will swirl around and wash down the sides, cleansing them of syrup drops.

Because temperature is such a crucial factor in successful sugar cooking, a candy thermometer is more than just a handy gadget — it's downright indispensable. Look for one with large, easy-to-read numbers arranged in increments of 10°F. Many candy thermometers come labeled with the various stages of sugar cooking — a feature that's particularly helpful. Most can be washed in the dishwasher, but abrupt exposure to heat is apt to break a thermometer. It's therefore a good idea to either warm it in a pan of gently boiling water or place it in the sugar syrup before it begins to boil, letting it warm right along with the syrup.

As sugar cooks, it goes through various stages, which are commonly referred to in recipes as thread (223° to 234°F.), soft ball (235° to 240°F.), firm ball (244° to 248°F.), hard ball (250° to 266°F.), soft crack (270° to 290°F.), hard crack or light caramel (300° to 310°F.), and hard caramel (320° to 350°F.). Since sugar retains a tremendous amount of heat, it's wise to remove the pan from the burner as soon as the lower degree of each temperature span is reached; cooking will continue to take place from the residual heat, and you can easily move into the next stage without realizing it.

One of the most popular forms of cooked sugar is caramel syrup or glaze. Caramel can be produced by cooking a sugar-water mixture through all the intermediate phases, until nearly all the water is evaporated and the mixture colors. Or you can make it by cooking the sugar dry. This eliminates some of the middle steps, but it must be done *slowly* over low heat; consequently, you really don't save any time.

To form caramel by the dry method, place a thick-bottomed saucepan on a heat diffuser (see Heat Diffuser). Add enough sugar to the pan to cover the bottom. Regulate the heat until it's just hot enough to melt the sugar in its own moisture, and stir continuously. You can add lemon juice for flavor, or as insurance against crystallization, but it isn't really necessary. In the process of becoming caramel, sugar is exposed to heat intense enough to cause it to decompose. When this happens, acids are released that invert the sucrose and prevent crystal formation (see Invert Sugar).

Cook the melted sugar, stirring continuously, until it begins to turn the color of maple syrup. Then slowly sprinkle in more sugar and cook, stirring, until the syrup develops a darker, amber tone. If you want more caramel than you see there, gradually sprinkle in more sugar until you arrive at the quantity you desire. Halt the cooking process immediately when you're through by placing the pan in a large container of ice water.

Preparing caramel by the dry-sugar method is a procedure I have reservations about recommending. There are just too many ways to get into trouble. You absolutely must have a thick-bottomed pan that heats evenly; you must use a heat diffuser or a burner capable of providing extremely low, even heat; and you must have patience — *tons* of it. Sugar cooked in its own moisture burns quickly and is apt to overcook in spots if it gets ahead of you. The safer approach to preparing caramel is by cooking the sugar in water.

RECIPE: Caramel Flan.

SUSPENSION

An obvious example of a suspension is chicken and rice soup, where heavy particles of rice are dispersed throughout a liquid. This is called a coarse suspension, because the particles are so large and so heavy that they will stay suspended only as long as the liquid is stirred or shaken. Once agitation ceases, the particles fall to the bottom.

A second type of suspension occurs when extremely fine particles, only a bit larger than molecules, are dispersed throughout a liquid. Because they're so small and weigh so little, these particles can remain suspended indefinitely without any stirring to keep them dispersed. This is called fine suspension or a colloid.

A colloid often resembles a solution, for it seems like all the particles have dissolved in the liquid. But if you shine a flashlight through a clear glass bowl containing a colloid, the tiny particles will act like mirrors and reflect the light so you can see the beam as it passes through. Unclarified stock is a colloid, because microscopic particles float throughout the liquid without settling (see Clarifying Stock).

A third type of suspension occurs when one liquid is suspended in another. Oil and vinegar dressing is just such a liquid-in-liquid suspension. Because neither liquid will dissolve the other, a solution can't be formed; but if you agitate a mixture of oil and vinegar (which is essentially water), the oil droplets will break up and disperse throughout the vinegar.

However, oil droplets would much rather be with other oil droplets than with water, and the instinct for oil droplets to seek each other is very strong. So once the agitation ceases, the oil droplets slither through the water, joining together and floating to the top. Meanwhile, the water settles to the bottom. This kind of liquid-in-liquid suspension is also called a temporary suspension. To form a longer-lasting suspension, you have to add an emulsifier, which will create a permanent suspension, or emulsion (see Emulsifiers; Emulsion).

T

THERMOMETERS

For anyone who wants to be successful in the kitchen, thermometers are essential equipment. A thermometer gives you a sense of security. It can cut guesswork to a minimum and help you produce dependable, consistent results.

All sorts of specialized thermometers exist. There are dough thermometers, yogurt thermometers, cheese-making thermometers, egg-cooking thermometers; for every task, it seems, there's a thermometer. But three basic thermometers will handle nearly every cooking situation.

First there's the instant-read thermometer, which registers the temperature of food immediately. Therefore, you don't have to leave it in a roast throughout the entire cooking period. This is an outstanding advantage, because the rod of a thermometer can act just like a potato nail, conducting heat along the metal to the interior of the roast and causing the area around the rod to overcook (see Heat: Conduction).

An instant-read thermometer is an extremely versatile tool. Because it measures temperatures from 0° to 220°F., you can use it for any preparation that falls within that range. Don't let the fact that it was designed for roasting meat stand in your way. Use it when making yeast dough, for testing pastry to see if it's sufficiently chilled, and for maintaining control over delicate sauces.

A second type of thermometer measures temperatures within the 100° to 400°F. range.

It is often referred to as a candy or jam thermometer, because using one makes it possible to accurately determine the various cooking stages of sugar syrup. This thermometer is also advertised as a deep-frying thermometer. Whatever it's called, its temperature range and design make it ideal for all three projects. The handiest model to use is about 12 inches long (including the plastic handle) and comes with a clip on the back so it can be attached to a pan or kettle. It also has large, easy-to-read numerals.

The third type of thermometer is just about indispensable. Every serious cook needs an oven thermometer, because most oven thermostats are off by 25° to 50°F. (I'm not exaggerating), and that's a considerable margin of error.

An oven that is not heating accurately can cause you an untold number of cooking disasters, so it's wise to test the heat of your oven cavity with a thermometer every time you bake or roast. Set the thermometer on the same rack with the pan. Then regulate the heat by altering the setting of the dial.

By the way, an oven thermometer can also detect hot spots in an oven. They're quite common but usually not too severe. If you find they do exist, you can rotate food in such a way as to even out browning. Just be sure, especially in the case of cakes and breads, to wait until the crumb structure is set before you do any major moving. Otherwise, you'll precipitate a collapse.

When purchasing kitchen thermometers, you can't go wrong with Taylor or H-B Instrument products. Both are reliable and highly respected brands. The best oven thermometers are those that operate on the principle of mercury rising in a glass tube (as opposed to those that work on a spring-based mechanism). My favorite oven thermometer is a model that unfolds to create a wide sturdy stand. It's called the Serviceman's Folding Oven Test Thermometer and is manufactured by Taylor. This particular thermometer has a large mercury-filled tube and widely spaced increment markings of 25°F. that are exceptionally easy to read from outside the oven (see Appendix).

It's important to note that variations in temperature can occur depending on where you live and what the weather conditions are on any given day. The boiling point of water is commonly considered to be 212°F. But that's at sea level, and since many people don't live at sea level, it's necessary to consider possible deviations that may take place.

Test the situation in your own kitchen by filling a saucepan with water to the depth of 4 or 5 inches. Bring it to a full rolling boil and insert an instant-read or candy thermometer. (Do not allow the bulb to touch the bottom of the pan.) One of the things you'll notice is that the temperature climbs to a certain point and stops there. That's because no matter how fast water boils, it can never get any hotter than its boiling point (see Boiling and Simmering).

It's entirely possible that the mercury will not reach 212°F. This could be caused either by the fact that you live at a high enough altitude to lower the temperature of the boiling point, or by the fact that a weather system has brought low atmospheric pressure to your area. Another thing you're bound to see is a marked fluctuation in temperature as you move the thermometer around the inside of the pan. (If you ever suspected that your burner had hot spots or that your saucepan heated unevenly, this is the way to find out. All of which illustrates the need for constantly stirring certain mixtures to distribute heat evenly during cooking on a stove-top burner.)

Once you know what the boiling point is in your kitchen, you'll be able to make adjustments when you're cooking sugar syrup or making jam, or whenever the temperature of a mixture is critical to its success. For example, if the boiling point is 210°F. in your kitchen, simply deduct 2°F. from the stated temperature.   ❧

THICKENERS

Thickeners play a critical role in the success or failure of many recipes. Puddings, custards, pie fillings, soups, and all types of sauces both sweet and savory are considered acceptable only if (in addition to good taste) their consistency is correct.

Starch is probably the first thing that comes to mind when you think "thickener," but it is only one of several elements you can use to increase the viscosity of a mixture. Eggs, cream, butter, purées, and reduced sauces may also be helpful.

All starches thicken liquid in the same way. Heated in the presence of water, the starch granules swell slightly and begin to absorb liquid. As they continue to heat, the granules go on swelling and absorbing until they burst, spilling starch molecules into the surrounding liquid (see Gelatinization). However, the various types of starches possess different characteristics.

Flour, for example, has a pasty, unpleasant flavor when raw. It's best to use it only in situations where it will be thoroughly cooked (which explains why a beurre manié should only be incorporated into dishes containing robust flavor elements, such as wine, that are strong enough to compete with the taste of uncooked flour).

Flour stabilizes egg protein, so you can slowly bring a mixture containing flour and eggs, like cream pie fillings, to the boil without curdling the eggs.

Flour has its share of pluses and minuses in the area of sauce making, too. All-purpose flour contains 10 to 11 percent protein. When flour is heated, these proteins denature, imparting a rich-looking, opaque appearance to the completed sauce. Flour-thickened sauces are quite durable. Except in the presence of a strong acid (vinegar or tomato), you can keep a sauce bound with flour at a medium bubble for a relatively long period of time without it thinning. You can also chill or freeze a flour-bound sauce and reheat it without difficulty. Any separation that might have occurred will disappear as you stir the sauce over moderate heat.

On the minus side, flour-thickened sauces don't cool graciously. Since amylose starch molecules have the tendency to group together and squeeze out the liquid that has been held in the spaces between them, you can expect a starch-bound sauce to congeal and weep if it sits on the plate too long (see Starch Molecules). To alleviate this problem, many sauce recipes suggest that you blend in an egg-yolk-and-cream liaison (see Liaison).

Cornstarch and arrowroot are also used as thickening agents. They contain very little protein; consequently, they produce a translucent sauce. Of the two, cornstarch is the more stable. A cornstarch-thickened sauce can be chilled or frozen, then reheated. Unlike flour, cornstarch cannot be held at high temperatures; it tends to lose its thickening power after 1 minute of boiling. Arrowroot reaches its maximum thickening ability far below the boil (about 160° to 170°F.), so it is an excellent choice to use with delicate eggs or cream, but it thins out if brought to the bubble. Arrowroot produces an exceptionally brilliant, sparkling sauce; it is more reliable than flour in the presence of acid and has no discernible flavor of its own — all of which makes it a superior thickener for fruit glazes. Both cornstarch and arrowroot sauces cool without weeping; however, their viscosity increases significantly as the temperature decreases (a fact you might want to consider if your sauce is going to stand for a while).

Potato flour, which is dried, pulverized potato, is similar to arrowroot in that it reaches its thickening potential far below the boil (160° to 170°F.) and will thin if subjected to intense heat. Cornstarch and potato flour have approximately twice the thickening power of wheat flour, so use half as much if you're substituting for flour.

Tapioca is often used for fruit pie fillings, because it is even more stable in the presence of an acid than arrowroot. Tapioca takes 15 to 20 minutes to fully absorb liquid, so you might consider mixing it with the fruit and letting it stand for a while before filling the crust.

Eggs thicken mixtures by coagulating. When the egg proteins are heated, they uncoil and become firm, joining together to create the sturdy weblike network that increases the viscosity of a liquid (see Coagulation). To a lesser extent, cream also thickens by coagulation. Sometimes it is blended with egg yolks to form a liaison, a combination that lends a particularly rich texture as it thickens. On other occasions, cream is reduced to a thick consistency before being added to a sauce. *Crème fraîche,* which is naturally thickened by the denaturing action of lactic acid, can also be used to increase the viscosity of a mixture.

Butter contains a natural emulsifier and is used to thicken sauces in special circumstances (see Finishing A Sauce). Actually, what happens is not so much a thickening as it is a binding. If a flour-thickened sauce begins to separate, you can pull it back together by removing it from the heat and swirling in chunks of cold butter.

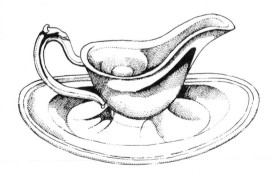

Reduced sauces, such as *Glace de Viande,* and flour-bound sauces like *Demi-Glaze* are already thick, so it's easy to see how their addition to a sauce increases its viscosity. Puréed vegetables and beans, as well as pastes made from nuts, are often stirred into soups and sauces to make them more viscous. They thicken by a principle similar to that of reduction — adding solids (instead of evaporating liquids) thickens a mixture by reducing the amount of available liquid.   ◄੭

TRUSSING POULTRY

Trussing poultry is a technique that has pretty much gone the way of the dodo bird. Turkeys come all done up with wire contraptions to hold the legs in place, and roasting chickens are packaged with string thingamajigs you can use to lift the bird in and out of the pan. So why bother with a technique that isn't necessary any more?

If you plan to present a whole bird to be carved at the table, you'll want it to look as nice as possible. Trussing poultry positions the drumsticks up against the body and back toward the breast, which tends to give the bird a plump, compact appearance. The wing tips are folded back behind the shoulders, the neck skin is pulled taut, and the flap over the body cavity is secured under the legs. All in all, a smart, tidy look.

Besides improving the appearance of poultry, trussing produces moist, flavorful meat because it prevents evaporation of juice from the cavity of the bird. It also keeps the skin from tearing. A compact shape encourages uniform heat penetration, so trussed poultry tends to cook more evenly. And the string gives you something to latch onto when you're lifting or turning a bird.

There are two ways to approach this task: the fairly complicated French method, which pierces the flesh with a trussing needle; or the English method, a quick and simple procedure using a single string and no needle at all (see illustration). The single-string method is often recommended only for small birds, but I've found it works well even with the largest turkey. A large bird requires what seems like a ridiculous length of string, but if you are fairly nimble-fingered, you'll manage without difficulty.

Use thin cotton or linen string, or the thicker cotton butcher's twine (see Appendix). Place the bird on its breast and pull the neck skin over the opening. Position the wing tips behind the shoulders to hold the neck skin closed (or fasten the skin to the back with a skewer). Turn the bird on its back so the tail is facing you. Cut a piece of string long enough to go around the circumference of the bird 2½ times. Double the string so you have an idea where the middle is.

Placing the string under the tail, position the tail in the middle of the string. Cross the strings and tie a knot over the tail. Wind the strings twice around the end of each leg, pulling them together over the cavity. Tie a knot

The single-string method of trussing works with large birds as well as small. It requires no trussing needle but does use a lengthy piece of string.

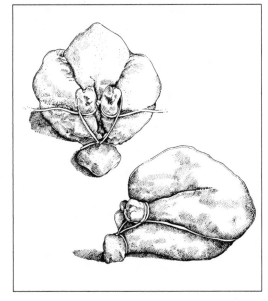

under the legs. Bring the string along the side of the bird, running it between the drumstick and the thigh (see illustration). Draw each string through the opening in the folded wings. Turn the bird over. Cross the strings, and bring each end over the wing and up through the space formed by the folded wing. This will hold the wings in place during roasting. Tie a final knot over the neck flap and cut off any excess string. ❧

TUBE PAN

A tube pan, or angel cake pan, is an ingenious device. The center tube speeds and evens cooking by allowing hot air to circulate up through the middle of the cake.

Cake batter cooks by conduction (see Heat: Conduction) — a slow, gentle heating process that takes a considerable length of time to reach the middle of an 8- or 9-inch pan. Cakes that are rich with fruit or dense with vegetable oil would develop soggy, heavy centers if cooked in a conventional cake pan; angel cake batter, with its abundance of whipped egg whites, would collapse before it cooked through. A tube pan solves these problems by eliminating the center and providing an efficient way for hot air to reach the batter in the middle (see illustration).

If you're in the market for a tube pan, choose one with a removable bottom. They're much easier to deal with when you're baking a coffee ring or some other cake that

A tube pan improves the baking of cakes that are either heavy and dense or egg-white lightened.

doesn't rise the full height of the pan and is therefore difficult to turn out.

Many tube pans come with three or four metal appendages that elevate the pan off the counter when you follow recipe instructions to "immediately invert." (This is done, by the way, because the structure of certain cakes — sponge, chiffon, and angel — is not set firmly enough to support its own weight. The structure of these cakes firms as it cools, so you hang them upside down to prevent them from falling in on themselves.) If your pan doesn't have legs, you can elevate it by setting the center tube on a narrow drinking glass. ❧

V

VINAIGRETTE SAUCE

Vinaigrette sauce is the basic French dressing. In addition to salads, it's used with hot and cold meat, fish, cold eggs, and cold vegetables. Vinaigrette is made by blending oil and water (vinegar or lemon juice) together.

A vinaigrette sauce is a temporary suspension, which means that as soon as you stop stirring or shaking it, the two incompatible elements, oil and water, will separate, and whatever herbs or other heavy ingredients it contains will sink (see Suspension).

A vinaigrette sauce usually consists of 3 parts oil to 1 part vinegar or lemon juice, but you can alter those proportions and the forms of the ingredients any way you wish to create your own vinaigrette variations. Try an aromatic vinegar like raspberry or tarragon, or substitute grapefruit or orange juice for the lemon juice. Experiment with the wide variety of oils that are available, too, such as olive, walnut, almond, sesame, or safflower; or use *crème fraîche* instead of oil. Add a single herb or combine two or three kinds. Keep in mind that fresh herbs are always more flavorful than dried, but if dried is all you have available, you can bring out their flavor by soaking them for a few hours in the vinegar or juice you plan to use.

RECIPES: Basic Vinaigrette Sauce, Red Wine Vinaigrette, Vinaigrette Sauce Variations I and II.   ✑

W

WHIPPING

Whipping is a technique designed to incorporate air into ingredients, such as egg whites and cream, for the purpose of making them light and fluffy. A large balloon whisk is the very best implement to use, and the more loops of flexible wire it possesses, the better job it will do of drawing in air and distributing bubbles.

Egg Whites

Most recipes that call for beaten egg whites instruct the cook to whip them to either the soft-peak stage or the stiff-peak stage. And therein lies a great deal of misunderstanding.

As egg whites whip, their physical characteristics undergo very distinct changes. Air bubbles, which start out large and irregularly shaped, grow smaller and smaller, until you can barely see them at all. A liquidlike surface becomes glossy and moist, then finally dull and dry. But the stages that recipes refer to don't come about abruptly; rather, a continuous, gradual progression takes place. Being able to recognize the different characteristics and knowing what change to expect next enables you to beat to precisely the right point, thereby avoiding recipe failures due to underbeating or overbeating.

The important features to keep your eye on are the size and uniformity of the air bubbles, the extent to which the surface looks moist or dry, the resistance you feel as the whisk passes through the whites, and, finally, the droopy or non-droopy condition of the peaks.

I don't want to imply that the only valid approach to whipping is by hand — I'm all for saving time and energy by using an electric mixer — but the only way to really experience what goes on during whipping is to whip egg whites by hand. Give it a try. Once you've seen and felt the different stages by hand whipping, you'll recognize them when they occur by machine. You'll know what to look for in the transformation that takes place from one stage to the next, and chances are you'll never overbeat or underbeat again.

Whether you beat by hand or by mixer, your choice of bowl and its condition are extremely important. Plastic is definitely out, because it retains grease from previous mixing jobs, and aluminum gives egg whites a greyish tint. Glass and porcelain are not only heavy and awkward to handle, but their slippery sides work against you. That leaves unlined copper and stainless steel.

Unlined copper is the best choice because it gives off a small amount of acid, which slightly denatures the whites, thereby stabilizing their consistency and speeding the whipping process. Not to mention the fact that those gorgeous copper bowls are purposely shaped so that the maximum amount of air is pulled through the whites with each stroke of the whisk. (When it comes right down to it, the shape of a bowl is as crucial to success as the material the bowl is made of.)

Second best is a stainless steel bowl. It should have a rounded bottom and be wide enough to accommodate circular strokes with a whisk. A small amount of cream of tartar, added to the whites at the foamy stage, will make up for the acid that's lacking. You can also squeeze a few drops of lemon juice into a bowl and wipe it over the surface with a paper towel. (Many recipes suggest adding salt, which encourages egg whites to stiffen and provides protection against the gumminess caused by humidity, but salt tends to toughen meringue, so it has been omitted from the meringue recipes in this book. If you prepare meringue on a rainy day, however, feel free to add a pinch of salt.) Use a 10- or 12-inch-long wire whisk with lots of wires; this too should be made of stainless steel to avoid the greyish tinge that aluminum can impart.

The bowl and whisk, or beater, should be free of all grease. And that means those tiny grease particles that float through the air — every house has them. Be sure to wash your utensils with hot, soapy water before you begin. Rinse thoroughly and dry with paper towels. It only takes a day or two for airborne grease to build up to the point where it can inhibit the successful whipping of egg whites.

Traces of egg yolk contain enough fat to prevent whites from whipping properly. Therefore, careful egg separation is essential. It's a good idea to separate each egg into two glass jars, putting the white in one jar and the yolk in the other. Then you can hold the jar containing the white up to the light to inspect for traces of yolk and bits of shell. This way, if one yolk breaks, you haven't contaminated the entire batch of whites.

Eggs separate more easily when they're cold, but whites whip to greater volume when they're warm. So separate the eggs while cold, then allow the whites to come to room temperature. (One hour is a good rule of thumb.) Place a folded kitchen towel on the countertop and set your bowl on top to discourage it from squirming around. Tilt the bowl at a 45° to 75° angle and begin to beat the whites, gently at first, using a wide, circular stroke with some lift to it. At first the whisk will meet considerable resistance from the whites; when it begins to move quite easily and the whites have turned opaque, you're approaching the foamy stage.

FOAMY STAGE: At this point, the egg whites will look like white, creamy foam. This stage is important, because it is here that you add the cream of tartar (or salt) to encourage volume. As you continue beating, more quickly now because there is very little resistance against the whisk, the air bubbles will become noticeably smaller.

Every time the whisk draws in more air, additional bubbles form and are shattered. The surface area of the bubbles continues to occupy more and more space within the egg whites. As the whites become filled with air bubbles, their volume increases and they become light and fluffy.

SOFT- OR DROOPY-PEAK STAGE: This is the most misunderstood stage. The surface of the whites is still quite moist-looking. Your whisk is once again meeting a considerable amount of resistance, and you can see lines left by the whisk as it passes through the whites. The air bubbles have increased greatly in number but decreased in size. When you lift the whisk gently, peaks with droopy tops will form.

At this point, the egg whites are firm enough in structure to support a batter or sauce, yet moist enough to blend in without breaking any air bubbles. It is the best time to fold them into another mixture (see Folding). If you are going on to form a meringue, this is the time to sprinkle in the required sugar (see Meringue).

But what about the stiffness element? What transforms egg whites from a flowing consistency to a firm consistency? Mechanical agitation, such as that provided by a moving whisk, causes protein molecules to denature, or change shape (see Denaturing). This change in shape enables the molecules to link together in a firm, weblike network. Thus, as air bubbles are drawn in, they are surrounded by firm, strandlike molecules that trap and hold the air in a stiff three-dimensional web.

STIFF- OR STRAIGHT-PEAK STAGE: With continued beating and the addition of sugar, the surface takes on a shiny gloss. The bubbles are so small you can barely see them, and when you lift the whisk gently, the peaks stand up straight. It's important to stop beating while the glossy surface still has a moist appearance. If a watery film appears between the whites and the side of the bowl, you've overbeaten.

DRY STAGE: Disaster. The whole business collapses, liquid is released, and the whites turn lumpy and grey. The reason why overbeaten egg whites turn lumpy and exude liquid is that excessive agitation causes protein molecules to aggregate. In other words, the protein molecules pull together in a group and squeeze out whatever air or liquid had been previously held within the web. This is the point at which you throw them out and try again.

Recipe failures involving egg whites are almost always due to overbeating. The philosophy that says if a little bit is good, then a lot must be better should not be applied to whipping egg whites.

RECIPES: Forgotten Cookies; Italian Meringue; Meringue Shells Melba; Sachertorte; Soft Meringue I, II, and III; Strawberry Mousse; Tortoni.

Whole Eggs

A technique far less familiar than the whipping of egg whites is the whipping of whole eggs to a fluffy golden foam. It is primarily done as the basis for that exquisitely delicate cake known as *Génoise*. Once you master the procedure of making a whole-egg foam, you can go on to prepare génoise batter, the foundation for a limitless variety of elegant cakes, tortes, and other delightful desserts.

The critical step in preparing a whole-egg foam is gently heating whole eggs and sugar over water warm enough to heat them, but not so hot as to cook them, and incorporating melted butter thoroughly and evenly.

Heating the eggs partially coagulates the protein, giving the molecules an elastic quality. This elasticity makes it possible for the molecules to trap and hold an extraordinary amount of air when the eggs are whipped. At the same time, since eggs contain a high percentage of water, the warmth will dissolve the sugar to produce a finely textured cake.

To make a whole-egg foam, break the eggs into a large bowl. Add the sugar and whisk slightly to blend. Set the bowl on a sturdy glass or mug placed in the center of a deep pan (see illustration). Pour in boiling water to the depth of 1½ inches. Regulate the heat of the burner so that steam continues to rise from the water, but the water must not bubble. Also, the bowl should never touch the water.

The warm water vapor rising up around the bowl of eggs and sugar will gently warm the eggs without any danger of curdling them. Stir the mixture occasionally with a rubber spatula to be sure it's heating evenly. You'll notice that, as the mixture warms, there's no longer a gritty sound as you stir. That indicates the sugar has dissolved.

When the mixture turns from pale yellow to deep yellow, the consistency is quite syrupy, and the mixture feels warm to the touch, remove the bowl and wipe the outside dry with a towel. Immediately begin to whip the warmed eggs, using a large whisk or a mixer

When warming whole eggs for whipping, regulate the heat so that steam continues to rise from the water but the water never bubbles.

with a balloon whisk attachment. Start at a fairly low speed and increase gradually until you're whipping at full speed. The mixture will triple in volume, and become a pale yellow foam resembling whipped cream. Use a whole-egg foam right away, as it deflates very quickly.

RECIPES: Génoise, Torte Sylvia.

Cream

When whipping cream, the whisk draws in a small amount of air as it travels through the cream and creates bubbles — just as in whipping egg whites. Repeated strokes of the whisk draw in more air and, at the same time, break those bubbles already present into thousands of tinier bubbles. As these tiny air bubbles occupy more and more area within the cream, it becomes light and fluffy.

But whipping cream differs from whipping egg whites because there's an additional factor involved — the splitting of fat particles. As the whisk passes through the cream, it not only incorporates air, but the wire loops also shatter the butterfat particles into thousands of tinier particles. Consequently, the surface area of the fat particles increases, and, since fat particles are fairly firm, the cream not only grows in volume, but also becomes stiff.

Whipped cream should not be excessively beaten. The best consistency for folding or spooning atop desserts is usually described as "lightly whipped." This stage occurs just after you see the whisk leave tracings in the cream. The texture is smooth and the cream is thick enough to stand with droopy peaks when dropped from a spoon. For piping from a pastry bag, you'll need a somewhat stiffer consistency in order for the design to hold its shape. However, stiffly whipped cream develops a granular mouthfeel that's less than ideal.

Overbeaten cream, like overbeaten egg whites, will turn lumpy and exude liquid, but the reason for it is different. Cream is basically an emulsion consisting of butterfat particles suspended in milk. The fat particles are surrounded by a membrane that contains the emulsifier lecithin. Lecithin holds the butterfat in suspension, but excessive agitation (like overbeating) ruptures the membrane surrounding the fat, and the butterfat particles begin to coalesce. Tiny lumps of butter form, and the emulsion breaks.

RECIPES: Coconut Bavarian Cream, Coconut Custard Cream Pie, Essence of Fresh Orange Mousse, Tortoni.   ◄ぅ

WHITE SAUCE

A white sauce is basically a white roux blended with a white liquid, and the liquid used determines the kind of sauce that results (see Chart, this page). A roux mixed with milk or cream creates a béchamel; mixed with white stock, a velouté. And it's possible to create three different veloutés depending on the flavor of the white stock you use. White stock can be made from veal, chicken, or fish. The veal- and chicken-based veloutés are fairly versatile and can be interchanged in most recipes, but the fish-based velouté has a distinctively fishy flavor and should only be used for dishes incorporating fish.

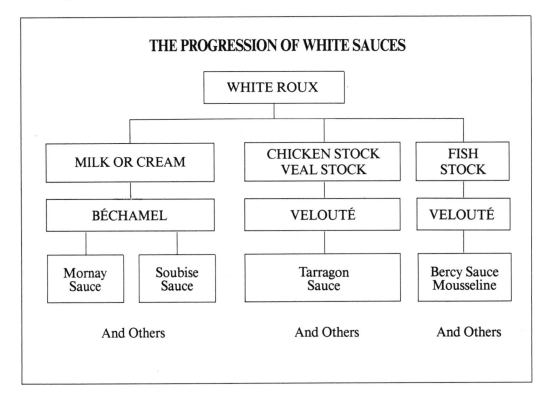

THE PROGRESSION OF WHITE SAUCES

WHITE ROUX

MILK OR CREAM — CHICKEN STOCK / VEAL STOCK — FISH STOCK

BÉCHAMEL — VELOUTÉ — VELOUTÉ

Mornay Sauce — Soubise Sauce — Tarragon Sauce — Bercy Sauce / Mousseline

And Others   And Others   And Others

There are many variations on either of these basic sauces. Adding cheese to a béchamel yields *Mornay Sauce;* adding cooked onion creates *Soubise Sauce.* Puréed shrimp blended into a fish-based velouté produces *Sauce Nantua.* Feel free to be flexible and creative. If you have some béchamel in the freezer (and it freezes very well), there's no reason why you can't use it in place of velouté and vice versa. Unless, of course, the velouté has been made with fish stock.

RECIPES: Bercy Sauce Mousseline, Chicken Stock, Fish Stock, Mornay Sauce, Sauce Nantua, Soubise Sauce, Tarragon Sauce, White Sauce with Milk, White Sauce with Stock.   ❧

YEAST

Working with yeast can be compared to handling a newborn baby. Not because it's so fragile, but because most people think it is. In fact, both are sturdier and more flexible than we give them credit for.

Yeast is a living, single-celled organism. Given the right environment and something to eat, it will grow and reproduce. Cold temperatures inactivate yeast and excess heat kills it, but you don't need special thermometers, fancy rising bowls, or thermostatically controlled boxes to work successfully with yeast — just a little knowledge and a lot of common sense.

It doesn't make much difference whether you buy yeast in a moist, compressed cake or in the form of dried granules. It's inactive, or dormant, in either case. Compressed cakes must be kept under refrigeration and don't keep nearly as long as dried yeast, but some cooks insist on their superiority over dried. The only advantage I can see is that the small amount of moisture that the compressed cake contains makes it a bit easier to dissolve.

Dried yeast comes in a strip of two or three foil packets and will keep for months on the pantry shelf. It also comes in jars and should be refrigerated after opening. Most types and brands of yeast are stamped with an expiration date. If you check the package before you buy, you shouldn't have any problems with freshness. Feel free to store dried yeast in the freezer; I've kept it this way for up to a year beyond its expiration date without any signs of diminished potency.

Many recipes suggest that you proof yeast before using it as insurance against dough that refuses to rise. This procedure, which involves combining yeast with water and some form of sugar, is usually carried out to determine whether or not the yeast in question is capable of becoming active. The vitality of yeast approaching its expiration date or of that purchased in bulk (and therefore lacking an expiration date) is uncertain. Yeast is also proofed to accelerate the fermentation process in rapid-rise breads and to give an added boost to dense, heavy doughs.

The first step in activating yeast is to rehydrate it. This is usually done by combining

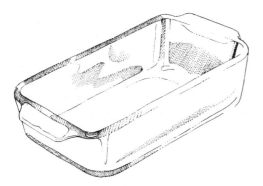

yeast with water. (Recipes that direct you to dissolve yeast in milk overlook the fact that butterfat contained in milk coats the yeast cells and seals them, significantly slowing the dissolving process. Skim milk, which is low in fat, is sometimes specified in an attempt to cope with this situation.)

Nourishment is also an important part of the activating procedure. Consequently, after the yeast has been hydrated, it must be supplied with some form of sugar to feed on so it can grow and multiply. Its favorite food is the simple sugar glucose, but glucose is only occasionally among the ingredients used in baking bread. Most yeast bread recipes do call for a certain portion of wheat flour, however, and many also suggest the addition of a sweetener. Honey consists of fructose and glucose, but granulated sugar, molasses, brown sugar, and maple syrup are all forms of sucrose, a complex sugar; flour also contains sucrose. In order to have the simple sugar it needs, yeast must break down sucrose into glucose and fructose, and it does this through the action of an enzyme it contains called invertase. This is why some directions for proofing yeast recommend using a flour-sugar combination and others suggest flour alone. Yeast can derive glucose from either source in about the same length of time, so it makes little difference which method you use. If, however, you want especially fast results, dissolve the yeast in water that has been used for cooking potatoes, because the potato sugar in the water is exceptionally easy for yeast to digest.

As yeast consumes sugar, it gives off alcohol and carbon dioxide as waste. This is the chemical reaction known as fermentation, during which yeast produces the gas that leavens dough and the alcohol that contributes flavor and aroma to bread (see Fermentation). While fermentation is taking place, yeast cells continue eating, growing, and reproducing. As the number of yeast cells increases, so do the levels of carbon dioxide and alcohol.

The critical element is temperature. Yeast activates best in liquid that's between 100° and 110°F. Since body temperature is 98.6°F., you can test the temperature by dropping some of the liquid on the inside of your wrist. If it feels just slightly warm, the liquid is perfect for dissolving yeast.

There are some rapid-mix recipes that direct you to use a liquid heated to 120° to 130°F. But yeast begins to die at 120°F., and is completely destroyed by 140°F., so this method is risky. A safer approach is to heat ¼ cup of the liquid to 100°F. and use it to dissolve the yeast. Set it aside while you heat the remaining liquid as directed. Then blend the warmer liquid into the dry ingredients. Test the mixture with your finger or with a thermometer to make sure the temperature has dropped to at least 110°F. before stirring in the dissolved yeast.

Fermentation takes place most efficiently between 70° and 80°F. Placing yeast dough on the hearth, or near another heat source, results in a fast, spectacular rise, but when fermentation occurs too quickly, it weakens the gluten structure and thus causes bread to collapse when you place it in the oven. Rapidly fermented dough also produces a loaf with a coarse, crumbly texture, and doesn't give dough time to develop full-bodied flavor. That's why you'll notice a distinct difference in taste between single-rise or rapid-rise bread and a loaf that has been allowed to rise slowly at least a couple of times. Since yeast dough develops the best texture and flavor from slow, gradual fermentation, don't worry about not having an exceptionally warm spot in which to raise bread or rolls. All you need is a draft-free area that's neither too hot nor too cold.

Then what about the cool-rise method, or refrigerator dough? Since cool temperatures deactivate yeast, any rising that occurs takes place very slowly. Here again, you'll notice a difference in the flavor of the final product, because when fermentation takes place this slowly, less alcohol is produced, and a decrease in the level of alcohol means a reduction in flavor.

When a recipe calls for 1 package of yeast, use 1 of the packets from the strip of dried yeast. One package of dried yeast equals 1 cake of compressed yeast. If you're measuring from a jar of dried yeast, 1 scant tablespoon equals 1 package.

Recipes that call for 2 packages of yeast are attempting to accomplish one of three things: produce a quick, spectacular rise; counterbalance the slowing effect a high proportion of sugar has on fermentation; or give a boost to dough containing a high ratio of flour that is low in gluten-producing proteins. In the latter case, a double dose of yeast will speed up the production of carbon dioxide, which will lighten the dough. (Dough that is low in gluten tends to be dense and heavy.) In any event, you can almost always get by using 1 package of yeast, if you don't mind the time it takes for a packet to grow and reproduce.

Dough that contains a high proportion of sugar will rise slowly, too, but don't panic. When yeast consumes large quantities of sugar, it produces excessive amounts of alcohol, which in turn slows down the action of the yeast cells. For this reason, sweet yeast breads tend to be heavier and more densely textured. You can compensate for this to a limited degree by adding extra yeast.

Salt retards the fermentation process and helps to keep it under control. Consequently, unsalted bread tends to rise very rapidly, which can result in a weak crumb structure. (The rise of unsalted bread can be controlled by reducing the amount of yeast or by placing the dough in a cool spot to ferment.) Adding salt to yeast dough will counterbalance the increased rate of fermentation that occurs in hot, humid weather, a fact that lends credence to the old adage that a pinch of salt makes better bread in the summer.

Brewer's yeast is often found in health food stores and is a nutritional supplement, not a leavener. You can add 1 to 3 teaspoons of brewer's yeast per cup of flour to bread dough to increase its nutritional value, but it has no effect on the way bread rises.

Instant yeast is the result of new developments in food technology. A form of fast-acting yeast, it comes already combined with sugar, so activation occurs immediately upon contact with warm liquid. Dough fermented with this new type of yeast is supposed to rise 50 percent faster, but my experiments with it confirmed my suspicions — using it involves a compromise in flavor. Better not to rush Mother Nature. Slow, gradual fermentation is still the only way to produce full-bodied, great-tasting bread.   ◄§

YOGURT

At the beginning of this century when the Russian scientist Metchnikoff came to the conclusion that Bulgarians live longer because they eat yogurt, he decided to name the strain of bacteria that produces yogurt *Lactobacillus bulgaricus*.

This bacteria transforms milk into yogurt in much the same way that *Streptococcus lactis* and *S. cremoris* ferment milk into buttermilk and light cream into sour cream (see Sour Cream). By feeding on milk sugar (lactose) and giving off lactic acid as waste, these helpful bacteria provide the acidic flavor characteristic of fermented dairy products. At the same time, the lactic acid also denatures the milk protein and coagulates the milk, changing it from a liquid to a custard-like consistency.

Yogurt is made from pasteurized milk inoculated with lactic-acid–producing bacteria. It possesses a more assertively acidic flavor than sour cream, and because it's lower in calories, it is often used as a substitute for sour cream in diet recipes. If you want to increase the thickness of yogurt so it will more closely resemble sour cream, line a sieve with a double thickness of cheesecloth, pour in the yogurt, and place over a bowl in the refrigerator for 8 to 12 hours, allowing the whey to drain off. Like sour cream, yogurt curdles if carelessly added to a hot sauce, so warm it gradually and never allow it to boil (see Curdling).

Z

ZEST

The rind, or peel, of citrus fruit is made up of two distinct layers — a colorful outer skin and the white, spongy pulp between the skin and the fruit.

When a recipe calls for zest (usually from a lemon or an orange), remove only the thin, outermost layer of colored skin, leaving the white part of the peel behind. It pays to be fussy, because the zest is full of sweet, flavorful oils, but the white layer of skin is quite bitter.

A specially designed tool called a zester (which looks like a shallow-pronged rake) makes the job easy. Pull it firmly across the surface of the fruit to create delicate, thin shavings of zest. In lieu of a zester, a swivel-blade peeler works almost as well. Apply light pressure as you draw the peeler over the skin, and remove only the outer layer of zest. Then proceed to chop or slice it thinly according to your recipe. Avoid using a grater to remove zest because the teeth cut too deeply into the rind and lift away a considerable amount of the bitter white portion.

Recipes sometimes fail to make the fine distinction between rind, or peel, and zest. When in doubt, use only the zest for sauces and other delicate preparations. Baked goods like breads, muffins, and cakes often develop a sweeter, more pronounced fruit flavor if you use the zest alone.

Citrus fruits are frequently sprayed with a fine coating of wax to prolong freshness, so it's a good idea to wash fruit before using the zest. Use a few drops of lemon juice or vinegar and a stiff brush. Scrub briefly, and hold under cold running water to rinse. This is especially important for those recipes that direct you to rub a cube of sugar over the surface of the skin. Since this procedure is designed to collect the flavorful oils of the zest on the sugar cube, it's important to remove as much wax as possible before you begin.

RECIPES

Appetizers

create a rough purée. Transfer to a plastic container. Lay a piece of plastic wrap directly on the surface of the mixture, smoothing out any air bubbles with your fingertips. Refrigerate for 2 hours to allow the flavors to meld.

3. Fry the bacon in a large skillet until browned. Transfer to a double thickness of paper toweling to drain and crisp. Crumble into small bits. Lay whole wheat bread on a baking sheet and slide under the broiler. Toast on both sides. Lightly spread one side of the toast with butter and cut each slice into 4 triangles. (Remove the crusts if you wish.) Arrange, buttered side up, on a serving tray. At the last minute, blend the avocado and bacon bits together and spoon into a small bowl to set in the center of the toast points.

NOTE: The correct texture can be achieved only by mashing the ingredients. Using a food processor or blender liquefies them. ◄੨

Avocado and Bacon Spread

SERVES 6

Puréed avocado, accented with Worcestershire sauce and blended with crisp bacon bits, is spread on triangles of whole wheat toast.

2 ripe avocados
2 medium shallots, finely chopped (or substitute
  1½ teaspoons freeze-dried)
2 tablespoons fresh lemon juice
¼ teaspoon salt
Generous amount of freshly ground black pepper
½ teaspoon Worcestershire sauce
½ pound sliced bacon
6 slices whole wheat bread
3 tablespoons butter, slightly softened

1. Halve each avocado, remove the seeds, and lift off the skin. Cut each half into large chunks and place in a shallow bowl, on a plate, or on any flat surface that will facilitate mashing.

2. Add the shallots (if you're using freeze-dried shallots, crush them to a coarse powder with a mortar and pestle), lemon juice, salt, pepper, and Worcestershire sauce. Combine the ingredients, mashing them with a fork to

Herbed Cheese

MAKES ABOUT 1 POUND

Serve this versatile cheese as an appetizer with crackers or toasted rounds of French bread. Or use it to stuff ribs of celery, to spoon over grilled hamburgers, or to spread on hot roast beef sandwiches.

8 ounces cream cheese
8 ounces feta cheese
2 garlic cloves, pressed
1 tablespoon chopped fresh chives (or substitute
  freeze-dried)
1 teaspoon dried tarragon leaves
½ teaspoon dried leaf thyme
½ teaspoon dried rosemary leaves, pulverized
  with a mortar and pestle
¼ teaspoon salt
⅛ teaspoon ground cayenne
1 bay leaf

1. Place the cream cheese in a large mixing bowl. Add the feta by forcing it through a coarse sieve. Set the cheeses aside at room temperature for 30 minutes to soften.

2. Beat the cheeses until well combined. Add the garlic, chives, tarragon, thyme, rosemary, salt, and cayenne. Beat to blend thoroughly. Place the bay leaf in the bottom of a 1-quart plastic container or 3-cup ceramic crock. Spoon in the cheese, packing it down tightly. Cover and refrigerate for 3 days before using to allow the flavors to meld. ◄₹

Baked Camembert

SERVES 4 TO 12, DEPENDING ON THE SIZE OF THE ROUND

Cutting into a melting round of Camembert and tasting the interplay of flavors between the delicate cheese and its coating of toasted almonds is an unforgettable experience.

1 round Camembert cheese (or substitute Brie)
2 tablespoons to ½ cup sliced almonds
2 to 4 tablespoons butter

1. Preheat the oven to 425°F. Place the cheese round on an ovenproof serving plate. (Do not remove the greyish rind because it is edible and it keeps the cheese from oozing out as it heats.) Starting at the outer edge of the round, arrange the sliced almonds in concentric circles, allowing the nuts to overlap and creating a petaled effect over the top of the cheese.

2. Consider the size of the round and melt enough butter to pour over most of the surface. Drizzle the melted butter over the almonds. Place in the oven and bake for 15 to 20 minutes or until the almonds are richly browned and you can hear sizzling sounds. The sides of the cheese should bulge gently. Serve immediately with thin slices of French bread or mildly flavored crackers. ◄₹

Sautéed Cheese Wedges

SERVES 4

These delightful morsels of hot cheese, known as Saganaki *in the Greek cuisine of their origin, may also be served as a luncheon or light supper. If you have a shallow chafing pan of the sort used to flame crêpe suzettes, you might enjoy preparing this exciting dish at the table.*

12 ounces Kasseri or Kefalotiri cheese
½ cup unsalted butter, clarified (see entry for Clarifying Butter)
Juice of 1 lemon
⅓ cup Metaxa (or substitute cognac)

1. Cut the cheese into 12 wedges about ½ inch thick. Place on a baking sheet lined with paper towels and cover the cheese with another layer of paper towels. Place in the freezer for 1 hour prior to sautéing.

2. Melt the butter in a 12-inch skillet or shallow chafing dish. Blot the surface of the cheese to make sure it's perfectly dry. When the butter begins to foam, add the cheese wedges and cook over high heat. Sauté briefly on each side (about 1 minute). When the cheese begins to soften, sprinkle the lemon juice over the wedges. Pour on the Metaxa and wait for the sauce to bubble up again. When you can smell alcohol rising from the pan, ignite with a wooden match and remove the pan from the heat. Immediately begin to place the cheese wedges on serving plates and spoon on the flaming sauce. Serve with toasted rounds of French bread. ◄₹

Potted Lobster

SERVES 6 TO 8

A dash of cognac adds drama to this captivating essence of lobster. Serve lightly chilled with toast points.

6 tablespoons unsalted butter, melted and clarified (see entry for Clarifying Butter)
1½ cups (about 8 ounces) cooked lobster, coarsely chopped
1 medium shallot, cut into quarters (or substitute the white portion of 2 green onions)
1 tablespoon cognac
2 teaspoons tomato paste
2 large egg yolks

½ cup heavy cream
½ teaspoon dried tarragon leaves
¼ teaspoon salt
Freshly ground white pepper or cayenne

1. Measure 4 tablespoons of the melted butter into the container of a blender or processor. Add the lobster, shallot, cognac, and tomato paste. Whirl until smooth, but do not liquefy.

2. In a thick-bottomed saucepan, whisk together the egg yolks and cream. Stir in the lobster purée. Add the tarragon, salt, and pepper and place over medium-low heat. Cook, stirring constantly, until the egg yolks coagulate and thicken the mixture. Do not allow it to boil. Transfer to a generously buttered 2½-cup ramekin or ceramic crock. Smooth the surface and pour on the remaining 2 tablespoons of melted butter. Refrigerate for 2 hours or until the layer of butter is solidified.   ❧

Shrimp Pâté Canapés

MAKES 24 CANAPÉS

Complexly flavored, yet not overwhelming, these hot canapés provide just the right anticipatory note for the meal to come.

1 cup dry white vermouth
½ cup water
2 sprigs fresh parsley
1 bay leaf, broken in half
4 black peppercorns
12 medium-size fresh shrimp, unpeeled
½ cup heavy cream
¼ cup unsalted butter
¼ cup freshly grated Parmesan cheese
1 tablespoon cognac
¼ teaspoon salt
Generous amount of freshly ground nutmeg
12 slices thin white bread

1. Combine the vermouth, water, parsley, bay leaf, and peppercorns in a nonreactive 4½-quart saucepan and bring to a boil. Add the unpeeled shrimp and toss to coat with

liquid. Regulate the heat so that the liquid barely simmers. Cover the pan and steam the shrimp for 5 to 7 minutes. It's important not to overcook shrimp. When done, they take on a pinkish hue, a curved shape, and a firmness to the touch. Empty the shrimp and the liquid into a bowl to cool.

2. Peel the cooled shrimp and discard the intestinal vein. Cut into quarters and place in the container of a food processor. Add the heavy cream, butter, Parmesan cheese, cognac, salt, and nutmeg. Pulse 10 or 12 times until the mixture is smooth. (In lieu of using a processor, whirl the cream, butter, cheese, cognac, salt, and nutmeg in a blender until well mixed. Then add the pieces of shrimp and whirl to incorporate.)

3. Cut 24 circles or triangles from the bread and toast one side. Spread the shrimp pâté on the untoasted side and bake at 350° F. for 8 to 10 minutes to warm.   ❧

Polenta Crostini with Gorgonzola

SERVES 6 TO 8

Rounds of polenta are fried until crisply crusted and then spread with a creamy blend of butter and Gorgonzola cheese.

2 cups yellow cornmeal
9 cups water
1 teaspoon salt
½ cup freshly grated Asiago or Parmesan cheese
4 tablespoons butter
6 ounces Gorgonzola cheese (preferably the sweet, green-veined variety)
3 tablespoons unsalted butter
Vegetable oil

1. Generously butter a 10×15-inch jelly roll pan. In a 4-cup measure, disperse the cornmeal in 1 cup of the water to prevent lumping.

2. Bring the remaining water and the salt to a boil in a 4½- to 6-quart saucepan. With the water bubbling vigorously, pour in the corn-

meal-water mixture. Stir continuously. When the mixture boils, reduce the heat and cook uncovered at a gentle bubble for 20 minutes. Stir occasionally during the first 10 minutes, but as the water evaporates and the polenta thickens, stir continuously to prevent the mixture from scorching.

3. Blend in the grated Asiago cheese, and continue cooking, stirring continuously. Polenta is thickened completely when a spoon will stand upright in the center without being held. Remove from the heat and stir in the 4 tablespoons butter. Pour into the prepared pan, smoothing the top with a knife. Refrigerate until cool and firm (about 4 hours).

4. Set out the Gorgonzola and the 3 tablespoons unsalted butter and allow them to soften. Turn the chilled polenta out onto a work surface. Using a 2-inch biscuit cutter, cut rounds from the sheet of polenta (you'll get about 32 to 35 rounds). Heat the vegetable oil in a 12-inch skillet and fry the polenta rounds over medium-high heat until their surfaces develop a slightly puffy, deep golden appearance. Transfer to absorbent paper with a slotted spoon. (The rounds may be prepared ahead to this point and refrigerated.)

5. Preheat the oven to 425°F. Force the Gorgonzola through a coarse sieve. Add the softened butter and beat with a wooden spoon until creamy. Arrange the polenta rounds on an ungreased baking sheet. Place in the oven for 8 to 10 minutes or until heated through. Immediately spread with the Gorgonzola mixture and serve hot.   ◄§

Caponata with English Muffin Melba

SERVES 8

Chunks of bright red sweet bell pepper and glossy-skinned purple eggplant are tossed together to create this stunning relish that tastes every bit as good as it looks. English muffins sliced thinly and crisped in the oven (see Note) *provide an interesting accompaniment for caponata and other kinds of relish spreads.*

3 or 4 small eggplants (about 1½ pounds)
2 large red sweet bell peppers
¼ cup olive oil
1 large onion, cut in half from stem end to root end, and then sliced crosswise
2 ribs celery, diagonally sliced
2 garlic cloves, minced or pressed
1 can (16 ounces) Italian-style plum tomatoes, drained
2 tablespoons red wine vinegar
1 tablespoon sugar
1 tablespoon capers, nonpareille variety, drained and rinsed
10 pitted black Greek or Italian olives, coarsely chopped
½ teaspoon salt
Generous amount of freshly ground black pepper
English Muffins (p. 232)

1. Wash the eggplants and blot dry. Trim off the ends but do not peel. Cut into ¾-inch cubes. (Small, young eggplants don't contain any bitter juices, so there's no need to salt and drain the cubes.) Core and seed the red peppers and cut into ¾-inch chunks.

2. Heat the oil in a 12-inch skillet. Add the red peppers, onion, celery, and garlic. Toss to coat with oil and stir over medium heat until the onion is tender. Blend in the eggplant cubes and stir over medium heat until they soften (about 5 minutes).

3. Remove the pan from the heat and add the tomatoes by pressing them with a wooden pestle through a coarse sieve. Discard the seeds and bits of tomato left in the sieve. Add the vinegar, sugar, capers, black olives, salt, and pepper. Stir to combine and place over medium heat. Cook uncovered for 10 to 15 minutes, stirring occasionally. When most of the liquid has evaporated and the vegetables are tender, transfer the caponata to a serving dish and surround with English Muffin Melba toasts. Serve hot or at room temperature.

NOTE: To prepare English Muffin Melba, slice English Muffins (p. 232) into 4 or 5 very thin slices. (English Muffins sold in supermarkets are usually halved and consequently difficult to work with. If you want to use store-bought muffins, look for a brand that doesn't come already split.) Arrange the muffin slices on a baking sheet and place in a 350°F. oven for 10 to 15 minutes or until crisp and lightly browned.   ❧

Basil Torta

SERVES 16

With its alternating layers of creamy white cheese and brilliant green pesto, this cheese torta makes a stunning addition to an hors d'oeuvre buffet. Cut into slim wedges or slices and serve with toasted rounds of French bread or crackers.

1 pound Robiola cheese (see Note)
1 pound Mascarpone cheese (see Note)
2 generous handfuls of fresh basil leaves, rinsed and dried
¼ cup unsalted butter, softened
⅓ cup olive oil
¾ cup freshly grated Asiago or Parmesan cheese
2 garlic cloves
½ cup pine nuts (or substitute walnuts)
¼ teaspoon salt

1. Set the Robiola and Mascarpone cheeses in separate mixing bowls. Allow them to sit at room temperature until soft enough to spread easily (about 1 hour).

2. Meanwhile, prepare the mold by lining a 6-cup charlotte tin or loaf pan with cheesecloth. (Cut a 17- or 18-inch square from a double thickness of cheesecloth. Moisten with water and lay the cheesecloth inside the mold, letting the corners hang out over the side.) Then prepare the pesto by whirling the basil, butter, olive oil, cheese, and garlic to a paste in a blender or processor. Add the nuts and salt and whirl only briefly so that the nuts retain a coarse texture.

3. Beat the Robiola and Mascarpone cheeses until they reach a light, spreadable consistency like that of cream cheese. Divide each cheese into 3 almost equal portions.

(Since a charlotte tin tapers slightly, each successive layer will require slightly more cheese.) Divide the pesto into 5 portions.

4. Using your fingers or the back of a spoon, spread one-third of the Mascarpone into the lined mold. Spread on a thin layer of pesto, then top with a layer of Robiola. Repeat twice, ending with a layer of Robiola. (You will have 6 layers of cheese, alternating with 5 layers of pesto.) Bring up the corners of the cheesecloth and lay them over the surface of the cheese. Press down firmly to set the layers. Refrigerate for 1½ to 2 hours. As soon as the cheese feels firm to the touch, invert onto a serving platter and remove the cheesecloth. If you don't plan to serve the *torta* immediately, lay plastic wrap directly on the surface of the cheese and return it to the refrigerator. (The indentations left by the cheesecloth are considered an integral part of a *torta*; however, if you prefer a smooth surface, you can remove the lines by smoothing them out with a knife or metal spatula heated in boiling water.) Garnish with fresh basil leaves if you like.

NOTE: If you're unable to purchase Robiola and Mascarpone cheese, this basil *torta* can be created from equal parts of cream cheese and unsalted butter. Allow 1 pound of cream cheese and 1 pound of unsalted butter to soften, and then blend together thoroughly. Layer with basil pesto as described above.   ❧

Herbed Cheesecake

SERVES 12

A savory, herb-flavored cheesecake to serve as an appetizer.

1 pound cream cheese
8 ounces soft, white goat cheese (chèvre), such as Montrachet
6 green onions
3 large eggs
2½ cups sour cream
2 garlic cloves, minced or pressed

1 teaspoon dried tarragon leaves
1 teaspoon dried basil
½ teaspoon dried oregano
½ teaspoon dried rosemary leaves, pulverized
   with a mortar and pestle
½ teaspoon dried leaf thyme
½ teaspoon salt
Generous amount of freshly ground white pepper

1. Combine the cream cheese and goat cheese in a large mixing bowl. Allow to soften for 30 minutes. Thinly slice the green onions, including most of the green portion. (Reserve the green slices for garnishing the finished cheesecake.) Generously butter a 9-inch springform pan. (No crust is needed, but if you wish, you may line the pan with Press-In Pastry, p. 294. Bake as you would a pie shell in a 350°F. oven for 20 minutes.)

2. Preheat the oven to 325°F. Beat the cheese at high speed until light and fluffy. Add the eggs, one at a time, beating continuously. Blend in 1 cup of the sour cream. Add the white portion of the green onions and the garlic, tarragon, basil, oregano, rosemary, thyme, salt, and pepper. Blend thoroughly.

3. Pour into the prepared pan and bake for 50 to 60 minutes or until a quarter-size area in the center barely jiggles when you nudge the pan. Remove from the oven and spread the remaining 1½ cups sour cream over the top. Return to the oven for 10 minutes. Turn off the oven and allow the cheesecake to cool inside with the oven door left ajar. Scatter the reserved green onion over the top and serve at room temperature. (If made ahead and chilled, allow the cheesecake to warm at least 2 hours.) Spread on crackers or small bread rounds, or offer in slim wedges.   ◄❧

Falafel

MAKES ABOUT TWENTY-FOUR 1½-INCH
PATTIES OR WALNUT-SIZE BALLS

Puréed chickpeas, or garbanzo beans, form the basis for these flavorful tidbits. Shape into small patties and stuff inside pita bread with shredded lettuce and chunks of fresh tomato, or make into tiny balls and present as an appetizer with a dipping sauce, such as Fiery Sauce (p. 353) or Yogurt Sauce (p. 354).

2 cups canned garbanzo beans, drained and
   rinsed
1 large egg
½ cup whole wheat bread crumbs
1 medium onion, finely chopped
2 garlic cloves, minced or pressed
1 tablespoon fresh lemon juice
2 tablespoons chopped fresh parsley
½ teaspoon salt
½ teaspoon ground cumin
½ teaspoon ground coriander leaves (cilantro)
¼ teaspoon freshly ground black pepper
¼ teaspoon ground turmeric
Vegetable oil

1. Purée the garbanzo beans in a food mill, blender, or food processor.

2. Combine with the remaining ingredients, except oil, and beat until smooth. The mixture will be moist and sticky. Shape into walnut-size balls or 1½-inch patties. (If the mixture sticks to your hands, flour them with whole wheat flour.)

3. Pour the oil into a 12-inch skillet to a depth of ½ inch. Heat until the surface ripples and cook 8 to 10 pieces at a time. Turn frequently to encourage even browning, and then transfer to absorbent paper to drain. Serve hot or warm.   ◄❧

Glazed Meatballs

MAKES SIXTY ¾-INCH BALLS

Because these appetizer meatballs are made primarily from ground pork, they are exceptionally moist and flavorful. Serve with the zesty glaze that appears here or with a double recipe of Sweet and Sour Sauce (p. 354).

2 large eggs
1 medium onion, minced
½ cup dry, unseasoned bread crumbs

1½ teaspoons dried leaf thyme
1 teaspoon salt
Generous amount of freshly ground black pepper
⅓ cup chopped fresh parsley
1½ pounds ground pork
½ pound ground beef

GLAZE
1 teaspoon sugar
2 tablespoons dry mustard
⅓ cup cool water
⅓ cup ketchup
3 tablespoons molasses
2 tablespoons red wine vinegar

1. Preheat the oven to 375°F. Lightly grease a 9×13-inch baking pan. Beat the eggs in a large bowl. Add the onion, bread crumbs, thyme, salt, pepper, and parsley. Stir to blend.

2. Add the pork and beef, breaking the meat apart with your fingers. Blend well, take up by teaspoonfuls, and shape into tiny balls. Arrange in a single layer in the prepared baking pan. Cover with aluminum foil and bake for 20 minutes. Remove the foil and continue baking for 10 to 15 minutes or until slightly browned. Turn occasionally to promote even browning.

3. Prepare the glaze by dispersing the sugar through the dry mustard in a small bowl. Add the cool water and stir to dissolve. In a 1½-quart nonreactive saucepan, combine the dissolved mustard and sugar, ketchup, molasses, and vinegar. Place over low heat and simmer uncovered for 10 minutes. Using a slotted spoon, transfer the meatballs to a 12-inch skillet. Pour on the glaze and toss to coat the meatballs evenly. Place over low heat, cover, and cook slowly for 30 minutes to mellow the mustard.   ⋖ఢ

Gingered Chicken Wings

SERVES 8 TO 10

Chicken parts have become so specialized that you can often find the first section of the

wing packaged separately. These meaty wing segments, labeled "drumettes," make succulent (but messy) appetizers.

4 pounds chicken wings (3-segment style or drumettes)
Oil for deep frying
⅔ cup naturally brewed soy sauce
½ cup light brown sugar
½ cup dry sherry
2 garlic cloves, minced or pressed
2 tablespoons finely chopped fresh ginger root
1 tablespoon cornstarch
2 tablespoons red wine vinegar

1. Divide the wings by cutting at both joints. Discard the wing tips or freeze for stock. If you're using drumettes, simply pat them dry with a paper towel. ˉ

2. Heat the oil to 370°F. Add 8 to 10 wings at a time and fry for about 8 minutes or until the skin is crisp and golden. Transfer to absorbent paper to drain. Repeat until all the chicken wings are cooked.

3. Preheat the oven to 350°F. In a 2½-quart nonreactive saucepan, combine the soy sauce, brown sugar, sherry, garlic, and ginger root. Place over high heat and stir until the sugar dissolves. Remove from the heat. In a glass measuring cup, dissolve the cornstarch in the vinegar. Add to the soy sauce mixture and return to high heat. Stirring continuously, cook until the sauce bubbles and thickens slightly.

4. Generously butter two 9×13-inch baking dishes. Arrange the chicken wings in the two pans and pour the hot sauce over the wings, dividing it between the two pans. Place in the preheated oven and bake uncovered for 15 minutes. Turn the wings over and continue cooking for an additional 15 minutes.   ⋖ఢ

Ham Biscuits

MAKES 25 BISCUITS

Shaped into small squares and stuffed with slivers of ham, these delicate biscuits make an elegant appetizer.

2 cups all-purpose flour, scoop measured

3 teaspoons baking powder

½ teaspoon salt

¼ cup cold butter

2 teaspoons snipped fresh chives (or substitute freeze-dried)

1 cup heavy cream

¼ pound prosciutto or Westphalian ham, thinly sliced

1. Preheat the oven to 425°F. Sift the flour, baking powder, and salt into the largest bowl you have. Combine thoroughly by blending with a fork or wire whisk.

2. Cut the cold butter into 16 small chunks and add to the dry ingredients. Using a table knife, or an 8-inch palette knife, cut the butter into the flour until the pieces resemble tiny peas. Stir in the snipped chives.

3. Gradually pour in the cream, tossing the mixture constantly with the knife. Add only enough liquid to form a soft, malleable dough. When the dough begins to hold together, gather it into a ball with your fingertips and roll it around the inside of the bowl to pick up any stray particles.

4. Turn out onto a *lightly* floured board and dust the top of the dough with flour. Knead with 20 to 25 strokes. Lightly press the dough into a flat square, ½ inch thick. Roll with a rolling pin to smooth the top, striving for a 10-inch square. Trim the edges with a floured chef's knife using a firm downward motion: do not pull the knife through the dough; lift it straight up. Flour the knife and cut the dough (in the same way) into 5 strips. Then divide the strips into 5 equal portions to form 25 squares, each measuring slightly less than 2×2 inches.

5. Transfer the squares to an ungreased baking sheet without sides. Place them 1½ inches apart so the sides of the biscuits will crisp. Place in the preheated oven and bake for 10 to 12 minutes or until nicely browned. Cool on a rack and split gently with a fork. Place ham between the biscuit halves and serve warm or at room temperature.   ❧

Goat Cheese Beignets

MAKES 36 SMALL OR 12 LARGE BEIGNETS

These crisp, deep-fried cheese puffs are enhanced by the tang of crumbly goat cheese. Drop the batter by teaspoonfuls to create small appetizer puffs or by tablespoonfuls for larger puffs to serve as luncheon. Large puffs may be served on a pool of Summer Sauce (p. 352) or Buttered Tomato Sauce (p. 351).

1 cup cold water

4 tablespoons unsalted butter, cut into 16 small chunks

¼ teaspoon salt

1 cup all-purpose flour, scoop measured

6 ounces soft goat cheese (chèvre), such as Montrachet, crottin, or bûcheron

4 large eggs

Vegetable oil for deep frying

1. In a thick-bottomed saucepan, combine the water, butter, and salt. Stir over medium heat until the butter melts. Stop stirring and allow the mixture to come to a rolling boil. Immediately remove the pan from the heat and add the flour. Beat vigorously with a wooden spatula. Return to medium-low heat and cook, stirring, until the batter pulls together into a smooth, shiny mass. When the dough pulls away from the sides of the pan, test for doneness by pinching with two fingers. The batter is cooked when it no longer sticks to your fingers. Immediately empty into a large bowl. Allow the batter to cool for 5 to 10 minutes (or to below 140°F.), stirring occasionally to prevent a skin from forming.

2. Meanwhile, crumble the cheese and set aside. Add the eggs to the cooled batter one at a time, beating vigorously after each addition to create a smooth, shiny batter. Blend in the cheese.

3. Heat the oil to 370°F. Dip a teaspoon into the fat to grease it. Then take up the dough by rounded teaspoonfuls. Gently push the dough from the spoon into the hot fat and cook the *beignets* until they are crisply crusted and golden brown. Serve hot.

(See entry for Cream Puff Pastry.)   ❧

King Crab Puffs

MAKES ABOUT 3 DOZEN

Serve these delicate crab puffs with Sweet and Sour Sauce (p. 354) or your favorite seafood cocktail sauce. They may be made ahead of time and frozen.

1 cup cold water
4 tablespoons butter, cut into 16 small chunks
½ teaspoon salt
Generous pinch of ground cayenne
1 cup all-purpose flour, scoop measured
½ teaspoon Worcestershire sauce
1 tablespoon chopped fresh chives (or substitute freeze-dried)
4 or 5 large eggs
12 ounces cooked fresh king crabmeat (or frozen crabmeat, defrosted)
Vegetable oil for deep frying

1. Prepare *pâte à choux* (cream puff pastry) by combining the water, butter, salt, and cayenne in a thick-bottomed 1½-quart saucepan. Stir over medium-high heat until the butter melts. Stop stirring and allow the mixture to come to a vigorous boil. Immediately remove the pan from the heat and add the flour. Beat vigorously with a wooden spatula. Return to burner and cook over medium-low heat, stirring, until the batter pulls together into a smooth, shiny mass. Continue stirring the dough *(panade)* over medium-low heat to dry it. A white granular film will appear on the bottom of the pan. Do not allow it to burn and don't attempt to incorporate it into the dough. Test the *panade* for doneness by pinching with two fingers. When it no longer sticks to your fingers and takes on a putty-like consistency, the *panade* is cooked. Immediately empty it into a large bowl and allow to cool for 5 to 10 minutes (or to below 140°F.), stirring occasionally to prevent a skin from forming. Beat the Worcestershire sauce and chopped chives into the *panade.*

2. Lightly whisk 4 eggs and pour into a measuring cup. If necessary, whisk the remaining egg and add enough of it to form 1 cup of eggs.

3. Using a wooden spatula or the paddle attachment of an electric mixer, beat one-quarter of the whisked eggs into the *panade.* Continue beating until the *panade* accepts the eggs and the mixture smoothes out. Repeat twice. Add the last portion of the eggs in a thin stream. Check for proper consistency by lifting the beater or allowing the dough to drop from a spoon. It should fall in a thick, heavy ribbon and leave a peak that stands stiff. Keep in mind that the goal is to add as much egg as possible without overly thinning the dough. (Cream puff pastry [*pâte à choux*] may be made to this point and refrigerated for 2 or 3 days, but for best results it must be brought to room temperature before shaping.) Flake the cooked crabmeat and make certain it is well drained. Blend into the completed *pâte à choux.*

4. Heat the vegetable oil to 370°F. Take up the pastry by rounded teaspoonfuls (using the teaspoon that belongs to a measuring spoon set tends to produce a more rounded effect). Gently push the dough from the spoon into the hot fat. Cook only 5 or 6 puffs at a time and turn frequently with a slotted spoon to promote even browning. Transfer to absorbent paper to drain. Serve immediately, keep warm in a 350°F. oven with the door left ajar, or freeze in an airtight plastic bag. (If using frozen, let them defrost, and then heat in a 375°F. oven for 8 minutes. Turn off the oven, leave the door ajar, and let sit inside for 3 to 5 minutes to dry and crisp slightly.)   ❧

Cheese-Filled Rice Croquettes

MAKES FIFTEEN 2½-INCH CROQUETTES

In Rome, these rice croquettes are called suppli al telefono *because the hot stringy mozzarella hidden inside forms "telephone lines" when the croquette is broken apart. It's important to use starchy Arborio rice in this recipe so that the croquettes will hold together during frying.*

¾ cup raw Arborio rice (or substitute 2¼ cups leftover **Risotto Milanese, p. 316**)

2 cups chicken broth

Small pinch saffron threads, pulverized with a mortar and pestle (optional)

4 tablespoons butter

1 small onion, finely chopped

¼ cup dry white wine

Salt and freshly ground black pepper to taste

¼ cup freshly grated Parmesan cheese

2 large eggs

4 ounces mozzarella cheese, cut into ½-inch cubes

¾ cup dry, unseasoned bread crumbs

Vegetable oil for deep frying

1. If you're using leftover Risotto Milanese, allow it to warm to room temperature and then skip to step 6; otherwise, prepare the rice by bringing the broth to a boil in a 1½-quart saucepan. Ladle ½ cup of the hot broth into a small bowl. Stir in the saffron and allow it to steep. Set aside. Reduce the heat until the broth barely simmers.

2. In a wide, thick-bottomed sauté pan or deep skillet, melt 2 tablespoons of the butter over medium-high heat. Add the onion and cook, stirring, until it is soft.

3. Blend in the rice, stirring to coat the surface of each kernel with butter. Continue stirring over medium-high heat until the rice turns opaque. Blend in the wine and the reserved ½ cup saffron-broth. Stir continuously until all the liquid is absorbed.

4. Add the simmering broth to the rice and onion mixture one ladleful at a time. Stir over medium-high heat with a wooden spoon or spatula until the rice absorbs all the liquid. When the bottom of the pan is dry and the rice appears ready to stick to the pan, stir in another ladleful of broth. Repeat this procedure for about 20 minutes, in which time nearly all the broth will be used up. Test the rice by biting a kernel. It should be tender but still resistant to the teeth. Continue stirring in hot broth until the rice is done. Season with salt and pepper to taste.

5. Remove the rice from the heat. Allow it to stand uncovered for 1 minute. Meanwhile,

cut the remaining 2 tablespoons butter into small chunks. Gently blend into the rice the chunks of butter and the Parmesan cheese until the butter is melted. The rice should be slightly sticky and intact (do not mash the kernels as you stir). Allow the rice to cool to room temperature.

6. Whisk the eggs in a small bowl and blend into the cooled rice. Scoop up a scant tablespoon of rice and place it in the palm of your hand. Place a cube of mozzarella in the center and top with another tablespoonful of rice. Press into a ball and roll in the bread crumbs. Place on a baking sheet lined with waxed paper. Repeat until all the mixture is shaped into croquettes. Chill the rice balls for 30 to 45 minutes or until they feel firm to the touch. Deep fry in oil heated to 370°F. When golden brown, drain on absorbent paper and transfer to a 250°F. oven to keep croquettes warm until all are cooked. Serve as an appetizer, first course, or side dish. ◄₰

Fried Pork Packets

MAKES ABOUT 50 PACKETS

In this recipe, won-ton wrappers create a crispy outer crust for an oriental-style pork and mushroom filling. Because the wrappers are folded into triangles, you can stuff them with a generous amount of filling. Serve hot with Hot Mustard Sauce (p. 354) or Sweet and Sour Sauce (p. 354).

1 medium head romaine lettuce

6 green onions

Peanut oil (or substitute vegetable oil)

12 large fresh mushrooms, coarsely chopped

1 garlic clove, minced or pressed

1 pound ground pork

4 tablespoons peach jam

2 tablespoons naturally brewed soy sauce

1 teaspoon freshly grated ginger root

½ teaspoon salt

Generous amount of freshly ground black pepper

1 tablespoon cornstarch

2 tablespoons cold water
50 won-ton wrappers
Vegetable oil for deep frying

1. Prepare the romaine by rinsing the leaves and blotting them dry. Stack them one on top of the other and slice thinly across the ribs, creating fine shreds. Slice the green onions, including three-quarters of the green portion.

2. Pour enough oil into a 12-inch skillet to cover the bottom of the pan. Place over high heat. Add the onions, mushrooms, and garlic. Cook, stirring constantly, until the onions are limp and the mushrooms have given up their moisture.

3. Add the pork and cook, stirring, for 3 or 4 minutes or until the pork is no longer pink. Add the romaine and stir, tossing to combine with the other ingredients. Continue cooking over high heat until the romaine is limp. Stir in the peach jam, soy sauce, ginger root, salt, and pepper. Empty into a bowl to cool.

4. In a small bowl, blend the cornstarch and water. Remove 4 won-ton wrappers from the package and twist the package closed so the remaining wrappers won't dry out. Lay them on the counter, each turned in a diamond shape, with 1 point near you. Place a

To seal Fried Pork Packets, brush with a cornstarch mixture, then fold into triangles.

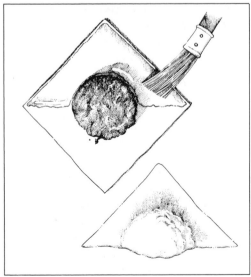

generous teaspoonful of filling in the center of each one. Brush the cornstarch mixture over the edges of one-half of the wrapper, proceeding from the left-hand point around to the right-hand point (see illustration). Bring up the point nearest you to form a triangle and seal. Refrigerate for 1 hour. Deep fry 4 or 5 at a time in oil preheated to 370°F. Turn with tongs to encourage even browning. When golden brown, transfer to absorbent paper. Serve immediately or chill and then freeze in an airtight plastic bag. Reheat for 15 minutes in a 375°F. oven in a single layer without defrosting.

NOTE: This filling and the one that appears in Shrimp-Filled Egg Rolls (p. 302) may be used interchangeably.   ☙

Flaky Cheese Triangles (Tiropetes)

MAKES 60

These cheese-filled multilayered pastries are easier to make than they appear to be. Best of all, they can be prepared weeks in advance and frozen in airtight plastic bags. A few minutes in the oven turns them into crisp, flaky triangles of melted cheese.

½ pound filo dough
8 ounces feta cheese
8 ounces cream cheese
½ pound plus 2 tablespoons butter
1 medium onion, finely chopped
2 garlic cloves, minced or pressed
1 large egg
½ cup freshly grated Parmesan cheese
½ teaspoon dried leaf thyme
½ teaspoon dried oregano
½ teaspoon dried basil
¼ teaspoon salt

1. Set the wrapped filo dough out to warm to room temperature. (Sheets of chilled filo tear when you try to separate them.) Place the feta and cream cheese in a large mixing bowl to soften.

2. Meanwhile, melt 2 tablespoons of the butter in a 6-inch skillet. Add the onion and garlic, tossing to coat. Place over medium-low heat and cook, stirring constantly, until the onion is tender. Do not allow the onion or garlic to brown. Beat the softened cheeses together until light and fluffy, and beat in the egg. Add the cooked onion and garlic, Parmesan cheese, thyme, oregano, basil, and salt. Blend in thoroughly.

3. Melt the remaining ½ pound butter and set aside. Tear off two 14-inch lengths of plastic wrap and lay them on a counter so that they overlap and cover an area about 14×18 inches. Unwrap the filo and lay it on the plastic wrap. Smooth the sheets of filo out flat with your fingertips. Tear off 2 more 14-inch pieces of plastic wrap and lay them over the dough, smoothing out any air bubbles with your hands. (Because of its extraordinary thinness, filo dough dries out in minutes, so it's important to keep it protected at all times. Avoid covering it with a damp cloth because the moisture can cause the dough to disintegrate.)

4. Remove a sheet of filo from the pile and position it so that the longest edge is in front of you. Using a pair of scissors, cut the sheet of dough into five approximately 3-inch strips, each 12 inches long. Brush the strips with the melted butter. Place 1 heaping teaspoonful of the cheese mixture at the bottom of each strip. Lift the lefthand corner of the strip of filo and pull it over the cheese until the bottom edge lines up with the right-hand edge of the strip (see illustration). That will create the start of a triangular design. Brush the pastry covering the cheese with melted butter and continue to lift and fold the strip of dough from left to right as you would a flag. Brush the completed triangle with melted butter and place on an ungreased baking sheet. Repeat until all the filling is used. Bake the cheese triangles in an oven preheated to 400°F. for 10 to 15 minutes or until puffed and golden brown.

NOTE: To freeze the triangles, place the completed pastries on a baking sheet lined

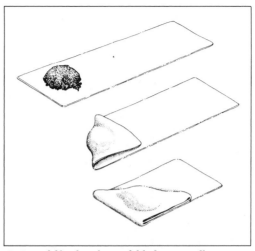

Strips of filo dough are folded repeatedly to enclose the filling for Flaky Cheese Triangles.

with waxed paper. Freeze, uncovered, in a single layer for 24 hours. Transfer to airtight plastic bags and set inside a large box to protect the pastry from being jostled. When ready to use, brush both sides of the frozen pastry with melted butter and place on an ungreased baking sheet. Bake while still frozen in a 400° oven for 20 to 25 minutes.

Mushroom Tarts

MAKES ABOUT 45 TARTS

Mushroom duxelles *flavored with thyme, refined with sour cream, and enveloped in tender, easy-to-prepare sour cream pastry.*

SOUR CREAM PASTRY

2 cups all-purpose flour, scoop measured
¼ teaspoon salt
1 cup cold butter, cut into small chunks
1 large egg
½ cup sour cream
1 tablespoon cold water

MUSHROOM FILLING

4 tablespoons butter
1 pound fresh mushrooms, finely chopped
12 green onions, thinly sliced (white portion only)
½ teaspoon dried leaf thyme

¼ teaspoon salt
Freshly ground black pepper
2 tablespoons chopped fresh parsley
½ cup sour cream

1. To form the pastry, measure the flour and salt into a large bowl and whisk or toss with a fork to combine. Add the butter and cut in with a pastry blender or knife. Separate the egg, reserving the white. Place the yolk in a small bowl and blend with the sour cream. Gradually add to the pastry mixture, tossing with a fork to combine. When the dough begins to hold together, form it into a ball with your fingertips. Drop into a plastic bag and seal airtight. Chill for 20 minutes to 2 hours.

2. Meanwhile, prepare the filling by melting the butter in a 12-inch skillet. Add the fresh mushrooms and onions and place over high heat. Cook, tossing and lifting continuously, until the vegetables begin to give up their juice. (If the mixture appears excessively dry and seems to refuse to give off liquid, pull the pan from the heat and wait until the sizzling dies down. The drop in temperature will encourage the release of moisture. Return to the heat and repeat if necessary.) Stir in the thyme, salt, and pepper, and cook, stirring continuously, until the vegetables are tender and all the moisture has evaporated. Remove from the heat. Transfer to a bowl to cool, and stir in the parsley and sour cream.

3. Preheat the oven to 375°F. Dust a work surface with sifted flour and roll the chilled pastry to a thickness of ⅛ inch. Using a 2-inch biscuit cutter, cut out as many rounds as possible (rerolling the scraps slightly toughens the pastry). Whisk the reserved egg white with 1 tablespoon of cold water. Spoon a generous teaspoonful of mushroom filling onto the center of a pastry round and moisten the edge of the dough with the beaten egg white. Close the dough, forming a semicircular tart, and crimp with the tines of a fork to seal.

4. Arrange the tarts on a lightly greased baking sheet and place in the preheated oven. Bake 15 to 20 minutes or until golden brown and slightly puffed. Serve hot.   ❧

Leek and Ham Tart

SERVES 8

Cream-cheese puff pastry forms the top and bottom crusts of this thin, delicately flavored pie filled with slivers of tender leek and ham. This makes a great picnic appetizer.

CREAM-CHEESE PUFF PASTRY

1¼ cups butter (see Note)
1¼ cups cream cheese (about 10 ounces)
¾ cup confectioners' sugar, sifted and then scoop measured
½ teaspoon salt
2½ cups flour, sifted and then scoop measured
1 large egg, separated
2 tablespoons water

LEEK AND HAM FILLING

3 medium leeks
4 tablespoons butter
2 tablespoons flour
½ teaspoon dried leaf thyme
½ cup medium, or whipping, cream
Freshly ground nutmeg
Salt and freshly ground black pepper to taste
8 ounces Westphalian ham (or other German smoked ham)
8 ounces Gruyère cheese

1. To make the pastry, place the butter and cream cheese in a large mixing bowl and allow them to warm for 30 minutes. Whip until light and fluffy. Beating continuously, sprinkle in the sugar and salt. Remove the bowl from the mixer stand. Add the flour and incorporate by using a fork. Blend with quick, light strokes. When the mixture is still quite crumbly, turn out onto a lightly floured surface and complete the blending by pushing small clumps of the dough away from you with the heel of your hand.

2. Sprinkle the dough with sifted flour. When the dough is cohesive and feels like moist clay, shape it into a large, flat rectangle measuring 6×10 inches. Wrap the dough in waxed paper and chill for 45 minutes. Remove from the refrigerator and roll into a rectangle measuring 11×18 inches. (Using an

18-inch rolling pin enables you to refer less often to a ruler.) Fold the dough in thirds like a business letter and turn so that the folded edges are to the right and left. Once again, roll the dough into an 11×18-inch rectangle and fold into thirds. Wrap in waxed paper and chill for 30 minutes. Repeat the procedure of rolling the dough into an 11×18-inch rectangle, then folding it into thirds. Again, wrap and chill the dough for 30 minutes. After the second 30-minute chilling segment, the pastry is ready to be used.

3. To prepare the tart filling, remove the roots from the leeks and cut off the dark green portion of the leaves. (Use the light green portion.) Cut each leek in half lengthwise and rinse under cold running water, separating the layers to rinse away hidden sand and dirt. Pat dry and slice.

4. In a 2½-quart saucepan, melt the butter and add the sliced leeks, tossing to coat. Cover the pan and cook over low heat for 10 to 15 minutes or until the leeks are tender. Sprinkle the flour and dried thyme over the leeks and increase the heat. Stir constantly over medium-high heat for 1 minute to cook the flour. Add the cream and continue stirring until the mixture bubbles and thickens. Blend in the nutmeg and season with salt and pepper. Transfer to a bowl and allow to cool to room temperature.

5. Roll up the sliced ham and cut across the roll to produce thin slivers. Shred the cheese and set aside. Roll the chilled dough into a large rectangle as before. When the rectangle becomes too large to work with easily, cut it in half, setting 1 piece aside and covering it with plastic wrap. Continue rolling half the dough until you have a 12-inch square. Trim the corners with a pastry wheel to form a 12-inch round.

6. Preheat the oven to 400°F. Transfer the 12-inch pastry round to a greased baking sheet. Distribute the cooked leeks over the dough to within 1 inch of the edge. Scatter the ham slivers and grated cheese over the leeks. Whisk the egg white with 1 tablespoon of the water. Roll out the remaining dough. Apply

egg white around the vegetables near the edge of the first pastry. Place the second pastry atop the filling, sealing the edge to the bottom dough with the egg white. Crimp the crust. Whisk the egg yolk with the remaining 1 tablespoon of water and brush over the surface of the tart to encourage browning. Cut a few decorative vents in the center, place the tart in the preheated oven, and bake for 20 to 25 minutes or until well browned. Loosen the edges with a metal spatula if necessary and slide onto a flat serving plate. Serve hot or at room temperature.

NOTE: This Cream-Cheese Puff Pastry creates an exceptionally cooperative dough. The confectioners' sugar interferes with gluten development just enough to prevent toughening of the dough without creating an overly sweet taste. The result is a multilayered pastry with a lively flavor and texture that lies somewhere between the crisp Viennese type and the softer Danish variety. You can use it in any recipe calling for puff pastry. For the sake of economy, feel free to use salted butter or one of the recently marketed butter-margarine blends when preparing this puff pastry to use in savory dishes. Use unsalted butter when preparing dough to use as dessert or breakfast pastry.   ❧

Pizza Appetizers

SERVES 8

The original pizzas were rounds of bread dough spread with relish, usually made of sliced or chopped leftovers, such as cabbage, onions, mushrooms, or eggplant. In towns near the sea, fish and shellfish often made up the pizza topping. The relishes used varied from region to region according to what was available, but only in a few areas were tomatoes included.

You can offer an intriguing appetizer by recreating these unusual relishlike pizza toppings and spreading them on small rounds cut from bread dough with a biscuit cutter.

1 recipe for Pizza Dough (p. 297)

RED SWEET BELL PEPPER TOPPING

2 pounds red sweet bell peppers, rinsed, cored, and seeded
2 garlic cloves, minced
6 tablespoons olive oil
½ cup water
½ cup chopped fresh parsley
2 tablespoons red wine vinegar
2 teaspoons sugar
½ teaspoon salt
Freshly ground black pepper

1. Coarsely chop the bell peppers and transfer to a large mixing bowl. Add the garlic and pour on the olive oil, stirring to coat.

2. Pour the water into a 12-inch skillet or wide saucepan. Bring to a boil and stir in the chopped pepper mixture. Reduce the heat to low and cover the pan. Cook for 30 minutes, stirring occasionally. Sprinkle on the parsley, vinegar, sugar, salt, and pepper. Increase the heat to high and cook, stirring continuously, until the pepper mixture takes on a relishlike consistency. Use immediately or refrigerate. (See Note below for baking instructions.)

ZUCCHINI TOPPING

2½ pounds slender zucchini
2 medium onions
2 garlic cloves, minced
6 tablespoons olive oil
½ cup water
1 tablespoon fennel seed
1 tablespoon chopped fresh basil (or substitute 1 teaspoon dried)
1 tablespoon chopped fresh oregano (or substitute 1 teaspoon dried)
½ teaspoon salt
Freshly ground black pepper

1. Coarsely chop the zucchini and onions and transfer to a large mixing bowl. Add the garlic and pour on the olive oil, stirring to coat the vegetables.

2. Pour the water into a 12-inch skillet or wide saucepan. Bring to a boil and stir in the chopped zucchini mixture. Blend in the fennel seed and dried herbs if you're using them.

Reduce the heat to low and cover the pan. Cook for 30 minutes. Sprinkle on the fresh herbs if you're using them and add the salt and pepper. Increase the heat to high and cook, stirring continuously, until the zucchini mixture takes on a relishlike consistency. Use immediately or refrigerate. (See Note below for baking instructions.)

ANCHOVY AND TOMATO TOPPING

4 tablespoons olive oil
1 medium onion, coarsely chopped
1 garlic clove, minced
12 anchovy fillets
1 can (28 ounces) crushed tomatoes
1 tablespoon chopped fresh basil (or substitute 1 teaspoon dried)
½ teaspoon salt
Generous amount of freshly ground black pepper
Capers, nonpareille variety, drained
Pitted black Greek or Italian olives

1. Heat the olive oil in a 12-inch skillet or wide saucepan. Add the onions, tossing to coat. Stir over medium heat until the onion is translucent. Add the garlic and anchovies. Continue to stir over medium heat, crushing the anchovies with a wooden spoon.

2. Add the tomatoes, basil, salt, and pepper. Stir over medium heat until the mixture begins to bubble. Reduce the heat to low and cook uncovered for 20 minutes. Stir occasionally. Use immediately or refrigerate. (Slice or quarter the black olives and distribute along with the capers over the Anchovy and Tomato Topping when ready to serve.)

NOTE: To assemble appetizer pizzas, roll out pizza dough to the desired thinness. Using your fingertips, rub the surface of the dough with olive oil for thin pizzas, or leave unoiled for thicker, puffy pizzas. Cut out 2- or 3-inch rounds with a biscuit cutter and place on a greased baking sheet (preferably made of black steel). Spread each dough round with a spoonful of topping and place in a preheated 450°F. oven. Bake for 10 to 12 minutes or until the crust is lightly browned. Serve hot.   ❧

Soups

Beef Broth

MAKES 10 TO 12 CUPS

For those times when you want a truly robust beef broth, try this recipe. The leeks, garlic, and mushrooms lend a depth of flavor not attained in more traditional recipes. And because the meat is roasted first, very little fat is left to rise to the surface, so there's hardly any need to skim the broth during cooking.

4 pounds low-priced beef (heel of round, shank cuts, or stew beef — whatever is on sale)
2 ounces prosciutto
2 large onions
8 whole cloves
3 medium carrots
3 leeks
2 ribs celery
2 garlic cloves
2 tablespoons dried Porcini mushrooms (optional)
12 ounces fresh mushrooms
4 tablespoons butter
1 can (28 ounces) Italian tomatoes, undrained
1 cup dry red wine
3 sprigs fresh parsley
2 bay leaves, broken in half
1 teaspoon dried leaf thyme
½ teaspoon dried marjoram
1 teaspoon salt
4 whole peppercorns

1. Cut the beef into large chunks and chop the prosciutto. (Most of the flavor and nutrients will be cooked out of the beef during the preparation of this broth, so you won't have much choice but to discard it at the end.) Arrange the beef and prosciutto in a roasting pan and place in a 375°F. oven for 20 minutes. Stir to distribute whatever fat is released and cook 20 minutes more.

2. Quarter the onions and stud each quarter with a clove. Cut the carrots into ½-inch lengths. Remove the roots and dark green portion of the leaves from the leeks and wash thoroughly, separating the layers to expose hidden sand and dirt. Pat dry and slice. Cut the celery into ½-inch lengths. Cut the garlic into thirds. Cover the dried mushrooms with water to soften. Wash and quarter the fresh mushrooms.

3. When the meat has roasted for a total of 40 minutes, scatter the onions and carrots over the top. Toss to coat the vegetables with fat and meat juice and roast 30 to 40 minutes or until vegetables have begun to color. Do not allow vegetables to char.

4. Meanwhile, melt the butter in a 6- or 8-quart stockpot. Add the leeks, celery, and garlic. Toss to coat with butter. Cover the pot and cook over low heat until leeks are wilted, but not browned.

5. Transfer the roasted meat and vegetables to the stockpot. Cover with cold water from the tap and bring to a boil. Break up the tomatoes and stir them in. Lift the rehydrated mushrooms from their soaking liquid with a fork and add to the broth. Strain the soaking liquid through a cheesecloth-lined sieve to eliminate any sand and pour into the broth. Stir in the fresh mushrooms. Blend in the wine, parsley, bay leaves, thyme, marjoram, salt, and peppercorns. Cook at a gentle bubble for 3½ to 4½ hours, adding more water when necessary to keep the contents of the pot covered.

6. When the vegetables are soft and the meat falls apart in shreds, pour the broth through a colander into a large bowl. Refrigerate overnight. Degrease by lifting the hard-

ened fat off the surface of the broth. Empty into a 3- or 4-quart saucepan, leaving behind the layer of herbs and other debris that has fallen to the bottom of the bowl. Heat gently to melt, then increase the heat and cook at a brisk boil. Reduce to 12 cups (or less, depending on the intensity of flavor you desire). Strain through a cheesecloth-lined sieve and refrigerate or freeze.

NOTE: You can add cooked noodles to this broth and serve as beef-noodle soup, or use it as a base for Minestrone (p. 200). It can also be reduced to 6 cups, garnished in any way you desire, and served as consommé. ◄ઙ

Chicken Broth

MAKES 4 TO 6 CUPS

This casual approach to chicken broth makes use of the carcass and leftovers from a roast chicken. The result is not a refined stock, but rather a full-bodied broth suitable for use as a hearty soup base. (Use the less assertive Chicken Stock on p. 343 when you want a more delicate flavor.)

If you're not in the habit of serving roast chicken, or you want to supplement leftovers from a smaller chicken, purchase chicken legs when they're on sale and keep them in the freezer to use in this broth. (Legs contribute a deeper flavor than wings or backs and are only slightly higher in price when on sale.) Roast uncooked legs by placing them in a shallow pan and baking at 375°F. for 1 hour.

1 carcass plus meaty scraps from a 5½- to 6-pound chicken (or substitute 4 to 5 roasted chicken legs, including thighs and drumsticks)
2 medium carrots, sliced
1 large onion, cut into eighths
3 sprigs fresh parsley
1 teaspoon dried leaf thyme
1 teaspoon dried sage leaves (or substitute ½ teaspoon ground sage)
1 teaspoon salt
4 whole peppercorns
Any leftover gravy or pan drippings (see Note)

1. Break up the carcass or separate the thighs from the drumsticks on the roasted legs. Distribute over the bottom of a roasting pan. Add scraps of meat and skin. Scatter the carrots and onion over the chicken and place in a 350°F. oven. Cook for 20 minutes. Then stir the contents of the pan to coat the vegetables with whatever fat has been released. Cook for another 20 to 30 minutes, stirring occasionally. The vegetables should develop some color, but don't allow them to become overly brown or blacken because that results in a harsh, scorched flavor.

2. Transfer to a 6- or 8-quart stockpot and cover with cold tap water. Add the remaining ingredients and bring to a gentle bubble. Cook uncovered until the vegetables are tender and the meat falls away from the bone (about 2½ to 3 hours). Add water, when necessary, to keep the contents of the pot covered. Pour through a colander into a large bowl. Refrigerate overnight.

3. Remove the fat by lifting it off the top with a shallow spoon. Empty the chilled broth into a 3- or 4-quart saucepan, being careful to leave behind the layer of herbs and other debris that has fallen to the bottom. Heat gently to melt, then increase the heat and cook at a brisk boil. Reduce to 4 or 6 cups, depending on the intensity of flavor you desire. Strain through a cheesecloth-lined sieve and refrigerate or freeze.

NOTE: When you roast a chicken, plan ahead to make this broth by roasting the neck and giblets alongside. Save the pan juices if you don't use them for gravy, for everything goes into this broth. ◄ઙ

Chilled Pineapple Soup

SERVES 6 TO 8

A special-occasion soup of chilled pineapple purée laced with champagne and served with a garnish of fresh mint.

2 fresh pineapples
1½ cups plus ⅔ cup water

⅔ cup sugar

2 cups champagne (use a moderately priced
champagne or other white sparkling wine)

6 to 8 sprigs fresh mint

1. To peel and core the pineapple, slice off the top and base, removing about 1 inch from both. Stand the pineapple up and remove the skin by slicing downward. Cut out any eyes that remain. Cut the pineapple into quarters and remove the fibrous section of core from each piece. Place all the trimmings, except the top and base, in a 4½-quart saucepan and add 1½ cups water. Bring to a boil. Reduce the heat and cook covered for 15 minutes.

2. Meanwhile, coarsely chop the pineapple and set aside. Make a sugar syrup by combining the sugar and ⅔ cup water in a 1½-quart saucepan. Stir over medium-high heat until the mixture boils and the sugar is completely dissolved.

3. Strain the liquid containing the boiled trimmings through a cheesecloth-lined sieve. Return liquid to the 4½-quart saucepan. Add the chopped pineapple and the sugar syrup. Bring to a boil. Reduce the heat and simmer uncovered for 30 minutes or until the pineapple is soft enough to mash against the side of the pan.

4. Put through a food mill and chill. Just before serving, blend in the wine. Ladle from a clear glass tureen or punch bowl, garnishing each serving with a sprig of fresh mint.   ◦ঽ

Fresh Green Pea Soup

SERVES 6

Based on a purée of fresh peas, this chilled soup epitomizes the spirit of spring. Serve in clear glass bowls. A green onion chrysanthemum placed in the center of each serving makes an attractive presentation (see Note).

6 green onions, plus 6 more if needed for
garnish

2 cups water

3 cups green peas (shelled from 3 to 3½ pounds
fresh peas)

8 mint leaves

2 tablespoons butter

3 cups half-and-half

2 tablespoons flour

½ teaspoon salt

Generous amount of freshly ground white pepper
(or substitute a pinch of ground cayenne)

1 tablespoon lemon juice (optional)

1. Slice the green onions, including all the green portions. Bring the water to a rapid boil. Stir in the peas and green onions and add the mint. When the water returns to a boil, cook uncovered for 4 to 8 minutes, depending on the size of the peas.

2. When the peas are soft enough to mash against the side of the pan, remove from the heat. Transfer to the container of a blender or processor, liquid and all. Whirl until smooth.

3. Melt the butter in a 2½-quart saucepan. Meanwhile, warm the half-and-half in a small pan on another burner until bubbles appear. When the butter is melted, remove from the heat and blend in the flour. Return to medium-high heat and cook, stirring, until the mixture foams. Remove from the heat. Pour the hot half-and-half into the mixture and beat vigorously with a wire whisk. Return to medium-high heat and stir until the mixture bubbles and thickens.

4. Blend in the pea purée and cook over medium-high heat until the mixture bubbles. Season with salt and white pepper and chill. Just before serving, blend in lemon juice and garnish with green onions if desired.

NOTE: To make green onion chrysanthemums, select 6 green onions with well-developed bulbs. Remove the roots and cut into 2½- to 3-inch lengths. You should have the white bulb plus approximately ½ inch of green for each one. Using the tip of a very sharp knife, make several lengthwise cuts in the bulb. Then give it a quarter turn and make several more lengthwise cuts, creating a series of thin strands. Leave about ¾ inch intact at the green end. Drop into a bowl of ice water and refrigerate. The bulb will open and the strands will curl outward like a delicate flower. Place on absorbent paper to drain.   ◄୧

Cream of Spinach Soup

SERVES 6

Freshly grated nutmeg, often used to underscore the flavor of spinach, works its usual magic in this cold soup.

1½ pounds fresh spinach
6 green onions
4 tablespoons butter
4 cups Chicken Broth (p. 193) or Chicken Stock (p. 343)
2 tablespoons flour
½ teaspoon salt
⅛ teaspoon freshly grated nutmeg
Pinch of ground cayenne
2 large egg yolks
1 cup medium, or whipping, cream
2 tablespoons cold water

1. Wash the spinach and separate the leaves from the tough stems. Discard the stems or save for another use. Slice the leaves into thin shreds. Set aside. Thinly slice the green onions, including 2 to 3 inches of the green portion.

2. Melt the butter in a 4½-quart saucepan and add the green onions, tossing to coat. Cover the pan and cook the onions slowly for 10 minutes or until they are tender and translucent. Don't allow them to brown.

3. Pour the broth into a 2½-quart saucepan and bring to a boil. Reduce the heat to the lowest possible setting to keep the broth warm. Sprinkle the flour over the cooked onions and stir to blend. Cook over moderate heat until the mixture foams. Remove from the heat. Immediately add the warm broth, stirring vigorously. Add the spinach, salt, nutmeg, and cayenne. Regulate the heat so that the soup bubbles gently, and cook uncovered for 10 minutes. The spinach should be wilted, but not soft, and should display a vibrant green hue. Remove from the heat.

4. Whisk together the egg yolks and cream in a large bowl to form a liaison. Blend in the water to dilute the mixture. Measure out 1 cup of hot soup and slowly pour it into the liaison, stirring continuously to warm the egg-yolk-and-cream combination gradually. Stir the warmed liaison into the remaining soup and return to low heat. Cook for 8 to 10 minutes, stirring continuously, until the soup thickens slightly. Don't allow it to boil or the eggs will curdle. Serve hot or refrigerate it and serve chilled, garnished with gratings of nutmeg.

NOTE: Chilled soups made with homemade stocks tend to solidify somewhat because of the natural gelatin in broth. To adjust the consistency, stir a small amount of cream into the chilled soup before serving.

(See entry for Liaison.)   ◄୧

Chilled Sweet Potato Soup

SERVES 6

Like most cold soups, this offering is basically a thin purée tempered with cream. It makes a light and appealing introduction to a dinner of roast game such as pheasant or wild duck.

6 medium-size sweet potatoes
1 small onion
1 rib celery
4 tablespoons butter
6 cups Chicken Broth (p. 193) or Chicken Stock (p. 343)
¼ teaspoon ground cinnamon
Freshly grated nutmeg
3 tablespoons Cointreau
½ teaspoon salt
Generous amount of freshly ground white or black pepper
½ cup medium, or whipping, cream

1. Peel and coarsely chop the sweet potatoes. Cover with cold water to prevent discoloration and set aside. Coarsely chop the onion and celery.

2. Melt the butter in a 4½-quart saucepan. Add the onion and celery and cook over medium heat until the onion is wilted. Do not allow the onion to brown.

3. Stir in the broth or stock and sweet potatoes. Blend in the cinnamon and nutmeg. Cover and cook for 30 minutes or until the potatoes are soft enough to mash against the side of the pan. Remove from the heat and blend in the Cointreau. Allow the soup to cool for 20 minutes.

4. Pour into the container of a blender or processor and whirl to purée. Refrigerate until chilled. Season with salt and pepper and blend in the cream. Serve chilled, garnished with freshly grated nutmeg.   ◄ð

Fresh Tomato Soup

SERVES 6

Orange zest is the ingredient responsible for the elusive quality of this fresh tomato soup.

3 medium leeks
1 large red onion
3 ribs celery
2 medium carrots
1 garlic clove
2 tablespoons olive oil
4 tablespoons butter
4 pounds fresh tomatoes
6 cups Chicken Broth (p. 193) or Chicken Stock
  (p. 343)
3 strips (3 to 4 inches long) orange zest (do not
  substitute dried orange peel)
1 tablespoon chopped fresh basil (or substitute 1
  teaspoon dried)
1 teaspoon chopped fresh leaf thyme (or
  substitute ¼ teaspoon dried)
½ teaspoon fennel seeds
Generous pinch of saffron threads, pulverized
  with a mortar and pestle, then steeped in ¼
  cup boiling water (optional)
1 teaspoon salt
Generous amount of freshly ground black pepper
Whipped cream or whipped Crème Fraîche (p.
  361) and chives for garnish

1. Prepare the leeks by removing the roots and cutting off the dark green portions of the leaves. (Use the light green part.) Cut each leek in half lengthwise and rinse under running water, separating the layers to expose hidden sand and dirt. Pat dry and slice thinly. Slice the onion, celery, and carrots. Peel and mince the garlic.

2. Heat the oil and butter in a 6½-quart saucepan. When the butter is melted, add the prepared vegetables and toss to coat. Cover the pan and regulate the heat so that the vegetables cook slowly.

3. Meanwhile, peel the tomatoes, remove the cores with a grapefruit knife, and cut into wedges.

4. When the onions are translucent, stir in the broth or stock. Add the prepared tomatoes. Remove the zest from an orange with a swivel-blade peeler and drop in. Add the basil, thyme, fennel seeds, and the saffron plus its steeping liquid. Simmer uncovered for 1½ to 2 hours or until the vegetables are soft enough to mash against the side of the pan.

5. Put through a food mill in order to purée the vegetables and eliminate the tomato seeds. (Do not use a blender or processor.) Season with salt and pepper and return to the heat. Simmer uncovered for 30 minutes. Refrigerate and serve cold garnished with a dollop of chilled whipped cream or whipped *crème fraîche*. Sprinkle with snipped chives.   ◄ð

Cream of Celery Soup

SERVES 6

Served hot, this soup makes an elegant prelude to a meal of roast chicken or roast veal. It's also smashing served cold with chilled lobster salad.

2 medium leeks
8 green onions
2 medium carrots
2 stalks or bunches celery plus leaves (see Note)
4 tablespoons butter
2 cups water

4 cups Chicken Broth (p. 193) or Chicken Stock
(p. 343)
1 tablespoon lemon juice
1 teaspoon dried tarragon leaves
½ teaspoon salt
Generous amount of freshly ground white pepper
or a pinch of ground cayenne
½ cup medium, or whipping, cream
Twists of lemon peel for garnish

1. Prepare the leeks by removing the roots and cutting off the dark green portions of the leaves. (Use the light green part of the leaves.) Cut each leek in half lengthwise and rinse under running water, separating the layers in order to wash thoroughly. Slice thinly. Cut the roots from the green onions. Wash and remove the outer membrane. Slice thinly, including 3 to 4 inches of the green portion. Slice the carrots and celery, including the celery leaves. (Remember that thinner slices cook in less time than thicker slices.)

2. Melt the butter in a 4½-quart saucepan. Add the vegetables and toss to coat with butter. Cover the pan and regulate the heat so that the vegetables cook slowly.

3. When the onions are translucent, add the water and broth or stock. Simmer uncovered for 1½ to 2 hours or until the vegetables are soft enough to mash against the side of the pan.

4. Put through a food mill in order to purée the mixture and eliminate the celery strings at the same time. (Do not use a blender or processor because neither will disintegrate the strings.) Stir in the lemon juice and tarragon. Season with salt and pepper. Return to the heat and simmer uncovered for 30 minutes. Remove from the heat and stir in the cream. Heat briefly to warm the cream, but do not allow the soup to boil. Serve garnished with twists of lemon peel.

NOTE: There is great confusion in the terminology concerning celery. Strictly speaking, a *bunch* of celery is also a *stalk* of celery. The stalk is composed of leaved branches called *ribs*. Therefore, 1 or 2 pieces of celery should be referred to as *ribs*.   ◅ঽ

Leek and Potato Soup

SERVES 6

This delicious soup is made in two easy steps. Half the leeks and potatoes are cooked in chicken broth until tender and then puréed in the blender to create a thickened consistency without using any flour. The remaining leeks and potatoes are then simmered in the purée until tender. The finished soup is enhanced with cream and spiked with lemon juice.

2 medium onions
4 tablespoons butter
4 medium leeks
6 medium potatoes
6 cups Chicken Broth (p. 193) or Chicken Stock
(p. 343)
1 tablespoon lemon juice
½ teaspoon salt
Generous amount of freshly ground white pepper
or a pinch of ground cayenne
½ cup medium, or whipping, cream

1. Peel the onions and cut them into quarters. Turn each quarter on its side and slice thinly. Melt the butter in a 4½-quart saucepan. Add the onions and toss to coat with butter. Cover the pan and cook over low heat until tender and translucent.

2. Meanwhile, prepare the leeks by removing the roots and cutting off the dark green portions of the leaves. (Use the light green parts of the leaves.) Cut each leek in half lengthwise and rinse under cold running water, separating the layers to expose hidden sand and dirt. Pat dry and slice. Add half the sliced leeks to the onions. Peel the potatoes, cut into ½-inch slices, and then cut into cubes. Add half the cubed potatoes to the combined onions and leeks. Cover the remaining potatoes with water to prevent browning and set aside. Stir the onions, leeks, and potatoes, cover the pan, and continue cooking over low heat for 20 minutes.

3. Stir in the broth. Regulate the heat so that the soup simmers gently and cook uncovered for 1 hour or until the potatoes are soft enough to mash against the side of the pan. Transfer to the container of a blender or

processor and whirl until smooth. Return the puréed soup to the saucepan. Add the reserved leeks. Drain the reserved potatoes in a colander or sieve and stir in. Bring to a gentle simmer and cover the pan. Cook covered about 40 to 45 minutes or until the potatoes are tender.

4. Remove from the heat. Stir in the lemon juice, and season with salt and pepper. Blend in the cream and return to low heat for 10 minutes. Serve hot or cold. (If you serve this soup cold, you may want to increase the amount of lemon juice and salt.)   ◄ఇ

Avgolemono Soup

SERVES 6

Eggs play a significant role in creating the outstanding texture of this famous chicken and lemon soup from Greece. Egg yolks, assisted by the acid in lemon juice, cause the soup to thicken, while the whipped whites lighten the consistency.

6 cups Chicken Broth (p. 193) or Chicken
  Stock (p. 343)
¼ cup long grain rice
4 large eggs
4 tablespoons lemon juice
½ teaspoon salt
Generous amount of freshly ground white pepper
  or a pinch of ground cayenne
Chopped fresh mint

1. Pour the chicken broth into a 4½-quart saucepan. Bring to a boil and sprinkle in the rice. Cover the pan and cook over low heat for 20 minutes or until the rice is tender. Remove from the heat and measure out 1 cup of the broth.

2. Separate the eggs, placing the yolks in a small bowl and the whites in a large bowl. Add the lemon juice to the yolks and whisk until they are light in color. Beat the whites until soft peaks form. Pour the yolks over the whipped whites and whisk in very gently. (The object is to combine them without deflating the whites any more than necessary.)

3. Slowly pour in the cup of broth to gradually warm the eggs without curdling them. Whisk gently but constantly. Switch to a wooden spoon or heat-resistant rubber spatula and blend the contents of the bowl into the remaining stock. Stir in salt and pepper. Place over the lowest possible heat and cook, stirring continuously, until the soup is slightly thickened. Serve immediately to prevent the rice from becoming soggy and to avoid curdling. Garnish with chopped fresh mint.   ◄ఇ

Hazelnut Cream Soup

SERVES 6

An infusion of toasted hazelnuts plus a fillip of Frangelico produces the seductive flavor of this soup.

8 ounces hazelnuts
3 tablespoons butter
4 cups Beef Broth (p. 192) or Dark Brown
  Stock I or II (p. 340 or p. 341)
3 tablespoons flour
2 tablespoons Frangelico liqueur
3 large egg yolks
1 cup medium, or whipping, cream
2 tablespoons cold water
½ teaspoon salt
Generous amount of freshly ground black pepper

1. Preheat the oven to 350°F. Prepare the nuts by spreading them in a single layer on a baking sheet. Toast in the oven for 10 minutes. When the skins become brittle, remove from the oven. Peel by transferring the nuts onto an abrasive kitchen towel. Fold the towel over, and rub the nuts back and forth until the skins fall away. Remove stubborn bits of skin with your fingers. Finely chop the nuts and set aside.

2. Melt the butter in a 4½-quart saucepan. At the same time, warm the broth on another burner until bubbles begin to appear. When the butter is melted, remove from the heat and add the flour all at once. Blend well to coat each flour particle. Return to medium-high heat and cook, stirring constantly, until

the mixture foams. Remove from the heat. Pour the hot broth in all at once and beat vigorously with a wire whisk. Return to medium-high heat and stir until the soup bubbles and thickens slightly.

3. Stir in the prepared nuts and simmer, uncovered, for 30 minutes. Strain into a large bowl and add the Frangelico.

4. In another bowl, form a liaison by whisking the egg yolks and cream together. Blend in the water to dilute the mixture. Stirring constantly, pour the strained liquid into the egg-cream combination. Return to the saucepan and place over low heat. Cook, stirring constantly, until smooth and slightly thickened. Do not allow it to boil. Season with salt and pepper and serve hot.

Cream of Onion Soup

SERVES 6

Slowly cooked onion rings are combined with a thin white sauce and chicken stock. Cream and mace contribute richness and additional flavor.

4 large sweet onions (Bermuda or Vidalia)
8 tablespoons butter
3 cups milk
4 tablespoons flour
2 cups Chicken Broth (p. 193) or Chicken Stock (p. 343)
⅛ teaspoon ground mace
1 cup medium, or whipping, cream
½ teaspoon salt
Generous amount of freshly ground white pepper or a pinch of ground cayenne
Snipped chives for garnish

1. Peel and thinly slice the onions, separating the slices into rings. Melt 4 tablespoons of butter in a wide thick-bottomed saucepan. Add the onion rings and toss to coat with butter. Reduce the heat to its lowest setting, cover the pan, and slowly cook the onions until they are translucent and have taken on a rich golden hue. Do not allow them to brown.

2. Meanwhile, melt the remaining butter in a 1½-quart saucepan. Pour the milk into another small saucepan and heat gently, but do not allow it to boil. Stir the flour into the melted butter and stir over medium heat until the mixture foams. Remove from the heat and immediately whisk in the warm milk. Return to the heat and cook, stirring constantly, until the mixture thickens and boils. Remove from the heat.

3. Whisk in the chicken broth or stock. Then stir in the mace. When the onions are cooked, transfer them to the container of a blender or processor. Add the white sauce base and whirl to purée. (If your blender is too small to accommodate the entire amount at one time, purée in small amounts.) Pour into a clean saucepan. Blend in the cream. Season with salt and pepper and heat briefly over medium heat. Serve with a few snipped chives floating in the center.

Mushroom Soup

SERVES 6

Although this soup is finished with cream, its flavor is so rich and complex that you won't think of it as a creamed soup. Make every effort to use either fresh or dried sage leaves. Ground sage can be substituted, but the overall effect is not nearly as spectacular. To use dried sage leaves, measure out a generous teaspoonful and gently rub it through a coarse sieve. Discard any stubborn sticks or stems.

2 cups water
2 tablespoons dried Porcini mushrooms (optional)
6 tablespoons butter
2 medium onions, sliced
3 cups Chicken Broth (p. 193) or Chicken Stock (p. 343)
2 tablespoons flour
12 ounces fresh mushrooms, rinsed and quartered, plus 3 or 4 mushrooms set aside to use as garnish

15 fresh sage leaves, coarsely chopped, or 1
   teaspoon dried sage leaves (or substitute ½
   teaspoon ground sage)
1 large bay leaf
1 teaspoon dried chervil
½ teaspoon dried leaf thyme
½ teaspoon salt
Generous amount of freshly ground black pepper
2 tablespoons lemon juice
½ cup medium, or whipping, cream
Fresh parsley for garnish

1. Combine the water and dried mushrooms. Set aside to soften. (The water should
be added later in the recipe even if you don't
include the dried mushrooms.)

2. Melt the butter in a 4½-quart saucepan.
Add the onion slices and toss to coat with
butter. Reduce the heat to low and cover the
pan. Cook slowly for 15 to 20 minutes or
until onions take on a deep golden color.
Don't rush this step or the onions will burn.
It's the slow cooking that imparts a uniquely
rich onion flavor to this soup.

3. Meanwhile, bring the broth to a boil in a
1½-quart saucepan, and then lower the heat
to keep the broth warm. When the onions are
golden, sprinkle on the flour and cook, stirring, over medium heat until the mixture
foams. Don't allow the flour to brown. Remove from the heat and add the chicken
broth, stirring to blend. Add fresh mushrooms and pour in the water and rehydrated
mushrooms, if you're using them, taking care
to leave behind any sand or sediment that has
fallen to the bottom.

4. Blend in the dried sage leaves (if using
dried) by rubbing the leaves through a coarse
sieve. Break the bay leaf in half to release its
flavor and drop in. Add the chervil, thyme,
salt, and pepper. Cover and cook over low
heat for 1½ to 2 hours or until mushrooms
are tender. (If using fresh sage, add it during
the last half hour.)

5. Remove the bay leaf pieces. Pour the
mixture into the container of a blender or
processor and add the lemon juice. Blend until smooth, return to the pan, and stir in the
cream. Return to low heat for 10 minutes.
Serve hot garnished with thin slices of raw
mushrooms or chopped fresh parsley.   ❧

Walnut, Basil, and Spinach Soup

SERVES 6

*This soup derives its marvelous flavor and
slightly thickened consistency from a walnut,
garlic, and basil paste — a version of the
popular pesto sauce.*

1 pound fresh spinach
20 medium to large fresh basil leaves
¼ cup olive oil
¼ cup butter
1 garlic clove
¼ cup freshly grated Parmesan cheese
⅓ cup chopped walnuts
6 cups Chicken Broth (p. 193) or Chicken Stock
   (p. 343)
Salt and pepper to taste

1. Wash the spinach and remove the tough
stems. Tear into bite-size pieces. Set aside.
Wash the basil and blot dry.

2. In the container of a blender or processor, combine the oil, butter, garlic, and Parmesan. Whirl until smooth. Add the walnuts
and basil and whirl until the mixture is a vivid
green. Transfer to a small bowl.

3. Heat the broth in a 4½-quart saucepan
over medium heat. When the broth bubbles
gently, slowly add the basil paste, whisking
constantly.

4. Stir in the spinach and cook briefly over
medium heat until the spinach is wilted. Season with salt and pepper if desired and serve
immediately with additional Parmesan.   ❧

Minestrone

SERVES 10

*Puréed beans provide a slightly thickened,
stick-to-your-ribs consistency, and because*

canned beans are used in place of dried, this can be made in a relatively short time. If you happen to have a piece of the rind or hard outer edge of a chunk of Parmesan cheese, let it simmer in the soup. It adds immeasurable flavor.

3 tablespoons olive oil
3 tablespoons butter
2 medium-size red onions, coarsely chopped
2 medium carrots, thinly sliced
3 ribs celery, thinly sliced, plus ⅓ cup celery
    leaves, chopped
2 garlic cloves, minced
2 ounces prosciutto, finely chopped
4 cups Beef Broth (p. 192)
8 cups water
2 small zucchini, unpeeled but scrubbed and
    thinly sliced
2 cups spinach leaves, loosely packed
1 can (28 ounces) Italian tomatoes, undrained
¼ cup tomato paste
2 cups canned garbanzo beans
1 cup canned kidney beans
1 cup canned cannellini beans
½ cup ditali (a short, tubular pasta)
¼ cup chopped fresh parsley
2 tablespoons chopped fresh basil (or substitute
    2 teaspoons dried)
1 tablespoon chopped fresh oregano (or
    substitute 1 teaspoon dried)
1 teaspoon dried rosemary leaves, pulverized
    with a mortar and pestle
1 teaspoon salt
Generous amount of freshly ground black pepper
½ cup frozen peas
Freshly grated Parmesan cheese

1. Heat the olive oil and butter in a 6-quart saucepan or Dutch oven. When the butter is melted, add the onions, carrots, celery slices, garlic, and prosciutto. Toss to coat. Cover the pan and regulate the heat so that the vegetables and prosciutto cook slowly.

2. When the onions are translucent (about 20 minutes), add the broth, water, zucchini, and celery leaves. Cook uncovered at a gentle bubble for 1½ hours or until the vegetables are tender.

3. Snip or slice the spinach into shreds and add to the soup. Stir in the tomatoes, breaking them apart with your fingers. Blend in tomato paste. Drain the garbanzo beans in a sieve and place half the beans in the soup and the other half in the container of a blender or food processor. Do the same with the kidney and cannellini beans. Add the ditali to the soup, and then blend in the herbs and season with salt and pepper. Cover and cook over low heat for 30 minutes.

4. Meanwhile, purée the reserved beans. When the ditali are tender, blend the bean purée into the soup. Add the frozen peas and cook uncovered until the peas are tender. Serve sprinkled generously with Parmesan cheese.

Vegetable Bean Soup

SERVES 6

Here's a real snowy-day soup. Flavored with prosciutto and thickened with a purée of navy beans, this comforting soup is topped with a layer of melted cheese.

½ pound dried navy beans
Olive oil
2 ribs celery, sliced
2 medium carrots, sliced
2 medium onions, chopped
2 medium potatoes
1 teaspoon sugar
½ teaspoon salt
Generous amount of freshly ground black pepper
¼ pound prosciutto, thinly sliced
2 garlic cloves, minced or pressed
1 medium head romaine, rinsed
8 cups water
1 can (28 ounces) tomatoes, undrained
2 tablespoons tomato paste
1 tablespoon chopped fresh basil (or substitute 1
    teaspoon dried)
1 tablespoon chopped fresh parsley
6 one-inch-thick slices French bread
¼ cup freshly grated Parmesan cheese
¼ cup grated Gruyère cheese

1. Rinse beans and remove any that are discolored. Place in a 4½-quart saucepan and cover with cold water. Discard any beans that float to the surface. Bring the water to a moderate boil and cook uncovered for 10 minutes. Drain and rinse the beans under cold running water. (Don't save the cooking liquid. This method of cooking beans civilizes them so they don't come back to haunt you. The amount of nutrients lost in the cooking water isn't enough to worry about, and this way you don't have to soak them overnight.)

2. Return the beans to the pan and pour in enough cold water to cover the beans by 2 inches. Bring to a moderate boil. Then reduce the heat so that the water barely bubbles. Cover the pan and cook for 2 hours. Check occasionally to see if more water is needed to keep the beans covered at all times. When the beans are tender, drain them. Purée two-thirds of the beans by blender or processor. Reserve the remaining beans.

3. Pour enough oil into a 6-quart Dutch oven or casserole to cover the bottom. Add the celery, carrots, and onions. Toss to coat with oil. Cover the pan and cook over low heat until the onions are translucent. Peel the potatoes, cut into ½-inch slices, and then cut into cubes. Add to the simmering vegetables and sprinkle on sugar, salt, and pepper. Coarsely chop the sliced prosciutto and stir in. Add the garlic. Cover the pan and continue cooking over low heat for 20 minutes.

4. Meanwhile, prepare the romaine by placing the leaves on top of one another in a pile and slicing across into thin shreds. Add the water to the cooked vegetables and bring to a boil. Blend in the bean purée. Stir in the remaining one-third of the whole beans, the shredded romaine, and the tomatoes, breaking them up with your fingers. Add the tomato paste and basil. Regulate the heat so that the mixture bubbles gently. Stir in the parsley and cook uncovered for 1 hour or until the carrots are tender.

5. Slide the inch-thick bread slices under the broiler to toast. Turn and toast the other side. Preheat the oven to 450°F. Sprinkle Parmesan cheese over the soup and immediately (before the cheese sinks) arrange toasted bread over the top of the soup. Sprinkle Gruyère cheese on top of the bread slices. Place in the oven and bake uncovered until the cheese melts. Turn on the broiler for a minute or two to brown the melted cheese. To serve, scoop out a cheese-covered bread slice and place it in the bottom of a soup bowl. Ladle soup over the bread. Pass additional Parmesan cheese if you like.   ◅ঽ

Chinese Cabbage Soup

SERVES 6

A light, elegant soup that can be made in less than half an hour. The Chinese cabbage should be tender but remain crunchy, providing an interesting textural contrast to the broth. As the meatballs cook in the broth, foam or scum will rise to the surface, which you'll need to skim off with a slotted spoon or shallow skimmer.

1 large egg
½ pound ground pork
1 teaspoon sherry
½ teaspoon freshly grated ginger root
½ teaspoon salt
6 green onions
2 ounces shirataki (or substitute other translucent noodles commonly referred to as "cellophane" noodles)
6 cups Chicken Broth (p. 193) or Chicken Stock (p. 343)
1 medium Chinese cabbage

1. Prepare the meatballs by beating the egg and mixing in the ground pork, sherry, ginger root, and salt. Thinly slice the green onions, tops and all. Set aside the green portions and blend the white slices into the meat mixture. Take up by teaspoonfuls and shape into tiny meatballs.

2. Place the noodles in a bowl. Pour on enough boiling water to cover and allow them to stand for 10 minutes.

3. Pour the broth into a 4½-quart saucepan and bring to a boil. Add the meatballs. Regulate the heat so that the broth bubbles gently. As foam forms on the surface, remove it with a slotted spoon or skimmer. Cook uncovered for 10 minutes.

4. Meanwhile, slice across the cabbage, cutting it into inch-wide pieces. Add it to the bubbling broth. Stir in the reserved tops of the green onion and cook for 10 minutes or until the cabbage is tender but still crisp. Drain the noodles and add to the soup. Cook briefly (the soaked noodles will soften almost instantly) and serve very hot.　　　　◄ই

3. Remove the mushrooms with a fork and strain the liquid through a cheesecloth-lined sieve. Add the liquid to the simmering broth. Slice the mushrooms into thin slivers.

4. Strain the pork broth into a bowl and return it to the saucepan. Add the mushroom slivers and reserved ½ cup green onions. Stir in the noodles and season with salt and pepper. Simmer for 20 minutes or until the noodles are tender. The green onions should retain a certain degree of crispness. Serve hot in colorful porcelain bowls.　　　　◄ই

Pork and Mushroom Soup

SERVES 6

The next time you have bones and scraps left over from a pork roast, try this Oriental-style soup. It not only tastes great, but also looks beautiful in the bowl.

8 cups water
2 tablespoons dried mushrooms (Chinese Shiitake or Italian Porcini)
10 green onions
2 pounds pork bones and meat scraps (include as little fat as possible)
1½ teaspoons freshly grated ginger root
1 two-inch strip lemon zest
2 ounces cellophane noodles (or substitute other very thin noodles)
½ teaspoon salt
Freshly ground black pepper

1. In a small bowl, pour ½ cup of the water over the mushrooms and set them aside to soften. Slice the green onions, including all of the green portion. Set aside ½ cup.

2. Place the bones and meat scraps in a 4½-quart saucepan. Add the remaining 7½ cups water, all but the reserved green onions, the ginger root, and lemon zest. Bring to a boil. Reduce the heat and simmer uncovered for 2½ hours, skimming off any fat that rises to the surface.

Hearty Pea and Sausage Soup

SERVES 8 TO 10

Dried peas soften and form a purée as they cook, so there's no need to put this soup through a mill or into a processor. For tastiest results, use a full-flavored sausage like kielbasa or cervelat.

1 pound dried green split peas
8 cups cold water
3 medium onions
2 medium carrots
2 medium potatoes
½ teaspoon dried leaf thyme
1 to 1½ pounds kielbasa
½ teaspoon salt
Generous amount freshly ground black pepper

1. Empty the dried peas into a sieve and rinse under running water. Pick out any that are discolored. Place the peas in a 5- to 6-quart saucepan or casserole. Add the water and bring to a boil. Lower the heat so that the water simmers gently, and cover the pan.

2. Meanwhile, prepare the vegetables by cutting the onions into quarters, then into eighths. Cut the carrots into ¼-inch slices. Cut the potatoes into ½-inch slices, and then cut the slices into cubes. Stir the vegetables into the simmering liquid. Add the thyme. Regulate the heat so that the water simmers

gently and cover the pan. Cook for 1 hour, stirring occasionally, for as the peas soften, they have a tendency to stick to the bottom of the pan and scorch.

3. With a fork or skewer, prick the sausage over its entire surface so the juices will escape and flavor the soup. Submerge the sausage in the liquid and continue simmering uncovered for 45 minutes. Season with salt and pepper. Lift the sausage out with a fork and remove the skin if you wish. Cut into ¾-inch slices and return to the soup. Serve with a warm dark bread. ◄ð

Albóndigas Soup

SERVES 6

Albóndigas *is the Mexican word for meatball, and the following recipe is a zesty example of what Mexican meatball soup is all about. For maximum flavor, toast whole cumin and coriander seeds at 375°F. for 20 minutes. Allow them to cool and pulverize with a mortar and pestle. (See entry for Spices.)*

Vegetable oil
2 medium onions, chopped
2 garlic cloves, minced or pressed
8 cups Beef Broth (p. 192) or Dark Brown Stock I or II (p. 340 or p. 341)
1 can (28 ounces) whole tomatoes
½ cup tomato purée
1 can (4 ounces) green chilis, finely chopped
4 to 5 drops Tabasco sauce
1 teaspoon ground cumin
1 teaspoon ground coriander
1 large egg
1 pound ground beef
1 pound ground pork
½ cup long grain rice, uncooked (don't use converted rice)
1½ tablespoons chopped fresh mint (or substitute fresh basil or, if necessary, 1 teaspoon dried basil)
½ teaspoon salt
Generous amount of freshly ground black pepper

1. Pour enough oil into a 4½-quart saucepan to cover the bottom of the pan. Add the onions and toss to coat. Cover the pan and cook slowly for 15 minutes or until the onions are tender and translucent, but not browned. Stir in the garlic. Add the broth and tomatoes, breaking the tomatoes up with your fingers. Blend in the tomato purée, green chilis, Tabasco sauce, cumin, and coriander. Bring to a boil, and then lower the heat so that the soup bubbles gently. Cook uncovered for 30 minutes.

2. Meanwhile, prepare the meatballs. Beat the egg lightly and add the ground beef, ground pork, rice, mint, salt, and pepper. Knead the mixture with your hands to make certain that it's well mixed. Scoop out by heaping teaspoonfuls and shape into small balls about the size of unshelled walnuts.

3. Add the meatballs to the simmering broth and stir gently. Regulate the heat so that the soup bubbles gently and cook uncovered for 45 minutes. Skim off any foam that appears on the surface as the meatballs heat and release fat and protein elements. Serve steaming hot. ◄ð

Turkey Soup

SERVES 6 TO 8

This soup might be more aptly named Hunter's Stew because of its rich flavors. You can assuage your guilt for including wild rice by using the meat and carcass of a turkey left over from the holidays.

1 carcass plus the scraps from an 18- to 25-pound turkey (supplement smaller carcasses with 2 turkey legs roasted at 350°F. for 1½ hours)
6 ounces baked ham, coarsely chopped
2 bay leaves
2 large onions
2 medium carrots
4 ribs celery, including leaves
8 ounces fresh mushrooms
1 can (28 ounces) tomatoes, undrained
1½ cups dry red wine

2 tablespoons tomato paste
1 cup leftover stuffing, regular seasoning or
   chestnut (optional; see Note)
½ cup leftover gravy (optional)
3 tablespoons wild rice (or substitute ¼ cup long
   grain)
2 tablespoons chopped fresh parsley
1 tablespoon chopped fresh sage (or substitute 1
   teaspoon ground dried)
1 teaspoon dried leaf thyme
½ teaspoon dried marjoram
1 teaspoon salt
Generous amount of freshly ground black pepper

1. Break up the carcass, picking off 1 to 2 cups of meat. Set the meat aside. Place the carcass in a 6- to 8-quart stockpot. Scatter the chopped ham over the turkey carcass and add enough water to cover completely. Break the bay leaves in half and drop in. Bring to a boil, and then lower the heat so that the water bubbles gently. Cover and cook 2½ to 3 hours or until the remaining meat falls away from the bones. Strain the broth through a colander and return it to the stockpot.

2. Meanwhile, prepare the vegetables by coarsely chopping the onions, thinly slicing the carrots and celery (leaves and all), and cutting the mushrooms into quarters. Refrigerate until the broth is ready.

3. Bring the strained broth to a boil. Add the prepared vegetables and canned tomatoes, breaking the tomatoes apart with your fingers. Blend in the red wine, tomato paste, and leftover stuffing and gravy. Cut the reserved meat into bite-size pieces and stir in. Add the rice, parsley, sage, thyme, marjoram, salt, and pepper. Regulate the heat so that the soup simmers gently, and cook uncovered for 1½ hours or until the vegetables are tender.

NOTE: Do not use oyster stuffing. If you do add regular or chestnut stuffing, the bread will create a slightly thickened consistency. You may substitute ½ cup fresh bread crumbs in lieu of the stuffing if you want a thickened broth, but they must be freshly made. Store-bought crumbs will not create the same effect.   ❧

Mediterranean Fish Soup

SERVES 6

A magnificent soup, thickened by simmering a whole potato with the other ingredients. When the potato is tender, it is used to form a flavorful thickening agent known as a rouille.

3 medium leeks
2 large onions
3 garlic cloves
4 tablespoons olive oil
4 cups water or substitute 6 cups Fish Stock or
   Quick Fish Stock (p. 344; see also Note, p.
   345)
2 cups clam juice
1 cup dry white wine
1 can (35 ounces) Italian tomatoes, undrained
3 two-inch strips of fresh orange zest
3 sprigs fresh parsley
2 bay leaves, broken in half
1 teaspoon dried leaf thyme
Pinch of saffron threads, pulverized with a
   mortar and pestle, then steeped in ¼ cup
   boiling water
10 fennel seeds
6 black peppercorns
1 medium Idaho or other mealy potato, unpeeled
3 pounds of lean white fish (combine any two or
   more — haddock, cod, flounder, rockfish,
   sole, perch)
2 roasted red sweet bell peppers (fresh or from a
   jar)
½ cup freshly grated Parmesan cheese
15 fresh basil leaves (or substitute 1 teaspoon
   dried)
6 drops Tabasco sauce
Salt and pepper to taste

1. Prepare the leeks by removing the roots and cutting off the dark green portion. (Use the light green part.) Cut each leek in half lengthwise and rinse under running water, separating the layers to expose hidden dirt and sand. Pat dry and slice thinly. Peel and thinly slice the onions and mince 2 of the garlic cloves.

2. Heat the olive oil in a thick-bottomed 8-quart, nonreactive stockpot. Add the prepared vegetables, tossing to coat. Cover and cook slowly for 20 to 30 minutes or until they begin to take on a golden hue. Do not allow the vegetables to brown.

3. Stir in the water, clam juice, and wine. Add the tomatoes, breaking them up with your fingers. Stir in the orange zest, parsley, bay leaves, thyme, saffron with its steeping water, fennel seeds, and peppercorns. Scrub the potato and drop it into the stockpot. Regulate the heat so that the liquid bubbles gently and cook uncovered for 45 minutes.

4. Lift out the potato with a slotted spoon. Peel immediately and break up with a fork to release the interior steam. Set aside. Put the broth with vegetables through a food mill and return to the heat. Cut the fish into 2-inch chunks and add to the broth. Cover and cook slowly for 10 to 15 minutes or until the fish flakes apart.

5. Meanwhile, purée the roasted peppers in a blender or processor. Add the potato, cheese, remaining garlic clove, basil, and Tabasco sauce. Whirl until smooth. The mixture should be quite thick (add a few drops of olive oil to thin if necessary). Transfer half the potato purée to a small bowl. Blend in ½ cup of the hot broth. Stir until smooth and add to the simmering soup. Taste to check for seasoning. Clam broth tends to be excessively salty, so you may not want to add more salt. Blend in salt and pepper as desired. Serve within 15 minutes because the fish will disintegrate if cooked too long. Pass the remaining half of potato purée in a small bowl. ❧

Sea Bass Chowder

SERVES 6

A splash of dark rum and a bit of Worcestershire set this chowder apart from all others.

2 whole sea bass, scaled and gutted (about 6 pounds)
1 teaspoon dried leaf thyme
6 whole cloves
2 bay leaves, broken in half
2 medium onions
3 ribs celery
1 green sweet bell pepper
4 tablespoons butter
1 can (35 ounces) Italian tomatoes, undrained
2 tablespoons tomato paste
¼ cup dark rum
1 teaspoon Worcestershire sauce
5 to 6 drops Tabasco sauce
¼ teaspoon curry powder
2 tablespoons chopped fresh parsley
Lemon wedges for garnish

1. Remove the heads and tails from the fish. Discard the tails. Place the heads and bodies in a large stockpot and cover with cold water from the tap. Add the thyme, cloves, and bay leaves. Cover and cook slowly for 30 minutes.

2. Lift out the fish, discarding the heads, and set aside to cool slightly. Pour the liquid through a cheesecloth-lined sieve and transfer to a 4½-quart saucepan. Bring to a moderate boil and cook until reduced to 6 cups.

3. Meanwhile, chop the onions, celery, and green pepper. Melt the butter in a 6-quart saucepan. Add the vegetables, tossing to coat. Cover and cook slowly for 15 to 20 minutes or until tender.

4. Remove the skin from the fish and flake the cooked flesh away from the bones.

5. Using your fingers, break up the tomatoes and add them to the cooked vegetables. Stir in the reduced broth. Add the tomato paste, rum, Worcestershire sauce, Tabasco sauce, curry powder, and fresh parsley. Gently stir in the flaked fish. Simmer uncovered for 10 to 15 minutes. Serve with wedges of lemon. ❧

Salads and Dressings

Shredded Lettuce Salad

SERVES 4

Iceberg lettuce has suffered some bad press recently. Never mind that it's a reliable friend — it isn't chic. But shredded and lightly dressed, iceberg can keep up with the newcomers anytime.

½ cup sliced almonds
2 medium carrots
1 medium head iceberg lettuce

VINAIGRETTE SAUCE
¼ teaspoon salt
½ teaspoon sugar
1 tablespoon Dijon mustard
2 tablespoons fresh lemon juice
6 tablespoons olive or corn oil
2 tablespoons chopped fresh chives (or
   substitute freeze-dried)
Generous amount of freshly ground black pepper

1. Scatter the almonds in a shallow baking pan and toast in a 350°F. oven for 8 minutes or until lightly browned. Cool to room temperature. Grate the carrots and refrigerate. Remove the core of the lettuce and shred finely with a knife. (Iceberg lettuce, like cabbage, is composed of tightly packed leaves and therefore seldom needs rinsing.)

2. In a small bowl or glass jar with a screw-on lid, make the vinaigrette by combining the salt, sugar, and mustard into a smooth paste. Add the lemon juice and stir with a fork until well blended.

3. Gradually whisk in the oil, or add it all at once, covering the jar and shaking vigorously to blend. Stir in the chives and black pepper. Use immediately or set aside at room temperature to allow the flavors to meld. Whisk again to combine if necessary and pour over the shredded lettuce. Sprinkle on the carrots and toasted almonds and toss lightly. Serve on chilled plates.   ☙

Cole Slaw

SERVES 6 TO 8

To achieve a wilted, yet crunchy, consistency, pour the hot dressing over shredded cabbage. Then cover the bowl tightly with aluminum foil and refrigerate for 2 hours.

1 large head cabbage

COOKED DRESSING
¼ cup sugar
1 teaspoon salt
2 tablespoons flour
1 tablespoon dry mustard
¼ teaspoon paprika
4 large egg yolks
1½ cups milk
4 tablespoons butter, melted
⅓ cup cider vinegar

1. Cut the cabbage into long, thin shreds by slicing thinly with a serrated knife, or shred according to your favorite method. Transfer to a large mixing bowl.

2. Whisk the sugar, salt, and flour together in the top of a double boiler. Whisking disperses the flour and makes it easier to dissolve. Blend in the mustard and paprika. Add water to the bottom of the double boiler and bring it to a boil. Regulate the heat so that the water bubbles gently.

3. Whisk the egg yolks in a medium-size bowl. Add the milk and slightly cooled melt-

ed butter and blend thoroughly. Gradually whisk into the dry ingredients and place the upper container over the bubbling water.

4. Stirring constantly with a rubber spatula or wooden spoon, slowly pour in the vinegar. Continue to stir until the mixture develops a smooth, slightly thickened consistency. Immediately pour the hot dressing over the shredded cabbage. Toss to coat evenly and cover with aluminum foil. Refrigerate at least 2 hours.   ◄ॐ

Spring Carrot Salad

SERVES 4

Use the first carrots of the season, slender and sweet, to present whole in this stunning salad.

1 pound slender first-of-the-season carrots
12 sprigs of watercress

VINAIGRETTE SAUCE
¼ teaspoon salt
¼ teaspoon paprika
1 small shallot, minced (or substitute 1½
   teaspoons freeze-dried, crushed with a mortar
   and pestle)
2 tablespoons fresh lemon juice
6 tablespoons olive or corn oil
1 tablespoon chopped fresh chervil or parsley
1 teaspoon chopped fresh basil

1. With a soft-bristled brush, scrub the carrots under cold running water. Trim off the stem ends and round them attractively with a swivel-blade peeler. Leave the carrots whole. Place in a wide saucepan and cover with cold water. Set over high heat and bring to a boil. Regulate the heat so that the water bubbles gently and cook uncovered for 10 to 30 minutes (depending on the size and quality of the carrots). Cook until the blade of a knife slides in easily, yet meets some resistance.

2. Drain the carrots and immediately cover with cold water. Rubbing the submerged carrots between your fingers, remove the thin outer skins. Rinse under cold running water and place on a double thickness of paper towel-

eling to drain. Blot dry. Refrigerate for 1 hour. The carrots should be slightly chilled, but not cold. Rinse the watercress and blot dry.

3. To make the vinaigrette, combine the salt, paprika, and shallot in a small bowl or glass jar with a screw-on lid. Add the lemon juice and stir with a fork to dissolve the salt and paprika.

4. Gradually whisk in the oil, or add it all at once, covering the jar and shaking vigorously to blend. Stir in the chervil and basil with a fork. Set aside at room temperature to allow the flavors to meld. Shake or whisk to combine and pour over the chilled carrots. Arrange on a chilled salad plate with the sprigs of watercress.   ◄ॐ

Watercress and Walnut Salad

SERVES 4

A felicitous combination of watercress, walnuts, and goat cheese.

1 bunch watercress (about 5 ounces)
½ teaspoon Dijon mustard
¼ teaspoon salt
⅛ teaspoon ground cayenne
2 tablespoons red wine vinegar
6 tablespoons vegetable oil
2 tablespoons finely chopped walnuts
4 half-inch-thick rounds ash-coated or plain
   Montrachet cheese

1. Rinse the watercress under cold running water and cut away the darkened ends of the stems. Scatter over a kitchen towel and blot dry. Roll up the towel jelly-roll fashion and place in the refrigerator to chill.

2. Meanwhile, combine the mustard, salt, and cayenne in a small bowl. Blend together with a fork or small whisk. Add the vinegar, oil, and walnuts, stirring briskly to combine. Cover and set aside at room temperature for 30 minutes to allow the flavors to meld.

3. Arrange the sprigs of watercress in the shape of a fan on individual salad plates.

Place a slice of Montrachet cheese on the watercress at the point where the stems converge at the base of the fan. Stir the dressing to combine the ingredients and pour over the watercress and cheese.   ❧

Pear Salad with Gorgonzola Dressing

SERVES 4

The combination of ripe pears and Gorgonzola cheese forms a traditional duo in the cuisine of Northern Italy. Although it usually makes its appearance during the dessert course, here the classic partnership is served as a salad.

2 ounces Gorgonzola cheese
2 ripe pears
4 tablespoons Marsala
2 tablespoons fresh lemon juice
6 tablespoons heavy cream
¼ teaspoon salt
Generous amount of freshly ground black pepper
12 leaves of ruby lettuce (also called red leaf)
2 tablespoons finely chopped pine nuts (or substitute walnuts)

1. Crumble the Gorgonzola into a small bowl and allow it to come to room temperature. (Crumbled, the cheese will fill ½ cup lightly packed.)

2. Meanwhile, peel the pears and cut them in half. Remove the cores with a large melon baller. Then, cutting a narrow groove into each pear, take out the center filaments and remove the stem. Cut each half into 6 thin lengthwise slices. Place in a shallow baking dish and sprinkle with Marsala. Toss gently to coat the surface of each slice. Cover and refrigerate.

3. With a hand mixer or wooden spoon, beat the softened Gorgonzola with the lemon juice until the mixture is smooth and fluffy. Beating continuously, add the cream in a thin stream. Blend in the salt and pepper.

4. Wash the lettuce and blot dry. Place 3 leaves on each plate. Arrange 6 pear slices atop the lettuce in a fanlike configuration. Pour what remains of the Marsala over the pear slices and lettuce leaves. Spoon on the dressing and sprinkle with the pine nuts.   ❧

Endive and Red Onion Salad

SERVES 4

Pale green spears of endive interleaved with rings of red onion make a sensational-looking salad when served in a tall, narrow glass bowl.

3 medium-size Belgian endive
1 large red Spanish or Italian onion, thinly sliced and separated into rings
8 medium-size fresh mushrooms, thinly sliced
6 tablespoons vegetable oil
2 tablespoons tangerine juice (or substitute orange juice)
¼ teaspoon salt
Generous amount of freshly ground black pepper
2 tablespoons chopped fresh chives

Endive and Red Onion Salad adds a colorful, elegant touch to a dinner party.

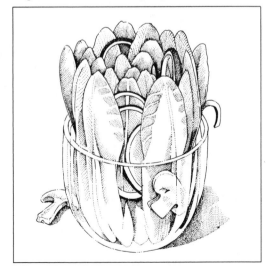

1. Cut off the darkened ends of the endive and discard any withered outer leaves. Peel the leaves away from the head and rinse under cold running water. (Heads of Belgian endive are so tightly packed that rinsing the inner leaves is often unnecessary.) Lay the leaves on a kitchen towel and blot dry.

2. Arrange the leaves in a narrow glass bowl by standing them in concentric circles. Place the onion rings between the leaves and tuck the mushroom slices in among the onions (see illustration).

3. In a 1-cup glass jar with a screw-on lid, combine the vegetable oil, tangerine juice, salt, and pepper. Shake vigorously to mix and pour over the salad. Scatter the chopped chives over the moistened leaves. ◄੨

Spinach and Mushroom Salad

SERVES 4

A lighter alternative to heavier versions of this popular salad.

1½ pounds fresh spinach
¼ pound sliced bacon
8 medium-size fresh mushrooms

CREAMY DRESSING
¼ teaspoon salt
1 teaspoon sugar
1 tablespoon freshly grated Parmesan cheese
1 tablespoon Dijon mustard
1 teaspoon Worcestershire sauce
2 tablespoons fresh lemon juice
6 tablespoons corn oil
1 large egg yolk
Generous amount of freshly ground black pepper

1. Rinse the spinach in cold water. Turning each leaf over, remove the center stem by pulling it away from the underside. Drain thoroughly, and then arrange in a single layer on a clean kitchen towel. (You may need to use two towels.) Gently roll up the towel to absorb excess moisture from the spinach. Refrigerate the spinach, towel and all.

2. Fry the bacon in a large skillet. Drain on a double thickness of paper toweling, and then break into bite-size pieces. Slice the raw mushrooms and set aside.

3. In a small bowl, combine the salt, sugar, Parmesan cheese, and mustard into a smooth paste. Add the Worcestershire sauce and lemon juice and blend well with a fork.

4. Gradually whisk in the oil. Add the egg yolk by passing it through a fine sieve. Sprinkle on the black pepper and whisk vigorously to develop a smooth, creamy texture. Use immediately or refrigerate. (Since chilling attenuates the flavor of this dressing, plan to warm it slightly by lowering the bowl into a pan of warm water. Whisk continuously during warming.) Pour over chilled spinach leaves. Add the mushroom slices and bacon. Toss lightly to coat the leaves. ◄੨

Spinach Salad with Hot Dressing

SERVES 4

If you like your spinach salad to retain some of its crunch, pour the hot dressing over the leaves and serve immediately. To wilt the leaves, toss the salad in a large bowl and then place a flat skillet cover on the bowl for a minute or two, allowing the steam to soften the spinach.

1½ pounds fresh spinach
¼ pound sliced bacon
8 medium-size fresh mushrooms, sliced
½ avocado, peeled and cubed
2 large eggs, hard-boiled and chilled
2 tablespoons bacon fat
¼ cup white wine vinegar
2 tablespoons cognac
4 green onions, thinly sliced (white portion only)
Generous amount of freshly ground black pepper

1. Rinse the spinach in cold water. Turning each leaf over, remove the center stem by pulling it away from the underside. Drain thoroughly, and then arrange in a single layer on a clean kitchen towel. (You may need to use two towels.) Gently roll up the towel to absorb excess moisture from the spinach. Refrigerate the spinach, towel and all.

2. Fry the bacon in a large skillet. Drain on a double thickness of paper toweling, and then break into bite-size pieces. Discard all but 2 tablespoons of the bacon fat. Prepare the mushrooms and avocado. Slice the chilled eggs and set aside.

3. In the skillet used to fry the bacon, combine the bacon fat, vinegar, cognac, and onions. Place over high heat and cook, stirring, until the onions are limp. Unroll the kitchen towel and empty the spinach into a large salad bowl. Pour on the hot dressing and sprinkle with black pepper. (Salt is not needed because the bacon fat is quite salty.) Add the bacon bits, raw mushroom slices, avocado cubes, and hard-boiled eggs. Toss gently to combine.   ❧

Hot Potato Salad with Bourbon

SERVES 4

Potato salad is one of America's all-time favorites. And what could make it any more American than a dash of Kentucky bourbon?

6 small California or other waxy potatoes
2 slices bacon, each cut into 8 pieces
1 small onion, finely chopped
1 tablespoon flour
½ cup hot water from the tap
2 tablespoons bourbon
1 teaspoon sugar
¼ teaspoon salt
Generous amount of freshly ground black pepper
¼ teaspoon dry mustard

1. Place the potatoes in a 6-quart pan and cover with cold water. Bring to a moderate boil. Cook uncovered until the potatoes can be easily pierced with a metal skewer.

2. Meanwhile, fry the bacon in an 8-inch skillet until browned. Transfer to absorbent paper to drain. Stir the onion into the bacon fat and cook over low heat until tender. Sprinkle on the flour and increase the heat to medium-high. Stir continuously. When the mixture foams, add the water and stir until smooth. Add the bourbon and cook, stirring, until thickened. Remove from the heat.

3. In a small mortar or bowl, blend the sugar, salt, pepper, and dry mustard. Be sure to completely disperse the mustard throughout the other ingredients. Add to the mixture in the skillet and place over medium heat. Cook, stirring, until the sugar dissolves and the mustard is well incorporated. Allow to cool to room temperature.

4. When the potatoes are tender, lift them from the water with a slotted spoon. Peel them while they are hot and slice into quarters to allow interior steam to escape. Allow the potatoes to cool to room temperature, and then cut each quarter into thin slices. Pour on the bourbon-flavored sauce. Add the cooked bacon and toss together. Serve at room temperature or heat in a 325°F. oven for 15 to 20 minutes.   ❧

Sara's Potato Salad

SERVES 6

This salad is named for my daughter, who would filch a tablespoonful every time she passed the refrigerator, so it never did serve six in our house.

2½ pounds California or other waxy potatoes
2 fresh shallots, minced, or 3 teaspoons freeze-dried shallots (or substitute 1 small onion, minced)

¼ teaspoon dry mustard
¼ teaspoon salt
¼ teaspoon sugar
2 tablespoons red wine vinegar
½ cup vegetable oil
½ teaspoon dried tarragon leaves
2 tablespoons chopped fresh parsley
Freshly ground black pepper
¾ to 1 cup mayonnaise

1. Place the potatoes in a 6-quart pan and cover with cold water. Bring to a moderate boil. Cook uncovered until the potatoes can be easily pierced with a metal skewer.

2. Meanwhile, slightly crush the freeze-dried shallots with a mortar and pestle.

3. Prepare a vinaigrette by dispersing the dry mustard throughout the salt and sugar with a fork or small whisk. (This enables the mustard to dissolve without lumping.) Whisk in the vinegar and oil. Measure the dried tarragon into your hand. Crush it with your fingertips to release the maximum flavor and add it to the dressing. Blend in the shallots and set aside.

4. When the potatoes are tender, lift them from the water with a slotted spoon. Spear a potato with a fork and peel quickly. Cut into ¾-inch cubes and transfer to a large bowl. Stir the dressing briefly and pour a small portion over the potato. Toss gently with a rubber spatula to coat every surface. Repeat until all the potatoes are peeled, cubed, and dressed. Sprinkle on the chopped parsley and freshly ground pepper. Drizzle on any remaining vinaigrette. Blend well so that the vinaigrette will be evenly absorbed by the potatoes. Cover the bowl with a piece of waxed paper. Then place a sheet of aluminum foil on top of that and secure tightly by folding down over the rim of the bowl. (Foil has a peculiar quirk — it occasionally leaves flecks of aluminum on the surface of potato salad. The waxed paper prevents that from happening.) Refrigerate for 3 to 4 hours.

5. Uncover the salad and gently blend in enough of the mayonnaise for the consistency you prefer. Test for seasoning. (You might want to add more salt at this point.) Cover and chill for at least 2 hours; however, it's best if made the day before serving to give the flavors time to meld.　　　　🖎

German Potato Salad

SERVES 6

Although most potato salads rely on waxy potatoes for their consistency, this one uses baking, or mealy, potatoes to create a less distinct, somewhat creamy texture. The full, lusty flavor is most intense when served at room temperature, but it can also be enjoyed when it is cold. A great companion for highly seasoned sausages, corned beef, or pastrami sandwiches.

2½ pounds Idaho or other mealy potatoes
¼ pound sliced bacon
1 large sweet onion, thinly sliced and separated
　into rings
3 tablespoons flour
1 cup water
1 cup sugar
¾ cup cider vinegar
1 teaspoon Dijon mustard
¼ teaspoon salt
Generous amount of freshly ground black pepper

1. Place the potatoes in a 6-quart pan and cover with cold water. Bring to a moderate

boil. Cook uncovered until the potatoes can be easily pierced with a metal skewer.

2. Meanwhile, fry the bacon in a 12-inch skillet until browned. Transfer to absorbent paper to drain. Stir the onion rings in the bacon fat and cook over low heat until tender. Sprinkle on the flour and increase the heat to medium-high. Stir continuously. When the mixture foams, blend in the water and stir until smooth. Blend in the sugar. In a small bowl, whisk the vinegar and mustard until well blended. Add to the hot mixture. Blend in the salt and pepper and cook, stirring, until the sugar is dissolved and the mixture is thickened. Reduce the heat and simmer for 20 to 30 minutes while the potatoes finish cooking.

3. When the potatoes are tender, lift them from the water with a slotted spoon. Peel while hot and slice thinly. Do not be alarmed if some of the slices crumble and break apart — that contributes to the unique texture of this salad. Place approximately one-third of the potato slices in a large bowl, pour on one-third of the simmering sauce, and crumble on one-third of the bacon. Repeat twice. (This procedure makes it possible to combine the potatoes and dressing without excessively breaking the potato slices.) Gently give the salad a final tossing. Serve immediately or, for even more pronounced flavor, cover and allow to stand at room temperature for 2 hours.   ◄¿

White Bean and Tuna Salad

SERVES 6

Here's a refreshing, yet substantial, salad to serve as a luncheon dish or as part of a soup-and-salad supper. Strips of red sweet bell pepper add flavor and color.

1 red sweet bell pepper, seeded and cut into thin strips
4 cups (two 20-ounce cans) cannellini beans
2 cans (6½ ounces each) solid white tuna
5 green onions
2 tablespoons chopped fresh basil (or substitute fresh parsley)
1 teaspoon grated lemon zest

VINAIGRETTE SAUCE
½ teaspoon salt
1 garlic clove
2 tablespoons fresh lemon juice
6 tablespoons olive oil
Generous amount of freshly ground black pepper
Boston or romaine lettuce
Pitted black Greek or Italian olives for garnish

1. Place the strips of red pepper in a 1½-quart saucepan. Add water to cover and place over high heat. Bring to a boil and cook uncovered for 1 minute. Drain and set aside.

2. Empty the cannellini beans into a colander and rinse under cold running water. Shake off the excess water, and then scatter the beans over a double thickness of paper toweling to dry.

3. Drain the oil from the tuna and flake into a large bowl. Thinly slice the onions, including most of the green portion. Add to the tuna. Gently stir in the beans, red pepper strips, and basil. Sprinkle on the lemon zest.

4. In a small mortar, combine the salt and garlic and work into a paste with a pestle. Add the lemon juice and stir with the pestle until the salt is dissolved. Transfer to a small bowl. Place the bowl on a kitchen towel folded into quarters to keep it from moving around as you whisk.

5. Gradually whisk in the oil and add the black pepper. Pour over the bean mixture and toss to combine. Spoon onto a bed of Boston or romaine lettuce and garnish with black olives cut into quarters. Serve chilled or at room temperature. ◄◊

Red Wine Vinaigrette

MAKES 1½ CUPS

Capers add pungency and an Italian flair to this zippy vinaigrette dressing. Purchase the smaller capers often described as nonpareille (larger capers are called capote). You can usually find them packed in vinegar and sold in glass jars in the specialty food sections of supermarkets. Rinse capers if you like; however, the brine adds an interesting taste.

1 garlic clove
1 small shallot
½ teaspoon sugar
½ teaspoon salt
2 anchovy fillets
1 teaspoon Dijon mustard
6 capers, nonpareille variety, drained
¼ teaspoon Worcestershire sauce
¼ teaspoon celery salt
⅓ cup red wine vinegar
1 cup olive oil (or substitute half corn, half olive oil)
Generous amount of freshly ground black pepper

1. Using a mortar and pestle, combine the garlic, shallot, sugar, and salt. Pound into a smooth paste with a pestle. Add the anchovy fillets, mustard, capers, Worcestershire sauce, and celery salt, and work into a paste. Blend in 1 tablespoon of the red wine vinegar. Transfer to a large bowl and combine with the remaining red wine vinegar.

2. Whisking continuously, add the oil in a thin stream. Season with pepper and serve immediately or cover and refrigerate. This dressing will keep for 2 to 3 weeks. ◄◊

Basic Vinaigrette Sauce

MAKES ½ CUP

This recipe is for the light classic vinegar and oil dressing that customarily contains no emulsifying agent. The sauce is considered a temporary suspension because the oil and water-based components separate almost immediately. Here mustard has been added to create a transitory emulsion — one that will hold the components together for a minute or two. Minced garlic or shallot and a variety of herbs may be added to a vinaigrette for flavor.

¼ teaspoon salt
⅛ teaspoon ground cayenne
¼ teaspoon dry mustard
2 tablespoons red or white wine vinegar (or substitute lemon juice)
1 small shallot, minced
1 teaspoon dried herbs, such as basil, tarragon leaves, chervil, or a combination (or 1 tablespoon chopped fresh herbs)
6 tablespoons vegetable oil of your choice

1. Using a small mortar and pestle, disperse the salt and cayenne throughout the dry mustard to enable the mustard to dissolve more easily. Add the vinegar and blend until the salt and mustard are dissolved. Transfer to a small bowl.

2. Stir the minced shallot and herbs into the vinegar mixture. Then, whisking continuously, add the oil in a thin stream. Use immediately or cover and allow to stand at room temperature so that the flavors will meld. Whisk again before serving. ◄◊

Vinaigrette Sauce Variations I

MAKES ½ CUP

Using the basic proportions of 1 part acidic element to 3 parts oil, you can devise your own "house" dressing. If you like, an egg yolk may be incorporated to supply the lecithin needed for a creamy consistency and a more stable suspension.

¼ teaspoon salt

⅛ teaspoon ground cayenne (or substitute a generous amount of freshly ground black pepper)

¼ teaspoon dry mustard (optional; see Note)

2 tablespoons of one of the following acidic ingredients: red wine vinegar, white wine vinegar, sherry vinegar; *or* strawberry vinegar, raspberry vinegar, another aromatic vinegar such as the specially aged wine vinegar known as Aceto Balsamico; *or* lemon juice, lime juice, orange juice, grapefruit juice

1 large egg yolk (optional)

6 tablespoons of one of the following oils: sunflower oil, safflower oil, corn oil, peanut oil, olive oil; *or* almond oil, walnut oil, hazelnut oil

1 teaspoon dried herbs, such as basil, tarragon leaves, chervil, or a combination (or substitute 1 tablespoon chopped fresh herbs)

1. Using a small mortar and pestle, disperse the salt and cayenne throughout the dry mustard to enable the mustard to dissolve more easily. Add the acidic ingredient and blend until the salt and mustard are dissolved. Transfer to a small bowl.

2. If you're adding the egg yolk, force it through a sieve and whisk into the acidic mixture until smooth in appearance. Slowly pour in the oil in a thin stream. Whisk continously until creamy and well blended. Whisk in the herbs. Use immediately or cover and refrigerate for an hour to allow the flavors to meld. Whisk again before serving if necessary.

NOTE: The mustard is an optional ingredient that you may prefer to omit, especially with fruit-flavored vinegars such as strawberry and raspberry. In such a case, blend the salt and cayenne with the acidic ingredient in a small bowl and proceed to step 2. Keep in mind that in creating a dressing you're actually orchestrating flavors. To bring out the

taste of the acidic component, combine it with one of the soft, unobtrusive oils (sunflower or safflower); to mellow or counterbalance the acidic element, use a more aggressive oil (corn or olive). On the other hand, if you want the flavor of the oil to predominate, pair a stronger flavored oil (olive or hazelnut) with a less assertive acid (lemon or lime juice). Herbs should be chosen to complement the balance of flavor. If in doubt, use chervil and parsley.   ❧

Creamy Caesar Dressing

MAKES ¾ CUP

There's no egg to coddle with this Caesar dressing. Whisking a raw egg yolk into a vinaigrette base creates the type of creamy dressing described under Vinaigrette Sauce Variations I (p. 215). Pour this over romaine torn into bite-size pieces, scatter on some toasted croutons, and toss to combine.

½ teaspoon salt

1 garlic clove

4 anchovy fillets

2 tablespoons freshly grated Parmesan cheese

1 tablespoon Dijon mustard

1 teaspoon Worcestershire sauce
3 tablespoons fresh lemon juice
1 large egg yolk
½ cup plus 1 tablespoon olive oil
Generous amount of freshly ground black pepper

1. Using a mortar and pestle, work the salt and garlic into a smooth paste. Add the anchovy fillets, Parmesan cheese, and mustard. Blend into the garlic paste with the pestle. When the mixture is smooth, work in the Worcestershire sauce and lemon juice until the salt is dissolved (you'll no longer detect a grittiness). Transfer to a medium-size bowl.

2. Add the egg yolk by passing it through a fine sieve. Whisk vigorously to incorporate. Gradually pour in the oil, whisking continuously, until all the oil is blended in and the dressing develops a creamy consistency. Then add the black pepper.

NOTE: If you place the bowl on top of a folded kitchen towel, the bowl will not move around while you are pouring the oil in with one hand and whisking it with the other. ◄೩

6 tablespoons sour cream, Crème Fraîche (p. 361), buttermilk, yogurt, or whipped heavy cream
1 teaspoon dried herbs, such as basil, tarragon leaves, chervil, or a combination (or substitute 1 tablespoon chopped fresh herbs)

1. Using a small mortar and pestle, disperse the salt and cayenne throughout the dry mustard to enable the mustard to dissolve more easily. Add the vinegar or lemon juice and blend until the salt and mustard are dissolved. Transfer to a small bowl.

2. Whisking continuously, slowly blend in the creamy ingredient. Stir in the herbs. Cover and refrigerate for 1 hour to allow the flavors to meld.

NOTE: In dressings of this type, the mustard is incorporated for flavor, not for its emulsifying properties; consequently, it may be omitted according to your taste. If you leave the mustard out, blend the salt and cayenne with the vinegar or lemon juice in a small bowl and proceed to step 2. ◄೩

Vinaigrette Sauce Variations II

MAKES ½ CUP

Another method of achieving a creamy vinaigrette is by substituting a creamy ingredient in place of the oil component. Buttermilk, sour cream, yogurt, heavy cream, or crème fraîche are all possibilities. The result is a rather thick, creamy consistency that will hold together well without the use of an egg yolk.

¼ teaspoon salt
⅛ teaspoon ground cayenne (or substitute a generous amount of freshly ground black pepper)
¼ teaspoon dry mustard (optional; see Note)
2 tablespoons red or white wine vinegar, or lemon juice (or substitute one of the other acidic ingredients listed under Vinaigrette Sauce Variations I, p. 215).

Green Goddess Dressing

MAKES ½ CUP

An outstanding dressing that tastes best when made with fresh herbs.

¼ teaspoon salt
⅛ teaspoon cayenne
½ teaspoon sugar
¼ teaspoon dry mustard
1 garlic clove
2 anchovy fillets
2 tablespoons lemon juice
6 tablespoons sour cream
1½ teaspoons chopped fresh chives (or substitute ½ teaspoon dried)
1½ teaspoons chopped fresh parsley (or substitute ½ teaspoon dried)
1½ teaspoons chopped fresh tarragon leaves (or substitute ½ teaspoon dried)

1. Using a small mortar and pestle, disperse the salt, cayenne, and sugar throughout the mustard to enable the mustard to dissolve more easily. Add the garlic and anchovy fillets. Work into a paste with the pestle. Add the lemon juice and blend in until the salt, mustard, and sugar are dissolved. Transfer to a small bowl.

2. Whisking continuously, slowly blend in the sour cream. Stir in the herbs. Cover and refrigerate for 1 hour to allow the flavors to meld.   ⊷

Herbed Buttermilk Dressing

MAKES 1 CUP

Try this dressing on tomato slices interspersed with rings of sweet onion, or serve with cold roast beef or thinly sliced cold steak.

½ cup buttermilk
2 tablespoons lemon juice
1 medium shallot, cut into quarters
1 garlic clove, cut in half
2 tablespoons chopped fresh parsley (or
    substitute 2 teaspoons dried)
1 tablespoon chopped fresh basil (or substitute 1
    teaspoon dried)
1½ teaspoons chopped fresh tarragon leaves (or
    substitute ½ teaspoon dried)
1½ teaspoons chopped fresh oregano (or
    substitute ½ teaspoon dried)
¼ cup mayonnaise
½ teaspoon salt
Generous amount of freshly ground black pepper

1. In the container of a blender or processor, combine the buttermilk, lemon juice, shallot, garlic, and herbs. Whirl to blend and pulverize the shallot and garlic.

2. Add the mayonnaise, whirling briefly to incorporate. Season with salt and pepper. Cover and refrigerate for 1 hour to allow the flavors to meld.   ⊷

Mint Salad Dressing

MAKES ½ CUP

Yogurt provides the creamy base for this delightful dressing. Serve over chilled romaine or spears of Belgian endive.

¼ teaspoon salt
½ teaspoon sugar
1 garlic clove
6 tablespoons unflavored yogurt
1 tablespoon chopped fresh mint
Generous amount of freshly ground black pepper

1. Using a small mortar and pestle, combine the salt and sugar. Then add the garlic and work to a paste. Add 1 tablespoon yogurt and blend well. Transfer to a small bowl.

2. Whisking continuously, incorporate the remaining yogurt. Stir in the mint. Season with pepper and cover. Refrigerate 1 hour to allow the flavors to meld.   ⊷

CREAM-STYLE SALAD DRESSINGS

Cream-style salad dressings are immensely popular in America, but the commercial varieties often possess an unpleasant plastic consistency and a stale, lackluster taste. There are several fairly uncomplicated ways to make your own creamy dressings. For example, a light creamy consistency can be produced by adding an egg yolk to a basic vinaigrette (see Vinaigrette Sauce Variations I, p. 215); or a thicker, creamier texture can be achieved by using a creamy ingredient in place of the oil component (see Vinaigrette Sauce Variations II, p. 217).

A third technique for creating cream-style dressing relies on starting with a mayonnaise base, and then adding the flavorful ingredients characteristic of different kinds of dressing. You can prepare the following recipes by beginning with the base described, by substituting ⅔ cup of homemade mayonnaise (see p. 354 or p. 356), or by using ⅔ cup of high-quality commercial mayonnaise.

Creamy Italian Dressing

MAKES ABOUT ¾ CUP

MAYONNAISE BASE
1 large egg yolk
½ teaspoon Dijon mustard
½ teaspoon salt
1 tablespoon fresh lemon juice
½ cup olive oil, corn oil, peanut oil, or a combination

FLAVORING INGREDIENTS
1 garlic clove, cut into quarters
½ teaspoon dried rosemary leaves
½ teaspoon sugar
2 tablespoons red wine vinegar
2 tablespoons white distilled vinegar
1 teaspoon dried basil
½ teaspoon dried oregano
Salt and freshly ground black pepper (optional)
2 to 4 tablespoons light cream (optional)

1. In a large, wide bowl, prepare the base by combining the egg yolk, mustard, salt, and lemon juice. Whisk lightly to blend. Cover the bowl with a kitchen towel and allow the contents to come to room temperature (about 30 minutes). Remove the towel and fold it into quarters. Place the bowl on top of the folded towel to keep the bowl from moving around as you whisk. Whisk vigorously until the egg mixture thickens slightly. Continue to whisk, adding the oil drop by drop at first and then in a thin stream.

2. When all the oil is incorporated and a stiff base is formed, set the mixture aside. In a small mortar, combine the garlic, rosemary, and sugar. Work into a paste with the pestle.

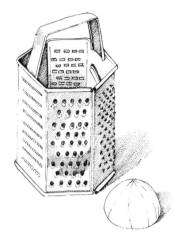

Add the wine vinegar and stir with the pestle until the sugar is dissolved. Blend into the base. Add the white vinegar, basil, and oregano. Stir to blend and taste for seasoning. Add salt and pepper if you wish. To thin, add light cream. Serve as a dressing for green salad or toss with cold shrimp. ⌇

Creamy Roquefort Dressing

MAKES ABOUT ¾ CUP

¼ cup finely crumbled Roquefort cheese (or substitute Stilton or other blue-veined cheese to create a different effect)
Mayonnaise Base (see previous recipe)
2 tablespoons sour cream
1 tablespoon fresh lemon juice
Salt and freshly ground black pepper (optional)
2 to 4 tablespoons light cream (optional)

1. Set out the Roquefort cheese in a small bowl and allow it to come to room temperature so that it will soften.

2. Prepare Mayonnaise Base.

3. After a stiff base is formed, beat the softened Roquefort with a wooden spoon until it becomes light in texture. Add the sour cream and fresh lemon juice to the cheese and beat. Blend with the base. Taste for seasoning, add-

ing salt and pepper if you wish. To thin, add light cream. Serve as a dressing for green salad or spread on hot steak sandwiches.   ✌

Creamy Russian Dressing

MAKES ABOUT ¾ CUP

Mayonnaise Base (see Creamy Italian Dressing, p. 219)
3 tablespoons ketchup
1 tablespoon red pepper relish
1 teaspoon minced onion
½ teaspoon Worcestershire sauce
Salt and freshly ground black pepper (optional)
2 to 4 tablespoons light cream (optional)

1. Prepare Mayonnaise Base.
2. After a stiff base is formed, stir in the ketchup, red pepper relish, minced onion, and Worcestershire sauce. Taste for seasoning, adding salt and pepper if you wish. To thin, add light cream. Serve as a dressing for green salad, spoon over hard-boiled eggs, or use as an accompaniment to cold chicken or turkey.   ✌

Breads

Maple Whole Wheat Bread

MAKES 1 LOAF

Baking 100 percent whole wheat bread can be tricky. Because whole wheat flour is absorbed by liquid quite readily, cooks often add more flour than they should and end up with a dense, heavy loaf. The secret to success is to knead lightly, using as little additional flour as possible. Allowing the dough to rise 3 times gives it an opportunity to develop full flavor.

1¼ cups water
¼ cup cold milk
3 tablespoons maple syrup
3 tablespoons butter
1 teaspoon salt
1 package dry yeast
¼ cup warm (100°F.) water
4 to 4½ cups whole wheat flour, scoop measured

1. Bring 1¼ cups of water to a boil in a 2½-quart saucepan. Remove from the heat. Add the milk, maple syrup, butter, and salt, stirring until the butter melts. The mixture should then be lukewarm.

2. In a large mixing bowl, dissolve the yeast in the warm water. Blend in the warm butter mixture. Add 3½ cups of flour and beat vi-

gorously with a wooden spoon until the dough pulls away from the bowl in ropy strands.

3. Measure out ¼ cup of flour onto a work surface and spread the flour out in a large circle. Empty the dough onto the flour. Sift ¼ cup of flour over the dough and knead until all the flour has been absorbed. Use very light movements. Place in a greased bowl and cover with plastic wrap. Secure the wrap with an elastic band to keep the dough moist. Set in a draft-free place to rise.

4. When the dough is double in size (about 1½ hours), turn it out onto a floured surface and press-knead 4 or 5 times according to the directions on p. 225. Shape it into a ball, dust it lightly with flour, and return it to a greased bowl. Cover with plastic wrap and allow it to rise a second time.

5. When the dough is double in size (60 to 70 minutes), turn it out onto a floured surface. Without kneading, shape into a loaf and place in a well-greased 9×5-inch loaf pan. Cover with a kitchen towel and allow to rise.

6. When the dough has doubled in size (45 to 55 minutes), but is still resilient to the touch, place in a preheated 400°F. oven. Bake for 40 to 50 minutes or until the loaf sounds hollow when you tap the top of it. Turn out and set on a cooling rack.

NOTE: For a dark, shiny crust, brush on the following glaze while the loaf is still hot: In a small saucepan, combine 2 tablespoons butter, ½ teaspoon water, and a few grains of instant coffee. Heat to melt the butter and dissolve the coffee.

One-Hour French Bread

MAKES TWO 17½-INCH LOAVES

In this recipe, yeast is proofed to get things going so the bread will rise in 1 hour. Since the proofing takes place in 1 cup of water, the mixture won't double or foam the way it does when you proof yeast in only ¼ cup of water.

1 cup warm (100°F.) water
¾ teaspoon sugar
1 package dry yeast
3 cups bread flour (preferably bromated), scoop
   measured
¾ teaspoon salt
Lightly salted water

1. Set the oven dial to "Warm" or 150°F. Stir the water and sugar together in a 2-cup glass measure until the sugar is almost completely dissolved. Sprinkle on the yeast and stir to moisten all the granules. Place in the oven. Turn the heat off and close the door. When the mixture is murky, remove it from the oven.

2. In the bowl of a processor, pulse the flour and salt with the steel blade until well blended. With the motor running, pour the yeast mixture through the feed tube. Add 1 or 2 tablespoons additional water if needed to form a ball. Remove the dough from the processor and dust with flour. Knead for 1 minute.

3. Divide the dough in half. With the palms of your hands, roll the dough away from you, shaping it into two 17½-inch French loaves. Dust with flour and lay in 2 well-greased baguette pans. Cover with a kitchen towel and allow to rise until double (45 to 60 minutes).

4. Slash the loaves across the tops with a razor blade and brush with lightly salted water. Place in a preheated 450°F. oven for 30 to 40 minutes or until nicely browned. Turn out and cool on a rack.   ❧

Country-Style Italian Bread

MAKES ONE 8-INCH LOAF

This recipe makes a hefty round loaf of the best coarsely textured bread you've ever eaten. The ingredient that makes the difference is semolina. Look for "100 percent pure durum semolina" in Italian grocery stores and ethnic food shops. Pale yellow, this semolina has a granular texture resembling that of cream of wheat. It is more coarsely ground than the semolina flour used in making pasta.

2 cups warm (100°F.) water
2 packages dry yeast
1 teaspoon sugar
2 cups coarse semolina
1 teaspoon salt
2¼ to 3 cups bread flour (preferably bromated),
   scoop measured

1. In a large mixing bowl, combine the water, yeast, and sugar. Stir to dissolve the yeast and sugar. Set aside for 5 minutes.

2. Add the semolina, salt, and 1 cup of the flour. Beat vigorously with a wooden spoon until the dough pulls away from the bowl in ropy strands.

3. Measure out 1 cup of flour onto a work surface and spread the flour out in a large circle. Empty the dough onto the flour. Sift ¼ cup of flour over the dough and knead until all the flour has been absorbed and the dough springs back when you poke it with your finger. Place in a greased bowl and cover with plastic wrap. Secure the wrap with an elastic band to keep the dough moist. Set the bowl in a draft-free place to rise.

4. When the dough is double in size (about 1½ hours), turn it out onto a floured surface and press-knead 4 or 5 times according to the directions on p. 225. Shape it into a ball, dust it lightly with flour, and return it to a greased bowl. Cover with plastic wrap and allow it to rise a second time.

5. When the dough is double in size (60 to 70 minutes), turn it out onto a floured surface. Press-knead 3 times. This unusual kneading technique has a dual advantage that comes in especially handy when you're forming a free-standing loaf — it not only incorporates less flour (which results in a moist crumb), but all the folding and layering it involves encourages the dough to acquire a high, round shape.

6. Form the dough into a ball and dust with sifted flour. Lay a piece of extra-heavy aluminum foil on a flat cookie sheet. Grease the

foil and sprinkle with cornmeal or semolina. Place the dough in the center of the foil and loosely drape a piece of plastic wrap over the surface. When the dough is nearly double in size, preheat a baking stone at 475°F. for 10 minutes. Using a razor blade held at a 45° angle, make 2 slashes in the loaf — 1 from east to west, the other north to south. Lightly sift flour over the loaf. Slide the foil with dough on top onto the hot baking stone. Bake for 10 minutes at 475°F. to firm the loaf. Pull the foil out from under the loaf and reduce the oven temperature to 450°F. Bake for 45 minutes or until nicely browned.

NOTE: This bread may be baked in a greased 8-inch round pan (black steel is best) or 1½-quart Pyrex casserole with rounded sides.   ◄୬

American-Style Italian Bread

MAKES TWO 17½-INCH LOAVES

This recipe contains a high ratio of liquid to flour — 1 part water to 2 parts flour — which produces the light, delicately textured loaf favored by Americans. It also produces an exceptionally moist, sticky dough that requires an unusual kneading technique. Traditional forms of kneading incorporate a considerable amount of flour that would upset the moisture balance of this dough, so I've outlined the steps for the Press Method of Kneading — a technique that involves pressing and folding the dough without working in excessive flour.

1½ cups warm (100°F.) water
1 package dry yeast
Small pinch of sugar
3 cups bread flour (preferably bromated), scoop measured
¾ teaspoon salt
¾ teaspoon sugar

1. In a large mixing bowl, combine the water, yeast, and pinch of sugar. Stir to dissolve the yeast and sugar and set aside.

2. In another large bowl, combine the flour, salt, and ¾ teaspoon sugar. Whisk or toss with a fork to blend thoroughly.

3. Pour two-thirds of the flour mixture into the water and dissolved yeast mixture. Beat vigorously with a wooden spoon until the dough pulls away from the bowl in ropy strands. The mixture will be very wet.

4. Dump all but 2 tablespoons of the remaining flour mixture onto a work surface and spread the mixture out in a large circle. Empty the dough onto the flour mixture and sprinkle the remaining 2 tablespoons of flour over the dough. Using a pastry scraper (because the dough is so moist), lift and fold the dough over on itself. Press down to work the flour in. Repeat the process of folding and pressing with the pastry scraper until the flour is entirely absorbed. Shape the dough into a ball (actually it's more like a flabby mass), lightly dust with flour, and place in a greased bowl. Cover with plastic wrap and secure with an elastic band to keep the dough moist. Set in a draft-free place to rise.

5. When the dough is double in size (about 1½ hours), turn it out onto a floured surface. Sift on a small amount of flour and distribute it over the surface with your hand. Then knead according to the Press Method of Kneading (see Notes).

6. After press-kneading 4 or 5 times, shape the dough into a ball, dust it lightly with flour, and return it to a greased bowl. Cover with plastic wrap and allow it to rise again.

7. When the dough is double in size (60 to 70 minutes), turn it out onto a floured surface, and press into a large circle. (Do not knead.) Cut the dough in half with a serrated knife to form 2 semicircles. Turn one piece of dough so that the rounded edge is nearest you. Roll up the dough, starting at that rounded edge, pressing and shaping into a long, slender loaf. Pinch the dough to seal the seams together and repeat with the other loaf. Place in 2 well-greased baguette pans that have been sprinkled with cornmeal if you like. Drape plastic wrap loosely over the loaves and allow to rise.

8. When the dough is double in size (45 to 55 minutes), but still resilient to the touch, make 3 diagonal slashes with a razor blade and brush with a cornstarch glaze or spray with a plant mister filled with salt water (see Notes). Place in a preheated 450°F. oven and bake for 25 minutes or until nicely browned. Remove from the pans immediately and cool on a rack.

NOTES: To make cornstarch glaze, dissolve 1 teaspoon cornstarch in ½ cup cold water in a small saucepan. Bring to a boil and cook, stirring, until the mixture is clear. Cool for 5 minutes. Brush on the uncooked loaves and bake for 10 minutes. Apply a second coat, and bake for 15 minutes more.

If you have the patience and prefer a salt-water crust, combine 1 cup warm water with 1 teaspoon salt and stir to dissolve. Pour it into a mister. (I keep a well-cleaned, pump-style hair spray container for this purpose.) Open the oven and spray the loaves at 5-minute intervals for the first 20 minutes of the baking time.

PRESS METHOD OF KNEADING

Using both hands, press down on the dough to evenly distribute the bubbles of carbon dioxide. Form the dough into a flat circle approximately ½ inch thick. Dust any sticky spots with flour. Fold the circle in half and dust the surface. Press down over the entire surface of the dough until the 2 layers are well joined and the dough is ½ to ¾ inch thick.

Fold the semicircle of dough in half to form a triangle. Dust the surface if necessary and press down once again. Continue pressing over the entire surface until the 2 layers are well joined and the dough is ½ to ¾ inch thick.

Bring up the 3 points of the triangle, placing one on top of the other. Dust any sticky spots and press down to join the 3 layers together. At this point, you will have a somewhat irregular circle of dough. Turn the circle over and go on with the recipe. (Recipes usually direct you to continue to knead by repeating all the steps or to shape the dough into a ball and return it to a greased bowl for another rising.)　　　　　　　　　　🥨

Hawaiian Sweet Bread

MAKES TWO 9-INCH ROUNDS

Because this dough contains an exceptionally high proportion of sugar, the customary amount of yeast has been doubled. This doubling is to compensate for the inhibiting effect excess sugar has on the growth of yeast. You can use 1 package of yeast if you like, but the dough will take much longer to rise.

½ cup leftover mashed potatoes (or substitute ⅓ cup instant mashed potato granules softened in ⅓ cup boiling water)
¼ cup milk
½ cup butter, cut into small pieces
2 packages dry yeast
⅓ cup warm (100°F.) water
⅔ cup sugar
3 large eggs
1 teaspoon tap water
1 teaspoon salt
½ teaspoon vanilla
4½ to 5 cups all-purpose or bread flour, scoop measured

1. In a small saucepan warm the leftover mashed potatoes with the milk, or prepare the instant mashed potato and blend in the milk. Stir the pieces of butter into the hot potato mixture until melted. Return briefly to the heat if necessary to melt the butter. Transfer to a large bowl and set aside.

2. Dissolve the yeast in warm water, stirring in a pinch of sugar taken from the ⅔ cup.

3. Blend the sugar minus the pinch into the potato mixture. Beat the eggs in a small bowl. Remove 2 tablespoons of the eggs and combine with 1 teaspoon water in a glass jar. Refrigerate until needed for glazing the loaves. Add the salt, vanilla, and dissolved yeast to the remaining eggs. Beat into the potato mixture with a wooden spoon.

4. Add 2 cups of flour and beat vigorously

until the dough pulls away from the bowl in ropy strands. Work in another cup of flour.

5. Measure out 1 cup of flour onto a work surface and spread the flour out in a large circle. Empty the dough onto the flour. Sift ¼ cup of flour over the top and knead until all the flour has been absorbed and the dough springs back when poked with your finger. Add more flour if necessary to form a smooth, nonsticky dough. Place in a greased bowl and cover with plastic wrap. Secure the wrap with an elastic band to keep the dough moist. Set in a draft-free place to rise.

6. When double in size (2 to 2½ hours), turn the dough out onto a floured surface. Dust with flour and press the dough into a rectangular shape with the palms of your hands. Roll into a cylinder and distribute the carbon dioxide bubbles by pressing down and rolling the dough at the same time. Divide the roll of dough in half and allow it to rest while you grease two 9-inch pie pans. (Cake pans can be used if necessary, but the slanting sides of a pie pan produce a more attractive loaf.) Using the palms of your hands, roll each piece of dough into a 30-inch rope. Hold one end of the rope in place with one hand while twisting the rope by repeatedly rolling the other end of the dough away from you. As you twist, the rope of dough will become shorter and fatter. When it measures about 13 inches long, lay the dough around the outer edge of the pie pan, leaving ½ inch between the dough and the side of the pan. Coil one end into the center in a snail-like fashion. (Leave space in the coil for the dough to expand.) Repeat with the second loaf. Cover loosely with plastic wrap and set aside to rise.

7. When the loaves are nearly doubled (50 to 60 minutes), brush them with the reserved egg-and-water mixture and bake in an oven preheated to 350°F. for 30 minutes or until the top is nicely browned. Turn out and cool on a rack. Serve warm or cooled. (To fully enjoy the unique consistency of this bread, pull it apart rather than cut pieces.)   ⌐ನ

Old-Fashioned Sourdough Starter (Water-Based Starter)

MAKES 8 TO 9 CUPS

You've probably heard it said that "real" sourdough can only be made in San Francisco. That's because the yeasts and bacteria living in the air and water of San Francisco are different from those living in Minneapolis or Hartford, and therefore they produce their own uniquely flavored dough. But that doesn't necessarily make it any more "real" than dough flavored by microorganisms in other areas. If you want to try making sourdough bread unique to your area, leave out the yeast in the following recipe and let the native yeasts and bacteria do the work. Using commercial yeast yields more dependable results, but because it is more active, it crowds out the wild yeasts and your dough loses its individuality. Potato starch is easily converted to the glucose that yeasts need as food, which explains why most starter recipes of the non-milk variety include some form of potato.

2 large mealy potatoes, peeled and halved
2 tablespoons sugar
3 cups flour, scoop measured
1 package dry yeast plus ¼ cup warm water (optional)
1 cup warm (100°F.) water

1. Place the potatoes in a 4½-quart saucepan. Cover with water and bring to a boil. Cook potatoes uncovered, boiling at a brisk pace, until they fall apart. Do not drain. Beat the potatoes into a purée or force through a sieve. Cool to room temperature.

2. Add more water if necessary to form 3 cups of potato purée and pour into a large glass or ceramic bowl. Using a wooden spoon, stir in the sugar and 2 cups flour. Dissolve the yeast, if you're using it, in ¼ cup of the warm water. Add to mixture and beat until it is smooth and creamy.

3. Since the object is to attract wild yeasts in the air and eventually to lure the airborne

bacteria that convert alcohol to acetic acid, loosely cover the bowl of starter with a porous cloth towel. Set in a warm spot (80° to 85°F.) to begin fermentation. When the mixture begins to bubble, move it to a cooler place (65° to 70°F.) so that it will not ferment too rapidly.

4. In 24 hours, the starter should be bubbly and have a pleasantly sour smell. You could use it at that point, but flavor develops with time. So for best results "feed" it the remaining 1 cup flour and 1 cup warm water. Stir it down, cover with a towel, and let it stand for 2 to 3 more days. Once a day stir in the colorless liquid that rises to the surface. If the mixture turns pink or orange, that means unwanted molds have dropped in. You'll have to toss it out. Green, black, or blue molds are harmless, so just skim them off.

5. When ready to use, take out what you need and replenish it with an equal amount of flour and water combined. (For example, if you remove 1 cup of starter, replace it with ½ cup flour and ½ cup warm water.) Store sourdough starter in a glass or plastic container with a tightly fitting lid. Kept refrigerated, a starter will last indefinitely. But flavor develops best when a starter is replenished often, so periodically take some out and give it to a friend if you find that you use your starter infrequently.

NOTE: Always allow sourdough starter to come to room temperature before using. ◄੨

Herman Starter (Milk-Based Sourdough Starter)

MAKES 6 TO 7 CUPS

Like the Old-Fashioned Sourdough Starter (p. 226), this mixture achieves a tangy, acidic flavor through the process of fermentation. However, the fermentation process in a water-based sourdough starter is accomplished by bacteria feeding on the alcohol given off as waste when yeast consumes sugar. In this recipe, the fermenting is primarily done by bacteria feeding on the sugar in milk. Yogurt is included because it contains lactic-acid-producing bacteria that feed on lactose. (See entry for Sourdough Starter.)

2 cups milk
3 tablespoons unflavored yogurt
1 package dry yeast
¼ cup warm (100°F.) water
2 cups flour, scoop measured

1. In a 1½-quart saucepan, heat 1 cup of the milk over moderate heat until it registers 98°F. on a thermometer. Remove from the heat and stir in the yogurt. Pour into a glass or ceramic bowl. Cover with plastic wrap and secure airtight with an elastic band. Set in a warm spot (80° to 85°F.) to begin the fermentation process.

2. In 24 hours, the mixture should be about the consistency of yogurt. Dissolve the yeast in the warm water. Stir 1 cup of the flour and the dissolved yeast into the starter with a nonmetal spoon. Cover tightly and allow to stand at room temperature for 3 to 5 days. (The length of time is determined by how sour you want the starter to be.) The mixture should give off a pleasantly sour smell and have a bubbly consistency. If the bubbles have deflated, it means that the yeast cells are resting. They will become active again when you add more flour.

3. Warm the remaining 1 cup milk to 98°F. and add to the starter along with the remaining 1 cup of flour, using a nonmetal spoon. Cover tightly and allow to stand at room temperature for 24 hours. Uncovering the starter gives mold a chance to sneak in, so don't lift the plastic wrap more often than necessary. If at any point the starter turns pink or orange, discard it and start over; green, black, or blue spots are harmless mold and can be lifted off. Clear liquid that is given off should be stirred back in.

4. Take out whatever starter you need and replenish it with equal portions of flour and milk. (For example, if you remove 1 cup of starter, replace it with ½ cup flour and ½ cup

warm milk.) Store the starter in a glass or plastic container with a tightly fitting lid. Kept refrigerated, a starter will last indefinitely, but flavor develops best when a starter is replenished often. If you use your starter infrequently, periodically take some out and give it to a friend.

NOTE: To provide the warm environment needed in step 1, set the oven to its lowest setting. When the set temperature has been reached and the heat goes off, place the starter inside the oven, close the door, and turn the oven off. After the yeast is added, a slightly cooler climate is needed to prevent the yeast from multiplying too rapidly. Normal room temperature (about 70°F.) is fine.   ◆⅔

Sourdough Banana Bread

MAKES 1 LOAF

The outstanding flavor of this quick bread is the result of using a milk-based, or lactic acid, sourdough starter. (See entry for Sourdough Starter.)

1 cup Herman Starter (p. 227)
2¼ cups whole wheat flour, scoop measured
1 teaspoon baking powder
½ teaspoon baking soda
½ teaspoon salt
¾ teaspoon ground cinnamon
¼ teaspoon freshly ground nutmeg
1 large egg
¼ cup granulated sugar
½ cup light brown sugar
¼ cup butter, melted
3 medium or 2 large bananas, mashed (about 1 cup)
½ cup chopped walnuts

1. Preheat the oven to 350°F. Set out the sourdough starter and allow it to come to room temperature. Meanwhile, sift the flour, baking powder, soda, salt, cinnamon, and nutmeg into a small bowl and stir with a fork or whisk to blend thoroughly.

2. In a large mixing bowl, beat the egg and the sugars until mixture is smooth and slightly thickened. Add the cooled melted butter, mashed bananas, and sourdough starter. Blend well. With the mixer on low speed, or by hand, blend in the dry ingredients until they are moistened. Do not overbeat. Stir in the walnuts.

3. Pour into a greased 9×5-inch loaf pan and bake for 50 to 60 minutes. Test for doneness by inserting a metal skewer into the center of the loaf. When the skewer comes out clean, the bread is done. Cool on a rack for 10 minutes, and then turn out.

NOTE: This bread should develop a handsome crack in the top crust. To encourage it to form down the center of the loaf, run the blade of a kitchen knife through the batter just before baking. Draw the knife from one end of the pan to the other and cut through the batter to the bottom of the pan.   ◆⅔

Sourdough French Bread

MAKES TWO 15-INCH LOAVES

This is the crusty sourdough loaf for which San Francisco is famous. Just keep in mind that the microorganisms in your air, water, and flour will produce bread that tastes entirely different from that made in San Francisco — and who knows, maybe better.

2 cups Old-Fashioned Sourdough Starter (p. 226)
1 cup warm (100°F.) water
3 teaspoons sugar
1 package dry yeast
1 teaspoon salt
4 to 5 cups bread flour (preferably bromated), scoop measured

1. Allow the sourdough starter to warm to room temperature. Pour the warm water into a large mixing bowl and stir in 1 teaspoon of sugar. Add the yeast and stir to dissolve.

2. When the yeast looks murky and bubbles begin to form, blend in the remaining 2 teaspoons of sugar, salt, and sourdough starter. Add 2 cups of flour and beat until smooth. Add another cup of flour and beat vigorously until the dough pulls away from the bowl in ropy strands.

3. Measure out ¾ cup of flour onto a work surface and spread the flour out in a large circle. Empty the dough onto the flour and sift ¼ cup of flour over the dough. Knead until all the flour has been absorbed and the dough springs back when you poke it with your finger. Add more flour if necessary to form a smooth, nonsticky dough. Place in a greased bowl and cover with plastic wrap. Secure the wrap with an elastic band to keep the dough moist. Set aside in a draft-free place to rise.

4. When the dough is double in size (about 1½ hours), turn it out onto a floured surface. Dust with flour and knead briefly to evenly distribute the bubbles of carbon dioxide. Return the dough to the greased bowl to rise.

5. When the dough is double in size (about 60 to 70 minutes), turn out onto a floured surface. Dust with flour and press into a flat rectangular shape using the palms of your hands. Roll into a cylinder and distribute the bubbles of carbon dioxide by pressing down and rolling at the same time. Divide the roll in half. Shape the ends so they taper and roll into two 15-inch loaves. (Or shape and bake as described in steps 7 and 8 under American-Style Italian Bread, p. 224.)

6. Lay a piece of extra-heavy aluminum foil on a flat cookie sheet. Grease the foil and sprinkle with cornmeal or semolina. Dust the loaves with sifted flour and transfer to the greased foil. Cover loosely with plastic wrap. When the dough is nearly double in size, place a baking stone on an oven rack set at the level next to the lowest. Heat the baking stone for 10 minutes at 475°F. Make 3 diagonal slashes down each loaf with a razor blade. Lightly sift flour over the loaves and slide the foil with the dough on top onto the hot baking stone. Bake for 10 minutes at 475°F. to firm the loaves. Pull the foil out from under the loaves and reduce the temperature to 450°F. Bake for 35 to 45 minutes or until nicely browned.

NOTE: Sifted flour draws moisture from the loaves like a blotter and produces a rather thick, exceptionally crusty exterior. If you wish, you can develop the crust by spraying with water instead. Use a plant mister filled with salted water and spray the loaves before they go in the oven, and then at 5-minute intervals for 20 minutes. ❧

Sour Caraway Rye

MAKES 2 ROUND LOAVES

Because the basis for this recipe is a form of sourdough starter (see entry for Sourdough Starter), it produces rye loaves with that extraordinary sour taste usually found only in bread from European-style delicatessens. Burying a peeled onion in the starter for 12 hours is an optional step, but one that lends a flavor too good to miss.

STARTER
1 package dry yeast
1½ cups warm (100°F.) water
¼ cup molasses
1½ cups medium or dark rye flour, scoop measured
1 small onion (optional)

BREAD DOUGH
All the starter
1 cup warm water
2 teaspoons salt
1 tablespoon caraway seeds
3 tablespoons butter, melted
2 cups medium or dark rye flour, scoop measured
2¼ to 3 cups bread flour (preferably bromated), scoop measured
1 large egg white plus 1 teaspoon water

1. Prepare the starter the night before. In a large glass or ceramic bowl dissolve the yeast

in 1½ cups warm water. Stir in the molasses and 1½ cups rye flour. Lumps may form, but they'll break down as the starter sits. Peel the onion and bury it in the mixture. Cover the bowl with plastic wrap and secure with an elastic band or tie with string. Place in a fairly cool spot, not near a heat source. The starter will foam and triple in size so use a bowl that can accommodate this increase. If the starter has fallen back to its original size by the time you go to use it the next day, don't worry. The yeast cells are simply waiting for something else to eat.

2. Remove the onion from the starter and pour the starter into a large clean bowl. Stir in 1 cup warm water, the salt, caraway seeds, and melted butter. Using a wooden spoon, stir in the 2 cups of rye flour and 1 cup of the white bread flour. Beat vigorously until the dough pulls away from the bowl in ropy strands.

3. Measure out 1 cup of flour onto the work surface and spread the flour into a large circle. Empty the dough onto the flour. Sift ¼ cup flour over the dough and knead until all of the flour has been absorbed and the dough springs back when poked with your finger. Place in a greased bowl and cover with plastic wrap. Secure airtight with an elastic band to keep the dough moist and set in a draft-free place to rise.

4. When the dough is double in size, turn it out onto a floured surface. Since these are going to be free-standing loaves, sufficient kneading is of the utmost importance. The gluten must be developed so that it forms a network strong enough to support high, nicely rounded sides. (An underkneaded loaf will flatten out.) If you knead by the traditional method, plan to keep at it for 6 to 8 minutes. This approach, however, works in quite a bit of flour and is apt to produce an overly dry loaf. For a moister loaf, press-knead 4 or 5 times according to the directions on p. 225. Then form the dough into a ball and return it to the greased bowl. Cover with plastic wrap, secure with an elastic band, and allow to rise a second time.

5. When the dough is double in size, turn it out onto a floured surface and divide in two. Shape into 2 balls. Place in two 8-inch round pans that have been greased and sprinkled with cornmeal. (Or follow the directions under step 6 for Country-Style Italian Bread [p. 223] for placing on greased aluminum foil in preparation for using a baking stone.)

6. When the loaves are double in size, but still somewhat resilient, slash with a razor blade in 3 parallel lines. Whisk the egg white with 1 teaspoon water and brush over loaves. Bake in a preheated 425°F. oven for 10 minutes. Reduce the heat to 375°F. and bake for 45 minutes or until the bread sounds hollow when tapped on the top.   ❧

Grammy's Rolls

MAKES 42 TO 44 ROLLS

These irresistible rolls have been served in our family on important holidays for as long as I can remember. Being able to prepare them was a rite of passage for the girls — not until you got them just right were you considered capable.

2 large eggs
1 cup milk
½ cup butter
¼ cup sugar
1 teaspoon salt
1 package dry yeast
¼ cup warm (100°F.) water
4 cups all-purpose flour, scoop measured

1. Beat the eggs lightly in a large mixing bowl and set aside.

2. Heat the milk in a 1½-quart saucepan until the surface wrinkles or to 160°F. on a thermometer. Remove from the heat. Cut ¼ cup of the butter into 4 large chunks. Add the sugar, salt, and butter chunks to the milk, stirring until the butter melts. The mixture should then be lukewarm.

3. Dissolve the yeast in the warm water.

4. Test the beaten eggs with your finger. They should feel slightly cool to the touch. Stirring continuously, slowly pour the milk mixture into the beaten eggs. The resulting blend should feel slightly warm.

5. Stir in the dissolved yeast. Add 2 cups of the flour and beat vigorously with a wooden spoon until the dough pulls away from the sides of the bowl in ropy strands. Beat in another cup of flour. Lightly dust a work surface with flour. Turn out the dough and knead in the remaining cup of flour. The dough should feel soft, slightly moist, and somewhat sticky. Form into a ball, dust with flour, and place in a greased bowl. Cover the bowl with plastic wrap and secure with an elastic band. Let rise until double (about 1½ hours).

6. Turn the dough out onto a floured surface and press down into a flat round about 8 inches in diameter. Do not knead. Roll into a circle measuring 16 inches across. Using a 2-inch biscuit cutter, cut out 42 to 44 two-inch rounds. Take up a round of dough, place a small dab of the remaining ¼ cup butter in the center, and fold over to form a semicircle. Arrange in 3 concentric circles inside 2 well-greased 9-inch cake pans. Placing the straight edge of the rolls against the rim of the pan, form an outer circle of 11 or 12 rolls, a second circle of 7 rolls, and a third circle of 3 rolls. Cover with a clean towel and allow to rise until doubled (about 1½ hours).

7. Bake in a preheated 375°F. oven for 25 minutes or until nicely browned. Brush the tops with solid shortening that has been melted. Cool on a rack for 5 minutes and turn out. Serve warm.

NOTE: The trimmings may be kneaded together into a round and placed in a greased 1-quart Pyrex casserole to rise. Or shape into a small loaf and set inside a loaf pan (3×5 inches) to rise. Bake alongside the pans of rolls.　　　　　　　　　　　　　　　☙

Quick Poppy-Seed Rolls

MAKES 17 ROLLS

Proofing yeast gives dough a head start. So these one-step rolls are ready to eat in half the time it usually takes to make dinner rolls.

¼ cup plus 1 teaspoon water
2 tablespoons plus a pinch sugar
3 to 3½ cups plus a pinch all-purpose flour,
  scoop measured
1 package dry yeast
½ cup milk
2 tablespoons butter, cut into chunks
½ teaspoon salt
1 large egg
1 large egg white
Poppy seeds

1. Set the oven to "Warm" or 150°F. Stir ¼ cup water and the pinch of sugar together in a 1-cup measure until the sugar is almost completely dissolved. Sprinkle on the pinch of flour and stir to dissolve. Add the yeast. Stir to moisten all the granules. Place in the oven. Turn the heat off and close the door. When the mixture foams, or bubbles, remove it from the oven.

2. Meanwhile, heat the milk in a 1½-quart saucepan until the surface wrinkles or to 160°F. on a thermometer. Remove from the heat and stir in the butter, 2 tablespoons sugar, and salt until the butter is melted and the sugar and salt are dissolved.

3. In a large bowl, whisk the egg slightly. Slowly pour in the warm milk, stirring continuously. Blend in the proofed yeast.

4. Add 2 cups of flour and beat with a wooden spoon until smooth. The dough should be somewhat ropy-looking as it pulls

away from the sides of the bowl. Turn out onto a floured surface and knead in additional flour until the dough is stiff and has a satiny finish. Toward the end of the kneading step, begin to form the dough into a sausage shape. Then, pressing down with the palms of your hands, continue rolling it until it measures 17 to 18 inches long.

5. Cut the roll into 17 one-inch-thick slices and form each slice into a ball by pressing and rolling between the palms of your hands. Place in a greased 9-inch round cake pan. Arrange 10 balls of dough just inside the rim of the pan, 6 balls in a second circle, and 1 ball in the center. Cover loosely with plastic wrap and let rise 1 hour.

6. Preheat the oven to 375°F. Whisk the egg white and 1 teaspoon water. Brush the rolls with the mixture (see entry for Egg Wash) and sprinkle with poppy seeds. Tap the seeds against the dough lightly with the back of a spoon to make sure they stick. Bake for 25 minutes or until golden brown. Cool on a rack for 5 minutes before removing the rolls from the pan.   ◄ও

English Muffins

MAKES 12

If you think homemade bread outshines store-bought, wait till you try homemade English muffins. Cooked on a griddle, the outsides of these muffins develop a familiar deep brown color. A light sprinkling of corn-meal adds authenticity to the exterior while yeast produces the carbon dioxide that creates all those nooks and crannies inside.

½ cup water
3 tablespoons butter, cut into 6 chunks
2 tablespoons sugar
1 teaspoon salt
1 package dry yeast
¼ cup warm (100°F.) water
1 large egg
2½ to 3 cups bread flour (preferably bromated),
    scoop measured

1. Bring ½ cup of water to a boil in a 1½-quart saucepan. Remove from the heat. Add the butter, sugar, and salt, stirring until the butter melts. The mixture should then be lukewarm.

2. Dissolve the yeast in ¼ cup warm water.

3. Beat the egg in a large mixing bowl. Blend in the butter mixture, and then stir in the dissolved yeast. Add 1½ cups of flour and beat vigorously with a wooden spoon until the dough pulls away from the bowl in ropy strands.

4. Measure out ¾ cup of flour onto a work surface and spread the flour out in a large circle. Empty the dough onto the flour. Sift ¼ cup of flour over the dough and knead until all the flour has been absorbed. Continue kneading for 5 minutes, sprinkling with additional flour if needed to prevent sticking. Place in a greased bowl and cover with plastic wrap. Secure the wrap with an elastic band to keep the dough moist. Set in a draft-free place to rise (about 1½ hours).

5. When the dough is double in size, turn it out onto a floured work surface and knead for 2 minutes. Dust with flour and cover with a piece of plastic wrap. Let the dough rest for 20 minutes to facilitate rolling.

6. Roll the dough to a ½-inch thickness. Cut into 3-inch rounds with a biscuit cutter and place on a baking sheet sprinkled with cornmeal. Sprinkle cornmeal over the tops of the muffins and cover with a kitchen towel. Let rise for 45 minutes.

7. Lightly grease a griddle with solid shortening or spray shortening. Warm the griddle over medium-high heat for 10 minutes. Test the temperature of the griddle by sprinkling a few drops of cold water onto the surface. The drops of water should bead and jump around 3 or 4 times before evaporating. (If they evap-

orate instantly, the griddle is too hot.) Transfer the muffins to the hot griddle and cook for 3 minutes. Turn and cook 3 minutes on the other side, then cook 5 to 7 minutes more on each side. Brush or scrape excess cornmeal from the cooking surface between batches. Cool cooked muffins on a rack. Split with a fork and toast to serve.　　　　　◄ぅ

Orange Quick Bread

MAKES 1 LOAF

Because this bread is made with the zest, or outermost layer of the rind, it possesses an exceptionally delicate orange flavor with no bitter overtones.

2 bright-skinned oranges
1 cup sugar
2 cups all-purpose flour, scoop measured
1 teaspoon baking powder
½ teaspoon baking soda
½ teaspoon salt
3 tablespoons butter, melted
1 large egg
½ cup finely chopped walnuts

1. Preheat the oven to 350°F. Grease a 9×5-inch loaf pan.
2. Cut the oranges in half and squeeze to remove the juice. Reserve ⅔ cup of juice. Using a swivel-blade peeler, remove the zest of the oranges. Scatter 2 tablespoons of the sugar over a cutting board. Lay the strips of zest over the sugar. Sprinkle an additional 2 tablespoons of sugar over the zest. Using a large chef's knife, finely chop the zest.
3. Sift the remaining sugar, flour, baking powder, baking soda, and salt into a large bowl. Blend thoroughly with a fork or a few passes of the electric beater.
4. Pour the melted butter into a small bowl and stir in the reserved ⅔ cup of orange juice. Add the egg and blend with a whisk or fork. Add the liquid mixture, all at once, to the dry ingredients. Blend only until the dry ingredients are moistened. Add the prepared zest and chopped nuts. Stir briefly to combine.

5. Pour into the prepared pan and bake for 45 to 50 minutes or until a metal skewer inserted into the middle comes out clean. Place on a cooling rack for 10 minutes, and then turn out. Stand the loaf upright to avoid unsightly rack marks on the side of the loaf. Cool completely before slicing.　　　◄ぅ

Gingered Pear Bread

MAKES 1 LOAF

Occasionally you'll see quick-bread recipes that direct you to begin by creaming the butter and sugar together rather than adding melted butter later in the procedure. This approach creates a loaf that is more cakelike in texture because the creaming step incorporates air into the batter. To transform the following bread into a lovely tea cake, invert it and frost with a vanilla butter cream.

½ cup butter or solid shortening
2 cups flour, scoop measured
1 teaspoon baking powder
½ teaspoon baking soda
½ teaspoon salt
½ teaspoon ground ginger
1 cup sugar
2 large eggs
1 teaspoon vanilla
¼ cup sour cream
3 medium pears, peeled, cored, and coarsely chopped (about 1 cup)

1. Preheat the oven to 350°F. Grease a 9×5-inch loaf pan. Place the butter in a large mixing bowl to soften.
2. Sift together the flour, baking powder, baking soda, salt, and ginger. Toss with a fork or whisk to blend thoroughly.
3. Beat the butter until creamy. Gradually sprinkle in the sugar, beating continuously until the mixture is light and fluffy. Add the eggs, one at a time. Beat in the vanilla. Add half the dry ingredients, and then blend in 2 tablespoons of sour cream. Repeat with the remaining dry ingredients followed by the

rest of the sour cream. Gently stir in the chopped pears.

4. Pour into the prepared pan and bake for 45 to 50 minutes or until a metal skewer inserted into the middle comes out clean. Cool on a rack for 10 minutes, then turn out. Cool completely before slicing.   ❧

Blueberry Buttermilk Muffins

MAKES 12 MEDIUM MUFFINS

After washing the berries, scatter them on a double thickness of paper toweling to drain. Allow them to air dry for 15 to 20 minutes. Then lay a paper towel over the berries and gently roll them around to dry completely. Adding wet berries to muffin batter causes soggy muffins and dredging wet berries with flour makes the berry pockets gluey.

1 cup fresh blueberries
2 cups all-purpose flour, sifted
¼ cup sugar
3 teaspoons baking powder
½ teaspoon baking soda
¼ teaspoon salt
⅛ teaspoon ground mace
1 large egg
1 cup buttermilk
¼ cup butter, melted
1½ teaspoons finely grated lemon zest

1. Preheat the oven to 400°F. Grease muffin tins or line with paper cups. Wash the berries and pick off any stray stems. Drain in a colander, and then scatter the berries over a double thickness of paper toweling. Allow them to air dry, then blot with another paper towel.

2. In a large mixing bowl, combine the flour, sugar, baking powder, baking soda, salt, and mace. Stir with a fork or whisk to evenly distribute the ingredients.

3. Whisk the egg and buttermilk until well blended. Stir in the cooled melted butter and lemon zest. Make a well in the dry ingredients and pour in the egg mixture. Blend with a

wooden spoon or rubber spatula until the dry ingredients are moistened. The batter will be *very* lumpy.

4. Fold in the berries, being careful not to break them. Spoon into muffin tins, filling the cups no more than two-thirds full. Immediately place in the hot oven and bake 20 to 25 minutes or until the tops are nicely browned. Muffins baked directly in the tin will show signs of pulling away from the sides when they are done. Cool 5 minutes, then tilt the muffins on their sides or transfer to a rack to prevent soggy bottoms.   ❧

Cranberry-Walnut Muffins

MAKES 12 MEDIUM MUFFINS

These muffins, made with whole-berry cranberry sauce, are exceptionally moist and flavorful. Don't attempt to thoroughly blend in the cranberry sauce. Rather, leave it in little blobs that will melt when heated and create a dazzling cranberry ripple effect.

2 cups all-purpose flour, sifted
¾ cup sugar
1 teaspoon baking soda
½ teaspoon salt
¼ cup butter, melted
⅔ cup cold milk
1 large egg
1 cup whole-berry cranberry sauce
½ cup finely chopped walnuts

1. Preheat the oven to 400°F. Grease muffin tins or line with paper cups.

2. In a large mixing bowl, combine the flour, sugar, baking soda, and salt by stirring with a fork or a whisk to blend thoroughly.

3. Pour the melted butter into a small bowl. Stir in the cold milk. Add the egg and beat with a whisk. (The cold milk will reduce the temperature of the butter so the egg won't curdle.)

4. Make a well in the dry ingredients and pour in the egg mixture. Blend with a wooden

spoon or rubber spatula until the dry ingredients are moistened. The batter will be *very* lumpy.

5. Break up the cranberry sauce by stirring with a fork, then add to the batter. Mix gently so that you don't break the berries, and don't attempt to blend in the sauce completely. Stir in the walnuts and spoon the batter into the muffin tins. Fill the cups no more than two-thirds full. Place immediately in a hot oven and bake 20 to 25 minutes or until the tops are nicely browned. Cool 5 minutes, and then tilt muffins on their sides or transfer to a rack to prevent soggy bottoms.　　　　◄ᢒ

Fresh Raspberry Muffins

MAKES 11 LARGE MUFFINS

Because sugar interferes with gluten development, the high ratio of sugar in this recipe produces finely textured, cakelike muffins.

1 cup fresh raspberries
1½ cups all-purpose flour, sifted
½ cup sugar
2 teaspoons baking powder
¼ teaspoon salt
1 large egg
½ cup milk
¼ cup butter, melted

1. Preheat the oven to 400°F. Grease muffin tins or line with paper cups. (If you're using a cast-iron pan, you can achieve crustier sides by greasing the cups with solid shortening and then preheating the pan. Place it in a cold oven and set the dial to 400°F. When the oven reaches 400°F., the pan will be sufficiently hot.)

2. Wash the berries and pick off any stray stems. Drain in a colander, and then scatter the berries over a paper towel. Gently blot them dry.

3. In a large mixing bowl, combine the flour, sugar, baking powder, and salt with a fork or a whisk to distribute the ingredients.

4. Whisk the egg and milk until well blended. Stir in the cooled melted butter. Make a well in the dry ingredients and pour in the egg mixture. Blend with a wooden spoon or rubber spatula until the dry ingredients are moistened. The batter will be lumpy (but not as lumpy as batters containing less sugar).

5. Fold in the berries, being careful not to break them. Spoon into muffin tins, filling the cups no more than two-thirds full. (If you're using a preheated cast-iron muffin tin, take it from the oven and spoon the batter into the hot cups. Don't forget to use pot holders to protect your hands.) Immediately place in the hot oven and bake 20 to 25 minutes or until the tops are nicely browned. Muffins baked directly in the tin will show signs of pulling away from the sides when they are done. Cool 5 minutes, then tilt the muffins on their sides or transfer to a rack to prevent soggy bottoms.　　　　◄ᢒ

Blueberry Pancakes

MAKES 8 TO 10 PANCAKES

To obtain an even distribution of berries throughout each pancake, drop the berries onto the cakes as they cook rather than stirring them into the batter.

1 cup fresh blueberries
1½ cups all-purpose flour, scoop measured
2 tablespoons sugar
1 teaspoon baking powder
½ teaspoon baking soda
1 cup plus 2 to 6 tablespoons buttermilk
1 large egg
2 tablespoons butter, melted
¼ teaspoon ground mace
½ teaspoon grated lemon zest

1. Rinse the blueberries under cold running water and drain in a colander. Scatter over a double thickness of paper toweling and blot dry. Set aside.

2. In a large mixing bowl, combine the flour, sugar, baking powder, and baking soda. Toss with a fork or a whisk to blend evenly. In

a small mixing bowl, beat the 1 cup of buttermilk, egg, and cooled melted butter.

3. Make a well in the dry ingredients by pushing them up the sides of the bowl. Pour in the liquid mixture. Add the mace and lemon zest. Stir with quick, light movements to blend, but do not beat. There should be numerous lumps. Cover and refrigerate for 10 minutes. Gently stir in 2 or more tablespoons of buttermilk until the batter develops the consistency of thick heavy cream.

4. Place a griddle over medium-high heat. Brush the surface with vegetable oil or rub with a strip of uncooked bacon as the griddle warms. Test the temperature of the griddle by sprinkling a few drops of cold water onto the surface. The drops of water should bead and jump around 3 or 4 times before evaporating. Using the ¼-cup measure from a set of nesting measuring cups, pour on ¼ cup of batter for each pancake. Take up a handful of blueberries and drop them evenly over the surface of the pancake as it cooks. When the undersides of the pancakes are nicely browned (2 to 3 minutes) and half the bubbles on the surface are broken, turn the pancakes and cook the other side.   ◅◌

Heavenly Pancakes

MAKES 12 TO 15 PANCAKES

Egg whites gently folded in, plus the carbon dioxide in the club soda turn these into exceptional, lighter-than-air griddle cakes.

1 cup sifted confectioners' sugar
2 cups all-purpose flour, scoop measured
4 teaspoons baking powder
½ teaspoon salt
2 large eggs
3 tablespoons butter, melted
1⅓ cups plus 2 to 6 tablespoons club soda

1. Sift the confectioners' sugar, and then scoop measure and level off the cup measure with the blade of a knife. Combine in a large mixing bowl with the flour, baking powder,

and salt. Toss with a fork or a whisk to blend thoroughly.

2. Separate the eggs, placing the yolks in a small mixing bowl and whipping the whites to the soft-peak stage. Add the cooled melted butter and 1⅓ cups club soda to the yolks and stir to blend.

3. Make a well in the dry ingredients by pushing them up the sides of the bowl. Immediately pour in the club soda mixture. Stir with quick, light movements to blend, but do not beat. There should be numerous lumps. Cover and refrigerate for 10 minutes. Remove and gently stir in 2 or more tablespoons of club soda until the batter develops the consistency of thick heavy cream, then fold in the whipped egg whites.

4. Place a griddle over medium-high heat. Brush the surface with vegetable oil or rub with a strip of uncooked bacon as the griddle warms. Test the temperature of the griddle by sprinkling a few drops of cold water onto the surface. The drops of water should bead and jump around 3 or 4 times before evaporating. Using the ¼-cup measure from a set of nesting measuring cups, pour on ¼ cup of batter for each pancake. When the undersides of the pancakes are nicely browned (after 2 to 3 minutes) and half the bubbles on the top are broken, turn the pancakes and cook the other side.   ◅◌

Jelly Doughnuts

MAKES 24

Because these doughnuts are filled before they are fried, they hold an unusually generous amount of jelly. The trick to avoiding heavy, grease-laden doughnuts is to have the dough and fat at the correct temperature. Dough that is too warm (over 80°F.) readily absorbs fat; dough that's too cold (below 70° F.) takes longer to cook, giving excess fat time to soak in. (See entry for Frying: Deep-Fat).

1 package dry yeast
¼ cup warm (100°F.) water
¾ cup milk

¼ cup granulated sugar
¼ teaspoon salt
4 tablespoons butter, cut into 8 chunks
¼ teaspoon vanilla
2 large eggs
1 teaspoon finely grated lemon zest
3½ to 4 cups all-purpose flour, scoop measured
⅔ cup grape, plum, or apricot jam
1 teaspoon tap water
Vegetable oil for deep frying
Confectioners' sugar

1. Sprinkle the yeast into the ¼ cup warm water. Stir to dissolve and set aside.

2. Heat the milk in a saucepan until the surface wrinkles or to 160°F. on a thermometer. Remove from the heat. Add the granulated sugar, salt, and butter. Stir to dissolve the sugar and salt. Continue stirring until the butter is melted. Blend in the vanilla.

3. Separate an egg, setting aside the white to use in sealing the dough. Whisk the remaining yolk and whole egg in a large mixing bowl. Stirring continuously, pour in the slightly cooled milk. Blend in the dissolved yeast and the grated zest.

4. Add 2 cups of flour and beat vigorously with a wooden spoon until the dough pulls away from the sides of the bowl in ropy strands. Measure out 1 cup of flour onto a work surface and spread the flour out in a large circle. Empty the dough onto the flour. Sprinkle ½ cup of flour over the dough and knead until the dough is smooth and elastic and no longer sticks to the work surface. Sprinkle on additional flour if necessary, but the dough should be light and soft. Place in a greased bowl and cover with plastic wrap. Secure with an elastic band to keep the dough moist. Set in a draft-free place to rise.

5. When the dough is double in size (1½ hours), turn it out onto a lightly floured surface. Dust with flour and pat into a rectangle. Then roll out to ½-inch thickness. Cut out 3-inch rounds with a biscuit cutter. Spoon a generous dollop of jam onto the center of half of the rounds. Whisk the egg white and 1 teaspoon water until foamy, and then lightly brush the dough surrounding the jam. Top with the remaining dough rounds and press to seal. Transfer to a baking sheet. Loosely cover with a kitchen towel and allow to rest for 10 minutes.

6. Heat the fat to 370°F. Lower the doughnuts into the fat 2 or 3 at a time. Cover the pan and fry for 1 minute (the moist heat will increase the rising). Uncover and fry until the underside is golden brown; turn and fry the top side. Do not turn more than once. Remove from the fat with a slotted spoon and drain on absorbent paper. Dust with sifted confectioners' sugar.   ◈

Dropped Doughnuts

MAKES 36

These easy-to-make doughnuts are Yankee cousins to French beignets. *Spoonfuls of batter dropped into hot fat puff and swell to light brown nuggets. And since they don't contain yeast or require rolling, they can be made in the morning without too much fuss. Serve hot with maple syrup or dusted with confectioners' sugar.*

2½ cups all-purpose flour, sifted
1¼ cups sugar
3 teaspoons baking powder
1 teaspoon salt
1 teaspoon ground mace
Generous amount of freshly ground nutmeg
¾ cup milk
¼ cup vegetable oil
1 large egg
½ teaspoon almond extract
Vegetable oil for deep frying

1. In a large mixing bowl, combine the dry ingredients and toss with a fork or a whisk to thoroughly blend the leavening agent and spices.

2. Whisk the milk, oil, egg, and almond extract together in a small bowl.

3. Begin to heat the oil to 370°F. so you can start to cook the doughnuts as soon as the baking powder has been moistened.

4. Make a well in the dry ingredients and pour in the milk mixture. Stir until smooth but don't overbeat. When the oil is hot, drop the batter from rounded teaspoonfuls. Turn the doughnuts as they puff to encourage even browning. Transfer to absorbent paper with a slotted spoon to drain.   ⊷

Buttermilk Biscuits

MAKES FIFTEEN 2-INCH BISCUITS

The lactic acid contained in buttermilk produces an exceptionally flaky texture — a fact that explains the long-standing popularity of buttermilk as a traditional biscuit ingredient.

2 cups all-purpose flour, scoop measured
½ teaspoon baking soda
½ teaspoon baking powder
½ teaspoon salt
¼ cup cold butter or lard
¾ cup buttermilk

1. Preheat the oven to 425°F. Sift the flour, baking soda, baking powder, and salt into the largest bowl you have. Combine thoroughly by blending with a fork or wire whisk.

2. Cut the cold butter into 16 small chunks by dividing the half stick into quarters and then cutting the quarters into 4 equal portions. Add the butter to the dry ingredients. Using a table knife, or an 8-inch palette knife, cut the butter into the flour until the butter bits resemble tiny peas.

3. Gradually pour in the buttermilk, tossing the mixture constantly with the knife. Add only enough liquid to form a soft, malleable dough. When the dough begins to hold together, gather it into a ball with your fingertips and roll it around the inside of the bowl to pick up any stray particles.

4. Turn out onto a *lightly* floured board and dust the top of the dough with flour. Knead with 20 to 25 strokes. Lightly press the dough into a flat circle, ½ inch thick. Roll with a rolling pin to smooth the top. Cut out with a 2-inch biscuit cutter using a firm

downward motion. Do not twist the cutter from side to side — lift it straight up.

5. Transfer the biscuits to an ungreased baking sheet without sides. Place in the preheated oven and bake for 12 to 15 minutes or until nicely browned. Cool on a rack or serve hot with whipped butter.

NOTE: Using lard instead of butter lends biscuits a slightly smoky flavor. (See entry for Biscuits.)   ⊷

Shortcake Biscuits

MAKES TWELVE 2½-INCH BISCUITS

Freshly grated nutmeg lends a tantalizing accent to these biscuits. Somewhat sweeter than dinner biscuits, they are a light and delectable foundation on which to build a strawberry or blueberry shortcake.

2 cups all-purpose flour, scoop measured
¼ cup sugar
3 teaspoons baking powder
¼ teaspoon salt
Generous amount of freshly ground nutmeg
¼ cup cold butter
¾ cup milk

1. Preheat the oven to 425°F. Sift the flour, sugar, baking powder, and salt into the largest bowl you have. Add the nutmeg and combine thoroughly by blending with a fork or wire whisk.

2. Cut the cold butter into 16 small chunks by dividing the half stick into quarters and then cutting the quarters into 4 equal portions. Add the butter to the dry ingredients. Using a table knife, or an 8-inch palette knife, cut the butter into the flour mixture until the butter bits resemble tiny peas.

3. Gradually pour in the milk, tossing the mixture constantly with the knife. Add only enough liquid to form a soft, malleable dough. When the dough begins to hold together, gather it into a ball with your fingertips and roll it around the inside of the bowl to pick up any stray particles.

4. Turn out onto a *lightly* floured board and dust the top of the dough with flour. Knead with 20 to 25 strokes. Lightly press the dough into a flat circle, ½ inch thick. Roll with a rolling pin to smooth the top. Cut out with a 2½-inch biscuit cutter using a firm downward motion. Do not twist the cutter from side to side — lift it straight up.

5. Transfer the biscuits to an ungreased baking sheet without sides. Place in the preheated oven and bake for 12 to 15 minutes or until nicely browned. Cool on a rack. Split gently with a fork and spoon on fresh berries. Top with sweetened whipped cream. (See entry for Biscuits.) ঌ

Herbed Popovers

MAKES 12 POPOVERS

When you want a quick and unusual bread to serve with dinner, try this herb-flavored variation on a breakfast classic. Use dried herbs if you don't have fresh, and feel free to substitute your favorite combination of herbs in place of those listed.

1 cup all-purpose flour, scoop measured
½ teaspoon salt
1 cup milk
3 large eggs
2 tablespoons butter, melted
1½ teaspoons chopped fresh leaf thyme (or substitute ½ teaspoon dried)
1½ teaspoons chopped fresh oregano (or substitute ½ teaspoon dried)

1. After positioning a rack in the center, preheat the oven to 400°F. In a large mixing bowl, combine the flour and salt. Stir with a whisk or fork to blend thoroughly.

2. Whisk the milk, eggs, and cooled melted butter in a small bowl. Make a well in the center of the dry ingredients by pushing them up the sides of the bowl. Beat with a wooden spoon while slowly pouring in the milk mixture. Continue beating for 2½ to 3 minutes or until the mixture is smooth and free of lumps. Stir in the chopped herbs.

3. Pour into well-greased popover cups or Pyrex custard cups. Fill the cups no more than half full. Place on the centered rack and immediately lower the heat to 375°F. Bake for 35 to 45 minutes or until puffed and browned. Serve straight from the oven with whipped Unsalted Butter (p. 240). ঌ

Bacon-Cheese Popover

MAKES ONE 10- to 11-INCH POPOVER

Here's a hearty variation on Yorkshire pudding. Flavored with bacon fat and Cheddar cheese, this giant popover makes a great partner for robust soups.

1 cup all-purpose flour, scoop measured
½ teaspoon salt
1 cup milk
4 large eggs
½ cup grated Cheddar cheese
4 tablespoons bacon fat

1. After positioning a rack in the center, preheat the oven to 400°F. In a large mixing bowl, combine the flour and salt. Stir with a whisk or fork to blend thoroughly.

2. Whisk the milk and eggs in a small bowl. Make a well in the center of the dry ingredients by pushing them up the sides of the bowl. Beat with a wooden spoon while slowly pouring in the milk mixture. Continue beating for 2½ to 3 minutes or until the mixture is smooth and free of lumps. Stir in the grated cheese.

3. Put the bacon fat in a 10-inch skillet with an ovenproof handle, a 10-inch paella pan, or a specially designed oven pancake pan with curved sides (see Appendix). Place inside the warm oven and heat until the fat is melted. Tilt and rotate the pan to coat the bottom. Pour in the batter and place on the centered rack. Bake for 15 minutes. Lower the heat to 350°F. and bake for 35 to 45 minutes or until puffed and browned. Slide out onto a serving dish and cut into wedges to serve. ঌ

Individual Yorkshire Puddings

MAKES 12 INDIVIDUAL PUDDINGS

Created from popover batter, Yorkshire pudding is flavored with roast beef drippings rather than melted butter. Bake in a popover pan or Pyrex cups for individual servings. A single Yorkshire pudding may be cooked in an 11-inch black steel pan designed for baking oven pancakes (see Appendix) or, more traditionally, in an 8-inch-square aluminum pan.

1 cup all-purpose flour, scoop measured
½ teaspoon salt
1 cup milk
3 large eggs
½ cup heated roast beef drippings

1. After positioning a rack in the center, preheat the oven to 400°F. In a large mixing bowl, combine the flour and salt. Stir with a whisk or fork to blend thoroughly.

2. Whisk the milk and eggs in a small bowl. Make a well in the center of the dry ingredients by pushing them up the sides of the bowl. Beat with a wooden spoon while slowly pouring in the milk mixture. Continue beating for 2½ to 3 minutes or until the mixture is smooth and free of lumps.

3. Place 2 teaspoons of hot roast beef drippings in each baking cup. Tilt and rotate the cups to completely coat the bottoms with fat. Fill the cups no more than half full with batter. (If you're baking a single large pudding, pour in enough roast beef fat to generously coat the bottom of the pan. You won't need the full amount.)

4. Place on the centered rack and bake for 20 to 30 minutes for individual puddings. Bake a single large pudding at 400°F. for 15 minutes and then at 350°F. for 35 to 45 minutes. When the puddings are puffed and browned, take them from the oven and serve immediately.   ‹ᴈ

Unsalted Butter

MAKES ½ TO ⅔ CUP

If this delicately flavored butter is not readily available in your area, you can make your own with very little fuss. Homemade butter is the crowning touch for your special holiday breads.

8 ice cubes
1 cup cold water
2 cups heavy cream, preferably *not* ultrapasteurized

1. Place the ice in the cold water and set aside.

2. Cut a circle of aluminum foil to fit the circumference of the top of the bowl of your electric mixer. Place it loosely over the bowl so the mixture won't splatter all over the place. Make a hole in the foil and insert the beaters. (If you're using the type of mixer where the beater moves around the inside of the bowl, don't crimp the foil over the rim of the bowl. Just let it move around the bowl with the beater. Use the paddle beater.)

3. Pour the cream into the bowl. Begin to churn by beating at medium speed. When the butterfat starts to form tiny clots (it takes about 4 to 6 minutes), stop the mixer. Pour ¼ cup of ice water through the hole in the foil and beat again at medium speed for another 4 to 6 minutes.

4. When full separation has taken place, there will be globs of fat around the beaters and a watery liquid in the bottom of the bowl. Pour off the liquid and reserve for adding to soup.

5. Add ½ cup of ice water to the butter and beat again at medium speed to wash out any excess buttermilk. Pour the mixture into a fine sieve. Transfer the butter to a bowl and knead to extract remaining water. If necessary, add the final ¼ cup of ice water and continue kneading until the liquid given off is clear. Pack the butter in a crock or a screw-top jar and refrigerate.   ‹ᴈ

Poultry, Fish, and Meat

Poultry, Fish, and Shellfish

Breast of Chicken Cacciatore

SERVES 4

This hearty dish derives extra zip from paper-thin slices of pepperoni. Instead of a whole chicken, it uses only the breast meat and can be prepared in 45 minutes.

2 large whole chicken breasts
2 tablespoons vegetable oil
½ cup dry white wine
4 tablespoons butter
12 medium-size fresh mushrooms, rinsed, dried, and quartered
1 large sweet onion, sliced
1 green sweet bell pepper, seeded and cut into ½-inch strips
1 garlic clove, minced or pressed
1 can (35 ounces) Italian tomatoes, undrained
½ cup Basic Brown Sauce (p. 346 or p. 348)
3-inch piece of pepperoni, peeled and very thinly sliced
1 teaspoon dried basil
½ teaspoon dried oregano
½ teaspoon dried rosemary leaves, pulverized with a mortar and pestle
½ teaspoon salt
Generous amount of freshly ground black pepper
2 tablespoons chopped fresh parsley

1. Bone and skin the chicken breasts and cut them in half. Divide each breast half into 8 pieces. Blot dry with paper towels but do not flour. Set aside.

2. Preheat a wide burner to its highest setting. Pour the oil into a thick-bottomed 12-inch skillet, tilting and rotating the pan to film the entire surface of the bottom. Place the chicken on the film of cold oil. Set over the preheated burner. Tossing continuously with 2 wooden spatulas, keep the meat in constant motion. (The tossing action speeds the evaporation of moisture.) When the chicken is well browned, transfer it to a platter. Deglaze the pan with ¼ cup of the wine and pour the pan liquid over the chicken.

3. While the pan is off the burner, add the butter. Tilt the pan to start the butter melting. Add the mushrooms. Return to high heat and cook, stirring continuously to keep the mushrooms in motion. When they begin to brown around the edges, stir in the onion, green pepper, and garlic. Reduce the heat to medium-low and continue to stir until the vegetables release their moisture. Cover and cook for 5 minutes.

4. Add the tomatoes, breaking them up with your fingers. Stir in the remaining ¼ cup wine, the brown sauce, pepperoni, basil, oregano, rosemary, salt, and pepper. Return

the chicken and deglazing liquid to the pan. Regulate the heat so that the mixture bubbles gently and allow the cacciatore to simmer uncovered until the consistency thickens (about 30 minutes). Blend in the parsley and serve.

Creamed Chicken and Mushrooms

SERVES 4

Spoon each serving over a single large crouton made by toasting thickly sliced homemade bread. Accompanied by chilled champagne, this constitutes an elegant late-night supper.

2 whole chicken breasts, split
6 tablespoons butter
12 ounces fresh mushrooms, sliced
½ teaspoon dried leaf thyme
1 cup White Sauce with Milk (substitute 1 cup
  medium, or whipping, cream for milk, p. 348)
1 cup medium, or whipping, cream
Salt and freshly ground white pepper
4 one-inch-thick slices of white bread,
  preferably homemade

1. Place the chicken breasts in a 6-quart saucepan and cover with cold water from the tap. Set over medium heat and bring to a gentle bubble. Cook uncovered for 20 minutes, stirring occasionally to promote even cooking. Transfer the cooked chicken to a double thickness of paper toweling to drain.

2. When the chicken is cool enough to handle, remove the skin and lift the meat from the bones. (If the breasts are exceptionally large, you may find pink undercooked spots in the interior. Don't be alarmed; the sautéing will complete the cooking.) Cut the chicken into bite-size chunks and refrigerate.

3. Melt 3 tablespoons butter in a 10-inch skillet. Add the mushrooms and toss to coat. Sprinkle on the thyme and cook over high heat, tossing and lifting constantly. When the mushrooms are tender, remove from the heat. (Whether or not you allow the mush-

rooms to brown is very much a matter of personal preference. Lightly browned mushrooms contribute a taste significantly different from that of those cooked just until tender. You might want to experiment to find which flavor you prefer.) Set the cooked mushrooms aside.

4. Prepare the white sauce according to the directions, but in place of the milk, heat 1 cup of medium cream and whisk it into the roux. Remove the completed sauce from the burner and gradually whisk in another cup cream. Return to medium heat and cook, whisking, until the mixture is bubbly and smooth. Season generously with salt and freshly ground white pepper.

5. In a 12-inch skillet melt the remaining 3 tablespoons butter and add the chicken. Place over high heat and cook, stirring constantly and shaking the pan, until the pieces of chicken are lightly browned around the edges. (Because the meat completely absorbs the melted butter, there is no risk of burnt milk solids ruining the final flavor.) Add the mushrooms and any juice they have released and cook briefly to warm through. Combine the chicken and mushrooms with the white sauce and place over low heat. Cover and keep warm.

6. Trim the crusts from the bread. Cut into neat rectangles or squares. Place on a baking sheet and slide under the broiler. Toast lightly on both sides. Serve the creamed chicken and mushrooms over the toasted croutons.

Chicken Veronique

SERVES 6

Boned chicken breasts in wine sauce creates a dinner-party dish that's ready in minutes. The combination of orange marmalade and seedless grapes lends a unique flavor.

3 whole chicken breasts, split, skinned, and
  boned
2 tablespoons butter
12 ounces fresh mushrooms, sliced

2 tablespoons vegetable oil
2 tablespoons flour (preferably granulated, see
    entry for Flour)
1 cup dry white wine
½ teaspoon dried tarragon leaves
2 tablespoons orange marmalade
1 cup medium, or whipping, cream
½ pound seedless grapes
Salt and freshly ground black pepper to taste

1. Cutting across the grain, divide each breast half into 4 or 5 large pieces. Set aside.

2. Melt the butter in a 12-inch skillet or sauté pan. Add the mushrooms, tossing to coat. Place over high heat and cook, stirring and lifting constantly, until the mushrooms are tender. Transfer mushrooms to a plate.

3. With the pan off the heat, pour in the vegetable oil. Distribute the pieces of chicken evenly over the bottom of the pan and sprinkle with flour. Place over high heat and cook, stirring constantly, until the chicken is well browned. Take the pan from the heat and immediately add the white wine. Return to high heat and cook, stirring, until the sauce bubbles and thickens slightly. Remove from the heat. Stir in the mushrooms (and whatever liquid they've released), the tarragon, marmalade, and cream. Place over medium heat and stir until the marmalade melts and is incorporated into the sauce. Continue cooking at a brisk bubble until reduced to about half the original amount.

4. Stir in the grapes and reduce the heat so that the sauce bubbles gently. Cook for approximately 5 minutes to allow the grapes to exude some of their flavor. (It should be released through the tiny hole where the stem was once attached. Do not allow the grapes to burst their skins.) Season with salt and pepper to taste. Serve with brown or wild rice.

NOTE: It isn't necessary to peel the grapes. If you must use grapes with seeds, select a white or green variety and slit one side of each grape. Pry out the seeds with the blade of a paring knife.

(See entry for Sautéing.)

Chicken Breasts in Saged Cream

SERVES 4

This recipe is an example of one way to use the reduction sauce known as meat glaze or, more specifically in this case, Chicken Glaze (p. 351). If you've never experimented with meat glaze before, you'll be astonished at the full-bodied chicken flavor that comes through. As you rapidly cook the cream and Chicken Glaze together, the sauce will thicken without the use of any starch.

2 whole chicken breasts
2 tablespoons vegetable oil
⅓ cup dry white wine
1½ teaspoons freeze-dried shallots (or substitute
    1 fresh shallot, minced)
2 tablespoons butter
8 ounces fresh mushrooms, sliced
Juice of half a lemon
1 cup medium, or whipping, cream
2 to 3 tablespoons Chicken Glaze (depending on
    its strength, p. 351)
1 tablespoon chopped fresh sage (or substitute
    ½ teaspoon dried sage plus ½ teaspoon dried
    chervil)
Salt and pepper to taste

1. Bone and skin the chicken breasts and cut them in half. Lay the breast halves between two pieces of waxed paper. Pound thicker portions to flatten so that the breasts are of equal thickness. Blot dry with paper towels, but do not flour.

2. Heat the oil in a 12-inch skillet. Add the chicken and cook over high heat until well browned. Shake the pan back and forth so that the meat won't stick to the pan. Transfer the cooked chicken to a heat-resistant plate and place in a 250°F. oven to keep warm.

3. Deglaze the pan with the wine. (If using freeze-dried shallots, stir them in now to rehydrate.) Pour the mixture into a bowl.

4. Melt the butter and add the mushrooms. Cook over high heat, stirring constantly. (If using a fresh shallot, add now and cook briefly with the mushrooms.)

5. When the mushrooms are tender, pour in the deglazing liquid. Add the lemon juice and cook over high heat for 1 minute. Remove from the heat. Blend in the cream, chicken glaze, and sage. Place over medium-high heat and bring to a boil. Cook, stirring, until the sauce is reduced and slightly thickened. Season with salt and pepper and pour over the chicken breasts to serve.   ◄ৡ

Baked Chicken Thighs

SERVES 4

The thigh meat of poultry is more strongly flavored than breast meat, but not quite as assertive as the meat of the drumstick. In this recipe, thigh meat provides a flavorful counterpoint to the Oriental-style sauce that accompanies it.

1 cup dry white wine
¼ cup naturally brewed soy sauce
2 tablespoons fresh lemon juice
1½ teaspoons Chinese five-spice (see Note)
8 green onions, thinly sliced (including most of the green portion)
4 chicken thighs
2 tablespoons cornstarch
¼ cup cold water

1. Prepare a marinade by combining the wine, soy sauce, lemon juice, Chinese five-spice, and sliced onion in a 7×11-inch baking dish. Prick the chicken thighs in several places with the long tines of a meat fork, and add the thighs to the marinade, turning to coat on all sides. Cover the baking dish with aluminum foil and refrigerate for 6 to 8 hours to marinate. Turn occasionally to promote even absorption of the marinade.

2. Preheat the oven to 350°F. Place the covered baking dish in the oven and cook for 30 minutes. Uncover and turn the chicken thighs in the marinade. Bake uncovered for 15 to 20 minutes or until the chicken is tender when pierced with a fork. Transfer the cooked chicken to a warmed platter.

3. Pour the contents of the baking dish into a 2½-quart saucepan. Dissolve the cornstarch in the cold water and add to the liquid. Place over high heat and cook, stirring, until the sauce bubbles and thickens. Pour sauce over warm chicken and serve.

NOTE: Commercially prepared Chinese five-spice seasoning is readily available in large supermarkets and Oriental grocery shops. If necessary, you can approximate its flavor by combining ½ teaspoon cinnamon, ½ teaspoon ground ginger, ¼ teaspoon ground allspice, ¼ teaspoon crushed anise seed (or substitute fennel seed), and ⅛ teaspoon ground cloves.   ◄ৡ

Rock Cornish Hens with Rice and Pecan Stuffing

SERVES 4

Lightly toasted pecans and golden raisins add a memorable touch to this succulent stuffing of wild and brown rice. If you can find California wild rice, by all means try it. The kernels are somewhat larger than those of the rice grown in the Midwest, and the price is slightly more reasonable.

½ cup wild rice
½ cup brown rice
3 cups plus 2 tablespoons water
1 teaspoon salt
⅓ cup coarsely chopped pecans
4 Rock Cornish hens (about 1 pound each)
½ cup golden raisins
4 tablespoons butter, melted
½ cup orange marmalade
1 tablespoon white vinegar

1. Place the wild rice and brown rice in a sieve and rinse thoroughly under hot running water. Drain well. In a 2½-quart saucepan, bring 3 cups of water to a boil. Add the rice and ½ teaspoon of the salt. When the water returns to a boil, stir once and reduce the heat to low. Cover the pan. Cook for 35 to 45 min-

utes or until most, if not all, of the water has been absorbed and the kernels are crunchy but tender. (Rice used as a stuffing should be slightly undercooked because it will continue to absorb moisture during roasting.)

2. Meanwhile, preheat the oven to 350°F. Scatter the pecans over a baking sheet and place in the oven for 10 minutes to toast lightly. Remove the pecans and increase the oven temperature to 425°F. Prepare the hens by rinsing them thoroughly under cold running water. Pat them dry with paper towels and sprinkle the cavities with the remaining ½ teaspoon of salt.

3. Drain the rice if necessary and transfer to a large mixing bowl. Add the raisins and pecans, and toss to combine. Lightly stuff the cavities of the hens no more than two-thirds full, and close each opening with toothpicks. Truss the hens with butcher's twine (see p. 164) and place on a roasting rack set inside a shallow pan. Brush the hens with melted butter and roast for 10 minutes. Reduce the oven temperature to 350°F. and continue cooking for 50 minutes.

4. In a 1½-quart saucepan, combine the orange marmalade, 2 tablespoons water, and vinegar. Bring to a vigorous bubble. Stir in any remaining melted butter and brush over the hens. Continue to roast for 15 to 20 minutes longer, basting twice. Test for doneness by inserting a meat thermometer through the cavity aperture and into the center of the stuffing. The temperature should read 165°F. when the hens are finished roasting.   ◆

Mexican-Style Red Snapper

SERVES 4

The juices of lemons and oranges combine to lend a sunny, sparkling air to this exquisite, creamy-fleshed fish.

1 red snapper, cleaned (about 2 pounds)
Juice of 2 lemons
Juice of 2 oranges
1 medium onion, coarsely chopped
1 garlic clove, minced or pressed
1 red sweet bell pepper, coarsely chopped
1 tablespoon capers, nonpareille variety, drained and rinsed
2 tablespoons chopped fresh coriander leaves (cilantro)
2 large hard-boiled egg yolks, crumbled
½ cup pine nuts (or substitute almonds)
¼ teaspoon salt
Generous amount of freshly ground black pepper
10 pitted green olives, sliced

1. Rinse the cavity of the snapper under cold running water. Pat dry with paper towels. In a 9×13-inch baking dish, combine the lemon juice, orange juice, onion, garlic, red pepper, capers, and coriander. Place the snapper in the baking dish. Spoon some of the mixture inside the cavity and turn the fish to coat both sides. Marinate, refrigerated, for 2 to 3 hours, turning occasionally.

2. Preheat the oven to 375°F. Place the baking dish in the preheated oven and bake uncovered for 35 to 45 minutes or until the fish is opaque and separates easily when flaked with a fork.

3. Transfer the cooked fish to a warmed serving platter and pour the marinating liquid into the container of a blender or processor. Add the crumbled egg yolks, pine nuts, salt, and pepper. Whirl to purée and pour over the fish. Sprinkle on the sliced green olives. Serve with rice.   ◆

Trout with Kasha and Hazelnut Stuffing

SERVES 6

Toasted buckwheat kernels, known as kasha, are becoming readily available in most supermarkets and health-food stores. Surprisingly easy to prepare, kasha provides an engaging alternative to rice.

4 ounces hazelnuts
6 trout, boned (about 8 ounces each)
1 large egg
1 cup coarsely ground uncooked kasha
¼ cup olive oil
1 medium onion, coarsely chopped
½ teaspoon salt
Generous amount of freshly ground black pepper
2 cups boiling water
2 tablespoons lemon juice
2 tablespoons chopped fresh coriander leaves
(cilantro)
½ cup golden raisins
Butter

1. Scatter the hazelnuts in a baking pan and place in a 350°F. oven for 10 to 15 minutes or until aromatic. Rub the nuts briskly with a kitchen towel to remove the brown skins. Chop coarsely and set aside. Rinse the cavities of the boned fish and pat dry with a paper towel. Place in a generously buttered baking dish.

2. In a large mixing bowl, beat the egg and add the kasha, stirring to coat the individual kernels with egg. Heat the oil in a 12-inch skillet and add the onion, tossing to coat. Cook over medium heat, stirring constantly until the onion is tender. Remove from the heat. Add the egg-coated kasha to the pan and return to medium heat. Stir constantly for 3 to 4 minutes or until the egg coating has set. Sprinkle with the salt and pepper and stir in the boiling water. Reduce the heat to low

and cover the pan tightly. Cook for 15 to 20 minutes or until the kernels are tender and most of the liquid is absorbed. Stir in the lemon juice, coriander, raisins, and nuts.

3. Preheat the oven to 400°F. Spoon the stuffing into the cavities of the trout. Place a pat of butter on top of each fish and put in the preheated oven. Bake uncovered for 15 to 18 minutes or until the fish is opaque and firm to the touch.

Perch Fillets with Chive Butter

SERVES 4

Crisply sautéed fillets are dressed with a silken sauce of butter, wine, and lemon juice.

8 perch fillets
Flour for dredging
4 tablespoons vegetable oil
½ cup dry white wine
2 tablespoons fresh lemon juice
1 tablespoon chopped fresh chives (or substitute freeze-dried)
4 tablespoons cold butter, cut into 16 chunks

1. Dredge the perch fillets with flour. Heat the oil in a 12-inch skillet. Add the fish and cook over medium-high heat, turning to brown on both sides. Using a perforated metal spatula, transfer the cooked fish to a warmed serving platter. Pour off the excess oil from the skillet.

2. Add the wine to the pan, stirring to dislodge any particles of flour. Blend in the lemon juice and chives. Continue cooking over medium-high heat until the liquid almost entirely evaporates. (Leave about 2 tablespoons in the pan.) Remove the pan from the heat and whisk in 2 chunks of butter. If it refuses to melt completely, hold the pan over the heat for 1 or 2 *seconds*. The object is to warm the mixture only enough to melt the butter. Continue to whisk in the remaining butter, one chunk at a time, holding the pan off and on

the heat. The result will be a pale creamy sauce. (Excessive heat will melt the butter past the creamy stage, creating an acceptable chive-flavored butter, but one that is lacking the silky, creamy texture.) Spoon over the perch fillets to serve.

NOTE: An 8-inch whisk works best when you're whisking a small amount of liquid spread over a wide area. A fork may also be used. An alternate approach is to swirl in the chunks of butter.

Turbans of Sole in White Wine Sauce

SERVES 6

The trick to preparing rolled fillets of fish successfully is to position the skin side on the interior curve of the turban. Then as the skin contracts during cooking, it will pull the roll into shape.

6 large sole fillets (about 6 ounces each)
2 medium leeks
4 tablespoons butter
8 ounces fresh mushrooms, coarsely chopped
¾ cup dry white wine
¾ cup bottled clam juice
2 tablespoons chopped fresh parsley
¼ teaspoon dried leaf thyme
1 bay leaf, broken in half
2 whole peppercorns
2 tablespoons all-purpose flour
¼ teaspoon salt
¼ teaspoon ground cayenne
½ cup medium, or whipping, cream
2 tablespoons fresh lemon juice
Fresh parsley or watercress to garnish

1. Preheat the oven to 350°F. Lay the fillets in front of you, skin side up. Starting at the tapered end, roll each fillet firmly, taking care to align the roll so that one edge is more or less straight. Secure the roll with toothpicks or bamboo skewers, or tie gently with butcher's twine. Prepare the leeks by removing the roots and cutting off the dark green portion of the leaves. Cut the leeks in half lengthwise and rinse under cold running water, separating the layers to expose hidden sand and dirt. Pat dry. Thinly slice the white and pale green portion and set aside.

2. Generously butter a glass baking dish. Arrange the rolled fillets in the dish, standing them on the side with the straighter edge. Place in the preheated oven and bake uncovered for 10 to 15 minutes or until the fish is opaque and flakes in the center when nudged with a fork.

3. Meanwhile, in a nonreactive 2½-quart saucepan, melt 2 tablespoons of the butter. Add the leeks and mushrooms, tossing to coat. Reduce the heat to low and cover the pan. Cook for 8 to 10 minutes or until the vegetables are tender. Pour in the wine and clam juice and bring to a gentle bubble. Stir in the parsley, thyme, bay leaf, and peppercorns. Regulate the heat so that the liquid bubbles briskly, and cook uncovered until reduced to 1 cup. Pour the liquid through a cheesecloth-lined sieve, pressing to extract all the flavorful essence.

4. When the fish is cooked, transfer the turbans to an ovenproof serving platter and reserve the liquid in the bottom of the baking dish. Reduce the oven temperature to 250°F. and return the fillets to the oven to keep warm. In a 1½-quart saucepan, melt the remaining 2 tablespoons of butter over medium heat. Blend in the flour, salt, and cayenne. Cook, stirring constantly, until the mixture foams. Remove from the heat and whisk in the sieve-strained, reduced liquid. Return the pan to medium heat, whisking constantly. Cook until the sauce bubbles and thickens. Pour in the cream and reserved juices from the bottom of the baking dish. Continue whisking until the sauce bubbles. Remove from the heat and stir in the lemon juice. Take the turbans of sole from the oven and remove the toothpicks or cut the string with scissors. Pour on the sauce and garnish with fresh parsley or watercress. Serve with rice.

Sole Française

SERVES 2

A sauce of reduced wine and lemon butter provides the final flourish for these batter-coated fillets.

4 sole or flounder fillets
½ cup all-purpose flour
1 teaspoon salt
Generous amount of freshly ground black pepper
2 large eggs
2 teaspoons cold water
Vegetable oil
½ cup dry white wine
1 tablespoon lemon juice
1 tablespoon chopped fresh parsley
2 tablespoons cold butter, cut into 4 pieces
Fresh lemon

1. Lay the fish fillets on a double thickness of paper toweling and pat dry. Set aside. Season the flour by blending in the salt and pepper. Whisk the eggs and water to blend, but don't incorporate too many air bubbles. Pour into a wide, shallow dish such as a pie pan.

2. Pour vegetable oil into a 12-inch, thick-bottomed skillet to a depth of ½ inch. Place over high heat until the oil begins to ripple. Meanwhile, coat each piece of fish with flour and place on a rack set inside a jelly roll pan.

3. When the oil is heated, place a floured fillet in the beaten egg. Coat with egg on both sides and transfer to the hot oil. Repeat as quickly as possible with the remaining fillets. Reduce the heat to medium-high to avoid overbrowning. Cook uncovered for 3 to 4 minutes or until the underside is nicely browned and the egg coating on top looks as if it's beginning to set. Turn and cook the other side. Transfer to a warm platter.

4. Pour off the oil and return the pan to high heat. Add the wine, lemon juice, and parsley and cook rapidly until reduced by half. Pull the pan from the heat. Immediately add the butter, tilting and rotating the pan to swirl it in. Pour over the cooked fish and serve with slices of fresh lemon.

NOTE: A simple garnish may be made by

Twisted slices of fresh lemon make attractive garnishes for fish and seafood dishes.

cutting half way through a slice of lemon (that is, from the perimeter to the center) and twisting the edges of the cut in opposite directions until the slice will sit in an S-shaped squiggle (see illustration).   ◄₂

Halibut Steaks en Papillote

SERVES 4

Halibut steaks, spread with ginger-lime butter and sprinkled with chopped coriander leaves, are individually wrapped in parchment and baked. Referred to as en papillote, *this method of preparing fish allows it to steam gently while absorbing the essence of flavorful elements accompanying it. The result is moist, succulent fish of unparalleled texture and consistency.*

8 tablespoons butter
Vegetable oil
4 one-inch-thick halibut steaks
Salt and freshly ground black pepper
2 tablespoons fresh lime juice
2 teaspoons grated lime zest
1 tablespoon freshly grated ginger root
1 medium shallot, minced
2 tablespoons chopped fresh coriander leaves (cilantro)

1. Place the butter in a large mixing bowl and set aside to soften at room temperature.

Tear off or cut 4 pieces of parchment large enough to envelop the steaks. Lay the 4 sheets out and brush a steak-size area in the center with oil. Place a fish steak on the center of each oiled paper and sprinkle with salt and pepper.

2. Preheat the oven to 500°F. Whip the butter until light and fluffy. Slowly add the lime juice by drops, beating continuously. Beat in the lime zest, grated ginger, and minced shallot. Spread generously over the entire surface of the halibut steaks. Sprinkle on the chopped coriander and seal the packets by bringing up both edges of the parchment as you would to wrap a sandwich. Make 2 folds, drawing the paper taut against the fish. Fold the ends twice and tuck securely under the steak. Set the packets on an ungreased baking sheet and brush the tops with vegetable oil. Place in the preheated oven and bake for 10 minutes. (It isn't necessary to turn the packets during baking.) To test for doneness, make a tiny slit in the paper near the center of a steak and insert the blade of a paring knife. The fish is done when the flesh is opaque. Place the individual packets on serving plates. At the table, cut the packets open with scissors or slit with a knife. The fish is eaten directly from the paper packet.

NOTE: Aluminum foil may be used in place of parchment. However, because parchment is porous, a certain amount of steam is allowed to escape during cooking, producing superior results; nonporous foil tends to create an overly moist consistency. If you decide to substitute foil, reduce the oven temperature to 450°F.

(See entry for Parchment Paper and Appendix for sources.)

Poached Medallions of Salmon

SERVES 2

Poaching a whole salmon is fine for feeding a crowd, but poached salmon steaks are every bit as delightful and are easy to manage. Serve salmon steaks whole or separate them into medallions by removing the skin and lifting out the center bone.

2 tablespoons butter
Juice of half a lemon
2 fresh salmon steaks
Two sprigs of parsley
Whipped Butter Sauce (p. 360)

1. Coat the bottom and sides of a 10-inch stainless steel or other nonreactive skillet with the butter. Leave any excess butter in a lump in the pan. Add the lemon juice.

2. Fill the pan with cold water to a depth of 1 inch. Arrange the salmon steaks in the poaching liquid and lay the sprigs of parsley around the side. Add enough water to completely cover the fish.

3. Place over medium heat. When you can see the water begin to shimmer or move reduce the heat to a point at which the water gives off steam but doesn't bubble. Lay a piece of parchment or buttered waxed paper cut to the size of the pan on the surface of the water. Cook for 5 minutes or until the flesh is light pink and flakes easily.

4. Transfer to a double thickness of paper toweling to drain. Then serve whole or separate into medallions. Spoon Whipped Butter Sauce onto a plate and arrange the medallions on top of the sauce.

Sautéed Tuna Steaks with Fresh Tomato Sauce

SERVES 4

Full-flavored tuna with a lusty sauce of tomatoes, garlic, anchovies, and black olives.

1 large tuna steak (about 2 pounds)
Flour for dredging
¼ cup olive oil
1 cup dry white wine
1 medium onion, coarsely chopped

1 garlic clove, minced or pressed
4 anchovy fillets
6 medium-size ripe tomatoes (about 2 pounds),
  peeled, seeded, and chopped
1 tablespoon chopped fresh basil (or substitute 1
  teaspoon dried)
1½ teaspoons chopped fresh oregano (or
  substitute ½ teaspoon dried)
1½ teaspoons chopped fresh rosemary leaves (or
  substitute ½ teaspoon dried, pulverized with a
  mortar and pestle)
¼ teaspoon salt
Generous amount of freshly ground black pepper
8 pitted black Greek or Italian olives, quartered

1. Cut the tuna into 4 individual steaks, and dredge with flour. Heat the olive oil in a 12-inch skillet. Add the tuna steaks and cook over high heat for 3 to 5 minutes, turning to brown both sides. Using a perforated metal spatula, transfer the cooked fish to a platter.

2. Add the wine to the skillet and stir over high heat to dislodge any particles of flour. Blend in the onion and garlic and cook uncovered until the wine is reduced to ½ cup. Add the anchovies, tomatoes, basil, oregano, rosemary, salt, and pepper. Stir to break up the anchovies, and continue cooking over high heat until the tomatoes have softened and most of the liquid has evaporated. Reduce the heat to medium and return the tuna steaks to the pan. Cover and cook for 20 to 25 minutes or until the tuna separates easily when flaked with a fork.

3. Transfer the tuna steaks to a warmed serving platter. Increase the heat to high, add the black olives, and cook, stirring constantly, for 1 minute. Spoon the sauce over the tuna steaks to serve. ᜒ

Codfish Steaks in Mustard Cream

SERVES 4

Firm-fleshed cod in a simple, yet dramatic, wine sauce that is thickened and enriched with cream.

4 one-inch-thick codfish steaks
1 cup dry white wine
1 tablespoon Dijon mustard
1 tablespoon chopped fresh basil
¼ teaspoon salt
Generous amount of freshly ground black pepper
2 tablespoons butter, cut into 4 chunks
1 cup heavy cream

1. Preheat the oven to 375°F. Arrange the codfish steaks in a generously buttered baking dish. In a small bowl, whisk the wine and mustard together. Blend in the basil, salt, and pepper. Pour the mixture over the fish. Add the butter to the liquid and place in the preheated oven. Bake uncovered for 30 to 40 minutes or until the fish is opaque and separates easily when flaked with a fork.

2. Meanwhile, pour the cream into a thick-bottomed 1½-quart saucepan. Place over medium heat and cook uncovered until reduced to ½ cup. Remove from the heat, but do not refrigerate. When the fish is cooked, transfer to a warmed serving plate. Off the heat, whisk the reduced cream into the pan juices. Then pour the mixture into the saucepan and place over medium heat. Stirring constantly, bring the sauce to a gentle bubble and immediately pour over the codfish steaks to serve. ᜒ

Batter-Fried Nuggets of Cod

SERVES 6

The exceptionally light batter coating possesses the same marvelous flavor and aroma as freshly baked bread.

1 cup milk
1 tablespoon butter
1½ teaspoons sugar
½ teaspoon salt
1 package dry yeast
1 large egg, separated
1 cup all-purpose flour, scoop measured, plus
  seasoned flour for dredging

Vegetable oil for deep frying

1½ pounds fresh cod, cut into large chunks (or substitute another firm-fleshed fish such as haddock or pollock)

1. Heat the milk in a 1½-quart saucepan until the surface wrinkles or to 140°F. on a thermometer. Remove the pan from the heat and add the butter, sugar, and salt. Stir to melt the butter and dissolve the sugar and salt. Pour into a large mixing bowl. When the milk feels slightly warm to the touch (about 100°F.), sprinkle the yeast over the surface and stir to dissolve. Since the fat in milk interferes with the dissolving process, don't be alarmed if the yeast forms small lumps. They will break down as the batter stands.

2. Add the egg yolk and stir briskly with a fork to blend. Place the egg white in a large bowl and set aside to warm to room temperature. Add the 1 cup flour to the yeast mixture all at once and stir with a wooden spoon until the flour is moistened but still rather lumpy. Cover the bowl with a kitchen towel and let stand at room temperature for 30 minutes. The batter will develop a spongy consistency.

3. Stir the batter gently to smooth it out. Do not beat. Whisk the egg white until soft peaks form, and fold it into the batter. Heat the vegetable oil to 375°F. Coat the fish nuggets with flour that has been seasoned with salt and pepper. Using a metal or bamboo skewer, take up a cube of fish and dip it into the batter. Transfer to the hot fat and fry, turning with a slotted spoon, until golden brown. Fry 5 or 6 nuggets at a time and transfer them to absorbent paper to drain. Serve immediately.

(See entry for Batter Coating.)

Flounder Quenelles au Gratin

MAKES 16 QUENELLES

Fish dumplings are poached in a mushroom-flavored broth; topped with a rich, creamy sauce; and browned briefly under the broiler.

2 cups cold water

4 tablespoons butter

1 teaspoon salt

1 cup all-purpose flour, scoop measured

Generous pinch ground cayenne

Freshly ground nutmeg

4 large eggs

1¼ pounds flounder fillets (or substitute skinless, boneless halibut, pike, or cod)

1 cup dry white wine

1 bay leaf, broken in half

16 medium shrimp, peeled and deveined

1 large fresh shallot, coarsely chopped (or substitute 2 teaspoons freeze-dried)

8 ounces fresh mushrooms, coarsely chopped

¾ cup medium, or whipping, cream

MUSHROOM SAUCE

4 tablespoons butter

3 tablespoons flour

1¼ cups medium, or whipping, cream

Salt and freshly ground white pepper to taste

2 ounces Gruyère cheese, grated

1. Prepare an unsweetened *pâte à choux* (cream puff pastry) by combining 1 cup of the water, 4 tablespoons of butter, and 1 teaspoon salt in a thick-bottomed saucepan. Stir over medium-high heat and bring to a rolling boil. Remove the pan from the heat and immediately add 1 cup flour, the cayenne, and nutmeg. Beat vigorously with a wooden spatula. Return to medium-low heat and cook, stirring, until the batter pulls together into a smooth, shiny mass. When the dough pulls away from the sides of the pan, test for doneness by pinching the mixture with two fingers. The *panade* is cooked when it no longer sticks to your fingers (see entry for *Panade*). Immediately empty into a large bowl. Allow to cool for 5 to 10 minutes (or to below 140°F.), stirring occasionally to prevent a skin from forming.

2. Separate 2 of the eggs, setting aside the whites and reserving the yolks. One at a time, incorporate the 2 whole eggs into the *panade*. Beat vigorously with a wooden spoon after each addition. The mixture should be smooth and glossy. Set aside.

3. Place the reserved egg whites in the container of a food processor or blender. Cut the fish into 1-inch pieces and add to the egg whites. Pulse briefly to purée the fish. At this point, you should have approximately 2 cups of fish purée and 2 cups of *pâte à choux*. Packing firmly, measure out equal amounts of both. (Whether or not you come up with a total of 4 cups is not important. The significant factor is combining equal portions of both elements.) Using a wooden spoon or the paddle attachment to an electric mixer, vigorously beat the fish purée and *pâte à choux* together. Cover and chill thoroughly (at least 4 hours).

4. Meanwhile, combine the remaining 1 cup water, wine, and bay leaf in a nonreactive saucepan. Bring to a boil and add the shrimp. Regulate the heat so that the liquid simmers gently. Cook uncovered until the shrimp become firm (3 to 5 minutes). Lift out the shrimp with a slotted spoon and refrigerate to use as a garnish. Stir in the shallot and mushrooms. Bring to a gentle boil and cook uncovered until the mushrooms are tender. Remove and discard the bay leaf and strain the liquid, reserving the cooked shallot and mushrooms.

5. Take the chilled mixture from the refrigerator and gradually beat in approximately ¾ cup cream. This step establishes the proper consistency of the quenelles: too much cream will cause them to break apart during poaching; too little cream creates a dense, heavy texture. As the cream is absorbed, the mixture will lighten and become soft. To test, take up a heaping tablespoonful. The mixture should stand in a high mound without drooping or collapsing. It may not be necessary to add the total ¾ cup of cream.

6. Butter a 12-inch sauté pan or skillet. Pour in the strained broth and regulate the heat so that it barely simmers. In a teakettle, bring additional water to a boil. Using 2 wet tablespoons, shape a quenelle by scooping out a heaping spoonful with 1 spoon and smoothing the top of the quenelle with the other spoon. Slide the quenelle from the spoon into the simmering broth. Positioning the quenelles in a single layer, poach 8 at a time. Refrigerate the remaining mixture.

7. Add boiling water to the pan by pouring it onto the back of a spoon so the turbulence won't disturb the quenelles. You should have 2 to 3 inches of water simmering in the pan. Cook the quenelles uncovered for 15 to 20 minutes, maintaining the temperature of the water between 170° and 180°F. Turn once with a slotted spoon. Quenelles are done after they puff and nearly double in size. Lift out with a slotted spoon and drain on paper towels. Using the same procedure, poach the remaining quenelles.

8. Transfer the cooked quenelles to a generously buttered gratin dish or rimmed platter. Strain the poaching liquid through a cheesecloth-lined sieve and place over high heat. Cook at a brisk boil until reduced to 1½ cups. Transfer to the container of a blender or processor. Add the reserved shallot and mushrooms and whirl to purée.

9. Prepare the sauce by melting 4 tablespoons butter in a thick-bottomed saucepan. Using a heat-resistant rubber spatula, blend in 3 tablepoons flour and cook over medium heat until the butter foams. Remove from the heat and whisk in the puréed mushroom broth. Increase the heat and bring to a boil. Add 1¼ cups cream, whisking continuously. Adjust the seasonings by blending in salt and white pepper if necessary.

10. Whisk the 2 reserved yolks. Slowly add one-half of the hot sauce to warm the eggs, whisking continuously. Blend the mixture into the sauce remaining in the pan. Place over medium-high heat and cook, stirring, until a plopping sound indicates that the mixture has reached the boiling point. On the second plop, remove the saucepan from the heat. Pour the sauce over the quenelles. Sprinkle on the grated cheese and place in a 400°F. oven for 15 minutes. Broil briefly to brown the surface.

(See entry for Au Gratin.)

Portuguese-Style Bay Scallops

SERVES 4

Clarifying the butter insures that these sweet, tender scallops will cook at high heat without inheriting the harshness caused by burnt milk solids.

8 tablespoons unsalted butter, cut into 8 pieces and clarified
1 pound fresh bay scallops
Flour for dredging
2 garlic cloves, minced
¼ cup chopped fresh parsley
Salt and freshly ground black pepper to taste
2 tablespoons fresh lemon juice

1. Melt the butter in a small saucepan. Clarify and set aside. Place the scallops in a large sieve and rinse under cold running water. Shake vigorously and scatter over a kitchen towel in a single layer. Blot dry with a paper towel.

2. Put a generous amount of flour into a large bowl. Add the dry scallops and toss with your fingertips to coat. Transfer the scallops to a dry sieve and shake vigorously to dislodge any excess flour.

3. Pour the clarified butter into a 12-inch skillet. Place over high heat and warm until the butter ripples (about 15 seconds). Add the floured scallops and stir constantly to keep them in motion. When they begin to become firm (about 2 minutes), sprinkle on the garlic and parsley. Continue to stir over high heat for 2 to 3 minutes or until the scallops are lightly browned. Remove from the heat. Sprinkle with salt and pepper and drizzle on the lemon juice. Serve immediately.
(See entry for Clarifying Butter.)   ◄₂

Lobster in Sherry Cream

SERVES 4

Blending sweet paprika into the cream sauce colors this dish a magnificent hue.

2 lobsters (about 1½ pounds each)
4 tablespoons butter
1 medium shallot, finely chopped
1 tablespoon flour
2 teaspoons sweet Hungarian paprika
2 cups medium, or whipping, cream
2 large egg yolks
¼ cup dry sherry
2 tablespoons chopped fresh parsley

1. Fill a 12-quart kettle with enough water to completely cover the lobsters (about 8 quarts). Bring to a vigorous boil. Seize the lobsters behind the head and plunge them, head first, into the boiling water. Cover the kettle to enable the water to return quickly to a boil. When the water is again boiling vigorously, uncover the kettle and cook for 12 minutes. Immediately remove the cooked lobsters from the hot water so they won't continue to cook. Set them aside to cool slightly.

2. When the lobsters are cool enough to handle, lay them on their backs and slit each undershell from the tail to the head with a chef's knife or poultry shears. Reach in with a fork and pry out the cooked tail meat, removing and discarding the dark intestinal vein. Crack the claws and lift out the meat. Cut the lobster meat into bite-size chunks and set aside.

3. Melt the butter in a 12-inch skillet. Add the shallot, tossing to coat, and stir over medium heat until tender. Sprinkle on the flour and paprika and continue stirring over medium heat until the mixture begins to foam. Remove from the heat and blend in 1½ cups of the cream. Return to medium heat and cook, stirring, until the sauce bubbles gently and thickens slightly.

4. Reduce the heat to low, add the lobster meat, and stir to coat with sauce. In a small bowl, whisk the egg yolks with the remaining ½ cup cream. Transfer about ½ cup of the hot sauce to the egg-yolk mixture, adding it in a thin stream and whisking constantly. Slowly pour the warmed egg-yolk mixture into the pan. Stir constantly until the sauce thickens,

but do not allow it to boil. Blend in the sherry and parsley. Cook for 30 seconds to dissipate the alcohol in the sherry and spoon over rice or toast points.

NOTE: Whether you salt the cooking water for lobster or not is a matter of personal taste; however, lobster meat cooked in unsalted water is apt to be more tender.　　　　◄ঽ

Shrimp and Mushroom Sauté

SERVES 2

Shrimp and sliced mushrooms sautéed in butter and then bathed in wine make a quick, yet elegant, entrée.

18 medium shrimp
Flour for dredging
6 tablespoons butter
8 ounces fresh mushrooms, sliced
½ cup dry white wine
1 garlic clove, minced or pressed
2 tablespoons fresh lemon juice
A few drops of Worcestershire sauce
2 tablespoons chopped fresh parsley
1 tablespoon chopped fresh basil
Salt and freshly ground white pepper to taste

1. Rinse the shrimp under cold running water. Carefully remove the shell so the tail remains intact. Devein the shrimp and set on a double thickness of paper toweling to drain. Blot dry and dredge with flour.

2. In a 12-inch skillet, melt 2 tablespoons of the butter. Add the mushrooms, tossing to coat. Place over high heat and cook, stirring and lifting constantly, until the mushrooms are tender. Transfer to a platter.

3. Melt the remaining 4 tablespoons of butter in the skillet. Add the flour-coated shrimp and place over medium-high heat. Cook, stirring or shaking the pan to keep the shrimp in constant motion. When the shrimp become firm and the flour begins to brown, immediately pour in the wine. Add the garlic, lemon juice, Worcestershire sauce, parsley, and ba-

sil. Stir over high heat until the wine is reduced and slightly thickened. Add salt and white pepper and serve immediately.　　◄ঽ

Baked Shrimp Stuffed with Mushrooms

SERVES 4

Baked stuffed shrimp customarily appear on the plate in a gracefully curved position with the tails arching over the stuffing. To give your shrimp this look, make a deep cut in the flesh when you remove the intestinal vein from the back of the shrimp. Then spread the flesh apart and press down with the flat blade of a knife until the tail rises.

16 jumbo shrimp
4 one-inch-thick slices of French bread
8 tablespoons butter
8 ounces fresh mushrooms, coarsely chopped
1 medium shallot, minced
1 garlic clove, minced or pressed
2 tablespoons fresh lemon juice
1 tablespoon chopped fresh basil (or substitute 1 teaspoon dried)
¼ teaspoon salt
Freshly ground black pepper

1. Holding each shrimp under a gentle stream of water from the tap, peel off the shell. Secure the tail of the shrimp firmly between your thumb and forefinger so you can tear the body segments of the shell away, leaving the tail shell intact. Cut down the curve of the back with kitchen scissors and remove the intestinal vein. Repeat until all the shrimp are cleaned. Using a sharp knife, deepen the cut in the flesh until it goes almost all the way through the shrimp. Lay each shrimp on a sheet of waxed paper and spread the cut flesh open. Using the wide blade of a chef's knife, press down on the cut flesh to flatten the shrimp and force the tail to rise (see illustration). If necessary, secure the tail in place with a toothpick. Arrange the shrimp, cut side up,

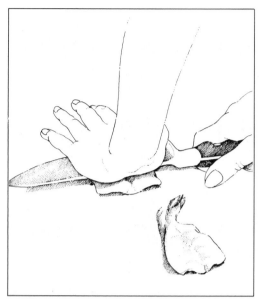

To flatten shrimp and make the tails arch, remove the intestinal veins, spread the flesh apart, and press down on the shrimp with the flat side of a knife blade.

in 4 buttered ovenproof serving dishes or in a buttered shallow baking pan. Refrigerate them and prepare the stuffing.

2. Break each of the 4 slices of bread into 6 or 8 pieces and drop them into the container of a blender or processor. Make fresh bread crumbs by whirling the chunks of bread with brief spurts of power to shred the bread without matting it. Set the bread crumbs aside. Melt the butter in a 10-inch skillet. Add the mushrooms, tossing to coat. Cook, stirring constantly, over high heat until the mushrooms begin to release their moisture. Stir in the shallot and garlic and reduce the heat to medium. Continue stirring over medium heat until the minced shallot is tender. Blend in the lemon juice, basil, salt, and pepper and cook briefly to soften the basil. Stir in the bread crumbs and blend, moistening the bread crumbs and combining the ingredients. Remove from the heat and cool slightly.

3. Preheat the oven to 350°F. Take up the stuffing by heaping tablespoonfuls. Cupping your hand over the stuffing, compress it slightly, then mound it on the prepared

shrimp. Place in the preheated oven and bake uncovered for 15 or 20 minutes or until the shrimp are light pink and firm to the touch. Slide under the broiler for a minute or two if you wish to crisp the surface of the stuffing. Serve with lemon wedges.

NOTE: You can create a more cohesive stuffing if you wish by stirring in a beaten egg just before spooning the mixture onto the shrimp. The resulting stuffing will have a heavier consistency and a denser texture. ◆੨

Mussels Broiled in Garlic Butter

SERVES 4

Minced garlic and shallots are cooked slowly in wine to temper their harshness and then whipped into softened butter laced with Pernod. When heated under the broiler, a dollop of this flavored butter melts to bathe each mussel-on-the-half-shell.

½ pound butter
48 fresh mussels
½ cup water
1 cup dry white wine
4 garlic cloves, minced
2 medium shallots, minced
¼ teaspoon salt
Freshly ground black pepper
¼ cup chopped fresh chervil (or substitute parsley)
1 tablespoon Pernod
4 wedges of fresh lemon

1. Place the butter in a large mixing bowl and set aside to soften. Scrub the mussels with a stiff brush under cold running water. Discard any that do not snap shut when you hold them under the water. Pull or cut off the threadlike beard, or byssus. (You may find remnants of this beard inside when the mussel shells open. Just pull them off.)

2. Transfer the cleaned mussels to a 6-quart pot. Pour in the water and ½ cup of the wine.

Cover the pot and place over medium-high heat for 5 to 8 minutes or until the mussels have steamed open.

3. Meanwhile, combine the remaining ½ cup of wine and 2 tablespoons of the softened butter in a nonreactive 1½-quart saucepan. Heat until the butter melts, and then stir in the minced garlic, shallots, salt, and pepper. Regulate the heat so that the liquid barely bubbles, and cook uncovered for 5 minutes or until the shallots and garlic are tender and the liquid is reduced to ¼ cup. Remove from the heat and let cool to room temperature.

4. When the mussels have opened, scoop them out with a slotted spoon and place them on a jelly roll pan to cool slightly. When they are cool enough to handle, remove the mussels from their shells and break the shells apart at the hinge. Discard half the shells and arrange the remaining half shells in a single layer on 4 ovenproof serving plates or in a shallow baking dish.

5. Preheat the broiler. Whip the remaining butter until light and fluffy. Beating continuously, gradually pour in the cooled reduced liquid. Beat in the chervil and Pernod, adding the Pernod by droplets. Put a small dab of garlic butter in each shell. Lay the mussels on top and cover with a generous dollop of the flavored butter. Place 4 inches from the broiler and cook for 4 to 6 minutes or until the butter is bubbly. Serve with wedges of lemon.　　　　　　　　　　　　　　　　⋖ও

Steamed Clams and Spanish Sausage

SERVES 4

Cherrystone clams steam open and release their juices, which intermingle with the heady flavor of sliced chorizo sausage. Serve in deep bowls with linguine or offer thick slices of crusty bread for sopping up the broth.

36 cherrystone or medium-size hard-shell clams
1 chorizo sausage (about ¾ pound)

Generous pinch of saffron threads, pulverized with a mortar and pestle
¼ cup olive oil
1 medium onion, coarsely chopped
1 green sweet bell pepper, coarsely chopped
1 red sweet bell pepper, coarsely chopped
2 garlic cloves, minced or pressed
1 can (28 ounces) crushed tomatoes
1½ cups dry white wine
2 tablespoons fresh lemon juice
1 tablespoon chopped fresh coriander leaves (cilantro)
½ teaspoon salt
Generous amount of freshly ground black pepper
1 bay leaf, broken in half
1 two-inch strip of orange zest

1. Scrub the clams with a stiff brush under cold running water, taking special care to dislodge any sand that may be caught in the seam between the two shells. Discard any clams that are open or have chipped shells. Cut the sausage into ½-inch slices. Place the saffron in a small bowl, add ¼ cup boiling water, and set aside to steep.

2. Heat the oil in a 6-quart Dutch oven. Add the chopped onion, green and red bell peppers, and garlic, tossing to coat. Cook over medium heat, stirring slowly, until the onions are translucent. Add the sliced sausage and continue stirring until the peppers are tender. Add the tomatoes and increase the heat to high. Stir in the wine, lemon juice, saffron and steeping liquid, coriander, salt, and pepper. Submerge the bay leaf and orange zest in the sauce. Regulate the heat so that the sauce bubbles gently and cook uncovered for 30 minutes.

3. Arrange the clams in the sauce and reduce the heat to low. Cover the pan and cook for 10 to 12 minutes or until the clams have opened. Using a slotted spoon, transfer the clams to a serving platter or individual bowls. (Discard any that have refused to open.) Stir the sauce to thoroughly incorporate the clam juice. Retrieve and discard the orange zest and bay leaves. Spoon the sauce and sausage slices over the clams to serve.　　　⋖ও

Clam Fritters

SERVES 4

Minced onion and green pepper add a spark of unexpected flavor to these New England favorites.

30 medium or cherrystone clams (about 2 cups shucked)
⅓ cup juice from clams
⅔ cup milk
2 large eggs, beaten
1 tablespoon melted butter
1 small onion, minced (about 1 tablespoon)
2 one-inch strips green sweet bell pepper, minced (about 1 tablespoon)
2 teaspoons fresh lemon juice
½ teaspoon salt
Generous amount of freshly ground black pepper
1 cup all-purpose flour, scoop measured
1 teaspoon baking powder
Vegetable oil for deep frying

1. Scrub the clams with a stiff brush under cold running water. Discard any that are open or have chipped shells. Open the clams, allowing the juice to collect in a bowl. When the debris has settled to the bottom of the bowl, pour or spoon off ⅓ cup of the juice and set aside. Scatter the clams on a double thickness of paper toweling and blot dry to facilitate chopping. Using a chef's knife, chop the clams finely. (A food processor or blender will not produce the correct consistency.)

2. Transfer the chopped clams to a large bowl. Stir in the reserved clam juice, milk, beaten eggs, and melted butter. Add the onion, green pepper, lemon juice, salt, and pepper. In another bowl, combine the flour and baking powder and toss with a whisk or fork to blend thoroughly. Sprinkle the dry ingredients over the clam mixture and stir with light strokes to combine.

3. Heat the vegetable oil to 375°F. Drop the fritter batter by generous tablespoonfuls into the hot fat. Cook 5 or 6 fritters at a time. Turn frequently with a slotted spoon to promote even browning. When the fritters are crisp and attractively browned, transfer them to absorbent paper to drain. Serve with Tartar Sauce (p. 356) or wedges of lemon. ❧

King Crab Flamed with Cognac

SERVES 4

Chunks of crabmeat and sliced mushrooms are flamed with cognac and then bound with a light tomato cream. Makes a delightful repast to serve after the theater.

4 tablespoons butter
8 ounces fresh mushrooms, sliced
1 medium shallot, finely chopped
¼ cup cognac, slightly warmed
1 pound king crabmeat, cut into bite-size chunks
1½ cups medium, or whipping, cream
2 tablespoons tomato paste
2 tablespoons chopped fresh parsley
1½ teaspoons chopped fresh basil (or substitute ½ teaspoon dried)
1½ teaspoons chopped fresh tarragon leaves (or substitute ½ teaspoon dried)
¼ teaspoon salt
Generous amount of freshly ground black pepper
2 large egg yolks
1 tablespoon fresh lemon juice

1. Melt the butter in a 12-inch skillet. Add the mushrooms, tossing to coat. Place over medium-high heat and cook, stirring constantly, until the mushrooms begin to release their liquid. Add the shallot and continue stirring until the mushrooms are tender.

2. Pour the cognac into a small pan and place over low heat to warm slightly. Mean-

while, add the crabmeat to the cooked mushrooms and increase the heat to high. Stir the mixture over high heat for 1 minute to warm the crabmeat through. Ignite the cognac and pour over the warm crabmeat, stirring and lifting constantly.

3. When the flame subsides, add 1 cup of the cream and the tomato paste. Reduce the heat to medium and stir to blend. When the mixture bubbles gently, stir in the parsley, basil, tarragon, salt, and pepper. Allow to bubble gently, uncovered, for 3 minutes.

4. Meanwhile, whisk the egg yolks with the remaining ½ cup of cream. Remove the pan from the heat and transfer about ¼ cup of the hot sauce to the egg-yolk mixture, adding it in a thin stream and whisking constantly. Then stir the warmed egg-yolk mixture into the pan. Place over low heat and cook, stirring slowly, until the sauce is slightly thickened. Blend in the lemon juice and spoon over wild rice.   ⤙

Valencian Stew

SERVES 6

The abundance and variety of ingredients in this stew nearly qualify it as a paella, that marvelous dish from the Levantine region of Spain. Chorizo, an essential element of this dish, is readily available now in most large supermarkets. If you can't find it, substitute kielbasa or another garlic-seasoned sausage.

3 tablespoons olive oil
6 chicken thighs
½ cup long grain rice
1 large onion, chopped
1 medium-size red sweet bell pepper, seeded and
　　coarsely chopped
1 garlic clove, minced
6 cups chicken broth or stock
2 cups water
12 small hard-shell clams (preferably littleneck
　　size)
6 mussels
12 medium shrimp

1 king crab leg (about ½ pound)
½ pound chorizo sausage
2 ounces Canadian bacon
1 can (35 ounces) Italian tomatoes, undrained
Pinch of saffron threads, pulverized with a
　　mortar and pestle, and then steeped in ¼ cup
　　boiling water
2 tablespoons lemon juice
½ teaspoon salt
Generous amount of freshly ground black pepper
½ cup frozen peas, defrosted

1. Heat the olive oil in a thick-bottomed 8-quart casserole or stockpot. Pat the chicken thighs dry with paper towels and add them to the hot oil. Cook over high heat, turning frequently, until nicely browned. Transfer to a platter. Stir the rice, onion, red pepper, and garlic into the oil in the pot. Cook, stirring continuously, until the rice becomes opaque. Add the chicken broth and water. Return the chicken to the pot. Regulate the heat so that the broth bubbles gently and cover the pan. Cook for 30 minutes.

2. Meanwhile, scrub the clams and mussels with a stiff brush under running water. Set aside. Shell and devein the shrimp. Using a chef's knife, cut the crab leg into 1-inch lengths, shell and all. (If the shell splinters excessively, remove it, but leaving it intact makes an attractive presentation.) Remove the casing from the chorizo and slice the sausage into ¼-inch rounds. Cut the bacon into bite-size pieces.

3. Add the tomatoes, breaking them up with your fingers, to the simmering broth. Stir in the clams, mussels, shrimp, crab, chorizo, and bacon. Blend in the saffron with its steeping water. Bring to a boil, and then reduce the heat so that the liquid simmers. Cover and cook for 15 minutes or until the clams and mussels have opened. Discard any that refuse to open.

4. Blend in the lemon juice, salt, and pepper. Add the peas and cook briefly, uncovered, until the peas are tender. Serve in large soup bowls with plenty of crusty bread to sop up every last bit.   ⤙

Beef, Veal, Pork, and Lamb

Italian-Style Meatballs

MAKES 24 TO 28 TWO-INCH MEATBALLS

Although it is customary to sauté meatballs in a skillet, this recipe suggests baking them instead. Not only is it a less messy approach, but baking meatballs gives them a light, moist texture.

4 one-inch-thick slices French bread
Milk (about ½ cup)
12 ounces fresh spinach
2 large eggs
2 tablespoons olive oil
2 pounds ground lean beef
2 four-inch links hot Italian sausage, casing
   removed
2 garlic cloves, pressed
⅔ cup freshly grated Parmesan cheese
Zest of 1 lemon, grated
¼ cup chopped fresh parsley
1 teaspoon salt
Generous amount of freshly ground black pepper
¼ teaspoon ground allspice
Vegetable oil

1. Place the inch-thick bread slices in a wide mixing bowl. Pour on enough milk to cover the bread and set aside. Wash the spinach and remove the tough stems. Cook in boiling water until limp and drain thoroughly under cold tap water. Squeeze dry with your hands and chop coarsely. Set aside.

2. In a large mixing bowl, whisk the eggs and olive oil together. Crumble in the beef and sausage. Add the garlic, Parmesan cheese, lemon zest, parsley, salt, pepper, and allspice. Mix well with a wooden spoon. Squeeze the milk from the bread and shred over the meat mixture. Add the spinach, crumbling it apart. Spreading your fingers wide, use your hands to blend the bread and spinach into the meat mixture. (Blending by hand results in a lighter texture than blending with a spoon.)

3. Preheat the oven to 375°F. Pour enough vegetable oil into two 9×13-inch baking dishes to film the bottoms. Take up the meat mixture by generous tablespoonfuls and shape into meatballs. Arrange inside the baking pans, leaving ample space between each meatball. Cover with aluminum foil and bake for 20 minutes. (If you're using separate oven racks, switch positions of the pans after the first 10 minutes to promote even cooking.) Remove the foil and bake uncovered for 15 to 20 minutes or until the meatballs are lightly browned. Coat with your favorite tomato sauce to serve or transfer with a slotted

spoon to a pot of simmering sauce and cook briefly to meld the flavors.

NOTE: Occasionally the fat contained in the sausage bakes out of the meatballs in a light yellowish foam. It's harmless, if somewhat unappetizing. Stirring the meatballs will cause it to fall away.   ◄₂

Burgundy Beef Patties

SERVES 4

Laced with Burgundy, these beef patties are sautéed, then blanketed with a mellow sour-cream sauce.

4 tablespoons butter
1 small onion, finely chopped
1 garlic clove, minced or pressed
1 large egg
¼ cup dry, unseasoned bread crumbs
¾ cup sour cream
½ cup plus 2 tablespoons Burgundy
½ teaspoon dried oregano
½ teaspoon salt
Freshly ground black pepper
1 pound ground lean beef
3 tablespoons chopped fresh parsley
2 tablespoons vegetable oil
½ cup beef broth
1 tablespoon Dijon mustard
2 teaspoons all-purpose flour

1. Melt 2 tablespoons of the butter in a 6-inch skillet and add the onion, tossing to coat. Stir over medium heat until the onion is translucent. Blend in the garlic. Continue stirring until the onion is tender, but don't allow the garlic to brown. Set aside.

2. Whisk the egg in a large mixing bowl. Blend in the bread crumbs, ¼ cup of the sour cream, 2 tablespoons of the wine, the oregano, salt, and pepper. Crumble in the ground beef and mix thoroughly with a wooden spoon. Add the cooked onion and garlic and 1 tablespoon of the parsley to the beef mixture. Incorporate thoroughly and form the mixture into 4 patties.

3. In a 12-inch skillet, heat the oil and the remaining 2 tablespoons of butter until the butter foams. Add the beef patties and cook over medium-high heat until well browned on both sides. Transfer to a warmed platter. Add the beef broth, remaining ½ cup wine, and Dijon mustard to the pan. Place over high heat and stir continuously until reduced to half the original amount. Remove from the heat.

4. In a small bowl, blend the remaining ½ cup sour cream with the flour. Off the heat, whisk the sour cream into the sauce. Stir in the remaining 2 tablespoons of parsley and place the pan over medium heat. Cook, stirring, until the mixture bubbles gently and thickens slightly. Pour over the beef patties to serve.   ◄₂

Beef Patties in Cognac Cream

SERVES 4

A smooth, creamy sauce transforms beef patties from simple to glorious fare.

1 large egg
¼ cup dry, unseasoned bread crumbs
½ teaspoon dried leaf thyme
⅛ teaspoon salt
Freshly ground black pepper
1 pound ground lean beef
4 ounces prosciutto, thinly sliced
All-purpose flour
2 tablespoons butter
2 tablespoons vegetable oil
¾ cup beef broth
1 tablespoon tomato paste
1 tablespoon fresh lemon juice
½ cup heavy cream
2 tablespoons cognac

1. Whisk the egg in a large mixing bowl. Blend in the bread crumbs, thyme, salt, and pepper. Crumble in the ground beef and mix well. Roll up the slices of prosciutto and cut across the roll to form shreds. Then cut the shreds into tiny pieces. Add to the beef mix-

ture and incorporate thoroughly with a wooden spoon. Form the mixture into 4 patties. Coat the patties with flour, pressing down to encourage the flour to adhere.

2. Heat the butter and oil in a 12-inch skillet until the butter melts. When the butter begins to foam, add the beef patties and cook over medium-high heat until well browned on both sides. Remove the pan from the heat and tilt so that the fat runs to one side. Spoon off 2 tablespoons of the fat and discard.

3. Place the pan over medium heat and pour the beef broth over the patties. Turn the patties frequently and move them around the pan until the broth bubbles vigorously. (As the cooked flour from the surface of the patties mingles with the hot broth, some thickening will take place.) Using a perforated metal spatula, transfer the patties to a warmed platter. Blend the tomato paste and lemon juice into the beef broth and stir over medium heat until the sauce is thickened. Remove from the heat and blend in the heavy cream and cognac. Return to medium heat and bring to a gentle bubble. Stir continuously until the sauce is slightly reduced and a desirable consistency is reached. Pour the sauce over the beef patties to serve.   ◦◦

Beef Stew

SERVES 6

Don't let the modest title fool you. This is not just any run-of-the-mill hodgepodge, but rather a sophisticated blend of complex flavors resulting in a truly stunning dish.

Vegetable oil

2½ pounds stew beef, cut into 1½-inch chunks (To obtain the best stewing beef, purchase a tip roast or bottom round roast and cut it into chunks yourself. Precut stew beef is often taken from the shank or plate and tends to be riddled with fat and connective tissue.)

1 tablespoon brown sugar

2 tablespoons flour

3 cups beef broth or stock

½ cup Madeira

1 garlic clove, minced or pressed

¾ teaspoon dried leaf thyme

¼ teaspoon dried tarragon leaves

3 bay leaves

½ teaspoon salt

Freshly ground black pepper

3 medium onions

12 large fresh mushrooms

3 medium carrots

6 small waxy potatoes (often called new potatoes)

1 cup Crème Fraîche (p. 361) or use regular heavy cream

1 tablespoon Dijon mustard

4 tablespoons butter

2 tablespoons chopped fresh parsley

1. Select a 12- to 14-inch thick-bottomed pan with a tight-fitting lid. A skillet, saucepan, or casserole — all are good choices. Pour in only as much oil as you need to cover the bottom of the pan. Pat the meat dry with paper towels to minimize spattering, but don't coat with flour. Quickly brown one-third of the meat in the oil over high heat. (Having too many pieces of meat in the pan at one time results in steaming the meat because a large amount of moisture is released.) Transfer to a platter and repeat with the remaining meat, adding a small amount of oil if necessary.

2. When all the meat is cooked, remove the pan from the heat and scatter the brown sugar over the bottom of the pan. Reduce the heat to low and cook the sugar, stirring, until it liquefies. Blend in the flour and continue cooking until the mixture is smooth and takes on a rich brown hue. Increase the heat and immediately whisk in the broth, wine, garlic, thyme, tarragon, and bay leaves (left whole). Add salt and pepper. Return the meat to the pan and bring the liquid to a boil. Regulate the heat so that the liquid barely bubbles, and cover the pan.

3. Meanwhile, prepare the vegetables by quartering the onions and mushrooms. Cut the carrots lengthwise into quarters, and then slice each quarter into 2-inch lengths. If the

potatoes are tiny, leave them whole; otherwise, cut them in half. Stir the meat to coat with braising liquid, and then arrange the vegetables over the top. Cover the pan and simmer for 1 to 1½ hours or until the vegetables are tender when pierced. (The vegetables actually are steamed rather than braised, so they maintain much of their own character while exuding juices that drip down and flavor the sauce.)

4. Transfer the vegetables and meat to a platter and arrange in an attractive pattern. Retrieve and discard the 3 bay leaves. Place in a warm oven while you make the sauce. Remove the pan from the heat and stir in the *crème fraîche.* Blend in the mustard and return to high heat. Boil, stirring constantly, until the sauce is reduced to about 1½ cups and takes on a thick, glossy appearance. Reduce heat to low and swirl in the butter, 1 tablespoon at a time. Tip and tilt the pan so that the butter melts slowly and is absorbed gradually. Sprinkle the chopped parsley over the meat and vegetables to serve and pass the sauce separately. ❧

Savory Pot Roast

SERVES 4 TO 6

Here's a hearty, full-flavored pot roast accompanied by a bouquet of vegetables and a robust sauce thickened with a beurre manié.

3½- to 4-pound beef brisket, bottom round, or rump roast
1 tablespoon dried leaf thyme
2 tablespoons bacon fat
2 cups beef broth
½ cup dry red wine
2 tablespoons tomato paste
1 can (28 ounces) Italian-style plum tomatoes, undrained
4 medium onions, quartered
3 medium carrots, cut into 1-inch lengths
12 medium-size fresh mushrooms, quartered
1 garlic clove, minced or pressed
1 teaspoon dried basil
½ teaspoon dried oregano
¼ teaspoon ground allspice
⅛ teaspoon ground cloves
1 bay leaf, broken in half
½ cup frozen peas
½ teaspoon salt
Generous amount of freshly ground black pepper
2 tablespoons all-purpose flour
2 tablespoons butter, at room temperature

1. Blot the meat with paper towels to dry. Prick the entire surface with the long tines of a meat fork, then rub the meat vigorously with leaf thyme.

2. Heat the bacon fat in a 6-quart pot or Dutch oven until the fat melts. Place the meat in the hot fat and cook over high heat until well browned. Turn the meat frequently to brown evenly on all sides. When a crusty, brown exterior has developed, immediately pour the broth over the meat. Add the wine, tomato paste, and plum tomatoes, breaking the tomatoes apart with your fingertips. Regulate the heat so that the liquid barely bubbles. Cover and cook while you prepare the vegetables.

3. Add the onions, carrots, mushrooms, and garlic. Stir in the basil, oregano, allspice, ground cloves, and bay leaf. Cover and continue to cook at a gentle bubble for 1½ hours.

4. Turn the meat and cook uncovered for 1 more hour or until the meat is tender when pierced with a fork. During the final 15 minutes, stir in the peas, salt, and pepper. Lift out the meat and transfer to a carving board. Allow the roast to rest for 10 minutes.

5. Meanwhile, prepare a beurre manié by blending the flour and softened butter to a smooth paste. Using a slotted spoon, scoop out the vegetables and transfer to a deep serving dish. Retrieve and discard the 2 pieces of bay leaf. Bring the sauce to a boil and gradually whisk in the flour-butter paste. When the sauce reaches the desired consistency (you may not need to use all the beurre manié), reduce the heat to its lowest possible setting to keep the sauce warm. (Do not cover.) Carve the meat by slicing against the grain and arrange the slices of pot roast on a serving

platter. Pour some of the sauce over the meat and pass the remainder in a sauce boat.

(See entries for Beurre Manié; Meat; Pot Roasting.)   ◂ᴗ

Skim the fat from the sauce with a shallow spoon and place sauce over low heat. Trim the fat from the meat. Break the meat into generous shreds. Return the meat to the pan and stir gently to coat with sauce. Heat briefly and serve.   ◂ᴗ

Barbecued Beef

SERVES 4 TO 6

A zesty dish to serve with rice or heap on crusty rolls for a cold-weather sandwich.

2 tablespoons vegetable oil
4½-pound beef brisket
2 large onions, coarsely chopped
1 green sweet bell pepper, coarsely chopped
2 ribs celery, coarsely chopped
2 garlic cloves, minced or pressed
1 cup ketchup
1 can (35 ounces) Italian-style tomatoes, undrained
¼ cup red wine vinegar
⅓ cup light brown sugar
½ teaspoon dried basil
½ teaspoon dried oregano
½ teaspoon ground cinnamon
½ teaspoon salt
½ teaspoon sweet paprika (or substitute hot paprika if you wish)
¼ teaspoon cumin
⅛ teaspoon ground cloves
⅛ teaspoon ground allspice

1. Heat the oil in a 6- to 8-quart casserole or Dutch oven. Pat the meat dry with paper towels and brown in the hot oil over medium-high heat. Transfer to a platter.

2. Reduce the heat and add the onions, green pepper, celery, and garlic. Stir to coat the vegetables with oil. Cover the pan and cook slowly until the onion is limp.

3. Add the remaining ingredients. Return the meat to the pan and turn to coat with sauce. Cover and place in a 325°F. oven. Cook for 3½ to 4 hours, turning the meat occasionally to promote even cooking.

4. When the meat falls apart if poked with a fork, transfer the brisket to a carving board.

Flank Steak with Mushroom Cream Sauce

SERVES 4

Cooked slowly in a small amount of wine and beef stock, flank steak emerges fork-tender. Mushrooms and onions simmered in the liquid are puréed in the blender or processor to create a rich, complexly flavored sauce.

2 tablespoons vegetable oil
1 flank steak (about 1½ pounds)
1 cup dry red wine
1 cup beef broth
1 teaspoon dried leaf thyme
1 tablespoon Dijon mustard
1 large onion, thinly sliced
2 tablespoons butter
8 ounces fresh mushrooms, quartered
½ cup medium, or whipping, cream
Salt and freshly ground black pepper to taste

1. Heat the oil in a 12-inch skillet. Add the flank steak and cook over high heat, turning frequently until both sides are well browned. Remove from the heat. Pour in the wine and broth, turning the steak to coat on both sides. Place over medium heat.

2. Stir in the thyme and mustard and scatter the onion slices around the meat. When the liquid bubbles vigorously, reduce the heat to its lowest possible setting and cover the pan with a tight-fitting lid. Cook for 1½ hours.

3. Melt the butter in an 8-inch skillet. Add the mushrooms, tossing to coat. Cook over high heat, stirring constantly, until the mushrooms brown lightly around the edges. Add to the liquid around the steak. Replace the

cover and cook for 1½ hours longer or until the meat is tender when pierced with a fork. Transfer the meat to a carving board.

4. Pour the braising liquid into the container of a blender or processor and whirl to purée the vegetables. Return the sauce to the skillet and place over low heat to keep warm. Stir frequently. (Whirling a sauce in the blender or processor often gives it an unattractive foamy look. This will disappear in about 10 minutes. Stirring the sauce helps to release the air bubbles.)

5. Carve the steak as you would a London broil: position the knife almost flat against the meat, and beginning one-third of the way back from the end of the steak, slice on an exaggerated diagonal, producing broad, thin slices.

6. Blend the cream into the sauce and increase the heat. Stir until the sauce bubbles. Season with salt and pepper. Arrange the slices of steak in an overlapping fashion and pour on the sauce to serve.

NOTE: Because this cut is essentially fat free, it makes an excellent meat to serve cold in salads or sandwiches. Cook according to the directions in steps 1–3, omitting the mushrooms if you wish. Refrigerate until thoroughly chilled, then slice thinly on the diagonal as described in step 5.　　　　⌒⌒

Rolled and Stuffed Flank Steak

SERVES 6 TO 8

Flank steak is a tough cut of meat; however, it's also exceptionally flavorful and inexpensive. By pounding the steak and then cooking it slowly in a moist environment, you can create a tender and delicious dish.

1 flank steak (about 1½ pounds)

STUFFING
3 slices stale French bread
Milk (about ½ cup)
12 ounces fresh spinach

3 tablespoons butter
12 ounces fresh mushrooms, thinly sliced
1 four-inch link hot Italian sausage
1 large egg, beaten
1 garlic clove, minced or pressed
½ cup freshly grated Parmesan cheese
12 pitted black Greek or Italian olives, finely chopped
1 teaspoon lemon zest
⅛ teaspoon ground allspice
½ teaspoon salt
Generous amount of freshly ground black pepper
12 thin slices prosciutto

SAUCE
1½ cups beef broth
½ cup dry red wine
3 tablespoons tomato paste
1 can (35 ounces) Italian-style plum tomatoes, undrained
1 teaspoon dried basil
½ teaspoon dried oregano
½ teaspoon dried rosemary leaves, pulverized with a mortar and pestle
1 bay leaf, broken in half
2 medium potatoes, peeled and quartered

1. Lay the flank steak between 2 pieces of waxed paper and pound with a wooden meat mallet to tenderize and thin. The muscle fibers in a flank steak are very large and easy to identify. Pound with the grain (in the same direction as the fibers), and then pound in the opposite direction, or against the grain. Turn the steak over. Replace the waxed paper if it's badly ripped, and repeat the pounding procedure until the steak is nearly twice its original size in both length and width. Roll up the meat in the same direction as the muscle fibers and place in a plastic bag to refrigerate.

2. To prepare the stuffing, place the bread slices in a wide mixing bowl. Pour on enough milk to cover the bread and set aside. Wash the spinach and remove the tough stems. Cook in boiling water until limp. Drain thoroughly and rinse under cold water from the tap. Squeeze dry with your hands and chop coarsely. Set aside.

3. Melt the butter in a 10-inch skillet. Add the mushrooms, tossing to coat, and place over high heat. Cook, stirring constantly, until tender. Transfer to a large mixing bowl. Add more butter to the skillet if necessary. Remove the casing from the sausage and crumble the sausage into the pan. Cook over medium heat until the sausage is no longer pink. Add the spinach and continue to stir over medium heat until the spinach dries and begins to stick to the bottom of the pan. Transfer to the mixing bowl containing the mushrooms. Add the beaten egg, garlic, Parmesan cheese, black olives, lemon zest, allspice, salt, and pepper. Squeeze the milk from the bread and shred the bread into the stuffing ingredients. Stir gently to combine.

4. Unroll the flank steak and place it on a fresh piece of waxed paper so that the muscle fibers are running from left to right in front of you. Lay 4 slices of prosciutto down the left side of the steak in such a way that they extend 2 inches over the side edge of the meat. They should overlap slightly. Repeat on the right side of the steak, then lay the remaining slices down the center. Spread the stuffing over the prosciutto and bring the ends of the slices up and over the filling so it won't ooze out during cooking.

5. Preheat the oven to 350°F. Using the waxed paper to help you, roll the flank steak away from you. The muscle fibers should be running the length of the roll. Tie securely, but not too tightly, with string in 4 or 5 places. (The stuffing will expand during cooking; tying the string too tightly causes the stuffing to bulge out the ends of the roll.) Place the meat roll in a 9×13-inch baking dish or shallow roasting pan. Drape a piece of aluminum foil over the meat and crimp along the sides of the pan to seal airtight. Place in the preheated oven and cook for 30 minutes. Uncover and increase the heat to 375°F. (save the foil for later). Cook uncovered for 30 minutes to brown the meat.

6. To prepare the sauce, add the broth, wine, tomato paste, and tomatoes to the pan, breaking up the tomatoes with your finger-

tips. Stir in the basil, oregano, rosemary, and bay leaf. Arrange the potatoes around the meat. Replace the foil and crimp the sides to seal. Cook for 15 minutes. Lower the oven temperature to 325°F. Prick several holes in the foil with the tines of a fork to allow some steam to escape. Cook for 1½ hours more, occasionally lifting the foil and basting the meat with the sauce.

7. Transfer the meat roll to a carving board. Pour the contents of the baking dish into the container of a blender and retrieve and discard the 2 pieces of bay leaf. Allow the fat to rise to the surface and skim off as much as possible with a spoon. Whirl to purée the cooked potato, which will slightly thicken the sauce. Cut the meat roll into 1-inch slices and arrange on a serving platter. Pour some of the sauce over the meat and pass the remaining sauce in a sauce boat.

(See entry for Pounding Meat.)   ◄ུ

Beef Rouladen

SERVES 4

Thin slices of beef rolled around sauerkraut and bacon are browned in the oven and then simmered in a richly flavored Burgundy sauce. Use a flank steak cut into 8 rectangles and pounded until thin or beef scallops cut from the eye of round roast (see Beef Scaloppine, p. 267).

8 beef scallops
Salt and freshly ground black pepper
1 cup sauerkraut (high-quality deli-style or the
    type sold in a plastic pouch)
½ pound sliced bacon, cut into 1-inch lengths
Pommery or other whole-grain mustard (or
    substitute Dijon)
2 large yellow onions, thinly sliced
2 tablespoons flour
2 cups beef broth
½ cup Burgundy
½ teaspoon dried marjoram
½ teaspoon dried leaf thyme

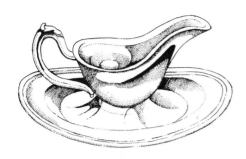

1. Lay the beef scallops on a double thickness of paper toweling and blot dry. Sprinkle with salt and pepper and set aside. Place the sauerkraut in a sieve to drain. In a 12-inch skillet or Dutch oven, cook the bacon until it browns. Transfer to absorbent paper to drain and crisp. Pour all but 2 tablespoons of the bacon fat into a 9×13-inch baking dish.

2. Preheat the oven to 375°F. Spread a small amount of mustard across the center of each beef scallop. Press down on the sauerkraut to remove the last traces of juice. Then, dividing it into 8 equal portions, arrange the sauerkraut in a mound across the center of each scallop. Top the sauerkraut with cooked bacon and roll up the beef scallops. Secure each with a metal skewer or long toothpick, or tie with string. Place the *rouladen* in the baking dish and brush each scallop's surface with the bacon fat from the bottom. Bake uncovered for 45 minutes, basting occasionally with bacon fat.

3. Meanwhile, add the onions to the reserved bacon fat in the skillet and toss to coat. Place over medium heat and stir until you hear sizzling sounds. Reduce the heat to its lowest possible setting and cover the pan. Cook the onions for 15 to 20 minutes or until tender and golden, but do not allow them to brown. Sprinkle on the flour and increase the heat to high. Cook, stirring, until the flour and fat foam together. (Do not be alarmed if the onions break apart.) Remove from the heat and stir in the broth. Return to medium heat and cook, stirring, until the liquid bubbles and thickens slightly. Blend in the wine, marjoram, and thyme. Regulate the heat so that the liquid bubbles gently.

4. Using tongs, transfer the browned *rouladen* to absorbent paper to blot excess bacon fat and then arrange in the bubbling sauce. Cover the pan and simmer for 30 to 45 minutes or until tender when pierced with a fork.

5. Transfer the *rouladen* to an ovenproof platter and remove the skewers or untie the strings. Place the *rouladen* in a 250°F. oven to keep warm. Pour the sauce into the container of a blender or processor and whirl until smooth. Pour over the *rouladen* and serve immediately with buttered noodles. ◄҉

Beef Scaloppine

SERVES 4

You can obtain beef scallops of excellent quality and save money in the bargain if you're willing to cut your own. Purchase an eye of round roast that's been cut in half (so that you can see it's free of gristle). Freeze the meat for 30 minutes to firm the muscle fibers and make slicing easier. Then cut the roast into ¼-inch slices and freeze what you aren't going to use. Trim the exterior fat and connective tissue from around each scallop. Place between two sheets of waxed paper and pound them with a meat mallet until they are thin. Use to prepare German-style rouladen *or cut into strips for stroganoff, stir-fry dishes, or the following Beef Scaloppine.*

1 pound thin beef strips (6 to 8 scallops cut into strips)
4 tablespoons butter
2 tablespoons vegetable oil
12 ounces fresh mushrooms, thinly sliced
1 tablespoon all-purpose flour
⅓ cup dry white wine
1 medium-size fresh shallot, finely chopped (or substitute 1½ teaspoons freeze-dried shallots)
1 cup beef broth
½ cup Marsala
1 teaspoon dried chervil
1 tablespoon capers, nonpareille variety, drained but not rinsed
½ cup heavy cream or Crème Fraîche (p. 361)
Salt and freshly ground black pepper to taste

1. Lay the beef strips on a double thickness of paper toweling and blot dry. Heat 2 tablespoons of the butter with the vegetable oil in a 12-inch skillet or sauté pan. Add half the beef strips and cook over high heat, stirring and lifting constantly with 2 wooden spatulas to make the moisture released by the meat evaporate as quickly as possible. Cook until lightly browned. Transfer to a platter using a slotted spoon. Sauté the remaining beef strips, adding more butter to the pan if necessary. Transfer to the platter.

2. Add the remaining 2 tablespoons of butter to the pan and melt over medium-high heat. Add the mushrooms and stir until they release their liquid. (Add the fresh shallot if you're using it and cook until tender.) Sprinkle the flour over the mushrooms and stir over medium heat for 1 minute to cook the flour. Add the white wine and bring to a brisk bubble.

3. Stir in the freeze-dried shallots, broth, Marsala, and chervil. Cook uncovered over high heat until the liquid is reduced to half the original amount. Drain but do not rinse the capers and blend into the bubbling sauce. Continue cooking until a fairly thick consistency is reached.

4. Remove the pan from the heat and stir in the cream. Return the beef strips to the pan and place over medium heat. Cook, stirring constantly, for 2 minutes to thoroughly warm the meat. Season with salt and pepper to taste (canned broth is exceptionally salty), and serve with rice or buttered noodles.   ◄ℨ

Tenderloin Tips Marsala

SERVES 4

This is one of those dishes that appear on restaurant menus all the time, but seldom show up in cookbooks. The reason why it is essentially a restaurant dish is that it's an excellent way to use up the odds and ends of a whole tenderloin strip. When the Châteaubri-

and, the filet mignon, and the tournedos are removed, the chef is left with a sizeable amount of meat at the tip and butt. These are frequently cut into bite-size pieces, sauced, and served as tenderloin tips.

Now that many supermarkets are selling the whole tenderloin at reasonable prices, you can obtain the tenderloin chunks used in this dish at a fraction of what it would cost you to buy individual steaks and cut them up. But you must be willing to buy the entire strip.

Ask the butcher to remove the side "strap" from the tenderloin and wrap it separately. This can be cut into strips for beef stroganoff. Then have the tenderloin cut into steaks, reserving 2 inches of the rounded butt and 4 to 6 inches of the tail. Or ask him to divide the strip into a Châteaubriand (which makes a lovely roast for 2), 2 fillet steaks, and 2 tournedos, leaving the butt and tip for preparing the following dish.

1 pound beef tenderloin (or substitute sirloin)
2 tablespoons vegetable oil
½ cup Marsala
2 tablespoons butter
12 ounces fresh mushrooms, sliced
1 garlic clove, minced or pressed
1 large shallot, minced (or substitute 2
**   teaspoons freeze-dried)**
4 anchovy fillets, chopped
¾ cup Basic Brown Sauce (p. 346 or p. 348)
½ cup canned crushed tomatoes
1 teaspoon dried chervil
Salt and freshly ground black pepper to taste
2 tablespoons lemon juice
1 tablespoon chopped fresh basil (or substitute 1
**   teaspoon dried)**

1. Cut the beef into 1-inch chunks and blot dry, but do not coat with flour. Set aside. (If you're using freeze-dried shallots, rehydrate them by soaking in ¼ cup of the Marsala.)

2. Preheat a wide burner to its highest setting. Pour the oil into a thick-bottomed 12-inch skillet, tilting and rotating the pan to film the entire surface. Place the meat on the film of cold oil. Set over the preheated burner. Tossing with 2 wooden spatulas, keep

the meat in constant motion. (The tossing action speeds the evaporation of moisture.) When the beef is well browned, transfer to a platter. Deglaze the pan with ¼ cup of the wine, then pour this liquid over the meat.

3. Add the butter to the pan. Tilt the pan to start the butter melting. Add the mushrooms. Return to high heat and cook, stirring continuously to keep the mushrooms in motion. When the mushrooms are entirely coated with melted butter, pull the pan from the heat and toss the mushrooms briefly to encourage them to release their juice. Stir in the garlic and the fresh shallot, if you're using it. Reduce the heat to medium-low and continue to stir until the vegetables are tender. Blend in the anchovies and cook briefly (they will disintegrate).

4. Add the brown sauce, tomatoes, remaining ¼ cup wine (and rehydrated shallots, if you're using them), chervil, salt, and pepper. Simmer uncovered for 10 minutes. Add the beef and deglazing liquid.

5. Blend in the lemon juice and fresh basil. Cook at a gentle bubble for 5 minutes. Serve immediately so that the interior of the beef will still be rare.　　　　　　　　　　⊷

Roasted Beef Tenderloin

SERVES 8

This roasted beef tenderloin, with its mushroom filling, makes a smashing entrée with which to celebrate a special occasion. To compensate for the lack of marbling (the interior fat that melts during roasting to flavor and moisten meat), ask the butcher for some trimmings from a rib roast of beef or porterhouse steak. Place the fat in a thick-bottomed saucepan and set over low heat until liquid fat is given off. Use the rendered beef fat to sear and baste the tenderloin.

1 two-pound piece of beef tenderloin (about 8 inches long)

⅓ cup vegetable oil
½ cup dry white wine
⅓ cup cognac
1 large onion, finely chopped
2 medium carrots, finely chopped
2 ribs celery, finely chopped
¾ teaspoon dried leaf thyme
¼ teaspoon dried sage
1 bay leaf, broken in half
3 whole cloves
1 cup beef broth
6 tablespoons rendered beef fat (or substitute clarified butter)
5 tablespoons butter
1 pound fresh mushrooms, finely chopped
2 tablespoons fresh lemon juice
¼ teaspoon plus a sprinkling of salt
Freshly ground black pepper
¼ cup chopped fresh parsley
⅓ cup Madeira
1 tablespoon cornstarch

1. Many supermarkets now sell whole beef tenderloins, which are also called beef fillets. The butcher will usually cut a tenderloin to order, but it's not a formidable project if you're forced to do it yourself. To obtain a center-cut roast, make a vertical cut approximately 4 inches from the larger end of the tenderloin. Then measure 8 inches and make a second vertical cut. You'll end up with an 8-inch roast, a 4-inch piece that can be sliced into steaks, and a somewhat longer strip that tapers to a point, which can be cut into medallions, cubes, or thin strips. Trim off the exterior fat and silvery membrane of the roast and tie securely, but not too tightly, in 5 places with butcher's twine. Pierce the roast in several places with the tines of a meat fork.

2. In a 1-gallon plastic bag, combine the oil, wine, cognac, onion, carrots, celery, ½ teaspoon of the thyme, the sage, bay leaf, and cloves. Place the beef inside the bag, turning to coat it on all sides with the marinade. Secure the bag with a metal twist and place inside a 9×13-inch baking dish. Refrigerate and allow to marinate for 6 to 8 hours. Turn frequently to encourage even absorption of the marinade.

3. Preheat the oven to 425°F. Lift the beef from the marinating liquid. Pat with a paper towel to remove any bits of vegetables and blot the meat dry. Transfer the marinating liquid to a 1½-quart saucepan. Add ½ cup of the broth and bring to a gentle bubble. Cook uncovered until the vegetables are tender and the liquid is reduced to half its original amount. Remove from the heat and skim off any fat that rises to the surface.

4. Meanwhile, spoon 3 tablespoons of the rendered beef fat into a roasting pan and place in the preheated oven to melt. Roll the beef in the hot fat to coat the entire surface and cook uncovered for 25 minutes. Turn the beef at 5- to 8-minute intervals to promote even browning.

5. Transfer the meat to a carving board. Add the remaining ½ cup of broth to the roasting pan and place over medium heat. Stir to dislodge any cooked-on particles and pour into a measuring cup. Allow to cool slightly. Skim off and discard the fat that rises to the surface; add broth to the vegetables.

6. In a 12-inch skillet, melt 3 tablespoons of the butter over medium heat. Add the mushrooms, tossing to coat. Cook, stirring constantly, until the mushrooms begin to give up their liquid. Add the lemon juice, the remaining ¼ teaspoon of thyme, ¼ teaspoon salt, and pepper, and continue cooking until all the liquid has evaporated and the mushrooms are tender. Add ¼ cup of the cooked mushroom mixture to the vegetable sauce and transfer the rest to a small bowl.

7. When the meat is cool enough to handle, cut away the string. Then measure off 8 equal 1-inch-thick portions, and slice vertically in 7 places, cutting two-thirds of the way through the meat. Pull the slices of tenderloin apart, sprinkling the surfaces with salt and pepper and spreading the mushroom mixture between the slices. (Apply a double portion between the first and second slices. Then, when you carve the roast to serve, the first slice will also be accompanied by stuffing.) Reshape the roast and tie it, end to end, with butcher's twine.

8. Reheat the oven to 350°F. Arrange the beef tenderloin on a rack set inside a roasting pan. Spoon the remaining 3 tablespoons of fat into the pan so it will melt, and place the beef in the reheated oven. Cook uncovered for 30 minutes, basting frequently with the melted fat. When the meat registers 140°F. on a meat thermometer (or 150°F. for medium), remove from the oven and transfer to a serving platter. Allow the roast to stand for 10 minutes before carving.

9. Meanwhile, skim any remaining fat from the vegetable mixture and pour through a sieve. Pick out the bay leaf and force the cooked vegetables through the sieve with a wooden pestle. Place the sauce over high heat and bring to a boil. Stir in the parsley. Combine the Madeira and cornstarch and stir to dissolve. Remove the sauce from the heat, blend in the cornstarch mixture, and return to high heat. Cook, stirring, until the sauce bubbles and thickens. Remove from the heat and swirl in the remaining 2 tablespoons of butter, 1 tablespoon at a time. Carve the tenderloin, placing a slice of mushroom-topped beef on each plate. Spoon the Madeira sauce over the mushrooms.   ❧

Veal Patties Stuffed with Herbed Cheese

SERVES 4

Soft cheese flavored with garlic and herbs provides a flavorful surprise when you cut into these tender patties. Use commercially prepared herbed cheese such as Boursin, or make your own (p. 176).

4 generous tablespoons herbed cheese
½ cup dry, unseasoned bread crumbs
¼ cup light cream
4 tablespoons butter
1 small onion, finely chopped
1 large egg
1 pound ground lean veal

Freshly ground nutmeg
½ teaspoon salt
Freshly ground black pepper
2 tablespoons vegetable oil
½ cup dry white wine
1 teaspoon cornstarch
1 tablespoon cold water
½ cup unflavored yogurt

1. Shape the cheese into four 1½-inch disks and refrigerate. Combine the bread crumbs and cream and allow the bread crumbs to soften. In a 6-inch skillet, heat 2 tablespoons of the butter. Add the onion and stir over low heat until the onion is translucent and tender.

2. In a large mixing bowl, whisk the egg. Add the veal, softened bread crumbs, cooked onion, nutmeg, salt, and pepper. Combine thoroughly and shape into 8 thin patties. Place a portion of chilled cheese on each of 4 rounds of veal. Top with a second patty and pinch around the sides to seal. Shape into fairly thick patties.

3. Heat the oil and remaining 2 tablespoons of butter in a 12-inch skillet or sauté pan. When the butter begins to foam, add the veal patties and cook over medium heat until well browned. Turn to brown the other side, and then transfer the patties to a heated platter. Add the wine to the pan and place over high heat. Cook, stirring, until the wine is reduced to 2 tablespoons. Remove the pan from the heat. Dissolve the cornstarch in the water and blend into the yogurt. (This stabilizes the yogurt so that it can be brought to a boil without curdling.) Stir the yogurt into the reduced wine and place over medium heat. Bring to a gentle bubble, then pour over the veal patties to serve.   ❧

Braised Veal Shanks

SERVES 6

This classic Italian dish, also called Osso Buco *(or "bone with a hole"), is customarily braised on top of the stove. However, braising the shanks of veal in the oven is an approach that some cooks prefer because it requires less supervision than stove-top braising. The flavoring secret lies in a blend of garlic, lemon zest, and fresh parsley known as a* gremolata.

2 veal shanks, each sawed into 2 or 3 two-inch pieces
Flour for dusting
1 tablespoon grated lemon zest
4 tablespoons chopped fresh parsley
1 teaspoon minced garlic (about 4 or 5 cloves)
⅓ cup olive oil
4 tablespoons butter
2 medium onions, finely chopped
3 medium carrots, finely chopped
3 ribs celery, finely chopped
1 can (35 ounces) Italian-style plum tomatoes, drained and broken apart
1 cup dry white wine
½ teaspoon salt
Generous amount of freshly ground black pepper
½ teaspoon dried basil
½ teaspoon dried leaf thyme
¾ cup beef broth

1. Because the meat has a tendency to fall away from the bone as the interior collagen melts during braising, it's a good idea to tie the shanks with string. Measure off a piece of butcher's twine long enough to go around the shank 2 times. Secure the meat firmly, but allow room for the expansion that will take place during cooking. Dust the entire surface of the veal with flour.

2. Preheat the oven to 425°F. Prepare the *gremolata* by combining the grated lemon zest, chopped parsley, and minced garlic. Toss with a fork to mix and set aside to allow the flavors to meld.

3. Pour the olive oil into a fairly deep roasting pan (an extra-heavy aluminum foil roasting pan works well), and place on the lowest rack in the oven to heat the oil. When the oil is sizzling hot, arrange the veal in the oil and cook uncovered for 30 to 40 minutes, turning the shanks at about 10-minute intervals to promote even browning.

4. Meanwhile, melt the butter in a 12-inch skillet and add the onions, carrots, and celery.

Place over medium heat and cook, stirring constantly, until the onions are tender. When the veal is well browned, remove the shanks from the roasting pan and distribute the partially cooked vegetables over the bottom of the pan. Add the tomatoes and the wine and stir to dislodge any particles that may have cooked to the bottom of the pan. Sprinkle with salt and pepper and return the shanks to the pan, arranging them so that the round bone faces upward. Stir the basil and thyme into the broth and pour over the veal. The liquid should come no more than halfway up the sides of the meat. Sprinkle on half the *gremolata* and cover the roasting pan with foil. Crimp around the sides to seal. Lower the oven temperature to 325°F. and raise the oven rack to the center of the oven. Cook the veal shanks for 1½ to 2 hours or until tender when pierced with a fork.

5. Transfer the cooked veal to a deep ovenproof platter and remove the twine. Place in a 250°F. oven to keep warm. Pour the pan juices through a sieve into a 2½-quart saucepan. Allow the fat to rise to the surface and remove with a spoon. Place the pan over medium heat and bring the liquid to a brisk bubble. Meanwhile, force the vegetables through the sieve with a wooden pestle. Add to the bubbling liquid and cook until a slightly thickened consistency is reached. Pour the sauce over the veal shanks and sprinkle on the remaining *gremolata* to serve. (Risotto Milanese on p. 316 makes an excellent partner for this dish.)

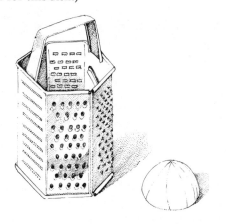

NOTE: The bone marrow is supposed to be scooped out and eaten as part of the meal. Spread it on toasted rounds of French bread. If you don't happen to have marrow spoons on hand, use seafood forks.

(See entry for Braising.)

Veal Chops in Lemon Cream

SERVES 4

Veal and the zesty tang of lemon juice are convivial companions. In this recipe, the familiar partnership is heightened by the lively accent of sour cream.

2 tablespoons vegetable oil
2 tablespoons butter
4 rib veal chops
Salt and freshly ground black pepper
⅔ cup dry white wine
2 tablespoons fresh lemon juice
1 medium shallot, finely chopped
½ teaspoon dried tarragon leaves
½ cup heavy cream
½ cup sour cream

1. Heat the oil and butter in a 12-inch skillet or sauté pan until the butter melts and begins to foam. Add the chops and cook over high heat, shaking the pan or moving the chops constantly to promote even browning. Sprinkle with salt and pepper to taste. Turn the chops and cook until well browned on both sides. Pour on ⅓ cup of the wine. Regulate the heat so that the liquid barely bubbles and cover the pan. Cook for 20 minutes or until the meat is tender when pierced with a fork. Transfer to a warmed platter.

2. Add the remaining ⅓ cup wine, lemon juice, and shallot to the pan juices and stir over high heat to dislodge any cooked-on meat particles. Cook until the chopped shallot is tender. Remove the pan from the heat. Whisk in the tarragon, heavy cream, and sour cream. Place over medium heat and bring to a brisk bubble. Cook, stirring, until the sauce

is reduced and slightly thickened. Pour over the cooked chops to serve. ❧

Veal Scallops Marsala

SERVES 2

Because the flavor of Marsala is a prominent element of this dish, it is important to select the wine that's pleasing to you. Experiment with various brands, both domestic and imported. You'll notice a marked difference in the level of sweetness and in the intensity of flavor derived from the addition of heated must, the component responsible for Marsala's unique nutty-caramel flavor.

6 medium veal scallops
6 tablespoons butter
1 medium shallot, finely chopped
6 ounces fresh mushrooms, sliced
Vegetable oil
Salt and freshly ground black pepper
Flour for dredging
½ cup beef broth
½ cup Marsala
1 teaspoon dried chervil

1. Select light pink scallops of veal in which the striations of muscle fiber are unnoticeable. Pound between sheets of waxed paper to a thickness of ¼ inch. Melt 2 tablespoons of butter in an 8-inch skillet and add the shallot. Cook over medium-high heat until limp. Add the mushrooms and cook, stirring constantly, until they release their liquid and become soft. Set aside.

2. Sprinkle the veal with salt and pepper and dredge with flour. Pour a small amount of oil into a 12-inch skillet. Tilt and rotate the pan so that the oil lightly coats most of the surface. Add 2 tablespoons of butter and place over high heat.

3. Cook the veal as soon as the butter foam in the skillet subsides. In order to cope with hot spots, keep the veal in continuous motion by shaking the pan or by gently pushing the veal around with a wooden spatula. The object is to cook the veal quickly and at the

same time to brown the flour without allowing it to burn. As soon as the undersides of the scallops are nicely browned, turn and cook the other sides. Transfer to a platter.

4. Pour in the broth and Marsala. Add the chervil and cook over high heat, stirring to dissolve the browned bits of flour. Depending on the amount of browned flour available, the sauce will begin to thicken. Stir in the cooked mushrooms and shallot. Add the remaining 2 tablespoons of butter. If the sauce seems slow to thicken, return the veal to the pan, arranging the scallops in a single layer. Gently shake the pan back and forth, dislodging just enough cooked flour from the undersides to encourage thickening. Do not turn the scallops. When the sauce reaches the desired consistency, transfer the veal to warmed plates, and slightly overlap the scallops. Pour the sauce over the top to serve.

NOTE: The success of this recipe depends on cooking a limited amount of veal at one time; therefore, in order to double the recipe, it's a good idea to use two 12-inch skillets.

(See entry for Pounding Meat.) ❧

Veal Scallops Saltimbocca

SERVES 2

Chopped fresh sage and authentic Italian fontina elevate this frequently prosaic dish to superlative heights. Look for imported Italian fontina cheese, which has a burnished-brown waxy rind; Danish fontina, which is more commonly available, has a red, waxy coating and an entirely different flavor.

6 medium veal scallops
6 tablespoons butter
1 medium shallot, finely chopped
6 ounces fresh mushrooms, sliced
Vegetable oil
Salt and freshly ground black pepper
Flour for dredging
½ cup beef broth
½ cup dry white wine

1 tablespoon lemon juice
1 tablespoon chopped fresh sage
6 thin slices prosciutto, cut to the size of the scallops
6 thin slices fontina cheese, cut to the size of the scallops

1. Select light pink scallops of veal in which the striations of muscle fiber are unnoticeable. Pound between sheets of waxed paper to a thickness of ¼ inch. Melt 2 tablespoons of butter in an 8-inch skillet and add the shallot. Cook over medium-high heat until limp. Add the mushrooms and cook, stirring constantly, until they release their liquid and become soft. Set aside.

2. Sprinkle the veal with salt and pepper and dredge with flour. Pour a small amount of oil into a 12-inch skillet. Tilt and rotate the pan so that the oil lightly coats most of the surface. Add 2 tablespoons of butter and place over high heat.

3. Cook the veal as soon as the butter foam in the skillet subsides. In order to cope with hot spots, keep the veal in continuous motion by shaking the pan or by gently pushing the veal around with a wooden spatula. The object is to cook the veal quickly and at the same time to brown the flour without allowing it to burn. As soon as the undersides of the scallops are nicely browned, turn and cook the other sides. Transfer to a platter.

4. Pour in the broth and wine. Add the lemon juice and sage and cook over high heat, stirring to dissolve the browned bits of flour. Depending on the amount of browned flour available, the sauce will begin to thicken. Stir in the cooked mushrooms and shallot. Reduce the heat so that the sauce simmers gently and return the veal to the pan, arranging the scallops in a single layer. Place a slice of prosciutto on each scallop, and then top with a slice of fontina. Gently shake the pan back and forth, dislodging just enough flour from the undersides to encourage thickening. Do not turn the scallops. The heat from the bubbling sauce will melt the cheese in 3 to 4 minutes.

5. When the cheese is melted and the sauce is thickened to the desired consistency, transfer the veal to warmed plates, slightly overlapping the scallops. Remove the skillet from the heat and swirl in the remaining 2 tablespoons butter by tilting and rotating the pan. Pour the sauce over the veal and serve.

(See entry for Pounding Meat.)   ◂ℨ

Pork and Chicken Stew Adobo

SERVES 6

Adobo *refers to a seasoning paste that gives much of Caribbean cooking its characteristic flavor. You can create the paste by mashing the garlic and other ingredients together with a mortar and pestle.*

2 garlic cloves
3 peppercorns
1½ teaspoons dried oregano
½ teaspoon salt
1 tablespoon lime juice
½ cup white wine vinegar
½ cup water
½ cup brown sugar
½ cup dry sherry
1 tablespoon ketchup
1 bay leaf
2 pounds pork stew meat (or cut a boneless shoulder roast into 2-inch cubes)
6 chicken thighs
3 tablespoons olive oil
2 medium onions, quartered
1 tablespoon flour
1 can (35 ounces) Italian tomatoes, undrained
2 tablespoons chopped fresh parsley

1. Combine the garlic, peppercorns, oregano, salt, and lime juice in a mortar. Mash to a smooth paste with the pestle.

2. Form a marinade by combining the vinegar, water, brown sugar, sherry, ketchup, and bay leaf. Stir to dissolve the sugar, blend in the garlic paste, and pour into a strong 1-gallon

plastic bag or shallow 9×13-inch baking dish. Add the pork cubes and chicken thighs. Marinate for 2½ hours in the refrigerator. Turn frequently to ensure even absorption of flavors.

3. Using a slotted spoon, remove the meat from the marinade and place on the rack of a broiling pan. Reserve the marinade. Slide the pork and chicken thighs under the broiler about 3 to 4 inches away from the coils or flame. Broil, turning the meat to expose all sides to the heat, until all surfaces are nicely browned.

4. Meanwhile, heat the olive oil in a 6-quart casserole and add the onions, tossing to coat. Cover and cook slowly for 15 to 20 minutes or until the onions begin to take on a golden hue. Remove from the heat and sprinkle on the flour. Return to medium heat and cook, stirring, until the mixture foams. Remove from the heat.

5. Remove the bay leaf from the marinade and pour the liquid into the casserole. Return to the heat and bring to a boil, stirring continuously. Add the tomatoes, breaking them up with your fingers. Transfer the broiled pork and chicken to the casserole. Regulate the heat so that the liquid simmers gently, stir in the parsley, and cook uncovered for 30 minutes. Serve with white or brown rice. ◀

Hungarian Stew

SERVES 6

Authentic Hungarian paprika comes in three styles — hot, half-sweet, and sweet. This recipe calls for sweet paprika, which is quite mild and the essence of a superb goulash. Check the Appendix for a mail-order source of Hungarian paprika.

1 pound sauerkraut (high-quality deli-style or
   the type sold in a plastic pouch)
2 tablespoons lard or vegetable oil
2 medium onions, coarsely chopped
1 garlic clove, minced or pressed
3 tablespoons Hungarian sweet paprika

2 cups chicken broth
¼ cup tomato purée
1½ teaspoons caraway seeds
2½ pounds pork stew meat (or cut a boneless
   shoulder roast into 2-inch cubes)
1 cup dry white wine
1 tablespoon cornstarch
2 tablespoons cold water
1 cup sour cream
½ teaspoon salt

1. Place the sauerkraut in a sieve. Rinse thoroughly under cold running water, lifting the sauerkraut with your fingers. Transfer to a large bowl and completely cover with cold water. Allow to stand for 30 minutes.

2. Melt the lard in a 6-quart casserole. Stir in the onions, tossing to coat. Cover the pan and cook slowly for 15 to 20 minutes or until the onions begin to take on a golden hue. Add the garlic and sprinkle on the paprika. Cook over medium heat for 1 minute, stirring constantly. Blend in the broth, tomato purée, and caraway seeds. Bring to a boil. Add the pork and stir to coat with liquid. Regulate the heat so that the liquid barely bubbles.

3. Drain the sauerkraut and squeeze dry with your hands. Arrange over the pork and pour on the wine. Cover the pan and simmer for 1½ hours.

4. Remove from the heat and, using a slotted spoon, transfer the sauerkraut and pork to a deep platter. Dissolve the cornstarch in the water and blend into the sour cream (this step stabilizes the sour cream so that it can be brought to a boil without curdling). Blend the sour cream into the stewing liquid and return to medium heat. Bring to a gentle bubble and add the salt. Pour over the pork and sauerkraut to serve. ◀

Barbecued Ribs

SERVES 4

Country-style pork ribs steeped in a Madeira-based marinade. When heat is applied, the surface of the ribs develops a delicious, dark brown, slightly syrupy crust.

4 pounds country-style pork ribs (or spareribs)
½ cup Madeira
½ cup naturally brewed soy sauce
¼ cup light brown sugar
2 garlic cloves, minced or pressed
1 tablespoon molasses
1 teaspoon Dijon mustard
¼ teaspoon ground cloves

1. Divide the ribs into 4 portions. Cut between the bones to facilitate even cooking, but don't separate the ribs completely.

2. Combine the remaining ingredients and pour into a 1-gallon plastic storage bag. Add the pork ribs and turn to coat all surfaces. Secure the bag and place inside a 9×13-inch baking dish. Refrigerate for 8 to 10 hours, turning the bag occasionally to promote even absorption of the marinade.

3. Preheat the oven to 350°F. Remove the ribs from the bag and arrange inside the baking dish. Reserve the marinade. Bake for 45 minutes, turning once.

4. Remove from the oven and barbecue over medium-hot coals for 20 to 30 minutes, turning and basting frequently with the reserved marinade. The ribs are done when the juices run clear and no traces of pink remain. The meat should be tender with a rich brown crust. (This last step may also be executed in the oven. Drain off any grease from the baking dish and increase the oven temperature to 425°F. Continue cooking the ribs, basting and turning frequently. The ribs will be done in 20 to 30 minutes but will not have a crust as crisp as that of ribs cooked over an open fire.)   ❧

Pork Chops Braised in Beer

SERVES 4

Cooking pork chops can be tricky. When fried or broiled, they often come out dry and greasy.

A better approach is to braise them, cooking the meat slowly in a moist environment. In this recipe, beer and sauerkraut provide both moisture and flavor to create juicy, fork-tender pork chops.

¼ pound sliced bacon, cut into 1-inch lengths
4 center-cut rib pork chops, ¾ to 1 inch thick
1 large onion, sliced
1 can (12 ounces) beer
2 teaspoons caraway seeds
Salt and freshly ground black pepper to taste
1 pound sauerkraut (high-quality deli-style or
the type sold in a plastic pouch), undrained

1. In a 12-inch skillet or Dutch oven, cook the bacon until browned. Transfer the bacon to a double thickness of paper toweling to drain and crisp. Add the chops to the bacon fat and place over medium heat. Cook, turning frequently, until lightly browned. Transfer the chops to a platter.

2. Add the onion slices to the fat and toss to coat. Reduce the heat to low and cover the pan. Cook the onion for 8 to 10 minutes or until tender but not browned. Using a slotted spoon, distribute the onion over the partially cooked chops. Drain the fat from the pan.

3. Pour in the beer and place over high heat to bring to a boil. Arrange the pork chops and onion in the bubbling beer. Scatter the cooked bacon and caraway seeds over the chops. Add salt and pepper to taste and reduce the heat to its lowest possible setting. Arrange the sauerkraut over the chops, taking care to cover the chops completely. Cover and cook for 20 to 30 minutes or until the meat is tender when pierced with a fork. Serve with small boiled potatoes or pumpernickel bread and a hearty mustard.

(See entry for Braising.)   ❧

Citrus-Braised Pork Chops

SERVES 4

Citrus juice, with its acidic composition, has a natural tendency to soften meat fibers. In this recipe, orange juice and lemon juice combine to work their tenderizing magic on pork chops. Freshly grated ginger root lends an oriental fillip to the final sauce.

2 tablespoons vegetable oil
4 center-cut rib pork chops, ¾ to 1 inch thick
½ cup chicken broth
¾ cup fresh orange juice
¼ cup lemon juice
⅓ cup naturally brewed soy sauce
3 tablespoons light brown sugar
1 garlic clove, minced or pressed
⅛ teaspoon ground cloves
6 green onions, thinly sliced (including most of
   the green portion)
1 teaspoon freshly grated ginger root
1 tablespoon cornstarch
2 tablespoons cold water
1 navel orange, peeled, split into segments, and
   membranes removed

1. Heat the vegetable oil in a 12-inch skillet or Dutch oven. Add the pork chops and place over medium heat. Cook, turning frequently, until both sides are lightly browned. Transfer the chops to a platter.

2. Pour the fat from the pan and add the broth, stirring to dissolve any particles that may have cooked to the bottom of the pan. Blend in the orange juice, lemon juice, soy sauce, brown sugar, garlic, and ground cloves. Increase the heat and bring to a brisk bubble.

3. Arrange the chops in the bubbling sauce. Reduce the heat to its lowest possible setting. Scatter the green onions and ginger root over the chops and cover the pan. Cook for 20 to 30 minutes or until the meat is tender when pierced with a fork. Remove the pan from the heat and transfer the chops to a platter.

4. Dissolve the cornstarch in the cold water and blend into the sauce. Place over high heat and cook, stirring constantly, until the sauce bubbles and thickens. Stir in the orange segments. Return the chops to the sauce and cook briefly to warm through. Serve with parsleyed rice.

NOTE: Navel oranges are virtually seedless, but do check the segments in order to remove seeds if they are present.

(See entry for Braising.)

Pork Scallops in Mustard Cream

SERVES 4

Tomato paste, blended with dry mustard, lends an elusive flavor to this smooth sauce.

6 center-cut rib pork chops, ¾ to 1 inch thick
3 tablespoons vegetable oil
3 tablespoons butter
½ cup dry white wine
2 tablespoons Madeira
1 cup heavy cream or Crème Fraîche (p. 361)
2 tablespoons tomato paste
1 tablespoon dry mustard
Salt and freshly ground black pepper to taste
2 tablespoons chopped fresh parsley

1. Cut the eye of the chop away from the bone. Trim off the fat and the small area of darker meat if there is one. (Freeze what you trim away to save for another purpose.) Slice in half horizontally to form 2 scallops. Place the scallops between 2 sheets of waxed paper and pound with a meat mallet to thin.

2. In a 12-inch skillet, heat the oil and butter until the butter melts. Add the pork scallops and cook over high heat until lightly browned on one side. Turn and cook to brown the other side. Transfer to a platter.

3. Pour the fat from the pan, leaving behind any cooked particles of meat. Add the white wine and place over high heat. Cook, stirring to dissolve the cooked particles, until the wine is reduced to ¼ cup. Blend in the Madeira and cream and regulate the heat so that the sauce bubbles gently. Combine the tomato paste and mustard into a smooth paste. Gradually stir the paste into the hot sauce and continue to cook at a gentle bubble until the cream mixture is reduced to half its

original amount and the harshness of the mustard is attenuated.

4. Return the pork scallops to the pan and cook briefly to warm through. Season with salt and pepper to taste and sprinkle the parsley over the top. Arrange 3 pork scallops on each serving plate and spoon the remaining sauce over the scallops.

(See entry for Pounding Meat.)   ⋙

Pork Scallops Chasseur

SERVES 4

This delightful dish is an example of the way thinly pounded pork can so easily masquerade as veal (see also Pork Scallops in Mustard Cream, p. 277). Purchase light-colored rib chops that have a generous eye and as little marbling as possible. Then create your own scallops according to the directions in step 1.

6 center-cut rib pork chops, ¾ to 1 inch thick
3 tablespoons vegetable oil
5 tablespoons butter
12 ounces fresh mushrooms, thinly sliced
1 medium shallot or 1 small onion, finely chopped
1 garlic clove, minced or pressed
3 fresh tomatoes, peeled, seeded, and coarsely chopped (or substitute 28 ounces canned, drained, and broken up)
1 tablespoon chopped fresh basil (or substitute 1 teaspoon dried)
1 tablespoon chopped fresh tarragon leaves (or substitute 1 teaspoon dried)
½ cup dry white wine
½ cup Basic Brown Sauce (p. 346 or p. 348)
Salt and freshly ground black pepper to taste
1 tablespoon chopped fresh parsley

1. Cut the eye of the chop away from the bone. Trim off the fat and the small area of darker meat if there is one. (Freeze what you trim away to save for another purpose.) Slice in half horizontally to form 2 scallops. Place the scallops between 2 sheets of waxed paper and pound with a meat mallet to thin.

2. In a 12-inch skillet, heat the oil and 3 tablespoons of the butter until the butter melts. Add the pork scallops and cook over high heat until lightly browned on one side. Turn and cook to brown the other side. Transfer to a platter.

3. Discard the grease in the pan. Add the remaining 2 tablespoons butter and place over high heat to melt. Add the mushrooms and cook, stirring constantly, until they begin to release their moisture. Add the shallot (or onion) and continue to stir over high heat until it is tender. Remove from the heat.

4. Blend in the garlic, tomatoes, basil, tarragon, and white wine. Place over medium heat and bring to a brisk bubble. Stir in the brown sauce and cook for 1 minute. Return the pork scallops to the pan and cook briefly to warm through. Season with salt and pepper to taste and sprinkle the parsley over the top. Arrange 3 pork scallops on each serving plate and spoon the remaining sauce on top.

(See entry for Pounding Meat.)   ⋙

Pork Medallions in Madeira Sauce

SERVES 6

Pork tenderloins are a tender, delicate cut of meat. Here they are sliced into medallions, sautéed briefly, and served with a rich, complex sauce.

2 pork tenderloins (about 1¾ pounds total)
2 tablespoons vegetable oil
4 tablespoons butter
⅓ cup dry white wine
¼ cup Madeira
¼ cup chicken glaze
3 tablespoons fresh lemon juice
3 tablespoons currant jelly
2 tablespoons chopped fresh parsley

1. Remove and discard the exterior fat from the tenderloins. Divide each tenderloin into 18 equal portions, and then slice across

the grain to form medallions approximately ¾ inch thick.

2. Heat the oil and 2 tablespoons of the butter in a 12-inch skillet until the butter foams. Add the pork medallions and cook over high heat, turning frequently. When the meat is lightly browned on both sides, transfer the medallions to an ovenproof platter, arranging them in an overlapping fashion. Place in a 250°F. oven to keep warm.

3. Pour the fat from the pan. Add the white wine, Madeira, chicken glaze, lemon juice, and currant jelly. Stir over high heat until the jelly melts and blends with the other ingredients. Add the parsley and continue stirring until a thickened, syrupy consistency is reached. When the surface of the sauce is alive with tiny bubbles, remove the pan from the heat. Swirl in the remaining 2 tablespoons of butter, 1 tablespoon at a time. The result is a shiny, jewel-like appearance. For maximum effect, pour the sauce on a white plate and set the medallions on top.

NOTE: As this sauce reduces, the bubbles become larger in size. Reducing it too far creates a sticky consistency. If you feel you have overreduced the sauce, add a few drops of water.

Rib Roast of Pork à l'Orange

SERVES 6 TO 8

À l'orange *is a style of preparation customarily associated with duckling; however, this flavorful sauce, based on a light caramel created from sugar and white wine vinegar, is equally appealing with roast pork.*

3½- to 4-pound center loin pork roast
2 tablespoons olive oil
1 garlic clove
1 teaspoon salt, preferably coarse sea salt
1 teaspoon dried rosemary leaves, pulverized
with a mortar and pestle
½ teaspoon dried leaf thyme

½ cup plus 2 tablespoons sugar
2 tablespoons white wine vinegar
Zest of 1 orange, cut into long, thin slivers
Zest of half a lemon, cut into long, thin slivers
1 cup fresh orange juice
1 tablespoon fresh lemon juice
½ cup Basic Brown Sauce (p. 346)
¼ cup Cointreau
1 tablespoon red currant jelly
3 tablespoons cognac

1. Have the butcher remove the chine, or backbone, from the roast. (Self-service meat departments usually prepare pork roasts by cracking between the ribs — an adequate procedure that makes it possible to carve the cooked roast into chops by slicing between the ribs. However, removing the chine creates a more attractive presentation because there's less bone on the plate.) Using a mortar and pestle, blend 2 tablespoons olive oil, the garlic, salt, rosemary, and thyme into a rough paste. Rub paste over the entire surface of the pork. Place the pork in a 1-gallon plastic bag and secure with a wire twist. Allow the pork to marinate in the refrigerator for 6 hours or overnight.

2. One hour before roasting, remove the pork from the refrigerator. Preheat the oven to 350°F. Arrange the pork, fat side up, in a shallow roasting pan or baking dish. (Since the ribs form a natural rack, a roasting rack isn't necessary.) Brush the entire surface generously with additional olive oil and place roast in the preheated oven. Cook uncovered

for 1½ to 2 hours (approximately 30 minutes per pound) or until a meat thermometer registers 170°F.

3. Meanwhile, prepare the orange sauce by combining 2 tablespoons of the sugar and the vinegar in a thick-bottomed 1½-quart saucepan. Place over medium heat and stir until the sugar is completely dissolved. Continue cooking over medium heat, without stirring, until the mixture develops a light caramel hue or registers 320°F. on a candy thermometer. Remove from the heat and set aside.

4. Place the slivers of orange and lemon zest in a wide saucepan. Add enough tap water to cover and place over high heat. Bring to a vigorous boil. Immediately remove from the heat and allow to steep for 3 minutes. Pour through a sieve, discarding the water. Transfer the zest to the saucepan containing the caramel. Add ½ cup of the orange juice, the lemon juice, brown sauce, Cointreau, and currant jelly. Place over low heat and stir constantly until the caramel begins to melt and blend with the other ingredients. When the mixture is well combined, remove the pan from the heat until the roast is done.

5. During the last hour of roasting, combine the remaining ½ cup sugar, ½ cup orange juice, and the cognac. Stir to blend. Baste the pork frequently with the cognac mixture to develop a glossy, dark brown coating. When the pork has finished roasting, transfer to a heated platter and allow to rest for 10 minutes before carving. Reheat the orange sauce and pour some over the roast, scattering the slivers of zest over the surface in an attractive manner. Pass the remaining sauce in a sauce boat.   ⤆

Curried Meatballs

SERVES 6

To fully experience the vivacity of curry dishes, try using freshly blended curry powder. You can prepare your own mixture from the recipe on p. 281.

MEATBALLS
1 large egg
1 garlic clove, minced or pressed
¼ teaspoon salt
Freshly ground black pepper
1½ pounds ground lean lamb or lean beef
½ cup dry, unseasoned bread crumbs
1 tablespoon chopped fresh coriander leaves
   (cilantro)

CURRY SAUCE
3 tablespoons butter
1 medium onion, finely chopped
1 garlic clove, minced or pressed
1 tart green apple, peeled, cored, and coarsely
   chopped
1 tablespoon curry powder (see following recipe)
2 tablespoons all-purpose flour
2 cups chicken broth
1 tablespoon fresh lemon juice
1 teaspoon grated lemon zest
¼ teaspoon salt
Freshly ground black pepper
½ cup heavy cream

1. Preheat the oven to 375°F. In a large mixing bowl, whisk the egg, garlic, salt, and pepper. Crumble in the meat. Add the bread crumbs and coriander leaves and mix thoroughly with a wooden spoon. Pour enough vegetable oil into a shallow roasting pan to film the bottom. Take up the meat mixture by generous teaspoonfuls and shape into 24 small meatballs. Arrange the meatballs in the oiled roasting pan. Cover with aluminum foil and place in the preheated oven. Bake for 15 minutes. Remove the foil and continue baking, uncovered, for 15 to 20 minutes or until the meatballs are lightly browned.

2. Meanwhile, prepare the curry sauce by melting the butter in a 12-inch skillet. Add the onion, garlic, and chopped apple, and toss to coat. Place over medium heat and cook, stirring, until the onions are translucent. Sprinkle on the curry powder. Continue to stir over medium heat until the onion is tender, but do not allow it to brown. Sprinkle on the flour and cook, stirring, for 1 minute.

Remove from the heat and add the chicken broth. Place over high heat and cook, stirring, until the sauce bubbles and thickens.

3. Stir in the lemon juice, lemon zest, salt, and pepper. Regulate the heat so that the sauce barely bubbles and cook uncovered for 10 minutes. Remove from the heat and blend in the cream. Add the cooked meatballs and return to low heat. Cook briefly to warm the cream. Serve with rice or buttered Orzo (p. 315).

CURRY POWDER

½ cup coriander seeds
4 tablespoons black peppercorns
2 tablespoons cumin seeds
2 tablespoons cardamom seeds, released from
   the pod
1 tablespoon whole cloves
½ cup ground turmeric
1 tablespoon ground mace
1 tablespoon ground cinnamon
1½ teaspoons ground ginger
½ teaspoon ground cayenne
1 tablespoon fenugreek seeds (optional; see
   Note)

1. Preheat the oven to 375°F. Sprinkle the coriander, peppercorns, cumin, cardamom, and cloves in a single layer in a jelly roll pan. Place in the preheated oven and toast for 15 to 20 minutes or until the aroma is quite prominent. Do not allow the spices to color.

2. When the seeds have cooled to room temperature, grind them in a spice mill, coffee mill, or mortar and pestle. (You can use a blender instead, but the seeds tend to whirl around inefficiently.) Combine the ground seeds with the turmeric, mace, cinnamon, ginger, and cayenne. Store the powdered spices in an airtight, opaque container.

NOTE: If you include fenugreek seeds, prepare them ahead of time by toasting them lightly, and then soaking them in water for 6 hours. Scatter on a paper towel and pat dry. Grind them and add to the powdered mixture. ❧

Lamb Loaf with Lemon-Yogurt Sauce

SERVES 6

A subtle hint of ouzo lends an air of mystery to this intriguingly flavored pâté. Serve thinly sliced at just below room temperature or present hot accompanied by the zesty Lemon-Yogurt Sauce.

2 one-inch-thick slices French bread
¼ cup ouzo (or substitute another anise-flavored
   liqueur)
2 tablespoons butter
1 medium onion, finely chopped
1 large egg
1 pound ground lean lamb (preferably ground at
   home)
½ cup crushed or finely ground almonds
1 garlic clove, pressed
1 teaspoon dried oregano
½ teaspoon dried leaf thyme
½ teaspoon salt
Freshly ground black pepper

LEMON-YOGURT SAUCE
3 large egg yolks
3 tablespoons fresh lemon juice
½ cup chicken broth
1 cup unflavored yogurt
Salt and freshly ground white pepper to taste

1. Preheat the oven to 350°F. Place the inch-thick bread slices in a wide mixing bowl. Pour the ouzo over the bread and set aside.

2. Melt the butter in a 1½-quart saucepan. Add the onion and stir to coat. Cover the pan and cook over low heat for 15 to 20 minutes or until the onion acquires a golden hue. (This slow cooking is essential to the development of its flavor.)

3. Meanwhile, whisk the egg in a large mixing bowl. Crumble in the ground lamb. Add the almonds, garlic, oregano, thyme, salt, and pepper. Mix thoroughly with a wooden spoon. Squeeze the ouzo from the bread and shred the bread over the meat mixture. Add the cooked onion and its butter. Spreading

your fingers wide, use your hand to blend the bread and onion into the meat. (Blending by hand results in a lighter texture than blending with a spoon.) Transfer to a lightly buttered 9×5-inch loaf pan and cover with aluminum foil. Place in the preheated oven and bake for 30 minutes. Remove the foil and continue baking for 15 to 20 minutes or until the top develops a light crust and the loaf begins to pull away from the sides of the pan.

4. To prepare the sauce, begin by combining the egg yolks and lemon juice in a mixing bowl. Whisk until slightly thickened. Bring the chicken broth to a boil in a 1½-quart saucepan. Whisking continuously, gradually add the hot broth to the egg yolks. Blend in the yogurt and transfer the mixture to the saucepan. Place over medium heat and cook, stirring constantly, until the sauce bubbles gently and thickens. (Keep in mind that excess heat will cause the egg yolks to curdle.) Season with salt and white pepper.   ◆

Lamb Medallions with Minted Hollandaise

SERVES 4

If you don't have access to the kind of butcher who will prepare fancy meats, that doesn't mean you have to forgo serving them. Medallions (sometimes called noisettes) of lamb are easy to prepare from rib chops offered in the supermarket meat case.

8 rib lamb chops with large meaty eyes
8 round slices French bread, each ½ inch thick
¾ cup hollandaise sauce
1 tablespoon finely chopped fresh mint

1. Prepare the medallions by cutting around the eye of each lamb chop. Remove the bone and all traces of fat and connective tissue, producing a disk of meat about 2¼ inches across. Trim the piece of fat removed from the outside of the chop into a thin strip. Wrap it around the edge of the chop and make it overlap by ½ inch. Tie the fat to the

chop securely with butcher's twine, but do not pull the string too tight or the meat will bulge out of the fat during cooking.

2. Preheat the broiler for 15 minutes. Meanwhile, toast the rounds of French bread on both sides and arrange on a serving platter. Adjust the oven rack so that the broiler pan will be as close as possible to the heating coils or flame. Broil the medallions for 4 minutes on each side or until the meat is well browned. Lower the oven rack to the next position and continue broiling for 3 to 5 minutes per side. Lamb is done when the center is a light pink.

3. Combine the prepared hollandaise sauce with the fresh mint. Cut the butcher's twine and remove from around the meat. Place a lamb medallion on each toasted bread round and pour on the minted hollandaise. Garnish the serving platter with sprigs of fresh mint if desired.

NOTE: Since medallions, or noisettes, are such small pieces of meat, they are usually served on a round platform of some nature to give them height. Toasted croutons, disks of sautéed eggplant, and round potato cakes are all possibilities. They serve the dual purpose of absorbing flavorful juices and creating the appearance of greater substance.   ◆

Marinated Lamb Steaks

SERVES 2

If you find that a whole leg, or even half a leg, of lamb is an overwhelming amount of meat, have the butcher slice two or three steaks from the center portion of the leg. Marinate them for extra moisture and flavor, and then broil or grill over an open fire.

½ cup olive oil
Juice of 1 lemon
2 garlic cloves, crushed
1 teaspoon dried rosemary leaves, pulverized with a mortar and pestle
2 lamb steaks (6 to 8 ounces each), cut from the center of the leg

1. Combine the olive oil, lemon juice, garlic, and rosemary in a 1-gallon plastic bag. Shake vigorously to mix well. One at a time, place the lamb steaks inside the bag, turning each one to coat evenly with the marinade. Secure the bag with a wire twist and place inside a 9×13-inch baking dish. Refrigerate and allow the lamb to marinate for 8 hours or overnight. Turn occasionally to promote even distribution of the marinade.

2. Preheat the broiler for 15 minutes. Adjust the oven rack so that the broiler pan will be as close to the coils or flame as possible. Remove the steaks from the marinade and place on the broiling pan. Slide under the heating element and broil until well browned. Turn the steaks and broil the other side until browned. Lower the rack to the next position and broil for approximately 4 minutes on each side. Lamb is done when the center is a light pink.

NOTE: Along with the lamb steaks, you might like to broil tomatoes cut in half or thick slices of sweet onion liberally brushed with the marinating liquid.   ◆∂

Shoulder Lamb Chops with Red and Green Peppers

SERVES 4

The combination of peppers, onions, mushrooms, and tomatoes lends a shish-kebab character to these lamb chops braised in white wine.

2 tablespoons butter
1 red sweet bell pepper, cored, seeded, and cut into strips
1 green sweet bell pepper, cored, seeded, and cut into strips
1 large onion, cut into 8 wedges
24 small fresh mushrooms, whole
1 garlic clove, minced or pressed
½ teaspoon dried basil
½ teaspoon dried rosemary leaves, pulverized with a mortar and pestle
2 tablespoons vegetable oil
4 shoulder or blade lamb chops
½ cup dry white wine
4 ripe tomatoes, peeled and quartered (or substitute 28 ounces canned, undrained)
¼ teaspoon salt
Freshly ground black pepper

1. Melt the butter in a 12-inch skillet or Dutch oven. Add the red and green bell peppers, onion, mushrooms, and garlic. Toss to coat. Reduce the heat to low and cover the pan. Cook the vegetables for 20 minutes, stirring occasionally. Blend in the basil and rosemary. Cover the pan and cook for 10 minutes more. Using a slotted spoon, transfer the vegetables to a platter.

2. Add the oil to the pan and place over medium heat. Add the lamb chops and cook, turning frequently, until both sides are lightly browned. Pour on the wine. Add the tomatoes. (Break them apart with your fingers if you are using canned ones.) Sprinkle with salt and pepper. Distribute the cooked vegetables over and around the chops. When the liquid begins to bubble, reduce the heat to its lowest setting and cover the pan. Cook for 20 to 30 minutes or until the meat is tender when pierced with a fork. Remove the chops from the pan. Increase the heat to high and cook, stirring constantly, until the liquid is almost completely evaporated. Serve the lamb chops with rice, arranging some of the cooked vegetables over each chop and spooning the remaining liquid over the rice.

(See entry for Braising.)   ◆∂

Roast Rack of Lamb with Currant Sauce

SERVES 4

A rack, or the rib section, of lamb provides a quick yet elegant roast. If you want to dress it up with paper frills, either ask the butcher to

"French" the bones, or do it yourself: Position your knife 1 inch in from the ends of the bones. Make a horizontal cut through the fat along the length of the roast and remove as much meat and fat as possible. Then, with a paring knife, cut in and around the bones to scrape them clean (see illustration).

8-rib rack of lamb
2 tablespoons olive oil
1 garlic clove
1 teaspoon coarse salt (or substitute regular salt)
1 teaspoon dried rosemary leaves, pulverized
    with a mortar and pestle

CURRANT SAUCE
Zest of half an orange
Zest of half a lemon
4 tablespoons fresh orange juice
2 tablespoons fresh lemon juice
½ cup red currant jelly
½ cup tawny port wine

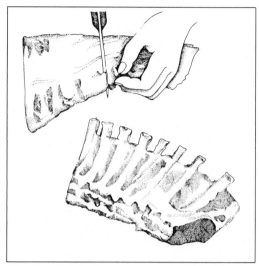

To "French" the bones on a rack of lamb, make a horizontal cut 1 inch in from the bone ends, running the length of the roast. Then cut away the meat and fat between and around each rib.

1. Have the butcher remove the chine, or backbone, from the roast. (Self-service meat departments usually prepare lamb roasts by cracking between the ribs — an adequate procedure that makes it possible to carve the cooked roast into chops by slicing between the ribs. However, removing the chine creates a more attractive presentation because there's less bone on the plate.) You might also want to request that he remove any of the shoulder blade that exists, or do it yourself: Lay the rack on its side, turning the end with the longest ribs toward you. Cut into the meat and probe with your finger until you locate a flat bone. Then pry it out with the tip of a knife.

2. Preheat the oven to 375°F. Using a mortar and pestle, blend the olive oil, garlic, salt, and rosemary into a rough paste. Rub the paste over the entire surface of the lamb. Arrange the roast, fat side up, in a shallow pan or baking dish. (Since the ribs form a natural rack, a roasting rack isn't necessary.) Place in the preheated oven and cook for 45 to 60 minutes or until a meat thermometer registers 140°F. or 160°F., depending on the measure of doneness you prefer.

3. Meanwhile, prepare the currant sauce by cutting the orange and lemon zest into thin slivers. Place in a 1½-quart saucepan and add enough tap water to cover. Set over high heat and bring to a vigorous boil. Immediately remove from the heat and allow the zest to steep for 5 minutes. Combine the orange juice, lemon juice, currant jelly, and wine in a 1½-quart saucepan. Stir over medium heat until the jelly melts and blends with the other ingredients. Drain the zest and add to the currant mixture. Bring to a gentle bubble and cook uncovered for 1 minute.

4. When the lamb has finished roasting, transfer it to a heated platter and allow it to rest for 10 minutes before carving. Serve by cutting between the bones. Place 2 rib chops on each serving plate and pass the currant sauce in a sauce boat.

Eggs, Cheese, Savory Pies, and Main Dishes

Pancetta and Bel Paese Frittata

SERVES 2 OR 3

In this open-faced Italian omelet, Bel Paese cheese and pancetta are the principal flavor components. Pancetta, a nonsmoked, salt-cured cut of pork, looks like strip bacon rolled tightly into a round cold cut or large sausage. You can find it in Italian grocery stores and the deli sections of large supermarkets. (There is no real substitute for pancetta, but you can make this frittata with any combination of ham and cheese that appeals to you.)

2 tablespoons butter
1 medium onion, thinly sliced
¼ pound pancetta
4 large eggs
½ cup light cream
Freshly ground black pepper
Freshly grated nutmeg
4 ounces Bel Paese cheese, grated (about 1 cup loosely packed)
2 tablespoons freshly grated Parmesan cheese

1. Melt the butter in a thick-bottomed 8-inch skillet (preferably with an ovenproof handle). Add the onion, tossing to coat. Place over low heat, cover the pan, and cook slowly until the onion rings are golden in color. (This slow cooking is essential to developing a smooth, mild flavor.)

2. Meanwhile, cut the pancetta into thin strips. In a large mixing bowl, whisk together the eggs and cream. Stir in the pepper and nutmeg. When the onions are cooked, transfer them with a slotted spoon to a plate. Add the pancetta to the pan and increase the heat to high. Cook, stirring constantly, for 2 or 3 minutes or until the edges of the pancetta begin to curl.

3. Remove the pan and reduce the heat to its lowest possible setting. Arrange the pancetta over the bottom of the skillet, scatter the onion over it, and evenly distribute the Bel Paese on top of that. Gently pour in the egg mixture, cover the skillet, and place over the low heat. Cook for 8 to 10 minutes or until about 2 inches of the outside edge are set. (The center will still be runny.) Sprinkle the Parmesan cheese over the surface and slide the frittata under the broiler. Cook for 2 to 3 minutes or until the center is firm. (If you're using a skillet with a plastic handle, remember to let the handle stick out from under the broiler so it won't be exposed to the heat.) A cooked frittata will pull away from the sides of the pan. Slide it onto a serving platter and cut into wedges.   ৵

Eggs Benedict

SERVES 4 OR 8

Eggs Benedict is one of America's favorite brunch dishes, but it has generally been regarded as an impractical dish to serve to a large group. This recipe, however, tells how to poach eggs ahead of time and then rewarm them at the last minute.

1 teaspoon salt
8 large, very fresh eggs (see Note, p. 288)
2 tablespoons butter
8 slices Canadian bacon
4 English Muffins (p. 232), split
8 fresh tomato slices, ¼-inch thick
3/4 cup hollandaise sauce

1. Prepare the poached eggs ahead of time by generously buttering the bottom and sides of a 12-inch skillet or large, wide saucepan. Fill the pan with water to the depth of 2½ inches. Add 1 teaspoon of salt to encourage the egg whites to set. Cover the pan and bring the water to a vigorous boil. Meanwhile, break 4 eggs into separate cups. When the water is boiling furiously, remove the pan from the heat. (Reduce the heat to low in case you need to return the pan to the burner.) Wait for the bubbling to subside. Lift the cover to see if the surface of the water is calm. When there are no signs of movement, quickly slip in the eggs by tilting the cups at the surface of the water. Immediately cover the pan and allow the eggs to poach off the heat for 3 to 4 minutes, depending on the degree of doneness you prefer. (If you need to apply gentle heat, return the pan to the burner for 30 seconds.) When the egg whites are opaque, lift the eggs from the water with a shallow skimmer and transfer them to a large bowl filled with cold water. Scoop out any pieces of cooked egg white from the pan of water and return to high heat. Bring the water to a vigorous boil. Repeat the above procedure to poach the remaining eggs. (Because the success of this method relies on the ratio of water to eggs, don't attempt to poach more than 4 at a time.) When all the eggs are cooked, lift them from the bowl of water and trim away ragged edges to give them a neater appearance. Return the eggs to the bowl of water and refrigerate for up to 24 hours.

2. In a 10-inch skillet, melt the butter and add the bacon, cooking over medium-high heat until both sides are lightly browned. Set aside. Bring a 6-quart pot of water to a vigorous boil. Cover and remove from the heat. When the surface of the water is calm, transfer the chilled, cooked eggs to the hot water with a shallow skimmer. Cover the pot. In 1 to 2 minutes the eggs will be warm to the touch.

3. Meanwhile, toast the split muffins under the broiler and top each half with a piece of Canadian bacon. Place a slice of tomato on the bacon. Lift the eggs from the hot water one at a time, and rest the bottom of the skimmer against a double thickness of paper toweling to draw off excess water. Place an egg on the tomato slice. Spoon warm hollandaise over the top and serve immediately.

(See entry for Eggs: Poaching.)　　　✑

Huevos Rancheros

SERVES 4

Poached eggs are served ranch style on sautéed polenta rounds covered with zesty tomato sauce and surrounded by wedges of fresh avocado. Melted Monterey Jack cheese provides a final flourish.

POLENTA ROUNDS

1 cup yellow cornmeal

5 cups water

½ teaspoon salt

¼ cup freshly grated Monterey Jack cheese

2 tablespoons butter

Vegetable oil

TOMATO SAUCE

2 tablespoons olive oil

1 medium onion, coarsely chopped

4 medium-size fresh tomatoes, peeled, seeded, and chopped

1 garlic clove, minced or pressed

1 can (4 ounces) peeled green chilis, seeded and chopped

1 tablespoon chopped fresh coriander leaves (cilantro)

1½ teaspoons chopped fresh oregano (or substitute ½ teaspoon dried)

¼ teaspoon salt

Generous amount of freshly ground black pepper

EGGS AND GARNISH

1 teaspoon salt

4 large, very fresh eggs (see Note)

2 ripe avocados at room temperature, peeled and cut into slim wedges

½ cup freshly grated Monterey Jack cheese

1. Generously butter an 8×8-inch baking pan and proceed to make the polenta by

combining the cornmeal, water, salt, Jack cheese, and butter according to the directions in steps 1–3 under Polenta Crostini with Gorgonzola (p. 178). Refrigerate the polenta until it is firm.

2. Meanwhile, prepare the tomato sauce by heating the olive oil in a 10-inch skillet. Add the onion, tossing to coat. Place over medium heat and cook, stirring, until the onion is translucent. Stir in the tomatoes, garlic, green' chilis, coriander leaves, oregano, salt, and pepper. Continue cooking over medium heat for 15 to 20 minutes or until most of the liquid has evaporated and the sauce has thickened.

3. Turn out the polenta onto a work surface and cut into four 3½-inch rounds with a biscuit cutter. Heat the vegetable oil in a 12-inch skillet and fry the polenta rounds over medium heat until the surfaces develop a slightly puffy, deep golden appearance. Using a perforated metal spatula, transfer the polenta to absorbent paper to drain. Generously butter four shallow 4-inch ramekins with sloping sides. Place a polenta round in each ramekin and set in a 250°F. oven to keep warm.

4. Generously butter the bottom and sides of a 12-inch skillet or large, wide saucepan. Fill the pan with water to the depth of 2½ inches. Add 1 teaspoon of salt to encourage the egg whites to set. Cover the pan and bring the water to a vigorous boil. Meanwhile, break 4 eggs into separate cups. When the water is boiling furiously, remove the pan from the heat. (Reduce the heat to low in case you need to return the pan to the burner.) Wait for the bubbling to subside. Lift the cover and when the water is calm, quickly slip in the eggs by tilting the cups at the surface of the water. Immediately cover the pan and allow the eggs to poach off the heat for 3 to 4 minutes, depending on the degree of doneness you prefer. (If necessary, you can return the pan to the heat for 30 seconds.)

5. When the egg whites are opaque, lift the eggs from the water with a shallow skimmer and transfer them to a double thickness of paper toweling to drain. Trim away the rag-ged edges with a sharp knife to give the eggs a neat appearance and place one atop each polenta round. Spoon the hot tomato sauce over the eggs and polenta. Arrange avocado wedges around the egg and sprinkle with the grated Jack cheese. Slide under the broiler to melt the cheese, and serve immediately.

NOTE: Extra-fresh eggs are compact and cohesive. They make the best candidates for successful poaching because they are less apt to spread. To poach more than 4 eggs at a time, use 2 pans or prepare 2 separate batches, setting the first batch aside until the second batch is done and has been transferred to absorbent paper. Then reheat the water until bubbles appear, take the pan off the heat, and return the first batch of eggs to the hot water for 30 to 60 seconds to rewarm them. To prepare poached eggs ahead of time, see Eggs Benedict (p. 286).

(See entry for Eggs: Poaching.)   ❧

Eggs Baked with Creamed Spinach and Bûcheron

SERVES 4

During baking, a nest of creamed spinach provides a moist protective environment for the eggs, shielding them from the harsh heat of the oven. Consequently, their final texture is light, delicate, and tender.

1 pound fresh spinach
3 tablespoons butter
¼ teaspoon salt
Generous amount of freshly grated nutmeg
2 tablespoons all-purpose flour
1 cup medium, or whipping, cream
4 large eggs
8 sun-dried tomato halves, cut into thin strips
    (or substitute canned pimientos)
4 ounces Bûcheron cheese, crumbled
Salt and freshly ground pepper to taste
2 tablespoons freshly grated Parmesan cheese

1. Submerge the spinach in a large quantity of cold water and jostle it to dislodge any sand that may be hidden in the leaves. Change the water and repeat if the spinach is excessively sandy. Remove the tough stems and discard any limp or discolored leaves. Fill a 6-quart pot with water and bring to a vigorous boil. Add the spinach and stir frequently to keep the leaves submerged. When the water returns to a boil, cook the spinach uncovered for 2 to 3 minutes or until limp.

2. Meanwhile, preheat the oven to 400°F. and generously butter 4 shallow ramekins or a 7×11-inch baking dish. Pour the cooked spinach into a colander set under cold water running from the tap. Lift the spinach in the colander with your fingers, allowing the cold water to reach the interior leaves. Drain thoroughly, and then squeeze the remaining water from the leaves with your hands. Chop coarsely and place in a wide, thick-bottomed saucepan or skillet. Place over medium heat. Stirring continuously, cook the spinach until most of the moisture has evaporated. Add the butter, ¼ teaspoon salt, and nutmeg, and stir over medium heat until the butter melts and is completely absorbed. Sprinkle on the flour and cook, stirring, for 30 seconds. Slowly blend in the cream and continue stirring over medium heat until the mixture bubbles. Remove from the heat and transfer to the prepared ramekins or baking dish.

3. Form a depression in the spinach to nestle each egg. Break 1 egg into a cup, then slip it into the depression in the spinach. (This maneuver ensures that the egg will get to the spinach without breaking.) Repeat for the remaining 3 eggs. Distribute the strips of tomato around the eggs and sprinkle the cheese over the tomato. Sprinkle the egg yolks with salt, pepper, and grated Parmesan. Cover the ramekins or baking dish with aluminum foil and place in the preheated oven. Bake for 10 to 12 minutes or until the eggs are set.

NOTE: The spinach may be prepared ahead of time and refrigerated. Add the eggs, tomato, and cheese at the last minute and bake as described above, but plan on a slightly longer baking time to compensate for the lower temperature of the spinach. ◄୬

Curry-Stuffed Eggs Baked in Shrimp Sauce

SERVES 4

Contrary to what their name implies, hard-boiled eggs should never be boiled. In fact, the best way to produce especially tender hard-boiled eggs is to cook them off the burner. The note following this recipe gives directions for using this technique, but keep in mind that the ratio of hot water to eggs is crucial to success. Be sure the eggs are not crowded in the pan and are covered by at least 3 inches of water.

SHRIMP SAUCE

2 cups water
½ cup dry white wine
2 medium shallots, cut in half
1 bay leaf, broken in half
2 one-inch-long strips lemon zest
6 black peppercorns
1 pound medium-size fresh shrimp
4 tablespoons butter
1 small onion, coarsely chopped
1 tablespoon curry powder
2 teaspoons sweet Hungarian paprika
¼ teaspoon salt
2 tablespoons all-purpose flour
1 cup medium, or whipping, cream
1/3 cup chopped chutney

CURRY-STUFFED EGGS

8 large hard-boiled eggs (see Note)
½ cup mayonnaise, commercially prepared or homemade (p. 354 or p. 356)
1 tablespoon fresh lemon juice
1 teaspoon curry powder
¼ teaspoon salt
Freshly ground black pepper

1. In a 2½-quart nonreactive saucepan, make the Shrimp Sauce by combining the water, wine, shallots, bay leaf, lemon zest, and peppercorns. Place over high heat and bring to a vigorous boil. Regulate the heat so

that the liquid bubbles gently and cook uncovered until the shallots are translucent. Stir in the shrimp and cover the pan. Cook gently for 3 to 5 minutes or until the shrimp have developed a light pink hue and are firm to the touch. Remove from the heat and, using a slotted spoon, transfer the shrimp to a large bowl. Return the pan to the stove and increase the heat. Cook uncovered until the shrimp broth is reduced to 1 cup. Pour through a cheesecloth-lined sieve and set aside.

2. Peel the shrimp; remove and discard the dark intestinal vein. Chop finely and set aside. In a 1½-quart saucepan, melt the butter over medium heat. Add the onion and continue stirring over medium heat until the onion is translucent. Blend in the curry powder, paprika, and salt. Add the flour and stir over medium heat until the mixture foams. Remove from the heat and whisk in the reserved shrimp broth. Return to the heat and cook, stirring constantly, until the sauce bubbles and thickens. Stir in the chopped shrimp and gradually pour in the cream. Continue to stir over medium heat until the mixture bubbles. Remove from the heat, stir in the chutney, and set aside.

3. Preheat the oven to 400°F. Generously butter 4 shallow ramekins or a large baking dish. Empty the hot water from the pan of eggs and add cold water from the tap. Peel the warm eggs, rinse them under cold running water, and blot dry with a paper towel. Cut the eggs in half lengthwise and turn the yolks out into a sieve set over a small bowl. Force the egg yolks through the sieve with a wooden pestle. Add the mayonnaise, lemon juice, curry powder, salt, and pepper and blend until smooth. Mound the filling into the egg-white cavities and transfer the stuffed eggs to the prepared ramekins or baking dish.

4. Place the shrimp sauce over medium heat. Cook, stirring constantly, until the sauce bubbles. Then pour the hot shrimp sauce over the stuffed eggs. Place in the preheated oven and bake for 5 to 8 minutes or until the sauce is bubbling hot.

NOTE: To produce tender hard-boiled eggs, take the eggs from the refrigerator and arrange them in a single layer in the bottom of a wide saucepan. Add cold water from the tap until the eggs are covered by at least 3 inches. Place the uncovered pan over high heat and gradually bring the water to a boil. Carefully rotate the eggs with a spatula to encourage the yolks to set in the center. When the water is boiling vigorously, add a generous pinch of salt to the water to raise the boiling point. When you see the water begin to boil faster, cover the pan and immediately remove it from the heat. Allow the eggs to stand for 30 minutes. Do not remove the cover of the pan during this time. The eggs will cook by steeping in the hot water. At the end of 30 minutes, empty the hot water from the pan and immediately replace it with cold tap water.

(See entry for Eggs: Boiling/Peeling.) ◄ৡ

Fonduta

SERVES 4

Although this Italian cheese dish is more authentically presented fondue style, it is every bit as enjoyable over toast points in the manner of Welsh rarebit. Imported fontina cheese from Northern Italy is essential to the light, nutty character of a true fonduta. *Shavings of white truffle are an elegant refinement but they are optional.*

1½ cups dry white wine
2 garlic cloves, cut in half
4 tablespoons butter
3 tablespoons flour
1 cup milk
¼ teaspoon salt
Generous amount of freshly ground white pepper
  (or substitute a pinch of ground cayenne)
10 ounces fontina cheese, grated
4 thin slices white bread
Generous shavings of fresh white truffle
  (optional)

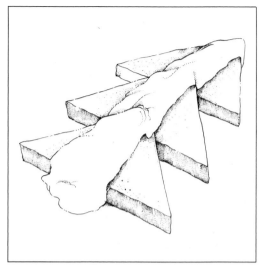

To serve, spoon the Fonduta *down the center of overlapping triangles of toast.*

1. Mix the wine and garlic in a 1½-quart nonreactive pan. Bring to a gentle bubble, and cook uncovered until reduced to ¾ cup.

2. Place the butter in the top container of a double boiler. Cover and set over hot water. When the butter is melted, blend in the flour. Cover and cook 3 to 5 minutes or until the mixture foams. Whisk in the milk and stir slowly until thickened. Blend in the salt and white pepper.

3. Stir in the grated cheese and cover the pan. Check to be certain that the water in the bottom pan isn't boiling. Excessive heat will cause the cheese to become tough and stringy. Cook for 3 to 5 minutes or until the cheese is melted. Stir with a fork to blend thoroughly.

4. Remove the garlic from the wine with a slotted spoon. Stirring the cheese mixture constantly with a fork, slowly pour in ½ cup of the reduced wine. If the consistency seems too thick (or if it thickens while you prepare the toast), stir in the remaining wine. Trim the crusts from the bread and toast on both sides. Cut into triangles. On each plate, overlap 4 triangles of toast in such a way that the points from the center of the slice all point in the same direction. Spoon the *fonduta* down the center of the toast triangles leaving both

ends of the triangles exposed (see illustration). Sprinkle on shavings of fresh white truffle, if desired.　　　　　　　　　◅∂

Cheese Soufflé

SERVES 4

This is a basic recipe incorporating the fundamental techniques of soufflé making. Once you've mastered it, you'll be able to tackle any soufflé that exists. You'll notice that in the recipe (and in other recipes in this book) I suggest stirring with a heat-resistant rubber spatula. It's not traditional and it's certainly not chic, but it works. The broad end of a spatula clears a wider path than a spoon or whisk and does a better job of getting into the curve where the bottom of the pan meets the sides, so there's far less danger of scorching small patches of a roux or sauce.

5 large eggs
4 tablespoons butter
2 tablespoons freshly grated Parmesan cheese
4 ounces Gruyère cheese
1 cup milk
3 tablespoons flour (if you're new to soufflé making, use instant, or granulated, flour such as Wondra to guarantee absolutely lump-free results)
½ teaspoon plus a dash salt
Freshly ground white pepper (or substitute a pinch of ground cayenne)
Freshly grated nutmeg
⅛ teaspoon cream of tartar

1. Separate the eggs, placing the whites in a grease-free stainless steel or unlined copper bowl. Set aside and allow to come to room temperature. Reserve 4 of the egg yolks in another bowl, refrigerating 1 yolk for another use. Using 1 tablespoon of the butter, grease a 6-cup soufflé mold or straight-sided baking dish. Sprinkle with grated Parmesan and tilt to coat the bottom and sides. Turn out excess cheese. Grate the Gruyère and set aside.

2. Preheat the oven to 400°F. Prepare the white sauce base by melting the remaining 3

tablespoons of butter in a 1½-quart sauce-pan. At the same time, warm the milk, but do not boil, on another burner. When the butter is melted, remove from the heat and add the flour all at once. Blend with a heat-resistant spatula, taking care to coat each flour particle with melted butter. Return to medium-high heat and cook, stirring constantly, until the mixture is foamy and deep yellow. Remove from the heat. Pour the warm milk into the mixture all at once and beat vigorously with a wire whisk. Add ½ teaspoon salt, the white pepper, and nutmeg. Return to medium-high heat and stir with a heat-resistant spatula un-til the sauce bubbles and thickens. Continue cooking for 1 minute. Remove from the heat and cool for 3 minutes.

3. Add the 4 egg yolks to the slightly cooled sauce by whisking them in one at a time. Beat vigorously after each addition. Stir in two-thirds of the Gruyère cheese and empty the sauce into a large bowl. The sauce must be warm when folded with the whites so proceed immediately to the next step.

4. Beat the egg whites until foamy. Add the dash of salt and the cream of tartar. Continue beating until the bubbles in the whites are very tiny and all the same size. Soft peaks will form when the beaters are lifted, and the sur-face should look very moist.

5. Scoop out 2 heaping serving spoons of the whipped whites and gently stir into the cheese mixture to lighten it. Add the remain-ing whites and fold in. Pour into the prepared dish and scatter the remaining Gruyère cheese over the top (or omit the cheese if you prefer a smooth brown surface). Place in the preheated oven. Reduce the temperature to 375°F. and cook 25 to 30 minutes. Do not open the oven door during the first 20 min-utes. Test for doneness by inserting a metal skewer. For a dry center, cook until no trace of liquid can be seen on the skewer; a soft-centered soufflé will produce tiny beads of moisture on the skewer. Serve immediately.

(See entries for Folding; Soufflés; Whip-ping: Egg Whites.)   ◄ఎ

Fresh Corn Soufflé

SERVES 4 TO 6

The vivid flavor of sweet, fresh corn is pro-nounced in this soufflé. Serve it as a main dish with sliced summer tomatoes or as an accom-paniment to grilled meat.

5 large eggs
1½ cups uncooked sweet corn (about 4 ears)
4 tablespoons butter
2 to 3 tablespoons unseasoned bread crumbs
2 ounces Gruyère cheese
1 cup milk
3 tablespoons flour
½ teaspoon plus a pinch salt
Freshly ground white pepper (or substitute a pinch of ground cayenne)
1 tablespoon cornstarch
2 tablespoons cold water
⅛ teaspoon cream of tartar

1. Separate the eggs, placing the whites in a grease-free stainless steel or unlined copper bowl. Set aside and allow to come to room temperature. Reserve 4 egg yolks in another bowl, refrigerating 1 yolk for another use. Remove the corn from the cobs and place it in the refrigerator.

2. Using 1 tablespoon of the butter, grease a 6-cup soufflé mold or straight-sided baking dish. Sprinkle with bread crumbs and tilt to coat the bottom and sides. Turn out the ex-cess crumbs. Grate the Gruyère cheese and set aside.

3. Preheat the oven to 400°F. Prepare the white sauce base by melting the remaining 3 tablespoons of butter in a 1½-quart sauce-pan. At the same time, warm the milk, but do not boil, on another burner. When the butter is melted, remove from the heat and add the flour all at once. Blend with a heat-resistant spatula, taking care to coat each flour particle with melted butter. Return to medium-high heat and cook, stirring constantly, until the mixture is foamy and deep yellow. Remove from the heat. Pour the warm milk into the mixture all at once and beat vigorously with a wire whisk. Add ½ teaspoon salt and the

white pepper. Return to medium-high heat and stir with the spatula until the sauce bubbles and thickens. Continue cooking for 1 minute. Remove from the heat and allow to cool for 3 minutes.

4. Add the 4 egg yolks to the slightly cooled sauce by whisking them in one at a time. Beat vigorously after each addition. Stir in the corn and return to medium heat. Cook, stirring, for 3 minutes. Do not allow the mixture to boil. Remove from the heat. Dissolve the cornstarch in the cold water. Blend it into the corn mixture and place over medium-high heat. Stir continuously until the mixture bubbles. Transfer to a large bowl.

5. Beat the egg whites until foamy. Add a pinch of salt and the cream of tartar. Continue beating until the bubbles in the whites are very tiny and all the same size. Soft peaks will form when the beaters are lifted, and the surface should look very moist.

6. Scoop out 2 heaping serving spoons of the whipped whites and gently stir into the corn mixture to lighten it. Add the remaining whites and fold in. Pour into the prepared dish and scatter the Gruyère cheese over the top. Place in the preheated oven. Reduce the temperature to 375°F. and cook 25 to 30 minutes. Do not open the oven door during the first 20 minutes. Test for doneness by inserting a metal skewer. For a dry center, cook until no trace of liquid can be seen on the skewer; a soft-centered soufflé will produce tiny beads of moisture on the skewer. Serve immediately.　　　　　　　　　　　　　🍲

Strata of Bel Paese and Fresh Tomato Sauce

SERVES 6 TO 8

Layers of French bread, melted cheese, and fresh tomato sauce are enveloped with a combination of eggs and milk and baked until puffy and brown.

FRESH TOMATO SAUCE

2 tablespoons olive oil
1 medium onion, coarsely chopped
8 large fresh tomatoes, peeled, seeded, and chopped
1 garlic clove, minced or pressed
1 teaspoon sugar
¼ teaspoon salt
Freshly ground black pepper
1 tablespoon chopped fresh parsley
1 tablespoon chopped fresh basil (or substitute 1 teaspoon dried)

1 loaf French bread cut into ½-inch rounds
1½ pounds Bel Paese cheese, grated
2 tablespoons chopped fresh basil
6 large eggs
2½ cups milk
⅓ cup freshly grated Parmesan cheese
¼ teaspoon salt
Freshly ground black pepper to taste

1. Prepare the tomato sauce by heating the olive oil in a 12-inch skillet or wide saucepan (to allow evaporation to take place as rapidly as possible). Add the onion, tossing to coat. Place over medium heat and cook, stirring constantly, until the onion is translucent. Pour or spoon off the excess oil. Add the tomatoes, garlic, sugar, salt, and pepper. Increase the heat to high and stir in the parsley and basil. Cook, stirring constantly, over high heat until all of the liquid has evaporated and the sauce has thickened. (Or cook at a lower temperature, stirring occasionally, if you aren't pressed for time.) With a wooden pestle force the tomato sauce through a sieve and set aside.

2. Generously butter a 9×13-inch baking dish. Line the bottom of the dish with bread slices. (Do not overlap the slices: lay them flat.) Pour half the tomato sauce over the bread. Sprinkle with half the grated Bel Paese and scatter 1 tablespoon of chopped fresh basil over the cheese. Arrange another layer of bread over the chopped basil and repeat the procedure. Top with a final layer of bread slices arranged in an attractive overlapping fashion.

3. Using a metal skewer, pierce deep holes into the bread. Whisk the eggs and milk together in a large bowl. Stir in the grated Parmesan, salt, and pepper and gently pour over the top layer of bread. Cover with aluminum foil and refrigerate for 2 hours (or overnight) to allow the bread to fully absorb the egg mixture. Uncover the baking dish and place in an oven preheated to 375°F. Bake for 40 to 50 minutes or until the strata is puffed and the top layer of bread is well browned. Allow to stand for 10 minutes to facilitate slicing. Cut into squares to serve.   ❧

Four-Cheese Tart

SERVES 6 TO 8

Equal portions of Bel Paese, fontina, Gorgonzola, and Parmesan cheese blend to create this dramatic, open-face pie. Serve with a crisp green salad and slices of fresh tomato.

Pastry for a 9-inch pie shell
1 cup light cream
2 large eggs
¼ teaspoon salt
⅛ teaspoon ground cayenne
Freshly grated nutmeg
4 ounces Bel Paese cheese, grated (see Note)
4 ounces fontina cheese (preferably imported Italian), grated
4 ounces Gorgonzola cheese, crumbled
4 ounces Parmesan cheese, grated

1. Preheat the oven to 425°F. Prick the bottom and sides of a 9-inch pie shell with the tines of a fork. Fit waxed paper or aluminum foil inside the pastry and weight with 1 pound of dried beans or metal weights. Place on the middle oven rack and bake for 8 minutes.
2. Meanwhile, whisk the cream and eggs in a large mixing bowl. Add the salt, cayenne, and nutmeg. Stir in the grated Bel Paese, fontina, Gorgonzola, and Parmesan.
3. Take the partially baked shell from the oven and reduce the oven temperature to 375°F. Remove the paper or foil liner and the

weights. Do not prick the crust a second time. Pour in the egg-and-cheese mixture, distributing the cheese evenly with a fork. Place in the preheated oven and bake for 25 to 35 minutes or until slightly puffed and browned. Allow the tart to stand at room temperature for 10 minutes and serve.

NOTE: Four ounces of grated cheese, loosely packed, equals approximately 1 cup.   ❧

Mediterranean Tart

MAKES ONE 9-INCH TART

Open-face tarts are a breeze to make when you use press-in pastry. There's no need to chill and roll; just blend the dough together in the traditional way, crumble it over the bottom of a tart shell or quiche pan, and pat it into place. The filling in the following recipe combines the subtle sweetness of roasted red sweet bell peppers with the mysterious flavor of hot feta cheese.

PRESS-IN PASTRY
1¼ cups all-purpose flour, scoop measured
½ teaspoon salt
8 tablespoons cold butter, cut into 32 chunks
2 large egg yolks
1 tablespoon cold water

FILLING
6 large red sweet bell peppers
½ cup olive oil
6 tablespoons water
3 tablespoons butter
3 large sweet onions, cut into ⅛-inch slices
2 garlic cloves, minced
½ teaspoon dried oregano
¼ teaspoon salt
Freshly ground black pepper
12 anchovy fillets
8 ounces feta cheese, crumbled
2 tablespoons chopped fresh basil
16 large pitted black Greek or Italian olives

1. Preheat the oven to 350°F. Measure the flour and salt into a large bowl and whisk or toss with a fork to combine. Add the butter

and cut in with a pastry blender or knife. In a small bowl, whisk the egg yolks and water together. Sprinkle over the pastry mixture, tossing with a fork to combine. When the dough begins to hold together, form it into a ball with your fingertips. Then crumble the ball over the bottom of a buttered tart pan or quiche dish and pat into a thin, even layer. Press against the sides and trim off the pastry flush with the rim. Prick the bottom with the tines of a fork and bake in the preheated oven for 10 minutes. Prick a second time and return to the oven for another 10 to 15 minutes or until the tart shell is lightly browned.

2. Prepare the peppers by laying them directly on the oven rack under the broiler. Broil until the skins blister and turn black in spots. Turn the peppers and broil on all sides. Transfer to a bowl and cover with a kitchen towel folded in half. When the peppers are cool enough to handle, slip off the outer skins and tear the peppers into wide strips. Discard the inner membranes and seeds. Place the strips of pepper in a bowl and add the olive oil. Toss to coat the peppers with oil.

3. In a wide saucepan, combine the 6 tablespoons of water and 3 tablespoons of butter. Place over medium heat. When the butter melts, add the onions, separating the slices into rings. Sprinkle on the garlic, oregano, salt, and pepper. Increase the heat to high and cook, stirring constantly, until the water is completely evaporated and the onions are tender.

4. Preheat the oven to 350°F. Spread the cooked onions over the tart shell. Arrange the anchovy fillets on top of the onions in a spoke-like fashion. Crumble half the feta cheese over the anchovies and sprinkle on the chopped fresh basil. Lay the strips of oil-coated red pepper over the cheese in an attractive pattern, then crumble the remaining half of the feta on top. Turning the olives on their sides, place them around the perimeter of the tart. Place in the preheated oven and bake for 20 to 25 minutes or until heated through. Serve immediately or at room temperature.   ◄ঽ

Ratatouille Pie

MAKES ONE 9-INCH DEEP-DISH PIE

The hearty fillings of entrée pies can hold their own when enveloped within assertively flavored crusts. Lard and butter are always good choices for these crusts, but you can also feel free to experiment with unusual fats like beef drippings, chilled bacon fat, or chilled chicken fat.

3 tablespoons olive oil
1 medium eggplant, peeled and thinly sliced
3 slender zucchini, scrubbed and thinly sliced
1 large sweet onion, thinly sliced
2 green sweet bell peppers, cored and cut into narrow strips
2 garlic cloves, minced or pressed
Pastry for double-crust pie
3 large ripe tomatoes, peeled, seeded, and cut into strips
12 pitted black Greek or Italian olives, coarsely chopped
2 tablespoons chopped fresh basil (or substitute 2 teaspoons dried)
1 tablespoon chopped fresh parsley
½ teaspoon salt
Generous amount of freshly ground black pepper
6 ounces Gruyère cheese, grated
½ cup freshly grated Parmesan cheese
1 large egg
1 tablespoon water

1. Heat the olive oil in a 12-inch skillet. Add the eggplant slices and cook over medium heat until they brown lightly. Using a slotted spoon, transfer the eggplant to a large bowl. Add the zucchini to the hot oil and cook, tossing and lifting continuously, until lightly browned. Transfer with a slotted spoon to the large bowl. Add the onion and peppers to the hot oil and stir briefly over medium heat. Return the zucchini and eggplant to the skillet. Sprinkle on the garlic and cover the pan. Reduce the heat to low and cook about 15 minutes or until the vegetables have begun to soften and release their juices.

2. Meanwhile, prepare the pastry and chill. Remove the cover from the softened vegeta-

bles. Add the tomatoes and increase the heat to high. Cook, stirring continuously, until most of the liquid has evaporated. Blend in the black olives, basil, parsley, salt, and pepper. Remove from the heat and set aside.

3. Preheat the oven to 375°F. Line a deep-dish pie pan or quiche dish with pastry. Combine the vegetable mixture, Gruyère, and Parmesan cheese by tossing with two forks. Pour into the prepared crust and distribute evenly. Whisk the egg and water together and brush over the rim of the pastry.

4. Roll out the remaining dough and arrange over the vegetable filling. Trim the edges of the crust and flute or crimp to seal. Cut a generous steam vent in the center of the top crust with a 1-inch biscuit cutter. Brush the surface of the pastry with the remaining egg wash. Place in the preheated oven and bake for 50 to 60 minutes or until the crust is richly browned.

NOTE: If what seems like an excessive amount of liquid appears at the steam vent, siphon it with a bulb baster.

(See entry for Pie Baking: Main Course Pies.)   ◆⟆

Pork and Apple Pie

MAKES ONE 9-INCH DEEP-DISH PIE

A robust meat pie with a middle layer of grated apple. Serve hot or offer chilled as satisfying tailgate fare.

2 pounds ground pork
1 medium onion, finely chopped
2 garlic cloves, minced or pressed
½ cup dry white wine
¼ cup chopped fresh parsley
½ teaspoon dried leaf thyme
½ teaspoon dried sage
2 bay leaves, broken in half
⅛ teaspoon allspice
Pastry for double-crust pie
2 tart green apples, peeled, cored, and grated
3 large eggs
¾ cup dry, unseasoned bread crumbs

1 teaspoon salt
Generous amount of freshly ground black pepper
1 tablespoon water

1. In a large mixing bowl, combine the pork, onion, garlic, wine, parsley, thyme, sage, bay leaves, and allspice. Blend thoroughly. Cover the bowl and refrigerate for 12 hours or overnight.

2. Prepare the pastry and chill. Take the meat mixture from the refrigerator and remove and discard the bay leaves. Transfer the mixture to a colander, pressing to thoroughly drain off excess liquid. Grate the apple and set aside.

3. Preheat the oven to 375°F. In a large bowl, whisk the eggs, measure out 3 tablespoons, and set aside. Place the meat mixture in the bowl containing the beaten eggs and blend in the bread crumbs, salt, and pepper. Line a deep-dish pie pan or quiche dish with pastry. Spoon in half the meat mixture and spread evenly over the prepared crust. Scatter the grated apple over the meat. Cover with the remaining half of the meat mixture.

4. Roll out the remaining dough. Whisk the reserved egg with 1 tablespoon of water and brush over the rim of the pastry. Arrange the top crust over the meat filling. Trim the edges of the crust and flute or crimp to seal. Cut a generous steam vent in the center of the top crust with a 1-inch biscuit cutter. Brush the surface of the pastry with the remaining egg wash. Place in the preheated oven and bake for 50 to 60 minutes or until the crust is richly browned.

NOTE: If what seems like an excessive amount of liquid appears at the steam vent, siphon it with a bulb baster.

(See entry for Pie Baking: Main Course Pies.)   ◆⟆

Pizza

MAKES ONE 14-INCH PIZZA

A light, puffy pizza with a crisp crust. It's extremely important that you use high-gluten bread flour in preparing the dough because regular all-purpose flour won't produce as light and crisp a crust.

PIZZA DOUGH

1 cup warm (100°F.) water
1 package dry yeast
Small pinch plus ½ teaspoon sugar
2 cups bread flour (preferably bromated), scoop measured
½ teaspoon salt

SAUCE

1 can (35 ounces) Italian plum tomatoes, undrained
1 teaspoon dried basil
½ teaspoon dried oregano
½ teaspoon dried rosemary leaves, pulverized with a mortar and pestle
½ teaspoon sugar
Pinch of thyme
1 bay leaf, broken in half
1 garlic clove, halved
Salt and freshly ground black pepper to taste

OPTIONAL TOPPINGS

Sliced red or green sweet bell pepper, raw or roasted
Finely chopped Italian sausage or thinly sliced pepperoni
Sliced fresh mushrooms, raw or sautéed
Coarsely chopped onion, raw or sautéed
Grated Parmesan cheese
Grated mozzarella, Monterey Jack, or Meunster cheese

1. In a large mixing bowl, combine the water, yeast, and pinch of sugar. Stir to dissolve the yeast and sugar and set aside.

2. In another large bowl, combine the flour, salt, and ½ teaspoon sugar. Whisk or toss with a fork to blend thoroughly.

3. Pour two-thirds of the flour mixture into the dissolved yeast. Beat vigorously with a wooden spoon until the dough pulls away from the bowl in ropy strands. The mixture will be very wet.

4. Dump out all but 2 tablespoons of the remaining flour onto a work surface and spread the flour out in a circle. Empty the dough onto the flour and sprinkle the re-maining 2 tablespoons of flour over the dough. Using a pastry scraper, lift and fold the dough over on itself. Press down to work the flour in. Repeat the process of folding and pressing with the pastry scraper until the flour is entirely absorbed. Shape the dough into a ball (actually it's more like a flabby mass), lightly dust with flour, and place in a greased bowl. Cover with plastic wrap and secure with an elastic band to keep the dough moist. Set in a draft-free place to rise (about 1½ hours).

5. Meanwhile, prepare the sauce. In a wide saucepan, combine the tomatoes, basil, oregano, rosemary, sugar, thyme, bay leaf, and garlic. Place over medium heat and cook uncovered until the mixture bubbles vigorously. Reduce the heat and continue to cook uncovered for 2 hours or until the excessive moisture has evaporated and the sauce has thickened. Stir occasionally to break up the tomatoes. Test for doneness by spooning a dollop of sauce onto a plate. The sauce has thickened sufficiently when only a negligible amount of liquid seeps out around the edge of the dollop. Season with salt and pepper.

6. When the dough is double in size, turn out onto a floured work surface. Pat down into a flat circle, dusting any moist spots with flour. Press the circle as flat as you can, working out any air bubbles you see. Fold the dough in half, dust with flour, and press into a flat semicircle. Fold into quarters, dust with flour, and press flat. Tucking the corners underneath, form the dough into a ball. Dust with flour and return to the bowl. Cover with plastic wrap and secure with an elastic band. Allow the dough to rise until doubled (about 1 hour).

7. Twenty minutes before you plan to assemble the pizza, set the oven rack in its lowest position (or higher for a less crispy crust). Line the rack with unglazed quarry tiles or a baking stone. Set the oven temperature to 500°F. and preheat for 20 minutes.

8. Cover a large pastry board with 18-inch extra-heavy aluminum foil. Grease the foil generously with solid shortening. Sprinkle

with coarse semolina or cornmeal if you like. Turn the dough out onto a lightly floured surface and flatten into a large circle by pressing down with your hands. Fold in half and then into quarters and transfer to the greased foil. Unfold the dough and shape into a 14-inch circle, forming a rim around the outside edge. (For a thin crust, lightly rub the surface of the dough with olive oil.) Spoon hot sauce over the dough and arrange other topping ingredients over the sauce. Do not sprinkle on grated cheese.

9. Open the oven door and pull out the rack. Lift the pastry board and pizza onto the rack and tilt slightly. Holding the board with one hand, use the other hand to pull the foil onto the hot tiles. Cook for 5 minutes.

10. At that point, the crust will be partially set, allowing you to lift the pizza with a long spatula and pull the foil out from underneath. Continue baking the pizza directly on the hot tiles for 5 to 8 minutes. When the crust has begun to brown and the sauce is bubbling, sprinkle the pizza with grated Parmesan. Cook for 3 minutes. Again sprinkle the pizza with grated mozzarella or other cheese. Cook until the cheese is completely melted. Slide onto a pastry board to cut.

NOTE: Allow the quarry tiles or baking stone to cool completely inside the oven before removing them. They retain so much heat that they will destroy a wooden or formica surface. When completely cool, scrub under hot running water but do not use soap. Do not be alarmed if the tiles or stone develop an untidy appearance. It's to be expected that grease and oil will leave markings on their absorbent surfaces.

(See entry for Pizza.)

Pizza Rustica

SERVES 8 TO 12

A distant cousin of the more familiar single-crust pizza, this deep-dish, double-crust pie is hearty fare, reminiscent of robust country dinning. It may be served hot, or cool as part of a picnic supper.

DOUBLE CRUST

1½ cups warm (100°F.) water
1 package dry yeast
Small pinch plus ¾ teaspoon sugar
3 cups bread flour (preferably bromated), scoop measured
¾ teaspoon salt

FILLING

6 red sweet bell peppers
2 pounds fresh spinach
1 pound sweet Italian sausage
2 tablespoons olive oil
2 garlic cloves
½ pound mozzarella cheese, grated
½ pound caciocavallo or provolone cheese (preferably smoked), grated
½ cup freshly grated Parmesan cheese
3 large eggs
¼ cup milk
¼ teaspoon salt
Generous amount of freshly ground black pepper

1. Combine the ingredients for the crust according to steps 1–4 under Pizza (p. 297). Allow the dough to rise, and then knead it according to the directions in step 6 (p. 297). Allow the dough to rise until double in size.

2. Rinse the sweet bell peppers under cold running water and blot dry with paper towels. Arrange directly on the oven rack and broil until the skin blisters and small areas of pepper become charred. Turn the peppers and broil on all sides, including the tops and bottoms. Using tongs, transfer the roasted peppers to a bowl and cover with a kitchen towel. Let them sit at room temperature for 45 minutes.

3. Meanwhile, rinse the spinach under cold running water and remove the tough stems. Place the spinach in a colander and drain thoroughly. Chop coarsely and set aside. Remove the casing from the sausage and chop or break apart with your fingers. Remove the blistered skin from the peppers. Cut them in half and gently remove the seeds and cores, but do not rinse them under running water

because that would dilute their flavor. Tear the pepper halves into wide strips.

4. Heat the olive oil in a 12-inch skillet. Add the garlic cloves and stir over low heat until the garlic develops a golden hue. Using a slotted spoon, remove the garlic and discard. Add the chopped spinach to the oil and increase the heat to high. Stirring constantly, cook for 2 to 3 minutes or until the spinach is limp. Transfer the cooked spinach to a bowl with a slotted spoon. Add the crumbled sausage to the hot oil and reduce the heat to medium. Cook, stirring constantly, until the sausage is no longer pink. Using a slotted spoon, transfer the sausage to a bowl.

5. When the dough is double in size, break off one-third of it and set it aside. Generously butter a 9-inch springform pan. On a lightly floured surface, roll out the larger piece of dough until it measures 14 inches in diameter. Roll the dough up onto the rolling pin and transfer to the buttered pan. Fit the dough inside, allowing it to hang out over the edge of the pan.

6. Preheat the oven to 375°F. Scatter half the cooked sausage over the dough and top with half the cooked spinach. Sprinkle on half of the grated mozzarella, half of the grated caciocavallo, and half of the Parmesan. Lay on half of the red pepper strips. Repeat this procedure in the same order, ending with strips of red pepper. In a small bowl, whisk the eggs and milk together. Blend in the salt and black pepper. Pour the egg mixture over the filling, piercing deep holes in the filling with a metal skewer to guarantee that the egg mixture is distributed evenly.

7. Roll out the remaining smaller portion of the dough and lay it over the filling. Bring up the side dough and roll it together with the top crust to seal the pie and form a ropelike border around the outer edge. Cut a decorative steam vent in the center of the top crust and brush with an egg-yolk wash if you want a deeply colored top. Place in the preheated oven and bake for 55 to 65 minutes or until the crust is well browned. Remove from the oven and cool on a rack or serve hot.

NOTE: To serve hot, let the pie stand for 10 minutes at room temperature. Then remove the sides of the pan and allow it to stand for 10 minutes more. This gives the filling an opportunity to settle and facilitates slicing. ◖◗

Pastitsio

SERVES 12

A savory casserole from the Greek cuisine. Allow it to rest for 15 minutes at room temperature after baking to give the custard an opportunity to firm slightly before cutting into squares.

1 pound ungrooved ziti or elbow macaroni
2 tablespoons vegetable oil
1 large onion, coarsely chopped
1 pound ground beef (or substitute lamb)
1 garlic clove, minced or pressed
1 teaspoon dried oregano
½ teaspoon ground cinnamon
½ teaspoon salt
Generous amount of freshly ground white pepper
2 tablespoons butter, cut into 8 pieces
8 ounces feta cheese, crumbled
8 ounces Kasseri cheese, grated
½ cup freshly grated Parmesan cheese
6 large eggs
2 cups milk

1. Fill a 6-quart pot with water. Cover and place over high heat. Bring to a vigorous boil. Stir in the ziti with a wooden fork to separate the pieces. Return to a moderate boil and cook uncovered until tender.

2. Meanwhile, heat the vegetable oil in a 12-inch skillet. Add the onion and toss to coat. Stir over medium heat until the onion becomes limp. Add the beef and increase the heat. Stir over high heat until the meat is browned. Add the garlic, oregano, cinnamon, salt, and pepper. Cook, stirring, for 1 minute.

3. Preheat the oven to 325°F. Generously butter a 9×13-inch baking pan. Drain the cooked ziti in a colander and transfer to a large bowl. Toss the hot ziti with the butter

until the butter melts. Add the feta, Kasseri, and Parmesan cheese. Toss to combine.

4. Line the baking dish with one-third of the cooked ziti mixture. Spoon on one-third of the meat mixture. Repeat 2 more times, ending with the meat mixture. Whisk the eggs and milk together and pour over the casserole, parting the ziti in several places with the blade of a knife to guarantee that the custard mixture is evenly distributed. Place in the preheated oven and bake for 50 to 60 minutes or until slightly puffed.   ◄২

Middle Eastern Stuffed Eggplant

SERVES 4

In this recipe, scoring and prebaking the eggplants make the flesh easier to remove, and using the curved, serrated blade of a grapefruit knife further simplifies the task.

2 medium eggplants (each about 7 inches long)
2 tablespoons olive oil
2 tablespoons butter
1 large onion, thinly sliced
1 pound ground lean lamb (preferably ground at home)
½ cup dry red wine
1 can (28 ounces) crushed tomatoes
1 garlic clove, minced or pressed
1 teaspoon dried leaf thyme
¼ teaspoon allspice
½ teaspoon salt
Freshly ground black pepper
¼ cup whole pine nuts, toasted (or substitute coarsely chopped walnuts)
¼ cup freshly grated Parmesan cheese
2 tablespoons chopped fresh parsley
1 cup White Sauce with Milk (p. 348)
½ cup grated Kasseri cheese (or substitute Cheddar)
2 large egg yolks
¼ cup cold water

1. Preheat the oven to 425°F. Rinse the eggplants and cut in half lengthwise. Using a curved grapefruit knife, cut around the perimeter of the eggplant about ¼ inch in from the skin (see illustration). Then with a paring knife score the exposed surface of the flesh (do not cut into the ¼-inch rim). The object of this procedure is to hasten cooking, so make your cuts no deeper than 1 inch. Rub the exposed flesh and the skin with olive oil. Arrange, skin side up, on a jelly roll pan or baking sheet. Place in the preheated oven and bake for 20 to 30 minutes or until the flesh is somewhat tender. When the eggplant halves are cooked, transfer them, skin side up, to a double thickness of paper toweling to cool.

2. Meanwhile, prepare the stuffing by melting the butter in a 12-inch skillet. Add the onion and toss to coat. Cover the pan and cook over low heat until the onion is tender. Stir occasionally to break the onion into small pieces. Crumble in the ground lamb and increase the heat. Cook, stirring, until the lamb is no longer pink. Tilt the pan and spoon off the excess fat. Blend in the wine, tomatoes, garlic, thyme, allspice, salt, and pepper. Cook uncovered over medium heat until nearly all the liquid has evaporated. Remove from the heat.

3. When the eggplants are cool enough to handle, use a grapefruit knife to loosen the

Cut around the perimeter of the eggplant with a curved grapefruit knife. Then, using a paring knife, score the surface of the flesh.

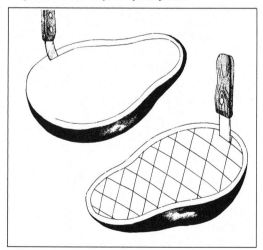

flesh. Scoop it out, taking care not to break through the skin and leaving a ¼-inch rim around the outside. Chop the flesh coarsely and add to the lamb mixture. Stir in the pine nuts, Parmesan cheese, and parsley and continue cooking until the remaining liquid evaporates. The mixture should have substantial body and be capable of being mounded on a spoon.

4. Reheat the oven to 350°F. Generously butter a 9×13-inch baking dish. Arrange the eggplant shells in the dish and spoon equal amounts of the stuffing into each shell.

5. In a 1½-quart saucepan, stir together the white sauce (either hot or cold) and the grated Kasseri cheese. In a small bowl beat the yolks and water. When the sauce and cheese are well combined, stir in the egg yolks and water. Place over medium heat and cook, stirring constantly with a heat-resistant rubber spatula, until the cheese is melted and the sauce has begun to bubble. Remove from the heat and pour over the eggplant, masking the stuffing. Place in the preheated oven and bake uncovered for 30 to 45 minutes or until a metal skewer slides into the eggplant easily and the sauce is lightly browned.   ◅҉

Spinach and Ricotta Pie (Spanakopita)

SERVES 12

Folding in whipped egg whites lends an especially light texture to the filling in this pie.

8 sheets of filo dough (each measuring 12×16 inches)

2 pounds fresh spinach

1 pound ricotta cheese

3 large eggs

3 tablespoons olive oil

8 green onions, thinly sliced, including most of the green portion

½ pound feta cheese, crumbled

2 tablespoons chopped fresh parsley

1 tablespoon chopped fresh oregano (or substitute 1 teaspoon dried)

½ teaspoon salt

Generous amount of freshly ground black pepper

1 cup butter, melted

1. Set the filo dough out to warm to room temperature. Make certain that it's sealed airtight. Wash the spinach and drain in a colander. Remove the tough stems and scatter the leaves over a clean kitchen towel in a single layer (you'll need more than 1 towel). Roll up tightly to dry. Unroll and stack 12 or so leaves on top of one another. Slicing across the leaves, shred the spinach into ¼-inch-wide strips.

2. Force the ricotta through a sieve, then return it to the sieve and let any liquid drain off. Separate the eggs, allowing the whites to warm to room temperature.

3. Heat the olive oil in a 12-inch skillet. Add the shredded spinach and toss to coat. Stir over high heat, tossing and lifting continuously, until the spinach becomes limp. Stir in the green onions and cook in the same manner for 1 minute.

4. Whisk the egg yolks in a large mixing bowl. Add the strained ricotta, feta, parsley, oregano, salt, and pepper. Blend well, then stir in the cooked spinach and green onions. Whip the egg whites to the soft-peak stage and fold into the cheese mixture.

5. Preheat the oven to 350°F. Brush the bottom and sides of a 9×13-inch baking dish with melted butter. Cut the sheets of filo in half to create sixteen 8×12-inch sheets. Lay the sheets of dough on a piece of plastic wrap. Cover with a second sheet of plastic wrap and smooth out the air bubbles with your hands. (Keep the filo sheets covered with plastic wrap at all times so they won't dry out.)

6. Lay one sheet of filo inside the baking dish. Brush with melted butter using light strokes. Place a second sheet of filo on top and again brush with melted butter. Repeat this procedure until you have 6 sheets of buttered filo in the bottom of the pan. Spread half the spinach-cheese mixture over the filo, leaving about ¼ inch of dough uncovered all around the perimeter. Layer on 5 sheets of

filo, brushing each with butter. Spread on the remaining half of the spinach-cheese mixture and top with the 5 remaining sheets of filo brushed with melted butter. (Be sure to butter the top sheet.) Place in the preheated oven and bake for 45 to 55 minutes or until slightly puffed and golden brown. Serve at once.

(See entry for Layered Pastry.)   ◀₂

Shrimp-Filled Egg Rolls

MAKES 12 LARGE EGG ROLLS

The availability of ready-made wrappers in most large supermarkets makes it not only possible but also easy to prepare homemade egg rolls.

1 pound medium-size fresh shrimp, peeled and deveined
1 medium head Chinese cabbage
6 green onions
Peanut oil (or substitute vegetable oil)
6 large fresh mushrooms, coarsely chopped
1 garlic clove, minced or pressed
3 tablespoons duck sauce, see Note (or substitute apricot jam)
½ teaspoon salt
Generous amount of freshly ground black pepper
1 tablespoon cornstarch
2 tablespoons cold water
1 package large egg-roll wrappers (6- or 7-inch squares)
Vegetable oil for deep frying

1. Coarsely chop the shrimp and set aside. Prepare the Chinese cabbage by thinly slicing across the ribs to create fine shreds. (The leaves of Chinese cabbage are tightly packed and seldom need washing; however, if you do rinse them, blot dry and stack them to slice.) Slice the green onions, including three-quarters of the green portion.

2. Pour enough oil into a 12-inch skillet to cover the bottom of the pan. Place over high heat. Add the onions, mushrooms, and garlic. Cook, stirring constantly, until the onions

are limp and the mushrooms have given up their moisture.

3. Add the shrimp and cook, stirring, for 1 minute or until slightly pink. Add the Chinese cabbage and stir, tossing to combine with the other ingredients. Continue cooking over high heat until the cabbage is limp. Stir in the duck sauce, salt, and pepper. Empty into a bowl to cool.

4. In a small bowl, blend the cornstarch and water. Remove 1 egg-roll wrapper from the package and twist the package closed so that the remaining wrappers won't dry out. Lay the wrapper on the counter in a diamond shape — 1 point near you, 1 point to the left, 1 point to the right, and 1 point away from you. Place 2 tablespoons of the cooled filling slightly below the center of the wrapper and spread horizontally into a 3-inch-long strip. Bring the point nearest you up and over the filling. Then brush the cornstarch mixture over the edges of the wrapper, proceeding from the left-hand point around to the right-hand point. Also brush the wrapper encasing the filling. Bring the left-hand point over to the center and press so that it will adhere. Repeat with the right-hand point. Then roll to complete shaping. Place on a baking sheet with ample space between egg rolls so that they won't stick together. Refrigerate for 1 to 6 hours. Deep fry 2 at a time in vegetable oil preheated to 370°F. Turn with tongs to encourage even browning. When golden brown, transfer to absorbent paper. Serve immediately with Hot Mustard Sauce (p. 354) or Sweet and Sour Sauce (p. 354).

NOTE: Duck sauce is a spicy condiment customarily served with oriental-style duckling. It can be purchased in jars or cans, or you can make a reasonable facsimile by heating ½ cup plum jelly, 2 teaspoons sugar, 2 teaspoons white wine vinegar, and ¼ cup finely chopped chutney.

This recipe's filling may be used interchangeably with the one for Fried Pork Packets (p. 185).

(See entry for Frying: Deep-Fat.)   ◀₂

Pasta, Rice, Beans, and Grains

Egg Pasta I

MAKES ABOUT 1 POUND

Although some regions of Italy create pasta dough from flour and eggs only, this recipe includes water and olive oil. Water activates the gluten in flour and results in a dough that is easier to knead. It also lends a degree of tackiness that enables you to shape and seal the dough efficiently. Olive oil lubricates the gluten strands to facilitate rolling and stretching the dough, and it also inhibits drying, which gives you extra time to fill and shape intricate pieces.

This recipe's by-hand approach to creating pasta dough is often called the crater method because flour is measured directly onto a work surface and the liquid ingredients are poured into a well or crater formed in the center. The advantage of this technique is that only a limited amount of flour is pulled into the liquid at a time.

2 cups unbleached all-purpose flour, scoop measured
½ teaspoon salt
3 large eggs
2 tablespoons warm water
1 tablespoon olive oil

1. Measure the flour and salt directly onto a work surface. Resist the temptation to use a bowl even if you're the fastidious type — it doesn't work nearly as well. Stir with a fork to mix the salt into the flour. Then form a crater in the center of the flour, but don't expose the work surface at the bottom of the depression. Leave it covered with a thin layer of flour.

2. In a small bowl, whisk the eggs, water, and oil together. Pour into the crater. Using a fork, begin to slowly incorporate the flour from the sides of the crater by using an up-and-over stroke of the wrist (see illustration). Each stroke will pull away only as much flour as the liquid can readily absorb. Don't rush and take large amounts of flour, for the quality of your dough depends on doing this step slowly.

3. When the dough becomes too stiff to mix with a fork, gather it into a ball and begin to knead, working in whatever flour is left from the sides of the crater. Knead for about 20 minutes, dusting the dough with additional flour if it becomes sticky. As you knead, the dough should begin to feel like fine soft leather. When you make a depression with your finger, it should spring right back. If you hear faint popping sounds, that's a good sign. It means you're incorporating air as you knead (a characteristic of high-quality pasta). To determine if you've kneaded long enough, poke your index finger into the center of the

Using a fork and an up-and-over motion of the wrist causes the moist mass in the center of the crater to pull away only as much flour as the liquid can readily absorb.

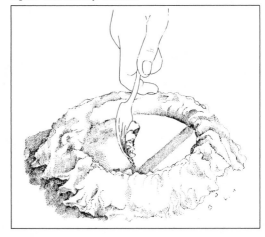

dough; it should feel damp, but not sticky or overly moist.

4. Cut the dough in half. Check the cut surface. If you've kneaded the dough enough to develop the gluten to its fullest capacity, you'll see hundreds of tiny air pockets. Drop the dough halves into separate plastic bags and seal airtight. Allow the dough to rest for 24 hours, refrigerated, or place in the freezer overnight. Bring dough to room temperature before rolling it out, but let frozen dough defrost in the refrigerator first. (Pasta dough can be chilled for only 4 hours but it won't handle as well as dough that has rested for a longer period.)

5. Before you begin to roll it, divide the dough into as many parts as you used cups of flour. A 1-cup batch rolls out to about an 18-inch circle. Anything larger than that is wider than the average work area and difficult to manage. Keep any dough you're not working with in an airtight plastic bag to prevent it from drying out. (Once pasta dough begins to dry, it's difficult to roll and impossible to seal.) Use a straight pasta pin for the best control — a conventional rolling pin with handles is not as efficient for this job.

6. Place the dough on an unfloured surface. Flour it only if the dough seems excessively sticky, and add it by sifting instead of sprinkling. (Here's an excellent place to use granulated flour because it isn't as apt to be taken in by the dough, yet it will alleviate sticking.) Actually, a limited amount of stickiness is helpful. It makes it possible for the dough to adhere slightly to the work surface, enabling you to roll it out without having it roam all over the place.

Roll the dough using away-from-you strokes. Be fairly assertive, but don't press down. And don't roll over the edge because that will cause it to dry out. Roll the dough, lift it a quarter turn, and roll again. Continue rolling, lifting, and turning until you reach the desired thinness. Generally speaking, you should roll pasta dough until it is so thin that you can begin to see the faint outline of the wood grain or pattern on the work surface

through the dough. However, many people prefer homemade pasta to be a bit thicker than that, especially for lasagna or fettuccine.

7. As soon as the dough is thin enough, immediately cut out the necessary strips or rounds. If you're forming intricate shapes, work with only 3 or 4 pieces of dough at a time. Keep the remaining dough covered with damp paper towels. The thinner the dough, the faster it dries out, so work as quickly as possible. You will notice several variations in color as you work with pasta dough. Freshly cut pasta is a bright, cheery yellow. As it dries the color deepens to a dark, rich yellow, and cooked pasta is almost white. (This change in color is one of the ways you can tell pasta is nearly cooked.)

8. Cook the pasta immediately, dry it for storage, or freeze it in an airtight plastic bag. Filled pasta may be refrigerated for 24 hours or frozen for up to 4 months. Keep in mind that the condition it's in when it goes into the pot determines how long it will need to cook. Frozen, stuffed, or dried pasta takes longer to cook than freshly cut or unstuffed pasta. Test for doneness by inserting a metal skewer or toothpick. It should easily pierce the pasta. If you're in doubt, bite into a piece. The proper consistency of cooked pasta is such that your teeth meet some resistance. Pasta should never be mushy.

(See entries for Pasta; Kneading; Gluten.) ❧

Egg Pasta II

MAKES ABOUT 1 POUND

In a fraction of the time it takes to make by hand, the food processor turns out pasta dough of excellent quality. It not only blends the dough in seconds, it does most of the kneading for you, too.

2 cups unbleached all-purpose flour, scoop measured
½ teaspoon salt
3 large eggs
1 tablespoon warm water
1 tablespoon olive oil

1. With the metal blade in place in a food processor, measure the flour and salt directly into the work bowl. Pulse to evenly distribute the salt.

2. Whisk the eggs, water, and oil in a small bowl. Have some additional warm water ready to use if you need it. With the machine running, slowly pour the egg mixture through the feed tube. The dough should form a ball on top of the processor blade. If it doesn't, drizzle in additional water until a ball forms. On the other hand, if the dough is sticking to the sides of the bowl, remove the cover of the processor and sprinkle 1 tablespoon of flour over the dough. Replace the cover and process until the dough comes away clean. Repeat with more flour if necessary. When the ball of dough rattles freely around inside the work bowl, begin to count off 15 seconds, then immediately turn the machine off.

3. Remove the dough from the work bowl and knead for 5 to 10 minutes, dusting with sifted flour if the dough becomes sticky. As you knead, the dough should begin to feel like fine soft leather. When you make a depression with your finger, it should spring right back. If you hear faint popping sounds, that's a good sign. It means you're incorporating air as you knead (a characteristic of high-quality pasta). To determine if you've kneaded long enough, poke your index finger into the center of the dough; it should feel damp, but not sticky or overly moist. Continue according to the directions in steps 4–8 for Egg Pasta I (p. 304).

(See entries for Pasta; Kneading; Gluten.) ◄ℨ

Salmon-Filled Agnolotti with Dilled Butter Sauce

SERVES 4

Strictly speaking, the difference between ravioli and agnolotti *is one of shape and type of filling. Traditionally, ravioli are square or rec-* *tangular pasta packets filled with cheese, eggs, or vegetables;* agnolotti, *which literally means "little fat lambs," are round pockets stuffed with meat. But recent innovative approaches to pasta cookery have blurred these distinctions and led to new and exciting variations. This recipe suggests forming* agnolotti *in the classic manner, that is, by folding rounds of pasta into turnoverlike semicircles. It also gives directions for creating circular envelopes by topping one pasta round with another.* Agnolotti *may be served in hot broth, tossed with meat juices or melted butter and cheese, or sauced in a variety of ways. Serves 8 as a first course.*

SALMON FILLING
3 tablespoons unsalted butter
1 medium shallot, finely chopped
1 pound raw salmon, bones and skin removed
½ cup dry white wine
2 tablespoons fresh lemon juice
1 teaspoon dried chervil
½ teaspoon salt
Freshly ground white pepper
2 large egg whites
3 tablespoons heavy cream

PASTA
1 tablespoon cornstarch
2 tablespoons cold water
1 pound prepared pasta dough (p. 304 or p. 305)

DILLED BUTTER SAUCE
8 tablespoons unsalted butter
2 tablespoons fresh lemon juice
1 teaspoon grated lemon zest
1 tablespoon fresh dill leaves

1. Make the filling by melting 3 tablespoons of butter in a 10-inch skillet. Add the shallot and toss to coat. Add the salmon and place over medium heat. Blend in the wine and cook, stirring continuously with a fork to flake the salmon as it cooks.

2. When the wine is almost completely evaporated, add the lemon juice, chervil, salt, and white pepper. Continue stirring over medium heat until the mixture is dry enough to

stick to the bottom of the pan. Transfer to a large mixing bowl.

3. In another bowl, whip the egg whites to the soft-peak stage. Add the cream and whipped egg whites to the salmon mixture and beat vigorously with a wooden spoon. The consistency of the mixture should be smooth, but not homogeneous.

4. Combine the cornstarch and water and stir to dissolve. Set aside. Roll out half the prepared pasta dough and return the remaining half to an airtight plastic bag. Using a 2½-inch biscuit cutter (larger cutters may be used if you wish), cut the dough into rounds. Immediately cover all but 6 rounds with a damp paper towel (a cloth towel provides too much moisture). Drop a small amount of filling in the center of each pasta round (a level ¼ teaspoonful works well, although experienced pasta cooks will be able to use more). Pick the round up and hold it in the fingertips of one hand. With the thumb of the opposite hand, moisten the edge of half the circle, using the cornstarch mixture. Guide the edges of pasta together and seal by pressing together with your fingertips. Place on a baking sheet sprinkled with coarse semolina or cornmeal. Repeat with the remaining pasta rounds. Refrigerate the *agnolotti* or drop into gently boiling water and cook until a metal skewer can be inserted with slight resistance. With a slotted spoon, transfer the cooked *agnolotti* to a double layer of paper toweling to drain. Blot dry.

5. Prepare the sauce. Melt 8 tablespoons of butter in a 12-inch skillet or wide saucepan. Stir in the lemon juice and lemon zest and blend in the feathery leaves from fresh dill. Add the cooked *agnolotti* and toss over medium heat to warm briefly.

NOTE: A more generous amount of filling can be enveloped if you use 2 pasta rounds of different sizes to form the *agnolotti*. Cut half the rounds with a 2½-inch cutter and the remaining half with a 3-inch cutter. Shape a spoonful of filling into a small ball and place it in the center of the smaller round. Moisten with the cornstarch mixture and lay the larger round over the top, patting around the mound of filling and working out any air bubbles with your fingertips. Trim the edges by cutting through both pasta layers with a scalloped pastry cutter or biscuit ring. ◄֎

Agnolotti Variations

GOAT CHEESE FILLING: Allow 4 ounces of dry, white goat cheese to soften. Force through a coarse sieve into a bowl. Add ½ cup ricotta cheese, also forced through the sieve. Blend in 1 large beaten egg yolk, 2 tablespoons freshly grated Parmesan cheese, 2 tablespoons chopped fresh parsley, 1 teaspoon dried leaf thyme, ½ teaspoon salt, and freshly ground white pepper. Fill and cook *agnolotti* as described above. Serve in shallow bowls of beef broth and sprinkle on freshly grated Parmesan cheese.

PORK AND MUSHROOM FILLING: Cover ½ ounce of dried Porcini mushrooms with warm water and set aside to rehydrate (see Note, p. 311). In an 8-inch skillet, melt 2 tablespoons of butter. Add ½ pound finely ground lean pork, and stir over medium heat until no longer pink. Chop the softened mushrooms and add to the pork. Pour in the mushroom liquid and add ½ teaspoon dried rosemary leaves, pulverized with a mortar and pestle; ½ teaspoon salt; and freshly ground black pepper. Transfer to a bowl and combine with 1 large beaten egg, 2 tablespoons freshly grated Parmesan cheese, and a generous amount of freshly grated nutmeg. Fill and cook *agnolotti* as described above. Prepare Creamed Leek Sauce by slowly cooking the white portion of 2 sliced leeks in a covered pan with 4 tablespoons of butter. Stir in 2 cups of medium cream and heat gently until bubbling. Whirl in a blender until smooth, then reheat briefly. Pour over the cooked *agnolotti* to serve.

SQUASH AND KALE FILLING: Bake a 1-pound acorn squash and scoop out the flesh.

Mash and cook over low heat until the squash is dry enough to stick to the bottom of the pan. Add 2 tablespoons of butter, 2 tablespoons freshly grated Parmesan cheese, ½ teaspoon salt, and a generous amount of freshly grated nutmeg. Beat until the butter melts. Remove stems from ½ pound of kale. Cook leaves in boiling water, drain, and chop coarsely; combine with squash mixture. Fill and cook *agnolotti* as described above. Serve with hot melted unsalted butter and freshly grated Parmesan cheese.   ◆੨

Cannelloni

SERVES 6 TO 8

Frequently confused with manicotti, a large tubular macaroni, cannelloni are delicate squares of egg pasta wrapped around a filling, which in this case is composed of cheese and spinach. The filled cannelloni are then masked with a balsamella *(a thin white sauce), topped with a light tomato sauce, and baked slowly to meld the flavors.*

Although this recipe looks like a real project, you can easily prepare it in stages, freezing the various elements as you make them and assembling the final dish at the last minute. You might, for example, stuff and roll the cannelloni and freeze them in an airtight plastic bag, and make and freeze the two sauces at separate times.

1 pound prepared pasta dough (p. 304 or p. 305)

MARINARA SAUCE
6 tablespoons butter
2 large onions, coarsely chopped
2 medium carrots, coarsely chopped
2 garlic cloves, minced or pressed
2 cans (35 ounces each) Italian plum tomatoes, undrained
1½ teaspoons dried basil
½ teaspoon dried oregano
Pinch of sugar
½ teaspoon salt

Generous amount of freshly ground black pepper
3 tablespoons chopped fresh parsley
Freshly grated Parmesan cheese

CHEESE AND SPINACH FILLING
1 pound fresh spinach
1½ pounds ricotta cheese
½ cup freshly grated Parmesan cheese
Freshly grated nutmeg
½ teaspoon salt
Generous amount of freshly ground black pepper

THIN WHITE SAUCE
4 tablespoons butter
2 tablespoons all-purpose flour
½ teaspoon salt
2 cups hot milk
Freshly ground white pepper
Freshly grated nutmeg
1 bay leaf, broken in half
½ teaspoon dried leaf thyme

1. Roll out half the prepared pasta dough and return the remaining half to an airtight plastic bag. Cut the rolled pasta into 4-inch squares. Arrange them in a single layer on a surface coated with cornmeal. Roll and cut the remaining pasta. Set aside the pasta squares in a single layer.

2. Meanwhile, prepare the Marinara Sauce. Melt the butter in a wide saucepan or Dutch oven. Add the onions, carrots, and garlic, and toss to coat. Cover the pan and cook over low heat for 30 minutes or until the vegetables are tender.

3. Add the tomatoes, breaking them up with your fingers. Stir in the basil and oregano. Regulate the heat so that the sauce bubbles gently and cook uncovered for 30 minutes. Stir in the sugar, salt, pepper, and parsley. Cook uncovered for 30 minutes more. Put the sauce through a food mill and refrigerate or freeze until needed.

4. To form the filling, wash the spinach and remove the tough stems. Plunge into boiling water and stir frequently to keep the spinach submerged. Cook uncovered until the water

returns to a vigorous boil. Transfer the spinach to a colander and drain under cold running water. Take up the cooled spinach by handfuls and squeeze dry. Chop coarsely. Place in an 8-inch skillet and cook, stirring constantly, until no more steam rises and the spinach begins to stick to the bottom of the pan. Remove from the heat.

5. In a large mixing bowl, combine the ricotta, Parmesan, nutmeg, salt, and pepper. Add the spinach and blend thoroughly. Cover the bowl and refrigerate until needed. (Some recipes for this filling call for a whole egg or an egg yolk and grated mozzarella cheese, but the resulting texture of the filling will be heavier and more dense.)

6. Prepare the Thin White Sauce by melting the butter over medium heat in a 1½-quart thick-bottomed saucepan. Remove from the heat and blend in the flour and salt. Return to medium heat and cook, stirring continuously, until the mixture foams. Remove the pan from the heat and immediately whisk in the hot milk. Stir in the white pepper and nutmeg. Return the sauce to the burner and reduce the heat to its lowest possible setting. Create a bouquet garni by enclosing the bay leaf and thyme inside a piece of clean cheesecloth and tying it securely with string. Drop into the simmering white sauce and cover the pan. Cook for 15 minutes, stirring occasionally. Lift out the bouquet garni and refrigerate or freeze the sauce. (Frozen or chilled white sauce should be heated before using to attain the proper consistency. Add 1 or 2 tablespoons of milk if necessary to thin the sauce.)

7. To assemble the final dish, begin by bringing a large pot of salted water to a vigorous boil. Drop in the pasta squares and stir gently with a wooden fork to separate the pieces. Return to a moderate boil and cook uncovered until tender. Halt the cooking abruptly by running cold water into the pot. When the water in the pot is cool to the touch, reach in and lift out the squares. Lay them on a double thickness of paper toweling to drain. Blot gently.

8. Preheat the oven to 375°F. Place a heaping tablespoon of filling on the lower third of a pasta square, dabbing it in a thin line from one edge of the square to the other. Roll up the pasta rather tightly, smoothing out the filling as you go.

9. Pour enough Marinara Sauce into a 9×13-inch baking dish to cover the bottom. Arrange the cannelloni on top of the sauce, seam side down. Pour the Thin White Sauce over the cannelloni, covering all surfaces completely.

10. Pour on the remaining Marinara Sauce and cover the pan with aluminum foil. Place in the preheated oven and bake for 15 minutes. Remove the foil and bake for 15 to 20 minutes more or until bubbling hot. Sprinkle with freshly grated Parmesan to serve.

(See entries for Pasta; White Sauce; Bouquet Garni.) ◄ʑ

Lasagne Verdi Bolognese

SERVES 8 TO 10

In this dramatic preparation, layers of green spinach pasta alternate with a savory meat sauce, punctuated by the earthy flavor of finely chopped chicken livers. This particular sauce, or ragù, *is commonly referred to as Sauce Bolognese and may be served in its own right over fettuccine or as an accompaniment to sautéed veal scallops.*

½ pound fresh spinach
1 pound fresh pasta dough (p. 304 or p. 305)

SAUCE BOLOGNESE
6 tablespoons butter
¼ pound prosciutto, coarsely chopped
1 large onion, finely chopped
2 medium carrots, finely chopped
3 ribs celery, finely chopped
1 garlic clove, minced or pressed
1 ounce dried Porcini mushrooms (see Note)
2 tablespoons vegetable oil
¾ pound ground extra-lean beef

¼ pound ground extra-lean pork
½ cup dry white wine
2 cups beef broth
1 can (35 ounces) Italian plum tomatoes, drained and chopped
1 teaspoon dried marjoram
½ teaspoon salt
Generous amount of freshly ground black pepper
2 chicken livers, finely chopped
3 tablespoons chopped fresh parsley

THIN WHITE SAUCE
1 recipe Thin White Sauce (p. 308)
¾ cup freshly grated Parmesan cheese
¾ cup freshly grated mozzarella

1. Wash the spinach and remove the tough stems. Plunge the spinach into boiling water and stir frequently to keep it submerged. Cook uncovered until the water returns to a vigorous boil. Transfer the spinach to a colander and drain under cold running water. Take up the cooled spinach by handfuls and squeeze dry. Mince finely. Place in an 8-inch skillet and cook, stirring constantly, until no more steam rises and the spinach begins to stick to the bottom of the pan. Remove from the heat.

2. Prepare the pasta dough according to the directions under Egg Pasta I (p. 304) or Egg Pasta II (p. 305), stirring the prepared spinach into the egg mixture and working it into the dough along with the egg.

3. Roll out half the dough and return the remaining half to an airtight plastic bag. Cut the rolled pasta into 3×4-inch strips. Arrange them in a single layer on a surface coated with cornmeal. Roll and cut the remaining pasta. Set aside the strips in a single layer.

4. Meanwhile, prepare the Sauce Bolognese. Melt 4 tablespoons of the butter in a wide saucepan or Dutch oven. Add the prosciutto, onion, carrots, celery, and garlic, tossing to coat. Cover the pan and cook over low heat for 30 minutes or until the vegetables are tender. Cover the dried mushrooms with warm tap water and set aside to soften.

5. In a 12-inch skillet, heat the vegetable oil and add the ground beef and pork. Cook over high heat, stirring continuously, until the meat is no longer pink. Do not allow it to brown. Pour in the wine and continue stirring over high heat until the wine is completely evaporated. Add the meat to the cooked vegetables. Stir in the broth, tomatoes, marjoram, salt, and pepper. Lift the softened mushrooms from their liquid with a fork and chop finely. Add to the simmering sauce. Pour in the mushroom liquid, straining if necessary to eliminate particles of sand. Regulate the heat so that the sauce bubbles gently and cook uncovered for 45 minutes or until thickened.

6. Melt the remaining 2 tablespoons of butter in a 6-inch skillet. Add the chicken livers and place over medium heat. Cook, stirring constantly, until the liver turns tan and begins to disintegrate. When the sauce reaches the desired thickness, stir in the cooked chicken liver and parsley. Simmer uncovered for 10 minutes.

7. Prepare the Thin White Sauce according to the directions in step 6 under Cannelloni (p. 308). Combine the grated Parmesan and mozzarella in a large mixing bowl. Toss to combine thoroughly. Set aside.

8. To assemble the dish, begin by bringing a large pot of salted water to a vigorous boil. Drop in the pasta strips and stir gently with a wooden fork to separate the pieces. Return to a moderate boil and cook uncovered until tender. Halt the cooking abruptly by running cold water into the pot. When the water in the pot is cool to the touch, reach in and lift out the strips of pasta. Lay them on a double thickness of paper toweling to drain. Blot gently.

9. Preheat the oven to 425°F. Generously butter the bottom and sides of a 9×13-inch baking dish. Cover the bottom with a thin coating of Sauce Bolognese. Arrange a layer of pasta strips over the sauce in such a way that they hang out about 3 inches over the edge of the dish on all four sides. Don't be concerned if some of the pasta strips overlap.

10. Spoon Sauce Bolognese over the strips of pasta in a thin layer. Sprinkle on one-third

of the grated cheese and pour a thin coating of Thin White Sauce over all. Cover with additional pasta strips, cutting them to fit inside the dish, and repeat the layering procedure two more times, ending with a layer of Thin White Sauce. Fold in the overhanging pasta strips on both ends of the baking dish, then fold in the strips down each side. Pour a final coating of Thin White Sauce over the top and dot with butter. Place in the preheated oven and bake for 30 to 40 minutes or until the lasagna has puffed and developed a golden crust. Allow the dish to rest at room temperature for 15 minutes to facilitate cutting into serving portions.

NOTE: Dried Porcini mushrooms, imported from Italy, are available from gourmet shops or by mail order. (See Appendix.)   ◁

Fettuccine with Pesto Sauce

SERVES 2

Unlike many recipes for basil-based pesto, this version produces a creamy sauce with a lighter-than-usual basil flavoring. Presented as a first course, it will serve 4.

Generous handful of fresh basil leaves (about
    eighteen 2½-inch leaves)
¼ cup butter
¼ cup olive oil
¼ cup freshly grated Asiago or Parmesan cheese
¼ cup pine nuts (or substitute walnuts)
1 garlic clove
¼ teaspoon salt
Generous amount of freshly ground black pepper
½ pound fettuccine
½ cup reserved hot pasta cooking water

1. Wash the basil leaves and pat dry with paper towels.

2. Combine the butter, olive oil, cheese, nuts, garlic, and salt in the container of a processor or blender or in a mortar. Whirl or pound to a paste. Incorporate the basil leaves until the paste takes on a bright green hue. Blend in the pepper. Refrigerate.

3. Cook the fettuccine in boiling salted water until tender. Remove ½ cup hot pasta water and drain the fettuccine.

4. Transfer the cooked fettuccine to a large skillet. Stir 2 tablespoons of the hot pasta water into the pesto sauce to lighten it. Pour the remaining water over the fettuccine and toss to coat. Place over medium-low heat, add the pesto sauce, and continue tossing until the sauce smoothly coats the pasta. Serve immediately, accompanied by additional grated cheese.   ◁

Fettuccine Verdi with Prosciutto Sauce

SERVES 4

Not only does this simple dish taste great, it looks beautiful. Green noodles topped with a vivid red sauce is a feast for the eye as well as the palate. Serves 8 as a first course.

½ pound prosciutto, thinly sliced
2 tablespoons olive oil
2 tablespoons butter
1 garlic clove, halved crosswise
2 cans (35 ounces each) Italian tomatoes,
    undrained
1 teaspoon sugar
2 tablespoons chopped fresh basil (or substitute
    2 teaspoons dried)
2 tablespoons chopped fresh parsley
Generous amount of freshly ground black pepper
1 pound spinach fettuccine

1. Starting from the wide edge, roll up the slices of prosciutto. Cut the rolls into thin slices and set aside.

2. In a thick-bottomed saucepan, heat the oil and butter over medium heat. When the butter is melted, add the garlic and cook, stirring, until the garlic begins to turn golden. Do not allow it to brown because that would create a bitter taste. Remove the garlic with a slotted spoon and discard.

3. Stir the slivered prosciutto into the hot fat and cook over medium heat until the

prosciutto fat begins to curl. Add the tomatoes, breaking them up with your fingers as you add them. Blend in the sugar. Cook uncovered for 30 minutes or until the sauce is slightly thickened. Add the basil, parsley, and pepper, and cook uncovered for 15 to 20 minutes or until the herbs have released all their flavor.

4. Meanwhile, cook the fettuccine in boiling salted water until tender. Drain and serve immediately, topped with the hot sauce. ◅

Linguine Carbonara

SERVES 2 OR 4

In this recipe, I've taken the unconventional liberty of suggesting that you break the strands of linguine in half. I found, quite by accident, that it's much easier to coat each strand with the thick, creamy sauce if they aren't so tangled, and the difference in length is scarcely noticeable. This version is exceptionally rich and creamy because of the number of eggs and the use of heavy cream. Consequently, a small portion makes an adequate luncheon dish or after-theater snack.

½ pound sliced bacon
1¼ teaspoons salt
½ pound linguine (or substitute fettuccine if you
    prefer)
4 large egg yolks
1 cup heavy cream
½ cup freshly grated Parmesan cheese
1½ teaspoons chopped fresh sage (or substitute
    ½ teaspoon dried)
Generous amount of freshly ground black pepper

1. Fry the bacon in a large skillet. Drain on a double thickness of paper toweling, and then break into bite-size pieces. Set aside.

2. Fill a 6-quart pot with water. Add 1 teaspoon of salt and cover. Bring to a rolling boil. Break the linguine in half and drop into the water. Immediately stir with a wooden fork to separate the strands. Return to a moderate boil and cook uncovered until tender.

3. Meanwhile, pass the egg yolks through a sieve into a medium-size bowl. Add the heavy cream and whisk until well blended. Stir in the Parmesan, sage, remaining ¼ teaspoon salt, and pepper.

4. Drain the cooked linguine in a colander and transfer to a 12-inch skillet. Pour on the egg mixture and toss to combine. Place over medium heat. Cook, tossing the linguine continuously, until the mixture begins to thicken. Scatter the bacon pieces over the linguine. Toss to incorporate the bacon. When the sauce reaches a thick, creamy consistency, serve immediately. ◅

Linguine Marinara

SERVES 4

Serve this aromatic dish with sourdough bread and a crisp green salad.

4 tablespoons olive oil
2 tablespoons butter
1 large onion, coarsely chopped
8 ounces fresh mushrooms, quartered
2 garlic cloves, minced or pressed
1 cup dry white wine
1 cup clam juice
1 can (28 ounces) crushed tomatoes
2½ pounds haddock (or substitute other firm
    white fish)
Two 2-inch strips of fresh orange zest
2 bay leaves, broken in half
⅛ teaspoon saffron threads, pulverized with a
    mortar and pestle, and then steeped in ¼ cup
    boiling water
1 king crab leg, cooked (or substitute 6 ounces
    frozen)
12 medium shrimp
12 littleneck clams
2 tablespoons Pernod
20 large fresh basil leaves, chopped (or
    substitute 1 teaspoon dried)
2 tablespoons chopped fresh parsley
1½ teaspoons salt
Generous amount of freshly ground black pepper
1 pound linguine
Freshly grated Asiago or Parmesan cheese

5. Remove the orange zest and bay leaves from the sauce. Stir in the remaining 1½ pounds haddock, crabmeat, shrimp, and clams. Cook at a gentle bubble until the clams open and release their juices. (Discard any that refuse to open.) Serve over linguine in large, shallow bowls or rimmed plates. Pass freshly grated Asiago or Parmesan cheese.   ❧

Cavatelli with Gorgonzola Sauce

SERVES 4

Shops selling fresh pasta in larger cities often carry these short curled noodles, and a frozen version is also available in many supermarkets. If you can't find them, use the dried, commercial variety. Serves 8 as a first course.

1 pound *cavatelli*
½ cup butter
8 ounces Gorgonzola cheese
2 cups medium, or whipping, cream
2 tablespoons cognac
½ cup pine nuts
½ teaspoon salt
Generous amount of freshly ground black pepper
1 cup freshly grated Parmesan cheese
15 medium to large fresh basil leaves, finely chopped

1. Fill a 6-quart pot with water. Cover and place over high heat. Bring to a vigorous boil. Stir in the *cavatelli* with a wooden fork to separate pasta. Return to a moderate boil and cook uncovered until tender.

2. Meanwhile, melt the butter in a 12-inch skillet. Crumble in the Gorgonzola and add the cream. Cook over medium heat until the cream bubbles gently and the cheese is melted. Blend in the cognac and nuts. Season with salt and pepper. Reduce the heat and continue cooking until slightly thickened.

3. Drain the cooked pasta and transfer to the skillet. Sprinkle on the Parmesan and toss to coat the noodles with sauce. Serve immediately, sprinkled with the chopped basil.   ❧

1. In a thick-bottomed Dutch oven or 6-quart saucepan, heat the olive oil and butter until the butter melts. Add the onion, mushrooms, and garlic and toss to coat. Reduce the heat to its lowest setting. Cover the pan and cook about 20 minutes or until the mushrooms are tender.

2. Add the wine, clam juice, and tomatoes. Increase the heat until the liquid bubbles gently. Cut the haddock into 1-inch chunks and add about 1 pound to the mixture. Set aside the rest. Remove the orange zest with a swivel-blade peeler and drop in. Stir in the bay leaves and softened saffron with its steeping water. Simmer uncovered for 45 minutes.

3. Remove the crabmeat from the shell and cut into bite-size chunks. Peel the soft shell from the shrimp, leaving the tail intact. Cut down the back of the shrimp and remove the dark intestinal vein. Scrub the clams under running water using a toothbrush to remove sand from the seam where the shells meet. Set aside.

4. Add the Pernod, basil, parsley, ½ teaspoon salt, and pepper to the simmering sauce. Continue cooking for 15 minutes. Meanwhile, fill a 6- to 8-quart pot with water and bring to a boil. Add 1 teaspoon salt and the linguine.

Conchiglie with Vegetables and Ham

SERVES 4

Conchiglie, *or conch shells, are the perfectly shaped pasta for this quick, easy-to-prepare dish. As you toss the pasta, the shell cavities collect and hold generous amounts of cheesy rich sauce.*

3 cups small shells (about ¾ pound)
4 slender carrots
8 ounces fresh mushrooms
1 cup frozen peas
6 thin slices prosciutto or baked ham
2 large egg yolks
2 cups medium, or whipping, cream
½ cup freshly grated Parmesan cheese
3 tablespoons olive oil
3 tablespoons butter
¼ teaspoon salt
Generous amount of freshly ground black pepper

1. Cook the shells in boiling salted water until tender. Drain and use immediately, or rinse with cold water to remove excess starch and set aside.

2. Meanwhile, prepare the vegetables by peeling the carrots with a swivel-blade peeler and cutting them into julienne strips about 2 inches long. Wash, dry, and slice the mushrooms. Set out the peas to defrost. (They don't need to be cooked before adding.) Roll up the ham, starting from the wide edge, and slice thinly.

3. Pass the egg yolks through a sieve into a small bowl. Add 1 cup of the cream and whisk to blend. Stir in the cheese.

4. In a 12-inch skillet, heat the olive oil and butter over medium-high heat. When the butter is melted, add the carrots and cook, stirring continuously (as you would stir-fry). When the carrots are tender, but still crunchy, add the mushrooms and continue stirring until tender. Add the ham and cook, stirring, until warmed through. Remove the pan from the heat and stir in the defrosted peas.

5. Blend in the cream mixture, salt, and pepper and return to low heat. Stir constantly and bring to a simmer. Increase the heat gradually until the mixture is bubbly and begins to thicken. Slowly pour in the remaining cup of cream to thin the sauce to a light, creamy consistency. Add the cooked shells and toss to combine.   ❧

Farfalle with Walnut Sauce

SERVES 4

Similar in consistency to the well-known basil-flavored pesto, this sauce may be served with any form of egg pasta, boiled potatoes, or gnocchi. Serves 8 as a first course.

4 tablespoons olive oil
8 ounces walnut halves or pieces
½ cup butter
½ cup freshly grated Asiago or Parmesan cheese
1 garlic clove
¼ teaspoon salt
Generous amount of freshly ground black pepper
1 pound farfalle (small bow-shaped egg pasta)
⅔ cup medium, or whipping, cream

1. In a 12-inch skillet, heat the olive oil and add the walnuts. Cook over medium heat, stirring continuously, until the walnuts are lightly browned (5 to 8 minutes). Do not drain. Set aside to cool.

2. Transfer the cooled walnuts and oil to the container of a blender or processor or to a mortar. Add the butter, cheese, garlic, and salt. Whirl or pound to a paste. The final consistency should be smooth but somewhat grainy. Blend in the pepper and refrigerate.

3. Cook the farfalle in boiling salted water until tender. Meanwhile, warm the cream, but don't allow it to boil.

4. Drain the cooked farfalle and transfer to a large skillet. Stir 2 tablespoons of the warm cream into the walnut sauce to lighten it. Pour the remaining cream over the farfalle and toss to coat. Place over medium-low

heat, add the walnut sauce, and continue tossing until the sauce smoothly coats the pasta. Serve immediately with additional grated cheese. ◄ॐ

Baked Macaroni and Cheese

SERVES 4

Considered by most cooks to be a humble, thoroughly American dish, this is essentially pasta dressed with a Mornay sauce. One of my favorite variations is made with Monterey Jack cheese, but Cheddar, the traditional choice, also makes a delicious casserole. You might want to experiment with using Edam, Gouda, Danish fontina, Havarti, Muenster, or brick, which like Monterey Jack is one of the few truly American cheeses.

½ **pound elbow macaroni**
2 **cups White Sauce with Milk (p. 348)**
Salt and freshly ground white pepper
½ **pound Monterey Jack, Cheddar, or other**
  cheese, grated
2 **tablespoons butter**
4 **tablespoons dry, unseasoned bread crumbs**

1. Preheat the oven to 375°F. Fill a 6-quart pot with water. Cover and place over high heat. Bring to a vigorous boil. Stir in the macaroni with a wooden fork to separate the pieces. Return to a moderate boil and cook uncovered until tender. Pour into a colander and *rinse thoroughly* under cold running water. Shake the colander gently from side to side to drain. Set aside.

2. Meanwhile, prepare a double recipe of White Sauce with Milk. Season generously with salt and freshly ground white pepper. Stir in the grated cheese and blend over medium heat until melted. (The sauce should be thin enough to pour smoothly from a spoon. If it seems too thick, blend in additional milk.) Combine the sauce and drained macaroni and transfer to a generously buttered 2½-quart casserole.

3. In a 6-inch skillet, melt the butter and add the bread crumbs, tossing to combine. Scatter the buttered crumbs over the top of the macaroni. Bake uncovered for 30 minutes, or until the sauce is bubbly and the bread crumbs are nicely browned.

NOTE: Baked macaroni that has a consistency like library paste is often caused by not rinsing the surface starch from the cooked pasta. To achieve the proper consistency, rinse the macaroni thoroughly before combining with the sauce. ◄ॐ

Orzo

SERVES 6

This rice-shaped pasta may be cooked in boiling water and drained like pasta or sautéed in fat and baked in broth as you would prepare rice pilaf.

4 **tablespoons butter**
1 **medium onion, finely chopped**
1½ **cups orzo**
3 **cups chicken broth**
1 **teaspoon dried chervil**
6 **tablespoons freshly grated Parmesan cheese**

1. Preheat the oven to 350°F. Melt the butter in a wide 1½-quart stove-top-to-oven casserole. Add the onion and toss to coat. Cover the pan and cook over low heat for 5 minutes or until the onion is translucent. Add the orzo and stir to coat the pasta grains with butter. Stir briefly over low heat.

2. Meanwhile bring the broth to a vigorous boil. Pour the hot broth over the butter-coated orzo and bring to a boil. Stir in the chervil. Cover immediately and place in the preheated oven. Bake for 10 minutes. Uncover and continue cooking for 5 to 10 minutes or until the pasta is tender and has absorbed the chicken broth. Stir the cheese into the hot orzo and serve immediately.

NOTE: To serve boiled orzo, begin by bringing a pot of water to a vigorous boil. Add the pasta and cook uncovered at a gentle bubble for 10 to 15 minutes. Drain in a colander and toss with butter or cheese. Like rice, properly cooked orzo should offer some resistance to the teeth.   ❧

Risotto Milanese

SERVES 4

To achieve the proper consistency of this Northern Italian rice dish, use the slightly starchy Arborio rice, a short-grain variety imported from Italy. The traditional cooking technique involves constant stirring, which ruptures the surface starch molecules, producing the desired creamy consistency.

4½ cups chicken broth
⅛ teaspoon or a generous pinch saffron threads, pulverized with a mortar and pestle
6 tablespoons butter
2 tablespoons beef marrow, coarsely chopped
1 medium onion, finely chopped
1½ cups Arborio rice
½ cup dry white wine
⅓ cup freshly grated Parmesan cheese
Salt and freshly ground black pepper to taste

1. Bring the broth to a boil in a 2½-quart saucepan. Ladle ½ cup of hot broth into a small bowl. Stir in the pulverized saffron and allow it to steep. Set aside. Reduce the heat under the pan until the broth barely simmers.

2. In a wide, thick-bottomed sauté pan or deep skillet, melt 3 tablespoons of the butter over medium-high heat. Add the marrow and cook, stirring, until the marrow is translucent and has broken up into very small pieces. Stir in the onion and cook until soft.

3. Blend in the rice, stirring to coat the surface of each kernel with butter. Continue stirring over medium-high heat until the rice turns opaque. Blend in the wine and the ½ cup of reserved saffron-broth. Stir continuously until all the liquid is absorbed.

4. Add the simmering broth to the rice one ladleful at a time. Stir over medium-high heat with a wooden spoon or spatula until the rice absorbs all the liquid. When the bottom of the pan is dry and the rice appears ready to stick to the pan, stir in another ladleful of broth. Repeat this procedure for about 20 minutes, in which time nearly all the broth will have been used. Test the rice by biting a kernel. It should be tender but still resistant to the teeth. Continue stirring and adding hot broth until the rice is done. (You may not need to add the entire amount.)

5. Remove the rice from the heat. Allow it to stand uncovered for 1 minute. Meanwhile, cut the remaining 3 tablespoons of butter into small chunks. Gently blend in the chunks of butter and the cheese until the butter is melted and a creamy consistency develops. Season with salt and pepper to taste; however, reduced broth can be extremely salty, so you may not need additional salt at this point.   ❧

American-Style Risotto

SERVES 4

By using converted rice, it's possible to produce a risotto that cooks without constant stirring. The result is a drier, less creamy consistency than that of the traditional risotto.

2 tablespoons olive oil
4 tablespoons butter
1 medium onion, finely chopped
6 thin slices prosciutto, coarsely chopped
1 cup converted rice
½ cup dry white wine
1¾ cups chicken broth
Generous pinch saffron threads, pulverized with a mortar and pestle
¼ cup boiling water
½ cup freshly grated Parmesan cheese
Salt and pepper to taste

1. In a wide, thick-bottomed saucepan, heat the oil and 2 tablespoons of the butter until the butter melts. Add the onion and toss to coat. Cook over low heat, stirring constantly, until the onion is wilted. Stir in the prosciutto and rice. Increase the heat slightly

and cook, stirring, until the prosciutto fat begins to curl and the rice turns opaque.

2. Add the wine and cook over high heat until all the moisture evaporates. Stir in the broth and bring to a boil. Immediately reduce the heat to its lowest setting and cover the pan. Cook for 15 minutes.

3. Meanwhile, in a small bowl, steep the saffron in ¼ cup boiling water. When the rice has cooked for 15 minutes, stir in the softened saffron and water. Replace the cover and continue cooking for 5 to 7 minutes or until tender, but still resistant to the teeth.

4. Remove from the heat and gently stir in the remaining 2 tablespoons of butter and the Parmesan cheese. (Using the blade of a kitchen knife to stir helps keep the rice intact.) Season to taste with salt and pepper only if needed. ❧

Lemon Rice

SERVES 4

Laced with fresh lemon juice, this zesty rice dish is the perfect partner for broiled fish or chicken.

2¼ cups water
½ teaspoon salt
1 cup converted rice
3 large eggs
2 tablespoons fresh lemon juice
¾ cup freshly grated Asiago or Parmesan cheese
3 tablespoons butter
Generous amount of freshly ground black pepper
Lemon slices and fresh parsley to garnish

1. Bring the water to a boil in a wide, thick-bottomed saucepan and add the salt. Gradually pour in the rice, stirring to separate the kernels. Reduce the heat to its lowest setting and cover the pan. Cook for 17 to 20 minutes or until tender but still resistant to the teeth.

2. Meanwhile, whisk the eggs and lemon juice together in a small bowl until slightly thickened. Blend in the cheese. Set aside.

3. Remove the cooked rice from the heat and stir in the butter until it is melted and

absorbed. Pour in the egg mixture. Add the pepper and mix gently with a heat-resistant rubber spatula to avoid crushing the rice.

4. Return to medium heat and cook, stirring with the spatula, until the eggs thicken the rice to a creamy consistency. Garnish with lemon slices and fresh parsley if you wish and serve immediately.   ❧

Rice Fritters

MAKES 12 FRITTERS

Flavored with finely chopped mushrooms and thyme, these rice pancakes make a delightful accompaniment for roasted or grilled meats.

2 tablespoons vegetable oil
2 tablespoons butter
1 medium onion, finely chopped
6 ounces fresh mushrooms, finely chopped
1 cup converted rice
2¼ cups chicken broth
½ teaspoon dried leaf thyme
½ teaspoon dried chervil
1 bay leaf, broken in half
3 ounces Gruyère or fontina cheese, freshly grated
Salt and freshly ground black pepper to taste
1 large egg
¾ cup dry, unseasoned bread crumbs

1. In a wide, thick-bottomed saucepan, heat the oil and butter until the butter melts. Add the onion and toss to coat. Cook over medium heat until the onion is translucent. Add the mushrooms and cook, stirring, until they release most of their moisture and become soft.

2. Add the rice and cook, stirring, until it turns opaque. Add the broth all at once and bring to a boil. Stir in the thyme, chervil, and bay leaf. Reduce the heat to its lowest setting and cover the pan. Cook for 20 minutes or until tender yet resistant to the teeth.

3. Remove from the heat. Lift out the bay leaf and stir in the grated cheese. Season with

salt and pepper and empty into a bowl. Allow to cool to room temperature.

4. Whisk the egg and blend into the cooled rice. Scoop out by ¼ cupfuls and form into patties on a baking sheet lined with waxed paper. Chill for 30 to 45 minutes or until firm to the touch. Coat the patties with bread crumbs and cook on a hot griddle lightly brushed with vegetable oil. When the underside is nicely browned, turn and cook the second side.   ◄ℨ

Baked Beans with Bacon

SERVES 6 TO 8

No matter how sophisticated food preferences become, certain dishes will always remain popular because they are comforting, sustaining, and, in most cases, part of our heritage. The following recipe is a spicy, robust variation of the traditional New England baked bean casserole.

1 pound dried navy beans (also called pea beans)
½ pound sliced bacon, cut into 1-inch lengths
1 large onion, coarsely chopped
1 garlic clove, minced or pressed
1 teaspoon dry mustard
½ cup cold water
½ cup molasses
⅓ cup ketchup
⅓ cup light brown sugar
½ teaspoon salt
⅛ teaspoon ground cloves
Generous amount of freshly ground black pepper

1. Pour the dried beans into a colander and rinse under cold running water. Pick through the beans, discarding any small stones or discolored beans. Transfer the beans to a large bowl and soak overnight according to the directions in step 1 under White Beans Baked with Fruit (p. 319), or place the rinsed beans in a 2½-quart saucepan. Add enough warm water from the tap to cover the beans by 2

inches, and quick-soak by placing the pan over medium heat and bringing the water to a gentle bubble. Boil uncovered for 2 minutes, then cover the pan and remove from the heat. Allow the beans to soak in the hot water for 1 hour without removing the cover to the pan.

2. Drain the softened beans in a colander and return them to the saucepan. Once again, add enough warm water to cover the beans by 2 inches. Place over medium heat and bring to a gentle bubble. Boil uncovered for 10 minutes. Regulate the heat so that the liquid barely bubbles, cover the pan, and cook slowly for 1½ to 2 hours or until a bean can be easily crushed between your thumb and forefinger. Drain in a colander and transfer to a deep 2½-quart baking dish or old-fashioned bean pot.

3. In a 12-inch skillet, fry the bacon until it is lightly browned. Remove the skillet from the heat and transfer the bacon to the baking dish with a slotted spoon. Add the onion and garlic to the bacon fat, tossing to coat. Place over medium-low heat and cook, stirring constantly, until the onion becomes limp. Remove the pan from the heat.

4. Preheat the oven to 375°F. In a small bowl, sprinkle the dry mustard over the cold water and stir to dissolve. Add the molasses, ketchup, brown sugar, salt, cloves, and freshly ground pepper. Blend thoroughly and add to the onions in the skillet. Place over high heat and bring to a vigorous boil. Pour the hot sauce over the beans and stir to distribute evenly. Cover the baking dish and place in the preheated oven. Bake for 1 hour. Remove the cover and bake uncovered for an additional 30 minutes.   ◄ℨ

Mexican Pinto Bean Casserole

SERVES 6 TO 8

A hearty one-dish meal to serve on a cold winter's night. Adjust the vibrancy of the

sauce by incorporating crushed red pepper and serve piping hot with squares of steaming cornbread.

1 pound dried pinto beans
2 tablespoons olive oil
¾ pound boneless lean pork, cut into 1-inch
 pieces
1 can (28 ounces) crushed tomatoes
½ cup dry red wine
1 large red onion, coarsely chopped
1 large green sweet bell pepper, seeded and
 coarsely chopped
2 garlic cloves, minced or pressed
1 can (7 ounces) green chili salsa
1 teaspoon dried oregano
½ teaspoon ground cumin
½ teaspoon salt
Generous amount of freshly ground black pepper
 (or substitute crushed red pepper)
½ teaspoon Worcestershire sauce

1. Pour the dried beans into a colander and rinse under cold running water. Pick through the beans, discarding any small stones or discolored beans. Transfer the beans to a large bowl and soak overnight according to the directions in step 1 under White Beans Baked with Fruit (p. 319), or place the rinsed beans in a 2½-quart saucepan and quick-soak according to the directions in step 1 under Baked Beans with Bacon (p. 318).

2. Drain the softened beans in a colander and transfer to a 2½-quart saucepan. Once again, add enough warm water from the tap to cover the beans by 2 inches. Place over medium heat and bring to a gentle bubble. Boil uncovered for 10 minutes. Regulate the heat so that the liquid barely bubbles, cover the pan, and cook slowly for 1 to 2½ hours, depending on the soaking method you used. When a bean can be easily crushed between your thumb and forefinger, drain the beans in a colander. Transfer to a deep 2½-quart baking dish.

3. Preheat the oven to 350°F. In a 12-inch skillet, heat the olive oil and add the pork, tossing to coat. Cook over high heat, stirring constantly, until the pork is well browned.

Add the tomatoes, wine, onion, green pepper, and garlic. Regulate the heat so that the mixture bubbles gently. Stir in the green chili salsa, oregano, cumin, salt, pepper, and Worcestershire sauce. Cook, stirring occasionally, for 10 minutes. Pour over the prepared beans and stir gently to combine.

4. Cover the baking dish and place in the preheated oven. Bake for 1 hour. If you prefer drier beans with a crusty surface, remove the cover and bake for 30 minutes more.　　⋐

White Beans Baked with Fruit

SERVES 6 TO 8

The following recipe describes the method used to rehydrate dried beans by soaking them overnight. A speedier approach, the quick-soak method, is described in step 1 under Baked Beans with Bacon (p. 318). These two preliminary techniques may be used interchangeably; however, beans that are soaked quickly do not absorb moisture evenly, so the overnight method of soaking is considered by most cooks to be superior.

1 pound dried white beans, such as Great
 Northern or baby lima
1 cup cold water
2 teaspoons Dijon mustard
1 medium onion, coarsely chopped
½ cup chutney, coarsely chopped
½ teaspoon salt
Generous amount of freshly ground black pepper
½ cup honey
¼ cup molasses
2 fresh tart apples, peeled, cored, and chopped
1 cup canned crushed pineapple, drained

1. Pour the dried beans into a colander and rinse under cold running water. Pick through the beans, discarding any small stones or discolored beans. Transfer the beans to a 2½-quart saucepan and quick-soak according to the directions in step 1 under Baked Beans with Bacon (p. 318), or place the rinsed beans

in a large bowl. Add enough warm tap water to cover the beans by 2 inches. Cover the bowl with a kitchen towel and set aside to soak for 12 hours or overnight.

2. Drain the softened beans in a colander and transfer to a 2½-quart saucepan. Once again, add enough warm tap water to cover the beans by 2 inches. Place over medium heat and bring to a gentle bubble. Boil uncovered for 10 minutes. Regulate the heat so that the liquid barely bubbles, cover the pan, and cook slowly for 1 hour or until a bean can be easily crushed between your thumb and forefinger. Drain in a colander and set aside.

3. Preheat the oven to 350°F. In a small bowl, combine the water, mustard, onion, chutney, salt, and pepper. Blend in the honey and molasses. Generously butter a deep 2½-quart baking dish. Pour in half the prepared beans and top with half of the chopped apple and half of the pineapple. Pour on the rest of the beans and top with the remaining fruit. Pour on the sauce, parting the beans in several places with the blade of a kitchen knife to insure that the sauce is evenly distributed. Cover the baking dish and place in the preheated oven. Bake for 1 hour. Remove the cover and bake uncovered for an additional 30 minutes. Serve as a side dish to baked ham or roast pork.   ◄ð

Kasha Pilaf

SERVES 4

The toasted ground kernels of buckwheat known as kasha can be cooked slowly in broth in the same manner as rice pilaf. In the following recipe, sautéed onions and chervil lend flavor while sliced mushrooms provide textural contrast.

4 tablespoons butter
8 ounces fresh mushrooms, sliced
1 medium onion, coarsely chopped
1 teaspoon dried chervil
2 cups chicken broth
1 large egg

1 cup coarsely ground, uncooked kasha
½ teaspoon salt
Generous amount of freshly ground black pepper

1. Melt the butter in a 12-inch skillet. Add the mushrooms, tossing to coat. Place over medium-high heat and cook, stirring, until the mushrooms begin to release their liquid. Add the onion and continue stirring until the onion is tender. Stir in the chervil and remove the pan from the heat.

2. Pour the chicken broth into a 1½-quart saucepan and place over medium heat. In a large mixing bowl, beat the egg and add the kasha, stirring to coat the individual kernels with egg. Add to the cooked mushrooms and return to medium-high heat. Stirring constantly, cook the kasha until the egg coating is set. Sprinkle with salt and pepper and remove from the heat.

3. Stir the hot broth into the egg-coated kasha and return to the heat. When the mixture begins to boil, reduce the heat to low. Cover the pan tightly and cook for 15 to 20 minutes or until the kernels are tender and most of the liquid is absorbed. Serve as an accompaniment to lamb or chicken.   ◄ð

Polenta Triangles

MAKES ABOUT 20 TRIANGLES

Thin slices of polenta, enriched with Bel Paese cheese, are sautéed in butter and oil until lightly browned. They can be served plain with roasted meat or poultry, or sauced with Buttered Tomato Sauce (p. 351) and served as a first course.

2 cups yellow cornmeal
9 cups water
1 teaspoon salt
6 ounces Bel Paese cheese, grated or diced
½ cup freshly grated Parmesan cheese
4 tablespoons butter
Equal portions of oil and butter for frying

1. Generously butter the bottom and sides of a 2-quart rectangular baking dish (about 7×11 inches). In a 4-cup measure, disperse

the cornmeal in 1 cup of the water to prevent lumping.

2. Bring the remaining 8 cups of water and the salt to a boil in a 4½- to 6-quart thick-bottomed saucepan. With the water bubbling vigorously, pour in the cornmeal-and-water mixture. Stir continuously. When the mixture returns to a boil, reduce the heat and cook uncovered at a gentle bubble for 20 minutes. Stir occasionally during the first 10 minutes, but as the water evaporates and the polenta thickens, stir continuously to prevent scorching.

3. Blend in the cheeses and continue cooking, stirring continuously. Polenta is thickened completely when a spoon can stand upright in the center without being held. Remove from the heat and stir in the butter. Pour into the prepared dish, smoothing the top with a knife. Refrigerate until cool and firm (about 4 hours).

4. Turn out onto a cutting board. Trim the perimeter by slicing off the slightly rounded edges. Then cut polenta into 10 rectangles, each measuring approximately 2×3½ inches. Cut each rectangle from corner to corner to form triangles.

5. Fry the triangles in a blend of vegetable oil and butter (equal portions of each). When lightly browned, drain on absorbent paper. ◆⋛

Polenta Pâté

SERVES 8

Layered with a wild mushroom and tomato sauce, this colorful, aromatic loaf can be

sliced and served as a first course or as an accompaniment to roast meat, poultry, or game.

POLENTA
2 cups yellow cornmeal
9 cups water
1 teaspoon salt
½ cup freshly grated Asiago or Parmesan cheese
4 tablespoons butter

SAUCE
1½ ounces dried Porcini mushrooms (see Note, p. 311)
4 tablespoons butter
1 medium onion, finely chopped
1 garlic clove, minced or pressed
8 ounces fresh mushrooms, coarsely chopped
1 can (35 ounces) Italian tomatoes, drained
2 tablespoons chopped fresh parsley
¼ teaspoon salt
Generous amount of freshly ground black pepper
4 ounces fontina cheese, grated

1. Generously butter a 9×5-inch loaf pan. In a 4-cup measure, disperse the cornmeal in 1 cup of the water to prevent lumping.

2. Bring the remaining 8 cups water and the salt to a boil in a 4½- to 6-quart saucepan. With the water bubbling vigorously, pour in the cornmeal-and-water mixture. Stir continuously. When the mixture boils, reduce the heat and cook uncovered at a gentle bubble for 20 minutes. Stir occasionally during the first 10 minutes, but as the water evaporates and the polenta thickens, stir continuously to prevent scorching.

3. Blend in the grated cheese and continue cooking, stirring continuously. Polenta is thickened completely when a spoon can stand upright in the center without being held by hand. Remove from the heat and stir in the butter. Pour into the prepared loaf pan, smoothing the top with a knife. Refrigerate until cool and firm (about 4 hours).

4. To prepare the sauce, place the dried mushrooms in a small bowl and cover with

warm water to soften. Melt the butter in a large skillet and add the onion, garlic, and fresh mushrooms. Cook, stirring, over medium heat until the vegetables are limp.

5. Add the drained tomatoes, breaking them up with your fingers as they are added. Simmer gently until most of the moisture has evaporated. With a slotted spoon, lift the softened mushrooms from the bowl and chop finely. Add to the simmering sauce. Pour the rehydrating liquid into the sauce through a cheesecloth-lined sieve. Add the parsley, salt, and pepper and continue cooking slowly until the sauce is thick and the mixture begins to dry. (It will begin to stick to the pan, so watch closely.)

6. Preheat the oven to 375°F. Unmold the chilled polenta and slice horizontally into 3 layers. Place the bottom layer back in the loaf pan, spoon half the sauce over it, and sprinkle with half the grated fontina. Top with the middle layer of polenta, taking care to replace the layers in the correct order. Spoon on the remaining sauce and sprinkle on the remaining cheese. Replace the top layer of polenta. Press down gently to set the layers. Cover with aluminum foil and bake for 30 to 40 minutes or until slightly puffed. Remove from the oven and allow to stand for 10 minutes. Unmold onto a warm platter and slice to serve.   ⮜ঽ

Vegetables

Asparagus Timbales with Lemon Mousseline

SERVES 8

If you're unaccustomed to peeling asparagus, the whole idea might seem overwhelming, but with a little practice, you can actually peel a pound in less than 5 minutes. The improvement in taste and texture is immeasurable.

2 pounds fresh asparagus
3 tablespoons butter
8 green onions, thinly sliced (white portion only)
4 large eggs
½ teaspoon salt
Freshly ground white pepper
Freshly grated nutmeg
⅔ cup dry, unseasoned bread crumbs
1 cup freshly grated Gruyère cheese
1 cup medium, or whipping, cream

LEMON MOUSSELINE
2 tablespoons unsalted butter
1 medium shallot, finely minced
½ cup chicken broth
½ cup dry white wine
2 tablespoons fresh lemon juice
1 tablespoon chopped fresh tarragon leaves (or substitute 1 teaspoon dried)

1½ teaspoons chopped fresh chervil (or substitute ½ teaspoon dried)
1 cup heavy cream

1. Wash the asparagus under cold running water. Slice off the tough, woody base of the stalk by making a cut where the color begins to lighten (usually 1 to 2 inches). Cradling the tip of the asparagus in the palm of your hand, draw a swivel-blade peeler away from you in light, gentle strokes to remove only the outermost layer of tough, fibrous stalk. (Leave about 2½ inches of the tender tip unpeeled.) Tie the asparagus in bundles of 10 or 12 stalks with butcher's twine or strips of cheesecloth (see Appendix).

2. Fill a 6-quart pot with water and bring to a boil. Add the bundles to the boiling water one at a time, waiting after each addition for the water to return to a boil. (Do not cover the pot at any time because that will cause the asparagus to lose its bright color.) Regulate the heat so that the water bubbles gently and cook uncovered for 10 to 12 minutes or until the tip of a paring knife will easily slide into the middle portion of the stalk. Have a large container of cold water ready. When the asparagus is cooked, bring the container of cold water to the stove. Lifting each bundle from the boiling water, immediately plunge the asparagus into the cold water to set its color. Transfer the bundles to absorbent paper. Untie the asparagus and lay the stalks on a kitchen towel to dry. Chop coarsely and set aside.

3. Preheat the oven to 325°F. and generously butter 8 ramekins or baba molds. Melt the 3 tablespoons butter in a thick-bottomed saucepan and add the onions, tossing to coat. Stir over medium heat until the onions are tender. In a large mixing bowl, whisk the eggs, salt, white pepper, and nutmeg. Blend in the bread crumbs, cheese, and cooked onion. Heat the cream in a 1½-quart saucepan until the surface begins to wrinkle. Beating continuously, add the hot cream to the egg mixture in a thin stream. Stir in the coarsely chopped asparagus. Pour the mixture into the prepared molds, filling them almost to

the top (a slight expansion will take place during baking.)

4. Cover each mold with a square of aluminum foil and crimp loosely. Line a shallow roasting pan with a kitchen towel folded in half. Place the molds on the towel and pour in hot, but not boiling, water to a depth of 1 inch. Bake for 30 to 40 minutes or until a metal skewer inserted near the center comes out clean. Transfer the molds to a cooling rack and remove the foil. Allow the custard to stand for 5 minutes, and then run the blade of a paring knife around the edge of each custard and invert onto a serving plate.

5. To prepare Lemon Mousseline, begin by melting the butter in a 1½-quart saucepan. Add the shallot, tossing to coat. Stir over medium heat until the shallot is translucent. Blend in the broth, wine, lemon juice, tarragon, and chervil. Cook over medium heat until reduced to ½ cup. Remove from the heat and stir in ½ cup of the cream. Return to medium heat and again cook until reduced to ½ cup. Whip the remaining ½ cup of cream and set it aside. Pour the reduced sauce through a sieve. Add the whipped cream and fold gently to combine. Spoon over each timbale to serve.

(See entry for Finishing A Sauce.)

Lemon-Buttered Broccoli with Sesame Seeds

SERVES 4

Cooking broccoli by the stir-fry method preserves the vegetable's brilliant emerald color and captures its exquisite flavor. To discourage spattering, be sure the broccoli has had ample time to air dry and use as little cooking oil as possible. Test for doneness by biting into a piece. It should be tender, but still retain a degree of crunchiness.

1 bunch fresh broccoli
¼ cup sesame seeds

2 large egg yolks
⅓ cup fresh lemon juice
¼ teaspoon salt
Freshly ground white pepper
6 tablespoons butter, cut into 6 pieces
1 tablespoon vegetable oil

1. Wash the broccoli and cut off the flowerets, placing them in a colander to drain. Peel the stems with a swivel-blade peeler and slice into ½-inch lengths. Remove any tough outer skin from the base of the flowerets with a swivel-blade peeler, and halve or quarter any large flowerets so that all the flowerets are about the same size. Distribute the trimmed, drained broccoli over kitchen towels, leaving space between the pieces, and allow to air dry (about 1 hour).

2. Scatter the sesame seeds over the bottom of a shallow baking pan and place in a 350°F. oven for 10 to 15 minutes or until lightly browned. Put the egg yolks through a sieve into a wide glass jar with a screw-top lid. Add the lemon juice, salt, and white pepper and blend with a fork or small whisk until the mixture is pale yellow and creamy. Cover the jar and set aside at room temperature.

3. Place the butter in a small saucepan and set over low heat to melt and keep warm. Meanwhile, add the oil to a 12-inch skillet with a nonstick surface. Place over high heat for 30 seconds. Gently add the broccoli, and immediately begin to stir, using two wooden spatulas. As the hot oil begins to coat the broccoli, it will turn a brilliant green and sizzle furiously. Immediately, drizzle 2 or 3 tablespoons of water over the broccoli. Add only enough to stop the sizzling sound. Continue stirring the broccoli with a lifting and tossing motion.

4. As the water evaporates, the broccoli will again begin to sizzle. When the sound is quite loud, once more drizzle on enough water to stop the sizzling. Continue stirring and lifting. Repeat this procedure until the broccoli is *al dente* — that is, tender yet resistant to the teeth. Transfer the cooked broccoli to a warmed serving dish.

5. Without waiting, add the warm butter to the lemon juice mixture all at once. Screw on the lid and shake vigorously until well blended. Pour over the hot broccoli and sprinkle on the toasted sesame seeds.   ✑

Oriental Vegetables

SERVES 4

This quick and delicious vegetable side dish combines the crunchy texture and fresh taste of stir-fried broccoli, mushrooms, and sweet onion rings with the tang of a ginger root sauce. Serve with roast chicken or broiled pork chops.

1 medium bunch fresh broccoli
8 ounces fresh mushrooms
1 large sweet onion, such as Bermuda or Vidalia
1 teaspoon minced or grated fresh ginger root (see Note)
1 garlic clove, minced or pressed
¾ cup chicken broth
¼ cup Madeira
2 tablespoons naturally brewed soy sauce
2 tablespoons red wine vinegar
2 tablespoons dark brown sugar
1 tablespoon cornstarch
Few drops Tabasco sauce
Vegetable oil

1. Prepare the vegetables by trimming the broccoli into flowerets, reserving the stalks for another use. Remove any tough outer skin with a swivel-blade peeler and cut the larger flowerets in half. Wash, dry, and slice the mushrooms. Peel and cut the onion into ¼-inch slices. Separate into rings.

2. Combine ginger root with the remaining ingredients, except the vegetables, to form a sauce.

3. Pour a scant amount of vegetable oil into a large skillet or wok. The oil should barely coat the surface. Place over high heat. When the oil shimmers, add the vegetables and toss to coat with oil. Use two wooden spatulas or spoons to keep the food moving constantly.

Scoop and turn the vegetables with both hands, cooking them over high heat, until the broccoli turns a bright green and the onion rings are slightly soft but still crunchy.

4. Pour on the ginger-root sauce and cook over high heat, stirring continuously, until bubbly and thickened.

NOTE: To prepare fresh ginger root, remove the thin brown skin with a swivel-blade peeler before mincing or grating.   ✑

Cabbage Braised in Apple Juice

SERVES 4

If you've been skeptical about serving cabbage, try this method of preparation. As the cabbage cooks, it absorbs the apple juice, tempering its strong flavor and producing a mild, slightly sweet result. Cook only until the cabbage is soft but retains its crunchy character, and serve with knockwurst or fresh ham.

1 medium head of cabbage
4 tablespoons butter
1½ cups apple juice
1 teaspoon sugar
¼ teaspoon salt
Generous amount of freshly ground black pepper

1. Remove the core and shred the cabbage finely.

2. Melt the butter in a 12-inch skillet set over medium heat. Add the shredded cabbage and toss to coat with butter. Increase the heat to high and continue tossing until the cabbage begins to wilt.

3. Pour in the apple juice. Sprinkle with sugar, salt, and pepper. Mix well and cover. Reduce the heat to its lowest possible setting and cook until the cabage is soft but retains its crunchy consistency. Using tongs, transfer the cooked cabbage to a bowl or serving plate. Increase the heat and cook the liquid until it is reduced to a lightly thickened sauce. Pour over the cabbage to serve.   ✑

Butter-Glazed Finger Carrots

SERVES 6

Finger carrots, also called baby carrots or Belgian carrots, are a sweet, tender variety about the length and breadth of a finger. Packed in 12-ounce plastic bags, they are becoming more readily available in most supermarkets. The easiest approach to removing the skins is to cook the carrots unpeeled and then lift off the skins under a gentle stream of tap water.

1½ pounds fresh finger carrots
1 cup water
2 tablespoons sugar
4 tablespoons butter
2 tablespoons chopped fresh parsley
Salt and freshly ground black pepper to taste

1. Rinse the carrots under cold running water. Cut off the ends and place in a 2½-quart saucepan. Add enough cold tap water to cover the carrots by 2 inches. Place over high heat and bring to a vigorous boil. Regulate the heat so that the water bubbles gently and cook uncovered for 45 to 60 minutes or until the carrots are tender when pierced with the blade of a paring knife.

2. Halt the cooking immediately by adding cold water to the pan. Adjust the tap water to run in a slow gentle stream. Holding each carrot under the water, gently pull and scrape off the skin with the blade of a paring knife held at an angle. The result will be smooth, brilliantly colored carrots.

3. Return the peeled carrots to the saucepan. Add the 1 cup of water, the sugar, and the butter. Place over medium heat and cook uncovered for 10 to 15 minutes or until most of the water has evaporated. Add the parsley and stir over medium-low heat until all the water has evaporated and the carrots are coated with a buttery sheen. Season with salt and pepper. ❧

Carrot Croquettes

SERVES 8

A satiny smooth interior provides just the right textural contrast to the crispy crust on these golden brown patties. And the hint of tarragon makes them the perfect companion for roast or grilled lamb.

2 tablespoons vegetable oil
4 tablespoons butter
2 green onions, thinly sliced (the white portion plus 3 inches of the green part)
2 cups shredded carrots (about ⅔ pound)
5 level tablespoons all-purpose flour
1 cup milk
2 large eggs
1 tablespoon freshly chopped tarragon leaves (or substitute 1 teaspoon dried)
½ teaspoon salt
Generous amount freshly ground black pepper
1 tablespoon water
1½ cups dry, unseasoned bread crumbs

1. Heat the oil and 2 tablespoons of the butter in a 12-inch skillet. When the butter foam subsides, add the green onions and stir over medium-high heat until the onion is limp. Add the shredded carrots and toss to coat with oil and melted butter. Using 2 wooden spatulas, stir and lift the carrots constantly over medium-high heat until they become limp.

2. Add the remaining 2 tablespoons butter and stir until melted. Remove from the heat. Sprinkle on the flour and stir to blend. Return to medium heat and cook, stirring, for 1

minute. Remove from the heat. Gently stir in the milk and return to medium heat. Cook, stirring, until the mixture thickens. Remove from the heat.

3. Separate the eggs, reserving the whites. Whisk the egg yolks. Stir in a heaping table-spoonful of the hot mixture to gradually warm the yolks. Stir in a second heaping ta-blespoonful and add the tarragon, salt, and pepper. Blend back into the remaining mix-ture in the pan. Place over medium-low heat. Stir gently until the mixture makes the plop-ping sound that indicates it has reached a boil. On the second plop, immediately re-move from the heat. Pour into an ungreased 8-inch square baking pan. Cool for 30 min-utes. Then lay a paper towel over the top to absorb any remaining condensation. Cover with aluminum foil and seal tightly. Chill for 4 hours or until firm.

4. Mark off 16 equal portions with the blade of a knife. Scoop out each square and shape it into a flat pattie about 1½ to 2 inches in diameter. (Flour your fingertips if neces-sary to prevent sticking.) Whisk the reserved egg whites with 1 tablespoon of water until foamy. Dip each pattie into the egg white, and then coat with bread crumbs, pressing with your fingertips to coat completely. Cover and chill 2 to 3 hours or until firm. Fry the chilled croquettes in 2 inches of vegetable oil heated to 370°F. Cook only 2 or 3 at a time because the cold temperature of the croquettes will drastically lower the temperature of the oil. Turn occasionally to promote even brown-ing. When nicely colored, transfer to absor-bent paper to drain. Serve immediately or keep warm in a 250°F. oven.

Batter-Fried Cauliflower

SERVES 4

Flowerets of cauliflower are parboiled until nearly tender, coated with a light batter, and deep fried to a crisp, golden turn.

1 cup all-purpose flour, scoop measured
2 large eggs
½ cup water
2 tablespoons olive oil
1 teaspoon salt
1 medium head cauliflower
Vegetable oil for deep frying
½ cup freshly grated Parmesan cheese
½ cup club soda
Lime slices for garnish

1. Place the flour in a large mixing bowl and make a well in the center. Whisk the eggs, water, olive oil, and salt in another bowl and pour into the well. Stir slowly with a wooden spoon to incorporate the liquid ingredients. Cover and set aside for 1 hour.

2. Meanwhile, rinse the cauliflower under cold running water and break into flowerets. Trim the stems of the flowerets to about ¾ inch. Fill a 6-quart pot with water and bring to a vigorous boil. Drop in the flowerets one at a time so that the water remains boiling. Cook uncovered for 3 to 5 minutes or until the blade of a paring knife meets only slight resistance when inserted into the stem of a floweret. Halt the cooking immediately by adding cold water to the pot. Place a colander under cold running water and pour the cauli-flower into the colander. Rinse thoroughly and allow to drain. Lay the cauliflower on a double thickness of paper toweling and blot dry. Allow to air dry until the batter is ready.

3. Heat the vegetable oil to 375°F. Add the Parmesan cheese and club soda to the batter and stir to blend. (If the batter seems too thick, stir in additional club soda.) Using a metal or bamboo skewer, take up a floweret by inserting the skewer lengthwise into the stem. Dip into the batter to coat and transfer to the hot fat. Fry 4 or 5 flowerets at a time, turning them occasionally with a slotted spoon. When they are nicely browned, trans-fer the cooked flowerets to absorbent paper to drain. Garnish with lime.

(See entries for Batter Coating; Frying: Deep-Fat.)

Sautéed Celeriac with Cheese

SERVES 4

Peeled celeriac should be immediately submerged in acidulated water because the exposed flesh darkens quickly.

3 tablespoons fresh lemon juice
2 or 3 medium celeriac (about 1 pound)
4 tablespoons butter
Salt and freshly ground white pepper to taste
4 tablespoons freshly grated Asiago or
   Parmesan cheese

1. Have ready a large bowl of cold water acidulated with 1 tablespoon of the fresh lemon juice. Rinse the celeriac under cold running water. Remove the peel with a paring knife or with short, firm strokes of a swivel-blade peeler. Cut out all the dark spots and creases in the flesh. Using the largest slits on your grater, shred the celeriac directly into the acidulated water.

2. Fill a 6-quart pot with water and bring to a boil. Add the remaining 2 tablespoons lemon juice. Drain the celeriac in a colander and stir into the boiling water. When the water returns to a boil, allow the celeriac to boil vigorously for exactly 3 minutes and then drain in a colander.

3. Melt the butter in a 12-inch skillet or wide saucepan. Add the drained celeriac, tossing to coat. Cover the pan and reduce the heat to low. Cook for 5 minutes. Remove the cover and increase the heat to high. Cook, stirring constantly, until most of the liquid evaporates and the celeriac is tender yet slightly crunchy. Season with salt and pepper and sprinkle on the grated cheese.

(See entry for Acidulated Water.)

Corn Fritters

SERVES 4

Freshly picked corn, cut from the cob and bound with just enough batter to hold the ker-nels together, produces these memorable fritters. For hearty, down-home flavor, brush the griddle with bacon fat before cooking. Serve with fried chicken or baked ham.

4 ears fresh corn (about 1½ cups of kernels)
½ cup all-purpose flour, scoop measured
2 teaspoons baking powder
2 teaspoons sugar
½ teaspoon salt
1 large egg
¼ cup milk
2 teaspoons melted butter
Bacon fat or solid shortening

1. Cut the corn from the cobs and set aside. In a large mixing bowl, combine the flour, baking powder, sugar, and salt. Stir with a whisk or fork to blend thoroughly. Beat the egg, milk, and melted butter in a small bowl. Make a well in the center of the dry ingredients and pour in the egg mixture. Stir with a wooden spoon to incorporate, then blend in the corn.

2. Brush a griddle with bacon fat and place over medium heat. Test the temperature of the griddle by sprinkling a few drops of cold water onto the surface. The drops of water should bead and jump around 3 or 4 times before evaporating. Using a large serving spoon, transfer the batter onto the hot griddle. Cook as you would pancakes. When bubbles form on the surface and break, check the underside of the fritter. Turn when nicely browned. (Fritters may be kept warm in a 250°F. oven until the entire batch is done.)

Cucumbers in Tarragon Cream

SERVES 4

Removing the seeds from a cucumber transforms this "obstreperous" vegetable into a refined, elegant dish. Serve in tomato shells warmed in the oven or in small glass dishes.

3 medium cucumbers, peeled
1½ cups medium, or whipping, cream

1 tablespoon chopped fresh tarragon leaves (or
   substitute 1 teaspoon dried)
½ teaspoon salt
Generous amount of freshly ground white pepper

1. Cut the cucumbers lengthwise into quarters. Using the serrated blade of a grapefruit knife, remove the strip of seeds that runs the length of each quarter. Cut the cucumber into 1-inch pieces, rounding the corners if you have time.

2. In a 2½-quart saucepan, combine the cucumbers, cream, tarragon, salt, and pepper. Place over medium heat and bring to a gentle bubble. Cook uncovered for 8 to 10 minutes or until the cucumbers are tender and the cream is slightly reduced.   ✑

Braised Endive with Grapefruit Sauce

SERVES 4

Endive braised in water retains its own compelling flavor. A simple finishing touch is provided by reduced grapefruit juice and a fillip of butter.

4 large or 8 small Belgian endives
½ cup water
6 tablespoons butter
1 teaspoon sugar
Salt and freshly ground black pepper
½ cup fresh grapefruit juice, strained

1. Rinse the endives under cold running water. Cut off the darkened ends of each. Then remove the cone-shaped core by inserting the tip of a paring knife into the base of the endive and cutting out the small woody portion.

2. Heat the water, 4 tablespoons of butter, and sugar in a deep skillet or shallow casserole until the butter melts. Add the endive, turning to coat. Regulate the heat so that the liquid barely bubbles and cover the pan tightly. Cook for 20 to 30 minutes, depending on the thickness of the endives. When the blade

of a paring knife slides in easily, season the endives with salt and pepper and transfer to a warmed platter.

3. Add the grapefruit juice to the pan and increase the heat to high. Cook, stirring constantly, until the liquid is reduced to ½ cup. Remove the pan from the heat and swirl in the remaining 2 tablespoons of butter 1 at a time. Pour the sauce over the endives to serve.   ✑

Escarole Sautéed in Garlic Oil

SERVES 4

When garlic is cooked slowly in olive oil, it develops a deep golden hue and imparts a distinctive, almost sweet flavor to the oil. Chopped escarole, veiled with this oil, is sautéed briefly over high heat.

1 large head escarole (about 1 pound)
4 tablespoons olive oil
6 garlic cloves, peeled
Salt and freshly ground black pepper to taste
4 wedges fresh lemon

1. Separate the leaves of escarole, pulling them away from the central core. Rinse the leaves under cold running water and place in a colander to drain.

2. Fill a 6-quart pot with water and bring to a rolling boil. Add the escarole and stir, pressing down to submerge the leaves. When the water returns to a boil, reduce the heat so that the water bubbles gently. Stir, pressing down frequently to promote even cooking. Cook until the escarole is completely limp (about 5 minutes), then pour into a colander set under cold running water. Allow the escarole to drain, then squeeze out the excess water with your hands. Chop coarsely and set aside.

3. In a 12-inch skillet, stir the oil and garlic over medium heat. When the garlic makes a faint sizzling sound, reduce the heat to low and cook, stirring slowly, until the garlic is

tender and golden. (Do not allow it to brown.) Using a slotted spoon, transfer the garlic to a small plate.

4. Add the chopped escarole to the hot oil and increase the heat to high. Stirring and tossing constantly, cook the escarole for 2 minutes. Return the garlic to the pan. Continue stirring over high heat for 2 to 3 minutes or until tender. Season with salt and pepper to taste. You may discard the garlic cloves or place 1 atop each serving. Garnish each serving with a lemon wedge.

Creamed Leeks au Gratin

SERVES 4

In this dish, the liquid in which the leeks are braised becomes the foundation for their accompanying sauce, an approach that is similar to the salsa bianca *of the Italian cuisine because it consists of a white sauce made with vegetable broth.*

8 medium leeks
4 tablespoons butter, cut into chunks
½ teaspoon salt
1 bay leaf, broken in half
½ teaspoon dried leaf thyme
4 whole peppercorns
1 cup White Sauce with Stock (p. 349),
   substituting leek broth for stock
1 cup medium, or whipping, cream
½ cup heavy cream

1. Prepare the leeks by removing the roots and cutting off most of the green portion of the leaves. You should be left with leeks about 6 inches long. Make a 2-inch horizontal cut in the white portion of each leek, and then make a 2-inch horizontal cut in the green portion, slicing completely through the leek. This leaves a center segment of the leek intact. Rinse under cold running water, separating the layers to expose hidden sand and dirt. Place the leeks in a buttered 12-inch skillet.

2. Pour on enough warm tap water to barely cover the leeks. Place over high heat. Add the butter, salt, bay leaf, thyme, and peppercorns. Bring to a boil, and then regulate the heat so that the liquid barely bubbles. Cover the skillet and cook gently for 30 minutes or until the blade of a knife can be inserted easily into the centers of the leeks. Lift out the leeks and drain them on a double thickness of absorbent paper.

3. Increase the heat and reduce the broth to 1 cup. Pour through a cheesecloth-lined sieve into a 1-quart saucepan. Place over low heat to keep warm. Generously butter a shallow gratin dish or 9×13-inch baking pan and arrange the leeks in the bottom. Preheat the oven to 350°F.

4. Prepare White Sauce with Stock (p. 349), whisking in the hot leek broth instead of the stock. Bring to a boil and cook, stirring with a heat-resistant rubber spatula, for 1 minute. Remove from the heat and whisk in medium cream. Return to medium-high heat and whisk until bubbly and smooth. Pour over the prepared leeks. Cover loosely with aluminum foil and bake for 30 minutes.

5. Whip the heavy cream until soft peaks form. Spread lightly over the surface of the hot sauce and slide under the broiler to brown.

Roasted Red Pepper Flan

SERVES 8

The distinctive flavor of roasted peppers permeates this delicate custard. Bake in an 8-inch cake pan and serve in slim wedges as an accent for roast chicken or broiled fish.

4 large red sweet bell peppers
6 large egg yolks
¼ teaspoon salt
Freshly ground white pepper
2 cups medium, or whipping, cream

1. Rinse the peppers under cold running water and blot dry with paper towels. Arrange the oven rack as close to the broiler as possible. Place the peppers directly on the rack and broil until the skins blister and small areas of pepper become charred. Turn the peppers and broil on all sides, including the top and bottom. (This broiling will take 20 to 30 minutes total time.) Using tongs, transfer the roasted peppers to a large bowl. Fold a kitchen towel in half and drape over the bowl. Allow the peppers to sit at room temperature for 45 minutes.

2. Remove the blistered skin from the peppers. Cut each in half and gently remove the seeds and core. Do not hold the peppers under running water because that would dilute their flavor. Tear the pepper halves into strips and drop into the container of a blender or food processor. Whirl briefly to purée, but do not liquefy.

3. Place an oven rack as near the middle of the oven as possible. Preheat the oven to 325°F. and generously butter an 8-inch cake pan. Put the egg yolks through a sieve into a large mixing bowl. Add the bell pepper purée, salt, and pepper and blend. Pour the cream into a 1½-quart saucepan and place over medium heat. When the surface begins to wrinkle, slowly add the warm cream to the egg-yolk mixture, stirring constantly.

4. Line a roasting pan with a kitchen towel folded into quarters to protect the bottom of the custard from the heat of the roasting pan. Place the buttered cake pan on the folded towel and pour the custard mixture into the cake pan. Place the roasting pan on the centered oven rack. Add enough hot tap water to the roasting pan to cover the towel and come half way up the sides of the cake pan. Bake for 20 minutes. Then increase the oven temperature to 350°F. and bake 20 to 30 minutes more. Test for doneness by inserting the blade of a paring knife half way between the center and the rim of the pan. When the blade parts the custard neatly, removing no traces of liquid egg mixture, take the roasting pan from the oven.

5. Transfer the cooked flan to a cooling rack and let stand for 10 minutes. Run the blade of a knife around the outside edge of the flan to loosen it if necessary. Invert onto a flat serving plate.   ◅₂

Baked Stuffed Potatoes

MAKES 6

Almost an American classic, these ever-popular potatoes are too often poorly prepared. Many times the potatoes are cooked in aluminum foil, a maneuver that traps steam inside the flesh rather than allowing it to escape. The result is overmoist, lumpy potatoes. For best results, bake Idaho or other mealy potatoes unwrapped. Then force the cooked flesh through a food mill, ricer, or sieve to release the last traces of steam and allow the flesh to dry and fluff.

6 Idaho or other mealy potatoes
2 tablespoons olive oil
Coarse salt (or substitute regular)
½ cup warm (130°F.) medium, or whipping, cream
6 tablespoons butter, melted
1 cup grated sharp Cheddar cheese
2 teaspoons chopped fresh chives (or substitute 2 teaspoons freeze-dried)
1 teaspoon salt
¼ teaspoon ground cayenne
Paprika or Parmesan cheese

1. Preheat the oven to 375°F. Scrub the potatoes under cold running water and blot dry. Rub the potato skins with olive oil and coat with salt. Prick each potato in 3 or 4 places with a metal skewer to allow steam to escape during baking. (As the interior moisture converts to steam, the starch cells absorb a certain degree of moisture and expand, transforming the flesh into a fluffy mass.)

2. Place the potatoes directly on the rack in the center of the oven and bake for about 1 hour, depending on their size. Check after 30 minutes to make sure the steam vents are still

open. Test for doneness by draping a pot holder or towel over a potato and squeezing gently. If the flesh gives under your touch, the potato is done. Remove from the oven.

3. Using a serrated knife, immediately cut a thin slice off the top of each potato. Fluff the inside of the potato with a fork to release the steam. (Do not wait for the potatoes to cool because that allows the steam to condense and creates a heavy, densely textured consistency.) When all the potatoes are open, proceed to scoop out their flesh with a small spoon. Force the hot flesh through a food mill, ricer, or sieve.

4. Beat in the warm cream and 4 tablespoons of the melted butter. Add the grated cheese, chives, salt, and cayenne. Spoon the mixture back into the shells or pipe in with a pastry bag. Make attractive peaks or ridges in the surface and refrigerate or return to the oven. Before baking a second time, drizzle the remaining melted butter over the exposed flesh. Sprinkle with paprika or Parmesan cheese and place in a 375°F. oven for 15 to 20 minutes or until the surface is pleasantly browned.   ◖⟩

Potatoes Dauphine

SERVES 4

These puffy balls of fried potato are so exceptionally good and so easy to make that it is surprising they aren't served more often. The pâte à choux *base (see entry for Cream Puff Pastry) can be made ahead of time, warmed to room temperature, and combined with an equal portion of warm or room temperature mashed potatoes. Frying is the only last-minute procedure required.*

1 cup cold water
4 tablespoons butter, cut into 16 small chunks
1 cup all-purpose flour, scoop measured
4 to 5 large eggs
1 pound Idaho, Maine, or other mealy potatoes
(makes about 2 cups plain mashed potatoes)
1 teaspoon salt

Generous amount of freshly ground white pepper (or substitute a pinch of ground cayenne)
Grated cheese (see Note)
Vegetable oil for deep frying

1. Prepare the *pâte à choux* (or cream puff pastry) by combining the water and butter in a thick-bottomed 1½-quart saucepan. Stir over medium-high heat until the butter melts. Stop stirring and allow the mixture to come to a vigorous boil. Immediately remove the pan from the heat and add the flour. Beat vigorously with a wooden spatula. Place over medium-low heat and cook, stirring, until the batter pulls together into a smooth, shiny mass. Continue stirring the dough *(panade)* over medium-low heat to dry it. A white granular film will appear on the bottom of the pan. Do not allow it to burn and don't attempt to incorporate it into the dough. Test the *panade* for doneness by pinching with two fingers. When it no longer sticks to your fingers and takes on a putty-like consistency, the *panade* is cooked. Immediately empty it into a large bowl. Allow the *panade* to cool for 5 to 10 minutes (or to below 140°F.), stirring occasionally to prevent a skin from forming.

2. Lightly whisk 4 eggs and pour into a measuring cup. If necessary, whisk the remaining egg and add enough of it to make 1 cup eggs.

3. Using a wooden spatula or the paddle attachment of an electric mixer, beat in one-quarter of the whisked eggs. Continue beating until the *panade* accepts the eggs and the mixture smooths out. Repeat twice. Add the last portion of the eggs in a thin stream. Check for proper consistency by lifting the beater or allowing the dough to drop from a spoon. It should fall in a thick, heavy ribbon and leave a peak that stands stiff.

4. Peel the potatoes and place them in a 6-quart pan. Cover with cold water and bring to a moderate boil. Cook uncovered until the potatoes can be easily pierced with a metal skewer. Drain in a colander and put through a food mill while still hot. Beat with a wooden spoon to mash.

5. Measure the mashed potato and combine with an equal portion of *pâte à choux*. Season with salt and pepper and blend in grated cheese if you like. If either component has been prepared ahead and chilled, be sure the final mixture is at room temperature before frying.

6. Heat the oil to 370°F. Take up the batter by rounded teaspoonfuls. Gently push the potato mixture from the spoon into the hot fat. Cook about 5 or 6 at a time, turning them with a slotted spoon to promote even browning. Transfer to absorbent paper to drain. Salt and serve immediately or keep warm in a 350°F. oven with the door left ajar. (They will soften if left to stand for too long.)

NOTE: To create a cheesy flavor, blend in 2 ounces of grated Gruyère, Cheddar, or Monterey Jack cheese. ◀?

Spinach and Ricotta Soufflé

SERVES 6

Sautéing spinach in olive oil contributes an aggressive, earthy flavor to this lightly textured vegetable side dish.

Dry, unseasoned bread crumbs
2 pounds fresh spinach
½ cup olive oil
4 large eggs, separated
⅓ cup freshly grated Parmesan cheese
1 pound ricotta cheese
½ teaspoon salt
Generous amount of freshly ground black pepper
Freshly grated nutmeg

1. Preheat the oven to 350°F. Generously butter the bottom and sides of a round 6-cup casserole or soufflé dish and coat with bread crumbs. Wash the spinach, remove the tough stems, and chop coarsely. Heat the olive oil in a 12-inch skillet and add the spinach, tossing to coat. Cook over high heat, stirring constantly, until the spinach becomes limp. Remove from the heat.

2. In a large mixing bowl, whisk together the egg yolks and Parmesan cheese. Stir in the ricotta and blend thoroughly. Using a slotted spoon, transfer the spinach to the ricotta mixture, leaving any excess oil behind. Add the salt, pepper, and nutmeg and mix well.

3. In another bowl, whip the egg whites until soft peaks form. Transfer 2 heaping tablespoons of the whipped whites to the spinach mixture and stir in gently to lighten. Add the remaining egg whites and fold in. Pour into the prepared baking dish and place in the preheated oven. Bake for 30 to 40 minutes or until the blade of a paring knife inserted in the center comes out clean. ◀?

Purée of Yellow Squash with Toasted Pecans

SERVES 4

Tender, young summer squash creates a beautifully colored silken purée. A garnish of coarsely chopped toasted pecans enhances the taste as well as the texture.

6 small yellow squash (about 1¾ pounds)
½ cup coarsely chopped pecans
4 tablespoons butter, cut into 4 equal pieces

1. Small yellow squash is pale yellow and has smooth, delicate, blemish-free skin that doesn't need scrubbing or scraping. Rub the skin gently under cold running water and cut away the blossom and stem ends. Slice into ¼-inch-thick rounds and set aside.

2. Fill a 6-quart pot with water and bring to a boil. Drop in the sliced squash, stirring with a wooden spoon. Cover the pot to encourage the water to return quickly to a boil. Remove the cover and regulate the heat so that the water bubbles gently. Cook uncovered for 15 to 20 minutes or until the squash is tender when pierced with the tip of a paring knife. Meanwhile, scatter the chopped pecans over the bottom of a baking pan and place in a

350°F. oven for 10 to 15 minutes or until their aroma is discernible.

3. Transfer the cooked squash to a colander and drain thoroughly. Place the well-drained squash in a wide saucepan and purée with a potato masher. (You can also force the squash through a food mill, but do not purée in a blender or processor because that will liquefy the squash.) Set the pan over medium heat. Stirring constantly, gently cook the squash until it is dry enough to begin to stick to the bottom of the pan. Remove from the heat and stir in 1 tablespoon of butter. Repeat this procedure, adding butter a tablespoon at a time until all is used. (Drying the squash and then gradually blending in the butter encourages the squash to totally absorb the butter.) Transfer to a serving dish and garnish with the toasted pecans. ◅ঽ

Zucchini and Fresh Tomato Strudel

SERVES 6

Layers of crisp filo dough envelop zucchini slices and chunks of fresh tomato. Serve as a light luncheon or as an accompaniment for grilled beef.

12 sheets filo dough (each 12×16 inches)
6 small slender zucchini (about 1½ pounds)
2 tablespoons olive oil
3 large fresh tomatoes, peeled, seeded, and
   coarsely chopped
1 garlic clove, minced or pressed
2 tablespoons chopped fresh parsley
1 tablespoon chopped fresh basil (or substitute 1
   teaspoon dried)
¼ teaspoon salt
Freshly ground black pepper
¼ cup freshly grated Parmesan cheese
¼ pound butter, melted

1. Set the filo dough out to warm to room temperature. (Sheets of chilled filo tear when you try to separate them.) Rinse the zucchini under cold running water and blot dry with paper towels. Cut off the ends, and then slice into ¼-inch-thick rounds. Set aside.

2. Heat the olive oil in a 12-inch skillet. Add the zucchini and toss to coat. Cook over high heat, stirring and lifting constantly with 2 wooden spatulas. When the zucchini becomes limp, add the coarsely chopped tomatoes to the pan and reduce the heat to medium. Stir in the garlic, parsley, basil, salt, and pepper. Cook, stirring slowly, until all the moisture evaporates. Transfer to a bowl and blend in the Parmesan cheese.

3. Melt the butter and set aside. Tear off two 14-inch lengths of plastic wrap and lay them on the counter so that they overlap and cover an area about 14×18 inches. Unwrap the filo and place the stack on the plastic wrap. Smooth the pile of filo out flat with your fingertips. Tear off 2 more 14-inch pieces of plastic wrap and lay them over the dough, smoothing out any air bubbles with your hands. (Because of its extraordinary thinness, filo dough dries out in minutes, so it's important to keep it protected at all times. Avoid covering it with a damp cloth because the moisture can cause the dough to disintegrate.)

4. Preheat the oven to 400°F. Remove a sheet of filo from the pile and position it so that the shortest edge is in front of you. Brush

Transfer about ½ cup of the vegetable mixture to a sheet of filo dough, fold in the sides, and roll up.

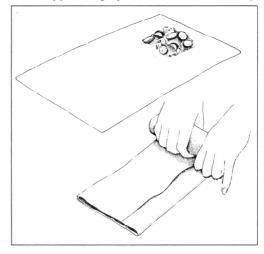

the surface with melted butter, top with another sheet of filo, and brush the surface of the second sheet. Using a slotted spoon, transfer about ½ cup of the zucchini mixture to the middle of the dough, distributing it across the bottom third of the pastry in a 4-inch line. Lift the left-hand side of the pastry over the filling and brush with melted butter. Bring over the right-hand side of the pastry, brush with butter, and roll firmly to create a 4-inch strudel (see illustration). Brush with melted butter and place on an ungreased baking sheet. Repeat with the remaining filo dough. (As you get to the end of the vegetable mixture, you'll probably find liquid at the bottom of the bowl. Continue to take the vegetables up with a slotted spoon and leave the liquid behind.) Place the strudels on a greased baking sheet in the preheated oven and bake for 15 to 20 minutes or until the pastry is puffed and golden brown.   ◅

Spaghetti Squash

SERVES 4 TO 6

This versatile vegetable can be baked in the oven like a giant potato, then pulled from its shell and served with melted butter, grated Parmesan cheese, and a sprinkle of nutmeg. Or present it as you would pasta — sauced with a light fresh-tomato purée or a rich mushroom mélange.

1 two-pound spaghetti squash

MUSHROOM SAUCE
2 ounces prosciutto, thinly sliced
4 tablespoons butter
8 ounces fresh mushrooms, coarsely chopped
4 green onions, thinly sliced (white portion only)
⅓ cup Madeira
Salt and freshly ground black pepper to taste

1. Preheat the oven to 350°F. Wash the squash and pat it dry with a paper towel. Set the squash directly on the oven rack and pierce the upper portion of the shell in several places with a metal skewer. Bake for 45 to 60 minutes or until the squash yields to the pres-

sure of your fingertips. Remove from the oven and allow it to cool for 15 minutes.

2. Meanwhile, coarsely chop the prosciutto. Melt the butter in a 10-inch skillet and add the mushrooms. Stir over high heat until the mushrooms begin to release their moisture. Add the green onions and prosciutto. Continue stirring over high heat until the mushrooms have browned slightly. Add the Madeira, salt, and pepper and stir over high heat until most of the liquid evaporates.

3. Cut the squash in half across its width (not lengthwise). Holding the squash in a folded towel, scoop out the seeds and discard them. Using the tines of a kitchen fork, pull the strands of squash from the cavity, allowing them to mound in a serving dish. Spoon the sauce over the squash and serve.   ◅

Sautéed Cherry Tomatoes

SERVES 4

Cherry tomatoes, which are usually served cold, take on a new personality when sautéed briefly in hot butter and fresh herbs. They make a delightful accent for scrambled eggs and breakfast steak.

1 pound small bright-red cherry tomatoes
4 tablespoons unsalted butter
2 tablespoons light brown sugar
1 tablespoon chopped fresh basil
1 teaspoon chopped fresh sage
¼ teaspoon salt
Freshly ground black pepper

1. Wash the tomatoes under cold running water and allow them to drain in a colander (there's no need to blot them dry).

2. Melt the butter in a 12-inch skillet and add the tomatoes, tossing to coat. Place over high heat and cook, stirring constantly, for 1 minute. Sprinkle on the brown sugar, basil, and sage and stir over high heat until the sugar melts and becomes somewhat syrupy. Season with salt and pepper.   ◅

Vegetable Pâté

SERVES 12

A vegetable pâté, more precisely termed a ter-rine because it is not encased in a crust, can be composed of a single vegetable or a combi-nation of many. In this recipe, purées of spin-ach, beets, and onions are layered to create a brilliantly colored assemblage of green, red, and white. The initial steps involve cooking the vegetables separately. Then they are pur-éed and bound with eggs and cream to form what is essentially a baked custard. For best results, chill the pâté thoroughly and then al-low it to come to room temperature to serve. A vegetable pâté makes a lovely addition to a buffet table or a delightful first course.

2 pounds fresh spinach
4 tablespoons butter
1 medium-size yellow onion, sliced
1½ cups medium, or whipping, cream
9 large eggs
1 cup dry, unseasoned bread crumbs
2 ounces Gruyère cheese, grated
Salt and pepper to taste
2 large sweet onions (such as Vidalia or
    Bermuda), coarsely chopped (about 1 pound)
Freshly ground nutmeg
9 or 10 medium-size beets (about 1¼ pounds)

1. To prepare the spinach layer, begin by washing the spinach and removing the tough stems. Submerge the leaves in boiling water. When the water returns to a boil, stir, pressing the spinach down, and cook uncovered for 2 minutes. Drain in a colander under cold tap water. Squeeze dry with your hands. In a 10-inch skillet, melt 2 tablespoons of the butter and add the sliced onion, tossing to coat. Cover and cook over low heat until tender. Do not allow the onion to color. Add the spinach and increase the heat to high. Stirring constantly, cook the spinach to evaporate its excess moisture. When the spinach begins to stick to the pan, transfer to the container of a food processor or blender. Add ½ cup of the cream, 3 of the eggs, and ⅓ cup of the bread crumbs. Pulse briefly to mix, but be careful not to liquefy the spinach. Blend in the grated cheese. Add salt and pepper to taste. Set aside.

2. Prepare the onion layer. Melt the re-maining 2 tablespoons of butter in a thick-bottomed saucepan. Add the chopped on-ions, tossing to coat with butter. Cover and cook over low heat until tender. Do not allow them to color. Stir in ½ cup of the cream and increase the heat. Stirring constantly, cook the onions until the cream is absorbed and the mixture is quite thick. Transfer to the container of a food processor or blender. Add 3 of the eggs and ⅓ cup of the bread crumbs. Pulse 3 or 4 times to blend. Stir in the nut-meg, and add salt and pepper to taste. Set aside.

3. Prepare the beet layer. Cut off the stem ends and place in a large saucepan. Cover with cold water and bring to a boil. Reduce the heat and simmer uncovered for 35 min-utes or until tender. Drain in a colander under cold tap water. Peel the beets if the skins seem tough. Slice the beets and return them to the saucepan. Stir over medium heat to help ex-cess moisture evaporate. When the beets ap-pear dry, transfer to the container of a food processor or blender. Add remaining ½ cup cream, last 3 eggs, and remaining ⅓ cup of bread crumbs. Pulse briefly to purée, but do not overprocess. Set aside.

4. Preheat the oven to 325°F. Assemble the pâté by generously buttering a 9×5-inch loaf pan. Line the bottom with parchment paper or buttered aluminum foil. Pour in the beet purée and spread evenly. Spoon on the onion purée, smoothing the top with the back of the spoon. Top with the spinach purée.

5. Cover with the buttered side of a piece of foil. Crimp the edges to seal. Line a roasting pan with a kitchen towel folded into quarters. Set the loaf pan on the towel. Pour in boiling water to a depth of 2 inches. Place in the lower third of the preheated oven and bake for 50 to 70 minutes. Test for doneness by inserting the blade of a knife half way be-tween the center and the rim of the pan. When the knife blade parts the custard neatly, removing no traces of liquid egg mixture, re-

move the pâté from the oven. Allow it to stand in the hot-water bath for 30 minutes to complete cooking by residual heat. Refrigerate to chill thoroughly. Unmold and peel off the parchment. Warm to room temperature. Slice and serve with mayonnaise blended with minced green onion, a few drops of lemon juice, and fresh herbs, such as chopped chives, tarragon leaves, parsley, or chervil. ◆

Mushroom Beignets

SERVES 8

Here's a delicious and unique way to include mushrooms as part of the main course. Since these beignets *are best when served immediately, plan to prepare the* pâte à choux *(cream puff pastry) ahead of time and allow it to warm to room temperature. Then all you have to do is fry them at the last minute.*

1 pound fresh mushrooms, finely chopped
1 small onion, finely chopped
1 teaspoon dried leaf thyme
1 tablespoon fresh lemon juice
4 tablespoons butter, cut into 16 small chunks
½ teaspoon salt
Generous pinch of ground cayenne
1 cup all-purpose flour, scoop measured
4 to 5 large eggs
Vegetable oil for deep frying

1. Place the mushrooms and onion in a 2½-quart saucepan. Add the thyme and lemon juice and pour in enough cold water to cover the vegetables. Bring to a boil. Regulate the heat so that the liquid simmers gently and cook uncovered for 8 to 10 minutes or until the mushrooms are tender. Strain the liquid, pressing down firmly on the mushrooms to extract as much juice as possible. Turn the vegetables out onto a double thickness of paper toweling to eliminate any remaining liquid. Measure the strained mushroom liquid. If you have more than 1 cup, place it over high heat and reduce until it measures 1 cup.

2. Prepare the *pâte à choux* (cream puff pastry) by combining the mushroom liquid, butter, salt, and cayenne in a thick-bottomed 1½-quart saucepan. Stir over medium-high heat until the butter melts. Stop stirring and allow the mixture to come to a vigorous boil. Immediately remove the pan from the heat and add the flour. Beat vigorously with a wooden spatula. Place over medium-low heat and cook, stirring, until the batter pulls together into a smooth, shiny mass. Continue stirring the dough *(panade)* over medium-low heat to dry it. A white granular film will appear on the bottom of the pan. Do not allow it to burn and don't attempt to incorporate it into the dough. Test the *panade* for doneness by pinching with two fingers. When it no longer sticks to your fingers and takes on a putty-like consistency, the *panade* is cooked. Immediately empty it into a large bowl. Allow the *panade* to cool for 5 to 10 minutes (or to below 140°F.), stirring occasionally to prevent a skin from forming.

3. Lightly whisk 4 eggs and pour into a measuring cup. If necessary, whisk the remaining egg and add enough of it to make 1 cup eggs.

4. Using a wooden spatula or the paddle attachment of an electric mixer, beat in one-quarter of the whisked eggs. Continue beating until the *panade* accepts the eggs and the mixture smooths out. Repeat twice. Add the last portion of the eggs in a thin stream. Check for proper consistency by lifting the beater or allowing the dough to drop from a spoon. It should fall in a thick, heavy ribbon and leave a peak that stands stiff. Blend in the cooked mushrooms.

5. Heat the vegetable oil to 370°F. Take up the pastry by rounded teaspoonfuls (or tablespoonfuls if you prefer larger puffs). Gently push the dough from the spoon into the hot fat. Cook, turning with a slotted spoon, until nicely puffed and golden brown. Transfer to absorbent paper to drain. Serve immediately or keep warm in a 350°F. oven with the door left ajar.

(See entries for Cream Puff Pastry; Frying: Deep-Fat.)   ◆

Stocks and Sauces

STOCK

The names that various stocks go by can be confusing because they are sometimes described in terms of color — such as brown stock or white stock — or in terms of their origin — beef stock, chicken stock, or veal stock. Generally speaking, a white stock is made from uncooked white meat or fish (although fish stock is traditionally known as *fumet*); brown stock is made from meat that has been browned in the oven before being simmered in water. Therefore, references to a brown veal stock indicate a stock made from browned veal; references to a white veal stock, a stock made from unbrowned veal.

As a result of the oven browning, brown stocks have a deep rich color and an assertive flavor, so they are usually included in full-bodied preparations such as brown sauces and hearty soups. White stocks are more delicately flavored and have an opaque white coloration. They are used in white sauces and light soups. (See entry for Stock.)

Dark Brown Stock I

MAKES 8 TO 12 CUPS

This is the hearty, full-flavored stock used as the base for brown sauces and meat glazes. It may be made from beef or a combination of beef and veal. Because veal bones release a considerable amount of gelatin-forming proteins, including them produces a smoother and more satisfying stock than one produced without them.

4 tablespoons vegetable oil
3 pounds meaty beef bones (shank crosscuts are best; rib bones are too fatty)
3 pounds meaty veal bones (shank crosscuts) or 3 more pounds meaty beef bones
2 pounds stew beef (or substitute shoulder steak or tip roast, cut into 2-inch cubes)
3 medium onions, quartered
3 medium carrots, cut into 1-inch pieces
1 teaspoon sugar
2 celery ribs, cut into 1-inch pieces
1 garlic clove, unpeeled but crushed
2 bay leaves, broken in half
½ teaspoon dried leaf thyme
8 whole peppercorns
4 whole cloves
3 sprigs fresh parsley
Salt and freshly ground black pepper to taste

1. Preheat the oven to 425°F. Pour the vegetable oil into a shallow roasting pan. Add the bones and meat and toss to coat with oil. Place in the oven and roast uncovered for 45 to 55 minutes or until the meat begins to brown. Stir occasionally to promote even browning.

2. Transfer the roasted bones and meat to a 12-quart stockpot, allowing any grease to remain in the roasting pan. Add the onions and carrots to the roasting pan, and sprinkle on the sugar. Stir to coat the vegetables with melted fat and oil. Return to the oven and roast uncovered for 30 to 45 minutes. The object is to cook the vegetables until they begin to color, but don't allow them to char as that imparts a bitter flavor to stock.

3. Add enough cold water to the stockpot to cover the bones and meat by 2 inches. Place over high heat. Do not cover, but bring to a boil slowly. Regulate the heat so that the liquid maintains a slow, gentle bubble. Skim the simmering stock with a shallow spoon to remove any scum that floats to the top. When the roasted vegetables have begun to color, transfer them with a slotted spoon to the pot and add more water to cover the contents by 2 inches. Pour the fat from the roasting pan and refrigerate if desired for later use. Deglaze the roasting pan with water and add to the stockpot. Stir in the celery and garlic (crushed with the blade of a chef's knife). Add the bay leaves, thyme, peppercorns, and whole cloves. Regulate the heat so that the liquid maintains a slow, gentle bubble and cook for 5 to 8 hours. (The length of time you simmer a stock is flexible and can be determined by your schedule. However, keep in mind that a long simmering period extracts the greatest amount of flavor from the meat and vegetables. Five hours of simmering will produce an acceptable stock, but 7 or 8 hours will produce one with increased intensity of flavor and a greater amount of natural gelatin.) As the liquid evaporates during simmering, add enough tap water to keep the contents of the pot covered at all times. Add the parsley about 1 hour before the end of the cooking time.

4. When the meat has fallen away from the bones and the vegetables are soft enough to disintegrate, pour the hot stock through a colander. Don't be alarmed if tiny particles pass through; the stock will receive a second straining in a later step. Refrigerate 12 hours or overnight.

5. Degrease the stock by lifting off the layer of solid fat that has formed on the surface. Remove the soft spongy layer underneath, then transfer the gel-like stock to a large saucepan. Be careful to leave behind any debris that has fallen to the bottom. Heat gently until the stock liquefies. Pour the warm stock through a cheesecloth-lined sieve and return to medium heat. Now that all traces of fat

have been removed, you can cook the stock at a brisk bubble without clouding the liquid. Boil gently uncovered for 1 to 2 hours to concentrate the flavor. When you have reduced the stock to the desired strength, adjust the seasoning by adding salt and pepper. Keep in mind that once a liquid is salted, any further reduction will cause an imbalance in the salt-liquid ratio and produce an overly salty taste. If the color of your stock is disappointingly pale, blend in a small amount of tomato paste or caramel coloring. This stock may be frozen.

NOTE: This recipe and the one for Beef Broth (p. 192) may be used interchangeably, although the blend of flavors is noticeably different. ◄ɕ

Dark Brown Stock II

MAKES 12 CUPS

Concentrated beef extract labeled "Bovril" provides an excellent way to quickly prepare a good-tasting brown stock.

1 jar (5.2 ounces) Bovril concentrated beef extract (or substitute 12 cups canned beef broth)
2 medium onions, quartered
2 medium carrots, sliced
2 celery ribs, sliced
1 garlic clove
2 bay leaves, broken in half
½ teaspoon dried leaf thyme
8 whole peppercorns
4 whole cloves
3 sprigs fresh parsley
Salt and freshly ground black pepper to taste

1. In a 6-quart pot, combine the beef extract with 4 quarts water and stir until well blended (or omit the beef extract and use canned beef broth plus 4 cups of water). Place over high heat and bring to a boil.

2. Add the onions, carrots, celery, garlic, bay leaves, thyme, peppercorns, and cloves. Regulate the heat so that the liquid bubbles

gently and cook uncovered for 2 hours. Add the parsley and continue cooking for 30 minutes or until the vegetables are completely tender and the stock is reduced to 3 quarts. Taste for seasoning and add salt and pepper if necessary.

3. Pour through a cheesecloth-lined sieve and use immediately or refrigerate. This stock may also be frozen.

NOTE: Because prepared products like beef extract and canned beef broth are inordinately salty, the safest approach is to wait until the end of the procedure before adding salt, if any.

Light Brown Stock

MAKES 8 TO 12 CUPS

This lightly colored stock, also called beef broth, white stock, or veal stock, is less assertively flavored than Dark Brown Stock I (p. 340) because it is made from raw, unroasted meat. It also differs in that the resulting liquid contains a substantial amount of gelatin because of the veal bones. Use it for braising rice and vegetables and as the basis for delicate soups and light-colored aspic.

2 pounds meaty beef bones (shank crosscuts are best)
4 pounds meaty veal bones (shank crosscuts are best)
3 medium-size yellow onions, quartered
3 medium carrots, cut into 1-inch pieces
2 celery ribs, cut into 1-inch pieces
6 green onions, sliced (including most of the green leaves)
2 bay leaves
½ teaspoon dried leaf thyme
8 whole peppercorns
4 whole cloves
3 sprigs fresh parsley
Salt and freshly ground black pepper to taste

1. When unroasted meats are initially heated in water, protein and fat that are released rise to the surface as scum, which can impart an unpleasant taste to stock if it is incorporat-ed. The following procedure alleviates this problem. Place the meat and bones in a 12-quart stockpot. Cover with cold tap water. Place over high heat and bring to a boil. When scum appears on the surface of the water, remove the pot from the heat. Pour off the water, emptying the meat into a colander. Rinse the stockpot and the meat thoroughly with warm water. Return the meat to the stockpot.

2. Add the onions, carrots, celery, and green onions. Pour in enough cold tap water to completely submerge the contents of the pot. Place over high heat. Do not cover, but bring to a boil slowly. Stir in the bay leaves, thyme, peppercorns, and cloves. (If the stock is to be used for consommé, aspic, or other preparations in which clarity is an important factor, enclose the bay leaves, thyme, peppercorns, and cloves in a double thickness of cheesecloth and tie securely.) Regulate the heat so that the liquid maintains a slow, gentle bubble. Cook uncovered for 6 to 8 hours, occasionally skimming off the foam that appears on the surface. As the liquid evaporates, add enough tap water to keep the contents of the pot covered. Add the parsley 1 hour before the end of the cooking time.

3. Strain the hot stock through a colander. Don't be concerned if tiny particles pass through; the stock will need a second straining anyway. Refrigerate overnight.

4. Degrease the stock by removing the layer of solid fat that forms on the surface. Remove the soft spongy layer underneath, then transfer the gel-like stock to a large saucepan. Be careful to leave behind any debris that has fallen to the bottom. Heat gently until the stock liquefies. Pour the warm stock through a cheesecloth-lined sieve and return to medium heat. Boil gently uncovered for about 1 hour to concentrate the flavor. When you have reduced the stock to the strength that you desire, adjust the seasoning by adding salt and pepper. Keep in mind that once a liquid is salted, any further reduction will cause an imbalance in the salt-liquid ratio and produce an overly salty taste.

NOTE: To clarify for use in clear soups or aspic, remove the stock from the heat and measure it into a large bowl to check the quantity. In another bowl, combine 1 egg white with 1 tablespoon of cold water for every quart or part of a quart of stock. Crumble the egg shells and set aside. (Reserve the yolks for another use.) Whisk the egg whites until frothy, then stir them into the stock. Add the crumbled egg shells and return the stock to the saucepan. Place over medium heat. Stirring slowly with a whisk, keep the liquid in constant motion to prevent the solidifying egg white from sticking to the bottom of the pan. As the liquid heats, streamers of solid egg white will appear throughout. Continue stirring until the liquid begins to bubble. Stop stirring and allow the solidified egg white to rise to the surface. Immediately remove from the heat and let stand for 15 minutes. Gently tilt the saucepan and pour the stock through a cheesecloth-lined sieve, allowing the egg whites to remain behind in the pan. For the clearest results, let the stock drip slowly through the cheesecloth. Do not attempt to hasten the process in any way. ◄᠗

Chicken Stock

MAKES 8 TO 12 CUPS

Sometimes referred to as chicken broth, this preparation is made from unroasted chicken and produces a pale, mild-flavored liquid that is considered a white stock. It is used to braise vegetables and as a foundation for. some of the white sauces. Chicken stock made from roasted chicken is more assertively flavored and darker in color. It is frequently used as a soup base, but seldom incorporated into white sauce.

3½-pound stewing chicken or fowl (or substitute
  5 pounds of chicken necks, backs, and wings)
3 medium leeks (including most of the green
  leaves)
3 medium onions, quartered
3 medium carrots, cut into 1-inch pieces
2 celery ribs, cut into 1-inch pieces
1 garlic clove, unpeeled but crushed
2 bay leaves, broken in half
1 teaspoon salt
½ teaspoon dried leaf thyme
6 whole peppercorns
2 whole cloves
3 sprigs fresh parsley
Salt and freshly ground white pepper to taste

1. Wash the chicken under cold running water. Remove the neck and package of organ meats from the cavity. Discard the liver or refrigerate it for another use. Set aside the neck, heart, and gizzard (a muscular portion of the alimentary canal).

2. Prepare the leeks by removing the roots and cutting off 2 inches of the dark green portion of the leaves. Cut each leek in half lengthwise and rinse under cold running water, separating the layers to expose hidden sand and dirt. Pat dry and cut into 3-inch lengths.

3. In a 12-quart stockpot, combine the whole chicken, the neck, heart, gizzard, leeks, onions, carrots, celery, and garlic. Add cold tap water until the contents are completely submerged. Place over high heat. Do not cover with a lid, but bring to a boil slowly. Stir in the bay leaves, 1 teaspoon salt, thyme, peppercorns, and whole cloves. Regulate the heat so that the liquid maintains a slow, gentle bubble. Cook uncovered for 3½ to 4 hours, occasionally skimming off the foam that appears on the surface. As the liquid evaporates, add enough tap water to keep the contents of the pot covered at all times. Add the parsley 1 hour before the end of the cooking time.

4. Lift out the chicken and pour the hot stock through a colander. Don't be concerned if tiny particles pass through; the stock will need a second straining anyway. Refrigerate overnight.

5. Degrease the stock by removing the layer of solid fat that forms on the surface. Remove the soft spongy layer underneath, then transfer the gel-like stock to a large saucepan, leaving behind any debris that has fallen to

the bottom. Heat gently until the stock liquefies. Pour the warm stock through a cheesecloth-lined sieve and return to medium heat. Now that all traces of fat have been removed, you can cook the stock at a brisk bubble without clouding the liquid. Boil gently uncovered for about 1 hour to concentrate the flavor. When you have reduced the stock to the desired strength, adjust the seasoning by adding salt and white pepper to taste. Keep in mind that once a liquid is salted, any further reduction will cause an imbalance in the salt-liquid ratio and produce an overly salty taste.

NOTE: Since a stewing chicken is customarily a tough old bird, you'll need to simmer this stock for a longer time than stocks made with younger chickens or chicken parts. The resulting flavor, however, is considerably stronger and more full-bodied. If you substitute a younger chicken or chicken parts, simmer for only 2½ hours. Stewing chicken cooked in this manner will be tender enough to make an excellent chicken salad.   ◄୬

Fish Stock

MAKES 8 TO 12 CUPS

Fish stock (or fumet*) is made from the heads, bones, and trimmings of nonoily fish, but avoid as much as possible using the skin because it colors the stock grey. Compared with other types of stock, fish stock can be cooked in a relatively short time because of the high water content and natural tenderness of fish. Therefore, the vegetables are precooked in this preparation to hasten the release of their flavor. See the note following this recipe for an even quicker fish stock.*

2 medium leeks
4 tablespoons butter
1 medium onion, thinly sliced
1 medium carrot, thinly sliced
8 medium-size fresh mushrooms plus stems,
  coarsely chopped
2 cups dry white wine

4 pounds nonoily fish, such as sole, flounder,
  haddock, or whiting, including the heads and
  bones
1 bay leaf
½ teaspoon salt
½ teaspoon dried leaf thyme
4 black peppercorns
3 sprigs fresh parsley
Salt and freshly ground white pepper to taste

1. Prepare the leeks by removing the roots and cutting off 2 inches of the dark green portion of the leaves. Cut each leek in half lengthwise and rinse under cold running water, separating the layers to expose hidden sand and dirt. Pat dry and slice thinly.

2. Melt the butter in a 6-quart nonreactive saucepan or Dutch oven. (Be sure to use a nonreactive pan to avoid the discoloration that results from simmering wine in an aluminum pot.) Add the sliced leeks, onion, carrot, and mushrooms. Toss to coat with melted butter. Cover the pan and cook over low heat until the onion is translucent.

3. Stir in the wine. Increase the heat and bring to a brisk bubble. Add the fish and enough cold tap water to completely cover the contents. Slowly bring to a boil uncovered. Stir in the bay leaf, ½ teaspoon salt, thyme, peppercorns, and parsley. Regulate the heat so that the liquid maintains a slow, gentle bubble. Cook uncovered for 45 to 60 minutes or until the fish bones begin to disintegrate. Skim occasionally. Add water if necessary to keep the contents of the pan covered at all times.

4. Pour the hot stock through a large sieve. Use immediately if desired or refrigerate overnight to solidify the butterfat. (If needed right away, strain a second time through a cheesecloth-lined sieve.)

5. Remove the thin layer of solidified fat from the surface. Transfer the gel-like stock to a large saucepan, leaving behind any debris that has fallen to the bottom. Heat gently until the stock liquefies. Pour the warm stock through a cheesecloth-lined sieve and return to medium heat. Cook at a brisk bubble for 10 to 30 minutes to concentrate the flavor.

When you have reduced the stock to the desired strength, adjust the seasoning by adding salt and white pepper to taste. Keep in mind that once a liquid is salted, any further reduction will cause an imbalance in the salt-liquid ratio and produce an overly salty taste.

NOTE: If you don't have time to prepare a traditional *fumet*, use this recipe for Quick Fish Stock. In a 4½-quart nonreactive saucepan, combine 1½ cups bottled clam juice; 3 cups water; ½ cup dry white wine; 1 fresh shallot, chopped (or 2 teaspoons freeze-dried); 2 sprigs fresh parsley; 1 bay leaf; ¼ teaspoon dried leaf thyme; 6 fennel seeds; and 3 peppercorns. Do not add salt because bottled clam juice is extremely salty. Bring to a boil. Drop in ½ pound of any fresh, nonoily fish that's inexpensive. Return to a gentle bubble and cook 30 to 45 minutes or until reduced to 3 cups. Strain through a sieve lined with a double thickness of cheesecloth to trap the herbs.

Do-Ahead Gravies

MAKES 5 TO 6 CUPS

Never enough gravy is a common problem associated with holiday cooking, but it need not be. You can make more gravy than you'll ever need by preparing a stock and thickening it. Use the bones and scraps from one meal to prepare and freeze gravy for the next.

DO-AHEAD TURKEY GRAVY
Bones, skin, and scraps of meat from an 18- to
   25-pound turkey
4 carrots, cut into 1-inch pieces
2 medium onions, quartered
4 ribs celery, cut into 1-inch pieces, plus a
   handful of leaves
2 teaspoons Bell's poultry seasoning
Leftover gravy
4 tablespoons turkey fat
4 tablespoons flour
Salt and freshly ground black pepper

1. Break up the turkey carcass and arrange it in a shallow roasting pan. Add any skin or meat scraps available. Prepare the carrots and onions and scatter them over the turkey. Place in a 375°F. oven and cook 20 to 30 minutes or until the turkey begins to release some fat. Stir to coat the vegetables with grease and cook 20 to 30 minutes to lightly color the vegetables.

2. Transfer the contents of the roasting pan to an 8-quart stockpot. Add the celery ribs and leaves. Pour in cold water to cover. Bring to a boil. Reduce to a gentle bubble and cook uncovered for 3 to 4 hours. Meanwhile, deglaze the roasting pan with a small amount of water and add to the simmering stock. Skim the surface as necessary and periodically add tap water to keep the bones covered. When the meat falls away from the bones and the vegetables are tender, stir in the poultry seasoning and any gravy you might have left over from another time. Reduce the heat so that the liquid isn't bubbling and cook for 1 hour. Strain through a colander and chill.

3. Degrease the stock by removing the layer of fat that has risen to the surface. Refrigerate 4 tablespoons of the cold fat. Transfer the cold stock to a large saucepan and bring to a boil. (The stock will contain small particles of meat and herbs that give the final product a home-style consistency. You can, however, warm the stock and put it through a cheesecloth-lined sieve if you wish to refine it.)

4. Adjust the heat so that the stock barely bubbles. Skim as necessary and cook uncovered for about 3 hours. At the end of that time, the liquid will be reduced to 4 or 5 cups of dark brown, rich-tasting broth.

5. In a large saucepan, prepare a roux by melting the reserved turkey fat and blending in the flour. Stir over medium heat until the mixture foams. Remove from the heat. Bring the turkey stock to a gentle, not vigorous, boil. Whisk in teaspoonfuls of the roux as you would a beurre manié. You might not need to add all of the roux. Stop when the mixture reaches a smooth, thickened, gravy-like consistency. Add salt and pepper to taste. Pour into plastic containers and freeze until your next turkey dinner. When you're ready

to use your frozen gravy, simply defrost in the refrigerator, and then heat in a saucepan.

NOTE: If you are cooking only a small turkey or part of a large one, see Do-Ahead Chicken Gravy below.

DO-AHEAD ROAST BEEF GRAVY: With the bones and scraps of a 4- or 5-rib roast, use the same amount of vegetables listed above (except omit the celery leaves). In place of the poultry seasoning, add 1 teaspoon dried leaf thyme and 2 tablespoons chopped fresh parsley. Reduce the final broth until the flavor is intense (about 2½ cups). For the roux, blend 4 tablespoons of melted beef fat with 4 tablespoons of flour. Whisk the roux in by teaspoonfuls because you may not need it all.

DO-AHEAD CHICKEN GRAVY: To use the bones and scraps of a roast chicken or small turkey, reduce the amount of vegetables to 2 slender carrots, 1 medium onion, and 2 ribs of celery (omit the celery leaves). Reduce the poultry seasoning to ½ teaspoon. Plan on a shorter cooking time because you'll be working with a smaller amount of liquid. Reduce the final broth until the flavor is intense (about 1½ cups). For the roux, blend 2 tablespoons of melted chicken fat with 2 tablespoons of flour. Whisk the roux in by teaspoonfuls because you may not need it all. ◄ৡ

BROWN SAUCES

Basic Brown Sauce (Espagnole)

MAKES 4 CUPS

The following approach is designed for the cook with little time to spend standing over the stove. It can be prepared in several stages and most of the cooking can go on without close supervision.

3 tablespoons vegetable oil
1 medium onion, quartered
1 medium carrot, sliced
1 rib celery, sliced
6 medium-size fresh mushrooms, sliced
4 tablespoons clarified butter (p. 38), vegetable oil, or melted beef fat from steak or roast beef trimmings
4 tablespoons flour
6 cups Dark Brown Stock I or II (p. 340 or p. 341) or Beef Broth (p. 192)
2 tablespoons tomato paste
½ cup dry white wine
1 bay leaf, broken in half
3 sprigs fresh parsley
¼ cup Madeira
Salt and freshly ground black pepper

1. Preheat the oven to 400°F. Pour the vegetable oil into a 9×13-inch baking pan. Add the onion, carrot, celery, and mushrooms. Toss to coat with oil. Place in the oven and roast uncovered for 30 minutes. Stir to redistribute the oil and encourage the vegetables to brown evenly. Roast uncovered for another 30 minutes or until they are tender and the onions have developed a light brown color; however, do not allow them to char.

2. In a 2½-quart thick-bottomed saucepan, combine the clarified butter and flour. Stir with a heat-resistant rubber spatula to blend well. Place over medium heat and cook, stirring continuously, until the mixture begins to bubble. Reduce the heat to its lowest possible setting and continue to cook, stirring with a heat-resistant rubber spatula, for 5 to 8 minutes or until the roux browns to the color of peanut butter. Keep in mind that it's safer to underbrown than to overbrown.

3. Meanwhile, in another saucepan, heat the stock or broth over medium heat. When it bubbles, remove the pan from the heat.

4. When the butter-flour mixture is nicely browned, remove the pan from the heat and immediately pour the *hot* stock into the *hot* roux. Whisk vigorously and return the pan to medium heat. Gradually increase the heat to high, whisking continuously, until the sauce

smooths out and thickens slightly. Bring to a boil and cook, stirring, for 1 minute.

5. Add the cooked vegetables, tomato paste, white wine, and bay leaf. Regulate the heat so that the liquid bubbles gently and cook for 2 hours. Skim occasionally during that time to remove the film that appears on the surface. You should have about 5 cups of sauce. Stir in the parsley and Madeira. Cook uncovered for 30 to 45 minutes or until the sauce is reduced to 4 cups and has developed a consistency similar to that of medium cream. Taste for seasoning and add salt and pepper. Strain the sauce and use immediately or freeze in 1-cup portions.

NOTES: Because reduction plays a significant role in the preparation of this sauce, salt should not be added until the end.

For a robust, casual brown sauce, purée the vegetables in the container of a blender or processor instead of straining them. Blended into the final sauce, they add hearty flavor and a degree of thickening.

This recipe for Basic Brown Sauce and the one for Demi-Glaze (see below) may be used interchangeably, but remember that Demi-Glaze is a stronger-flavored version of Basic Brown Sauce.　　　　　　　　　　✑

Variations on Basic Brown Sauce

DEMI-GLAZE: So named because it is half the thickness of meat glaze, this concentrated brown sauce may be frozen in an ice-cube tray and then transferred to an airtight plastic bag to be used later for enriching other sauces (1 ice cube equals approximately 2 tablespoons). In a 1½-quart saucepan, combine 1 cup Basic Brown Sauce with 1 cup Dark Brown Stock I (p. 340) or Beef Broth (p. 192). Simmer uncovered until the sauce is thickened and reduced to 1 cup. Skim occasionally if necessary.

BORDELAISE SAUCE: Combine 1 cup dry red wine, 1 minced shallot (or substitute

1½ teaspoons freeze-dried), ½ bay leaf, and ¼ teaspoon dried leaf thyme in a 1½-quart non-reactive saucepan. Place over medium heat and cook uncovered until reduced to ½ cup. Pour through a cheesecloth-lined sieve and set aside. Finely chop ¼ pound of beef marrow and place in a 1½-quart saucepan. Cover with tap water and place over high heat. Boil for 1 minute and strain. Stir the blanched marrow into 1 cup Basic Brown Sauce. Add the reduced wine and 2 tablespoons chopped fresh parsley. Heat until bubbling. Swirl in 1 tablespoon cold butter. Season with salt and freshly ground black pepper. Serve with grilled steak or veal chops.

SAUCE ROBERT: A zippy yet sophisticated sauce, this variation is smashing served over grilled hamburgers. Melt 2 tablespoons butter in a 1½-quart saucepan. Stir in 1 tablespoon finely chopped onion and cook over medium heat until translucent. Add 4 tablespoons red wine vinegar and ½ cup dry white wine. Simmer uncovered until reduced to ½ cup. Blend together 1 cup Basic Brown Sauce, 2 tablespoons ketchup, 1 tablespoon Dijon mustard, and 1 tablespoon finely chopped sweet pickle relish. Add to the reduced wine and heat until bubbling. Season with salt and freshly ground black pepper.

SAUCE CHASSEUR: Melt 2 tablespoons of butter in a 1½-quart saucepan. Stir in 6 finely chopped fresh mushrooms, 1 minced shallot, and 1 minced garlic clove. Cook over medium heat until the mushrooms are tender. Add ¾ cup dry white wine, 1 tablespoon to-

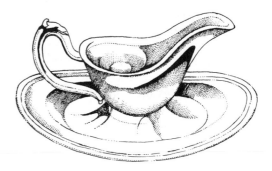

mato paste, 1 teaspoon dried tarragon leaves, and ½ teaspoon dried basil. Simmer uncovered until reduced to ½ cup. Blend in 1 cup Basic Brown Sauce and heat until bubbling. Serve with roast or grilled chicken, broiled pork chops, or sautéed veal.   ᴇᴈ

Basic Brown Sauce from Soup Mix

MAKES 4 CUPS

Here's a real shortcut that gives busy cooks the opportunity to have on hand a very acceptable substitute for Basic Brown Sauce.

1 box (2⅝ ounces) Knorr-Swiss dry oxtail soup
  mix
5 cups cold water
1 cup dry white wine
1 medium onion, quartered
1 medium carrot, sliced
1 celery rib, sliced
6 fresh mushrooms, quartered
1 garlic clove
2 sprigs fresh parsley
1 bay leaf, broken in half
½ teaspoon dried leaf thyme
2 tablespoons Madeira
Salt and freshly ground black pepper

1. In a 4½-quart saucepan, combine the soup mix and water and place over medium heat. Add the white wine and bring to a boil, stirring constantly, to break up the lumps of dry soup mix.

2. Stir in the onion, carrot, celery, and mushrooms. Add the garlic, parsley, bay leaf, and thyme. Regulate the heat so that the liquid barely bubbles. Cook uncovered for 1½ hours or until the vegetables are tender. Pour through a sieve and return to the pan.

3. Blend in the Madeira and cook uncovered at a gentle bubble until the liquid is reduced to 4 cups. Season with salt and pepper. Use immediately or freeze in 1-cup portions.   ᴇᴈ

WHITE SAUCES

Long considered a staple in American kitchens, this cosmopolitan sauce has venerable roots in the cuisines of France and Italy. In French cookery, it is called béchamel or velouté, depending on whether it's made with milk or stock, and in the cuisine of Italy it is differentiated as balsamella or salsa bianca on the same basis. All white sauces are exceptionally versatile and may be made in three degrees of thickness: 1 tablespoon of flour per cup of liquid produces a thin, or light, white sauce; 2 tablespoons of flour per cup of liquid produces a medium white sauce; 3 tablespoons of flour per cup of liquid produces a thick, or heavy, white sauce.

White Sauce with Milk (Béchamel or Balsamella)

MAKES ABOUT 1 CUP MEDIUM SAUCE

2 tablespoons butter
2 tablespoons flour
¼ teaspoon salt
¼ teaspoon ground cayenne
1 cup milk
Freshly ground nutmeg (optional)

1. Over medium heat, melt the butter in a 1½-quart thick-bottomed saucepan. Remove the melted butter from the heat. Add the flour all at once. Stir in the salt and cayenne and blend well. Return to medium heat and cook, stirring continuously, until the butter and flour begin to bubble. Continue stirring as the mixture froths for 2 to 3 minutes. Do not allow the roux to darken past the color of melted butter.

2. Meanwhile, in another saucepan, heat the milk over medium heat. When the surface wrinkles (it isn't necessary to bring it to a boil, but no harm is done if you do), remove the pan from the heat.

3. When the butter-flour mixture is cooked, remove the pan from the heat and immediate-

ly pour the *hot* milk into the *hot* roux. Whisk vigorously and return the pan to medium heat. Gradually increase the heat to high, whisking continuously, until the sauce smooths out and thickens. Blend in the nutmeg and bring to a boil. Cook, stirring with a heat-resistant rubber spatula, for 1 minute. Use immediately or lay a piece of plastic wrap directly on the surface of the sauce and refrigerate. White sauce may also be frozen.

White Sauce with Stock (Velouté or Salsa Bianca)

MAKES ABOUT 1 CUP MEDIUM SAUCE

2 tablespoons butter
2 tablespoons flour
¼ teaspoon salt
¼ teaspoon ground cayenne
1 cup Chicken Stock (p. 343), veal stock or
Light Brown Stock (p. 342), or Fish Stock
(p. 344)

1. Over medium heat, melt the butter in a 1½-quart thick-bottomed saucepan. Remove the melted butter from the heat. Add the flour all at once. Stir in the salt and cayenne and blend well. Return to medium heat and cook, stirring continuously, until the butter and flour begin to bubble. Continue stirring as the mixture froths for 2 to 3 minutes. Do not allow the roux to darken past the color of melted butter.

2. Meanwhile, in another saucepan, heat the stock over medium heat. When it bubbles, remove the pan from the heat.

3. When the butter-flour mixture is cooked, remove the pan from the heat and immediately pour the *hot* stock into the *hot* roux. Whisk vigorously and return the pan to medium heat. Gradually increase the heat to high, whisking continuously, until the sauce smooths out and thickens. Bring to a boil and cook, stirring with a heat-resistant rubber spatula, for 1 minute. Use immediately or lay a piece of plastic wrap directly on the surface of the sauce and refrigerate. White sauce may also be frozen.

Variations on White Sauce

MORNAY SAUCE: Although Gruyère and Parmesan are the traditional cheeses to use when forming this sauce, other types of cheeses create interesting effects. Try adding Italian fontina, Monterey Jack, herbed Boursin, Gorgonzola, Stilton, Bel Paese, or Montrachet. Grate or crumble 2 to 3 ounces per cup of sauce. Blend into White Sauce with Milk (p. 348) and heat gently to melt the cheese. (A thin white sauce containing melted Stilton tossed with fettuccine makes an outstanding first course or light luncheon.) Mornay Sauce can also be prepared by using White Sauce with Stock, in which case it's best to limit your choice of cheese to those with less competitive flavors.

SOUBISE SAUCE: A delightful onion sauce that can be used to particularly stunning effect in vegetable dishes like potatoes au gratin that are to be gratinéed. Peel and slice 3 large sweet onions. Melt 6 tablespoons of butter in a skillet or wide saucepan and add the onions, tossing to coat. Cover the pan and cook over low heat for 20 to 30 minutes or until the onions are tender and have taken on a yellow hue (do not allow them to brown). Sprinkle with ¼ teaspoon salt, freshly ground white pepper, and freshly grated nutmeg. Add 2 tablespoons medium cream and 2 cups of medium White Sauce with Milk (double the recipe on p. 348). Heat, stirring, until the mixture begins to bubble. Transfer to a blender or processor and whirl briefly to purée.

TARRAGON SAUCE: An exceptionally rich, flavorful sauce to serve with poached chicken or fish. In a 1½-quart nonreactive saucepan, combine ½ cup dry white wine, 1 minced shallot (or substitute 1½ teaspoons freeze-dried), and 1 teaspoon dried tarragon leaves. Place over medium heat and bring to a gentle bubble. Cook until the wine is reduced to half the original amount. Strain, returning the reduced wine to the saucepan. Stir in 1 cup medium, or whipping, cream. Add 1 cup medium White Sauce with Stock (p. 349) made with chicken stock, and 1 tablespoon lemon juice. Place over medium heat and whisk continuously until the mixture bubbles and smooths out. Season with salt and freshly ground white pepper.

BERCY SAUCE MOUSSELINE: In a nonreactive 1½-quart saucepan, combine ¾ cup dry white wine, 6 sliced fresh mushrooms, 1 minced shallot (or substitute 1½ teaspoons freeze-dried), and ½ teaspoon dried leaf thyme. Place over medium heat and bring to a gentle bubble. Cook until the wine is reduced to half the original amount. Strain, returning the reduced wine to the saucepan. Add 1 cup medium White Sauce with Stock (p. 349) made with fish stock and 1 tablespoon lemon juice. Place over medium heat and whisk continuously until the mixture bubbles and smooths out. Season with salt and freshly ground white pepper. Whip 1 cup of heavy cream and fold into the warm sauce. Pour over poached or baked fish fillets and slide under the broiler to brown lightly.

SAUCE NANTUA: Strictly speaking, the term *Nantua* denotes the inclusion of crayfish; however, shrimp, lobster, or crabmeat may be substituted. Place 6 ounces of cooked crayfish, shrimp, lobster, or crabmeat in the container of a blender or processor. Add 1 tablespoon tomato paste, 1 tablespoon lemon juice, and 1 cup medium cream. Whirl briefly to purée. Transfer to a 1½-quart saucepan and add 1 cup medium White Sauce with Stock (p. 349) made with fish stock. Place over medium heat and whisk until the mixture bubbles and smooths out.

Blend in 2 tablespoons of cognac and season with salt and freshly ground white pepper. Cook, stirring, for 1 minute. Serve over poached or baked scallops or fish fillets. Garnish with whole cooked shrimp or medallions of cooked lobster.   ◄៩

Cream Sauce

MAKES 2 CUPS MEDIUM SAUCE

This popular sauce is used to prepare cream-style dishes. You can proceed in one of two ways: make the richer, more velvety version by forming a white sauce with medium cream instead of milk and then thinning it further with additional cream; or produce a lighter sauce by forming the white sauce with milk and then thinning it with light or medium cream as described in the recipe below.

1 cup medium White Sauce with Milk (p. 348)
1 cup light or medium cream

1. Combine the white sauce and ½ cup of the cream in a 1½-quart saucepan. Place over medium heat and cook, stirring, until the mixture bubbles.

2. Gradually whisk in the remaining cream (there's no need to warm it). Increase the heat and continue whisking until the sauce bubbles and smooths out. Use immediately, or lay a piece of plastic wrap directly on the surface and refrigerate. Cream sauce may also be frozen.   ◄៩

Meat Glaze

MAKES 1 CUP

Beef glaze (glace de viande), *chicken glaze* (glace de volaille), *and fish glaze* (glace de poisson) *are flavorful essences all made the same way — a quantity of stock or broth is reduced to a concentrated syrup. When chilled, these glazes develop a rubbery, solidly gelled consistency. They may be stored in the refrigerator or frozen. In fact, you might want to cut the solidified glaze into teaspoon-size chunks and freeze them on a flat baking sheet. Transferred to an airtight bag, they can be frozen for up to 6 months.*

2 quarts Dark Brown Stock I (p. 340) or Light Brown Stock (p. 342) or Beef Broth (p. 192), Chicken Stock (p. 343) or Chicken Broth (p. 193), or Fish Stock (p. 344)

1. Degrease the stock completely by refrigerating it overnight and then lifting the solidified fat from the surface. Heat a metal spoon under hot water and draw the edge of the spoon over the chilled stock to remove every last trace of fat and spongy debris.

2. Transfer the stock to a thick-bottomed saucepan. Place over high heat and bring to a brisk bubble. Boil uncovered for 30 minutes. Skim off any foam that forms.

3. Reduce the heat to medium and continue to cook uncovered. Watch closely as the water evaporates and the stock becomes more concentrated. When the color of the liquid begins to darken and it develops a slightly thickened consistency, reduce the heat to low and cook slowly. Glaze reduces very rapidly toward the end and is apt to get away from you, so stir constantly to prevent burning during the final stages.

NOTE: Glaze may be prepared in any amount that's convenient. Four cups of stock reduces to ½ cup of glaze; or for a very small amount, 1 cup of stock reduces to 2 tablespoons. Should you wish to reconstitute glaze to make stock, add 7 parts water to 1 part glaze.   ◄ई

Chicken Glaze

MAKES 2 TO 3 TABLESPOONS

Here's a quick and easy way to obtain a small amount of full-bodied chicken glaze. This technique involves nothing more than cooking down the pan juices left over from roasting a chicken.

1 roasting chicken
2 cups water

1. After roasting the chicken, deglaze the pan with 2 cups of water, scraping up all particles of coagulated meat protein and bits of cooked meat. Empty into a glass jar, cover tightly, and refrigerate for at least 24 hours.

2. Remove the solidified fat from the surface and place the deglazing liquid in 1½-quart saucepan. Bring to a boil and cook briskly until reduced to 1 cup. Pour through a cheesecloth-lined sieve into a clean saucepan. Return liquid to medium heat and cook until reduced to a syrupy consistency. You'll have 2 to 3 tablespoons of full-flavored liquid. Pour into a glass jar and refrigerate. As the liquid cools, it will solidify and form a transparent gel with a rubbery consistency.   ◄ई

Buttered Tomato Sauce

SERVES 4 TO 6

Velvety is the only way to describe this ultra-rich sauce. Use it to enhance small portions of stuffed pasta served as a first course or to accent Polenta Triangles (p. 320).

2 tablespoons olive oil
8 tablespoons butter
1 medium onion, coarsely chopped
1 can (35 ounces) Italian tomatoes, undrained
1 teaspoon sugar
2 strips (each 2½ inches long) of orange zest (do not substitute dried orange peel)
1 large bay leaf, broken in half
1 tablespoon chopped fresh basil (or substitute 1 teaspoon dried)
¼ teaspoon salt
Generous amount of freshly ground white pepper

1. Heat the olive oil and 2 tablespoons of the butter in a thick-bottomed saucepan until the butter melts. Stir in the onion and toss to coat. Cover the pan and lower the heat to its lowest setting. Cook for 20 minutes or until the onion has taken on a golden hue.

2. Add the tomatoes, breaking them up with your fingers. Stir in the sugar. Remove

the zest from an orange with a swivel-blade peeler. Submerge the zest and the bay leaf in the tomato mixture. Stir in the fresh basil and salt. Bring to a gentle bubble and cook uncovered for 30 minutes.

3. Lift out the orange peel and bay leaf with a fork, and put the sauce through a food mill. Blend in the pepper and return to low heat. Divide the remaining 6 tablespoons of butter into 12 equal portions. Stirring constantly, add one piece of butter at a time. When it melts, add another piece. Continue until all the butter is incorporated. Refrigerate or use immediately.   ❧

Summer Sauce

SAUCE FOR 1 POUND OF PASTA

To achieve the most vibrant flavor, make this sauce during those last few weeks at the end of summer when native tomatoes are bursting at the seams and fresh basil appears in the supermarket. The natural sugar contained in fresh, sweet carrots counteracts the acidity of the tomatoes to produce an exceptionally smooth flavor. Tomatoes lose acidity as they ripen, so using tomatoes at the peak of ripeness adds to the smoothness of the sauce.

2 tablespoons olive oil
2 tablespoons butter
1 large sweet onion (Bermuda or Vidalia), cut
    into eighths
2 slender carrots, sliced
1 garlic clove, sliced
3 to 4 pounds ripe tomatoes
1 teaspoon sugar (optional)
½ teaspoon salt
Freshly ground black pepper
20 large fresh basil leaves

1. In a thick-bottomed saucepan or Dutch oven, heat the oil and butter together. Add the onion, carrots, and garlic, tossing to coat. Cover the pan and cook over low heat until the onion is translucent.

2. Meanwhile, begin preparing the tomatoes by placing them in the sink on their stem ends. (Leave the drain open.) Pour boiling water over them, washing them and loosening their skins. Peel immediately. Remove the stem-end cores with a grapefruit knife. Cut into quarters and transfer to the saucepan. Stir in sugar, salt, and pepper. Bring to a boil and adjust the heat so that the mixture bubbles gently. Cover and cook for 1 hour.

3. The secret of fine tomato sauce lies in avoiding the burnt flavor that results when bits of sauce cook to the side of the pan. Therefore, as the sauce thickens, reduce the heat of the burner so that the mixture won't splatter up onto the sides of the pan. Uncover and continue cooking until the carrots are tender (about 1 hour).

4. Put the mixture through a food mill. Pour the purée into a clean pan and place over moderate heat. When bubbles begin to appear, reduce the heat to its lowest setting. Chop the basil or snip with kitchen shears. Add to the sauce. Cook uncovered without bubbling for 1½ hours. When you stir, be certain not to leave any sauce on the sides of the pan; clear the sides with a heat-resistant rubber spatula. To test for proper consistency, spoon some onto a plate. When no ring of liquid appears around the edge, the sauce is sufficiently reduced. Serve over hot spaghetti or spinach fettuccine.

NOTE: This method produces a somewhat coarsely textured consistency that's in keeping with the informal spirit of this dish. If you would prefer a smoother, richer version, follow this procedure: Peel each tomato, remove the core with a grapefruit knife, and scoop out the seeds by running your index finger around the seed cavities. Break the tomatoes up into quarters and add to the simmering vegetables. Cook as described above (except that the reduction time will be much shorter because much of the tomato liquid has been removed with the seeds). When the carrots are tender, purée the mixture in a blender or processor and pour into a clean pan. Add the chopped basil and reduce over low heat until completely thickened. Just before serving, stir in 4 tablespoons of cold butter, 1 tablespoon at a time.

Tomato sauce containing seeds should never be puréed in a blender or processor because pulverized seeds lend a bitter, unpleasant flavor. If you want the more homogenized consistency provided by a blender, first remove the tomato seeds by putting the sauce through a food mill or by seeding the uncooked tomatoes.   ⁓

the sauce is reduced and able to coat the back of a spoon with a creamy film. Season with salt and white pepper. Refrigerate or chill by stirring over ice. When the sauce reaches a slightly thickened coating consistency, it is ready to spoon or pour. (It should have a pouring texture like that of maple syrup.)

NOTE: To create a creamy brown coating to use over cold beef or game, substitute Dark Brown Stock I or II (p. 340 or p. 341) in place of the chicken stock.   ⁓

Chaud-Froid Sauce

MAKES 2 CUPS

This is the elegant white coating seen on cold dishes displayed on extravagant buffet tables. In this recipe, which is easier to manage than the classic technique, cream is reduced with chicken stock, and then gelatin is added. The result is a creamy aspic that coats smoothly and firms when chilled. Try it over cold chicken breasts or use it to coat a whole ham. Decorate the surface with slivers of carrots or fine strands of green onion leaves.

5 tablespoons Madeira
½ teaspoon dried tarragon leaves
2 cups Chicken Stock (p. 343)
1 cup medium, or whipping, cream
2 teaspoons unflavored gelatin
¼ teaspoon salt
Freshly ground white pepper

1. Pour 4 tablespoons of the Madeira into a nonreactive 1-quart saucepan. Place over medium heat and warm until the surface ripples. Remove from the heat and stir in the tarragon. Set aside to steep.

2. In a 2½-quart saucepan, combine the stock and cream. Place over medium-high heat and bring to a boil. Reduce the heat so that the liquid barely simmers and cook uncovered for 15 minutes. Strain the Madeira and blend into the sauce.

3. Soften the gelatin in the remaining 1 tablespoon of Madeira, and then add to the creamy mixture. Stir over medium heat until

Fiery Sauce

MAKES ABOUT 1½ CUPS

This sauce may be served cold as a summer dressing for shrimp or crabmeat or hot as a dipping sauce for appetizers such as deep-fried cheese cubes or falafel. Adjust the potency of the sauce by blending in more or less Tabasco sauce.

1 cup tomato purée
1 green sweet bell pepper, cut into strips
1 small onion, quartered
1 small cucumber, peeled and cut into chunks
1 garlic clove, quartered
3 sprigs fresh coriander leaves (cilantro)
1 tablespoon light brown sugar
1 teaspoon salt
⅛ teaspoon ground cardamom
⅛ teaspoon ground cayenne
Drops of Tabasco sauce (optional)

1. Combine the ingredients in the container of a blender or processor and whirl until smooth. Refrigerate in a glass jar. Serve cold or hot.   ⁓

Hot Mustard Sauce

MAKES ½ CUP

Serve as a dipping sauce for egg rolls, fried won tons, barbecued ribs, and appetizers such as batter-coated chicken wings and shrimp.

4 tablespoons dry mustard
2 tablespoons cold water
½ teaspoon sugar
Generous pinch of ground cayenne
3 tablespoons mayonnaise

1. Combine the mustard, water, and sugar in a small bowl. Blend until smooth.

2. Add the cayenne and mayonnaise. Cover and let stand at room temperature for 2 hours to allow the mustard to mellow. Refrigerate in a glass jar with a screw-top lid. Serve at room temperature or chilled. ❧

Sweet and Sour Sauce

MAKES ABOUT 1½ CUPS

The elusive taste sensation known as sweet and sour is created by combining sugar, which is sweet, with vinegar, which is acidic and perceived as sour. The combination is then accented with various other ingredients to round out this flavorful sauce. Serve with Fried Pork Packets (p. 185) or use as a dipping sauce with King Crab Puffs (p. 184).

3 tablespoons sugar
3 tablespoons white vinegar
2 tablespoons naturally brewed soy sauce
1 tablespoon ketchup
1 tablespoon molasses
1 garlic clove, pressed
1 tablespoon cornstarch
¾ cup chicken broth

1. Mix the sugar and vinegar in a 1½-quart saucepan. Place over medium-high heat and cook, stirring, until the sugar is dissolved.

2. Add the soy sauce, ketchup, molasses, and pressed garlic. Dissolve the cornstarch in the chicken broth. Stir into the sauce and bring to a boil. Stir continuously until the sauce is thickened and transparent. ❧

Yogurt Sauce

MAKES ABOUT 1¼ CUPS

Here's an elegant, refreshing sauce to serve with cold chicken or to pour over falafel patties in a pita sandwich.

1 cup unflavored yogurt
2 tablespoons finely chopped fresh mint
1 tablespoon fresh lemon juice
1 garlic clove, pressed
¼ teaspoon salt
⅛ teaspoon ground cayenne

1. Combine the ingredients in a small bowl. Blend well and refrigerate in a glass jar. Serve cold or let come to just under room temperature. ❧

MAYONNAISE

Mayonnaise is considered a cold emulsion sauce because it consists of oil droplets held in a permanent suspension by the lecithin in egg yolks. Because the egg yolks are not heated, a cold emulsion is slightly less tricky to create than a warm emulsion. The acid-water component in mayonnaise is usually fresh lemon juice, although aromatic vinegars can be used to make sophisticated and elegant cold emulsion sauces.

Mayonnaise (Basic)

MAKES ABOUT 1⅓ CUPS

This recipe can be prepared by hand or by using an electric mixer with a balloon whisk attachment. A large eye dropper or a thin-spouted oil container greatly simplifies the task of adding the oil drop by drop. For best results, have all your ingredients and implements at room temperature.

2 large egg yolks
1 teaspoon Dijon mustard
1 teaspoon salt
2 tablespoons fresh lemon juice
1 cup olive oil, corn oil, or peanut oil (or use a combination)
1 tablespoon *boiling* water

1. Select a large wide bowl with plenty of room for a whisk to move around in. Place the egg yolks, mustard, salt, and lemon juice in the bowl. Whisk lightly to blend. Cover the bowl with a towel and allow the contents to come to room temperature (about 30 minutes). Or warm the bowl, whisk, and oil in a 250°F. oven for 5 minutes before beginning.

2. Remove the towel and fold it into quarters. Set the bowl on top of the folded towel to keep the bowl from sliding as you whisk. Whisk the contents of the bowl until they thicken slightly and you can begin to see traces left by the whisk.

3. Whisking continuously, add the room-temperature oil drop by drop. This is very important to the success of the emulsion because the object is to break the oil drops up into tiny droplets, each one surrounded by the lecithin in the egg yolk. If you add the oil faster than the drops can be broken into droplets, the oil drops will cling together and form puddles of oil.

4. As the emulsion forms, you should feel the mixture thicken. If you don't, you're adding the oil too fast. When half the oil has been added by drops, and the mixture is quite thick, it's safe to add the rest by pouring it in a thin stream. If oil puddles form at any time, you've poured too fast. Whisk vigorously for 1 minute. If the oil refuses to disappear, start over with a clean bowl and a fresh supply of lecithin in the form of an egg yolk. Whisk the yolk until it is light in color. Gradually whisk

in the mayonnaise. Then slowly incorporate any remaining oil.

5. Make a slight depression in the center. Add the boiling water all at once and whisk to blend thoroughly. (This will keep, refrigerated in a glass jar with a screw-top lid, for a week to 10 days.)

NOTE: When substituting vinegar for lemon juice, use 1 tablespoon of vinegar per egg yolk. Possibilities include sherry vinegar, raspberry or strawberry vinegar, tarragon-flavored vinegar, or Aceto Balsamico.

Adding other ingredients to mayonnaise transforms it into a variety of sauces.

AIOLI: To ¾ cup of Mayonnaise, add 2 pressed garlic cloves, 2 tablespoons white wine vinegar, and ½ teaspoon sweet Hungarian paprika. Serve Aioli with cold shrimp or poached fish. Stir it into fish stew or use as a dip for fresh vegetables.

AVOCADO SAUCE: To ¾ cup of Mayonnaise, add 2 tablespoons fresh lemon juice, 1 pressed garlic clove, 1 teaspoon minced onion, ½ teaspoon Worcestershire sauce, and a generous amount of freshly ground pepper. Mash half an avocado and blend in. Add 2 tablespoons crumbled bacon. Serve Avocado Sauce with grilled hamburgers or chilled tuna, or spoon over sliced tomatoes.

CURRY SAUCE: To ¾ cup of Mayonnaise, add 2 tablespoons unflavored yogurt, 1 teaspoon curry powder, ¼ cup chopped almonds, and 2 tablespoons raisins. Serve Curry sauce with cold chicken, turkey, lobster, crabmeat, cold hard-boiled eggs, or cucumber salad.

MALTAISE SAUCE: To ¾ cup Mayonnaise, add ¼ cup fresh orange juice and 1 teaspoon grated orange zest. Serve Maltaise Sauce over hot asparagus or cooked carrots.

TARTAR SAUCE: To ¾ cup Mayonnaise, add 1 tablespoon lemon juice, ¼ cup sweet pickle relish, 6 minced capers, 1 teaspoon Worcestershire sauce, and 6 drops Tabasco sauce. Season generously with salt and freshly ground pepper. Serve with hot or cold fish. ∙ᖹ

Mayonnaise by Blender or Processor

MAKES ABOUT 1½ CUPS

Mayonnaise made by machine isn't as light and exquisitely textured as mayonnaise made by hand because very little air is incorporated during the process; however, it certainly is quicker and easier. Both the processor and the blender homogenize the oil drops, breaking them into extremely tiny droplets, all the same size. This increases the volume of the mayonnaise to a limited degree and gives it a slightly rigid texture. Also, since mayonnaise made by processor or blender must include the white of an egg in order to achieve an acceptable consistency, it isn't quite as rich as mayonnaise made from egg yolks alone.

Excess agitation can break an emulsion. Therefore, if you use a blender, your safest approach is to set it at its lowest speed; if you use a processor, be sure to process no longer than absolutely necessary.

2 large eggs
1 teaspoon Dijon mustard
1 teaspoon salt
2 tablespoons fresh lemon juice
1¼ cups olive oil, corn oil, or peanut oil (or use a combination)
1 tablespoon *boiling* water

1. Set out all the ingredients at least 30 minutes ahead of time so that they will warm to room temperature.

2. Place the eggs, mustard, salt, and lemon juice in the container of a blender or processor equipped with a steel blade. Pulse briefly to combine. Then, with the machine running at low speed, add the oil by pouring it in a thin stream through the hole in the cover of the blender or through the feed tube of the processor.

3. When all the oil has been added, immediately stop the machine and check to see if it has been thoroughly incorporated. If it hasn't, scrape down the sides of the container with a spatula and pulse in very short spurts until the blending is complete. Take care not to overblend.

4. Empty the mayonnaise into a bowl. Make a slight depression in the center and add the boiling water all at once. Whisk vigorously to incorporate. (This will keep, refrigerated in a glass jar with a screw-top lid, for a week to 10 days.) ∙ᖹ

HOLLANDAISE SAUCES

If you've ever felt the least bit hesitant about attempting hollandaise sauce, try using the bowl-in-a-pan method rather than a double boiler. That, plus the incorporation of cold butter (instead of the melted butter many recipes call for), positively guarantees your success. The addition of cold butter repeatedly lowers the temperature of the mixture to help you avoid scrambling the eggs. As the butter melts, it's incorporated into the sauce in the most gradual manner possible.

The decision to use salted, unsalted, or clarified butter is determined by taste. Unsalted butter definitely produces a lighter flavor, but if you use top-quality fresh salted butter, you can nearly duplicate that flavor by omitting the salt called for in the recipe. Clarified butter is another matter. Most of the flavor elements associated with butter are in the milk solids that are separated out during the clarifying process. Therefore, sauces made with clarified butter are considerably milder — maybe even disappointing. If you decide to use clarified butter, chill the butter-fat until firm to use it in the following cold-butter technique.

Leftover hollandaise sauce can be chilled until firm, and then spooned in dollops onto a waxed-paper-lined baking sheet. Freeze until hard and transfer the dollops to an airtight plastic bag. Remove from the freezer 20 minutes before serving time. They will soften slightly. Placed atop hot food, the frozen sauce will melt to its original consistency. (This works so well, I frequently make up batches of sauce to keep on hand this way.)

Hollandaise Sauce (Bowl-In-A-Pan Method)

MAKES ABOUT ¾ CUP

This sauce is made by forming an emulsion with lemon juice as the acid-water component. Adding ground cayenne gives you the zip of pepper without the little black specks and intensifies the color of the sauce. Freshly ground white pepper may be used instead, but increase the amount because white pepper is milder.

8 tablespoons cold salted, unsalted, or clarified butter
2 large egg yolks
1 tablespoon lemon juice
½ teaspoon salt (optional)
Pinch of ground cayenne

1. Cut the cold butter into 24 small cubes by cutting the stick into quarters lengthwise and then dividing the quarters into 6 equal portions. (If you're using chilled clarified butter, cut it into 24 equal portions.) Return the butter to the refrigerator.

2. Select a stainless steel or glass bowl and a saucepan that accommodate each other so that the bowl sits no more than halfway down into the pan. There should be at least 2 inches between the water in the pan and the bottom of the bowl. Add water to the pan to a depth of ½ inch. Bring the water to a boil and reduce the heat so that the water is steaming but not bubbling. If you decide to use a double boiler instead, make certain that at least a 2-inch space exists between the water and the bottom of the upper container.

3. Put the egg yolks through a sieve to prevent tiny particles of coagulated egg white from marring the finished sauce. Combine the strained egg yolks with the lemon juice, salt, and cayenne in a bowl or the top of a double boiler. Whisk the mixture until it is slightly thickened and lemon colored. Place over the steaming water. Immediately drop in 4 butter cubes and whisk until they disappear. Repeat this procedure 1 cube at a time until you have 1 cube left. Around the ninth or tenth cube, the sauce will begin to thicken. As additional butter is incorporated, an even thicker consistency may develop. The final texture of the sauce should be firm, but pourable. If the sauce is too thick to pour, that's an indication that the moisture content is too low, and the sauce is almost certain to separate upon standing. A sauce that's unstable because of too little moisture develops a grainy appearance around the edge. The texture can be smoothed out by vigorous whisking, but the slightest increase in temperature (even pouring it over hot food) will cause the sauce to separate. Consequently, it's important to add moisture to a sauce that is too thick to pour. Whisk in a small amount of cream or cool water, drop by drop, until the sauce will run easily from a spoon.

4. When the proper consistency has been attained, remove the bowl from the hot water, set it on a folded towel, and whisk in the remaining cube of butter. Without waiting, pour the completed sauce into a bowl, sauce boat, or thermos. (The residual heat from the container it has been cooked in can cause the sauce to separate.) If for any reason you want to cover the sauce for a short time, loosely drape a paper towel over the bowl — it's

porous enough to allow steam to escape so that condensation will not form.   ❧

Saucepan Hollandaise

MAKES ABOUT ¾ CUP

Making hollandaise in a saucepan is a somewhat quicker method than making it the bowl-in-a-pan way, and there's only one pan to wash. Once you get accustomed to this method, you'll probably use it all the time, but the risk is that the eggs will overheat and therefore overcoagulate, releasing butterfat and whatever water they've been holding in suspension. It's important to work over very low heat (a heat diffuser is a great help) and to use a thick-bottomed pan.

Diluting the eggs with a small amount of water slows the coagulation of the protein molecules and provides a margin of safety against scrambling. As the mixture heats, the water evaporates as steam so the flavor of the completed sauce is not affected in any way.

An emulsion sauce in the first stages of separation can be rescued by sharply reducing the temperature; keep a cup of ice water or chips of ice nearby. If the butter starts to puddle on the surface of the sauce, pull the sauce off the heat and quickly whisk in a few drops of ice water or chips of ice.

8 tablespoons cold salted, unsalted, or clarified
   butter
2 large egg yolks
1 tablespoon lemon juice
1 tablespoon cold water
½ teaspoon salt (optional)
Pinch of ground cayenne

1. Cut the cold butter into 24 small cubes by cutting a stick into quarters lengthwise, then dividing the quarters into 6 equal portions. (If you're using chilled clarified butter, cut it into 24 equal portions.) Return the butter to the refrigerator.

2. Put the egg yolks through a sieve to prevent tiny particles of coagulated egg white

from marring the completed sauce. Combine in a 1½-quart nonreactive saucepan with the lemon juice, water, salt, and cayenne. Whisk until slightly thickened and lemon colored. Drop in 4 butter cubes and place the pan over low heat. Stir continuously with a heat-resistant rubber spatula, frequently clearing the outer edges of the pan. When the butter disappears, stir in the remaining butter cubes 1 at a time until you have 1 cube left. The sauce will thicken gradually. Remove the pan from the burner and stir in the remaining cube of butter.

3. Immediately pour into a bowl or sauceboat, straining if necessary, or transfer to a thermos bottle or other insulated container and seal.

NOTE: Hollandaise Sauce can be transformed into a variety of sauces by adding other ingredients.

SAUCE MALTAISE: Stir 1 tablespoon tangerine juice, or the juice of a blood orange, and 1 teaspoon tangerine zest into ¾ cup of Hollandaise Sauce. Serve with broccoli or asparagus.

SAUCE MOUSSELINE: Fold 2 heaping tablespoons of whipped cream or whipped Crème Fraîche (p. 361) into ¾ cup of Hollandaise Sauce. Serve with fish, fish soufflés, or poached eggs.

SAUCE CÂPRES: Drain 1 tablespoon capers and stir into ¾ cup of Hollandaise Sauce. Serve with poached salmon or broiled fish.

SAUCE SUPREME: Stir 1½ teaspoons melted and cooled Chicken Glaze (p. 351) into ¾ cup of Hollandaise Sauce. Serve over broiled or sautéed chicken.

SAUCE CURRIE: Stir ½ teaspoon of fresh curry powder (p. 281) into ¾ cup of Hollandaise Sauce. Serve over cold, sliced hard-boiled eggs or cold chicken.   ❧

Béarnaise Sauce

MAKES ABOUT ¾ CUP

Vinegar infused with tarragon and shallots is the acid used to form this warm emulsion. The dried tarragon and freeze-dried shallots suggested in this recipe will release their flavor when they're heated in the vinegar. Using the bowl-in-a-pan method instead of the traditional double boiler enables you to whisk in a greater amount of air and achieve a lighter, silkier texture.

¼ cup white wine vinegar
¼ cup dry white wine
1½ teaspoons freeze-dried shallots (or substitute
   1 fresh shallot, minced)
1 teaspoon dried tarragon leaves
½ teaspoon salt (optional)
Pinch of ground cayenne
8 tablespoons cold salted, unsalted, or clarified
   butter
2 large egg yolks

1. Measure the vinegar and wine into a 1½-quart stainless steel or other nonreactive saucepan. Add the shallots, tarragon, salt, and cayenne. Bring to a gentle bubble and cook over moderate heat until reduced to 2 tablespoons. Strain into a stainless steel or glass bowl (see step 2 under Hollandaise Sauce, p. 357) or the top of a double boiler. Pour water into a large saucepan or the bottom container of a double boiler. It should be 2 inches below the bottom of the upper con-tainer. To ensure the correct temperature conditions, bring the water to a boil, and then reduce the heat so that the water is steaming but not bubbling.

2. Meanwhile, cut the butter into 24 small cubes by cutting the stick into quarters lengthwise and then dividing the quarters into 6 equal portions. (If you're using chilled clarified butter, cut it into 24 equal portions.) Return the butter to the refrigerator.

3. When the infusion liquid is barely warm to the touch, or cools to below 120°F., put the egg yolks through a sieve to catch tiny particles of egg white that could coagulate when heated and mar the completed sauce. Then add the egg yolks to the mixture. Whisk until the mixture is slightly thickened and lemon colored. Place over steaming water. Immediately drop in 4 cubes of butter and whisk until they disappear. Repeat this procedure 1 cube at a time until you have 1 cube left. Around the ninth or tenth cube, the sauce will begin to thicken. As additional butter is incorporated, an even thicker consistency may develop. The final texture of the sauce should be firm, but pourable. If the sauce is too thick to pour, that's an indication that the moisture content is too low, and the sauce is almost certain to separate upon standing. A sauce that's unstable because of too little moisture develops a grainy appearance around the edge. The texture can be smoothed out by vigorous whisking, but the slightest increase in temperature (even pouring it over hot food) will cause the sauce to separate. Consequently, it's important to add moisture to a sauce that is too thick to pour. Whisk in a small amount of cream or cool water, drop by drop, until the sauce will run easily from a spoon.

4. Remove the bowl from the hot water, set it on a folded towel, and whisk in the remaining cube of butter. Without waiting, pour the completed sauce into a bowl, sauce boat, or thermos. (The residual heat from the container it has been cooked in can cause the sauce to separate.) If for any reason you want to cover the sauce for a short time, loosely

drape a paper towel over the bowl — it's porous enough to allow steam to escape so condensation will not form.

NOTE: This sauce can also be prepared in a saucepan. Follow the recipe for Saucepan Hollandaise (p. 358), reducing the vinegar and wine infusion in the saucepan first. Strain the liquid and return to the saucepan. Stir in 1 tablespoon cold water to cool the infusion, and put the egg yolks through a sieve and add. Whisk until slightly thickened and place over low heat. Incorporate the cold butter in the manner described above.

Béarnaise Sauce can be transformed into a variety of sauces by adding other ingredients.

SAUCE CHORON: Stir 1 tablespoon of tomato paste or purée into ¾ cup of Béarnaise Sauce. Serve with grilled fish or roasted veal.

SAUCE FOYOT: Blend 1½ teaspoons of melted and cooled Meat Glaze (p. 350) into ¾ cup of Béarnaise Sauce. Serve with small pan-fried steaks or broiled lamb chops.

BÉARNAISE MOUSSELINE: Fold 2 heaping tablespoons of whipped cream or whipped Crème Fraîche (p. 361) into ¾ cup of Béarnaise Sauce. Serve with grilled or roasted chicken.   ◈

2 large egg yolks
1 teaspoon lemon juice
½ teaspoon salt (optional)
Pinch of ground cayenne

1. Place fish stock in a 1½-quart nonreactive pan. Cook until reduced to ⅓ cup. Transfer to a stainless steel or glass bowl (see step 2 under Hollandaise Sauce, p. 357) or the top of a double boiler.

2. Meanwhile, cut the butter into 16 small cubes and return to the refrigerator.

3. When the stock is barely warm to the touch, or cools to below 120°F., put the egg yolks through a sieve to catch tiny particles of egg white that could coagulate when heated. Add the egg yolks, whisk in the lemon juice, and whip until foamy. Place over steaming water. Immediately drop in 2 butter cubes and whisk until they disappear. Repeat this procedure 1 cube at a time until you have 1 cube left. The sauce will thicken and become frothy. Remove the bowl from the hot water, wipe the bottom dry, and whisk in the remaining cube of butter. Taste and correct seasoning by whisking in salt and cayenne. Serve with baked or poached fillet of sole or other delicately flavored fish.

NOTE: Use chicken or veal stock when you want to serve sabayon with chicken or beef. Fold in 2 heaping tablespoons of whipped cream to create Sabayon Mousseline, a lighter, richer version.   ◈

Fish Sabayon

MAKES ABOUT 1 CUP

Similar in preparation to Béarnaise Sauce, this sabayon is based on reduced stock emulsified with egg yolks and cold butter. It is referred to as a sabayon because a greater proportion of liquid is incorporated, creating a final texture that's somewhat frothy.

1½ cups of Fish Stock or Quick Fish Stock (p. 344; see also Note, p. 345)
8 tablespoons cold salted, unsalted, or clarified butter

Whipped Butter Sauce (Beurre Blanc)

MAKES ABOUT ½ CUP

Shallots and a fine grade of white wine vinegar are the components essential to the quality of this sauce. As in other sauce recipes, the use of salted or unsalted butter is a matter of taste preference only.

2 tablespoons dry white wine
2 tablespoons white wine vinegar

1 medium shallot (or substitute 1½ teaspoons freeze-dried)
½ cup butter
Pinch of salt
Pinch of ground cayenne

1. Combine the wine, vinegar, and shallot in a nonreactive thick-bottomed 1½-quart saucepan. Place over medium heat and cook uncovered until the liquid almost completely evaporates. Stir the shallot during the final stages of reduction to prevent burning. The shallot will take on a golden hue. At that point only enough liquid will remain to moisten it. Immediately remove from the heat and allow to cool for 10 minutes.

2. Meanwhile, divide the stick (½ cup) of butter into 4 equal portions, and then cut each portion into 8 cubes to form 32 small cubes of butter. Return the butter to the refrigerator. Incorporating small cubes of cold butter is the secret to success with this sauce.

3. Fold a kitchen towel into quarters and lay it nearby to provide you with a place to securely rest the pan on its side. Heat a burner to medium. Drop 4 cubes of cold butter into the pan containing the cooled shallot. Whisking constantly (or stirring with a heat-resistant rubber spatula), place the pan over the heat. As soon as you see the butter begin to soften, pull the pan from the heat. Set it on the folded towel at a 45° angle and continue whisking or stirring until all the butter is incorporated. Repeat this procedure 7 more times, each time dropping in 4 butter cubes and briefly returning the pan to the heat (until the first signs of softening). Whisk or stir continuously, adding the salt and cayenne with the last 4 butter cubes. Serve the sauce warm.

NOTE: This technique is similar to the one used to prepare Saucepan Hollandaise (p. 358) except that an emulsion formed by butter alone is less stable than an egg-yolk emulsion. Consequently, you need to repeatedly take the pan off the heat to prevent the butter from overheating and separating. This method gives you finer control over the heat than using a double boiler.

Crème Fraîche

Proportions involved in making homemade crème fraîche *are very flexible. Since the flavor of your final product is determined by the culture you start with, your first decision is whether to use sour cream, buttermilk, or yogurt. The other thing to keep in mind is the butterfat content of the blend. From a health standpoint, you may want the lowest amount of fat possible, so use skim-milk yogurt to create a low-calorie* crème fraîche. *A high ratio of fat protects the protein molecules from curdling, so high-fat* crème fraîche *is the most reliable for finishing hot sauces. Heavy cream plus sour cream create the fattiest, and therefore the most stable,* crème fraîche.

HIGH-FAT CRÈME FRAÎCHE

MAKES 1½ CUPS

½ cup sour cream
1 cup heavy cream

MEDIUM-HIGH-FAT CRÈME FRAÎCHE

MAKES 1 CUP

1 tablespoon buttermilk or yogurt
1 cup heavy cream

EXTRA-LOW-FAT CRÈME FRAÎCHE

MAKES 2 CUPS

1 cup skim-milk yogurt
1 cup heavy cream

1. Blend the ingredients thoroughly by stirring with a fork or whisk. Pour into a glass jar.

2. Cover the jar (because lactic-acid fermentation is an anaerobic process) and set aside at room temperature — 75°F. is just about perfect. Under less favorable conditions, you can use a wide-mouth thermos to help you regulate the temperature. Rinse a thermos with hot water to compensate for a chilly room or with cold water to counterbalance the effects of an overly hot room. Check

the mixture after 8 hours. If it hasn't thickened and developed a slightly sour tang, stir and recover for another 2 hours. Continue to check at 2-hour intervals; mixtures containing less culture take longer to thicken.

3. Refrigerate the *crème fraîche* in a tightly covered glass jar. It will keep for 7 to 10 days.

NOTE: If your kitchen is especially cold or if you want to speed fermentation, you can blend the ingredients together and warm them slowly in a heavy saucepan until the mixture reaches 85°F. Immediately remove from the heat and pour into a glass jar to prevent any increase in temperature from residual heat.

Desserts

Basic Pie Crust

MAKES TWO GENEROUS 9-INCH CRUSTS

This recipe may be altered in several ways. If you're a beginning crust maker, use solid vegetable shortening because it's the most manageable fat with which to create a tender crust. More experienced cooks might want to substitute all lard or a blend of half lard and half solid shortening. (Allow the lard to warm to room temperature, beat it with the solid shortening, and chill the mixture for 2 hours before using.) To use butter in this recipe, increase the total amount of fat and plan to include slightly less water to compensate for the water contained in butter. One tablespoon of vinegar or lemon juice may be used in place of 1 tablespoon water to promote flakiness. Sugar, which is optional, encourages browning, and baking powder, also optional, encourages the flaky layers to puff apart.

⅔ cup solid vegetable shortening or lard, or a chilled blend of half lard and half solid shortening; or ⅔ cup butter, softened and blended with 3 tablespoons solid shortening and chilled until firm

6 tablespoons cold water (or substitute 5 tablespoons cold water plus 1 tablespoon vinegar or lemon juice)
2 cups all-purpose flour, scoop measured
½ teaspoon salt
2 teaspoons sugar (optional)
½ teaspoon baking powder (optional)

1. If you're using lard, butter, or a blend of chilled fats, cut the cold fat into pieces about the size of lima beans and place it back in the refrigerator. Solid shortening may be used at room temperature or chilled (although room temperature is easiest for beginners).

2. Measure the water into a glass measuring cup, blend in the vinegar or lemon juice if you wish, and place it in the freezer.

3. In a large mixing bowl or the bowl of an electric mixer fitted with a paddle beater, thoroughly combine the flour, salt, and optional sugar and baking powder by tossing with a fork or whisk. Add the fat to the dry ingredients. Using a table knife, an 8-inch palette knife, or a paddle attachment on a mixer set at lowest speed, cut the fat into the flour until the lumps of fat are reduced to the size of tiny peas. (For a sandy-textured crust, cut the fat in until the mixture resembles coarse cornmeal.)

4. Gradually sprinkle in the cold liquid, tossing the mixture constantly with the knife and adding only enough liquid to form a soft, malleable dough. Don't let this step intimidate you; remember that it's better to err on the side of too much liquid rather than too little. When the mixture begins to hold together, gather it into a ball with your fingertips and roll it around the inside of the bowl to pick up any stray particles.

5. Divide the dough into 2 portions and flatten into 3-inch disks. Wrap each disk in waxed paper, then place in a plastic bag and secure airtight with a twist. Refrigerate for 20 minutes or longer if you prefer. (When the dough's temperature falls to 65°F. on an instant-read thermometer — a process that takes almost 2 hours — it is sufficiently chilled, yet manageable. Dough chilled below that point is difficult to work with.) Dust

a work surface with sifted flour and roll the dough to a thickness of about ⅛ inch. Use as desired.

(See entries for Cutting-In; Fats; Pie Crust; Shortening.)

Egg and Vinegar Pie Crust

MAKES TWO GENEROUS 9-INCH CRUSTS

The yolk of an egg and a small amount of vinegar are the secret ingredients in this pie crust recipe. Protein in the egg yolk gives the dough extra strength and cohesiveness to make rolling and shaping easier. The acid in the vinegar promotes flakiness. If you'd like to experiment, try using lemon juice or wine instead of the vinegar. Both are acidic, but produce slightly different results.

⅔ cup solid vegetable shortening
3 tablespoons cold water
1 large egg yolk
2 teaspoons vinegar
2 cups all-purpose flour, scoop measured
1 teaspoon salt

1. Measure out the solid shortening and place it in the refrigerator to chill. In a small bowl, whisk together the water, egg yolk, and vinegar. Refrigerate to chill.

2. Proceed according to steps 3–5 under Basic Pie Crust (p. 364), omitting the sugar and baking powder.

(See entries for Cutting-In; Fats; Pie Crust; Shortening.)

Water-Whipped Pie Crust

MAKES TWO 9-INCH CRUSTS

This is my favorite nontraditional approach to short-flake pastry. It's so reliable that even a beginner can produce a respectable crust. The addition of boiling water causes the shortening to melt and become so thoroughly incorporated into the dough that the resulting texture is mealy but extremely tender. It isn't necessary to chill the dough before rolling.

¾ cup solid vegetable shortening at room temperature
1 tablespoon cold milk
¼ cup *boiling* water
1¾ cups all-purpose flour, scoop measured
¾ teaspoon salt

1. In a large mixing bowl, whip the shortening with a whisk or electric mixer until light and fluffy. Gradually add the cold milk, beating continuously. Then pour in the boiling water all at once and whip until the mixture resembles whipped cream. Don't worry if the shortening appears to melt or separate. Just keep beating; it will pull back together.

2. Add the flour and salt. Blend with a fork using quick, light strokes. When the dough begins to hold together, gather it into a ball with your fingertips and roll it around the inside of the bowl to pick up stray particles.

3. Shape the dough into 2 flat rounds. Without chilling, place each round between 12-inch squares of waxed paper and roll to a thickness of about ⅛ inch. You can hold the paper up to the light to check for even rolling, and feel free to roll on both sides — you won't do the pastry any harm.

4. Remove the top sheet of waxed paper. Invert the dough on the remaining sheet of paper and position over a pie plate. The pastry will adhere to the paper long enough for you to turn it over and lower it into the pan. Remove the waxed paper and ease the pastry into the pan without pulling or stretching it in any way.

(See entries for Pie Crust; Shortening.)

Processor Pie Shell

MAKES ONE 9-INCH PIE SHELL

The horizontal slicing motion of an electric processor incorporates fat not only more quickly, but to a more uniform degree than many experienced cooks can cut it in by hand. Consequently, making pie crust with a processor is a popular technique because it reliably produces a tender crust of excellent quality. The following recipe for a single pie shell can be easily doubled for two-crust pies.

6 tablespoons solid vegetable shortening, lard, or butter
3 tablespoons cold water
1 cup all-purpose flour, scoop measured
½ teaspoon salt

1. Measure out the solid shortening in 6 separate portions onto waxed paper (cut lard or butter into 6 equal portions). Freeze at least 4 hours. Refrigerate the water.

2. Place the flour, salt, and frozen fat in the container of a processor fitted with a metal blade. Pulse for approximately 10 seconds. When the mixture resembles coarse cornmeal, pour the water through the feed tube and pulse until the dough begins to hold together. Wrap in plastic wrap and refrigerate for 20 minutes.

3. Preheat the oven to 425°F. Dust a work surface with sifted flour and roll the dough to a thickness of about ⅛ inch. Transfer the pastry to a 9-inch pie or tart pan. Ease the pastry into the pan without pulling or stretching it in any way. Prick the bottom and sides of the pastry with the tines of a fork, making the pattern go in one direction. Line the pastry with waxed paper, parchment, or aluminum foil (see illustration, p. 124). Pour in 1 pound of dried beans or metal pie weights (see Appendix) and distribute them evenly.

4. For a *partially* baked shell, cook for 8 minutes. Remove the liner and weights. Do not prick a second time. Immediately fill with a prepared filling and return to the oven. If you're using an exceptionally runny filling, like pumpkin custard, you can give the crust additional protection against sogginess by brushing the surface with an egg-white wash (1 egg white whisked with 1 tablespoon water) and returning the pie shell to a 400°F. oven for 3 minutes to seal the pastry.

5. For a *fully* baked shell, cook for 8 minutes. Remove the liner and weights. Reduce the oven temperature to 375°F. Prick the bottom and sides of the pastry a second time with the tines of a fork, making the pattern go in the opposite direction. Brush the rim of the shell with an egg wash for color if you wish. Return the pie shell to the oven and bake for 15 minutes or until the pastry is nicely browned. Cool thoroughly on a rack before filling.

(See entry for Pie Crust: Baking Blind.) ◄₂

Blueberry Pie

MAKES ONE 9-INCH PIE

The amount of sugar you add to a blueberry pie has a direct effect on the consistency of the cooked filling. A high proportion of sugar produces a runny, juicy filling. To control the consistency, taste the berries before you begin. If they are at the peak of ripeness and naturally sweet, they will cook up extra juicy even without sugar, so add the smaller amount given in the recipe below. Tart berries give off significantly less juice; therefore, a greater amount of sugar can be added without creating an excessively watery filling. (If you use the maximum amount of sugar given below, also use the maximum amount of cornstarch or tapioca.)

4 cups fresh blueberries (about 1½ pounds of small berries)
⅔ to 1½ cups sugar
2 to 3½ tablespoons cornstarch (or substitute granulated, instant tapioca)
2-crust pastry dough (pp. 364-365)
1 tablespoon fresh lemon juice
Freshly grated nutmeg

1. Wash the berries and drain them thoroughly in a colander. Transfer to a large mixing bowl.

2. If you're using tapioca, sprinkle it over the damp berries and toss to distribute evenly. Let the berries and tapioca sit at room

temperature for 30 minutes to allow the tapioca to fully soften. If you're using cornstarch, combine it and the sugar in a small bowl. Whisk or toss with a fork to disperse the starch throughout the sugar. Do not add the sugar-cornstarch mixture to the berries until the last minute.

3. Preheat the oven to 450°F. Line a 9-inch pie pan with the prepared pastry. Sprinkle the lemon juice over the berries and toss lightly with a rubber spatula. Add the sugar-cornstarch blend, and toss to distribute evenly. Pour the berries into the pastry-lined pie pan and spread over the crust. Sprinkle with nutmeg. Roll out the remaining dough and arrange over the berries. Trim the edges of the crust and flute or crimp to seal. Cut a circular steam vent in the center of the top crust with a small canapé cutter or make V-shaped vents with a paring knife.

4. Place the pie on the lowest rack in the preheated oven and cook for 10 minutes. Transfer the pie to the middle rack, reduce the oven temperature to 375°F., and bake for 35 to 45 minutes or until the filling has begun to bubble. Remove the pie from the oven and cool on a rack.

NOTE: Waiting for the crust to brown often results in overcooked filling. For attractive browning, apply a whole-egg or egg-yolk wash.

(See entries for Pie Baking: Dessert Pies; Egg Wash; Cooling Rack.)

Coconut Custard Cream Pie

MAKES ONE 9-INCH PIE

A basic vanilla custard cream, which may be frozen and then defrosted and poured into a baked pie shell. To vary the formula, fold in chocolate bits, sliced fruit, or chopped nuts.

4 tablespoons flour
1 cup granulated sugar
⅛ teaspoon salt

2 cups milk
3 large egg yolks
1 cup heavy cream
4 tablespoons confectioners' sugar, sifted
1¾ teaspoons vanilla
9-inch baked pie shell
1 can (3½ ounces) flaked coconut (or substitute
** 1 cup freshly grated)**

1. In a thick-bottomed saucepan, combine the flour with 2 tablespoons of the granulated sugar and the salt. Stir with a whisk to disperse the flour. Slowly pour in 1½ cups of the milk, stirring continuously with a whisk. When the flour is dissolved, place the pan over medium-high heat and stir with a heat-resistant rubber spatula or a wooden spoon to keep the milk from scorching.

2. Cook until the mixture approaches 194°F. on a candy thermometer. Lift the spatula and listen for a plopping sound as the mixture approaches the boil. On the second plop, remove the pan from the heat. Stir in the remaining granulated sugar. Return to the heat and cook briefly to dissolve the sugar. You'll see the mixture thin out and then thicken again.

3. Put the egg yolks through a sieve to eliminate stray particles of egg white (called chalazae) that can cause tiny lumps to form. Whisk in the remaining ½ cup of milk. Then, stirring slowly with a heat-resistant rubber spatula or wooden spoon, gradually pour half of the hot mixture into the eggs. Pour the warmed egg mixture back into the pan and return to medium-high heat.

4. Cook, stirring, until the mixture approaches 180°F. If some lumps appear, stir vigorously to smooth them out, but do not whisk. Continue cooking to 190°F., listening for the first and then the second plop. Remove from the heat at once.

5. Pour into a bowl to cool. Do not stir to speed cooling. Lay a piece of plastic wrap directly on the surface of the hot custard cream. Smooth out any air bubbles with your fingertips. Press the excess wrap against the side of the bowl. Refrigerate until thoroughly

chilled. Meanwhile, whip the heavy cream until stiff. Blend in the confectioners' sugar and ¼ teaspoon of the vanilla.

6. Stir the remaining 1½ teaspoons of vanilla into the chilled custard cream filling and pour into the prepared pie shell. Sprinkle half the coconut over the filling. Spoon on the whipped cream and spread evenly over the pie. Sprinkle the remaining coconut over the top and refrigerate until serving time.

BANANA CUSTARD CREAM PIE: Follow the directions above for basic vanilla custard cream. When the filling is thoroughly chilled, stir in 1½ teaspoons vanilla and 2 ripe bananas, thinly sliced. Pour into prepared pie shell, top with whipped cream, and chill.

BUTTERSCOTCH-PECAN PIE: Follow the directions above for basic vanilla custard cream, substituting dark brown sugar for the granulated and adding 2 tablespoons of butter after the sugar has dissolved in step 2. Stir until the butter is melted and incorporated. When the butterscotch custard cream is thoroughly chilled, pour into the prepared pie shell. Top with whipped cream and sprinkle on 1 cup of coarsely chopped pecans.

(See entries for Cream Pie Filling; Pie Crust: Baking Blind.)   ◄෨

Triple Chocolate Cream Pie

MAKES ONE 9-INCH PIE

In this recipe, the amount of flour has been increased to form a thicker cream filling so that whipped cream can be folded in.

2 squares semisweet chocolate
½ cup flour, scoop measured
1 cup granulated sugar
⅛ teaspoon salt
2 cups milk
2 squares unsweetened chocolate

3 large egg yolks
2 cups heavy cream
½ cup confectioners' sugar, sifted
1½ teaspoons vanilla
1 tablespoon unsweetened cocoa
9-inch baked pie shell

1. Chop the semisweet chocolate into tiny pieces using a chef's knife or food processor. Set aside.

2. In a thick-bottomed saucepan, combine the flour with 2 tablespoons of the granulated sugar and the salt. Stir with a whisk to disperse the flour. Slowly pour in 1½ cups of the milk, stirring continuously with a whisk. When the flour is dissolved, place the pan over medium-high heat and continue stirring with a heat-resistant rubber spatula or wooden spoon to keep the milk from scorching.

3. Cook until the mixture reaches 194°F. on a candy thermometer. Lift the spatula and listen for a plopping sound. On the second plop, remove the pan from the heat. Stir in the remaining granulated sugar. Break the squares of unsweetened chocolate in half and add to the mixture. Return to medium-high heat. Cook, stirring, until the sugar is dissolved and the chocolate is melted. You'll see the mixture thin out and then thicken again.

4. Put the egg yolks through a sieve to eliminate stray particles of egg white (chalazae) that can cause tiny lumps to form. Whisk in the remaining ½ cup milk. Then, stirring slowly with a rubber spatula or wooden spoon, gradually pour half of the hot mixture into the egg yolks. Pour the warmed egg mixture back into the pan and return to medium-high heat.

5. Cook, stirring, until the mixture approaches 180°F. If some lumps appear, stir vigorously to smooth them out, but do not whisk. Continue cooking to 190°F., listening for the first and then the second plop. Remove from the heat at once.

6. Pour into a bowl to cool. Do not stir to speed cooling. Lay a piece of plastic wrap directly on the surface of the hot custard cream, smoothing out any air bubbles with

your fingertips. Press the excess wrap against the side of the bowl. Refrigerate until thoroughly chilled. Meanwhile, whip the heavy cream until stiff. Blend in the confectioners' sugar and ½ teaspoon vanilla.

7. Stir remaining 1 teaspoon of vanilla into the chilled chocolate custard. Divide the whipped cream into 2 equal portions. Blend the chopped semisweet chocolate gently into the chocolate custard. Fold in 1 portion of whipped cream and pour into the baked pie shell. Spoon on the remaining portion of whipped cream and spread over the pie, forming peaks and valleys. Dust the whipped cream with sifted cocoa. Refrigerate until serving time.

(See entries for Cream Pie Filling; Pie Crust: Baking Blind.)

Canadian Sugar Pie

MAKES ONE 9-INCH PIE

Before fresh fruit became available year-round, cooks devised a type of dessert known as winter pies. These pies were also called sugar pies because their essential ingredient was either dry sugar or some form of sugar syrup, such as molasses, cane syrup, maple syrup, or corn syrup. Canadian Sugar Pie, like its familiar cousins pecan pie and shoofly pie, is so tasty that it is nowadays served during the summer months as well.

9-inch unbaked pie shell
1¼ cups light brown sugar
¼ cup all-purpose flour, scoop measured
½ cup finely chopped walnuts
1 teaspoon maple extract
2 cups medium, or whipping, cream
2 tablespoons butter, cut into 16 small chunks
Freshly ground nutmeg
Sweetened whipped cream for garnish

1. Preheat the oven to 425°F. Prick the bottom and sides of the pie shell with the tines of a fork. Fit waxed paper or aluminum foil inside the pastry and weight with 1 pound of dried beans or pie weights. Place on the middle rack of the oven and bake for 8 minutes.

2. Meanwhile, combine the brown sugar, flour, and walnuts in a large mixing bowl. Stir with a fork to blend. In a small mixing bowl, blend the maple extract into the cream.

3. Take the partially baked shell from the oven and reduce the oven temperature to 350°F. Remove the paper or foil liner and the weights. Do not prick the crust a second time.

4. Immediately scatter the sugar mixture over the bottom of the partially baked pie shell. Pour on the maple-flavored cream and dot with butter. Sprinkle the surface with freshly ground nutmeg and place in the preheated oven. Bake for 40 to 50 minutes or until the filling is slightly puffed. The filling will not appear to be as set as a custard but will solidify as it cools. Remove from the oven and cool on a rack. Serve at room temperature topped with sweetened whipped cream.

(See entries for Pie Baking: Dessert Pies; Cooling Rack.)

Louisiana Pecan Pie

MAKES ONE 9-INCH PIE

Cane syrup, the concentrated sap of sugar cane, is the color and consistency of dark maple syrup. Produced in southern Louisiana, it lends a distinctive flavor to this pecan pie. Cane syrup is available in shops that specialize in Creole or Acadian food supplies or by mail (see Appendix).

½ cup unsalted butter
9-inch unbaked pie shell
1 cup sugar
4 large eggs
1 teaspoon vanilla
3 tablespoons dark rum
1¼ cups cane syrup (or substitute dark corn syrup)
1½ cups coarsely chopped pecans
Sweetened whipped cream

1. Set out the butter and allow it to warm to room temperature. Preheat the oven to 425°F. Prick the bottom and sides of the pie shell with the tines of a fork. Fit waxed paper or aluminum foil inside the pastry and weight with 1 pound of dried beans or metal pie weights. Place on the middle rack of the oven and bake for 8 minutes.

2. Meanwhile, whip the softened butter until creamy. Gradually sprinkle in the sugar, beating continuously, until the mixture is light and fluffy. Beat in the eggs, one at a time. Blend in the vanilla and 2 tablespoons of the dark rum. With the mixer on lowest speed, gradually pour in the cane syrup. Stir in the chopped nuts.

3. Take the partially baked shell from the oven and reduce the oven temperature to 350°F. Remove the paper or foil liner and the weights. Do not prick the crust a second time.

4. Immediately pour the prepared filling into the partially baked pie shell. Place in the oven and bake for 40 to 50 minutes or until the filling is slightly puffed. Remove from the oven and cool on a rack. Serve with sweetened whipped cream into which the remaining 1 tablespoon of the dark rum has been incorporated.

(See entries for Pie Baking: Dessert Pies; Cooling Rack.)

Double Strawberry Pie

MAKES ONE 9-INCH PIE

To protect the bottom crust of a fresh fruit pie against sogginess, brush a film of liquefied jelly over the inside of the baked pie shell. It's also a good idea to allow the glaze that goes over the fruit to cool thoroughly because warm glaze provokes uncooked fruit into releasing moisture.

9-inch unbaked pie shell
6 cups fresh strawberries
1 cup sugar
3 tablespoons cornstarch
½ cup cold water
Red food coloring (optional)
1 teaspoon butter
½ cup strawberry jelly
Sweetened whipped cream

1. Preheat the oven to 425°F. Prick the bottom and sides of the pie shell with the tines of a fork. Fit waxed paper or aluminum foil inside the pastry and weight with 1 pound of dried beans or metal pie weights. Place on the middle rack of the oven and bake for 8 minutes. Remove the paper or foil liner and the weights. Reduce the oven temperature to 375°F. Prick the crust a second time and bake the pie shell for 15 minutes or until nicely browned. Cool thoroughly on a rack.

2. Wash and hull the berries, setting them on a double thickness of paper toweling to drain. Lightly pat the berries dry with a paper towel. Sort out 2 cups of the least attractive berries. Place in the container of a blender or processor with ¼ cup of the sugar and whirl to purée.

3. In a 2½-quart saucepan, combine the remaining ¾ cup of sugar, cornstarch, and water. Stir to dissolve and place over medium heat. When the mixture is completely clear, blend in the strawberry purée. Continue heating, stirring constantly, until the mixture bubbles and thickens. Add drops of food coloring to intensify the color if you wish. Remove from the heat and swirl in the butter. Pour the glaze into a bowl to hasten cooling.

4. In a 1½-quart saucepan warm the strawberry jelly over medium heat until it melts and bubbles vigorously. Spread the liquefied jelly over the inside of the cooled pie shell. Allow the film of jelly to cool.

5. Arrange the remaining 4 cups of whole fresh berries inside the prepared pie shell. When the glaze is cool to the touch, pour over the fresh berries. Chill for at least 2 hours and serve with sweetened whipped cream. ◄℈

Chestnut Cream Tart

MAKES ONE 9-INCH TART

Here's an elegant tart to serve as a light, yet festive, finale for wintertime holiday meals.

9-inch baked tart shell
1½ pounds fresh chestnuts (or substitute 16 ounces roasted and shelled canned chestnuts; see Note)
½ cup sugar
1½ teaspoons vanilla
1 cup medium, or whipping, cream
1 cup heavy cream
Chocolate shavings for garnish

1. Set aside the fully baked tart shell to cool completely.

2. If you're using fresh chestnuts, cut a good-size cross into the flat or rounded side of each shell. (The flat side is easier to manage, but the rounded side gives better results because a greater amount of surface area is exposed.)

3. Place the chestnuts in a 4½-quart saucepan and cover them with hot tap water. Set over medium-high heat and boil gently for 10 minutes. Using a slotted spoon, lift 3 or 4 nuts from the hot water, allowing the remainder to soak. Peel away the shells and inner skins with a paring knife. If either the shell or skin refuses to come off, return the nuts to boiling water for 2 or 3 more minutes.

4. When all the chestnuts are shelled, pour the water from the pan. Place the nuts in the saucepan and cover with cold water. Set over medium-high heat and boil gently for 20 to 30 minutes or until they can be easily pierced with a metal skewer. Drain and allow to cool for 10 minutes. Purée the warm chestnuts by forcing them through a food mill or mashing with a potato masher. Do not use a blender or processor. Return the purée to the saucepan and place over low heat. Stirring constantly, cook until excess moisture evaporates. The purée should be thick and firm. Refrigerate until thoroughly chilled.

5. With an electric mixer set at high speed, briefly beat the chestnut purée to lighten it. Blend in the sugar and vanilla. Beating constantly, gradually add the medium cream in a thin stream. The final consistency should be light and fluffy.

6. Spoon the chestnut cream into the prepared tart shell. Whip the heavy cream until stiff peaks form. Using a pastry bag fitted with an open star tube, pipe a whipped cream border around the edge of the tart. Garnish the exposed purée with chocolate shavings if you like. Refrigerate until serving time.

NOTE: Roasted, shelled chestnuts and a chestnut knife (designed with a curved blade for incising the rounded sides of chestnuts) are available by mail (see Appendix). If you're using roasted, shelled chestnuts from a jar or can, warm the nuts in their liquid, or cover with water and bring to a gentle bubble. Cook 4 or 5 minutes to warm thoroughly. Drain and purée according to the directions in step 4. ◄℈

Lemon Meringue Pie

MAKES ONE 9-INCH PIE

I wouldn't have believed so many people still cared passionately about baking the perfect lemon meringue pie, but of all the cooking questions I've been asked, that's the one that heads the list.

3 large eggs
1½ cups sugar
3 tablespoons cornstarch
3 tablespoons all-purpose flour
¼ teaspoon salt
1½ cups cold water
2 tablespoons cold butter, cut into 8 chunks
⅓ cup fresh lemon juice
1½ teaspoons lemon extract
Soft Meringue I, II, or III for topping (pp. 372-374)
9-inch baked pie shell

1. Separate the eggs while they're still cold and set the whites aside to warm to room temperature. When whipped egg whites are spread over a warm filling, they coagulate on the underside of the meringue topping and set slightly, thus preventing liquid from forming between the meringue and the filling. Therefore, plan to prepare and apply the meringue immediately after the filling. (If you're using the recipe for Soft Meringue II, complete step 1 at this point.)

2. Place the egg yolks in a large mixing bowl, whisk lightly, and set aside. In a 1½-quart thick-bottomed saucepan, combine the sugar, cornstarch, flour, and salt. Stir with a fork or whisk to disperse the lump-causing flour throughout the more easily dissolvable sugar, salt, and cornstarch.

3. Gradually stir in the cold water. Continue stirring until most of the sugar dissolves. Place over medium heat and stir continuously with a heat-resistant rubber spatula or wooden spoon. As the mixture approaches 180°F., it will begin to thicken and its appearance will change from cloudy to translucent. Stir vigorously to avoid scorching, but pause occasionally to listen for the plopping sound that indicates the mixture has reached a boil. (The mixture will be too thick to truly bubble. Instead it heaves and plops.) When you hear the second plopping sound, immediately remove from the heat.

4. Whisking the egg yolks with one hand, slowly pour in half the hot mixture to gradually warm the yolks. With a heat-resistant spatula or wooden spoon, stir the warmed yolks into the hot mixture remaining in the pan. Do not whisk or beat excessively at this point because the incorporation of excess air will produce a grainy texture. Return to medium heat and cook, stirring, until the mixture again approaches 180°F. An enzyme present in egg yolks will break down starch and destroy its thickening power if the enzyme isn't deactivated by heat. Consequently, the mixture must be brought to a boil once more. Pause during stirring to watch for the heaving and plopping that indicate the mixture has reached the boiling point.

5. On the second plopping sound, remove the pan from the heat and stir in the cold butter. When the butter is melted and blended in, add the lemon juice and lemon extract. Leave the filling in the pan to keep warm while you prepare the meringue. Then, without stirring, pour the filling into the prepared pie shell and top with meringue. Bake in a 350°F. oven for 12 to 15 minutes to brown the meringue.

(See entries for Meringue; Thickeners.)

Soft Meringue I

MAKES MERINGUE FOR ONE 9-INCH PIE

Meringue that weeps, or beads, is a part of the dilemma facing cooks in search of the perfect meringue-topped pie. Since the chief cause of weeping is tiny particles of undissolved sugar, methods for alleviating the problem involve dealing with the sugar component.

The following recipe suggests the use of confectioners' sugar, which is not only finely textured, but also contains a limited amount of cornstarch. The cornstarch acts to absorb traces of moisture in the egg whites that would otherwise appear as beads on the surface of the baked meringue.

If you prefer to use granulated sugar instead, purchase the superfine variety or make your own superfine grade by whirling regular granulated sugar in a blender. Slowly beat it into the whipped whites as usual, but check by rubbing some meringue between your fingers to see if it has been thoroughly dissolved. If the meringue feels gritty, the sugar is not completely dissolved. Wait 15 seconds and then beat in 2 or 3 drops of warm water.

3 large egg whites
¼ teaspoon cream of tartar
8 tablespoons sifted confectioners' sugar (or
   substitute 6 tablespoons superfine granulated)
½ teaspoon vanilla

1. Place the egg whites in a grease-free stainless steel or copper bowl and allow them to come to room temperature (about 70°F.). Preheat the oven to 350°F. (or to 450°F. — see Note below). Whip the whites at medium speed until foamy. Add the cream of tartar and increase the speed of the beater to medium-high. Whip until the beaters begin to trace lines through the egg whites.

2. Gradually sprinkle in the sifted confectioners' sugar, beating continuously at medium-high. Then add the vanilla. Beat until the egg whites acquire a shiny gloss and stiff peaks stand straight when the beaters are lifted. Do not overbeat. (Whipping egg whites at a speed somewhere between medium and high, instead of at the highest possible setting, gives you more control, which reduces the possibility of overbeating.)

3. Lightly spread the meringue over the warm filling, taking care to push the meringue right up against the crust to completely insulate the filling from the heat of the oven. If the meringue doesn't adhere to the crust, it will contract during baking, allowing air to sneak under the meringue. This air will convert to steam (just like the steam that forms on the underside of a lid placed on a pot of hot food) and then condense to a watery film as the pie cools.

4. Swirl a knife through the meringue to form attractive peaks and place in the preheated oven. Bake for 10 to 12 minutes or until nicely browned, but do not overcook. Prolonged exposure to heat can cause the egg white proteins to denature and release moisture, creating a watery layer between the meringue and the filling. Remove the pie and cool on a rack out of the way of drafts. Do not refrigerate until completely cooled because any steam held inside the meringue will condense and turn to water.

NOTE: Although the topping on lemon meringue pie is customarily browned slowly at 350°F., you can achieve a lovely soft, marshmallowy consistency by browning the meringue quickly (3 to 4 minutes) at a higher temperature (450°F.). Because the interior of the meringue is exposed to less heat, the egg white proteins are not as apt to denature. (See entry for Whipping: Egg Whites.) ❧

Soft Meringue II

MAKES MERINGUE FOR ONE 9-INCH PIE

The following recipe incorporates a larger amount of cornstarch than is available in confectioners' sugar. Its presence creates a dense meringue that doesn't bead and slices without tearing.

1 tablespoon cornstarch
½ cup cold water
3 large egg whites
¼ teaspoon cream of tartar
6 tablespoons granulated sugar
½ teaspoon vanilla

1. Before you begin to make the pie filling, combine the cornstarch with the cold water in a 1½-quart saucepan. Stir to dissolve and place over high heat. Cook, stirring constantly, until the mixture bubbles, thickens, and becomes translucent. Pour into a small bowl and cool to room temperature.

2. Place the egg whites in a grease-free stainless steel or copper bowl and allow them to come to room temperature (about 70°F.). Preheat the oven to 350°F. (or 450°F. — see Note at the end of Soft Meringue I). Whip the whites at medium speed until foamy. Add the

cream of tartar and increase the speed of the mixer to medium-high. Whip until the beaters begin to trace lines through the egg whites.

3. Gradually sprinkle in the sugar, beating continuously at medium-high. Beat until the egg whites acquire a shiny gloss and stiff peaks will stand straight when the beaters are lifted. Stir the vanilla into the cooled cornstarch mixture. (Don't be alarmed if it has become congealed.) Beat the cornstarch mixture into the egg whites a tablespoonful at a time until well blended.

4. Lightly spread over the warm pie filling and bake according to the directions in steps 3–4 under Soft Meringue I (p. 373).   ᴇᓂ

Soft Meringue III

MAKES MERINGUE FOR ONE 9-INCH PIE

Another way to forestall weeping or beading of meringue is to dissolve the sugar in the egg whites' own moisture. Of course, this happens to a limited extent whenever sugar is added to egg whites, but gently warming the whites enables you to dissolve every last granule. The resulting meringue is exceptionally versatile. You can use it to top pies, make cookies, or form meringue shells.

3 large egg whites
6 tablespoons superfine or regular granulated
    sugar
½ teaspoon vanilla

1. Fill a 4½-quart saucepan or the bottom of a double boiler with water to a depth of 1½ inches. Bring the water to a boil, and then turn off the heat under the pan. Combine the egg whites and sugar in a large bowl, zabaglione pan, or the top of a double boiler. Stir together and set the bowl over the hot water. Do not allow the water to touch the bottom of the bowl at any time.

2. Continue to stir the egg whites and sugar. At first, you'll hear the "scritch-scratch" of undissolved sugar rubbing against the bottom of the bowl. As the mixture warms, the sugar will dissolve and you'll no longer hear that sound. Scrape down the sides of the bowl with a heat-resistant rubber spatula to chase any errant granules that linger there. (Egg white begins to coagulate at 145°F., so maintaining a low temperature is crucial. Don't attempt to hurry things by leaving the burner on under the water or you'll have scrambled egg whites.) As the mixture approaches 100° F., the whites will turn from cloudy to clear. At that point the sugar should be completely dissolved.

3. Remove the bowl or upper container of the double boiler from the pan of hot water. Immediately begin to whip the warmed whites with a large wire whisk or electric mixer set at medium-high. When the egg whites reach the foamy stage, add the vanilla. Continue whipping until the bubbles are so small you can barely see them and peaks stand straight when the beaters are lifted.

4. Spoon onto warm pie filling and bake according to the directions in steps 3–4 under Soft Meringue I (p. 373).   ᴇᓂ

Swiss Meringue

MAKES ABOUT 4 CUPS

In recipes for Swiss and Italian meringue, the ratio of sugar is increased to create a stiffer texture. The customary proportions for both types are 4 tablespoons (¼ cup) of granulated sugar per egg white, which is double the proportion for soft meringue (2 tablespoons per egg white). Swiss meringue is delicate and exhibits an especially light and tender quality. For this reason it is often preferred for meringue shells and elaborate pastries such as Pavlova and vacherin.

4 large egg whites
¼ teaspoon cream of tartar
1 cup superfine sugar (or substitute regular
    granulated sugar whirled in a blender to
    pulverize the granules)
½ teaspoon vanilla (optional; see Note)

1. Place the egg whites in a grease-free stainless steel or copper bowl and allow them to come to room temperature (about 70°F.). Preheat the oven to 250°F. (A low temperature is used because Swiss meringue is actually dried rather than baked.) Whip the whites at medium speed until foamy. Add the cream of tartar and increase the speed of the mixer to medium-high. Whip until the beaters begin to trace lines through the egg whites.

2. Gradually sprinkle in ½ cup of the sugar, beating continuously at medium-high. Then add the vanilla. When the egg whites acquire a shiny gloss and stiff peaks stand straight, stop beating and fold in the remaining ½ cup of sugar (this procedure insures a tender meringue). Immediately pipe or spoon into the desired shape and bake in a preheated oven. Meringue will deflate if left to stand.

NOTE: In order to achieve a vanilla flavor without the slight discoloration caused by adding pure vanilla extract, flavor the sugar ahead of time by burying a 1-inch piece of vanilla bean in 1 cup of sugar. Seal or cover tightly for at least 6 hours.   ◄঩

Italian Meringue

MAKES ABOUT 4 CUPS

Like Swiss meringue, this variety contains twice the amount of sugar used in soft meringue. Because the sugar is thoroughly dissolved in a water-based syrup, there is never a problem with beading on the surface; therefore, some cooks like to use it as a topping for pies. Italian meringue is more dense than Swiss meringue; but it keeps longer and bakes faster (see Note). Italian meringue may be used as a coating for Baked Alaska or dried as in Forgotten Cookies (p. 395) and Meringue Shells Melba (p. 375). Italian meringue also forms the basis for light buttercream frosting and frozen desserts such as Tortoni (p. 385).

4 large egg whites
1 cup sugar
⅓ cup cold water
¼ teaspoon cream of tartar
½ teaspoon vanilla

1. Place the egg whites in a grease-free stainless steel or copper bowl and allow them to come to room temperature (about 70°F.).

2. In a 1½-quart saucepan, combine the sugar and water and stir to partially dissolve. Set over medium-high heat and stir to completely dissolve the sugar. Increase the heat to high and bring the syrup to a boil. Cook uncovered and without stirring until the mixture reaches 238°F. on a candy thermometer or forms a soft ball when dropped into cold water.

3. Meanwhile, whip the whites at medium speed until foamy. Add the cream of tartar and vanilla and increase the speed of the mixer to medium-high. Whip until the beaters begin to trace lines through the egg whites. As soon as the sugar syrup reaches 238°F., slowly pour it into the whites in a thin stream. Beat constantly at medium-high. Do not be alarmed if the beaters throw beads of syrup against the sides of the bowl. Leave them there. By the time you have finished pouring in the syrup, the whites will be glossy and stiff peaks will stand straight when the beaters are lifted. Immediately pipe or spoon into the desired shape and place in a preheated oven (350°F. for baking a topping or 250°F. for drying cookies and shells). Meringue will deflate if left to stand.

NOTE: Because the addition of hot syrup warms egg whites and partially precooks them, Italian meringue takes less time to bake or dry. When substituting Italian meringue for other types, plan to reduce the oven time by approximately one-half.   ◄঩

Meringue Shells Melba

SERVES 6

You can create these meringue shells from Swiss Meringue (p. 374), Italian Meringue (p. 375), or, as in the recipe below, by using the warmed-whites technique for soft meringue that also appears under Soft Meringue III (p. 374). Fill them with any fresh fruit you like or spoon on ice cream and drizzle with fruit-flavored syrup. This recipe is one suggestion.

MERINGUE SHELLS

3 large egg whites
¾ cup superfine or regular granulated sugar
½ teaspoon vanilla

MELBA SAUCE

1 package (10 ounces) frozen red raspberries, undrained
½ cup currant jelly
1½ teaspoons cornstarch
1 tablespoon cold water
4 to 6 fresh peaches, depending on their size

1. Preheat the oven to 250°F. Prepare a cookie sheet by lining it with parchment. Fill a 4½-quart saucepan or the bottom of a double boiler with water to a depth of 1½ inches. Bring the water to a boil, and then turn off the heat under the pan. Combine the egg whites and sugar in a large bowl or the top of a double boiler. Stir together and set the bowl over the hot water. Do not allow the water to touch the bottom of the container.

2. Continue to stir the egg whites and sugar. At first, you'll hear the "scritch-scratch" of undissolved sugar rubbing against the bottom of the bowl. As the mixture warms, the sugar will dissolve and you'll no longer hear the sound. Scrape down the sides of the bowl with a heat-resistant rubber spatula to chase any errant granules that linger there. As the mixture approaches 100°F., the whites will turn from cloudy to clear. At that point the sugar is completely dissolved.

3. Remove the bowl or upper container of the double boiler from the pan of hot water. Immediately begin to whip the warmed whites with a large wire whisk or electric mixer set at medium-high. When the egg whites reach the foamy stage, add the vanilla. Continue whipping until the bubbles are so small you can barely see them and peaks stand straight when the beaters are lifted.

4. Immediately drop the meringue by large spoonfuls into 6 equal mounds on the parchment-lined cookie sheet. Using the back of a spoon, form each mound into a shell, hollowing out the center. Place in the preheated oven and allow the shells to dry for 45 to 60 minutes, but do not allow them to darken. (Meringue shells should be entirely white and not bear any traces of beige.)

5. Meanwhile, make the sauce. Combine the raspberries and currant jelly in a 1½-quart saucepan. Heat, stirring and slightly mashing the raspberries, until the mixture comes to a boil. Remove from the heat.

6. Dissolve the cornstarch in water and add to the raspberry mixture. Return to the heat and stir constantly until the sauce returns to a boil. Pour into a small bowl and cool to room temperature.

7. Peel and slice the peaches, discarding the pits. Fill the meringue shells with sliced peaches and drizzle on Melba Sauce, warm or chilled. (Or make a pool of sauce on each plate, center a peach-filled shell in the sauce, and top with sweetened whipped cream.) ◄₂

New York-Style Cheesecake

MAKES ONE 8-INCH CAKE

This is the lightly crusted cheesecake found in fine delicatessens. The secret to achieving the correct texture is to avoid beating in too much air. Excess air will cause a cheesecake to puff, weakening the surface and encouraging cracks. Use the best cream cheese you can afford; it does make a difference in the flavor.

1½ pounds cream cheese
Four ½-inch slices pound cake (use a high-quality frozen cake)
4 large eggs
½ cup plus 2 tablespoons heavy cream
1 large or 2 small lemons
1 orange

1 teaspoon vanilla
¾ cup plus 2 tablespoons sugar
2 tablespoons sour cream
2 tablespoons milk

1. Place the cream cheese in a large mixing bowl to allow it to soften for 45 minutes. Lay four ½-inch slices of pound cake directly on the oven rack. Bake at 350°F. for 10 to 15 minutes. Remove from the oven and break the cake up into a small bowl. The cake slices will appear quite moist, but crumbling them allows the interior steam to escape, drying the crumbs in the process. Whirl the cooled pieces of cake in a blender or processor to make crumbs (about ¾ cup).

2. Position a flat rack on the oven's second set of supports from the bottom and preheat to 375°F. Generously butter an 8-inch springform pan. Tear off an 18-inch piece of extra-heavy aluminum foil. (It comes 18 inches wide, so you will have an 18-inch square of foil.) Place the pan in the center of the foil. Using a pencil, mark an X on the foil 3 inches out from the side of the pan, and repeat every few inches around entire pan. Then connect the marks, thereby drawing a rough circle around the pan. Lift the pan off the foil and cut out the circle with scissors. You should have a piece of foil large enough to come up the sides of the pan. Once again place the pan in the center of the foil and bring up the edges, pressing and crushing the foil against the sides of the pan. (Don't attempt to accomplish this step by any shortcut method that involves folding the foil. Extra-heavy aluminum foil is brittle and creasing it creates tiny holes.) The foil serves a dual purpose — it not only keeps water from seeping in between the cracks of the springform pan, it helps to retain heat at the end of the baking period and to provide the slowest possible cooling.

3. Sprinkle the bottom and sides of the pan with cake crumbs, coating completely. Turn out the excess crumbs.

4. In a small bowl, beat the eggs and ½ cup of heavy cream. Very finely grate the zest from the lemon and orange and refrigerate the fruit for another use. With the mixer on low speed, blend the softened cream cheese, lemon zest, orange zest, and vanilla. Gradually sprinkle in the sugar, and then add the eggs-and-cream mixture. Combine the sour cream with the milk and remaining 2 tablespoons of heavy cream and slowly pour into the batter. Blend well, but don't beat on high speed. And don't be alarmed if tiny blobs of cheese remain unblended; they will melt and diffuse throughout the batter when heated.

5. Pour the mixture into the prepared pan. Set the springform inside a larger pan, which has been lined with a folded kitchen towel. Pour boiling water into the larger pan to a depth of 1 inch, creating a hot-water bath. Bake for 30 minutes. Reduce the oven temperature to 350°F. and bake for 30 to 45 minutes more or until the center of the cake barely quivers when you nudge the pan. To avoid cracking the cake, do not test for doneness by inserting a knife. Leave the door of the oven ajar and let the cake finish cooking by residual heat. After 2 hours, remove the cake from the oven and place on a cooling rack. As cooling continues, the sides of the cake will contract and pull away from the pan. Let the cake cool completely, and then remove the foil and release the sides of the springform. Store in the refrigerator. When the cake is completely chilled and the surface is no longer tacky, remove the cake from the bottom of the pan if you wish. Lay a sheet of waxed paper over the surface of the cake and invert onto a cake cardboard or cookie sheet. Remove the pan bottom and invert the cake again onto a serving plate. Top with fruit if you like.

NOTE: Don't be dismayed if you find some liquid inside the foil when you remove it. It's not unusual for a cheesecake to exude moisture as it cooks, and older springform pans that have lost some tension allow that moisture to seep out. It won't adversely affect your cheesecake.

(See entry for Cracking.)

Génoise

MAKES TWO 9-INCH LAYERS OR ONE 11×16-INCH SHEET

The following recipe is the classic formula for making this air-leavened butter sponge cake. To produce a moist cake with a fine crumb, use cake flour. All-purpose flour produces a drier texture, which some cooks prefer if the layers are to be brushed with flavored syrup.

½ cup unsalted butter (about 6 tablespoons
  clarified)
6 large eggs
1 cup sugar
1 teaspoon vanilla
1 cup all-purpose or cake flour, scoop measured

1. Clarify the butter (see entry for Clarifying Butter) and pour into a large mixing bowl. Set aside to cool to room temperature. Preheat the oven to 350°F. Prepare two 9-inch aluminum cake pans or one 11×16-inch jelly roll pan by buttering lightly and dusting with sifted flour or by lining with parchment. Fill a wide saucepan or skillet with water to a depth of 2 inches. Bring to a bubble, and then regulate the heat so that steam rises from the water but no bubbles appear. Using a peanut butter jar half filled with water or a soup can with both ends cut away, create a pedestal in the center of the steaming water.

2. Lightly whisk the eggs and sugar in a 3½-quart bowl. Place the bowl on the pedestal over the steaming water. The water should not touch the bowl. Stir slowly and continuously. When you no longer hear the undissolved sugar scratching against the bowl and the eggs are no longer cool to the touch, remove the bowl from the pedestal. The eggs will have developed a deep yellow color and syrupy consistency. Wipe the outside of the bowl dry and begin to whip the eggs. Start slowly and then gradually increase the whipping speed. Beat until the egg foam triples in volume and turns pale yellow.

3. Stir the vanilla into the slightly cooled butter. Scoop out a generous ½ cup of the whipped eggs and set aside. (Do not combine with the butter at this point because the mixture would stiffen.)

4. Sift one-third of the flour directly onto the egg foam in the 3½-quart bowl. Fold in lightly and rapidly using a rubber spatula. Repeat twice.

5. Add the reserved whipped eggs to the butter and stir with a whisk (the mixture will appear to curdle but continued whisking will smooth it out). Immediately transfer the egg foam to the bowl containing the lightened butter mixture and fold to incorporate the butter. The addition of the butter will cause the batter to deflate considerably, so immediately pour the batter into the prepared pans, minimizing the breakage of air bubbles by holding the bowl close to the pan as you pour.

6. Place in the preheated oven and bake for 25 to 30 minutes for 2 pans or 30 to 40 minutes for 1 large pan. The cake is done when it is lightly browned and has begun to pull away from the sides of the pan. The center should be springy when touched and a metal skewer inserted into the cake should come out clean. Allow to cool 5 minutes, and then turn out onto a lightly greased cooling rack. When the cake is thoroughly cool, split the layers and brush with flavored syrup, cover with a butter-cream frosting, or freeze in an airtight plastic bag.

NOTE: The texture of this cake can be regulated by the amount of butter you use. For a lighter, airier cake with a coarser crumb, use 4 tablespoons of melted clarified butter. Completely eliminating the butter produces an even lighter cake, considered a traditional sponge.

CHOCOLATE GÉNOISE: Substitute ½ cup unsweetened Dutch-process cocoa for ½ cup flour. Sift the cocoa with the remaining flour and incorporate as described in step 4 above. Split the cooled layers and fill with Coffee Butter Cream (p. 384). Frost the top and sides with Chocolate Butter Cream (p. 384). Garnish with finely chopped pistachios if desired.

ORANGE GÉNOISE: Reduce the vanilla to ½ teaspoon. Add 2 tablespoons fresh orange juice and 1 teaspoon grated orange zest to the melted clarified butter as described in step 3 above. Split the cooled layers, fill with Dark Chocolate Butter Cream (p. 384) and frost with Orange Butter Cream (p. 384). Garnish with whipped-cream rosettes and finely chopped candied orange peel.

PRALINE GÉNOISE: Prepare Praline Powder by combining 2 cups granulated sugar, ½ cup water, and 2 tablespoons lemon juice in a 1½-quart saucepan. Place over medium heat and cook, stirring, until the sugar is completely dissolved. Increase the heat and allow the mixture to bubble vigorously without stirring until the temperature reaches 320°F. and the mixture begins to turn the color of maple syrup. Immediately remove from the heat and stir in 12 ounces of coarsely chopped pecans. Pour onto a buttered marble slab or into a buttered jelly roll pan. Spread thinly with a buttered knife. When the mixture is hardened, break into small pieces and pulverize into powder by whirling in a processor or blender. Fold ½ cup Praline Powder into the Génoise batter after the flour has been incorporated as described in step 4 above. Split the cooled layers and fill with Praline Butter Cream (p. 384). Frost the top and sides with Coffee Butter Cream (p. 384) and garnish with Praline Powder.

NUTTED GÉNOISE: Spread 4 ounces of unsalted nuts — cashews, almonds, pecans, peanuts, walnuts, hazelnuts, or pistachios — over the bottom of a jelly roll pan. Place in a 350°F. oven and toast for 8 to 10 minutes or until the nuts color slightly and develop a heady aroma. Allow the nuts to cool completely to avoid excessive oiliness, and then grind in a nut grinder, coffee mill, or blender. (Do not use a processor.) Fold the ground nuts into the Génoise batter after the flour has been incorporated as described in step 4 above. Fill and frost the cooled layers with a compatible butter cream. For example, layers of walnut Génoise may be spread with Maple Butter Cream (p. 384) and garnished with chocolate shavings.

(See entries for Whipping: Whole Eggs; Clarifying Butter; Folding; Sifting.) ✑

Torte Sylvia

MAKES ONE 11×5-INCH LOAF

Creating a special cake is a truly personal way to celebrate a happy occasion or honor a close friend. This cake was inspired by the fiftieth birthday of someone very dear to me. Knowing how she loved apricots, I combined three hazelnut layers with rum-flavored syrup and apricot glaze and then frosted the torte with Coffee Butter Cream (p. 384).

If you would like to design your own special-occasion cake, begin by preparing the basic Génoise (p. 378) or one of its variations. Split round layers in half horizontally or bake 1 large loaf as described below. Brush with a flavored syrup if you like, apply a fruit glaze, and then spread with a compatible butter cream (see Note for variations). Garnish with whipped-cream rosettes, finely chopped nuts, chocolate shavings, or a combination of all three, depending on how extravagant you want to be.

HAZELNUT LAYERS
1 recipe Nutted Génoise (p. 379)

1. Toast 4 ounces of hazelnuts. Rub the warm nuts briskly with a kitchen towel to remove the brown skins. Allow to cool completely, and then grind in a nut grinder or blender. Fold into the Génoise batter.

2. Pour into an 11×16-inch jelly roll pan prepared according to the directions given in step 1 under Génoise (p. 378). Bake 30 to 40 minutes or until a metal skewer inserted into the center comes out clean. Cool on a rack and split into 3 equal portions, each measuring approximately 11×5 inches.

RUM SYRUP
1 cup sugar
¼ teaspoon cream of tartar
½ cup water
2 tablespoons dark rum

1. Combine the sugar, cream of tartar, and water in a 1½-quart saucepan. Place over medium heat and cook, stirring, until the sugar is completely dissolved. Increase the heat and allow the mixture to bubble vigorously, without stirring, until the temperature reaches 230°F. or a pinch of mixture spins a thread when dropped into cold water. Immediately remove from the heat and pour into a glass jar with a screw-top lid.

2. Stir in the rum and cover the syrup. Set aside at room temperature or refrigerate for up to 2 weeks. (Sugar syrup may also be frozen for up to 6 months.)

APRICOT GLAZE
⅔ cup apricot jam

1. In a 1½-quart saucepan, heat the jam over medium heat until it bubbles. Increase the heat and cook, stirring, for 3 minutes at a vigorous boil. Press through a fine sieve and return to the saucepan to be warmed briefly just before the cake is assembled.

COFFEE BUTTER CREAM
1 recipe Coffee Butter Cream (p. 384)

GARNISH
1 cup heavy cream, sweetened and whipped
2 tablespoons very finely chopped walnuts
Chocolate shavings

ASSEMBLY

1. Place 1 hazelnut layer on a piece of cardboard measuring 11×5 inches or directly on a rectangular serving plate (sometimes referred to as a sandwich tray). Brush the surface lightly, but completely, with Rum Syrup.

2. Reheat the Apricot Glaze if it has thickened excessively. Apply half of the warm glaze to the syrup-brushed layer. Top with Coffee Butter Cream. Place a second hazelnut layer on the butter cream and repeat the syrup-glaze-butter cream sequence.

3. Top with the third hazelnut layer. Frost the top and sides with Coffee Butter Cream. Using a pastry bag fitted with an open star tube, pipe a decorative border of sweetened whipped cream around the cake where it meets the plate and around the perimeter of the top layer. Sprinkle the top lightly with finely chopped walnuts and scatter chocolate shavings down the top center of the loaf. Serve by cutting into 1-inch-thick slices.

NOTE: A flavored syrup, though optional, provides moistness to cake layers and contributes additional flavor. You can substitute various liqueurs in order to create compatible effects. For example, Cointreau-flavored syrup with Orange Génoise, Tia Maria with Chocolate Génoise, and Nocello or Frangelico with Nutted Génoise. Frozen juice concentrate and fruit syrups, such as those served over ice cream, can also be blended into a sugar syrup with extraordinary results. Use 2 tablespoons per cup of sugar.

Different fruit glazes can be made by substituting various fruit jams. Strawberry, raspberry, peach, and pineapple all create outstanding glazes.

(See entries for Cake Baking; Nuts.)

Sachertorte

SERVES 12

This classic Viennese chocolate cake is leavened entirely by hot air. For that reason, it's imperative that the egg whites warm to room temperature in order to enable them to trap and hold as many air bubbles as possible. An apricot glaze is applied to the top and sides of the cake to provide a smooth, slightly tacky surface for the chocolate glaze to cling to.

CHOCOLATE CAKE

10 large eggs
¾ cup unsalted butter
7 ounces semisweet chocolate
¾ cup sugar
½ teaspoon vanilla
1 cup sifted all-purpose flour
⅛ teaspoon salt
¼ teaspoon cream of tartar

APRICOT GLAZE
½ cup apricot jam

CHOCOLATE GLAZE

6 ounces semisweet chocolate
¼ cup white corn syrup
1 tablespoon strong coffee (or substitute ½ teaspoon instant coffee dissolved in 1 tablespoon boiling water)

1. Begin by making the cake. Separate the eggs, reserving 2 yolks for another use. Refrigerate the 8 yolks and place the 10 whites in a large mixing bowl to warm to room temperature. Set the butter out to soften. Preheat the oven to 350°F. Prepare a 9-inch springform pan by greasing with solid vegetable shortening and dusting with sifted flour. Invert the pan to empty out excess flour.

2. Melt the chocolate in a saucepan over a heat diffuser or in the top of a double boiler set over hot, but not bubbling, water. Set aside to cool.

3. Whip the butter until light. Gradually sprinkle in the sugar, beating continuously until fluffy and lemon colored. Blend in the cooled chocolate and the vanilla. Add the 8 yolks, one at a time, beating vigorously after each addition.

4. Sift and then measure the flour. Sift about one-third of the flour over the batter and fold in gently, using a rubber spatula. Repeat until the flour is well incorporated.

5. Whip the 10 egg whites until foamy. Add the salt and cream of tartar and continue whipping until soft peaks form. Using a large serving spoon, scoop out 2 generous dollops of the whipped egg whites. Add to the chocolate mixture and stir in gently to lighten the batter. Fold in the remaining whites. Empty the batter into the prepared pan. Place in the preheated oven and immediately reduce the temperature to 325°F. Bake for 60 to 70 minutes or until a toothpick inserted into the center comes out clean.

6. Allow the cake to cool for 15 minutes on a cooling rack. Remove the sides of the pan and cool 15 minutes more. Invert the cake onto another rack and remove the bottom of the pan to complete cooling. (This gradual cooling produces a straight-sided cake.) When thoroughly cooled, brush stray crumbs from the surface with a pastry brush.

7. Make the apricot glaze by heating the apricot jam in a small saucepan until it boils. Cook over high heat for 3 minutes, stirring continuously. Remove from the heat and press through a fine sieve. While the glaze is still warm, brush it over the top and sides of the cake. Allow the glazed cake to stand for 1 hour to absorb most of the glaze.

8. Make the chocolate glaze by combining the chocolate, corn syrup, and coffee in a thick-bottomed saucepan. Cook over medium-low heat, stirring constantly until the chocolate is melted. (The presence of the corn syrup will prevent the chocolate from seizing.) Pour over the top of the cake. Heat a palette knife under hot tap water and dry with a towel. Spread the glaze over the top and sides of the cake. Reheat the blade of the knife as necessary to facilitate spreading. The glaze should take on a shiny, smooth-as-glass finish. Serve with generous dollops of sweetened whipped cream. ❧

Holiday Spice Cake

MAKES 1 DOUBLE-LAYER 9-INCH CAKE

Wait until you smell the marvelous aroma as this cake bakes. A blend of traditional spices accounts for the heavenly smell; buttermilk creates the melt-in-your-mouth texture.

You'll notice that this is one of those recipes that calls for both baking soda and baking powder. That's because, in this case, the amount of leavening needed to produce light layers is not balanced by a sufficient amount of naturally occurring acid. Therefore, baking powder, which contains its own acid, is included to boost both the leavening and acid levels.

½ cup butter
2½ cups sifted cake flour
1 teaspoon ground cinnamon
½ teaspoon ground ginger
½ teaspoon ground cloves
¼ teaspoon ground nutmeg
1 teaspoon baking powder
1 teaspoon baking soda
1 teaspoon salt
1 cup granulated sugar
½ cup light brown sugar
2 large eggs
1 teaspoon vanilla
1¼ cups buttermilk
Brown Sugar Frosting (recipe follows)

1. Set out the butter to soften. Preheat the oven to 350°F. Prepare two 9-inch cake pans by greasing with solid vegetable shortening and dusting with sifted flour. Invert pans to empty out excess flour.
2. Sift the cake flour and then measure. Sift again into a large mixing bowl with the spices, baking powder, soda, and salt. Combine by tossing with a fork or whisk.
3. Beat the butter until light. Gradually sprinkle in the granulated sugar, beating continuously until fluffy and lemon colored. Beat in the brown sugar. Add the eggs, one at a time, beating thoroughly after each addition. Blend in the vanilla.

4. With the mixer on low speed, add one-third of the dry ingredients to the mixture. Alternate with one-third of the buttermilk until both are completely incorporated.
5. Pour into the prepared pans and place in the preheated oven. Bake for 30 to 40 minutes or until a toothpick inserted into the center of both layers comes out clean. Cool on racks for 15 minutes. Then turn out onto other racks to complete cooling. Frost with Brown Sugar Frosting.   ❧

Brown Sugar Frosting

FROSTS TWO 9-INCH LAYERS

⅓ cup cold water
1 tablespoon light corn syrup
1 teaspoon vanilla
2 large egg whites, unbeaten
1½ cups light brown sugar
½ teaspoon salt

1. In the top container of a double boiler, combine the ingredients in the order given. Beat 1 minute at high speed.
2. Place over rapidly boiling water, beating continuously. Continue to beat for 7 minutes or until the frosting becomes stiff and well-defined peaks form. Remove the top container and wipe the bottom. Apply the frosting immediately to a cool cake.   ❧

Basic Egg-Yolk Butter Cream

MAKES ABOUT 2 CUPS

Butter-cream frostings are endlessly versatile, and because the sugar they contain is completely dissolved in a cooked syrup, they are flawlessly smooth. Basic Egg-Yolk Butter Cream is rich, full-bodied, and pale yellow.

1 cup (2 sticks) unsalted butter
5 egg yolks
⅔ cup sugar
⅛ teaspoon cream of tartar
⅓ cup water
1 teaspoon vanilla or other flavoring

1. Cut the butter into ½-inch-thick slices and set aside to soften. Place the egg yolks in a large mixing bowl.

2. In a 1½-quart saucepan, combine the sugar, cream of tartar, and water, stirring to partially dissolve the sugar. (The cream of tartar is included to minimize the risk of sugar crystals forming on the sides of the pan.) Place over medium heat and stir until the sugar is completely dissolved. Increase the heat and bring the syrup to a boil. Cook, without stirring, until the mixture reaches 238°F. (the soft-ball stage).

3. As the syrup cooks, whip the egg yolks until they are slightly thickened and light in color. When the sugar syrup reaches 238°F., immediately add it to the egg yolks by droplets while whipping continuously. After you have incorporated one-third of the syrup by droplets, you can begin to add it in a thin stream. The mixture will become fluffy and increase in volume. Allow the mixture to cool to room temperature, but do not refrigerate to hasten the process.

4. Gradually whip in the softened butter, one piece at a time. Blend in the vanilla or other flavoring (see Variations on Basic Butter Cream, p. 384). Chill to firm if necessary. ◄

Basic Egg-White Butter Cream

MAKES ABOUT 2 CUPS

Basic Egg-White Butter Cream, also called meringue butter cream, is lighter in both flavor and consistency than butter cream made with egg yolks. It is also almost purely white in color. For the finest, most delicate results in *any butter-cream recipe, use only unsalted butter.*

1 cup (2 sticks) unsalted butter
3 egg whites
1 cup sugar
⅛ teaspoon cream of tartar
⅓ cup water
1 teaspoon vanilla or other flavoring

1. Cut the butter into ½-inch-thick slices and set aside to soften. Place the egg whites in a large mixing bowl.

2. In a 1½-quart saucepan, combine the sugar, cream of tartar, and water, stirring to partially dissolve the sugar. (The cream of tartar is included to minimize the risk of sugar crystals forming on the sides of the pan.) Place over medium heat and stir until the sugar is completely dissolved. Increase the heat and bring the syrup to a boil. Cook, without stirring, until the mixture reaches 238°F. (the soft-ball stage).

3. As the syrup cooks, whip the egg whites until soft peaks form. When the sugar syrup reaches 238°F., immediately add it to the egg whites by droplets while whipping continuously. After you've incorporated one-third of the syrup by droplets, you can begin to add it in a thin stream. The mixture will become fluffy and begin to look like Italian meringue. Allow the mixture to cool to room temperature, but do not refrigerate.

4. Place the softened butter in a large bowl and whip until light and creamy. Gradually beat in the meringue mixture. Blend in the vanilla or other flavoring (see Variations on Basic Butter Cream, which follows). Chill until firm enough to spread.

NOTE: Both the egg-white and egg-yolk butter creams can be frozen. However, Basic Egg-White Butter Cream tends to develop a streaky texture as it defrosts, so it's best to use it between layers, where its appearance is not that important. Allow frozen butter cream to warm to room temperature, and then whisk vigorously before using. ◄

Variations on Basic Butter Cream

CHOCOLATE BUTTER CREAM: Prepare 2 cups of Basic Butter Cream according to either of the two preceding recipes, but reduce the vanilla to ½ teaspoon. Melt 2 ounces of unsweetened chocolate and allow it to cool to room temperature. Gradually blend into the Basic Butter Cream.

DARK CHOCOLATE BUTTER CREAM: Prepare 2 cups of Basic Butter Cream according to either of the two preceding recipes, but reduce the vanilla to ½ teaspoon. Melt 3 ounces of unsweetened chocolate and allow it to cool to room temperature. Pulverize 1 teaspoon instant coffee granules with a mortar and pestle. Add 1 tablespoon boiling water and stir to dissolve. Gradually blend the chocolate and coffee into the Basic Butter Cream.

COFFEE BUTTER CREAM: Prepare 2 cups of Basic Butter Cream according to either of the two preceding recipes. Pulverize 1 teaspoon instant coffee granules with a mortar and pestle. Add 1 tablespoon boiling water and stir to dissolve. Gradually blend the coffee and 2 tablespoons of dark rum into the Basic Butter Cream.

MAPLE BUTTER CREAM: Prepare 2 cups of Basic Butter Cream according to either of the two preceding recipes. Finely chop enough walnuts to make ½ cup. Gradually blend 6 tablespoons pure maple syrup into the Basic Butter Cream. Gently stir in the chopped walnuts.

ORANGE BUTTER CREAM: Prepare 2 cups of Basic Butter Cream according to either of the two preceding recipes, but omit the vanilla. Gradually whip in ⅓ cup orange juice by droplets. Blend in 2 tablespoons Cointreau and 2 teaspoons grated orange zest.

PRALINE BUTTER CREAM: Prepare 2 cups of Basic Butter Cream according to either of the two preceding recipes. Gradually whip in 2 tablespoons bourbon by droplets. Gently stir in ⅔ cup Praline Powder (p. 379).

CHESTNUT BUTTER CREAM: Prepare 2 cups of Basic Butter Cream according to either of the two preceding recipes, but increase the vanilla to 2 teaspoons. Gradually whip in ⅔ cup canned, unsweetened chestnut purée (or make from fresh chestnuts by following steps 2–4 under Chestnut Cream Tart, p. 371).

Coconut Bavarian Cream

SERVES 8 TO 12

Unlike more traditional Bavarian creams, this exceptional gelatin dessert is lightened by the addition of whipped egg whites and contains no custard base. Chilled in a 9-inch springform pan, it is served in wedges like a cake. Sliced fresh peaches or whole strawberries make a delightful accompaniment.

6 large eggs
2 cans (3½ ounces each) flaked coconut
2 envelopes unflavored gelatin
½ cup cold water
⅓ cup boiling water
2 cups heavy cream
1 teaspoon vanilla
⅛ teaspoon salt
⅛ teaspoon cream of tartar
¾ cup sugar

1. Separate the eggs, reserving the yolks for another use. Place the whites in a large mixing bowl and set aside to warm to room temperature.

2. Meanwhile, prepare a 9-inch springform pan by buttering generously. Coat the bottom and sides of the pan with the contents of 1¼ cans of coconut.

3. In a small bowl, sprinkle the gelatin over the cold water and stir to soften. Add boiling water and blend to dissolve. Set aside.

4. In a large mixing bowl, whip the cream until soft peaks form. Blend in the vanilla. Place in the refrigerator.

5. Whip the egg whites until foamy. Add the salt and cream of tartar, and whip until soft peaks form. Gradually sprinkle in the sugar, whipping continuously. Fold in the softened gelatin.

6. Empty the whipped cream into the egg-white mixture and fold gently. Pour into the coconut-coated pan. Smooth the surface, pushing the mixture firmly against the sides. Sprinkle the top with the remaining coconut. Chill overnight. To easily unmold the springform pan, set it on a sturdy container, such as a 1-quart mayonnaise jar. Release the sides and lower them to the counter. ◅੨

Tortoni

SERVES 12

It is more than mere coincidence that Italian meringue forms the basis for this creamy, almond-flavored delicacy. The technique for making frozen desserts of this kind originated in Italy.

3 large egg whites
¾ cup sugar
¼ cup cold water
⅛ teaspoon cream of tartar
½ cup slivered almonds
1½ teaspoons almond extract
1½ cups heavy cream
¾ teaspoon vanilla
12 candied cherries

1. Place the egg whites in a grease-free stainless steel or copper bowl and allow them to come to room temperature (about 70°F.).

2. Prepare Italian meringue by combining the sugar and water in a 1½-quart saucepan. Stir to partially dissolve the sugar and set over medium-high heat. Stir to completely dissolve the sugar. Increase the heat to high and bring the syrup to a boil. Cook uncovered and without stirring until the mixture reaches 238°F. on a candy thermometer or forms a soft ball when dropped into cold water. While the syrup is cooking, whip the whites at medium speed until foamy. Add the cream of tartar and increase the speed of the mixer to medium-high. Whip until the beaters begin to trace lines through the egg whites. As soon as the sugar syrup reaches 238°F., slowly pour it into the whites in a thin stream. Beat constantly at medium-high until the whites are glossy and stiff peaks stand straight when the beaters are lifted. Tightly cover the bowl of whipped whites with aluminum foil and refrigerate for 30 minutes.

3. Meanwhile, scatter the almonds over the bottom of a baking pan. Place in a 350°F. oven and toast for 8 to 10 minutes. Allow to cool slightly and transfer to the container of a blender or processor. Whirl to crush finely. Empty into a small bowl and stir in the almond extract. Set aside.

4. Whip the heavy cream until soft peaks form when the beaters are lifted. Blend in the vanilla.

5. Fold the whipped cream into the chilled meringue and spoon into twelve 2-inch paper muffin cups set inside a muffin tin for support. Sprinkle with the crushed almonds and top each with a candied cherry. Cover tightly with foil and freeze 6 hours or until firm. ◅੨

Strawberry Mousse

SERVES 6

Show off this exquisite dessert by serving it in a stemmed trifle bowl or crystal goblets. You can also spoon strawberry mousse into cream-puff shells and drizzle warm semi-sweet chocolate over the top.

2 large egg whites
1 quart (about ¾ pound) fresh strawberries
2 cups heavy cream

1¼ cups confectioners' sugar, sifted
¼ teaspoon cream of tartar
1 teaspoon gelatin
2 tablespoons cold water
1 teaspoon vanilla
Sweetened whipped cream and chocolate
   shavings to garnish

1. Place the egg whites in a large bowl and allow them to come to room temperature.

2. Wash, dry, and hull the strawberries. Purée them by mashing with a fork or whirling in a blender or processor. Measure out 2 cups and set aside at room temperature.

3. Whip the cream until you can see the lines traced by the beaters. Continue to whip, gradually sprinkling in ¼ cup of the sugar. Cover with aluminum foil and refrigerate.

4. Beat the egg whites at slow speed until foamy. Add the cream of tartar and increase whipping speed. Beat until soft peaks form. Gradually sprinkle on the remaining 1 cup of sugar, beating continuously until stiff peaks form when the beaters are lifted.

5. Fill a wide saucepan with water to a depth of 1 inch. Place over high heat and bring to a boil. In a 1-cup glass measure, combine the gelatin and cold water. Stir to soften the gelatin. Set into the boiling water and heat, stirring, until the gelatin dissolves. Lift out the measuring cup and dry with a kitchen towel. Blend in the vanilla. With the mixer at medium-low speed, slowly pour the warm gelatin into the whipped egg whites.

6. Pour the strawberry purée into a large mixing bowl. Add 2 generous dollops of the whipped whites and stir to lighten the mixture. Pour in the whipped cream and fold with light, rapid strokes. Add the remaining egg whites and once again fold lightly and rapidly. Lay a piece of plastic wrap directly on the surface of the mousse and refrigerate until serving time. Top with sweetened whipped-cream rosettes and chocolate shavings or serve inside cream-puff shells.

(See entry for Whipping: Egg Whites/ Cream.)

Essence of Fresh Orange Mousse

SERVES 6

Reduced fresh orange juice lends a seductive air to this refreshing mousse. To serve, mound inside chocolate cups; spoon into hollowed orange shells; or quarter fresh strawberries, marinate them in Cointreau, and spoon over each serving.

6 tablespoons unsalted butter, cut into 6 pieces
2 tablespoons Cointreau
⅔ cup fresh orange juice
3 large egg yolks
⅓ cup sugar
¼ cup water
1 cup heavy cream

1. Combine the butter and Cointreau in a small saucepan and stir over medium heat until the butter melts. Set aside to cool to room temperature.

2. Pour the orange juice through a sieve into a 1½-quart thick-bottomed saucepan. Place over medium-low heat and cook uncovered until reduced to ¼ cup (or slightly less). Stir frequently with a heat-resistant rubber spatula to prevent scorching. The use of gentle heat is extremely important here because the orange juice is apt to foam and adhere to the sides of the pan, where it will burn. Pour the reduced juice into a glass measuring cup and set aside.

3. Put the egg yolks through a sieve into the bowl of an electric mixer. Whip for 15 seconds to lighten their consistency. In a 1½-quart saucepan, combine the sugar and water and stir to partially dissolve the sugar. Place over medium heat and stir until the sugar is completely dissolved. Increase the heat and bring the syrup to a boil. Cook, without stirring, until the syrup reaches 238°F. on a candy thermometer (the soft-ball stage).

4. With the mixer on the highest possible speed, immediately add the hot syrup to the egg yolks a drop at a time. When the mixture begins to lighten in color, you may begin to

add the syrup in a thin stream. Don't be alarmed if a large amount of sugar syrup splashes up onto the sides of the bowl and adheres. Leave it there; don't scrape down the sides of the bowl.

5. Whipping continuously, add the warm, reduced orange juice in a thin stream. (If a considerable amount of sugar syrup has hardened to the saucepan, pour the orange juice essence into the pan, place over high heat, and stir for a few seconds to melt the syrup and incorporate it into the orange juice.) Still whipping, add the cooled butter in a thin stream. Make sure the butter gets thoroughly incorporated. The mixture will be light and fluffy and resemble the consistency of whipped cream. Whip the cream, either by hand or by mixer, and fold into the orange mixture. Cover and refrigerate for 4 to 6 hours.

NOTE: Because oranges vary widely in their natural sweetness, you may want to add more sugar than this recipe calls for. Taste the juice before you begin. If it seems to lack sweetness, incorporate 1 or 2 tablespoons of sugar during the final stages of whipping the cream.

(See entry for Whipping: Cream.)

Steamed Pumpkin Pudding

SERVES 8 to 12

Pumpkin, long considered a traditional component of fall menus, is presented here in a moist, cakelike steamed pudding. Serve warm with lightly whipped Crème Fraîche (p. 361) or Cream Cheese Sauce (see below).

6 tablespoons butter
1¼ cups all-purpose flour, scoop measured
1 teaspoon baking powder
¼ teaspoon baking soda
½ teaspoon salt
1 teaspoon cinnamon
½ teaspoon nutmeg
¼ teaspoon ground cloves
¼ teaspoon ground ginger
½ cup granulated sugar
½ cup light brown sugar
2 large eggs
½ cup milk
1 cup pumpkin purée (canned or fresh)
½ cup coarsely chopped pecans
¼ cup coarsely chopped candied orange peel

1. Set out the butter to soften. Generously grease a 2-quart pudding mold with a center tube. Arrange a rack inside a large kettle or canning pot. Put a teakettle of water on the stove to boil.

2. Sift together the flour, baking powder, baking soda, salt, cinnamon, nutmeg, cloves, and ginger. Combine thoroughly by tossing with a fork or whisk. Set aside.

3. Beat the softened butter until light. Gradually sprinkle in the granulated sugar, beating continuously until fluffy and lemon colored. Beat in the brown sugar. Add the eggs one at a time, beating thoroughly after each addition.

4. With the mixer on low speed, add one-third of the dry ingredients to the mixture. Alternate with one-third of the milk until both are completely incorporated. Blend in the pumpkin purée. Stir in the chopped pecans and chopped orange peel.

5. Pour into the prepared mold and cover with the lid of the mold or aluminum foil. (If using foil, secure it with string.) Place the mold on the rack set inside the kettle. Add hot water from the teakettle to a depth of 1½ inches. Bring the water to a vigorous boil. Cover the pot and lower the heat if necessary to prevent the cover from lifting, but keep the water boiling rapidly. Steam the pudding for 2½ to 3 hours, pouring in additional hot water if necessary to maintain the level at 1½ inches. Test for doneness by inserting a metal skewer into the center. When it comes out clean, the pudding is cooked. Transfer the mold to a cooling rack and allow to cool for

15 minutes. Unmold onto a serving plate. Drizzle Cream Cheese Sauce over the top or pass whipped *crème fraîche.*

CREAM CHEESE SAUCE

1 package (8 ounces) cream cheese, softened at room temperature
3 tablespoons confectioners' sugar, sifted
3 tablespoons milk
½ teaspoon vanilla
1 teaspoon finely chopped candied orange peel

1. In a small mixing bowl, beat the cream cheese until light and fluffy. Beat in the sugar, milk, and vanilla. Blend in the orange peel and pour over the warm pumpkin pudding. (If made ahead and refrigerated, allow the sauce to soften to room temperature, then beat vigorously until thin enough to pour smoothly.)   ❧

Maple-Bourbon Pudding

SERVES 6

To achieve a flawlessly smooth stirred pudding, disperse the cornstarch throughout the sugar, then add cold milk and stir constantly over medium-high heat. The native ingredients maple syrup and bourbon contribute an all-American flair to the following version of this popular dessert.

¾ cup light brown sugar
¼ cup cornstarch
¼ teaspoon salt
2¼ cups cold milk
½ cup pure maple syrup
3 tablespoons bourbon
1 teaspoon vanilla
2 tablespoons butter, cut into 8 chunks
1 cup heavy cream, whipped (optional)
Finely chopped pecans (optional)

1. In a thick-bottomed 2½-quart saucepan, combine the brown sugar, cornstarch, and salt with a whisk, stirring to disperse the cornstarch. (Don't be alarmed if some of the brown sugar remains in lumps.)

2. Slowly pour in the milk, stirring continuously with the whisk. When the cornstarch and most of the sugar are dissolved, place the pan over medium-high heat and continuously stir with a heat-resistant rubber spatula or a wooden spoon to keep the milk from scorching.

3. As the milk warms, portions of the mixture will begin to clump together. Pull the pan from the burner and stir off the heat for 15 to 20 seconds, then return to the heat. Repeat occasionally to slow the heating process. As thickening continues, the mixture will smooth out.

4. Lift the spatula and listen for the first plopping sound that indicates the mixture has reached the boil. On the second plop, remove from the heat. Stir in the maple syrup, bourbon, and vanilla. Return to medium-high heat and continue stirring for 1 minute. Remove from the heat at once and stir in the butter.

5. Pour into individual serving dishes or a large bowl. Do not stir to speed cooling. Lay a piece of plastic wrap directly on the surface of the hot pudding. Smooth out any air bubbles with your fingertips and press the excess wrap against the sides of the bowl or individual dishes. Refrigerate the pudding until thoroughly chilled. If desired, top with whipped cream and sprinkle on finely chopped pecans to serve.   ❧

Crème Brûlée

SERVES 6

Preparing Crème Brûlée is similar in technique to preparing stirred custard. The result is a velvety rich cream that thickens because of the coagulation of egg-yolk protein and then becomes firm as it chills. Residual heat is so often the cause of curdling in this type of mixture that the following recipe suggests adding 2 tablespoons of cold cream later to halt the cooking process abruptly at the end.

7 large eggs
2½ cups heavy cream
1 teaspoon vanilla
3 tablespoons granulated sugar
½ to ¾ cup light brown sugar, sifted

1. Separate the eggs, freezing the whites or reserving them for another use. Strain the yolks into the upper container of a double boiler to remove any traces of white that might coagulate and mar the final texture of the cream. Add water to the bottom container to the depth of ½ inch. Bring the water to a boil and reduce the heat so that the water is steaming but not bubbling. Do not place the upper container over the water yet.

2. Blend 2 tablespoons of the cream with the vanilla in a small bowl. Set aside. In a 1½-quart saucepan, combine the remaining cream and granulated sugar. Place over medium heat and stir to dissolve the sugar. Continue heating to 160°F. or to just below a boil.

3. Stir the egg yolks with a spatula or wooden spoon (or beat with a whisk to create an airier texture). Slowly pour the hot cream into the egg yolks, stirring (or whisking) constantly. Now place over the hot water and continue to stir slowly. Scrape down the sides of the pan frequently to avoid lumps of overcooked mixture. As the custard approaches 170°F., it will thicken considerably. Test for doneness by coating the spatula or the back of a spoon. Draw your finger through the mixture to create a path. The path should remain open for a few seconds. The custard will be completely cooked by the time it reaches 180°F. Immediately remove the upper container from the heat and blend in the reserved cream-and-vanilla mixture.

4. Pour, or strain if necessary, into six 4-ounce cups or an 8-inch baking dish (such as a quiche dish). Refrigerate 6 to 8 hours or until set. It isn't necessary to cover with plastic wrap if the custard is going to be served within 12 hours because the hot sugar that forms the caramel crust will dissolve any skin that might form; however, do lay plastic wrap directly on the surface if the custard is to be held longer than 12 hours.

5. Just before serving, generously sprinkle the top of each cream with sifted brown sugar. Set the custard cups in a large baking pan. Pour in *cold* water to a depth of 1 inch and add ample ice cubes to the pan to help keep the cups cold.

6. Slide the baking pan under the broiler as close to the heat as possible. In 2 to 3 minutes the sugar will caramelize and form a dark brown glaze. Serve immediately to fully appreciate the balance of sensations between the cold soft cream and the warm crisp glaze.

(See entry for Custard.) ᦰᦰ

Caramel Flan

SERVES 8

You can achieve perfect consistency in a baked custard, or flan, by baking at a moderate temperature and using a hot-water bath to buffer the heat of the oven. The object is to set up a warm environment that will cause the proteins to denature and coagulate, thereby firming the custard. To avoid incorporating air that gives baked custard a grainy texture, don't whisk the mixture or put it through a sieve. Instead, strain the egg yolks at the beginning of the procedure to remove traces of white that can cause pitting, and stir the mixture with a heat-resistant rubber spatula or wooden spoon. You'll notice that this recipe calls for egg yolks and cream rather than whole eggs and milk. The result is an extravagantly silky texture.

CARAMEL GLAZE
⅔ cup sugar
⅛ teaspoon cream of tartar
⅓ cup water

VANILLA RUM CUSTARD
8 large egg yolks
3 cups medium, or whipping, cream
6 tablespoons sugar
1½ teaspoons vanilla
2 tablespoons dark rum

1. Preheat the oven to 325°F. Place an 8-inch ungreased cake pan in the oven to warm.

2. To caramelize the sugar, begin by combining it with the cream of tartar and water in a 1½-quart thick-bottomed saucepan. Stir to dissolve the sugar and cream of tartar and place over low heat until the particles of sugar have completely disappeared. Increase the heat and bring the liquid to a boil. Cook without stirring until the mixture turns pale yellow. At that point, begin to stir slowly to even the coloring process. When the syrup reaches 320°F. on a candy thermometer, remove it from the burner long enough to take the preheated pan from the oven. Return the syrup to the burner and continue cooking until it reaches 338°F. Lifting the pan from the burner and returning it again, closely control the temperature of the syrup. As it passes the 340°F. mark, it will become the color of dark maple syrup. Immediately pour it into the heated cake pan and swirl slowly to coat the bottom and sides.

3. To make the custard, put the egg yolks through a sieve into a large mixing bowl and set aside.

4. Combine the cream and sugar in a 1½-quart saucepan and warm, stirring continuously over moderate heat to 140°F. Remove from the heat. Stirring gently, slowly pour the warm cream into the strained egg yolks. Blend in the vanilla and the dark rum.

5. Line a roasting pan with a folded kitchen towel to protect the bottom of the custard from the heat of the roasting pan. Place the caramel-coated cake pan on the folded towel and pour in the custard. Situate the oven rack as near the middle of the oven as possible. Place the roasting pan on the oven rack and add enough hot tap water to the pan to cover the towel and come halfway up the sides of the cake pan. Bake 20 minutes at 325°F. Then increase the oven temperature to 350°F. and bake 20 to 30 minutes more. Test for doneness by inserting the blade of a paring knife halfway between the center and the rim of the pan. (The "jiggle" method of testing [see p. 44] is difficult to use in this instance because the melted syrup allows the custard to move around.) When the knife blade parts the custard neatly, removing no traces of liquid egg mixture, remove the custard and water bath from the oven. Keep in mind that it's better to err on the side of undercooked than overcooked. Allow the custard to sit in the water bath until cooking is completed by residual heat (30 minutes).

6. Refrigerate until serving time or at least 6 hours. Run the blade of a knife around the outside edge of the flan to loosen it if necessary. (Usually it's sufficient to hold the pan at a 45° angle and let the custard pull away from the edges itself.) Select a large flat serving plate with a rim to contain the caramel glaze. Place the plate over the custard and invert. It will easily turn out, and the glaze will spill over the top and sides.

(See entry for Custard.)   ◅ঽ

Zabaglione
SERVES 6 TO 8

This light, frothy dessert, also called zabaione *in some regions of Italy and* sabayon *in France, is basically a warm emulsion sauce*

*consisting of wine (as the acid-water compo-
nent), sugar, and egg yolks. If you use the
unlined copper pan designed specifically for
making zabaglione (or an unlined copper
bowl), take a minute to wipe the inside with
an acid paste (see Note) or a commercial
cleaner. An unlined copper pan that is used
infrequently develops a film of copper carbonate, which can interact with the wine and turn
the mixture green.*

6 large egg yolks
½ cup superfine sugar
½ cup Marsala
**¼ cup dry white wine (for French-style *sabayon*,
use ¾ cup of a fruity sauterne in place of the
Marsala and white wine)**
1 teaspoon grated orange or lemon zest
**1 cup heavy cream, whipped and chilled
(optional)**

1. Fill a large saucepan or the bottom of a
double boiler with water to a depth of ½ inch.
Bring the water to a boil, and then reduce the
heat so that the water is steaming, not boiling. Keep in mind that just as in preparing a
warm emulsion sauce, the upper container
should be warmed by steam, not water.

2. Put the egg yolks into a zabaglione pan,
unlined copper bowl, or the top of a double
boiler by passing them through a sieve to
catch tiny particles of egg white that, when
heated, could coagulate and mar the final texture. Whisk in the sugar until the mixture is
slightly thickened and lemon colored. Place
over steaming water. Whisking constantly,
slowly pour in the wines. Add the grated zest
and continue whisking until the mixture
foams up to nearly triple its original volume.

3. Remove the pan from the hot water and
continue whisking for 30 seconds. Fold in the
optional whipped cream if you prefer a lighter version and pour into stemmed dessert
dishes or wine goblets. Zabaglione may also
be chilled and served cold. However, the liquid tends to settle out and the mixture deflates. To compensate for the loss of fluffiness
and to restore the light texture, fold in the
whipped cream right before serving.

NOTE: You can make an acid paste for
cleaning copper pans by blending 2 tablespoons vinegar, 2 tablespoons flour, and 1
tablespoon salt. Rub over the copper surface
and rinse well under running water. If the
paste turns green, that's the copper carbonate
coming off.   ◆♂

Tartufi

MAKES 12 TARTUFI

*A velvety chocolate dessert shaped to resem-
ble black truffles. This recipe contains a fairly
uncommon procedure — whipping a hot sugar syrup into egg yolks. It's possible to do
this without curdling the eggs if you add the
hot syrup by drops because the hot drops are
dispersed throughout a much larger quantity
of cold egg yolks. The yolks will warm gradually and actually cook. Then you can begin to
add the hot syrup in a thin stream.*

**12 ounces semisweet chocolate or real chocolate
bits**
6 ounces unsweetened chocolate
6 large egg yolks
1 cup water
1 cup sugar
2 cups heavy cream

1. Coarsely chop the semisweet chocolate
with a chef's knife or in a food processor (or
use chocolate bits). Melt the chocolate in a
pan placed on a heat diffuser or in the top of a
double boiler set over hot (140°F.) water.

2. Meanwhile, grate or finely chop the unsweetened chocolate in a processor or with a
hand-held grater. Set aside.

3. To prevent bits of coagulated egg white
from marring the final texture, put the egg
yolks through a sieve into a large mixing
bowl. Whip the yolks until slightly fluffy.
Combine the water and sugar in a 1½-quart
saucepan. Stir to dissolve the sugar and place
over medium-high heat. Cook, without stirring, until the syrup reaches 238°F. (the soft-
ball stage). Immediately add the hot syrup to

the yolks by droplets, whipping constantly. When the egg yolks begin to thicken, you can add the hot syrup in a thin stream.

4. Whipping continuously, pour in the melted chocolate. Then gradually add the heavy cream. Stop to scrape down the sides of the bowl, but don't be alarmed if some chocolate adheres to the sugar syrup that has stuck to the side. Whip again to blend well and cover the bowl with aluminum foil. Secure tightly and place in the freezer until firm (6 to 8 hours).

5. Remove from the freezer. Scoop out a generous tablespoonful and roll in the grated unsweetened chocolate, pushing and patting the mixture into an irregularly shaped ball that resembles a black truffle. As it is coated, transfer each *tartufo* to a pan lined with waxed paper. Repeat until the mixture is used up. Place in the freezer until firm (3 hours). Serve immediately, or wrap individually in plastic wrap for longer storage. ◄ぅ

Chocolate Truffles

MAKES FORTY-EIGHT 1½-INCH TRUFFLES

These elegant morsels are unbelievably easy to make. They're lovely as hostess or holiday gifts, and they freeze well. Be sure to use unsalted butter for its delicate, refined flavor and heavy cream for its high butterfat content. The setting of a truffle mixture depends on the firming of fat contained in chocolate, butter, and cream; consequently, a grade of cream with the highest possible fat content is necessary to the success of this recipe.

1 pound 3 ounces semisweet chocolate
2 cups heavy cream
½ cup unsalted butter, cut into large chunks
6 tablespoons sugar
6 tablespoons Grand Marnier or Cointreau
½ to ¾ cup unsweetened cocoa

1. Break the chocolate into pieces (since it is heated slowly in the cream, precise chopping or fine grating is unnecessary). Combine the chocolate with the cream, butter, and sugar in a thick-bottomed 2½-quart saucepan. Stir over medium heat to dissolve the sugar. Bring to a boil and cook, stirring continuously, until the butter and chocolate are melted.

2. Remove from the heat and stir in the liqueur. Pour the mixture into a stainless steel or copper bowl (glass or plastic will not work as efficiently). Fill a basin or large pan with cracked ice (ice cubes will also do the job, but not as quickly). Set the bowl in the ice and beat the mixture with a wooden spoon until it takes on the consistency of extremely thick frosting.

3. Line 2 baking sheets with waxed paper. Scoop up the mixture by level tablespoonfuls and drop in mounds onto the waxed paper. Refrigerate until firm but malleable — about 1½ to 2 hours.

4. Sift the cocoa into a small bowl. Take up a firm mound of chocolate and roll it lightly in the cocoa, pressing it over the entire surface to form an irregular truffle-shaped sphere. Place in a small, tea-size paper baking cup. Chill for 2 hours and serve, or freeze on a baking sheet and store them in an airtight plastic bag for up to 3 months. Serve chocolate truffles as you would petits fours or present after dinner with your favorite liqueur.

NOTE: It should go without saying that the quality of chocolate you use has a direct effect on the quality of truffles you create. Ordinary Baker's semisweet chocolate or Nestle's semisweet bits produce truffles that are quite good. But for depth of flavor, try Cailler Crémant or Callebaut, both exceptionally fine semisweet chocolates. ◄ぅ

Chips of Chocolate Toll House Cookies

MAKES 4 DOZEN 2-INCH COOKIES

When Ruth Wakefield baked the very first chocolate chip cookie, she didn't reach for the bag of bits — she chopped her own chips from

a chocolate bar. This recipe incorporates chocolate you chop yourself. The result is definitely a grownups-only version of this cookie.

½ cup butter (if you substitute solid vegetable shortening, add ¼ teaspoon water to the batter when you blend in the vanilla)
2 bars (3 ounces each) Tobler bittersweet or extra bittersweet chocolate
½ cup coarsely chopped pecans
1 cup plus 2 tablespoons all-purpose flour, scoop measured
½ teaspoon baking soda
½ teaspoon salt
6 tablespoons granulated sugar
6 tablespoons light brown sugar
1 large egg
¾ teaspoon vanilla

1. Set out the butter and allow it to soften for 30 minutes. Coarsely chop the chocolate with a chef's knife or by pulsing briefly in a processor. Chop the pecans.

2. Preheat the oven to 375°F. and generously grease 2 or 3 cookie sheets. Sift the flour, baking soda, and salt into a small bowl, then toss with a fork or whisk to be certain they are well blended. Set aside.

3. Whip the butter until light and fluffy. Gradually sprinkle in the sugars, beating continuously. Blend in the egg and the vanilla.

4. With the mixer at low speed or by hand, stir in the dry ingredients just until they disappear. Do not overbeat. Stir in the chopped chocolate and pecans. Drop by heaping teaspoonfuls onto greased cookie sheets and bake 10 to 12 minutes. Allow cookies to set for 3 minutes, then transfer to a cooling rack. (See entry for Cookies.)

Applesauce Chocolate Chip Cookies

MAKES 6 DOZEN 2-INCH COOKIES

This chocolate chip cookie owes its soft consistency to the use of solid shortening and applesauce.

2 cups all-purpose flour, scoop measured
1 teaspoon baking soda
½ teaspoon salt
½ teaspoon cinnamon
¼ teaspoon freshly ground nutmeg
⅛ teaspoon ground cloves
¾ cup solid vegetable shortening (try the butter-flavored)
1 cup light brown sugar
1 large egg
1½ teaspoons vanilla
1 cup applesauce
6 ounces semisweet chocolate chips (1 cup)
½ cup coarsely chopped walnuts

1. Preheat the oven to 375°F. and generously grease 2 or 3 cookie sheets. Sift the flour, baking soda, and salt into a small bowl. Add the cinnamon, nutmeg, and cloves and toss with a fork or whisk to blend the leavening agent and spices in thoroughly. Set aside.

2. Whip the shortening until light and fluffy. Gradually sprinkle in the sugar, beating continuously. Beat in the egg and vanilla.

3. With the mixer at low speed or by hand, blend in the dry ingredients, alternating with the applesauce. Do not overbeat. Stir in the chocolate chips and chopped walnuts. Drop by heaping teaspoonfuls onto greased cookie sheets and bake for 10 to 12 minutes. Allow cookies to set for 3 minutes, then transfer to a cooling rack.
(See entry for Cookies.)

Sourdough Oatmeal Cookies

MAKES 5 DOZEN 2½-INCH COOKIES

By incorporating sourdough starter into the batter, you can produce unusually soft, moist oatmeal cookies with a cakelike texture. Chopped dates add an unexpected dimension of flavor.

½ cup butter
1 cup all-purpose flour, scoop measured
1 cup whole wheat flour, scoop measured
1 teaspoon baking soda
1½ teaspoons ground cinnamon
½ teaspoon freshly ground allspice
¼ teaspoon ground cloves
¾ teaspoon salt
½ cup solid vegetable shortening
2 large eggs
½ cup honey
¼ cup molasses
2 cups Herman Starter (p. 227)
3 cups one-minute rolled oats
½ cup freshly chopped dates
½ cup chopped walnuts

1. Place the butter in a large mixing bowl and allow to soften at room temperature. Preheat the oven to 375°F. and lightly grease 2 or 3 cookie sheets. Sift together the all-purpose flour, whole wheat flour, baking soda, cinnamon, allspice, cloves, and salt. Toss with a fork or whisk to blend thoroughly and set aside.

2. Add the solid shortening to the softened butter and beat at high speed until light and fluffy. Beat in the eggs, one at a time. (The mixture will appear to curdle because no sugar has been incorporated into the butter. It will pull together when the honey is added.) With the mixer at medium speed, slowly pour in the honey and molasses. Add the sourdough starter and blend thoroughly.

3. Reduce the speed of the mixer to low and blend in the sifted flour and spices. Add the oats, dates, and walnuts and stir slowly to combine. Drop by generous tablespoonfuls onto prepared cookie sheets and flatten with the back of a spoon. Allow about 3 inches between cookies. Place in the preheated oven and bake for 12 to 15 minutes or until the bottoms are nicely browned. Transfer the cookies to a rack to cool.

NOTE: Honey that has hardened or formed large crystals can be smoothed out by heating. Place the jar of honey in a saucepan and add water to come halfway up the sides of the jar. Set over medium-high heat and warm until crystals disappear.

(See entry for Cookies.)

Almond Butterballs

MAKES 6 DOZEN COOKIES

Ball cookies are among the easiest to make. You don't have to cream the butter to incorporate air or spend hours rolling and cutting out dough. But there's still a trick or two involved in achieving tender, melt-in-your-mouth ball cookies. Stir gently and briefly when blending in the flour so that you don't agitate the gluten, and roll into balls using a light, quick touch. Otherwise, the warmth of your hands will encourage the gluten to develop and thereby toughen the cookies.

1 cup butter (don't substitute because the flavor is essential)
4 ounces blanched almonds
½ cup sifted confectioners' sugar
¼ teaspoon salt
1 teaspoon almond extract
2¼ cups all-purpose flour, sifted
Additional confectioners' sugar, sifted

1. Place the butter in a large mixing bowl and allow to soften for 30 minutes. Meanwhile, finely chop the nuts with a chef's knife or by pulsing briefly in a processor. Set aside.

2. Preheat the oven to 350°F. Beat the butter, ½ cup of sugar, salt, and almond extract together until light and fluffy.

3. Measure the flour by sifting it directly

into the cup, then gradually blend it into the butter mixture. Stir in the chopped nuts.

4. Take up by rounded teaspoonfuls and shape into balls by rolling lightly between the palms of your hands. Place on an ungreased cookie sheet and bake for 8 to 10 minutes or until firm but not brown. Roll the warm cookies in sifted confectioners' sugar and set on a cooling rack. When cooled, roll a second time in sifted confectioners' sugar.

(See entry for Cookies.)

Forgotten Cookies

MAKES 48 COOKIES

These delicate sweets are created by folding chopped nuts and chocolate into Swiss meringue. In keeping with the traditional techniques involving this particular meringue, these cookies are dried rather than baked. The oven is preheated, then turned off, so the cookies can remain inside for 12 hours or overnight — hence they are "forgotten."

4 large egg whites
¼ teaspoon cream of tartar
1 cup superfine sugar (or substitute regular granulated sugar whirled in a blender to pulverize the granules)
½ teaspoon vanilla
1 cup pecans, very finely chopped
4 ounces semisweet chocolate, very finely chopped

1. Place the egg whites in a grease-free stainless steel or copper bowl and allow them to come to room temperature (about 70°F.). Preheat the oven to 350°F. Prepare 2 cookie sheets by lining them with parchment or by buttering the pans lightly and then coating with flour. (Because the oven heat is extremely low, scorching the flour is not a problem here.)

2. Prepare Swiss meringue by whipping the whites at medium speed until foamy. Add the cream of tartar and increase the speed of the

mixer to medium-high. Whip until the beaters begin to trace lines through the egg whites. Gradually sprinkle in ½ cup of the superfine or regular granulated sugar, beating continuously at medium-high. Then add the vanilla. When the egg whites acquire a shiny gloss and stiff peaks stand straight, stop beating and fold in the remaining ½ cup of sugar (this procedure ensures a tender meringue).

3. Gently fold in the finely chopped nuts and chocolate. Immediately drop by teaspoonfuls or pipe into kisses onto the prepared cookie sheets. Place both sheets in the preheated oven and turn off the heat. Leave the cookies inside the oven for 12 hours or overnight. Do not open the oven door during that time or the cookies may deflate and crack.

Bananas Foster

SERVES 4

With its origins in New Orleans, this popular flaming dessert is truly a native American. The bananas are traditionally sliced in half lengthwise, but the diagonal cut suggested here is equally attractive and easier to manipulate without breaking. (Read the entry for Flaming before preparing this recipe.)

4 ripe bananas
2 tablespoons fresh lemon juice
1 pint vanilla ice cream
½ cup dark rum
¼ cup Cointreau
4 tablespoons unsalted butter
4 tablespoons light brown sugar
½ teaspoon ground cinnamon
Toasted sliced almonds

1. Peel the bananas and cut into ¼-inch-thick oval-shaped pieces by slicing on the diagonal. (Some Oriental cookbooks refer to this shape as "slanting slices.") Place the banana slices in a large mixing bowl. Sprinkle on the lemon juice and toss gently with a rubber spatula to coat.

2. Set the ice cream out to soften slightly. Combine the rum and Cointreau in a small bowl, and then pour half the mixture into a small saucepan. Melt the butter in a flambé pan or large skillet. When the butter begins to bubble, stir in the brown sugar and cinnamon. Add the banana slices and cook them in the bubbling mixture until the sauce begins to thicken slightly and the bananas soften. Turning the banana slices one at a time, move them continuously around the pan to promote even cooking.

3. Pour the rum and Cointreau from the bowl over the bananas and allow it to bubble, continuously spooning the hot sauce over the bananas. Meanwhile, set the saucepan containing the other half of the rum and Cointreau over medium heat and warm until the smell of alcohol becomes quite strong. Then, when the sauce with the bananas is bubbling vigorously, pour the warmed spirits on it. Wait for the sauce to return to a bubble and ignite with a long wooden match. Baste the banana slices with the flaming sauce until the alcohol is completely burned off and the flame subsides.

4. Spoon the cooked bananas and hot sauce over scoops of slightly softened ice cream and sprinkle with toasted almond slices.

(See Entry for Flaming.)   ✎

Cream Puffs

MAKES 12 LARGE OR 16 MEDIUM CREAM PUFFS

Traditional recipes for cream puff pastry rely solely on water as the liquid ingredient. However, a small portion of milk contributes protein to the skeletal structure of the pastry for added strength and provides elements that encourage superior color.

¾ cup cold water
¼ cup milk
4 tablespoons (¼ cup) butter, cut into 16 small chunks

1 teaspoon sugar
⅛ teaspoon salt
1 cup all-purpose flour, scoop measured
4 or 5 large eggs (see step 2)
Egg wash (1 egg whisked with 1 teaspoon water)

1. In a thick-bottomed 1½-quart saucepan, combine the water, milk, butter, sugar, and salt. Stir over medium-high heat until the butter melts. Stop stirring and allow the mixture to come to a vigorous boil. Immediately remove the pan from the heat and add the flour. Beat vigorously with a wooden spatula. Return to burner and cook over medium-low heat, stirring, until the batter pulls together into a smooth, shiny mass. Continue stirring the dough over medium-low heat to dry the *panade*. A white granular film will appear on the bottom of the pan. Do not allow it to burn and don't attempt to incorporate it into the dough. Test the *panade* for doneness by pinching with two fingers. When it no longer sticks to your fingers and takes on a putty-like consistency, the *panade* is cooked. Immediately empty into a large bowl. Allow it to cool for 5 to 10 minutes (or to below 140°F.), stirring occasionally to prevent a skin from forming.

2. Under optimum conditions, 1 cup of flour will absorb 1 cup of eggs. (Dry flour will absorb more liquid than flour that is already holding a degree of moisture.) Since egg-rich batter produces the largest puffs, try to incorporate as much egg as possible. Lightly whisk 4 eggs and pour into a measuring cup. If necessary, whisk the remaining egg and add enough of it to form 1 cup of eggs.

3. Using a wooden spatula or the paddle attachment of an electric mixer, beat in one-quarter of the whisked eggs. Continue beating until the *panade* accepts the eggs and the mixture smooths out. Repeat twice. Add the last portion of the eggs in a thin stream. Check for proper consistency by lifting the beater or allowing the dough to drop from a spoon. It should fall in a thick, heavy ribbon and leave a peak that stands stiff. Keep in mind that the goal is to add as much egg as

possible without overly thinning the dough. Cream puff pastry may be made to this point and refrigerated for 2 or 3 days, but for best results it must be brought to room temperature before shaping.

4. Preheat the oven to 425°F. Generously grease an aluminum cookie sheet. Drop the batter by rounded tablespoonfuls, or pipe into 12 or 16 mounds with a pastry bag. Allow 2½ inches between mounds to permit hot air to circulate efficiently around the sides of the puffs. Prepare an egg wash by whisking 1 egg with 1 teaspoon of water. Using your fingertips or a pastry brush, apply the egg wash to the tops of the puffs only. Flatten any peaks of batter and smooth the surface. Place on the rack nearest the middle of the oven and bake for 15 minutes. Lower the temperature to 375°F. and bake 10 to 15 minutes more. When the puffs are golden brown and sound hollow when tapped, tilt the baking sheet slightly and allow the puffs to slide off onto the oven rack. Turn off the heat and leave the oven door ajar. Allow the puffs to cool on the rack inside the oven for 30 minutes (too rapid cooling causes puffs to collapse).

5. Take the cream puffs from the oven and transfer to a cooling rack. The puffs produced by this recipe will be nearly devoid of the interior moist webbing that can cause the crisp shells to become soggy. Consequently, pricking the puffs during the cooling step is unnecessary.

6. Allow the puffs to cool completely. (They can stand, uncovered, for up to 48 hours.) Cut the puffs open with the serrated blade of a grapefruit knife. Pull out any webbing that may exist and fill with sweetened whipped cream. Dust with confectioners' sugar and refrigerate. Filled puffs may be kept for 6 to 8 hours in the refrigerator, but longer storage renders them soggy.

NOTE: Cream puff pastry may also be baked at 375°F. for the entire cooking period of 40 to 50 minutes. The initial baking at 425°F. recommended here produces a crisper exterior. ◄§

Beignets with Lemon Sauce

MAKES 12 LARGE BEIGNETS

A hint of Nocello, an Italian walnut liqueur, lends an intriguing note to these puffy spheres of fried pâte à choux. *To serve, center each* beignet *in a pool of warm Lemon Sauce and drizzle sweetened whipped cream over the top. Garnish with fresh raspberries if you wish.*

1 cup cold water
4 tablespoons butter, cut into 16 small chunks
1 teaspoon sugar
⅛ teaspoon salt
1 cup all-purpose flour, scoop measured
2 tablespoons Nocello (Italian walnut liqueur) or
   dark rum
4 or 5 large eggs
Vegetable oil for deep frying
Sweetened whipped cream for garnish

LEMON SAUCE
⅓ cup sugar
1 tablespoon cornstarch
Dash of salt
1 cup cold water
2 tablespoons fresh lemon juice
3 tablespoons butter

1. Prepare *pâte à choux* (cream puff pastry) by combining the water, butter, sugar, and salt in a thick-bottomed saucepan. Stir over medium-high heat until the butter melts. Stop stirring and allow the mixture to come to a vigorous boil. Immediately remove the pan from the heat and add the flour. Beat vigorously with a wooden spatula. Return to burner and cook over medium-low heat, stirring, until the batter pulls together into a smooth, shiny mass. Continue stirring the dough over medium-low heat to dry the *panade*. A white granular film will appear on the bottom of the pan. Do not allow it to burn and don't attempt to incorporate it into the dough. Test the *panade* for doneness by pinching with two fingers. When it no longer sticks to your fingers and takes on a putty-

like consistency, the *panade* is cooked. Immediately empty it into a large bowl and allow to cool for 5 to 10 minutes (or to below 140°F.), stirring occasionally to prevent a skin from forming. Beat the liqueur into the cooled *panade.*

2. Lightly whisk 4 eggs and pour into a measuring cup. If necessary, whisk the remaining egg and add enough of it to form 1 cup of eggs.

3. Using a wooden spatula or the paddle attachment of an electric mixer, beat one-quarter of the whisked eggs into the *panade* and continue beating until it accepts the eggs and the mixture smooths out. Repeat twice. Add the last portion of the eggs in a thin stream. Check for proper consistency by lifting the beater or allowing the dough to drop from a spoon. It should fall in a thick, heavy ribbon and leave a peak that stands stiff. Keep in mind that the goal is to add as much egg as possible without overly thinning the dough.

4. Heat the vegetable oil to 370°F. and dip the tablespoon in the fat to grease it. Take up the dough by rounded tablespoonfuls (using the tablespoon that belongs to a measuring-spoon set tends to produce a more rounded effect). Gently push the dough from the spoon into the hot fat. It will sink at first and then rise and begin to puff in an irregular manner. Each burst of expansion will propel the sphere of dough through the hot fat and may even cause it to turn over. Cook only 3 or 4 *beignets* at a time. Using a slotted spoon, turn the *beignets* over and over to promote even browning. Drain on absorbent paper. *Beignets* may be served at room temperature, but are best if eaten within 6 hours.

5. Begin to prepare Lemon Sauce by combining the sugar, cornstarch, and salt in a 1½-quart saucepan. Stir with a whisk to completely disperse the cornstarch. Gradually blend in the water. Add the lemon juice and place over medium-high heat. Bring to a boil, stirring constantly, and cook until thickened. Remove from the heat and stir in the butter 1 tablespoon at a time. This sauce may be made ahead and refrigerated for 2 or 3 days. Warm gently to serve with *beignets.* Garnish with sweetened whipped cream.   ◄੨

Appendix:
Mail-Order Sources

The following listing consists of sources you can contact for special food items and cookware if they are unobtainable in your local area. The items listed under each source are only those that are referred to in this text. Most of the sources carry a much wider variety than can be listed here, and will usually send a catalog upon request.

Brookstone Homewares
5 Vose Farm Road
Peterborough, NH 03460

Soft-bristled mushroom brushes, marble mortar and pestles, potato nails, pastry scrapers, crank-style flour sifters, Taylor thermometers, lemon zesters, rolling cookie cutters, Bel Cream Makers.

Cheeses of All Nations
153 Chambers Street
New York, NY 10007

Mail-order cheeses of all types.

The Chef's Catalog
3915 Commercial Avenue
Northbrook, IL 60062

One-degree interval thermometers for working with chocolate, black steel bakeware, Mouli stainless-steel food mills, battery-operated sifters, rolling cookie cutters, black steel popover pans, oven pancake pans, round (13-inch) baking stones, balsamic vinegar, black steel baguette pans, hazelnut and walnut oils.

Colonial Garden Kitchens
270 West Merrick Road
Valley Stream, NY 11582

Baking parchment; freeze-dried shallots, chives, and leeks; marble mortar and pestles; cast-iron muffin pans; heat diffusers; large (14×16-inch) baking stones; steamed pudding molds with center tubes.

Community Kitchens
P.O. Box 3778
Baton Rouge, LA 70821

Cane syrup; specialty teas, coffees, oils, and vinegars.

Fox Hill Farm
444 West Michigan Avenue
Parma, MI 49269

Fresh herbs by mail.

Garden Way Catalog
Charlotte, VT 05445

Pie birds, crocks and preserving supplies, nut crackers, mills for grinding flour.

Madame Chocolate
1940-C Lehigh Avenue
Glenview, IL 60025

Specialty chocolates for baking and candy making (3-ounce bars to 11-pound blocks).

Maid of Scandinavia
3244 Raleigh Avenue
Minneapolis, MN 55416

Extensive selection of baking tools and accessories, candy-making supplies, cookie cutters, parchment paper, heat-resistant rubber spatulas with wooden handles, rolling cookie cutters.

New England Cheesemaking Supply
PO Box 85
Ashfield, MA 01330

Equipment for making cheese, buttermilk, and yogurt; cultures and bacterial starters for blue cheese, camembert, Bel Paese, and mozzarella kits; Lactobacillus bulgaricus *for yogurt.*

Old Stone Oven Corporation
PO Box 141
Elmhurst, IL 60126

Baking stones.

Paprikas Weiss
1546 Second Avenue
New York, NY 10028

Whole spices, nut mills, spice mills, sweet Hungarian paprika, goose feathers.

G. B. Ratto and Company
821 Washington Street
Oakland, CA 94607

Arborio and basmati rice, kasha, chestnut purée, sun-dried tomatoes in oil, saffron threads.

S. E. Rykoff and Company
PO Box 21467
Market Street Station
Los Angeles, CA 90021

Freeze-dried shallots and chives, dried Porcini mushrooms from Northern Italy.

The Sausage Maker
177 Military Road
Buffalo, NY 14207

Cotton butcher's twine, sausage casing, and supplies for making homemade sausage.

Vermont Country Store
Weston, VT 05161

High-quality cheesecloth by the yard.

Villa/Cucina
74 Ashton Road
Stamford, CT 06905

Black steel bakeware, 6-cup and 12-cup popover pans.

Williams-Sonoma
PO Box 7456
San Francisco, CA 94120

Taylor thermometers, Bel Cream Makers, goose-feather brushes, linen butcher's twine, crank-style flour sifters, metal pie weights, Swedish nut mills, soft-bristled mushroom brushes, lemon zesters, gravy degreasing cups, rectangular (12×15-inch) baking stones, cast-iron muffin pans, pastry scrapers, steamed pudding molds with center tubes, black steel baguette pans, balsamic vinegar, roasted and shelled chestnuts, and chestnut knives.

The Wooden Spoon
Route 6
Mattopac, NY 10541

Round (13-inch) baking stones, nutmeg mills, oven pancake pans, gravy degreasing cups, Perfex spice mills, Bel Cream Makers, Solait Kitchen Dairy (crème fraîche maker), food mills, potato nails, black steel popover pans, crank-style flour sifters, mortar and pestles, Taylor thermometers (including Serviceman's Folding Oven Test Thermometers).

Index

(Italicized headings refer to the entries section of the book.)